STUDIES IN MYSTICAL RELIGION

STUDIES

IN

MYSTICAL RELIGION

BY

RUFUS M. JONES, M.A., D.Litt.

HAVERFORD COLLEGE, U.S.A.

Wipf & Stock
PUBLISHERS
Eugene, Oregon

Wipf and Stock Publishers
199 W 8th Ave, Suite 3
Eugene, OR 97401

Studies in Mystical Religion
By Jones, Rufus M.

ISBN: 1-59244-968-9
Publication date 10/28/2004
Previously published by Macmillan, 1909

PREFACE

No one doubts to-day that one of the main approaches to the meaning of religion is through the nature of the soul of man. It would no doubt be a mistake to push the method of the inner way to the exclusion of all other methods of studying religion, but it is certain that nobody can tell us what religion is until he has sounded the deeps within man, and has dealt with the testimony of personal consciousness.

The mystics have in all ages and in all lands—*semper et ubique*—been intent on finding a direct way to God. They have been voices, often crying in the wilderness, announcing the nearness of God, and calling men from the folly of seeking Him where, from the nature of the case, he could not be found. Their message strikes a note which appeals profoundly to our generation, and for obvious reasons there has been a revival of interest in them. I hope these studies of mine will contribute to this interest, and will throw positive light on the problems of mystical religion.

I have had before me, in all my labour on this volume, the desire to make my work advance the plans of my beloved friend John Wilhelm Rowntree, who is now in the unseen realm. He had set before himself as part of a larger purpose the task of writing the history of Quakerism, treating it as an experiment in spiritual religion, and even before I knew of his plans, I had chosen as my special field a study of the mystics of ancient and modern times. We each felt that our work was toward the same end, and we spent many joyous hours telling each other of our literary dreams, always putting all our emphasis on the way in which these unborn books of ours were to minister to the larger spiritual life of our age. His books, alas, must remain unwritten! We who were his friends know, though the world never can, what power they would have revealed.

> "The world which credits what is done
> Is dark to all that might have been."

Some of us who loved him are resolved that his work, so far as possible, shall go on to completion, and I have made my volume function, in every way I could do so, toward the fulfilling of his interrupted plans. There is no sectarian cast or bias in it, but it does prepare the way for an intelligent comprehension of the appearance in the English commonwealth of a society of Christians who seriously undertook to live by the Light within, and whose story will be told in later volumes.

I am under weighty obligations to many persons who have read and criticized some of the chapters. I desire to make particular mention of Professor Robert S. Franks, Principal T. M. Lindsay, William R. Inge, D.D., Professor Hastings Rashdall, Dr. J. Rendel Harris, T. Edmund Harvey, Joan M. Fry, and William Charles Braithwaite. I wish to express my debt also to Emily J. Hart, who assisted me in some of my researches, though she did not live to see the work completed. My greatest debt is due my dear wife, who has rendered invaluable help at every stage of my work, particularly in the sections dealing with German mystics, in the proof-reading, and in the preparation of the Index.

HAVERFORD, PENNSYLVANIA.

CONTENTS

INTRODUCTION

PAGE

THE NATURE AND VALUE OF FIRST-HAND EXPERIENCE IN RELIGION xiii

CHAPTER I

THE MYSTICAL ELEMENT IN PRIMITIVE CHRISTIANITY . 1

CHAPTER II

MINISTRY AND ORGANIZATION IN THE EARLY CHURCH . 20

CHAPTER III

MONTANISM: A RETURN TO PROPHECY 37

CHAPTER IV

ROOTS OF MYSTICISM IN CLASSICAL LITERATURE . . 57

CHAPTER V

MYSTICISM IN THE CHURCH FATHERS 80

CHAPTER VI

DIONYSIUS, "THE AREOPAGITE" 98

CHAPTER VII

PAGE

A Great Light in the Dark Ages—John the Scot, called Erigena 113

CHAPTER VIII

The Waldenses, an Anti-Sacerdotal Sect . . . 130

CHAPTER IX

St. Francis and the "Spiritual Franciscans" . . 150

CHAPTER X

A Group of Pantheistical Mystics 178

CHAPTER XI

Brotherhood Groups in the Thirteenth Century . 196

CHAPTER XII

Meister Eckhart 217

CHAPTER XIII

The Friends of God 242

CHAPTER XIV

The Brethren of the Common Life 298

CHAPTER XV

The Pre-Reformation in England—Wyclif and the Lollards 333

CHAPTER XVI

PAGE

The Anabaptists 369

CHAPTER XVII

Anabaptism in England 396

CHAPTER XVIII

The Family of Love 428

CHAPTER XIX

The Seekers and the Ranters 449

CHAPTER XX

Individual Mystics in the Period of the English Commonwealth 482

APPENDIX 501

INDEX 507

"The Kingdom of God is Within You."[1]

O world invisible, we view Thee,
O world intangible, we touch Thee,
O world unknowable, we know Thee,
Inapprehensible, we clutch Thee!

Does the fish soar to find the ocean,
The eagle plunge to find the air—
That we ask of the stars in motion
If they have rumor of Thee there?

Not where the wheeling systems darken,
And our benumbed conceiving soars!—
The drift of pinions, would we harken,
Beats at our own clay-shuttered doors.

The angels keep their ancient places;—
Turn but a stone, and start a wing!
'Tis ye, 'tis your estrangèd faces,
That miss the many-splendored thing.

But (when so sad thou canst not sadder)
Cry;—and upon thy so sore loss
Shall shine the traffic of Jacob's ladder
Pitched betwixt Heaven and Charing Cross.

Yea, in the night, my Soul, my daughter,
Cry,—clinging Heaven by the hems;
And lo, Christ walking on the water,
Not of Gennesareth, but Thames.

[1] From the Poems of Francis Thompson, with permission of John Lane Company, Publishers.

INTRODUCTION

THE NATURE AND VALUE OF FIRST-HAND EXPERIENCE IN RELIGION

TWO great tendencies come into prominence in the entire course of religious history,—the tendency, on the one hand, to regard religion as something permanent and unchanging, and on the other hand, the equally fundamental tendency to revivify and reshape religion through fresh and spontaneous experiences. It is natural that both tendencies should appear, for religion is both eternal and temporal—it is the child of permanence and change. No religion can live and be a power in this evolving world unless it changes and adjusts itself to its environment, and no religion can minister to the deepest needs of men unless it reveals permanent and time-transcending Realities.

Religion has many times lost its power because one of its two essential aspects has been ignored and the other aspect has been pushed to an absurd extreme. It will not do to forget or to overlook the advantages of habit, custom, and system—the storage of the gains of the race. The tendency to value what has worked well furthers order and stability, and keeps the future organic with the past. The conserving spirit, like an invisible mortar, binds the ages together and makes possible *one humanity*. It is the very basis of our social morality and the ground of all our corporate activities.

But, on the other hand, as soon as religion has closed up "the east window of divine surprise," and is turned into a mechanism of habit, custom, and system, it is killed. Religion thus grown formal and mechanical, though it may still have a disciplinary function in society, is no longer religion in the primary sense. The spring of joy which characterizes true religion has disappeared, the heightening, propulsive tone has vanished. It may linger on as a vestigial superstition, or a semi-automatic performance, but it is *live* religion only so long as it issues from the centre of personal consciousness and has the throb of personal experience in it.

The creative periods in religious progress have come when the crust of custom, the mechanism of habit, has been broken up by the impact of persons who were capable of fresh and original experiences, persons who have shifted the line of march and brought new energies into play, because they have gained new visions and new insights. The Church, it is true, has never in any period quite sunk to the level of tradition and the automatism of habit, for it has always had beneath its system of organization and dogma a current, more or less hidden and subterranean, of vital, inward, spiritual religion, dependent for its power of conviction, not on books, councils, hierarchies or creeds,—not upon anything kept in cold storage,—but on the soul's experiences of eternal Realities. But the main weakness of organized Christianity has been the tendency to settle into a "sacred" form and system.

Our generation has grown weary of ancient traditions and accumulated systems. We have discovered new worlds in all directions by following the sure path of experience, and we can never again settle down with a naive and childlike trust in the house which the past has builded. Our first question in any field is, not What do the scribes and schoolmen say? not What is the unbroken tradition? but, What are the facts? What data does experience furnish? This shifting of centre from "authority" to "experience" runs through all the pursuits of the human spirit in the modern world, and, as would be expected, religion has been profoundly affected by it. In religion as in other fields of inquiry, the questions of moment have come to be those which deal with life. We take slender interest in dogmatic constructions; we turn from these with impatience, and ask for the testimony of the soul, for the basis of religion in the nature of man as man. This profound tendency of the modern world has brought strongly into prominence a mystical type of religion, that is to say, a type of religion which is primarily grounded in experience,[1] and with the tendency has come a corresponding interest in the mystics of the past.

Mysticism is a word which cannot properly be used without careful definition. To many readers it carries no clear and concrete meaning; to others it has an ominous significance and a forbidding sound, as though the safe and beaten track, which the defenders of the faith have builded, were being left for will-o'-the-wisps and wandering lights. I shall use the word mysticism to express the *type of religion which puts the emphasis on immediate awareness of relation with God, on direct and intimate consciousness of the Divine Presence. It is religion in its most acute, intense, and living stage.*

Religion of this mystical type is not confined to Christianity, but belongs, in some degree, to all forms of religion, for first-hand experiences of a Divine and Higher Presence are as old as human personality. Dr Brinton is undoubtedly right in his contention that "all religions depend for their origin and continuance directly upon

[1] "The mystic is a thorough-going empiricist" (Josiah Royce, *The World and the Individual*, vol. i. p. 81).

inspiration," that is to say, upon direct intercourse.[1] The men who have made religion a living power for any people are, as he says, "persons who have been face to face with God, who have heard His voice and felt His presence."[2] Dr. Tylor has expressed much the same view in his account of the origin of religious experience in the primitive revealers.

"There are times," he says, "when powers and impressions out of the course of the mind's normal action and words that seem spoken by a voice from without, messages of mysterious knowledge, of counsel or warning, seem to indicate the intervention, as it were, of a second, superior soul."[3]

This quotation from Dr. Tylor puts the emphasis on an experience "out of the course of the mind's normal action," and raises the question whether mysticism is something normal or abnormal. Both positions have been strongly defended.

Canon R. C. Moberly says that "Christian mysticism is the doctrine, or rather the experience, of the Holy Spirit—the realization of human personality as characterized by and consummated in the indwelling reality of the Spirit of Christ, which is God." "It is Christ," he says, "who is the true mystic; or if the mode of expression be preferred, it is He who alone has realized all that mysticism and mystics have aimed at—with more, or with less, whether of disproportion or of success. And in Him that perfect realization evidently means a harmony, a sanity, a fitly proportioned completeness. It is an inward light which makes itself manifest as character; a direct communion of love which is also, to the fullest extent, wholly rational at once and wholly practical; it is as much knowledge as love, and love as knowledge;

[1] Brinton's *Religions of Primitive People*, p. 52. [2] *Ibid.* p. 58.

[3] Dr. E. B. Tylor, *Primitive Culture*, vol. i. p. 182.

it is as truly contemplation as activity, and activity as contemplation. In being the ideal of mysticism, it is also the ideal of general, and of practical, and of *all*, Christian experience. For the most practical type of Christian experience misconceives itself, until it conceives itself as an expression, in action, of a central truth,—that truth of transcendent fact, which practical Christians are too often content to call 'mystical,' and, so calling it, to banish, or to try to banish, from the region of practical life." [1]

In Canon Moberly's conception, mysticism is not a special, exceptional experience, but, rather, a life consummated in the practice of the Presence of God. It is life in its wholeness as over against a partial life, which is shut up to some *narrow compartment* of its true being. This meaning of mysticism is well brought out by President Henry Churchill King. He says: "The truly mystical may be summed up as simply a protest in favour of the whole man—the entire personality. It says that men can experience, and live, and feel, and do much more than they can formulate, define, explain, or even fully express. Living is more than thinking." [2]

Against this account of mysticism can be put a great array of testimony to show that it is an abnormal condition—a form of disease, a manifestation of hysteria.[3] The reason for this difference of view is easy to find. The two sets of writers are talking about two different things, though under the same name. For one group the *real* mystic is a person who, by conformity to the goal of life revealed in Christ, has realized his life upward in full union with God—a way of living which is as normal as healthy breathing. For the other group, the *real*

[1] Canon R. C. Moberly, *Atonement and Personality*, pp. 312-16.

[2] H. C. King's *Theology and Social Consciousness*, p. 77.

[3] Murisier, *Les Maladies du sentiment religieux*. Janet, "Une Extatique," in *Bulletin de l'Institut psychologique*, Paris, 1901. Leuba, "Tendances fondamentales des mystiques chrétiens," in *Revue philosophique*, vol. liv.

mystic is a person who exhibits a special form of psychical dissociation. He is "obsessed" with the idea that he is one with God, or he experiences a trance state, a state of "second personality," in which he loses the boundaries of his "primary self," or at least is subject to "incursions" from beyond the threshold of normal consciousness. Such experiences, we must admit, are not *normal*.

There is no question that there are "mystical experiences," *i.e.* experiences in which the subject feels the Divine Presence and has an assurance of union with God, which are abnormal and pathological, but there is no more reason for narrowing the word "mysticism" to cover this type alone than there is for using the word "love" for pathological love alone. Every form of human experience is capable of an exaggerated, an abnormal state, and there is always a shadowy borderland where it is extremely difficult to draw the line between the normal and the abnormal. This is peculiarly true of religious experience, and mystical experience may stretch over all the degrees from the most perfect sanity to utter disorganization of the self.

I shall first consider mysticism in its normal aspect, as a type of religion which is characterized by an immediate consciousness of personal relationship with the Divine. Something of this sort is familiar to the sanest and most matter-of-fact person among us. There is a mystical aspect in our highest moral moments. We never rise to any high level of moral action without feeling that the "call" of duty comes from beyond our isolated self. There is an augustness in conscience which has made men in all ages name it the voice of God; but however it is named, everybody in these high moments of obedience has an experience which is essentially mystical —an experience which cannot be analysed and reduced to "explanation" in terms of anything else. The great ethical writers of all schools recognize this. "What is good," says Paulsen, "will in the last analysis be decided by immediate incontrovertible *feeling, in which the innermost essence of the being* [*i.e.* the personality] *manifests itself.* It is as impossible to force a man by logical proofs to love and admire an ideal of life as it is to make his tongue feel the sweetness or bitterness of a particular fruit."[1] "The idea of the Good," says Hastings Rashdall, "is something simple, ultimate, and unanalysable." "Moral obligation is one of those immediate data of consciousness from which the idea of God may be inferred."[2] Professor Sidgwick says that, "Right and wrong as peculiar to moral cognition are unique and unanalysable."[3] "Duty," says Martineau, "involves the discovery of something higher than ourselves that has claims upon us."[4]

There is likewise a mystical element in prayer whenever it rises to the level of real communion, or, as Lowell puts it, when, "stirred below the conscious self," the soul feels

> "That perfect disenthralment which is God."[5]

Everybody who prays knows the difference between saying words and phrases, uttering requests, proffering petitions, and *coming into vital communion with God.* There are moments of prayer when the soul feels itself face to face with ultimate Reality and in joyous fellowship with perfect Personality. This latter experience is as normal as the lower form of prayer is, but they are worlds apart in significance and value. It is because prayer does rise to the height of actual fellowship with a Divine Companion that men who accept the conclusions of

[1] Paulsen, *A System of Ethics*, p. 11.

[2] Rashdall, *The Theory of Good and Evil*, vol. ii. pp. 103-106.

[3] *Mind*, vol. xxviii. p. 580.

[4] Martineau, *Types of Ethical Theory*, vol. ii. p. 104.

[5] Lowell, *The Cathedral.*

modern science go on praying, undisturbed by the reign of law. They are not concerned about the superficial question, whether prayers are answered or not; for prayer is its own reward, is an end in itself and carries the person who truly prays into a joyous state which transcends explanation. As S. T. Coleridge has well expressed it:—

> "A sense o'er all my soul impressed
> That I am weak, yet not unblessed,
> Since in me, round me, everywhere,
> Eternal strength and wisdom are."

These mystical experiences in a perfectly sane and normal fashion often come over whole groups of persons in times of worship. There are times when, in the hush and silence, with no appeal to the senses, and with nothing outward to stir emotion, low breathings of a diviner life are clearly felt and the entire group is fused and baptized into one spirit. There comes the experience of a great refreshing, a release of energy, as though a hidden circuit had been closed.

> "For a moment on the soul
> Falls the rest that maketh whole,
> Falls the endless peace."[1]

These are the times when the soul feels its real powers and when the possibilities of life are discovered, and they make the ordinary performances of religious service seem, in comparison, poor and dry. Such experiences are beyond explanation, but they are not abnormal.

There is, too, a mystical element of this normal type in any genuine *faith*. I am not speaking, of course, of a faith which consists in believing something on authority, for that is faith of a lower order. Faith in the primary sense is a way of corresponding with Realities which

[1] F. W. H. Myers' *Sunrise*.

transcend sense-experience. It is an inward power by which the soul lives above the seen and temporal, and "overcomes" the world of the causal, mechanical order. It is a conviction, arising apparently from the very rationality of the spirit in us, that there is an inner, unseen, spiritual universe—an eternal moral order. It is the soul's vision of *what ought to be* and its confidence in the reality and permanence of that estimate of worth—"the assurance of things hoped for and the evidence of things not seen." It is no mere product of sense-experience, but it is the very pinnacle of rationality and as normal a function as our responses to ocular vision.[1]

It is not an uncommon thing for persons who are entirely free from abnormality to have an experience in which the meaning, the significance, the worth, the richness of life, vastly transcends their concepts and descriptions—when life vastly overflows all that can be said about it. This experience is marked by the emergence of a sort of undifferentiated consciousness like that well known to us when we rise to a high appreciation of the beautiful in nature or art or music. At the highest moments of appreciation there comes, not a loss of consciousness, but the emergence of a new level of consciousness in which neither the *I* nor the *object* is focused in perception or thought.[2] There is in these experiences an absence of self-consciousness, and an absence, too, of the consciousness of any concrete, finite object contemplated, a

1 The question has been raised whether Mystical-religion is higher or lower than Faith-religion (see article by Dr. Lyman in *American Journal of Theology* for July 1904). It is hardly a fair question to raise, since mysticism at every point involves faith; and any faith which is really alive and dynamic is rooted and grounded in first-hand experience.

2 "The æsthetic object and the consciousness in which it arises are no longer held apart. The self becomes identified with the object as peculiarly its own." (Dr. W. D. Furry's *Aesthetic Experience: Its Nature and Function in Epistemology* (Baltimore, 1908), p. 49.)

penetration into a region more real and all-inclusive than that of finite "things."[1]

The poet Coleridge has in many passages called attention to a type of experience which is neither "feeling" nor "knowledge," but something much richer than either alone—an experience which he declares is "the very groundwork" of knowledge, and which arises "when we possess ourselves as one with the whole"—

"An experience deeper than science, more certain than demonstration, and from which flows the sap that circulates through every branch and spray of demonstration and knowledge, an experience which passeth all understanding."[2]

It is now a commonplace of psychology that what we *are* and what we experience vastly transcends our "knowledge"

[1] Wordsworth has described a personal experience in a beautiful passage:

"Sensation, soul and form
All melted into him; they swallowed up
His animal being; in them did he live,
And by them did he live; they were his life.
In such access of mind, in such high hours
Of visitation from the living God,
Thought was not; in enjoyment it expired.
No thanks he breathed, he proffered no request;
Rapt into still communion that transcends
The imperfect offices of prayer and praise,
His mind was a thanksgiving to the power
That made him; it was blessedness and love.

The Excursion, Book I.

There is no better first-hand account of such an unanalysable whole of experience than Mozart's description of the *coming* of a symphony into his consciousness.

"When and how my ideas come I know not, nor can I force them. Those that please me I retain in my memory and am accustomed, as I have been told, to hum them to myself. If I continue in this way, it soon occurs to me how I may turn this or that morsel to account. . . . All this fires my soul, and, provided I am not disturbed, my subject enlarges itself, becomes methodized and defined, and the whole, though it be long, stands almost complete and finished in my mind, so that I can survey it like a fine picture, or a beautiful statue at a glance. Nor do I hear in my imagination the parts *successively*, but I hear them as it were all at once. What a delight this is I cannot express. All this inventing, this producing, takes place in a pleasing, lively dream. But the actual hearing of the whole together is after all the best. And this is perhaps the best gift I have my Divine Master to thank for" (Holmes' *Life and Correspondence of Mozart* (London, 1845), pp. 317-18.)

[2] S. T. Coleridge's *The Friend*, Essay XI.

about it; reality overflows at every point our categories of description. Our full self, our *real* self, radiates out from a central pulse of consciousness, which is in the focus of attention, and the part of the self that gets focalized and reduced to conceptual knowledge is only a very tiny fragment. As Maeterlinck has declared: "There is in us, above the reasoning portion of our reason, a whole region answering to something different, which is preparing for the surprises of the future, and which goes on ahead of our imperfect attainments, and enables us to live on a level very much superior to that of those attainments."[1]

Now there are times when this underlying total whole of consciousness comes into power in us in unusual fashion, when the stored-up gains of a lifetime are at our command, and we seem to possess ourselves even down to the roots of our being. In truth, at times, we are aware of a More than "ourselves" impinging on the skirts of our being. There is no time in our lives, of course, when we do not draw upon this wider consciousness which is the matrix in which our "ideas" and concepts are born. We are all aware how often we arrive at conclusions and actions without reasoning or thinking; how often we deal wisely with situations, without being able to trace the source of our wisdom. The supreme issues of life are settled for us, all the way up and down the scale, by unreasoned adjustments, by intents rather than contents of consciousness, by value-responses, which far overflow any knowledge explanation which we can give. It may, I think, be said that all great work, all work which has the touch of genius on it, comes from persons who in special degrees draw upon this matrix consciousness. Such persons feel often as though a Power not themselves were working through them; as though, without tension or effort, the creation at

[1] Cited in Pratt's *Psychology of Belief*, p. 27.

which they are working was "given" to them or "brought" to them. There are, I repeat, times when in extraordinary ways the dualistic character of ordinary thought is transcended and the soul comes into possession of itself as a whole, when all we have been, or are, or hope to be, becomes real; and not only so, but in these deeper reaches of experience some higher Power than ourselves *seems* to work with us and through us—a larger life, continuous with ourselves, seems to environ us. Our own consciousness appears to be only an effective centre in a vast spiritual environment which acts along with us. As Matthew Arnold has finely said:

> "A bolt is shot back somewhere in our breast
> And a lost pulse of feeling stirs again.
>
> . . . . .
>
> And then he thinks he knows
> The hills where his life rose
> And the sea where it goes."[1]

There are persons seemingly as normal as the sanest tiller of the soil, who find themselves fused into union with a wider, diviner life than that of their common, everyday experiences, who have times when their soul takes hoilday from doubt and strain and perplexity. A great refreshing floods them, they are aware of a heightened energy, as though they had pushed out into a new compartment of being. It is like the aesthetic experience, in its lofty levels, only the impulse comes from within instead of from without. There could be no better account of this heightened life than Edward Dowden has given in his Sonnet on *Awakening.*

> "Suddenly, we know not how, a sound
> Of living streams, an odour, a flower crowned
> With dew, a lark upspringing from the sod,
> And we awake. O joy and deep amaze,

[1] Arnold's *Buried Life.*

> Beneath the everlasting hills we stand,
> We hear the voices of the morning seas,
> And earnest prophesyings in the land,
> While from the open heaven leans forth at gaze
> The encompassing great cloud of witnesses."

Such lofty æsthetic joy is perhaps unusual, though some degree of it has probably at some time swept the lives of the most prosaic of us, and so, too, these floods of religious refreshing from within, these mystical experiences, these times when we seem to possess the whole of ourselves, may be unusual, but they are not abnormal experiences, nor are they foreign to our true nature as men.

I have spoken of various types of experience which are in some degree mystical, and which yet are well within the line of normal healthy life. There are other types of mystical experience which may, and often do, pass over the border-line of normality and occasionally, at least, exhibit pathological phenomena. Among all peoples that have left any annals there have been persons of extraordinary powers; soothsayers, magicians, wizards, witches, medicine-men, sibyls, clairvoyants, seers, prophets, persons "possessed" by superhuman spirits. Such persons, sometimes called "divine," and sometimes called "demoniac," have played an enormous rôle in human history. Dr. Pierre Janet has well expressed the part such men and women have played: "In the development of every great religion, both in ancient and in modern times, there have always been strange persons who raised the admiration of the crowd because their nature seemed to be different from human nature. Their manner of thinking was not the same as that of the others; they had extraordinary oblivions or remembrances, they had visions, they saw or heard what others could not see or hear. They were illumined by odd convictions; not only did they think but they also felt in another way than the bulk of mankind; they had an extraordinary delicacy of certain senses joined to extravagant insensibilities, which enabled them to bear the most dreadful tortures with indifference or even with delight. Not only did they feel, but they also lived otherwise than other people; they could do without sleep, or sleep for months together; they lived without eating or drinking, without satisfying their natural needs. Is it not such persons who have always excited the religious admiration of peoples, whether sibyls, prophets, pythonesses of Delphi or Ephesus, or saints of the Middle Ages, or ecstatics, or illuminates? Now they were considered as worthy of admiration and beatified, now they were called witches or demoniacs and burnt; but, at the bottom, they always caused astonishment, and they played a great part in the development of dogmas and creeds."[1]

The literature of mysticism abounds with cases of ecstasy, of vision of "light," audition of "voices," and there are well-authenticated instances of automatisms and even of "stigmata." Again and again there have come to men and women sudden "incursions" or "invasions" from beyond the margin of personal consciousness, and these persons have *felt* themselves environed with God or even united in one life with Him.[2] Are these unusual and more or less abnormal experiences instances of

[1] Janet, *Major Symptoms of Hysteria*, New York, 1907, p. 8.

[2] It would be quite easy to make an entire volume of selections of instances. The four instances given below will illustrate the type I am discussing.

Eckhart declares: "I am as certain as that I live that nothing is so near to me as God. God is nearer to me than I am to myself (Meister Eckhart's *Mystische Schriften*, by Gustav Landaur, p. 96).

Jacob Boehme says: "In one quarter of an hour I saw and knew more than if I had been many years in a university. I saw and knew the being of all things, the Byss and Abyss." Jacob Behmen's [Boehme] *Theo. Phil.* by Edward Taylor (London, 1691), p. 425.

Madame Guyon, to whom mystic experiences were almost common occurrences, gives the following description of one of these: "My spirit disenthralled, became

pathology, cases of hysteria, or are they evidences of Divine Influence and Divine Presence? The mystic himself believes that he has an *experience of God* because (1) these experiences of his come from beyond the margin of his individual *me*; (2) there is something in the content of his experience which transcends anything that normally belongs to him in his finiteness; and (3) these experiences possess an impelling, coercive power, a higher unification of life than he ordinarily knows.[1]

But does this sort of subjective experience furnish empirical evidence of God? May not what, in his own personal vision, the mystic calls "an experience of God" be only the result of an unconscious "suggestion" and no more a proof of God than everyday, common experience is? Recent studies of hysteria and hypnotism have revolutionized all our ideas of the psychological range and scope and the subtle power of suggestion.[2] Society abounds with persons who are hyper-sensitive to suggestion and over-acute to imitate attitudes and experiences which occur within their environment, or are suggested by their reading, and there is no lack of persons who are swayed by impulses which seem to rise mysteriously within themselves by unconscious *auto-suggestion.*

united with and lost in God. And this was so much the case that I seemed to see and know God only, and not myself."

James Russell Lowell's "revelation," as he himself calls it, is a very good instance of this *experience*: "As I was speaking, the whole system (of the universe) rose up before me like a vague destiny looming from the Abyss. I never before so clearly felt the Spirit of God in me and around me. The whole room seemed to me full of God. The air seemed to waver to and fro with the presence of something, I knew not what. I spoke with the calmness and clearness of a prophet" (*Letters of Lowell*, vol. i. p. 75).

[1] See Delacroix, *Étude d'histoire et de psychologie du Mysticisme* (Paris, 1908), pp. 365-66. This is one of the most important books on mysticism that has appeared in recent years.

[2] The reader should consult Janet's *Major Symptoms of Hysteria*, New York, 1907.

Some aspects of the experience of mystics undoubtedly are due to suggestion. There have been mystics who have possessed abnormal constitutions, who were subject to strange psychical disturbances. It is certain that many of the abnormal phenomena reported in the lives of mystics are in no way distinguishable from similar phenomena in hysterical cases. Trances, losses of consciousness, automatisms, vision of lights, audition of voices, "stigmata," and such-like experiences, are evidences of hysteria, and they are not in themselves evidences of Divine Influence or of Divine Presence. In fact, many mystics have practised methods of asceticism which were adapted to turn them into abnormal persons and to produce in them hysterical constitutions. They have "worked themselves up" to abnormal states. In the light of these facts it has been contended that even those striking experiences of expansion, enlargement, absorption in the Infinite, freedom from all limits, ecstatic joy, which mystics exhibit, may be instances of auto-suggestion.[1] It is quite possible to be so absorbed in a single thought that all consciousness of body sensations, all awareness of an external world, all things of time and space, shall be unnoticed and be as though they were not, and when all strain and muscular tension are absent, peace and joy and fulness of life are the natural result. It is easy to produce such a state through hypnotic suggestion, and it seems plainly within the range of auto-suggestion.

We cannot, therefore, with implicit confidence, leap to the conclusion that every instance of so-called mystical experience furnishes us with a sure clue to the God Whom

[1] I am dwelling at some length on the place of "suggestion" and "auto-suggestion" because it has been assumed by some recent writers, notably by Professor Coe, that mystical experiences are only cases of "auto-suggestion" (see Professor Coe's article on "Sources of the Mystical Revelation" in the *Hibbert Journal* for January 1908, pp. 359-72).

our eager souls seek. To the mystic himself the experience is evidence enough. It lights his lamp and girds his loins for action; it floods him with new power; it banishes doubt and despair as the sunrise banishes darkness. He no more wants arguments now to prove God's existence than the artist wants arguments to prove the reality of beauty or the lover does to prove the worth of love.

But it is useless to claim that mystical experiences have such ontological bearing that they settle for *everybody* the reality of God. No subjective experience, however momentous and significant it may be for the person who has it, can settle for everybody else the question: Is there in the universe a God who is personal and all-loving? No empirical experience of any sort can ever answer that question, and to the end of the world men will be called upon to walk by *faith*, to make their venture in the light of what ought to be true, and in the light of what seems to them true, and to live by that faith.

But while these inward mystical experiences cannot be pushed to the extreme of being turned into compelling ontological proofs, they nevertheless do offer a very weighty ground for believing that there is a More of Consciousness continuous with our own—a co-consciousness with which our own is bound up, and that constructive influences do come into us from beyond ourselves.[1] We must not take fright at the word *auto-suggestion.* It is only a word, a phrase, which explains nothing. We have not eliminated God when we conclude, as we must do, that the physical universe has evolved. "Evolution" is only a fresh word for describing the method of making a universe. And when we have named these great spiritual crises, which carry men up to

[1] See James' *Varieties of Religious Experience,* p. 515.

new levels of life and power and service, "auto-suggestive experiences," we have only substituted one word for another. We called them "new births"; we call them "auto-suggestions"! The *fact* remains on our hands, and the fact is a momentous one.

There have been religious geniuses in all ages and in all countries, who have had experiences of spiritual expansion. They have been made aware of a Realm of Reality on a higher level than that revealed through their senses. They have sometimes felt invaded by the inrush of larger Life; sometimes they have seemed to push a door inward into a larger range of being, with vastly heightened energy. The experience is, as we have seen, always one of joy and rapture; in fact, it is probably the highest joy a mortal ever feels. But the significant fact is not the sense of expansion, or of freedom, or of joy. It is not something merely subjective. It is that such experiences minister to life, construct personality and conduce to the increased power of the race—*energy to live by actually does come to them from somewhere.* The universe backs the experience.

We cannot lightly pass over the spiritual service of mystics. Far from being the unpractical, dreamy persons they are too often conceived to have been, they have weathered storms, endured conflicts, and lived through water-spouts which would have overwhelmed souls whose anchor did not reach beyond the veil. They have discovered an inner refuge, where they enjoy the truce of God, even amid the din of the world's warfare. They have led great reforms, championed movements of great moment to humanity, and they have saved Christianity from being submerged under scholastic formalism and ecclesiastical systems, which were alien to man's essential nature and need. They have been spiritual leaders, they are the persons who shifted the levels of life for the race.[1] They have been able to render these services because they felt themselves allied inwardly with a larger personal Power than themselves, and they have been aware that they were in immediate correspondence with Some One—a Holy Spirit, a Great Companion—who was working with them and through them. This *furtherance of life* by incoming energy, the heightening of power by correspondence with what *seems* to be God, is, however, by no means confined to a few chosen spirits and rare geniuses; it is a wide-spread fact to be reckoned with everywhere. There are multitudes of men and women in out-of-the-way places, in backwoods towns, and on uneventful farms, who are the salt of the earth and the light of the world in their communities, because they have had experiences which revealed to them Realities which their neighbours missed, and powers to live by which the mere "church-goers" failed to find.

We have thus much more to account for and explain than a few rare, subjective experiences, a few cases of heightened *feeling*. We are bound to realize that mystic experiences have a life-value, and validify themselves in action. Those who are finely sensitive to wider spheres of Reality impinging on their inner realm, and who correspond and co-operate with that More which seems continuous and conterminous with their lives, gain not only in *capacity* to correspond and co-operate, but also in power to overcome difficulties, and to put their lives into constructive service. We have on our hands experiences which have opened to individuals and to the race as a whole wider realms of being, experiences which have heightened the quality of life and which have given new energy of survival, and we are compelled to conclude, either that the personal self is a bottomless affair, carrying

[1] Professor Royce has very well treated the social service of the Mystics in his *World and the Individual*, vol. i. pp. 85-87.

within itself infinite unexplored chambers and undreamed-of energies which sometimes come into play, or that the personal self is bosomed on a larger Realm of Consciousness from which we draw our being into the bounds of individuality, and with which we may *correspond.* It has been, as we shall see, the contention of mystics in all ages that God Himself is the ground of the soul, and that in the deeps of their being all men partake of one central Divine Life. The facts, at any rate, all point in this direction.

It is true that the great mystics have often possessed peculiar psychical constitutions. They have sometimes exhibited the phenomena of hysteria, and sometimes they have, beyond question, been pathological, and have experienced abnormal states due to an unstable nervous system. But it is also true that persons possessing such psychical constitutions have in unusual ways, and in heightened degree, been able to correspond with an environing Reality which built up and vitalised their personal lives. Again and again this "correspondence" has brought them health and a unified and ordered will. They *seem* to find themselves enveloped in a matrix-consciousness of far wider reach than that of which ordinary persons are conscious, and they demonstrate that their "correspondence" has life-value and a value for the race.

There is thus some co-relation between these inward experiences and the Eternal Nature of Things. They have functioned to the enlargement of personal life and to the expansion of human society. It is just these persons who have had first-hand experiences of dealing with inward Reality, that *seems* to be God, who have been the master builders of religion. Their testimony to unseen Realities gives the clue and stimulus to multitudes of others to gain a like experience, and it is, too, their testimony that makes God real to the great mass of men who are satisfied to believe on the strength of another's belief. They have, stage by stage, advanced the realm of spiritual life and the appreciation of it, just as great musicians have enlarged the realm of sound-harmonies and the appreciation of them.

It is no discredit to inward, mystical religion to show that social suggestion, or even auto-suggestion, has played a great part in the development of it. Both have played a great part in the development of all experiences. Our language, our moral ideals, our human fashions, are all what they are because of the conscious or unconscious influence of group-suggestion, for our lives are, to a greater extent than most persons realize, conjunct with our fellows. And "auto-suggestion" may be only another way of saying that God and man are conjunct, and that in the deeps of the soul, beyond our power of knowing how, Divine suggestions come to human consciousness. The fact is, that enlarging, expanding power, constructive spiritual energy, comes into certain persons, which makes them sure that they are allied to a Being who guarantees the ultimate goodness of the world. They hear

> "The bubbling of the springs
> That feed the world,"

and they live more dynamic lives because of these experiences which rise within them

> "as mysteriously as cape
> Of cloud grown out of invisible air."

But this experience, as soon as it is valued and appreciated, will, let us grant, show the influence of unconscious suggestion from the social environment, and will be found to have a temporal element in it. The actual mystical *views* of any given period, the symbolism through which these inward experiences are expressed, the "revelations" which come to mystical prophets, all bear the mark and colour of their particular age. There are no "pure experiences," *i.e.* no experiences which come wholly from *beyond* the person who has them:

> "For every fiery prophet in old time,
> And all the sacred madness of the bard,
> When God made music through him
> Could but make his music by the framework and the chord."[1]

The most refined mysticism, the most exalted spiritual experience is *partly* a product of the social and intellectual environment in which the personal life of the mystic has formed and matured. There are no experiences of any sort which are independent of preformed expectations or unaffected by the prevailing beliefs of the time. Every bit of our inner or outer life, however much it is our own, is shot through with lines of colour due to social and racial suggestions. All our ideals of goodness, all our instantaneous decisions of conscience, our most inward light, and our most instinctive wisdom, have come to be what they are because we have been organic with our particular social group at this identical period of human history. Mystical experiences will be, perforce, saturated with the dominant ideas of the group to which the mystic belongs, and they will reflect the expectations of that group and that period.[2]

It is this conformation of mysticism to the type of religion out of which it springs, and the fact that it is always imbedded in the life of a social group that gives it its sanity and safeguard from vagaries and caprices. The greatest danger from mysticism, and there are dangers, is just *this* of becoming relatively detached from the experience of the race, the illumination of the great revealers of the past. Religion and morality are the consummate gains of the travail of the ages, and no

[1] Tennyson's *Holy Grail.*

[2] This feature of mystical experience is well treated in Delacroix, *op. cit.*

person can cut loose from the spiritual group-life in which he is rooted without entailing serious loss. To sever one's roots in history and in the slowly-gathered content of religious faith, "to build all inward" and to have no light but what comes "pure" by the inward way, is to suffer shrinkage, and to run the tremendous risk of ending in moral and spiritual bankruptcy, with only vagaries and caprices for assets. The sane mystic does not exalt his own experiences over historical revelation, he rather interprets his own openings in the light of the master-revelations. He does not foolishly conclude, because he has a vision of his own, that "the glory of God in the face of Jesus Christ" is out-dated and unnecessary, any more than the artist, with a "gift" of his own, concludes that he has no need of the inspiring guidance of the old masters; or than the musician, who has an original creative power in himself, flies to the conclusion that he can ignore the men in the past who have revealed the nature and scope of music. Mystical religion, instead of making the soul independent of Christ and of earlier revelations, rather insists that every hint of the Divine meaning that has come in any age, through any person, is precious, and that the supreme unveiling of the nature and character of God, the highest exhibition of the range and scope of human possibility in the person of Jesus Christ, is unspeakably important for any one whose main concern is to be a son of God. This religion of first-hand experience is not a substitute for Christianity; it is Christianity alive and vocal in personal experience and in individual love.

There has undoubtedly been in many mystical movements an over-emphasis on ecstasy and moveless contemplation, and it is easy to see that individual mystics have, perhaps unconsciously, employed methods now familiar to us in hypnotic experiments. They have used short cuts and unspiritual aids to hasten their arrival at a state of joyous absorption. They have exhibited an over-fascination for a suspension of all desire and a loss of the strain and struggle, which go with that "slow, dead heave of the will" in the great moral issues of life. They have, too, sometimes been almost obsessed with the fixed idea that all the ills of life and the confusions of mutability would disappear if only they believed implicitly enough in the allness of God and the unity of all that is. This has led them to glorify abstraction and to choose the *via negativa*, the negative path; that is, to win their peace by refusing to take account of multiplicity and evil, sin and pain. They have found their line of least resistance to be withdrawal and negation, which is, at best, only the backstairs to the Upper Room.

But I prefer to dwell on the tremendous service of the Mystics. There are imperfections in all human undertakings, and there are blunderers wherever men seriously gird themselves for high endeavours. We do not scorn poetry, though there have been poetasters who became popular; we do not give up our appreciation of great music, though there have been poor performers who got the large gate receipts. We must recognise the limitations and the false trails, but we do well to keep in the goodly fellowship of those who have seen and heard and handled the Word of Life, and who have found the inner way home.

There is no attempt in the following chapters to give a complete history of Christian mysticism, nor are all the movements herein studied properly called mystical, though they have all helped to further religion of this inward and first-hand type. There have been momentous epochs when vital, dynamic religion has *flourished*, when men of creative power have made new discoveries of the soul's capacities, and have become so initiated into the mysteries of the kingdom of God that they could open for their fellows new doors into the spiritual life, and thus have become centres of spiritual groups. I shall study, in the following pages, some of these spiritual groups, these creative movements, and some of the persons who have been in a peculiar degree prophets of the soul by virtue of their own direct experience. It is not always possible to trace a *direct* historical connection between these spiritual groups, for the literary data which have survived are often meagre; but the following chapters will make it evident, I think, that there has been a continuous prophetical procession, a mystical brotherhood through the centuries, of those who have lived by the soul's immediate vision. Again and again, as will appear, the writings of a mystic, long dead and seemingly forgotten, with no school of disciples to disseminate his message, have reached an apt and ready soul, have kindled him to glowing life, and have made him again the centre of a new group; and so the torch has passed on to a new age.

I have begun with a brief study of the inward, free, and untrammelled type of religion which prevailed in the early period of the primitive Church, and I have, in the most compact way possible, sketched the growth and development of the ecclesiastical system which was gradually substituted for the free and organic *fellowship* of the first stage of Christianity. The studies of the mystical element in the Church Fathers and in Greek Philosophy are necessarily inadequate. I have confined myself to the task of gathering up the main lines of influence which reappear in the mystical sects of medieval Europe. I have included in these studies the Waldensian, the Wyclifite, and the Anabaptist movements, though they are mainly unmystical, because of their very great importance in the general movement of Christianity toward a more inward and personal form of religion, less ecclesiastical and sacerdotal, and depending more on the direct relation of man to God.

I propose, at some later time, to publish a volume on Jacob Boehme, and I have thought it best not to crowd his contribution into an inadequate chapter. My studies come down only to the end of the English Commonwealth, because this volume is intended to be an introduction to a series of historical volumes by myself and others devoted to the development and spiritual environment of a particular branch of modern Christianity—The Society of Friends—a religious body which has made a serious attempt to unite inward, mystical religion with active, social endeavours, and to maintain a religious fellowship without a rigid ecclesiastical system, and with large scope for personal initiative, immediate revelation and individual responsibility.

CHAPTER I

THE MYSTICAL ELEMENT IN PRIMITIVE CHRISTIANITY

I

THERE has been a persistent feeling, a perennially recurring faith throughout all centuries of the Christian Church, that the culminating period of religion was in the Galilean circle and in the apostolic age. Men have steadily looked back to that period as the "golden age," when the Divine and the human were completely united in one Life, and were brought into joyous fellowship in many lives. The supreme aspiration of the spiritual men and women who have travailed for the regeneration of humanity, has been for a return, a restoration, of that golden time. The cry, "Back to Christ," or "Back to apostolic Christianity," is not at all a new cry. Every profound movement toward a more spiritual and unfettered form of Christianity than that embodied in the dominant historical Church of the period has been initiated by a rediscovery of Christ, or by a fresh interpretation of the Gospel, and in nearly every instance the leaders of reform have asserted their particular movement to be a "revival of primitive Christianity."

We are now, however, well aware, through historical study, that there was in the first period of the Church no one well defined and fixed type of "apostolic Christianity." There were, even in the days of the apostles, many types and varieties of Christianity, almost as different from each other as our modern types are. Paul's interpretation was the first to receive literary expression, and through his dominating personality and his vast missionary and literary labours Pauline Christianity became a widespread form of early faith and practice.[1] A type very unlike that of Paul's finds expression in the short Epistle of James, and the conception expressed in that Epistle appears to have had many adherents and to have been "primitive Christianity" for a large circle of the followers of Christ. Johannine Christianity had many aspects unlike either that of Paul or that of James. Its perspective of Christ is different, its points of emphasis are very unlike those of the two apostolic interpreters already mentioned. The writer of the "Epistle to the Hebrews" is so unique in his interpretation of Christ, that no serious scholar can believe that Paul wrote this Epistle. The three synoptic writers, again, have made their particular selection of incidents and sayings because they have already formed their own conception of Christ, and because they have in mind the peculiar needs of the groups of Christians to which they belonged.

As Harnack has well said, "Jesus sought to kindle independent religious life, and He did kindle it; yes, that is His peculiar greatness, that He led men to God so that they lived their own life with Him."[2] Primitive Christianity was above everything else a way of living, and it exhibited, as life always does, freedom, variety, personality. It is vain to expect to *revive*—*i.e.* to bring back in its pristine form, the Christianity of the first century. There is no possibility, in an evolving world, of bringing back any age, however golden it may look in retrospect—the course of humanity is always forward. What we do want is to penetrate the secret of the power manifested in bygone times, and to discover, as far as may be, what

[1] It should be recognized, of course, that Paul himself had no fixed and unvarying system of doctrine or of practice. One who reads him in the historic spirit sees that Paul's "Christianity" is, throughout the Epistles, in process of making. His entire conception of the meaning of Christianity shows great advance between the writing of 1 Thessalonians and Philippians.

[2] *Das Wesen des Christenthums*, p. 7.

was the spring of energy, the vital spirit, which possessed men in ages when great things were done, and when men lived in joy and triumph.

The great epochs in religion, and particularly this greatest epoch, which we call the "apostolic age," are marked off and characterized by a peculiarly rich and vivid consciousness of the Divine Presence. They are times when in new, fresh, and transforming ways persons have *experienced* the real presence of God. Life is always raised to new levels, and receives a new dynamic quality whenever God becomes real in personal and social experience. The battle has raged long and bitterly over the metaphysical relation of Christ to God; great rallying cries have grown out of these battles, and different communions have gathered about the various formulations of doctrine upon these and other difficult metaphysical questions, but the much more important questions are questions of fact; namely, what were the significant features of Christ's *experience*, what gave Him His extraordinary power over those who were in fellowship with Him, and what was it that made His disciples in such effective ways "the salt of the earth, the light of the world"? and these questions have hardly been raised at all. The time is coming, however, when the emphasis will shift—it is already shifting—from questions of systematic theology to questions of religious experience, from metaphysics to psychology. It is a point of the first importance that the Gospels have given us little or no metaphysics; the language of theology is, too, quite foreign to them. They have given us instead the portrait of a Person who had a most extraordinary experience of God and of Oneness with Him. We may wish that we had more of the *very words* of this Person, and that our accounts of His life were not coloured by His reporters; but we ought rather to be grateful that these first century biographers have, with unstudied simplicity, given us so little of themselves, and have opened to us so many approaches to the real life and even the actual consciousness of the Person who originated in the world this new and intimate fellowship with God which we call Christianity.

We should be very far from depreciating the impressive efforts of scholars, ancient and modern, to gather up and formulate the teaching of Jesus, the original *message*, for no one can fail to recognize that He was a Master, that He taught disciples, and that His teachings, His dominant ideas, have enormously influenced human thought, and have formed a large factor in the moral evolution of the race; but no summary of Christ's teachings, no formulation of His dominant ideas can give us a full account of "primitive Christianity," for "primitive Christianity" is supremely this unique Person, Jesus Christ, with His experience of God, His insight into the meaning of Life, His consecration to the task of remaking man, and the extraordinary fellowship which His Spirit produced.

Christianity in the golden age was essentially a rich and vivid consciousness of God, rising to a perfect experience of union with God in mind and heart and will. It was a personal exhibition of the Divine in the human, the Eternal in the midst of time. When we get back to the head-waters of our religion we come ultimately to a Person who felt, and, in childlike simplicity, said that "No man knows the Father save the Son," and "I and the Father are one."

The direct impact and power of His life on His followers is the most extraordinary thing in the Gospels, and the continued power of His life over men is the most marvellous thing in human history. The source of this power is to be found in the fact that men have found through Him a direct way to God, that by His life and death they have been drawn themselves into a personal experience of God in some degree like His own. He always taught His disciples to expect this, and it was their attainment of this experience that made them the apostles of the new religion. Christianity is thus at its very heart a mystical religion—a religion which lives and flourishes because its members experience what its

Founder experienced, the actual presence of God as the formative Spirit of a new creation.[1] As I have said, every disciple was summoned to expect a direct and conscious incoming of the Divine Life. "Wherever two or three are gathered in My name, there am I in the midst,"[2] was the announcement of a mystical fellowship which has cheered the hearts of little groups of worshippers in all ages and in all lands where the words of the Gospel have come. "Lo, I am with you always"[3] was a promise which fed and watered the faith of men in the hard days of cross and stake, and in the long, uneventful years when no "sign" was given that the fellowship of the saints would finally overcome the world.

The members of this primitive group were taught in the most impressive way to avoid anxiety and worry, and, instead, to open their souls to the circulation of Divine forces of life which build up the inward life as noiselessly and yet as beautifully as the lily's robe is spun and the cubits are added to the care-free child.[4] They were told not to be disturbed about their defence before judges and authorities in times of strait, but to trust to the springs of wisdom that would flow into them from the larger Life of the Holy Spirit in which they lived.[5] The promise of direct and inward fellowship with Christ took on wider scope, according to the recently discovered "saying" of Jesus, "Wherever any man raises a stone or cleaves wood, there am I"; for whether this is a genuine "saying" of Jesus, or an early Christian reminiscence of an idea which He taught in a more general way, it undoubtedly expresses in graphic language one of the deepest truths which pervade the original teaching, namely that the disciple, whether gathered for

[1] The mysticism of the Gospels and so, too, that of the other New Testament writers is, of course, very far removed from that type of religion historically known as "mysticism." Strictly speaking, the New Testament is no more a mystical Book than it is a theological or metaphysical, or ecclesiastical Book. The mysticism in it is implicit and unconscious; it is never subjected to reflection or made explicit in thought. But, nevertheless, we have here throughout religion in the *intense stage*, as immediate and first-hand experience of God, which is mysticism at its best, and in its truest meaning—*initiation into the Divine secret.*

[2] Matt. xviii. 20.

[3] Matt. xxviii. 20.

[4] Matt. vi. 25-34.

[5] Luke xii. 11.

worship, or defending himself before the "authorities," or engaged in simple labour with his hands, is to share a direct fellowship with Christ, a fellowship which shall consecrate every spot of the earth and hallow every occupation.[1]

The pictorial description of "the Judgment Day" identifies God with the least member of the mystical fellowship. There is no other passage in the New Testament which announces more positively the solidarity of the race and the conjunct life of God and man. He, the Head of the Fellowship, drinks of the cup put to the lips of the thirsty child, and the slenderest ministry performed out of love circulates through the whole, and touches the Infinite Heart.[2] This description ought to have softened the lurid colours which have so often been used to paint the Judgment Day—supposed to be a *dies irae*; but there is unmistakable evidence that the idea of the solidarity of humanity, the announcement that God identifies Himself with the hungry and naked and persecuted—even the least—the teaching that every man in the deeps of his soul is bound in with God, which are expressed in this primitive narrative, have exercised a marked influence on those groups of Christians who have gone to the Gospel itself for their illumination.

The entire teaching of the Kingdom of God has its mystical aspect. It is a society, or fellowship, both in earth and in heaven, both human and Divine. Its capital is not in some foreign land, its King is not a distant Sovereign, for any member of the Kingdom at any spot of earth can see Him if his heart is pure. The person who belongs to the Kingdom is a person in whom God lives and rules, and through whom the contagion of a love, caught from above, spreads through the world. The Kingdom is the life of God exhibited in human fellowship, the

[1] This is Logion 5 of the *Oxyrhynchus Papyri*. It is in full as follows:—"Jesus saith, wherever there are (two), they are not without God, and wherever there is one alone, I say, I am with him. Raise the stone, and there thou shalt find Me; cleave the wood, and there am I." There is a profoundly mystical *saying* in the second collection of *Oxyrhynchus Papyri*, in which Jesus says: "Verily the Kingdom of Heaven is within you, and whoever *knoweth himself* shall find it."

[2] Matt. xxv. 31-46.

heavenly life appearing here in the midst of time, the sway of God in human hearts; it is a human society which grows on and flowers out and ripens its fruit, because its unseen roots are in God the Life.

Instead of founding a Church in the technical sense, Christ brought a little group of men and women into a personal experience of God, similar to His own, and left them baptized in a consciousness of the Spirit's presence to form the Church as the conditions and demands of different epochs and diverse lands should require. "I give unto you the keys," is said not only to Peter, but to every disciple who has reached the insight, not by flesh and blood, but by spiritual perception, that Christ is the Son of the living God—the personal realization of the life of God in a human life.[1]

The Church itself, then, as seen in its simplest conception, is a mystical fellowship, formed and gathered not by the will of man, nor schemes of flesh and blood, but by direct revelation from God to the soul. The first spiritual stone in the structure, which is to defy time and death, is a person who is *chosen* because by revelation he has discovered the Divine in the human; and with only one stone ready, Christ sees the spiritual building of the ages rising and reaching beyond the power of death. Each believer is a mystical stone. To each person who lives by his faith and vision of the Son of God the *key* is given. In a word, the authority is within the spiritual soul, and not external to it. Each member is crowned and mitred.[2]

The primitive Church, in its first stage, as it is described in Acts, was clearly a mystical fellowship, *i.e.* a fellowship bound together, not by external organization, but by the power of the experience of the Divine presence among the members. It is evident that many were drawn into the fellowship (*κοινωνία*, they called it) by their expectation of an imminent return of the Christ who, they believed, had disappeared for an interval, and would come

[1] Matt. xvi. 13-20.

[2] See Dante's *Purgatorio*, canto xxvii. lines 140-43.

soon "to restore all things" and "to give the Kingdom to Israel." But it is just as evident that there was at least a nucleus of persons in the group who were recipients of first-hand experiences of an extraordinary sort, and who lived, not on expectation, but on the actual experience of unwonted spiritual visitation.

At this stage of Christian consciousness the Holy Spirit was thought of as a power coming from without into the person. The Divine incoming was conceived as an invasion—as a mighty rushing wind—and the effects looked for were miraculous, sudden, and temporary.[1] The little group which gathered from house to house, eating their bread together in gladness and singleness of heart, lived in the borderland of ecstasy and exhibited the extraordinary phenomena which have appeared in some measure, wherever mystical groups have been formed, as we shall see in the course of this history.[2] "Speaking with tongues" was not confined to the one occasion when the little band felt the inrushing of the mighty wind. It was common in the primitive Church, and seems to have appeared wherever the first Christians went. Paul treats it in Corinthians as though it were a regular *gift*, which was to be looked for whenever the Spirit came upon men. The atmosphere was charged with wonder, and men expected incursions from the unseen world into the sphere of their daily lives.

There can be no question that these simple and unstudied accounts of the life of the primitive fellowship have played a great rôle in the history of the Church. The fellowship itself, with all things in common, the *agape* or love feast, the consciousness of Divine invasion, the expectation of the marvellous, the unconcern about the affairs of this life, the experiment to form a society governed from within and guided by ecstatic prophecy, have been in some degree repeated again and again.

[1] This view is perfectly natural. It always seems to persons who experience what may be called mystical consciousness, that the second self of which they become aware is a distinct *Other Self*, beyond the margin of their own personal life.

[2] These phenomena are due to the peculiar functioning of the central nervous system, and do not of themselves imply lofty inward spiritual experience.

The duration of the primitive fellowship, at least in its simple and mystical form, was short. The Jerusalem Church was soon organized under a visible head—James, the brother of the Lord—and the whole basis of the Church life and polity was powerfully affected by the remarkable missionary activity of Paul, and by the proclamation of what he himself called his "Gospel."[1]

II

It is possible to find in the writings of the Apostle Paul almost anything one is looking for. So universal a man was he, so deeply did he go down to the elemental springs of human life, that all the fundamental aspects of world religion are found in him. The person who comes to him with a well-defined theory can, with a little skill, generally prove by texts that *this* was Paul's "central idea," and the next person with an opposite theory can as conclusively prove that his own hobby was manifestly the "central idea of Paul." Whenever an elemental man appears in history he becomes the spiritual father of many very diverse children, and each child is apt to claim that he is the very own and only.

I shall not claim that Paul was exclusively a mystic, for that claim would be as partial and one-sided as the claim that has sometimes been made that he was exclusively a Rabbinical, scholastic theologian. But I shall maintain that there was a very marked mystical tendency in his nature, and that there is a strong mystical element in his writings. It is no straining of the facts to say that Paul's "Gospel" was deeply grounded in an immediate, personal experience of the Divine Being, who impinged upon him, invaded him, and finally became the inward principle and spirit of his very self. In a word, we have here a man whose religion was *first-hand*. I shall do little more in this short sketch than bring together the autobiographical passages, which show that he was subject to incursions from beyond the circle and margin of his

[1] "According to my Gospel," Rom. ii. 16.

own self, and that he attained a state of life in which he *felt* a unity of being with God, which made him "able to do all things."[1]

As a young man, fresh from the school of a great Rabbi, he came in contact with the strange new sect—"those of the way." Its teaching was abhorrent to him, and made him a persecutor. But the power exhibited in the lives of its saints, the assurance and triumph of its adherents whom he persecuted, the ecstatic vision and shining face of its first martyr, put goads in his soul.[2] He was aware of a dual nature within himself, for the seventh chapter of Romans has surely come out of his own actual experience. There was a dim glimmering of a new self not yet born, rising above an old self not yet dead, and nowhere could he find any "power of God," any dynamic of salvation, that would give him the victory. In this, the supreme issue of life, he felt himself defeated—"I know that in me dwelleth no good thing"; "what I would not that I do,"—and over against this continuous defeat stood the steady triumph of victory of those whom he was dragging to prison and to death. Through the closed lids of the man whom he helped to bring to martyrdom had come the vision of Christ at the right hand of God, and he had heard the vision announced in a way that burned into his soul. As he rode toward Damascus the goads became sharp within him, and suddenly the vision which had come to Stephen came to him; he too *saw* Jesus Christ. That it was an inward experience with powerful physical effects (such as often accompany mystical experiences), his own language makes almost certain. His own earliest account of it is in Galatians i. 15-16: "It pleased God to reveal His Son *in me*," and he is evidently referring to this great event in 2 Corinthians iv. 6: "God who said, 'Let light shine out of darkness,' *hath shined into our hearts* to give the light of the knowledge of the glory of God in

[1] Phil. iv. 3.

[2] See his speech before Agrippa: "It is hard for thee to kick against the goads" (Acts xxvi. 14). It is evident that his better self revolted from his course as persecutor.

the face of Jesus Christ."[1] We have, furthermore, his own testimony that the apprehension of Christ by sense is a very small matter in comparison with seeing Him inwardly and spiritually.[2]

There are other autobiographical passages which plainly show that Paul was subject to extraordinary experiences. Defending his apostleship to the Corinthians, he writes: "I will come to visions and revelations of the Lord. I knew a man in Christ above fourteen years ago (whether in the body, I cannot tell; or whether out of the body, I cannot tell: God knoweth);[3] such an one caught up to the third heaven. And I knew such a man (whether in the body, or out of the body, I cannot tell: God knoweth); how that he was caught up into paradise, and heard unspeakable words, which it is not lawful for a man to utter."[4] That this "such a man" was himself he forthwith tells us in verse 7. In his discussion of the relative importance of "speaking with tongues," he informs us that he possessed in high degree this extraordinary experience: "I speak with tongues *more than you all.*"[5] There are other indications in his epistles, strongly supported by definite passages in Acts, that he was the recipient of immediate and direct revelations of truths, whose origin he could not trace to books, or teachers, or to any human communications, and of positive practical guidance, which his own "wisdom" could not account for.

It requires no wrenching of texts to reach the conclusion that Paul was psychologically possessed of a constitution plainly adapted to experiences of an unusual sort. We have not only the extraordinary events of his sudden conversion with visual and auditory phenomena, we have not only the ecstatic experience of 2 Corinthians xii. 1 ff., which left him with his physical system permanently affected, but his entire biography is marked with similar events.

[1] The passage in 1 Cor. xv. 8, "Last of all He was seen of me also," is open to either a subjective or an objective interpretation, but there can be little doubt that he has his Damascus experience in mind.

[2] 2 Cor. v. 16.

[3] He would undoubtedly have said the same of his Damascus experience, for he wavers between the outward and the inward view.

[4] 2 Cor. xii. 1-4.

[5] 1 Cor. xiv. 18.

His first journey to Europe is motived by a "vision" which came at the close of a long strain of uncertainty. His journey from Antioch to Jerusalem to meet the apostolic fellowship and settle the basis of his own work among the Gentiles was the result of "revelation" coming after a mental tension. His "Gospel" is not a scholastic and carefully reasoned "system" of theology. It was "received" in a series of insights. His message surged up, without any conscious dialectic, from the deeps of his soul. He was eminently a person of the prophet type, speaking by inspiration, seeing with photographic intuition, and therefore never constructing a solid, consistent dogma, but producing instead a marvellous, many-sided ideal and method of life, in which are woven together all the strands of influence which shaped his own rich personal faith. Few more composite types have ever existed, and it is easy for the one-sided theorist to prove that Paul is always using the forensic conceptions of Jewish theology, or the imagery of the apocalyptic writers, or the animistic speech of popular usage, or the symbolism of the Greek mysteries, or the religious philosophy of the Hellenistic schools, or the pantheistic ideas of the Stoics, for all these elements of culture are combined in him, and are in evidence in his epistles.[1]

But it is also evident that Paul set slight value on extraordinary phenomena. His profound mysticism is not to be sought in glossolalia or in ecstatic vision. His real claim to be enrolled in the list of mystics is found in his normal experience. Over against a single experience of being "caught up into Paradise" in ecstasy, in the first stages of his Christian period, we can put the steady experience of *living* in heavenly places in Christ Jesus which characterised his mature Christian period. Over against the inrushing of a foreign power, which made his lips utter words which did not come from himself, we can put the calm but mighty transfiguration of personality which was slowly wrought in him during the fourteen years following

[1] See Pfleiderer, *Prim. Christ.* vol. i. p. 96.

his ecstasy: "With unveiled face, beholding as in a mirror the glory of the Lord, we are being transformed into the same image, from glory to glory (*i.e.* gradually) by the Spirit of the Lord."[1]

We must be very modest in making assertions about Paul's "central idea." But it is well on safe ground to say that his "Gospel" cannot be understood if one loses sight of this truth: The Christian must re-live Christ's life, by having Him formed within, as the source and power of the new life.

The autobiographical passages, to begin with his own first-hand experience, give the best illustration which we have of this normal mystical life. The earliest passage which we have comes out of the great contest with legalism. His opponents say that salvation comes through obedience to a divinely mediated and time-honoured "system" of rites and ordinances. *He* says: "Christ lives in me";[2] "I bear in my body the marks of the Lord Jesus";[3] "God hath sent forth the Spirit of His Son into our hearts, crying Abba, Father."[4] The Corinthian troubles called out another set of personal testimonies: "He hath given us the earnest of His Spirit in our hearts."[5] "We are transformed into the image of the Lord by the Spirit of the Lord."[6] "God hath shined into our hearts to give the light of the knowledge of the glory of God in the face of Jesus Christ."[7] "We are always bearing about in the body the dying of the Lord Jesus that the life also of Jesus may be seen in our body."[8] "Our inward self is renewed day by day,"[9] "If we have known Christ after the flesh, we know Him *so* no more."[10] To the Roman Christians who had not yet seen his face, he writes: "The law of the Spirit of Life in Christ Jesus hath made me free from the law of sin and death."[11] "The Spirit itself beareth witness with our spirit that we are sons of God."[12]

And finally, out of his prison in Rome he tells his

[1] 2 Cor. iii. 18. [2] Gal. ii. 20. [3] Gal. vi. 17.
[4] Gal. iv. 6. [5] 2 Cor. i. 22. [6] 2 Cor. iii. 18.
[7] 2 Cor. iv. 6. [8] 2 Cor. iv. 10. [9] 2 Cor. iv. 16.
[10] 2 Cor. v. 16. [11] Rom. viii. 2. [12] Rom. viii. 16.

Philippian friends: "For me to live is Christ,"[1] and he sets forth as the supreme attainment, the goal of hope, "to win Christ,"—which means, to "know Him (by inward experience) and the power of His resurrection and the fellowship of His sufferings, being made conformable to His death."[2]

The inward experience of a new creation, the actual formation of Christ, as the resident life within, "worked mightily" in *him*,[3] and he called everybody to a similar experience. Few words have ever borne a more touching appeal than that intimate personal call to his wavering friends in Galatia: "My little children, I am travailing in birth pains again for you until *Christ be formed in you*."[4] "As many of you as have been baptized into Christ have *put on Christ*."[5] To the Roman Christians he says: "If any man have not the Spirit of Christ, he does not belong to Him"; "*If Christ be in you*, the sinful body is dead"; "He that raised up Christ from the dead shall make your mortal bodies alive by His Spirit that dwelleth in you."[6] To the Corinthian believers he says: "He that is joined to the Lord is one Spirit with Him";[7] "Your body is a temple of the Holy Spirit which is in you";[8] "You are the body of Christ";[9] "By one Spirit we are all baptized into one body."[10] The Ephesian prayer carries us almost beyond what can be asked or thought, that "Christ may dwell in your hearts," and that "Ye may be filled to all fulness with God."[11] And the Colossian letter declares that the riches of the glory of the divine revelation is this: "Christ in you."[12]

It would be easy to multiply texts, but the mystical aspect of Paul's "Gospel" does not rest on isolated texts. It is woven into the very structure of his message. He cares not at all for the shell of religion. The survival of ceremonial practices are to him "nothing." Circumcision, which stands in his thought for the whole class of religious performances, "avails nothing." Everything turns on a "new creation." His aim is always the creation of

[1] Phil. i. 21.
[2] Phil. iii. 8-10.
[3] Col. i. 29.
[4] Gal. iv. 19.
[5] Gal. iii. 27.
[6] Rom. viii. 9-11.
[7] 1 Cor. vi. 17.
[8] 1 Cor. vi. 15 and 19.
[9] 1 Cor. xii. 27.
[10] 1 Cor. xii. 13.
[11] Eph. iii. 14-21.
[12] Col. i. 27

a "new man," the formation of the "inward man," and this "inward man" is formed, not by the practice of rite or ritual, not by the laying on of hands, but by the actual incorporation of Christ—the Divine Life—into the life of the man, in such a way that *he who is joined to the Lord is one Spirit.* Christ is resident within, and thereby produces a new spirit—a principle of power, a source of illumination, an earnest of unimagined glory.

The proof of this inwardly formed self is not ecstasy, tongue, or miracle. It is victory over the lower passions, —the flesh—and a steady manifestation of love. There are ascending stages of "spiritual gifts," *i.e.* of operations, which flow out from the new central self which Christ has formed within. Some are striking and spectacular, some seem extraordinary and "supernatural," but the best gift of all, the goal of the entire process of the Spirit, is the manifestation of love. It is "that which is perfect" and which supersedes knowledge, and tongues, and ecstatic prophecies which are "in part," and only mirror-reflections. Nobody else has ever expressed in equal perfection and beauty the fervour and enthusiasm of the initiated mystic, inspired by union with God, as Paul has expressed them in his two hymns of love—the hymn on the love of God,[1] and the hymn on the love of men.[2] Love *is* the Kingdom of God. It shows that, at length, the body has become a Temple, and that the human face and hands and feet, which move to exhibit love, are a visible façade of a holy place where God dwells. Paul's "Gospel" from beginning to end, whether his sacred word is "love" or "faith," presupposes a human person partaking of the Divine Life, which freely gives itself, and it points away to a consummation in which the Spirit and law of this Divine Life become the Spirit and law of "a new creature"—a man in whom Christ is re-lived. His "new man" is a supernatural inward creation wrought by the Spirit who is identical with Christ—"the Lord is the Spirit"—who enters into the man and becomes in him power, and life, and spiritualizing energy.

[1] Rom. viii. 31 f.   [2] 1 Cor. xiii.

III

Johannine Christianity has, by many writers, been regarded as the main source of Christian mysticism, and not infrequently the two expressions have been made synonymous, *i.e.* Christian mysticism and Johannine Christianity have been used interchangeably. It must, I think, be admitted that no other New Testament author has, to the same extent as John, made the world at large familiar with the principles of mystical religion, nor has any other furnished so many expressions which have become current coin in the mystical groups which have formed during the history of the Church. The Christianity of John has generally been taken as the type of "heart religion," a religion whose emphasis is upon inward and first-hand experience.

The fact is, however, that the term "mystic" does not as properly belong to John as to Paul. Paul's Christianity takes its rise in an inward experience, and from beginning to end the stress is upon Christ inwardly experienced and re-lived. John's emphasis is upon the Life and Work of a historical Person whose teaching and commandments are dwelt upon and urged as words of life. When he announces his own first-hand experience, it is *objective* experience: "We beheld His glory."[1] "We have seen with our eyes, and our hands have handled the manifested Word of Life."[2] The gaze turns back to a well-known Figure, and memory is busy with the face and form of Him who had, for John, been the tabernacle of God. And yet it is true that in the Fourth Gospel and the first Epistle of John we have a Christianity which is mystical, a religion, the central ideas of which are a Divine birth within, and the permanent presence of the Divine Spirit, imparting Himself to the human spirit. John's language is simpler than Paul's. The former puts the profoundest truth into a parable which may be taken at any height, according to the spiritual stature of the reader, and his

[1] John i. 14. [2] 1 John i. 1-2.

most important terms are themselves parables—"Light," "bread," "water," "seed"—and so, like the winged seeds of nature, his truths have floated across the world and germinated in multitudes of hearts, while Paul's deepest message has been missed and the world has got out of him only what the theologians formulated.

John has many ways of saying that spiritual life is the result of the incoming of God into human life. In fact, John's word, "Life," itself means always something divinely begotten. It is a type of Life, above the "natural" human life as that is above the animal, or as animal is above vegetable. It is Life "of God," or "from God"; Life "begotten of God," or "born of the Spirit." It is eternal Life, exhibited in time, and carrying within itself inexhaustible possibilities. It circulates out from God like light from a luminous body, and penetrates every person who comes into the world, but it becomes the *principle* of inward Life only for those who "receive" it by act of will, *i.e.* appropriate it by a positive response of faith.[1] I call this idea mystical because it is a direct and immediate experience by which the soul partakes of God.

No word which John uses conveys this truth better than "seed," a word, however, which he uses only once: "Whoever is born of God does not commit sin, for His seed (σπέρμα) is in him and he cannot sin because he is born of God."[2] It is a word which mystics have again and again adopted to express the implanting of the Divine Life within the human soul. It means that the *principle* by which a man lives unto God and resists the tendencies of the flesh is a Divine germ, something of God, "received" into the soul, a new life-principle which expands and becomes *the Life* of the person. The same idea is expressed in figure, by "water" and "bread"; "The water that I shall give him shall be in him a well of water springing up into everlasting life."[3] "I am the

[1] John i. 9.

[2] 1 John iii. 9. The same truth is expressed in 1 Peter i. 23: "Being born again not of corruptible seed (σπέρμα) but of incorruptible, by the word of God which liveth and abideth for ever."

[3] John iv. 14.

Bread of Life."[1] "If any man eat of this bread he shall live forever."[2] Through both figures—"you must drink me"; "you must eat me"—the profound truth is told that man enters into Life, or has Life in him, only as he partakes of God, for Christ is God in a form which man can grasp and assimilate. We are dealing with a process by which the believer takes into himself the Divine Life, and by an inward change makes it his own, so that he actually has "God abiding in him." This Lord's Supper calls for no visible elements, no consecrated priest. It calls only for a human heart, conscious of its needs, and ready to eat the Bread of God on the one momentous condition, of willing and loving what Christ wills and loves. It is actual transubstantiation, but it is not bread and wine changed to literal body and blood of Christ. It is finite human spirit feeding upon the bread and water of God—that is, upon God expressed to us in terms which fit our elemental human needs—and so being transformed into that very Divine Life itself: "As the living Father sent me, and I live because of the Father, so he that eateth me, he also shall live because of me." Indeed it is a "hard saying," for it takes us beyond all ordinary biology, beyond all traditional theology, and brings us to a new level of Life altogether—human life fed from within with the Life of God, and this is "Eternal Life."[3]

I shall speak of only one more aspect of John's mysticism, namely that of mystical union. It is now a well-known fact that "isolated" personality is an abstraction. Nobody can live absolutely unto himself. He who is to enjoy the privileges of personality must be conjunct with others. He must be an organic member in a social group, and share himself with his fellows. Christ shows that this truth which we know as a human principle is also

[1] John vi. 35-63.

[2] John vi. 35-63.

[3] Many modern scholars find in the sixth chapter of John evidence of the late authorship of the book. They suppose that it was written after the Lord's Supper had come to be thought of as a mystical Sacrament, an actual partaking of the Body and Blood of Christ, and they feel that in the light of the developed practice of the Sacrament the writer has consciously or unconsciously expanded a simple discourse of Christ into this final form. I am rather disposed to take it as a genuine saying and to see in it the utterance of a fundamental principle of spiritual life.

true of the Divine Life. God becomes conjunct with those who, by faith and love, and the practice of His will, *abide* in Him. The Divine-human conjunct Life is illustrated in the figure of the Vine and its branches.[1] The branch is a branch because it is in the vine, and the vine is a vine because it has branches. They share a common sap, and live by a common circulation. It is a parable of an organic union of God and men, an interrelation by which believers live in God and God expresses Himself through them—the Divine Life circulating through all who are incorporate with the Central Stock.

The great prayer of John xvii. drops figures and utters the naked truth of a Divine-human fellowship—a union of spiritual beings with a spiritual Head,

> "Two distincts, division none,
> Number there in love is slain."

We are here beyond the competitive basis of self-seeking individuals. The law is now each for other—"all mine are thine, and thine are mine." The very condition and basis of such a self-denying fellowship is incorporation in the Divine Life: "I in them, thou in me, that they may be made perfect in one." This is the Divine event towards which all true mystical Christianity moves.

[1] John xv.

CHAPTER II

MINISTRY AND ORGANIZATION IN THE EARLY CHURCH

ALL our New Testament sources [1] make plain the fact that in the first period "those of the way," to use the earliest name for the followers of Christ, formed a *fellowship* rather than a Church in the modern sense. In fact the writer of Acts has used this word "fellowship" (*κοινωνία*) to describe the group of Jerusalem Christians. The principle of union or fellowship was devotion to Christ, a belief in His Messiahship, a vivid expectation of his speedy return, and a consciousness of the continued presence of His Spirit. It was primarily fellowship with the Lord, whose presence, though invisible, made out of separate individuals one Church: "For in one Spirit were we all baptized into one body, and were all made to drink of one Spirit." [2] Christ Himself had promised, in a striking "saying," that His mystical presence should bind His believers into a living fellowship: "Where two or three are gathered together in My name, there am I in the midst of them." [3]

Each local church, in Paul's conception, was a body of which Christ was the living Soul and governing Head, while each particular member was "called to be a saint,"

[1] The earliest sources for an historical picture of the primitive Church are Paul's Epistles. The word "Church" is found in two sayings of Jesus, and the Book of Acts, though written considerably later than Paul's Epistles, throws much light both upon the character of the Jerusalem Church and upon the development of the Pauline churches, especially the one at Antioch, where the name "Christian" originated.

[2] 1 Cor. xii. 13. "In the earliest period the basis of Christian fellowship was a changed life. . . . It was the unity of a common relation to a common ideal and a common hope." Hatch, *The Organization of the Early Christian Churches*, p. 187.

[3] Matt. xviii. 20.

an actual habitation of the Spirit.[1] Each little society, thus vivified and dynamized by the streams of Life from above, was like "a tiny island in a sea of paganism." The visible bond of fellowship was a common meal together—in the earliest period a social meal, to which each member contributed his share. It was at first eaten from house to house and later in some central meeting-place. It was an occasion of joy and gladness—at its best a veritable love feast, an *agape*. Even in this common meal there was more than human fellowship. It was the Lord's Supper, and the partakers felt in a simple, mystical way that they were eating with Him and of Him.[2]

One characteristic feature of the Church in the early apostolic days was the consciousness of the believers that they were possessed and endowed by the Holy Spirit. The mysterious manifestation of tongues, the miracles which were worked among them and through them, the fact that they all felt themselves possessed with powers beyond their own—these things were unmistakable signs to them that the Spirit of God had come upon them in an unusual degree.

But an even more convincing proof of the Divine Presence—more convincing, at least, to the highest minds among them—was the directing and controlling power of the Holy Spirit in the ordinary religious exercises of the Church. While the high tide of the Pentecostal enthusiasm lasted, the meetings of the Church were extraordinary occasions. There was no machinery, no routine. An organization existed at all only so far as the life of the Church itself produced it; it was elastic and adjustable, and as fluid as the inward life of the Church itself.[3] Every believer was an organ of the Spirit, and every form of the manifestation of religious life, at least in the Pauline circle, was thought of as a direct *gift* of the

[1] For an illustration of the way in which Paul assumed the presence of Christ in a Church, see 1 Cor. v. 4.

[2] See 1 Cor. x. 16, 17. "The bread which we break is it not a communion of the body of Christ."

[3] The only officials we hear of in the earliest period of the Jerusalem Church are a committee of seven to distribute the supplies.

Divine Spirit. It was a central idea of Paul that "he that is joined to the Lord is one spirit" and so a partaker of Divine power and heavenly wisdom. To be of Christ's *way* was to become a spiritual organ of some sort, a person with a gift of some kind and some degree.[1] The ideal of the Church in the early apostolic days was unmistakably an organic fellowship of persons who were mutually helpful because they were all living in a common Divine Life.

Many of the earliest churches were "house-churches."[2] The believers frequently met in the house of some prominent member, and, until the fellowship grew too large for it, the meetings were held, and the common meal was eaten, in the large family room of a private house. The earliest church-buildings, as excavations are proving, were even modelled on the plan of the large audience hall of the wealthy burgher, and the earliest liturgies direct mothers when to take up their babies.[3] But it is a still more important fact that the Church itself was to a large degree modelled on the idea of the family group. The leaders in this primitive Church were not "officials" in the technical sense; they were persons who had influence and authority by reason of their age and spiritual qualifications, as a father has in his home. The "differences" of the members were not to be settled in Roman law courts but rather within the fellowship itself, as family "differences" were settled.[4]

There were of course from the first some who were peculiarly gifted, and they naturally came to the front. The apostles were for many reasons pre-eminent in whatever community they found themselves. They spoke with the authority which one who has seen and heard and handled always possesses. But they appear never to have had any authority beyond that which attached by right to their spiritual gifts and qualifications. The same can be said of the prophets and teachers, the evangelists

[1] "Unto each one of us was the grace given according to the measure of the gift of Christ" (Eph. iv. 7.)

[2] See Lindsay's *Church and Ministry in the Early Centuries*, chap. ii.

[3] Lindsay, p. 43.

[4] See 1 Cor. vi.

and pastors which appear in Paul's list of "gifts."[1] They are not officials—they are simply gifted members who are qualified for the work of "perfecting saints," and who edify the body, because in a peculiar way they make themselves channels for the Spirit. They are not elected officers; they are living personalities. Everywhere in Paul's writings (exclusive of Timothy and Titus) we find a Church composed of spiritual priests, a fellowship of brothers and equals in the faith—each person contributing, according to the measure of his gifts, to the life and power of the whole. Throughout the apostolic period leadership depended on edifying *service*, and capacity for service of every sort was considered a "gift" of the Spirit. All the names, which in a later time became official titles, were, at the period of which I am speaking, the names of "gifts." There was no laity; there was no clergy, and if the sense of the presence of the Holy Spirit, which filled the lives of the first Christians, had lasted, there never would have been a distinction of clergy and laity.

The most extraordinary of these "gifts," and the one placed by Paul next after the "apostolic gift," was that of the prophet. The New Testament prophet was a person gifted with an immediate revelation of the mind of the Spirit for the congregation. He was first and foremost a *revealer*, who uttered, by inspiration, truths which lay beyond the ken of his listeners, but which came with a conviction of reality when they were heard. The prophet's chief qualification was *vision*, rather than logical power or learning. He was a person who *saw* the way along which the Spirit wished individuals and the Church to go, but he was not a foreteller of events, or at least only rarely so. His speaking was apparently unpremeditated—a rapturous utterance, as though a power not himself were using him as a vehicle of communication.

Wherever Christianity went in the apostolic period there seems to have been an outbreaking of the spirit of prophecy. It was not confined to men, though the prophecy of women was apparently not encouraged. But

[1] 1 Cor. xii. 28-29; Eph. iv. 11.

there was a height of enthusiasm, a quality of faith, and a contagion of the Spirit which undoubtedly carried both men and women beyond their normal powers, and which resulted, so long as the flood was on, in an uninterrupted succession of prophecy, and this prophetic ministry was one of the great creative agencies in the formation and development of the early Church. Paul himself, from his own experience, has given us an impressive account of the power of this type of ministry: "If all prophesy, and if there come in an unbelieving person, or an unlearned one, he is convicted by all, he is judged by all; the secrets of his heart are made manifest, and so he will fall down on his face and worship God, declaring that God is among you."[1]

There were from the nature of the case dangers in this prophetic ministry. Enthusiasm always carries men up to the perilous edge. The difficulty is to unite calm judgment and balance with this subliminal activity and creative energy. So long as there was a high degree of spiritual life in the congregation, the prophet was "kept in his place" by the controlling power and common wisdom of the group. The spirit of a prophet was subject to the prophets.[2] There was a corresponding "gift of discernment" in the people, by which the prophet's message was tested. As this spiritual insight waned, many curious tests were formulated to "try" the prophets. "The Teaching of the Twelve Apostles" says:[3] "Not every one that speaketh in the Spirit is a prophet, but *only if he have the behaviour, or ways, of the Lord*,"[4] which is an excellent test. The "Didache," however, goes on to offer other tests: "No prophet that orders a table in the Spirit eats of it (himself) unless he is a false prophet"; "And every prophet who teaches the truth, if he does not practise what he teaches is a false prophet"; "Whoever says in the spirit: Give me money or any other thing,

[1] 1 Cor. xiv. 24-25.

[2] 1 Cor. xvi. 32.

[3] "The Teaching of the Twelve Apostles," often called, from the first Greek word of its title, the *Didache*, was discovered in Constantinople in 1873. It is one of the earliest and most valuable documents, outside the New Testament canon, for a study of the character and organization of the early churches.

[4] "Teaching," xi. 8.

ye shall not listen to him."[1] It is evident that by this time the waters of prophecy were beginning to run low.

The best example we have of early prophecy is our Book of *Revelation*, or The Apocalypse. The writer of it was in the Spirit, *i.e.* in ecstasy, on the Lord's day, and was granted a series of visions for the Churches. He does not speak as a man, in his own name or authority. His human personality is passive and merely transmissive. The real author is the Spirit, and what comes is a "revelation."[2]

While prophecy was at its height there was no fixed and rigid organization in the Church. It was held together by inspired personalities and not by officials. There was at least in the Corinthian circle an untrammelled liberty, and Paul declares, as a permanent principle, that "where the Spirit of the Lord is there is liberty." The one principle of restraint which Paul lays down is that every gift shall be exercised so as to *edify* believers and to construct the Church.[3] A Christian Church at this period, in so far as it had expanded beyond the family group, was a self-governing republic. The influences which came from without the local Church were suggestive and hortatory, not mandatory. There was plainly a peripatetic, or itinerant, ministry, which played a great part in the development of the Churches. The apostles "planted" and gave the little groups, or fellowships, their ideals, but under the Spirit, and, with the advice of the apostolic evangelist, they formed their own organization and worked out their own destiny.

Before considering the causes which led to the differentiation of a class of professional officials, we must consider first the persons who came the nearest to being officials in the primitive Church, namely, the bishops, presbyters, and deacons. Paul never uses any of these terms before the Philippian epistle. He alludes to the local ministers in Thessalonians as "those who labour among you," and

[1] "Teaching," xi. 9-12.

[2] See Wernle, *Beginnings of Christianity*, vol. i. p. 360.

[3] That principle would, if applied strictly, soon limit the exercises and work out a survival of the fittest.

"those who are over you in the Lord."[1] The Epistle to the Romans enumerates many kinds of ministry, but no technical terms are used to designate settled officials.[2] Philippians, however, makes use of two terms for local ministers which were destined to have a remarkable history. The words are, "To the saints in Christ Jesus, which are at Philippi with the Bishops and Deacons."[3] There is every reason for concluding that when this epistle was written these terms were used in a general way for the persons in the church who were especially gifted in guiding affairs, *i.e.* "overseeing" and in "serving" (which is the root meaning of *διακονία*). The names are not yet titles. Paul himself nowhere uses the term "presbyters" or "elders," though in the accounts which the Book of Acts gives of the founding of the Pauline Churches, Paul is everywhere represented as ordaining presbyters.[4] The difference between the accounts in Acts and the state of things revealed in Paul's own letters has always been felt to be a real difficulty. But the solution seems fairly easy. Those who are called "overseers" and "helpers" by Paul, *i.e.* those who were marked out as distinctively gifted for governing and ministering in the new Churches, would for the most part be those who were literally "elders"—the older members. So that during Paul's lifetime "overseers" and "elders" were synonymous terms, and "deacon" was a term used for less important helpers in the affairs of the Church. But when Acts was written, the word "presbyter" was already crystallizing into an official title, and is generally used in this book to designate the governing officials of the Church, who in chap. xx. 28 are also called "overseers," as if the two terms meant much the same thing.[5]

The word "pastor" is used in the letter to the Ephesians, but here again in a general and untechnical

[1] 1 Thess. v. 12.
[2] Rom. xii. 6-8.
[3] Phil. i. 1.
[4] The writer of Acts, looking back from his later standpoint, and viewing the natural growth and development in the Pauline Churches regarded it all as due to the direct appointment of Paul.
[5] See Hatch, *op. cit.* Lecture II., and A. V. G. Allen's *Christian Institutions*, chaps. iii. and vi.

sense, suggesting the duty of "feeding the flock," which had also been emphasized in Paul's farewell to the elders of Ephesus.[1] This word did not, however, become an official term in the early Church, because the bishop rapidly absorbed into himself all the functions which found expression in Paul's enumeration of gifts, and there was no place left for the ministry of a separate "pastor."

As soon as we turn to the Pastoral Epistles we are in another world—the entire situation has changed. The period of free, spontaneous, uprushing, spiritual life has passed away. The prophet with his message freshly breathed by the Holy Spirit has wellnigh disappeared, and the writers of these Epistles are busy with problems of organization and discipline. The "teacher," who was a person of importance in the early apostolic churches has fallen into disrepute (see especially I Tim.). Error, heresy, "false teaching," are the things which most concern the writer of First and Second Timothy and Titus.[2] The way out of these dangers seemed to the builders of the Church in that age to be the establishment of an authoritative hierarchy. The bishop here appears as a technical official, whose business it is to rule the Church and to teach as a pastor, and above everything he is to preserve untainted the faith which has been delivered. The Second and Third Epistles of John reveal a similar situation. In these Epistles the presbyter is an authoritative person, and Church organization is pretty well fixed.

We come now to the question why this free, spontaneous, enthusiastic Christianity, which we have been studying, changed into an ecclesiastical system? Why did this inward, spiritual faith—faith which was the immediate response of the soul to a Person—change into a *doctrine* which is henceforth called "the faith?" Why did the prophet speaking by revelation yield to the bishop ruling with authority?

[1] "Take heed to all the flock over which the Holy Spirit has made you overseers to feed the Church of the Lord which He purchased with His own blood" (Acts xx. 28).

[2] It is difficult to believe that the "Pastoral Epistles," often ascribed to Paul, can have been written at least in their entirety in his lifetime.

It would require an entire volume to write the answer. I can only roughly outline the reasons in this brief chapter:—

1. There is a fundamental principle of *habit*, both in individuals and in society, which always tends to organize any movement whatever into a fixed form of expression.

2. Christianity had to work itself out through the prevailing ideas of the world in which it was planted. It had to meet the Hellenic spirit and the Roman genius. It could satisfy the Greek only by developing a thought system. It could win the Roman only by the exhibition of an ecclesiastical system, suited to his genius for law and organization.

3. As time went on, prophecy itself degenerated, inspiration ran dry. Prophetic ministry grew weak and poor and "second-hand." The conviction of a direct fellowship with Christ waned. Little men, claiming infallible guidance, proved a menace, where men of the first rank in the preceding period had been creative. People began to be suspicious that under a claim of Divine inspiration prophets were uttering their own words and voicing their own wishes. Many of the prophets, too, fell below the lofty moral standard which befitted a prophet. An itinerant ministry of prophets had its dangers and difficulties.[1]

4. The fading away of the glowing expectation of an imminent return of Christ had much to do with the change which occurred in the character of the Church. While that expectation lasted it fused the Christian members together, and they saw no need of elaborate organization, but as this faith faded away they had to prepare for the work of the world.

5. The sacraments became indispensable rites by which Divine grace was believed to be mysteriously and magically conveyed, and as this view developed, the importance of the officials who administered them increased.

6. The early Church, even before it lost its first leaders,

[1] The reader will find plenty of confirmation of the above position in "The Teaching of the Twelve Apostles" and in "The Shepherd of Hermas."

was forced to meet a drift, or wave, of speculation which threatened to swamp the ship at the very beginning of its voyage.[1] The Church saw no way to meet this speculation except with a doctrine buttressed by hierarchical authority.

There are four great documents out of the early post-apostolic period, *i.e.* belonging to the first half of the second century, which show the gradual development of an official priesthood and the steady waning of the fundamental idea of the apostolic Church—the priesthood of believers, the ministry of "gifts." These documents are the Epistle of Clement of Rome to the Corinthians, "The Didache," or "Teaching of the Apostles," "The Shepherd of Hermas," and the Epistles of Ignatius. Clement, writing about the year 100, already makes the Jewish priesthood the analogy for the Christian, and he already speaks of the laymen as a class distinct from the ministers or priests. He declares that the Old Testament gives warrant for the system of bishops and deacons, and in confirmation he quotes Isaiah lx. 17, "I will appoint their bishops in righteousness and their deacons in faith."[2] His epistle is written to further the establishment of Church organization. Already the idea of the Church as a spiritual fellowship, a congregation of persons inspired by the invisible Christ, was yielding to the idea of a Church which was founded by Christ, and left in the care of vicars, whose authority came by ordination.

"The Shepherd of Hermas"[3] shows that the change was not effected without struggle. The old contest between prophet and priest, which ended so tragically in later Hebrew history, was repeated in the formative period of the Christian Church, with the same result—the suppression of the prophet. The author of "The Shepherd of Hermas" belongs to the order of the prophets. He makes known the will of God for the times, not

[1] I refer of course to Gnosticism.

[2] Epistle of Clement, chap. xlii.

[3] This is an allegory, or religious romance, written probably very early in the second century. It speaks of all the apostles as already dead (Sim. ix. 16), and it is quoted by Irenaeus (who lived between A.D. 120 and 200) as though it were Scripture. Harnack dates it between A.D. 140 and 145.

by reasoning or speculation, but by inward revelation. He has a series of "visions" for the illumination of the Church. His sympathies are with those who speak, not because they are appointed to speak, but because the Holy Ghost wishes to speak through them. He has discovered that "those who preside over the Church love the first seats," and even sometimes "plunder widows and orphans of their livelihood, and gain possessions for themselves from the ministry which they have received." "I speak" (the Church personified as a very old woman is speaking to him in a vision), "I speak unto you, the leaders and presidents of the Church, be ye not like unto sorcerers; for sorcerers carry their drugs in boxes, but you carry your drug and your poison in your hearts; ye are hardened and will not cleanse your hearts nor purify your minds in unity of spirit."[1] But it is clear through his pages that the prophets are dying out, and that the ordained priests are gaining the ascendancy.

There is every indication that the "Teaching of the Twelve Apostles" is a very early document, and that it comes out of a period, or at least a locality, in which the ministry was still fluid and the organization not rigidly formed.[2] The apostle and prophet and inspired teacher still have a dignified standing, and yet careful provision is also made for the more professional officials. The prophet's claim to inspiration is to be carefully sifted. We come across amusing tests for discerning the false and the true apostle and prophet, of which the following is a good example:

> "Every apostle who cometh to you, let him be received as the Lord; but he shall not remain more than one day; if, however, it need be, then the next day; but if he remains three days, he is a false prophet. When the apostle departeth let him take nothing except bread enough till he lodge again; but if he ask money he is a false prophet."
>
> "Whoever, in the Spirit, says, 'Give me money, or something

[1] Vision II. chap. ix.

[2] It does not seem probable that the "Teaching" can have been written later than A.D. 120. For the reasons for this conclusion see *Teaching of the Twelve Apostles*, edited by Hitchcock and Brown (London, 1885), Introduction, pp. xc.-xcix.

else,' ye shall not hear him; but if for others in need he bids you give, let no one judge him."[1]

The account goes on to deal with the case of the prophet who is not itinerant:

"But every true prophet who will settle among you is worthy of his support ('likewise the true teacher'). Every first fruit, then, of the products of the winepress or of the threshing floor, of oxen and of sheep, thou shalt take and give to the prophets; *for they are your high priests.* But if ye have no prophet, give it to the poor."[2]

The condition of the Church out of which this document came seems to have been such that a free, spontaneous ministry existed side by side with a system of Church officials who were to give large place for the prophet if he proved to be genuinely sent. The Church may appoint, as occasion requires, bishops and deacons, who apparently are to perform both the functions of governing the Church and of ministering to it as pastors.

"Now appoint for yourselves bishops and deacons worthy of the Lord, men meek and not avaricious, upright and proved; for they too render you the service of the prophets and teachers. . . . They are to be honoured of you, together with the prophets and teachers."[3]

It should be noted that up to this time there is a plurality of bishops in each Church, and the single bishop as head and pastor of the local flock has not yet appeared, either in practice or as the ideal for the Church.

When we pass over to the Epistles of Ignatius we leave prophets and inspired teachers in the dim background, for the entire stress of this impassioned man, who writes on his way to die in the Roman arena, is upon the establishment of the single bishop as the authoritative minister and head of the local Church.[4] Ignatius was

[1] "Teaching," chap. xi. [2] *Ibid.* chap. xiii. [3] *Ibid.* chap. xv.

[4] Ignatius' life and work is, as Westcott says, "enveloped in pitchy darkness." He was condemned to death in Antioch and sentenced to be exposed to beasts in the amphitheatre at Rome. The sentence was executed, as Westcott thinks, about A.D. 110. The seven Epistles believed to be genuine are: To the Ephesians; To the Magnesians; To the Trallians; To the Romans; To the Philadelphians; To the Smyrnaeans; To Polycarp. They were written on the journey from Antioch to Rome.

possessed of a passion to leave behind him an authoritatively organized Church. He had no faith that a body gathered together on the loose basis of brotherhood and fellowship and obedience to an invisible Head could survive in the midst of chaotic beliefs and growing heresies. He puts the bishop—who, according to his conception, is to be the head of the local Church—in the place of Christ. He even says, "Your bishop presides in the place of God."[1] And again: "Ye are subject to the bishop as to Jesus Christ."[2] Again: "Reverence the deacons as appointed by Jesus Christ, and the bishop *as* Jesus Christ."[3] He writes to the Philadelphians that, "the *Spirit proclaims these words*, 'Do nothing without the bishop.'"[4]

It takes little study of Ignatius to see that the thing which has raised the professional minister—*i.e.* the bishop—to such importance in the mind of Ignatius was the great importance which he attached to the sacrament of the Lord's Supper. Already, even as early as the first quarter of the second century, the sacramental bread is called "the medicine of immortality";[5] baptism is the medicinal bath of regeneration. It was vain to expect to maintain a spiritually conceived ministry when the loftiest figure in the Church had already laid the foundation for the substitution of an incomprehensible magic in place of the direct work of the Divine Spirit upon the human soul. It is a long way from Paul's conception of the believer as a living temple of the Holy Spirit to the belief that spiritual life is imparted in a magical way to those who eat the Lord's Supper at the hands of a divinely appointed priest who has taken the place of the absent Christ—but all that transformation came in one century.[6] As soon as the celebration of the Supper became the central point in worship there was no longer any possibility of maintaining the old order of a spiritually-directed community.

[1] Magnesians, chap. vi.
[2] Trallians, chap. ii.
[3] Trallians, chap. iii.
[4] Phil. chap. vii.
[5] Ephesians, chap. xx.
[6] It is not likely that the bishop was yet *explicitly* thought of as invested through his ordination with mysterious and miraculous power, as came to be the case in the third century.

A visible head was now a necessity. Note the logic of Ignatius: "There is but one Eucharist. For there is one flesh, and one cup into the unity of His blood; one altar, as there is one bishop."[1] "Let there be a proper Eucharist which is administered by the bishop, or by one to whom he has entrusted it." . . . "It is not lawful without the bishop either to baptize or to celebrate a love feast."[2]

Another influence which counted for almost more than did this exaggerated importance of the sacrament toward the complete change of the ministry, and the elevation of the minister to a priest with Divine authority, was the necessity which came upon the Church of dealing authoritatively with false doctrine. This tendency to formulate a fixed doctrine is already decidedly apparent in the Pastoral Epistles. Faith was beginning to be regarded as a definite body of doctrine to be held and handed on. The original idea of faith as the heart's attachment, and the obedience of the will, to Christ, was passing away and giving place to the lower view. Then, as in every age since, there were men who taught doctrine which did not ring true to the ears of those who were fighting the battles of the faith. The second century was remarkably prolific in speculation. New ideas sprang up like mushrooms. The air was full of fantastic theories. While the Church was still in its swaddling clothes it found itself in a life-and-death struggle with gnosticism. It was one of the most serious enemies which has ever confronted Christianity. It was certainly a part of the intellectual environment when the two Epistles to Timothy were written, and we hear already of the dangerous "*gnosis*, falsely so called."[3] How should this and kindred heresies

[1] Philadelphians, chap. iv. [2] Smyrnaeans, chap. viii.

[3] It is difficult to decide when Gnosticism first appeared in the Christian field, but Christianity is face to face with it in the Pastoral Epistles. For actual origin it goes back to the amalgamation of the religions of Babylonia and Persia after the conquests of Alexander. The world of Light, of Persian religion, became the "Pleroma" of the Gnostics, and the planetary gods of the Babylonian religion became the *aeons* of the descending emanations down to the lower, material world, so that it was from the beginning a purely dualistic system. It was an intellectual construction out of mythologies. There were many phases and types of Gnostic doctrine, not *one* consistent and orthodox form of it. It borrowed from Christianity a colouring and some ideas, but it remained throughout a form of

be met? was the problem. By the proclamation of the truth and the power of the light, Christ would have said. By the demonstration and power of the everliving Spirit, and by teaching and argument, Paul would have said. But already faith in the conquering power of the Spirit was dying out. Christians did not dare to rest their case on the mere announcement of truth which rested solely on their heart's conviction of its truth. They fell back to the basis of official authority and the authority of tradition. "The faith" assumed the importance of a fetish. It was the sacred thing which had come to the world from the heavens. Christ had tented among men for a few brief years, but the tent was folded and He was gone. But the one communication which God had made through Him was in the hands of the Church. The possession of it, they believed, made the Church a Church. Now, how could it be kept absolutely pure and unchanged in a world where error and heresy were as thick as thistle-down in the early summer? A way to accomplish that must be found.

The authoritative clergy seemed the only way. The appeal was first made to the authority of the apostles. But the apostles were mortal, and when they were dead it was possible to interpret their writings in diverse ways. There could be no ground of certainty unless there was somebody still in the Church who could speak with the same authority that the apostles possessed, and who could

thought. For the most part the Gnostic based his "knowledge" on the literature of revelation and mythology, which he interpreted by the allegorical method.

The main ideas of the movement may be summarized as follows:—

1. God is above all thought, and therefore an unknown and unknowable God, who is the *Pleroma*, or fulness.

2. Between this unknowable God and the visible universe there is a chain of spiritual beings—a descending hierarchy called *æons*. They are emanations from the *Pleroma*. The Jehovah of the Old Testament is only one of these *aeons*, and not God Himself.

3. There is an absolute dualism between good and evil. Good has its source in Spirit; evil is inherent in matter. This world of matter is the realm of evil, or Satan's world. Redemption can come only by enlightenment, which comes down from God by means of the *aeons*. Christ in some of the systems is one of these *aeons*.

4. The basis of their morality was asceticism, escape from evil matter, and particularly from body. For an exhaustive study of the movement see Bousset's *Hauptprobleme der Gnosis*, Göttingen, 1907.

guarantee that the doctrine of the Church had come down unchanged. Already in Irenaeus, who died at the end of the second century, we are told that "truth has come down by means of the succession of the bishops." When the Church emerged from its battle with Gnosticism the bishop was supreme, and the idea of his succession in the apostolic line was well established, and with it the view that faith is the deposit of truth received through the apostles and preserved by the hierarchy of the Church.[1]

There was, however, one great uprising during the first three centuries against the officialism and ecclesiasticism which was slowly taking the place of the immediate working of the Holy Spirit, and which was banishing the prophet and spiritual teacher from the Church.[2] There is some evidence that, in spite of the remarkable growth of the power and authority of the hierarchy, there still was, throughout the second century, a sporadic lay ministry and groups of persons who held for prophecy against priesthood. But one sees at once how difficult it would be for both to live in the same house. What is to happen if a prophet speaking with the inspiration of God conflicts with a priest who has the inherited authority of an apostle? How shall the Church exercises be orderly if the entire administration of worship may at any time be interrupted by the voice of a prophet who has received a message? The Apostolic Constitutions were apparently written to settle the final authority upon the clergy. Here is a passage from Book III. chap. x.: "We do not permit the laity to perform any of the offices belonging to the priesthood, as, for instance, neither the sacrifice, nor baptism, nor laying on of hands . . . for no one taketh this honour to himself but he that is called of God. A person who seizes upon such an office himself shall undergo the punishment of Uzziah." The punishment of Korah is also cited.

1 "The conception of a mutilated sacerdotalism, where one part of the Christian worship is alone thought of as the true sacrifice, and a small portion of the fellowship, the ministry, is declared to be the priesthood, did not appear until the time of Cyprian, and was his invention" (Lindsay, p. 37).

2 I shall study this uprising, under the title of Montanism, in the next chapter.

It needs but a word in conclusion. The Church became an ecclesiastic system, an order of priests, because men lost the experience of and faith in the continued presence of Christ through the Holy Spirit. So long as Christians knew that they were living and moving and having their being in God, they were all possessed of gifts, and they all had something to share. As soon as the sense of the Divine presence vanished from men's hearts, the religion which Christ had initiated underwent a complete transformation. Magic and mystery took the place of the free personal communication. The real presence of Christ was sought in the bread and wine and in the bath of regeneration, rather than within the soul itself. With this change of faith the administration of these rites became supremely important. Once the "Lord's Supper" had been a common joyous meal, now it became a mysterious rite by which immortality was imparted. Once faith had been the soul's response to a Divine Presence. Now it became the acceptance of a communication once delivered to men and passed on through a regularly ordained line. As faith changed to a deposit of doctrine, and as the Supper became a magic rite, the authoritative official became a necessity.

CHAPTER III

MONTANISM: A RETURN TO PROPHECY

WE saw in the last chapter the beginnings of tendencies which finally formed the imperial system of the Catholic Church. By gradual, but irresistible, movements — sometimes an unconscious drift, sometimes a purpose clearly conceived — the entire nature of Christianity underwent transformation. The simple fellowship of believers, held together by a common trust in Christ, their living Head, changed into a "sacred" and rigid ecclesiastical organization, which became the indispensable mediator of salvation. Faith, which at first was inward trust and immediate response to Christ, was turned into "the faith," which became a formulated set of doctrines, a fixed "deposit" of truth, the dogma of orthodoxy. The meal of love and fellowship, eaten in joyous memory of Christ's redeeming love and sacrifice, grew, partly under pagan influences, into a mysterious magical rite in which Christ's actual body and blood were believed to be miraculously reproduced and "sacrificed" on a priestly altar. The free and spontaneous exercise of spiritual "gifts" in the church-fellowship gave place to a new priesthood working under an inflexible system of form and ritual. Even before the third century opened the Church had begun to draw a sharp distinction between the epoch, or dispensation, of *revelation*, and all later, less divine epochs. The first period was set apart in an order all by itself as an unapproachable ideal. That extraordinary nearness of God, which the apostles knew, was regarded as a brief temporal span of excessive light, with darkness before it and twilight after it. The then present age was connected with this peculiar epoch of revelation by the line of bishops, and by holy Scripture, which was already coming to be thought of as *the* instrument of divine communication.[1]

But these momentous changes were not effected without protest and reaction. Our literary remains from the second century are too meagre to show conclusively that there was a continuous, even though slender, stream of simple, apostolic Christianity carrying steadily on the ideas and the spirit of the first epoch; but there are many internal indications in the literature which we possess that, at least in some districts, a Christianity something like that of the early days persisted. There were many, in districts remote from the large cities, who were "old-fashioned," and who clung to the freer ways which the traditions of country localities preserved. There was, however, no current of primitive faith sufficient to stem the steadily waxing power of ecclesiastical Christianity. In the middle of the second century, with the suddenness almost of a new Pentecost, a movement of reaction was inaugurated and a return to the supremacy of the prophet as against the priest attempted. The movement originated in Phrygia, not far from the region of Paul's Galatian churches, and it was started by a man named Montanus,[2] who is said to have been a native of Ardaban, in Phrygia, and who is reported, by those who denounced his prophecies, to have had an ante-Christian period when he was a pagan priest—possibly, as epithets imply, a priest of Cybele. The movement spread through Asia Minor with the rapidity of contagion. There was a sibylline strain in these simple, naive, rural people which made them ready for religious fervour and ecstatic visions, and entire communities received the new prophets with en-

[1] The "new prophecy" of Montanism had a decided influence in hastening the formation of the New Testament canon, as a fixed and final revelation (see Harnack's *History of Dogma*, vol. ii. p. 108).

[2] Those who took up the "new prophecy" are variously called "Montanists," "Kataphrygians," and "Priscillianians." Eusebius has preserved a contemporary account by an anonymous but very violent anti-Montanist (Eusebius, *Church History*, v. 16).

thusiasm. The movement first came to the attention of the Western Church in the year 177, when the Roman Bishop supported the Phrygian authorities in their condemnation of the new prophecy,[1] and it probably *arose* about the opening of that decade. Its spread, however, was not checked by opposition. It appealed powerfully to the common people, and it won to its support the greatest exponent of Christianity of that period, namely Tertullian (born about 145, died 220), whose writings give us about the only sympathetic account of the movement that has come down to us. It gathered a large following in North Africa where Tertullian lived, and it also developed strong centres of influence in Europe. Some scholars are inclined to make a pretty marked distinction between earlier and later Montanism, that is (1) the Montanism of "first-hand" prophecy, and (2) the Montanism which was content to accept at second-hand the "oracles" of the Montanist prophets who had spoken a generation or more earlier. This distinction is, however, true of all movements of a similar type in the history of the Church.

Montanism did not introduce new doctrines; it was not a new conception of God, nor of the world, nor of salvation. It was rather an attempt to realise in the Church the promise of Christ that the Paraclete should come to lead men into all truth and to enable them to do *greater things* than He did.[2] In the spirit of the Hebrew prophets they raised to a point of intensity the passion for purity and holiness in the people of God, and with this passion they joined a vivid expectation of the annihilation of the wicked pagan world by the miraculous arrival of the New Jerusalem from heaven.

Montanus was evidently a man subject to trance and

[1] The Bishop of Rome was at first on the point of recognizing the Montanists as in true and full communion with the Church, but he was influenced against them, according to Tertullian, by the false reports of a certain Praxeas (see Tertullian's *Treatise against Praxeas*).

[2] The Montanists took this promise in its naked literalness. There is a passage in a treatise, falsely ascribed to Tertullian, which says: "The Paraclete has revealed greater things through Montanus than Christ revealed through the Gospel" (*Pseudo-Tertullian*, 52).

ecstasy, and it is more than probable that his emphasis on the importance of ecstatic prophecy had its basis in personal experience—in the discovery, by an immediate experience, of unusual and extraordinary powers within himself. The anonymous opponent of the movement reported in Eusebius says of Montanus: "He became beside himself, and being suddenly in a sort of frenzy and ecstasy he raved and began to babble and utter strange things, *prophesying in a manner contrary to the constant custom of the Church*, handed down by tradition from the beginning."[1] This is evidently written with hostile animus, but it seems fairly certain that the fact of ecstasy is not fabricated, as it fits the teaching of Montanus.[2]

Among the few brief sayings of Montanus which have been preserved, there is one which gives his conception of prophecy so plainly that it is impossible to miss his meaning. "Man," he says, "is like a lyre, and I [the Holy Spirit] play on him like a plectrum [stick with which the lyre is struck]. Man sleeps; I [the Holy Spirit] am awake. See; it is the Lord who takes men's hearts out of their breasts and gives to men a heart."[3]

Montanus asserted that while in this ecstatic condition the Divine Spirit took the place of his own consciousness and spoke with his lips. There are three fragments to this effect: "Montanus said: 'I am the Lord God Almighty appearing in man'"; again he says, "Neither as angel or ambassador came I, but the Lord God, the Father"; "Montanus said: 'I am the Father and the Son and the Paraclete.'"[4] These "sayings" of

[1] Eusebius' *Church History*, v. 16.

[2] The contemporaries of Montanus seem to have had no idea that ecstatic prophecy existed in apostolic days. Clement of Alexandria regards ecstasy as the mark of a "false prophet" (*Stromata*, i. 17). Renan finds evidence of *Glossolalia* among the Montanists (see chapter on Montanists in his *Histoire des origines du christianisme*, tome vii.).

[3] Weinel in *Die Wirkungen des Geistes und der Geister* (1899), p. 92, makes the following comment on this saying: "It is with a man in this state as if he slept, or as if his heart, according to oriental ideas the seat of consciousness, was taken out of his breast and an alien power had put another into its place so long as this power speak from out him."

[4] The "sayings" of Montanus and the prophetesses are preserved by Epiphanius, whose two chapters, xlviii. and xlix., in *Contra Haereses* are the main source of our information.

Montanus are not to be interpreted in too literal a sense. They are not as blasphemous as they sound in their isolated nakedness. He does not mean that he, Montanus, a mere man, is God. He is rather asserting that the human can fall into the background, or fall off entirely, and that God can take the man's place and utter Himself through the lips that formerly were the man's, and Montanus declares that this substitution of selves has occurred in him.

He was soon followed in this manifestation of ecstatic utterance by two women, named Priscilla, or Prisca, and Maximilla, who became widely reverenced as prophetesses. These women left their husbands and became "virgins" in the Montanist Church, in which they gained an authority little short of infallible. Like their leader they believed in divine "possession," and absolute self-suppression. Priscilla had a vivid "vision," much like those which St. Catherine of Siena experienced later, in which she said that Christ assumed the form of a woman in bright apparel, and came to her side and put wisdom into her, and showed her that the place where she lived (Pepuza) was holy, and that there Jerusalem would come down from heaven. Of Maximilla's sayings we have only a few fragments: "Do not listen to me, listen to Christ"; "The Lord sent *me*[1] as the adherent in thy persecution and in the covenant and promise, and as their exponent and interpreter, and compelled willing and unwilling to learn the knowledge of God"; "I am pursued like a wolf among sheep, but I am no wolf; I am the Word, and the Spirit and power"; "After me there shall be no more prophetess, but the end shall come."[2]

The few actual sayings of the Montanist prophets

[1] The *me* in this saying refers to the Spirit.

[2] Bonwetsch, who has given us a very searching and valuable study of Montanism, holds that ecstatic speaking was probably confined to Montanus and the two prophetesses, Priscilla and Maximilla. He thinks that the "revelations" of later Montanism were received in visions during sleep, and communicated during waking condition. This position rests on slender evidence, but, even if it were well founded, it would introduce no new principle of revelation. The psychological basis is the same in both types, for Montanus and the two prophetesses were evidently subject to hypnotic or sleep "states" brought on by auto-suggestion (see Bonwetsch's *Montanismus*, pp. 67-68).

which have been preserved are so meagre and fragmentary that the student is tempted, on the face of the returns, to dismiss the movement as an aberration, or at least as of slight significance. Such a conclusion is, however, too hasty. The movement was widespread. It swept entire communities into fellowship with the new prophets, and we must remember that we can study it only from its fragments and in its cooled-down stage. It emphasized truths which the age needed. It developed a new type of Christianity which appealed to some of the best spirits of the age, notably Tertullian; it is a valuable historical illustration of the contagious character of ecstatic, or charismatic, manifestations; it grew into a powerful protest against a secularized Church; and it presents, with sharp emphasis, the mixture of truth and error, of divine illumination and human frailty, which were bound to appear in all early attempts to exhibit a religion of the Spirit.

The most striking feature of Montanism—the feature which first demands attention—is its revival of prophecy, the attempt to put the authority of the Christian Church in a succession of divinely inspired prophets. The Church was settling down on a basis of officialism. The sublime truth that God communicated His will directly to man as man was well-nigh lost. Church leaders were busy constructing an authoritative system, and were losing the vision of an unbroken procession of the Holy Ghost through human temples. Montanism once more returned to *prophecy* as the basis of Church fellowship, and as the method of arriving at fuller truth and purer life. Its prophets taught essentially the priesthood of believers, both male and female. They insisted that ministers are made by God alone, and they undertook to form a Church of saints—a Church which should be in truth the community of the faithful and holy. Surely a noble task in any age!

The movement claimed to be the beginning of a new dispensation—the dispensation of the Holy Ghost, the Paraclete, who was to be now and henceforth the

Head of the Church, governing, directing, and leading through divinely chosen prophets. It was now to be made plain that revelation was not finished but rather only well begun, and that the "greater things" promised by Christ were to appear in the dispensation of the Paraclete.

One of the names given to the movement by the originators of it themselves was "the Spirituals," or the "Spiritual people" They insisted on the progressive character of revelation, and they originated the idea of well-marked *stages* in revelation, an idea which comes up again and again with the rise of mystical societies in the history of the Church. They assumed three stages:—

(1) In the Old Testament revelation was in its infancy, and God dealt with men as parents do with children of feeble insight.

(2) Christ and the apostles advanced revelation to the stage of youth. The great Master was still unable to give the complete and final truth. He had many things to say, for which even His nearest followers were not ready, and He tempered His message and His commands to the weakness of flesh.

(3) In Montanus and his prophets, revelation comes to its culmination and full glory—it is the stage of manhood, and no "provision" is any longer made for the "flesh."

This progressive character of revelation gets its loftiest expression in the *Passion of Saint Perpetua*, a Montanist book of martyrdom and of prophetic visions, written early in the third century, possibly by Tertullian himself. This book describes the noble and heroic constancy of a little band of saints from the village of Thuburbo, near Carthage, who died in the arena for their faith. The narrative is the literary gem of Montanism, and has left behind an undying fragrance, and has put an indelible touch of glory on this early effort to realise on earth a Church of the Holy Spirit. Whatever criticism one may have in his head for Montanism, he must have a sympathetic beat of the heart for these "brave and blessed martyrs, called and selected to the glory of Christ."[1] The little group of Montanist martyrs (for I assume they were Montanists) from Thuburbo consisted of Saturninus and Secundus;[2] Revocatus and Felicitas; Saturnus and a noble lady, Vivia Perpetua. They were all young. Two of them, Perpetua and Felicitas, were women; and two of them, Felicitas and Revocatus, were slaves. A child was born to Felicitas in prison, and Perpetua was already a mother when she was apprehended.

The "Acts" or, as the narrative is more properly called, the *Passion of Saint Perpetua*, was evidently written by a contemporary Christian, and it supplies one of the most precious documents now in existence for the study of Montanism. The writer begins his narrative by insisting that the revelation of God is still going on, and that a new addition to this growing revelation has been made through the "visions" of Perpetua and her companions. He says:

"Let those look to it who judge of the Holy Spirit according to the successive ages of time; whereas they ought to regard what is new, nay, what is newest, as most full of power, inasmuch as it participates in that exuberance of grace which is promised for the latter days. 'And it shall come to pass in the last days (saith the Lord) that I will pour out of My Spirit upon all flesh; and their sons and their daughters shall prophesy, and upon all My servants and handmaids will I pour out of My Spirit, and the young men shall see visions and the old men shall dream dreams.' And therefore we who acknowledge and honour recent prophecies and visions as being as much the outcome of God's promise as the old, and who reckon all the operations of the Holy Spirit as part of the endowment of the Church—for to her was He sent, to administer all gifts to all members, according as God has apportioned to each—we, I say, of necessity both record these things and recite them in public to the honour of God; *lest men*

---

[1] Dr. Rendel Harris, in his valuable Introduction to the Greek text of *The Acts of the Martyrdom of Perpetua and Felicitas*, edited by himself and Dr. Seth K. Gifford (London, 1890), thinks that the martyrdom occurred in A.D. 203 (see *op. cit.* pp. 8-13). Dean J. Armitage Robinson holds that the martyrs here considered were from the city of Carthage, and not from the village of Thuburbo (see the *Passion of Saint Perpetua*, edited with notes, by J. Armitage Robinson (Cambridge, 1891), pp. 22-26).

[2] Secundus died in prison before the day of martyrdom arrived.

of weak or pusillanimous faith should suppose that the grace of God worked only of old either unto constancy in suffering or unto wonder of revelations; whereas He worketh always as He promised."[1]

Tertullian, too, who is very careful not to impair the full authority of the New Testament, nevertheless holds that there are stages of revelation, and he maintains that the dispensation of the Paraclete—the epoch of new prophecy—holds the same relation to the apostles as Christ does to Moses. He is very bold, and positively announces that a new Church Order has come—the final stage of revelation, the dispensation of the Paraclete. He says to those who will follow the new prophecy: "You will thirst for no instruction—no questions will perplex you."

The Church henceforth is to be "the Church of the Spirit by means of a spiritual man (*i.e.* the prophet); not the Church which consists of a number of bishops." He rises to the insight that the key was conferred upon Peter only because he was *spiritual*, and that the true successor in apostolic authority is the person who has the Holy Spirit. "The Church in the proper and pre-eminent sense is the Holy Spirit Himself, in whom is the trinity of the One Divinity—Father, Son, and Holy Spirit. . . . And thus from this time onward every collection of persons who have come together in this faith is accounted 'a church.'"[2]

Cardinal Newman finds overwhelming objection to the movement in the fact that "the very foundation of Montanism is development,"[3] and there can be no doubt that this was a central idea. Tertullian, in a remarkable passage, declares that truth is progressive, and the grace of God "operates and advances to the end."

"What kind of a supposition is it," he cries out, "that, while the devil is always operating and adding daily to the ingenuities of iniquity, the work of God should either have ceased or else

---

[1] *Passio S. Perpetuae*, i.

[2] Tertullian, *On Modesty*, chap. xxi. I have used the translation in the volumes of the *Ante-Nicene Fathers*.

[3] *An Essay on Christian Development*, pp. 349-50.

have desisted from *advancing*? The reason why the Lord sent the Paraclete was that since human mediocrity was unable to take in all things at once, discipline should, little by little, be directed and ordained, and carried to perfection, by that *Vicar of the Lord, the Holy Ghost*. Nothing is without stages, and the Holy Spirit is ever advancing towards better things." [1]

The stages of development are well defined. First, there was a rudimentary stage when men lived under "a natural fear of God." From that stage the race "advanced, through the law and the prophets, to infancy; from that stage it passed, through the Gospel, to the fervour of youth; now through the Paraclete it is settling into maturity. He will be, after Christ, the only one to be called and revered as Master. He is the only prelate, because He alone succeeds Christ. They who have received Him set truth before custom." [2]

According to the Montanist theory, the Holy Spirit may come upon any person, of any rank, and of either sex. In this respect it was a return to the freedom of apostolic days—to a priesthood not of flesh and blood, nor the will of man, but a priesthood of believers. Firmilian, Bishop of Cæsarea, in Cappadocia, in a letter cites the case of a prophetess who came into his diocese, and both baptized and consecrated the Eucharist. Tertullian gives a very interesting account of the performance of sacerdotal rites by a woman:

> "We have now among us a sister whose lot it has been to be favoured with sundry gifts of revelation, which she experiences in the Spirit by ecstatic vision amid the sacred rites of the Lord's day in the church: she converses with angels, and sometimes even with the Lord; she both sees and hears mysterious communications; some men's hearts she understands, and to them who are in need she distributes remedies. Whether it be in the reading of Scriptures or in the preaching of sermons, or in the offering up of prayers, in all these religious services matter and opportunity are afforded to her of seeing visions. . . . For her witness (of her vision) there was God; and the apostle most assuredly foretold that there were to be 'spiritual gifts' in the Church." [3]

---

[1] *On the Veiling of Virgins*, chap. i. [2] *Ibid.* chap. i.

[3] Tertullian, *Treatise on the Soul*, chap. ix.

Epiphanius says that in a Montanist church seven virgins used to come in, in white raiment, bearing torches; that they would then prophesy to the people, and move them to repentance and to tears by their powerful appeals. He says, further, that women were priests and even bishops. The first condition, however, of rising to place and position in the Montanist Church was the possession of spiritual power, *i.e.* ecstatic prophecy. The new Church was to be, as Tertullian said in the words already quoted, a Church of the Spirit, manifested through a spiritual person, who might be any person whom the Spirit selected.

The Montanist leaders were "possessed" with the idea that the promises in John xiv.-xvii. were now being fulfilled in them. The Holy Spirit was *now* given; He had come in wholly unique fashion, and the new prophets spoke in loftier tone and with higher assumption than any apostle in the primitive Church had done. The idea was lofty, the purpose of the movement was right, and the Montanist leaders were feeling after something which inherently belongs to the religion of Christ. But Montanist prophecy was not a *return* to the New Testament type, and it did not have in it the potentiality of a developing, conquering Christianity. Its type of prophecy was abnormal, and far too narrow. There was, to be sure, an element of ecstasy in the Apostolic Church, and the prophet of the first period sometimes received visions when he was "out of himself"; but in the main the New Testament prophet was a highly gifted, spiritually developed person who lived on a lofty level of experience, practised the truth which he knew, and he *saw*, by profound spiritual insight, the divine things which God had to reveal to his age. Instead of suppressing his powers and obliterating his reason, instead of sinking to a passive instrument to be played upon by an outside Force, he made himself an organ of an inward Spirit who had become the Life of his life, and who flooded all his faculties with energy. The prophet was a man still, using the powers which belonged to him as a man, and he was different from other men only in that he co-operated better than others did with the Divine Spirit, to Whom his life was consciously allied.

Montanist prophecy, on the other hand, was modelled on heathen oracles and frenzied soothsaying. In so far as it was a "return," it was a return to types which prevailed in most primitive religions—"the sacred madness of the bard," the type out of which Hebrew prophecy evolved, the type which Christian prophecy left far behind.[1]

The human recipient is, in the Montanist view, a mere passive *instrument*, swept and moved by the incoming Divine Spirit. Human reason must retire and consciousness must be absent before any revelation can come. The prophet is used as a *medium*. He imparts nothing of his own; he adds nothing. His one service is to take himself out of the way—to sleep—and let the Divine Spirit have his lips to use as the musician uses the lyre. Reason is thus thoroughly discredited, and is replaced by supernatural oracles. There is here a sharp dualism between the human and the divine, the natural and the supernatural. Every "natural" process, every mental activity, is undivine, and truth comes best when man himself has most withdrawn. Personality counts for nothing. There can be no "revelation" through a person in his normal activities. Finite nature, personal characteristics, must be suppressed for the time being, and then God can work unhindered. All the fragments preserved from Montanus and his followers support this view of prophecy as an overpowering of the soul by the Spirit, attended by a condition of motionless rapture or ecstasy.

Even in its most beautiful expression, in the visions of Perpetua, one feels that this is prophecy of the second, not of the first order. Perpetua's visions are excellent illustrations of the fact that in ecstatic vision the mind still uses, though sub-consciously, the material

[1] For a somewhat different estimate of Montanist prophecy, see Weinel, *op. cit.* p. 95.

of experience, and has by no means shaken off the human element.[1]

Montanus and his two prophetesses claimed that the Holy Spirit had come upon them in wholly unique fashion. They put themselves, as we have seen, even above the prophets of the primitive Church. They held themselves to be the bearers of the last and greatest revelation of divine truth. They figured as the instruments of the dispensation of the Paraclete. But, in fact, they exhibited a type of prophecy which was of a lower order than the primitive Christian one, and they proposed a basis of leadership no less dangerous than that which was being formed under the ecclesiastical system. They proposed a church guided by men and women, speaking in ecstatic states, whose "oracles" were to form "a new law," and whose utterances were to have the infallibility belonging to the last word of the Holy Spirit.[2] The door for caprice and vagary was wide open. The prophet suppressed his reason to become a passive lyre for the Spirit, and whatever might come through his lips in this state was *oracular*. His listeners were bound to suppress their reason, too, for the revelation was by hypothesis above reason, and they were to take the "word" without question as the will of the Paraclete. It was the oracular prophecy of Dodona and Delphi in a new dress and baptized with a new name. It gave extraordinary place to those pathological persons who abound in all ages and countries, and who, in response

[1] Perpetua says: "One day my brother said to me, 'Dear lady and sister, you are now in such high favour (with God) that if you ask for a vision it would be granted you, whereby you may know whether death or liberty awaits you.'" The beautiful "vision" which was granted her has undoubtedly an "other worldly" element in it, but it *comes* in the material and the setting of Perpetua's dominant ideas. For instance, when she is welcomed to heaven by "the white-haired man of great stature, in the guise of a shepherd, milking sheep," she is given "bread and cheese" to eat, which Rendel Harris, quite rightly, I think, believes is a reference to a simplified form of the Communion meal, which some of the Montanists wished to introduce; and "the kiss of peace," which holds an important place in the "visions," was another dominant idea in Montanist practice.

[2] It is quite likely, as Harnack says (*Hist. of Dogma*, vol. ii. p. 98, *n.* 4), that the Montanist prophets themselves did not intend their inspired words to be turned into precise "laws," but that is what actually happened in later Montanism, and it has, too, been the course in many other religious movements since!

to suggestion, and by the influence of imitation, fall into trance, or ecstasy, and utter words automatically. Not thus is the dispensation of the Paraclete realized. Not thus comes the Church of the Spirit to supplant the ecclesiastical Church.

The inherent weakness of Montanist prophecy lay in its suppression of personality, in the annihilation of those very faculties through which a personal God could reveal Himself. There was left no test of truth, no criterion of revelation, no principle of continuous expansion.[1] It gave no solid basis for historical development by the orderly unfolding of a steadily maturing plan. In short, it was non-spiritual, as any movement must be which undertakes to overleap the barriers of human nature and attain truth at a bound, instead of winning it as a possession of conscious personality by making it the inward spring and power of a transformed will. Ecstatic prophecy, calling for the annihilation of human reason and reducing the prophet to a blind instrument, was at best a dangerous experiment, and it would have been a feeble substitute for the imperial Church to which it was opposed.

There was another structural weakness in Montanism. Instead of receiving the message of its prophets as spiritual illumination, and as inspiration for free and continuous personal intercourse with God, the Montanist fellowship treated the communications as "oracles" to be obeyed as a *new law*. These new prophets did not conceive the Church as a living organism, penetrated and unified by an inward, formative Spirit, and growing continuously by conserving in a true spiritual way the gains of the past, so that the later members would be capable of higher insight as a result of the insight of their predecessors. The truth was, rather, to be found in the "oracle" of an ecstatic prophet, and this "truth" was to be accepted and practised as the will of the

[1] So far as a test was proposed, it was conformity to the revelations which had been given in the apostolic period, but the fundamental assumption of the "new prophecy" was that it was an advance upon all that was given in the past, and consequently the new could not consistently be judged by the old.

Paraclete. The entire collection of "revelations" would form the ultimate law of Christianity, higher than that of Sinai, and higher even than that of the Gospel.[1]

The radical error lay in the conception of Christianity as law. It was, of course, a well-nigh universal blunder. The religion of Christ which called for a new man, and which asked for a life in Christ Jesus, had already given place to *a substitute religion*, which was of a thoroughly legal character. It was submission to a *system* which regulated belief and practice. Montanism did not rise above this legalism. It only substituted another kind of legalism. Imperial Christianity was turning the Gospel and the apostolic teaching into a law-system, complete and final. Montanism put in the place of that law-system a "new law," composed of revelations of the Paraclete, spoken through prophets. It failed to introduce a truly spiritual religion, grounded in the direct relation of man as spirit to God as Spirit.

Montanism as a "new law" was a movement toward much sterner discipline and a very much stricter moral life. It pushed to the extreme the tendency already under way toward asceticism and toward severe Church discipline. The new law, which Montanist prophecy furnished, was to regulate daily life and purify the Church. The later writings of Tertullian are full of insistence on a strict moral life. In fact, it was the puritanic character of Montanism that attracted Tertullian to it. He was opposed to every pursuit of life which would bring Christians into contact with heathen idolatry, and he urged a complete separation from the contamination of the world. He emphatically declares the incompatibility of Christianity and war. It is unbecoming for any man "to range himself under the standard of Christ and also under that of the devil, to bivouac in the camp of light and also in the camp of darkness." "The Lord

[1] It must, however, be remembered that the *ideal* of the Montanist leaders was progressive development, unending revelation. Tertullian at his best, as we have seen, seems to have had an idea of a growing spiritual body of believers, but he also treats the "revelations" of prophets and prophetesses as final and authoritative.

disarmed Peter, and in doing so unbuckled the sword of every soldier."[1] He also opposes the exercise of public office as being contaminating. It is, he says, impossible to hold an office without presiding at spectacles, without taking an oath, without passing judgment of life or death.[2] Tertullian also urges that sinners guilty of gross immorality should not be reinstated in the Church, or, at least, should be absolved, not by official authority, but by the decision of the Spirit, speaking through a prophet.

But the two distinctly new regulations which Montanism introduced were (1) new laws about marriage, and (2) new laws about fasts. There is an "oracle" of Priscilla which says: "Only the holy minister can minister sanctity, for purity unites (with the Spirit), and they (the pure) see visions, and, bowing their faces downward, they hear distinct words spoken." This oracle means, according to Tertullian, that "purity," or virginity, is the true condition for receiving a revelation. Virginity is the highest stage of life, but, as marriage is permitted by Divine authority, and is essential to the propagation of the race, Montanism did not *require* celibacy. Its new command was that there should be single marriage. It allowed second marriage on no condition whatever. This custom of avoiding second marriage had already prevailed in the case of bishops; Montanism, on the basis that all Christians are under a Divine ordination, widened the custom into a law for all. The change of attitude worked in two ways. On the one hand, it raised marriage to a higher level by making it a union for time and eternity; on the other hand, by over-emphasizing the sexual side it led to the degradation of marriage, and prepared the way for the monstrosity of a celibate priesthood.

Montanists claimed that no complete system of fasts was laid down in the primitive Church, because the Church was then in its infant stage, and man "not able to bear" the whole system of religious perfection. This completer change was introduced through their prophets.

[1] Tertullian, *On Idolatry*, chap. xix. [2] *Ibid.* chap. xviii.

The revelations of the new prophecy provided that there should be a new fast of two weeks' duration (called the "Xerophagy," which means eating dry food). During this period there was to be abstinence not only from flesh and wine, and from bathing, but also from all succulent food and juicy fruit. Furthermore, the regular weekly "half-fast," which the Church observed only until three o'clock in the afternoon, was prolonged by the Montanists until evening. More than this, one finds in the Montanist movement an undue feeling of the importance of abstinence for its own sake. The strict Montanists felt that those who obeyed the new teaching belonged to a higher class than that to which the ordinary Christian belonged —they formed, in fact, a "peculiar people." They called themselves "Spirituals," and set themselves over against *ordinary* Christians, who were called "Psychical," or carnal. One serious outcome of this ascetic spirit was the tendency to set "this world" *over against* the Kingdom of God as a supernatural world. "That world" is to be reached only by escaping from "this world." This attitude led to an excessive zeal for the martyr's death —a zeal which lasted throughout the entire period of Montanism. Tertullian quotes with approval an "oracle" of the Paraclete through a Montanist prophet: "Let it not be your wish to die in your beds in the pains of childbirth, or in debilitating fever; but desire to die as martyrs, that He may be glorified who died for you."[1] In his treatise on the soul, Tertullian holds that departed souls are detained in Hades until the resurrection, but that the souls of martyrs are received at death directly into Paradise. He quotes in confirmation of this that Perpetua saw in a vision only those in Paradise who had died in martyrdom, and he adds: "The sole key to unlock Paradise is your own life's blood."[2]

Another outcome of their undue emphasis on the supernatural was their eager expectation of the millennium. "This world," with its temptations, its imperfections, its

[1] Tertullian, *On Flight in Persecution*, sec. 9; and *A Treatise on the Soul*, chap. lv.

[2] Id. *A Treatise on the Soul*, chap. lv.

evils, was to end, and the perfect reign of the heavenly King was to come by miracle—it was to come then and there. Montanus undertook to gather all those of his faith together into one great community about the town of Pepuza, in Phrygia. He named the locality "Jerusalem." The members were to sever their former connections with the world and society, to form an undivided Christian Commonwealth, where, living pure, holy lives, the "spiritual" were to wait for the descent of the new Jerusalem from above.[1] An oracle of Prisca says: "Christ came to me and showed me that this place (Pepuza) is holy, and here Jerusalem will come down from heaven." Maximilla also said: "After me there shall be no more prophetess, but an end." This glowing expectation of the visible coming of the heavenly Jerusalem appears with unabated vividness in the writings of Tertullian. Here is his extraordinary account of its imminent appearing:

"The word of the new prophecy, which is a part of our belief, attests how it foretold that there would be, for a sign, a picture of this very city exhibited to view previous to its manifestation. This prophecy, indeed, has been very lately fulfilled in an expedition to the East. For it is evident from the testimony even of heathen witnesses that in Judea there was suspended in the sky a city, early every morning for forty days. As the day advanced, the entire figure of the walls would wane, and sometimes it would vanish instantly."[2]

The movement, as we have already seen, early came into sharp collision with the Church. Its prophecy was pronounced not only contrary to that of the apostolic days, but a delusion of the evil spirit. Its "fasts" and its stricter discipline were denounced as innovations, and, when other "argument" failed, the moral character of the prophets was assailed. Like all contagious movements, it flourished on persecution, and, as we have seen, martyrdom grew into a holy passion. In the first stages, when the movement was borne on by an irresistible enthusiasm,

[1] See Eusebius' *Church History*, chap. xviii.; see also Harnack's *History of Dogma*, vol. ii. p. 95.
[2] Tertullian, *Against Marcion*, chap. xxv.

the Church made little headway in the effort to crush it out. But in the later stages, as it settled down into a *system* outside the "great Church," the merciless persecution which was made against it began to be effective. One gets in the story of the annihilation of Montanism startling exhibitions of ecclesiastical hate. An anonymous writer, quoted in Eusebius, says that when members of the "great Church" and Montanists were brought together in prisons, by a common anti-Christian persecution, the former refused all intercourse with the latter. Cyril of Jerusalem shows an *excess* of ecclesiastical slander. He reports that one of the rites of the Montanists is the sacrifice of an infant child, and the eating of his flesh! Under Constantine, edicts were issued depriving Montanists of their meeting-places and forbidding their form of worship. The penal laws against them were steadily increased in severity, and finally, in the reign of Justinian, the "sect" was practically crushed out of existence. Procopius has preserved an appalling picture of one of the last scenes in this spiritual drama. Surrounded everywhere by the coils of hate and persecution, the last little remnant of the "spiritual fellowship," in despair, gathered together—men, women, and children—in their own place of worship, set fire to the house, and so went to find the New Jerusalem, for which they had waited on earth in vain.

Montanism, as a movement, "failed"; its books were destroyed, its prophets were thrown to the beasts. Both the world and the "Church" arrayed themselves against it, and finally stamped it out. It would have "failed," however, without the stern methods which were used against it, for it had not within itself the inherent power of ministering to the condition of the world and the soul of man. It was, at best, a crude and imperfect type of the religion of the Spirit, and there were to be weary centuries of moral and spiritual discipline before the truth could set men free. But, in another sense, Montanism did not "fail"—the blood of its martyrs revivified faith in the real presence of the Holy Spirit, and its prophetic *word* about the unending development and progress of spiritual revelation was too quick and powerful to be silenced by the beasts of the arena. That word, once well uttered, was to grow in the hearts of men until a type of the religion of the Spirit could be born, virile enough to succeed.

CHAPTER IV

ROOTS OF MYSTICISM IN CLASSICAL LITERATURE

I HAVE already pointed out that primitive Christianity was mystical at its very heart and centre. The highest revelation which Christ makes is the exhibition of the fact that God's nature is such, and man's nature is such, that there can be a true union of God and man in a personal life. Paul and John set forth a type of religion grounded in the soul's own experience of God. There was, too, a strong mystical strain in the writings of the Church Fathers. Christianity, then, whenever it went back to its primitive literature for its inspiration, was almost certain to become mystical. But there were other powerful influences which largely determined the type of mysticism which actually appeared. The fact cannot be too often pressed that historical Christianity is a product of many movements, a religion woven out of many strands of faith and thought and practice. The river of water of life which flowed from Christ was eventually changed and coloured by streams from all lands and peoples and religions. What is true of ecclesiastical Christianity is also true of mystical Christianity. It has many sources, not one single source. No origin can ever be found for man's highest spiritual insights. Behind each apparent beginning there was an earlier movement ; at the back of every prophet there was some one whose human hand, however feebly, passed on the touch to him. Every person's experience, even in the highest reaches of it, is affected by what some other soul has already experienced, for human life is profoundly organic.

Platonic philosophy was by far the greatest pre-Christian influence. In fact it may be said that Plato is the father of *speculative*, as distinguished from simple, implicit, unreflective mysticism. It has fallen to the lot of few mortals to beget so large a spiritual progeny as this Greek who left no physical child to propagate his line, and one does not wonder that the Greek Christian Fathers put him in the list of the great prophets of the eternal Word, or that he was called "the Attic Moses."

The mysticism of the Platonic movement in reality goes back behind Plato himself, and had its creative source in Socrates, and to a lesser extent in Pythagoras and the Pythagorean school.[1] Socrates belongs to the order of the prophets. He is in that class of persons, appearing in all ages, who *feel* their connection with the Divine, and who speak and act with an insight far beyond the range of their own account of it. During his entire life he was conscious of an inner guide which he called "the divine something in his breast." Intimations, upon numerous occasions of his life, came to him with an inward compelling power, and he had direct revelations of the suitable course for him to pursue, and these experiences made him feel that he was in an unusual sense under divine care and under divine orders. Feelings, suggestions, incursions, whose origin he could not trace or discover, exercised over him irresistible control. There was, too, as many of his disciples declare, an extraordinary gift of personal magnetism in him, due in some measure to the belief of his contemporaries that he was in intimate relations with higher powers.

"When I hear him speak," says Alcibiades in the *Symposium*, "my heart leaps up far more than the hearts of those who

[1] There are many legends which connect Plato with the Far East, and there is no doubt that such a universal mind as Plato's was would absorb something from India, Persia, and Egypt, even though the stories of oriental travel are legendary. But the evidence of direct influence upon him from the religions of these countries is very slight.

celebrate the Corybantic mysteries; my tears are poured out as he talks—a thing I have seen happen to many others besides myself. . . . I stop my ears, therefore, as from the Sirens, and flee away as fast as possible, that I may not sit down beside him and grow old listening to his talk."

These inward experiences, however we may account for them now, were of very great importance to the foremost disciple of Socrates, Plato, who came to him in his youth and who, under the spell of his enchanting talk, burned his poems and turned all his powers to the problems of the soul. He did not himself possess a psychical constitution of the type of his master's; that is to say he was not in the same way subject to incursions and intimations which broke in upon him, and which seemed to come to him from a foreign source,—but he continued and carried still farther than his master the belief that there are germs of truth, dormant within all men, waiting only to be quickened and started growing to come into full power within the mind. Socrates had playfully called himself a mental midwife, whose service—a "divinely ordained service," he says—was to help men bring their own embryonic ideas and truths to full birth. This doctrine of the soul's native capacity to rise to truth and beauty and goodness, in short to find the realm of divine reality, suggested by Socrates, is vastly expanded by Plato and is one of his greatest religious contributions. Nobody has insisted with stronger emphasis than he on the divine *origin* of the soul. It is a presupposition of his entire philosophy that the soul, even while an alien in *this world*, is always within sight of the real, *i.e.* the eternal, world because it is unsevered from its source. He says (through the mouth of Socrates):

"Those who pass their time with me have never learnt anything from me, but have discovered for themselves *in their own minds* treasures manifold for their possession. Of this birth I *under heaven* am the cause."[1]

[1] *Theaetetus*, 150. It will be seen as this chapter progresses, that I do not consider the "two-world" interpretation, so frequently given, a correct understanding, but rather a misunderstanding of Plato's teaching.

Plato often seems to set the two worlds sharply against each other—the world of truth, of unity, of permanence yonder; the world of error, of variety, of mutability here. *There* is reality, *here* is only show; there is the pattern, here is only mimic copy; there the One, here the many.

As there are two worlds, so, too, there seem to be two distinct levels of experience. On the level of sense a person deals only with this show-world. Sense can give only the transitory, only the contingent, only what is in endless flux of becoming and decaying.

> "We must make a distinction," he says in the *Timaeus*, "of the two great forms of being, and ask: what is that *which is and has no becoming*, and what is that which *is always becoming and never is*? The latter, which is apprehended by opinion through irrational sensation, is ever coming into being and perishing, but never really is."

The other level is pure knowledge, or intelligence, by which the mind reaches the realities of the world yonder; the abiding, unchangeable realities which are freed from everything transitory and contingent. As Plato himself puts it in this same passage of the *Timaeus*: "The world apprehended by Reason or Thought is ever changeless and one with itself."

Plato used the word *Ideas* not to indicate something conceived in the mind as we use the word, but to indicate those permanent realities which stay unchanged in all the welter of mutation, like, for example, the Idea *man* or the universal *man*, regardless of the changes which happen to particular men, such as John and Peter and Henry; or like the law of gravitation through all the flux of infinite particles of matter. "Ideas" are in short types or laws. Sense never gives us these immutable, permanent realities—these "Ideas" which abide; it gives only a "this" or a "that," only a contingent something, nothing which *is just itself for ever*.

Where then did the mind get these permanent truths? It got them, Plato tells us in poetical and mythical language, from a supersensuous world where before birth it lived and dwelt in the presence of *pure being*, and where it contemplated every day these ultimate and unchanging realities. The soul was at home there in the real world and saw *that which is.* In a myth of exceeding beauty he has told us how the soul fared in that other realm, and how it *fell* from that world of reality to this world of shadows :

"The region above the heavens is the place of true knowledge. There colourless, formless, and intangible being is visible to the mind, which is the only lord of the soul. And as the divine intelligence and that of every other soul which is rightly nourished is fed upon mind and pure knowledge, such an intelligent soul is glad at beholding *being*; and feeding on the sight of truth is replenished."[1]

But whenever a soul is unable to maintain its vision of truth and fails to nourish its wings with the sight of pure being, that soul falls to this lower world and lives here among the shadows. But it never altogether forgets the realities it has seen in the eternal home. Deep in its memory it holds those realities it has known and, when it sees the shadow-image of the real thing, it remembers the "Idea" which it knew in the other sphere, so that all true knowledge is *reminiscence.*

In another figure[2] he has compared this *lower life* of sense experience to human beings

"living in an underground cave, with their faces turned toward the back of the cave; they have been there from their childhood, and have their legs and necks chained that they cannot move, and can only see before them ; for the chains are arranged in such a manner as to prevent them from turning round their heads. Above and behind them the light of a fire is blazing at a distance, and between the fire and the prisoners there is a raised way; and you will see, if you look, a low wall built along the way . . . over which puppets are shown."

The chained men within never see anything but the *shadows* of these puppets. Their world is "just nothing but the shadows of images."

Here in Plato, taken in a prosaic and literal sense, we

[1] *Phaedrus*, 247.

[2] *Republic*, opening of Book VII.

have the beginning of that tendency, which has played such a mighty part in Western speculation, and which appears in almost every school of mysticism — the tendency to treat the sense world as unreal, shadowy, and undivine. The temporal is in sharp antithesis to the eternal. The latter is the realm of *being*; the former is "the other"—a cave of shadows. But, even when taken at its face value and in its superficial meaning, Plato's doctrine is never consistently dualistic, for he finds it impossible to treat *this* world as a stubborn, foreign "other," unrelated to *that which is* and to the mind which perceives it. The soul—*i.e.* the spiritual principle in man—lives in both worlds and can always find a *suggestion* of *that which is* in that which appears. In the "cave-myth" some of the dwellers in the cave "turn their necks round" and "go up and look at the light." At first "the glare of the light distresses them" and they are unable to "see the realities of which they have before been seeing the shadows." But gradually "they grow accustomed to the sight of the upper world." And when they remember their "old habitation and the wisdom of the cave and their fellow-prisoners they felicitate themselves on the change," and they desire "to descend again among the prisoners of the cave" to help *them* to get liberated and "to see realities."

Plato tells us the entire allegory means that the prison is the world of sense, and that the ascent and vision of things above, *i.e.* realities, is "the upward progress of the soul into the intellectual world, where it gains beatific vision"; for "our argument shows," he adds, "*that the power of knowing reality is already in the soul when the eye of the soul is turned.*" Or as he puts it in the *Phaedo*:

> "When the soul returns into itself and reflects, it passes into another region (than that of the world of sense), the region of that which is pure and everlasting, immortal and unchangeable; and, *feeling itself kindred thereto*, it dwells there under its own control, and has rest from its wanderings, and is constant and one with itself as are the objects with which it deals."[1]

[1] The *Phaedo*, 79 C.

This means that the soul has within itself, whether by reminiscence or otherwise, the power of rising above the transitory to that which is permanent, and that there is something in the soul kindred to the Reality which it contemplates. He repeatedly says in the *Republic* that the essential thing in virtue and vice, in goodness and badness, is the disposition of the soul which they reveal.[1]

As Plato's conception developed, he dwelt more and more upon the one ultimate Reality which binds all subordinate realities into an organic whole—the supreme unity of all that is. This he called the "Idea of the Good." Through the "Idea of the Good" all special spheres of reality are united in *One Ultimate Real.* This is the Source and Goal of all things—the Alpha and Omega. Toward It all that is moves. It is the end and Final Cause in the entire circuit of the universe—"the one far-off divine event to which the whole creation moves." Whatever comes to any degree or stage of being does so through the attraction of the Idea of the Good. The universe in all its parts is realizing an End which is Good and the end or Goal functions in the entire process. As the idea of a loved one moves the lover toward her whom he loves, so the Idea of the Good moves the many parts of the universe toward Itself, the One Reality—the Absolute Good.

The great question now for the interpreter of Plato is this: Does Plato seriously mean that the permanent realities, and above all the One Reality, are actually off in another world, and that our only knowledge of them is by Reminiscence, or is the ultimate Reality, the Absolute Good, immanent in the universe, and immanent, too, in the mind that knows it? It is obvious to everybody who thinks about it, that, if through these Ideas, or permanent realities, we truly know anything, then there must be some organic unity between our minds and those things which we know. If they are apart from the mind in another world, they are of no use to us, and Plato cannot possibly have thought that they could have been actually

[1] The *Republic*, 358 B; 361 E; 367 E.

perceived by sense in some earlier world, or in some world higher up. An Idea to have any value must unify thought and being and be manifested in both; it must be both within and beyond the mind that knows it.

The passages I have already quoted show that Plato was fully aware of this: "When the mind returns into itself (from the confusion of sense) it is in the region of that which is pure and everlasting and is kindred thereto." The "Cave figure" leads to the same conclusion, namely that "the power of beholding Reality is already in the soul," and the ascent to the vision of the One Reality—"the beatific vision," he calls it—is always possible to the dwellers in the cave *if they turn the soul's eye.* Even the "Reminiscence myth" of the *Phaedrus* may have a much deeper meaning than that which is usually drawn from it. It may be a pictorial way of saying that the soul has a native power, or faculty, of apprehending the Real. The soul does not receive the truth *ab extra*, whether in this world or any other. As soon as it rises above sense and comes up to its real self it finds a permanent object of thought, *that which is*, which was always there, though only implicit or potential. It is called up from the soul's own deep, for if the soul had not this inherent capacity of rising to permanent truth, there could be no knowledge, only the welter of sense. There would be no gain in going *back* to a world before birth where the truth was *seen*, for this gives us a sense perception again only on a higher level. The myth suggests not a regress into the temporal past, but a regress into the soul's native capacity for truth, and so *native kinship and unity* with the Real.[1]

Plato very often implies that *this world*—the so-called shadow-world—is a real reflection of the truly Real, and so is more than a phantom; is in fact a divine world, with genuine beauty and goodness in it. In the *Timaeus* it is called a "second god"—an "only begotten son" of the first God. It is thus "an image of its Maker," and

[1] See Edward Caird's *Evolution of Theology in the Greek Philosophers*, vol. i. Lecture VIII.

"the most beautiful and perfect of all creatures." And he also implies that there is something in the very nature of the soul which enables it to find the eternal in the temporal, and to rise through the sight of the seen to the Reality, unseen and abiding. This faculty of soul he calls Love (ἔρως), a mystic passion which begins when the soul catches sight of the world of Reality through an object of beauty which opens a window into the eternal realm. The temporal object suggests the eternal, and the soul in a rapture sees through the transitory and contemplates absolute Beauty and so finds itself at home.

The steps of this divine, mystic passion are given in a beautiful passage of the *Symposium*. The lover soon gets beyond the satisfaction which physical nearness to the beloved object can give. There is still "an intense yearning," which "does not appear to be the desire of intercourse," but "something else which the soul desires and cannot tell, and of which she has only a dark and doubtful presentiment." The soul takes satisfaction in progeny only because it finds in offspring a visible image of some everlasting possession. It rises steadily to ever higher types of progeny—lofty thoughts, poems, statutes, institutions, laws—the fair creations of the mind. But the highest stage of Love comes when the soul sees Beauty itself which is everlasting, "not growing and decaying, not waxing and waning." He, who under the influence of Love rises to see that Beauty, *is not far from the end*, "for the true order of going to the things of Love is to use the beauties of earth as steps along which one mounts upward for the sake of that other Beauty, going from one to two, and from two to all fair forms, and from fair forms to fair actions, and from fair actions to fair notions until from fair notions he arrives at the notion of absolute Beauty and at last knows what the essence of Beauty is." This is the ascent of the soul from the temporal to the eternal, where it is one with that which it beholds. The final end toward which the soul moves is the Good—the Ultimate Reality—the apex of Being.

On this interpretation, the Good is the immanent rational principle which unifies all intelligible, *i.e.* thinkable, things and unites them in a living whole with the mind which knows them. It is the substance of all manifestation, the unifying principle of all finite experience. It is involved in all reality, and equally involved in all thought. It is never "beyond" except in the sense in which the life of any organism is "beyond" any single *member* of the organism. On this view the eternal world, the spiritual realm, is not "another world" to which we ascend by leaving "this world" behind; the Eternal world is rather the immanent Reality which is the ground and explanation of the temporal world.

Plato did not consistently develop this view, though it is possible to find it sketched and adumbrated throughout his later works, but there can be no doubt that he consistently and unvaryingly "keeps the faith" that *the soul has in itself an eye for divine Reality, and that the mind has a native capacity for beatific vision.* This doctrine has had mighty influence and is of vast import. The view which Plato's successors and the later mystics found in his teaching was rather an ultimate Reality "beyond" the universe, and "above" mind; "beyond being" and "above knowledge." It is to be reached only by a sublime process which *negates* all finiteness; all multiplicity, all particularity. On this basis the Absolute Reality is nothing knowable or thinkable—it is the Divine Dark to be reached only when the mind has transcended itself in ecstasy.[1]

[1] It should be said that Plato does not give in his Dialogues one consistent and unvarying exposition of a well-settled system. On the contrary his position constantly shifts, and his doctrine is always in the making, never a fixed system. He remains throughout a great artistic creator rather than a system-maker.

J. A. Stewart in his *Myths of Plato* (1905) holds that the mysticism of Plato is a *feeling* mysticism. Plato's myths—which J. A. Stewart very rightly says are organic parts of the dialogues in which they appear—are, he thinks, told to produce a state of "Transcendental feeling," through which the soul comes in contact with reality, with timeless existence, "that which the soul is and was and shall be." The myth induces, just as sublime poetry does, a dream-consciousness—a profound *feeling state*, by which the soul transcends the world of the senses, and scientific understanding, and has an experience of ultimate reality.

This theory is beautifully worked out in the work cited, and it has an important

Aristotle also exerted a profound influence on the types of mysticism which prevailed from the third to the fifteenth century. It is strange that this cold, analytic, unmystical philosopher, who would have none of Plato's myths, and who sought to bring everything in the universe under exact and scientific description, should have produced a great succession of mystics as his intellectual progeny, but such is the fact. It seems paradoxical that the beginner of exact observation of empirical phenomena should have inspired in his disciples a glowing passion for *contemplation*, but such, again, is the historical fact. Aristotle sharply separates God from the world. God is the Absolutely Real—remote from all that is finite, mutable, imperfect, and potential. He is not to be found here. He is wholly yonder, beyond the world, its "unmoved Mover." He is self-contained, one with Himself, a moveless Energy. He dwells in the peace of His own completeness. "He thinks His own thoughts." He feels nothing, needs nothing, seeks nothing, goes never out to find any "other." All things are drawn upward by His perfection and their imperfection. But man has one possible path open to God—it is the way of *pure contemplation* (*θεωρία*).

By pure contemplation the mind may rise above the transitory and contingent, may get beyond space and time and contemplate the Absolute. This attainment is possible because man possesses at the "top of his mind" an *active reason*, that is to say, "a pure self-consciousness." In his *De Anima*, or "Psychology," Aristotle distinguishes two *levels* of reason, which he calls the active and the passive reason. The active reason has no finite origin, is not bound up with, or dependent on, the body. It is "pure," *i.e.* not mixed with desire or passion, and does not receive its content

bearing on some types of mysticism, but it does not, I think, fit Plato's teaching. Plato always treats the *feeling experience* as a low stage. He puts its seat in the lower soul and reserves for Intellect alone a direct apprehension of *That which is.* Those who make mysticism consist in *feeling experience* cannot bring Plato into their category. For him the perception of the Divine is in the Intellect. We shall see, too, that his greatest interpreter, Plotinus, puts mind above heart in the ladder of ascent to God.

through sense. The lower or passive reason is wholly dependent for its content on the body. It begins with the body and ends with it. The *active reason*, not being dependent on sense impressions from without, is not determined by anything outside itself; does not proceed in its truth from finite aspect to finite aspect, as one proceeds in ordinary experience, but attains its "object," reaches its goal, by a supreme act of vision in which the mind sees the whole, the unity, without contrast or difference. It "thinks its own thoughts," like God. The particular disappears and the mind rises to the *unbroken one.* Some finite object may be the "occasion" for this ascent of reason, but sense does not supply the "object" which the mind beholds. The sense impression is only the "occasion" for a free activity of reason by which it mounts to a vision of forms and realities that are not in space and time, but are one with its own deepest nature. This "faculty" does not belong to man as finite man—as "mere man," but, as Aristotle says in his *Ethics*, it belongs to man only "as there is something divine within him."[1] He nowhere explains how there comes to be "something divine within man," but he implies that the *active reason* at the top of mind is one with that Divine Reason which in beholding beholds Itself, for in contemplation the mind is at home with itself and is one with what it beholds in unbroken unity.[2] The following is one of Aristotle's great passages in praise of contemplation as man's highest function :—

"If then reason is divine in comparison with man's whole nature, the life according to reason must be divine in comparison with human life. Nor ought we to pay regard to those who exhort us that, as we are men, we ought to think human things

[1] Weldon's *Ethics of Aristotle*, p. 337.

[2] Aristotle himself has nowhere worked out a consistent theory of the relation between the two types of reason, nor of the relation between the active reason and the Divine Reason. His great commentator, Alexander of Aphrodisias, who flourished about A.D. 200, took a very important step which was to have far-reaching consequences. Alexander explicitly identifies active reason with Divine Reason. Active reason, he holds, has no finite origin. It is of God and remains in God, and the ideas which it presents to passive human reason are in reality Divine Ideas—thoughts which God thinks. This interpretation of Aristotle had a remarkable history and will meet us again.

and to keep our eyes upon mortality: rather, as far as we may, we should endeavour to rise to that which is immortal in us and do everything to live in conformity with what is best for us; for if in bulk it is small, yet in power and dignity it far exceeds everything else which we possess. Nay, it may even be regarded as constituting our very individuality, since it is the supreme element, and that which is best in us. And if so, then it would be absurd for us to choose any life but that which is properly our own. . . . Such, therefore, to man is the life according to reason since it is this that makes him man."[1]

From this passage the natural inference is that that which makes man really man is something divine in him.

Aristotle's influence has always been in the direction of a negative mysticism, that is a mysticism which mounts upward towards reality by negativing all finite creatures and appearances. God is a One *beyond* the many. The soul attains its vision only when it leaves behind everything by which it could mark off and characterise the object of its vision. At the end of its ascent the soul finds that it has no way of distinguishing the *All* from the *Nothing*, because it has risen above all finites all the marks and names which give character and reality to our world of experience. *It has come home, but with empty hands*. We shall often enough find mystics travelling such a *via negativa*.

The influence of Stoic philosophy was far-reaching during the entire formative period of the Christian Church and the Christian ideas. Its doctrine of an immanent Spirit, alike in the world and in man—a soul of the universe—could not fail to impress the pillar Christians of the first centuries who came in contact with the doctrine.

"A divine force," writes Seneca, "has come down to earth, a heavenly power, by which the soul, with its splendid powers of thought, raises itself above all lower things. As the rays of the sun touch the earth indeed, but have their true home in that place whence they come forth, so it is with the great and holy Spirit which is sent down hither in order that we may learn to know the Deity better."[2]

---

[1] Weldon's *Ethics of Aristotle*, pp. 337-38.

[2] Ep. xli.

Again he says:

"God comes to man, yea, He comes closer, till He enters into men. No disposition is good apart from God. Seeds of the divine are planted in human bodies; if they are well tended, they germinate and grow up into the likeness of That from whence they sprang."[1]

The teaching that there is a germinative principle—a seed of God in the human soul—was a fundamental idea with the Stoics. This doctrine, interpreted at its best, offers a basis for mystical religion, and was very suggestive to the primitive Christians. Stoicism, too, proclaimed the doctrine that the inner spirit must free itself completely from everything individual and particular in order to identify itself with the Universal Reason. The path to the One and All is a path of surrender—one comes to the universal Spirit only by leaving behind all that is one's "own."

But the greatest outside influence in mystical directions was from the school of philosophy generally known as Neoplatonic. It became for many generations a necessary part of the intellectual environment of the Græco-Roman world, and most of the Christian thinkers knew their Plato, not directly but through the interpretation of Neoplatonism. We cannot understand the spiritual travail of later centuries without first coming to close quarters with this last great intellectual effort of paganism.

The master mind of the movement was Plotinus. He was the profoundest thinker between the flowering period of Greek philosophy and the creators of modern philosophy in the sixteenth and seventeenth centuries, and, though he lacked that peculiar quality of style which carries a system of truth into the very life-blood of humanity and makes it the possession of the race for ever, he has a passion and enthusiasm which makes his difficult book a live one even after more than fifteen centuries. He was born, as near as we can fix the date, at Lycopolis in Egypt in A.D. 205. His biographer Porphyry, a third century Boswell, has given us much detail and gossip, but

[1] Ep. lxxiii. 14.

he could not give the date of the birth of Plotinus for the reason that Plotinus himself refused to have it known. "He seemed ashamed of his body," and was unwilling that any one should ever celebrate the event of his birth. Origen, who was a fellow-student with Plotinus, had a similar objection to birthdays, and he supports the notion by pointing out that in the Bible only bad men are reported as having kept their birthdays! The teacher who first "spoke to the condition" of Plotinus was Ammonius Saccas of Alexandria. When the young inquirer found him he said, "This is the man I am seeking." Ammonius was a Christian in his youth, but turned from his religion to the pursuit of philosophy. His name "Saccas" means "porter" and tradition represents him as a self-taught man. We know almost nothing of him, or of his system, except through the effects of his ten years of teaching on his famous disciple. Plotinus settled in Rome in 244, where he became the centre of a group of eager seekers after truth. Porphyry has given us a human and charming picture of the man, who was evidently much more than a dry and bloodless metaphysician.

> "Many," he says, "of the noblest men and women, when death drew near, brought to him their boys and girls, and property, and entrusted all to him as to a holy and divine guardian. His house was full of boys and maidens, among whom was Polemo, for whose education he was so careful that *he would listen to his schoolboy verses*. He endured even to go through the accounts of his wards' possessions, and was most accurate and business-like, saying that, until they became philosophers, their property and revenues ought to be kept intact and secure."

Popular anecdotes about him give the impression that he was a man of unusual psychical disposition, which has important bearing on his teaching that the highest stage of truth is ecstasy—an experience which, Porphyry tells us, was four times granted to him. He wrote extensive treatises, which Porphyry collected into six books called *Enneads*. He died in the Roman Campagna in 269, saying to his companion as he passed away: "Now the divine in me is struggling to reunite with the divine in the All."

The attempt has often been made to trace the doctrines of Plotinus to oriental influences. It is true that he travelled through the Far East, and it is also true that Alexandria was a meeting-place for all types of men and of ideas; it is, further, true that Gnosticism, which was a semi-philosophy, partly formed by oriental speculation, was in the air at the time, as thick as thistledown in the summer breeze. His interpretation of his great Greek masters was no doubt coloured by the atmosphere of the time, but his system is, in the main, a direct development of classical Greek philosophy. He is the culmination of the movement whose three greatest exponents were Socrates, Plato, and Aristotle, though he brings together, as every great philosophical genius does, all the converging lines of thought before him, and, through the creative work of his own spirit, utters a *word* which is neither new nor old. It is not my purpose here to give any technical exposition of Plotinus. I shall point out, in as unscholastic language as possible, the mystical features of his system, and indicate how these Neoplatonic ideas come over into the stream of Christian thought.

"God is not external to any one." He is "the root of the Soul," the "centre" of the mind, and the way home to Him is within every person. This is the heart of the mysticism of Plotinus. There is in the universe, as he conceives it, a double movement—the way down and the way up. The way down is the eternal process of the Divine emanation, or outgoing of God towards the circumference.[1] At the centre of all is God, the One, the Good. The One is a Unity above all difference, an Absolute who transcends all thought, who is, in fact, even *beyond being*. Thought implies a contrast of knower and known; Being implies a substance with qualities or characteristics, and each quality limits the substance. For example redness necessitates the negation, or absence, of all other colours,

[1] These spatial words "centre" and "circumference" are used only metaphorically, not literally.

and so on with all qualities. The Perfect God, then, must be above all division of known and knower; beyond all limitation of qualities, *an undivided One*, too supreme and lofty to be expressed by any word, but containing in Himself All, with no contrasts of here or there, no oppositions of this and that, no separation into change and variation. He is divested of every likeness to anything in the heavens above, or in the earth beneath, or in the waters under the earth. He is dependent on nothing, in need of nothing, and every description of Him must be an everlasting Nay. From the Perfect One there flows or radiates out a succession of emanations of decreasing splendour and reality.

The first emanation from the One is Mind (Nous), which is the second name in the Trinity of Plotinus. This first sphere of being is an overflow from God—a "by-product," as it were, which leaves Him as He was before with no decrease. "Mind" radiates from God as light does from a luminous body, which floods the darkness, but loses none of itself by the outflow; or like goodness in a person, which by going out in service to others does not lessen the original amount of goodness. This highest circle of being is the world of Ideas—the universal principles, the archetypes and patterns, after which our world of things is framed. It is the Over-Mind of the Universe of whom all minds partake and in whom is everything which is real and intelligible. God, therefore, as the ground of the world is Intelligence.

Mind, again, overflows into a second sphere of being—the third name in this Trinity—Soul. This is Universal Soul, or Oversoul, and enfolds in itself all individual souls, so that all souls are both distinct and yet *one*. Soul is the outer rim of reality. It pours and streams out, and, as through myriad rivulets, it floods the world, in fact, makes the world. Matter by itself is nothing. It is the limit which Soul comes to, the outer husk or barrier—the dark into which the outflowing divine light rushes, so that what, in its origin, was one is splashed and broken into endless multiplicity. Soul has both a higher and a lower side, or, as a recent interpreter puts it, Soul is "an amphibious being who belongs to both worlds, and who, therefore, can climb to the highest or sink to the lowest." The lower soul *desires* a body and lives in the stage of sense and deals with objects seen partially and temporarily; in a word, is as far out at the rim of being as it is possible to go. The higher soul, on the other hand, transcends the body, "rides upon" it, as the fish is in the sea or as the plant is in the air. This higher soul never absolutely leaves its home, its *being* is not here but "yonder," or, in the language of Plotinus: "The soul always leaves something of itself above."

It is possible for every soul to retrace the process of its descent and return home. The first step on "the way upward" is for the soul to come to itself. "God is present," says Plotinus,

> "even with those who do not know Him, though they may escape out of Him, or *rather out of themselves*, and therefore are not able to see Him from whom they have exiled themselves. Having thus lost themselves, how shall they find another being? A child who is frenzied and out of his mind will not know his father. But he who has learnt to know himself will also know the Being from whom he comes."[1]

Again he says:

> "When we carry our views outside the Principle on which we depend, we lose consciousness of our unity, and become like a number of faces which are turned outward, though inwardly they are attached to one head. But if one of us, like one of those faces, could turn round either by his own effort, or by divine aid, *he would behold at once God, himself and the whole.* At first, indeed, he might be able to see himself as one with the whole, but soon he would find that there was *no boundary he could fix for his separate self.* . . . He would attain to the Absolute whole, not by going forward to another place, but by abiding in that Principle on which the whole universe is based."[2]

This means that the first stage on the journey home is for the soul to be completely restored to the unity of the universal soul, "attaching itself to that centre to which all souls ought to cling." The quest is furthered whenever

[1] *Ennead*, vi. 9, 7.

[2] *Ibid.* vi. 5, 7.

one realises that all souls have a common origin and ground: "When thou reverest the soul in another thou art revering thyself." But this is only the first stage. The next step is to rise to Mind (or Nous).

"Since, then," says Plotinus, "soul is so precious and divine a thing, believing that thou hast a strong helper in thy quest after God . . . go up to Him who is yonder. And of a truth *thou wilt find Him not far off, for there is not much between.* Grasp then what is diviner than this divine (*i.e.* diviner than Soul), the Soul's neighbour above (*i.e.* Mind), after whom and from whom the soul is."[1]

By withdrawal from desires, and from objects of sense to the contemplation of the true patterns of things, *i.e.* to the world of pure thought, one reaches a higher unity than was possible to the soul. Here in calm contemplation the highest unity is reached that is possible to a self-conscious being. It is a unity in which the thinker and the thought are not foreign to each other, though there still remains a distinction of subject and object, without which self-consciousness would cease.

The first *manifestation* of God is thought—the act by which He thinks the patterns of things—and so, too, the summit of human consciousness is thought, by which man arrives at the height of thinking God's thoughts. In this realm of pure thought the self finds its true ground of unity with the All. Each mind is like an open book to all other minds; each spirit is transparent to all the others.

"They see themselves in others," says Plotinus, "for all things are transparent, and there is nothing dark or resisting, but every one is manifest to every one internally. . . . For every one has all things in himself and again sees all things in another, so that all things are everywhere, and all is all, and each is all, the glory is infinite."[2]

But this is not the End; the soul is not yet at home, but where is the ladder to mount *above thought*, and so become one with the One? The last stage of the journey

[1] *Ennead*, v. 1, 3. [2] *Ibid.* v. 8, 4.

cannot be told in plain words. It can be divulged, says our mystic, only to those who are *initiated.* "Our teaching reaches only so far as to indicate the way in which the Soul should go, but the vision itself must be the soul's own achievement." There is in everybody a centre at the summit of the mind which is inalienably conjoined with the One, or, as Plotinus puts it, "God is not external to any one," so that the last mount is the complete return to this Divine centre, to a *vision* in which subject and object, known and knower, are one. But *that is a state beyond consciousness*; that is, beyond the subject-object type of consciousness.[1] Plotinus calls it "a mode of vision which is ecstasy," when the soul, "energising enthusiastically, becomes established in quiet and solitary union." It is, as he says, "the flight of the alone to the Alone," and in this highest experience of actual contact[2] and union with God, when the soul, one with what it loves,

"In undivided being blends,"

self-consciousness is transcended. This state is suggested rather than described in a great passage in *Ennead*, vi. 9, 10:—

"But to see and to have seen that vision is reason no longer, but more than reason, and before reason, and after reason; as also is that vision which is seen. And perchance we should not speak of sight. For that which is seen—if we must need speak of the seer and the seen as twain and not as one—that which is seen is not discerned by the seer nor conceived by him as a second thing; but becoming, as it were, other than himself, he of himself contributeth naught, but, as when one layeth centre upon centre, he becometh God's and one with God. Wherefore this vision is hard to tell of. For how can a man tell of that as other than himself which, when he discerned it, seemed not other, but one with himself indeed?"[3]

---

[1] We often have such experiences in some degree. All our high moments of experience of beauty, or of love, or of worship are experiences beyond the subject-object type of consciousness.

[2] He uses the phrase "intellectual contact" (νοερὰ ἐπαφή).

[3] It would be an error to suppose, as is often done, that the mind in ecstasy is *necessarily* a mental blank. To dispel such a view one needs only to study the personal experiences recorded by Tennyson where he came upon *That which is.*

It is not possible to follow in any detail, in this present study, the spiritual history of later Neoplatonism. There was an unbroken succession of teachers, or, as they themselves called it, "a Hermaic chain," from Plotinus to the closing of the Athenian school of Philosophy by order of Justinian in the year 529. The movement was marred by many vagaries, and it became so intimately allied with the vain effort to *revive* the ancient religion of the pagan world, and by it to conquer the ever-expanding religion embodied in the Christian Church, that it exposed itself to the corrupting influences of superstition and magic, and lost in some degree its lofty primitive mood. The movement had its moment of triumph in the person and in the reign of Julian, nicknamed "the Apostate." Many attempts were made to construct by myth and imagination a "philosophic master," who should captivate the imagination of the multitude and become a rival to Christ.[1] There is, however, a noble side to Neoplatonism even down to its end, and Eunapius, one of its chroniclers in later times, could say with some truth, "The fire still burns on the altars of Plotinus." It completely failed in its chief ambition to maintain the imperial spiritual supremacy of Rome, and Julian spoke words of truth and soberness when he said, "Thou hast conquered, Galilean," for the blood of youth was in the veins of Christianity, while Neoplatonism was an attempt to revivify a dead past. But the successive masters in the long line of Neoplatonic thought kept burning the torch which Plato had lighted, and passed it on for the Christian scholars to take up when they were ready for it.

The last great name in the "Hermaic chain" was Proclus (b. 410, d. 485), who taught once more in Athens, where the torch was first lighted. It is said that when he arrived in Athens, and came late at night to knock for

It is, however, true that no *description* can be given of anything which transcends subject-object experience. The rush of memory, by which a drowning man "sees his whole life," is doubtless a real, though certainly an indescribable, experience. Plotinus gives a wonderful description of the antecedent conditions of ecstasy in *En.* V. i. 2, 3, 4.

[1] The two most famous pagan "gospels" are the lives of "Apollonius of Tyana" and "Pythagoras."

admission into the school of philosophy, the porter said to him, "If you had not come, I should have shut the gates," which indicates that there was already a foreboding that the school was on the perilous edge of extinction. Proclus was a man of extraordinary mental powers, and under happier conditions might have *begun* an era instead of ending one.

He follows Plotinus in holding that everything emanates from the One, the Absolute First Principle, but this emanation is a much more complicated process than appears even in the system of Plotinus. Everything coming forth from the One differentiates into a descending *series of triads*, by which the manifestation of the finite is made. That which comes forth is both like and unlike its higher cause. In so far as it is like its cause, it remains in it; in so far as it is different from it, it goes out and separates from it; and can return only by becoming like that next above itself on the way back towards the One. The soul can always withdraw from those things which *separate it*, and return into its own inner sanctuary, where it finds an indwelling God. Life is at its best when it is caught up by the upward sweep of a *holy enthusiasm*, which Proclus often calls "faith," and sometimes "divine madness."

About forty years after the death of Proclus (in the year 527) the edict of a Christian emperor closed the doors of the Academy, and drove the little band of philosophers out into exile. There were seven of the band, and they took their beloved books and started out, from the famous seat of philosophy, to seek a quiet retreat in Persia—the wise men of the West going toward the East with no star for guide. It is a pathetic end. The mighty stream of truth seemed at last, after eight hundred years of luminous flood, to be losing itself in the desert sand. The Church would brook no rival in the field of truth, and it proposed to ban all unbaptized teachers, and to taboo all streams of truth which did not flow from the canon. The Christian emperor reckoned ill if he thought he could suppress the contribution of Greek wisdom by lock and key. He could banish the feeble relic of the school, and then settle down in the fond belief that the world was now rid of the philosophic brood. Not so. Before Justinian was in his grave, this Neoplatonic philosophy was, as we shall see, translated into Christian terms, and was made into the spiritual bee-bread on which many Christian generations fed.

CHAPTER V

MYSTICISM IN THE CHURCH FATHERS

THE Fathers were not "mystics" in the ordinary sense of the word. Their type of religion was mainly objective and historical, rather than subjective and inward. Their great task was the construction of an authoritative Church, and the formation of a permanent universal dogma, known as "the Faith." Some of them were pre-eminently of the statesman type; others were of the philosophical type; some of them combined both types. They all used the historical material which lay at their hands, and they built this material, as best they could, into the great world-structure, the Church—which was always in their thought. Very few of them have given us powerful descriptions of their own inward experience—Augustine is the striking exception—but there are scattered passages in the writings of almost all of them, from the earliest apostolic Fathers down, that express the kind of direct and inward religious experience which I have been calling "mystical."

There is a striking passage in the homily known as II. Clement, chapter xiv., which presents in a profound way the primacy of the *invisible Church*:

"Wherefore, brethren, if we do the will of God our Father, we shall be of the *first Church which is spiritual*, which was created before the sun and the moon. . . . So, therefore, let us choose to be of the Church of life, that we may be saved. And I do not suppose we are ignorant that the living Church is the body of Christ. . . . And the books of the apostles plainly declare that the Church existeth not now for the first time, but hath been from the beginning, for she was spiritual as our Jesus was spiritual."

The writer is contrasting the Church of Christ, thought of as pre-existing and eternal, with the Jewish Church, which was a temporal institution.

Irenaeus sets forth a lofty stage of religious experience —above the legal stage and the stage in which the dominion of the flesh renders the life imperfect—an attainment to the freedom of the spirit, wrought by the indwelling of the Divine Spirit in the man.

"The Lord," he says, "Who redeems us by His own blood gives us His soul for our soul, His own flesh for our flesh, and pours out the Spirit of the Father for the union and communion of God and man, imparting God to man through the Spirit, and raising man on the other hand to God."[1]

This higher life of spiritual religion he everywhere attributes to the direct "impartation of God," or to the soul's "participation in God." He says:

"It is impossible to live without life, but the means of life come from participation in God. But participation in God is to see God and to enjoy His goodness. . . . *The glory of God is a living man*, and the life of man is the vision of God."[2]

There is a noble passage in Tertullian which goes down beneath all the superficial grounds of evidence for the reality of Christianity, and which announces the soul's first-hand evidence:

"I call in," he writes,[3] "a new testimony; yea, one that is

---

[1] *Against Heresies*, Book V. chap. i. sec. 1.

[2] *Ibid.* Book IV. chap. xx. sec. 5-7. It must, however, be said that this "impartation of God to men" which Irenaeus teaches is not something mystical or spiritual, in our modern sense. He does not conceive of man, as the mystic does, as having a native capacity for God and as possessing within himself a meeting-place with God. He thinks rather of a miraculous impartation made possible through the Incarnation and mediated through the Eucharist. He is thinking of a way by which the *flesh* can be immortalized. Harnack sums up the teaching of Irenaeus as follows. He taught "restoration of the image of God in man, destruction of death, union of man with God, adoption of men to the status of sons of God and gods, communication of the spirit, imparting of knowledge, culminating in the vision of God, imparting of immortal life. All these goods are only the different sides of one and the same good, which, since it is of divine character, can only be brought to us by God and implanted in our nature" (Harnack's *Hist. of Dogma*, vol. ii. p. 292).

[3] Tertullian, *De Testimonio Animae*, chap. i.

better known than all literature, more discussed than all doctrine, more public than all publications, greater than the whole man—I mean all which is man's. *Stand forth, O soul*, whether thou art a divine and eternal substance, or whether thou art the very opposite of divine, and a mortal thing; whether thou art received from heaven, or sprung from earth; whether thine existence begins with that of the body, or thou art put into it at a later stage; from whatever source, and in whatever way, thou makest man a rational being, in the highest degree capable of thought and knowledge—stand forth and give thy witness."

He goes on to say that it is the soul's testimony in the "plain man," the ordinary, common man, that he wants:

"I call thee not as, when fashioned in schools, trained in libraries, fed up in Attic academies and porticoes, thou belchest forth thy wisdom. I address thee, simple and rude, uncultured and untaught, such as they have thee who have thee only; that very thing pure and entire, of the road, the street, the workshop. *I want thy experience.* I demand of thee the things thou bringest with thee into man, which thou knowest either from thyself, or from thy author, whoever he may be."

And then he draws out, with a flash of real prophetic fire, the soul's silent, subconscious witness to the God in whom it lives and moves, and has its being:

"Even with the garland of Ceres on thy brow, or wrapped in the purple cloak of Saturn, or wearing the white robe of Isis, *thou invokest God as Judge.* Standing under the statue of Aesculapius, adorning the brazen image of Juno, arraying the helmet of Minerva with dusky figures, thou never thinkest of appealing to any of these deities. In thine own forum thou appealest to a God who is elsewhere. . . . Though under the oppressive bondage of the body, though led astray by depraving customs, though enervated by lusts and passions, though in slavery to false gods; *yet, whenever the soul comes to itself, as out of a surfeit, or a sleep, or a sickness, and attains something of its natural soundness, it speaks of God.*"

And he ends his treatise with the sweeping declaration:

"There is not a soul of man that does not, from the light

that is in itself . . . proclaim God, though, O soul, thou dost not seek to know Him."[1]

The Greek Fathers were all influenced by the philosophy of Greece, and from the time of Origen (A.D. 185-254) there is a strong Neoplatonic flavour in all their work. The immanence of God is the very warp and woof of their thinking. "God mingles with humanity as the salt with the sea, as the perfume with the flower." God has always been in the world "working it up to better." The unwearied Divine Instructor has in all ages identified Himself with the growing, struggling race, and, in the fulness of time, became *incarnate* in one Life, and ever since has been the inward Spirit in all men who would receive Him. This Divine Word is ever being born anew in the hearts of saints.[2]

Clement of Alexandria carries his doctrine of immanence into every aspect of his religion. Prayer, he says, is direct intercourse with God. "Faith is a divine and human mutual and reciprocal correspondence." Clement's "harmonized man," the goal of human perfection here on earth, is a person who has the Divine Life so *formed within* that goodness and holiness have become "second nature"—the man is holy even in his dreams! Clement's Platonism comes out beautifully in the following passage, which is a good example of mysticism:

> "It is, then, the greatest of all lessons to know oneself. For if one knows himself he will know God, and knowing God, he will be made like God."[3]

It is possible to pick out such occasional passages in Clement, Origen, and Athanasius, but they do not prove that these men were mystics. They were, rather, profound thinkers, who were interpreting Christianity to the Greek mind through the historical forms of Greek thought, and who in high moods hit upon elemental facts

[1] I have greatly condensed Tertullian's "testimony," but the substance is accurately and correctly given.

[2] See *The Instructor* of Clement of Alexandria and the anonymous *Epistle to Diognetus*.

[3] *The Instructor*, Book III. chap. i.

of universal religious experience. Here is a famous passage from Athanasius which shows that, like Elias, he could be "very bold"—as bold as the highest mystic: "God became man that we might be made Divine,"[1] but the trend of Athanasius' thought was not that of a mystic.[2]

A somewhat better case can be made out for the great Cappadocian, Gregory of Nyssa (born about A.D. 335; died about 395). His famous brother, Basil, explained that he made him bishop of an insignificant place because he wanted Gregory to *confer* distinction on the city rather than receive it from the city, and Gregory fully justified the expectation. He came upon a stormy scene. Arianism was rending Christendom, and the Church was on a stormy sea when this lover of quiet thought was plunged into the tasks of active life. He was not over-wise in practical wisdom, but he was at home in the calmer occupation of formulating the truth for his age. His elaborate system of theology does not, fortunately, concern us now.[3] We are interested only in noting the mystical aspect of his Christianity, and the more so because his influence on later centuries was very great. Gregory's Christianity is still objective, and he does not ground it in the inward structure of the soul as the genuine mystic does, nor does he give any such profound analysis of consciousness as is frequent in Augustine.

[1] Athanasius, *De Incarnatione.* Irenaeus also said: "Jesus Christ our Lord, who, because of His great love, was made what we are, that He might bring us to be even what He is Himself." Irenaeus, *Against Heresies*, Book V., Preface.

[2] I have found it impossible in the limits of this book to include an extended study of the Greek Fathers. Their doctrine was not Mysticism in the proper sense of the word, but rather what the German scholars call "mystic-gnostic." Mysticism and Gnosticism are not in opposition in the Greek fathers, but just as in Neoplatonism (and the Greek mysteries whence the whole attitude is historically derived) closely associated. On the one hand we have the knowledge of God thought of as the highest thing possible to man; on the other, the feeling that such knowledge is different from ordinary knowledge and is communicated by mysterious and transcendent processes. There are differences, of course, among the Fathers. Clement and Origen are more of gnostics, and lay stress on the communion of God by the Logos. Athanasius thinks of a real and literal communication of God which, as with Irenæus, is mediated through the Eucharist. This idea is further elaborated by Gregory of Nyssa, whose view I shall briefly study.

[3] Ueberweg, in his *History of Philosophy*, says that Gregory of Nyssa "was the first who sought by rational consideration to establish the whole complex of orthodox doctrines."

But he does dwell with strong emphasis upon the possibility of a union of the Divine and the human, and he has put forth more forcibly than any other Christian Father the truth that the entire outward universe is a visible symbol, or parable, of a real, though invisible, world.

He holds, though not always clearly and consistently that a Divine element belongs to the original constitution of man—a mind's eye. This mind's eye, when not filmed by low passion, gets glimpses of the transcendent Good—"the first Good"—though no mortal lips can tell to other ears what has been beheld within the depths of consciousness. Gregory says that this is what the "great David" meant when he said: "All men are liars!" *i.e.* any attempt to tell the ineffable vision is a "lie!"[1] In a noble chapter,[2] in true Platonic spirit, he describes the spiritual ladder by which one climbs up to the prospect of Supernal Beauty, mounting into the heavens upon that "inward likeness to the descending Dove, whose wings David also longed for." The goal, he says, "is to become oneself as beautiful as the Beauty which he has touched and entered, and to be made bright and luminous oneself in communion with the real Light." "We can," he cries rapturously, "be changed into something better than ourselves." The eye, purged of all discolouring stain, can see God, the Archetype of all Beauty and of all Reality.

I will give only one illustration, among many, of the *kindred nature* of man and God:

> "As every being is capable of attracting its like, and humanity is, in a way, like God, as bearing within itself some resemblance to its Prototype, the soul is by a strict necessity attracted to *the kindred Deity*. In fact, what belongs to God must, by all means and at any cost, be preserved for Him."[3]

He goes on to tell in a graphic illustration how God draws and pulls the soul toward Himself.

> "The Divine Power, God's very love of man, drags *that which belongs to Him* from the ruins of the irrational and material, just

[1] *On Virginity*, chap. x.
[2] *Ibid.* chap. xi.
[3] *The Soul and the Resurrection*.

as after an earthquake bodies are drawn from mounds of rubbish —so God draws that which is His own to Himself."[1]

The actual *deification* of man, however, comes in Gregory's teaching, not by the mystical vision, nor by the successful drawing of God. It comes in a much more material way. It is effected, so he teaches, by the sacraments. An actual Divine nature is born within by the mediation of the baptismal water. The first birth is an allegory of this stupendous change. The first birth is mediated by moist seed in which no eye can detect the unborn person, but by Divine power that moisture becomes a human being. So, too, God uses water in an equally mysterious and miraculous way to recreate the "once born" man, and to produce in him Divine nature. The Divine process begun in baptism is carried on in the Eucharist. The bread and the wine are Divine body and blood, and they "nourish" the Divine life, which at *baptism* began within the man, so that by "communion with Deity mankind may be deified," and "by a union with the immortal may be a sharer in incorruption."

This magical, mystical view of the sacraments finally came to be, in one form or another, throughout Christendom the prevailing view. It was an attempt to satisfy two tendencies—the great material tendency of the age for something tangible, and the unstilled yearning of the soul for the "real presence" of God—for God within the personal life. This compromise seems to the modern mind woefully crude, but it seems much less so to one who studies it in its historical setting, and this is to be said for it: it enabled the Church to keep alive in the minds of multitudes of semi-Christians, who were at the same time semi-pagans, the *ideal* of having God within. This mystical view of Gregory is unquestionably a serious drop from Paul, or even from Plato, and it led to a low and perverted mysticism of a second order in his successors—some such degeneration as Neoplatonism underwent during the same period.

There is, however, a very lofty side to Gregory's

[1] *On the Soul and Resurrection.*

mysticism, and he must be judged in the light of his time—not in the light of these riper centuries. He is at his finest and loftiest when he strikes his great theme of the double universe—that which is seen and that which is not seen—the world within the world we see. The seen is a symbol of the unseen, the material a parable of the real. The visible world is the garment and drapery of God.[1]

The real father of Catholic mysticism, however, is St. Augustine.[2] He is, of course, the father of many other things also. He is one of those extraordinary persons who have dominated the minds of men with a sway which makes the rule of world conquerors look cheap and puny. He shows better than almost any other great religious teacher how impossible it is to separate "religion of authority" and "religion of the Spirit" into two sharply-divided groups. He is in both groups, and he is entirely unaware that they are inconsistent with each other. No other man has done more to construct an authoritative Church than he. The architectural plan was already there when he joined the Church, and he did not "create" the imperial design, but he saw with the genius of a statesman-philosopher how to *fulfil* the beginnings and the tendencies of the great Latin system. When his work was done the Roman Catholic Church was organized for its mighty task of making a new empire on the ruins of the old one.

While Rome was being sacked by hordes of barbarians, and the empire was tottering before the irresistible onset of races of vast potential power, St. Augustine, in his African retreat, was working out a new imperial system—a City of God—compared to which the old empire, even under the greatest Caesars, was a slender affair. St. Augustine's theology

[1] See especially *On Infants' Early Deaths*.

[2] Harnack says: "St. Augustine became the father of that mysticism which was naturalized in the Catholic Church, down to the Council of Trent" (*History of Dogma*, vol. v. p. 86). Harnack also speaks of Augustine as the first modern man and the first real *psychologist*. It is his psychological analysis that makes the peculiarity of his mysticism (see a long note in Harnack's *History of Dogma*, vol. v. p. 101).

made the Church—the City of God as it now is on the earth—the only door to the City of God as it is to be in the heavens. To Augustine the theologian, man as man was a depraved being, corrupt, root and branch—ruined, lost, possessed of nothing of his own which could minister to his salvation. The Church, with its mysterious sacraments, was an indispensable channel of Divine Grace.[1] In a world of sin and ignorance and error, in a world where no man could find any salvation for himself, it had pleased God to found and construct a City of Refuge, through which one might flee into the City of Eternal Rest.

It seems strange to call *him* a mystic. More than any other man he forged the iron system of dogma and authority. He taught that, since the "fall," the entire sphere and form of every (once born) man are sin and depravity. He made Saving Grace depend absolutely upon external channels. How is he a mystic? Like many another great man his life had two compartments. There were two "selves" within him—somewhat inconsistent with each other, though not recognized by him as being so.[2] He was first of all a living, throbbing *man*, facing life in his own human way. He had first-hand experiences of his own, and a wonderful power of penetrating and describing inward spiritual states. He has given us "a portrait of the soul," which in a profound and elemental way fits all generations of men. "I seem to be reading the history of my own wanderings and not another's," was Petrarch's penetrating comment as he read the *Confessions*.

On the other hand, he was a theologian-statesman, an architectural genius, whose supreme task was the construction of an imperial system—a Catholic Church—as the mysterious instrument of Grace in the midst of a ruined world. His mysticism was primary; his theology

[1] Augustine calls baptism "the water of salvation," and he says in his *Confessions* that his own most horrible and deadly sins were remitted in the holy water.

[2] Since writing this I have found the same thing said in Sabatier's *Religions of Authority*. "There were in this great doctor two men: the son of Monica and the orthodox bishop, the man of the Spirit and the man of authority." P. 484.

was secondary. I mean by that, that his mysticism belonged to his very nature as a man, and had no dependence upon his particular brand of theology. Theologically he held that man was depraved ; his own human *experience* told him that man and God are kindred, are meant for each other, and that man has within himself a direct pathway to the living God.

The famous sentence in the opening chapter of the *Confessions* announces a universal truth: "Thou hast made us for Thyself, and our heart is restless, until it rests in Thee." It is the announcement of a truth which grounds religion in the very nature of the soul itself, and annuls at once the depravity doctrine of the theologian. The positive, inward *push* of the soul Godward is frequently asserted in the *Confessions*, and Augustine bears steady testimony to an upward pull within himself which fits badly with the theory that man is a worm of the dust. Speaking of his life during his pre-Christian period, he says: "By inward goads Thou didst rouse me, that I should be ill at ease until Thou wert manifested to my inward sight."[1]

"Thou wert," again he says, during the period of his search, "more inward to me than my most inward part. I awoke in Thee and saw Thee infinite, and this sight was not derived from the flesh."[2] Nobody has more beautifully expressed the double nature of man—with the upward pull and the downward drag—than he has expressed it in the famous sentence: "I tremble and I burn ; I tremble, feeling that I am unlike Him ; I burn, feeling that I am like Him."[3]

No other man before modern times ever studied human nature with such profound insight as Augustine shows, and he constantly discovers not only these momentous yearnings towards God, but he finds also experiences which, to him, imply direct intercourse between the soul and God. He says that his mother could discern God's revelations to her by "a certain indescribable *savour*."[4] He

[1] *Confessions*, p. 121. The page references to the *Confessions* are to the edition of it in "Ancient and Modern Library of Theological Literature."

[2] *Ibid.* p. 126. [3] *Ibid.* Book VIII. chap. x. [4] *Ibid.* p. 107

himself, even before his actual "conversion," *beheld with the eye of his soul* the Light Unchangeable—the Light which Love knoweth, the knowledge of which is eternity.[1] He has thus, in the *Confessions*, used the sense-analogy of taste and sight; in the *City of God* he has a great passage in which the sense-analogy of hearing is used:

"God speaks with a man, not by means of some audible creature dinning in his ears, so that atmospheric vibrations connect Him that makes with him that hears the sound; nor even by means of a spiritual being with the semblance of a body, such as we see in dreams or similar states; for even in this case he speaks as if to the ears of the body, and *with the appearance of a real interval of space.* Not by these, then, does God speak, but by the truth itself, *if any one is prepared to hear with the mind* rather than with the body. He speaks to that part of man which is better than all else in him, and than which God himself alone is better."[2]

More commonly, however, he does not use sense-analogy. He was too much of a Platonist to put much emphasis on sense-experience. Consciousness in its very elemental structure may apprehend God. Sometimes it is the *heart* that finds Him—"I heard as the heart heareth, nor was there any room to doubt"—sometimes it is the *will*; sometimes, in true Platonic fashion, it is the *mind.* In his Epistles he says: "We cannot go to God afoot, but by our character" ("heart"). "He (Christ) departed from our eyes that we might return into our hearts and there find Him."[3] "Man is a huge abyss, and his hairs can be more easily counted than the affections and stirrings of his heart can be fathomed."[4] One of the finest of all his sayings is in one of his sermons: "Our whole work in this life is to heal the eye of the heart by which we see God,"[5] and in a passage which has a very modern note in it he says: "A good man is a man of good will."[6]

He says, in the *City of God*, that: God makes holy

1 *Confessions*, p. 123.
2 *City of God*, Book XI. chap. ii.
3 *Confessions*, p. 61.
4 *Ibid.* Book IV. chap. xiv.
5 Sermon xviii., *De Verb. Dom. secundum Matt.* chap. xxx.
6 *De Gratia*, xix.

souls His friends, and "noiselessly informs them" of His purpose.[1] It is strange to find the man who forged the doctrine of election making the *will*—"the momentous will," to use his own expression—the way to God. "Thither" (toward God), he says, in *Confessions*, p. 148, "one journeyeth not in ships, nor in chariots, nor on foot; for to journey thither, nay, even to arrive there, is nothing else but *to will to* go." There is no keener psychological analysis in all his writings than the penetrating study of "the momentous will" in Book VIII., especially chapters viii. and ix. He takes up the subject again in the *City of God*, Book XIV. chap. vi. Like Paul, he recognizes two wills; one the slave of habit,[2] the other the momentous will, which has the key to eternal reality. "*To will God entirely is to have Him!*"

The general type of his mysticism is, however, Platonic. The mind itself, or at least that which is "at the top of the mind," may directly apprehend God. There are many lofty passages which illustrate this aspect of Augustine's religion. Throughout the period of his search for God, Augustine's fundamental error was the conception of God as a substance which filled space, *i.e.* as a finer kind of material being. In one of his most powerful passages, describing his idea of God at this stage, he says:

"I set before the sight of my spirit the whole creation, whatsoever is visible in it, . . . and whatsoever in it is invisible. . . . And this mass I made huge, not as it was, which I could not know, but as large as I chose, yet bounded on every side (*i.e.* finite); but Thee, O Lord, I imagined on every part surrounding and penetrating it, but in every direction infinite: as if there were a sea, everywhere and on every side, through unmeasured space, one only infinite sea; and it contained within it some sponge, huge but finite; that sponge must needs, in all its parts, be filled from that unmeasured sea: So I imagined Thy finite creation full of Thee, the Infinite."[3]

"So did I endeavour," he says in another place,[4] "to

[1] *City of God*, Book XI. chap. iv.

[2] "Of a froward will a lust is made; by lust habit is formed; and habit not resisted becomes a necessity" (*Confessions*, p. 141).

[3] *Confessions*, p. 115.

[4] *Ibid.* p. 111.

conceive of Thee, Life of my life, as vast, through infinite space on every side penetrating the whole mass of the universe, and beyond it, through immeasurable boundless spaces; so that the earth would have Thee, the heavens have Thee, all things have Thee; they be bounded in Thee, and Thou bounded nowhere."

But he came to discover that the mind, which forms images of spatial objects, is itself not a thing of dimensions, and not to be conceived in terms of space; and that God is a substance of the same nature as mind, or spirit, "not present in the several portions of the world, piecemeal, large in the large, little in the little—not *such* art Thou."[1] And little by little he rose to the insight that God is the Eternal Reality, mirrored and veiled in the visible, changeable world, but to be found as He is with the eye of the mind. "In one trembling glance," he says, speaking of the mind's highest faculty, "*it arrived at That which Is.*"[2] At this period, which was before his conversion, he "lacked strength to fix his gaze thereon," but afterwards he learned "the way to that beatific country, which is not only to be gazed upon, *but to be dwelt in.*"[3]

The truth that God is the inner Reality, and so one with the hidden life of man, finds frequent utterance in his *Confessions*. He anticipates the great word of Pascal: "Thou wouldst not seek Me if thou hadst not already found Me." He tries to explain why men seek God and desire the blessed life, and, after a long, acute psychological analysis, he exclaims: "We could not love it unless we knew it!"[4]

"Thy God is unto thee, O my soul, even the Life of thy life," is the conclusion which he reaches after he has searched the universe for God. Here is a fragment of the noble passage which describes the search:

[1] See *Confessions*, Book VII. chap. i.

[2] *Ibid.* Book VIII. chap. xvii. Compare the τὸ ἔστιν ἀεί of Plotinus.

[3] Augustine says in *Confessions*, Book VIII. chaps. xviii.-xxi., that the new fact that enabled him to find the way to the blessed country was the Incarnation. As a *natural* mystic (Neo-Platonist) he could discern the land of Peace, but not find the way thither (see especially the close of chap. xxi.).

[4] *Confessions*, Book X. chap. xx.

"What do I love when I love Thee? Not beauty of the body, not harmony of line, nor brilliancy of light, so pleasant to these eyes, nor sweet melodies of every kind of song, nor the sweet scent of flowers and perfumes and spices, not manna and honey, not limbs inviting to fleshly embrace. Not these do I love when I love my God; and yet I love a kind of light and melody and fragrance and food and embrace, when I love my God—the light, melody, food, fragrance, embrace of my inward man: where there shineth upon my soul what space containeth not, and where resoundeth what time stealeth not away, where is fragrance which a breath scattereth not, where there is flavour that eating lesseneth not, and where there is an embrace that satiety rendeth not asunder. This I love, when I love my God.

"I asked the earth for God, and it answered me: 'I am not He'; I asked the sea and the depths and the creeping things, and they answered: 'We are not thy God, seek thou above us'; I asked the breezy gales, and the airy universe, and all its denizens replied: 'Anaximenes is mistaken. I am not God'; I asked the heaven, sun, moon, stars: 'Neither are we,' say they, 'the God whom thou seekest.' And I said unto all things which stand about the gateways of my flesh (the senses): 'Ye have told me of my God, that ye are not He; tell me something of Him.' And they cried with a loud voice: 'He made us.'"

And so the search goes on until the "inward self" is questioned, and the answer is, "Thy God is unto thee even the Life of thy life."[1]

There is another passage, even nobler still, in which St. Augustine describes how he and his mother, Monica, together climbed up through inner thought, came to their minds, and passed beyond them to *That which Is—the Self-Same*. I quote the passage in full.[2]

"As now the day drew near, on which she was about to depart out of this life, which day Thou didst know though we knew it not, it fell out, as I believe, through Thy Providence, working in Thy hidden ways, that she and I alone together, were standing leaning upon a certain window, from which there was a view of the garden within the house which sheltered us, there at Ostia, on the Tiber, where apart from the throng, from the fatigue of our long journey we were recruiting ourselves for our voyage. Together we, too, held converse very sweet, and

[1] *Confessions*, Book X. chap. vi.

[2] *Ibid.* Book IX. chap. x.

'forgetting those things which were behind, and reaching forth unto those things which were before' (Phil. iii. 13), we were discussing between us in the presence of the truth, which Thou art, of what kind would be that eternal life of the Saints, which 'eye hath not seen, nor ear heard, neither hath it entered into the heart of man' (1 Cor. ii. 9). But with the mouth of our heart we were panting for the heavenly streams of Thy fount, 'the fountain of life, which is with Thee' (Ps. xxxvi. 9), that besprinkled thence according to our capacity we might in some measure meditate upon so great a matter. And when our converse drew to such an end, that the utmost delight of the bodily senses, in the clearest material light, by the side of the enjoyment of that life seemed unworthy not only of comparison with it, but even to be named with it; raising ourselves with a more glowing emotion towards the 'Self-same' (Ps. iv. 8, Vulg.), we wandered step by step through all material things, and even the very heaven whence sun and moon and stars shed their light upon the earth. And further still we climbed, in inner thought and speech, and in wonder of Thy works, and we reached to our own minds, and passed beyond them, so as to touch the realm of plenty, never failing, where Thou feedest Israel for ever in the pasture of the truth, and where life is that Wisdom, by which all things are made, both those which have been, and those which shall be; and Itself is not made, but is now as it was and ever shall be; or rather in it is neither 'hath been' nor 'shall be,' but only 'is,' since It is eternal. For 'hath been' and 'shall be' spell not eternity. And while we thus speak and pant after it, with the whole stress of our hearts we just for an instant touched it, and we sighed, and left there bound the 'first fruits of the spirit' (Rom. viii; 23), and then returned to the broken murmurs of our own mouth, where the word hath its beginning and its end. And what is like unto Thy Word, our Lord, Who abideth in Himself, nor groweth old, and maketh all things new? We were saying then: If to any one should grow hushed the tumult of the flesh, hushed the images of earth, and of the waters, and the air, hushed, too, the poles, and if the very soul should be hushed to itself, and were by cessation of thought of self to pass beyond itself; if all dreams, and imaginary revelations, every tongue and every token, were hushed, and whatsoever falls out through change; if to any, such should be wholly hushed to silence, since could any hear them, they all say: 'We made not ourselves, but He made us, who abideth for ever,' and this said, if now they should cease to speak, because they had inclined our ears to Him, who made them, and He Himself by Himself should speak, not through them. but of

Himself, that so we should hear His Word, not uttered by a tongue of flesh, nor by a voice of angel, nor by thunders of a cloud, nor by a parable of comparison, but Himself, whom in these we love; if, I say, we should hear Him, without these, as now we strained ourselves, and in the flight of thought touched upon the Eternal Wisdom that abideth over all things; if this were continued, and other visions of a nature by far inferior were taken away, and this one alone should ravish, and absorb, and enwrap the beholder of it amid inward joys, so that life everlasting might be of such a kind, as was that one moment of comprehension for which we sighed; were not this an 'Enter thou into the joy of thy Lord'? (Matt. xxv. 21). And when shall that be? Shall it be when 'we all shall rise again, but shall not all be changed'?" (1 Cor. xv. 51, Vulg.).

It is clear from this great passage that Augustine looks for the truly Real above and beyond all that appears; a view which finds its plainest utterance in his well-known words: "God is best adored in silence; best known by nescience; best described by negatives."[1] This negative mysticism will meet us again and again, and can be permanently transcended only by a truer psychology than that which was possible in the ancient and medieval world.

The *vision* of God is, however, not the goal and end of Augustine's mystical striving. His highest word is *union*—union of being with the Eternal Reality: I heard, as the heart heareth, Thy voice, "I am the food of them that are full grown; grow and thou shalt feed upon Me, nor shalt thou transmute *Me* into thee, as thou didst food into thy flesh, but thou shalt be transmuted into Me."[2] In the *City of God*[3] he says that "the man Christ Jesus

[1] This view of the "self-same," to which the mind may rise as contrasted with the fleeting things which sense gives, is one of Augustine's inheritances from Platonic philosophy. He wrote in one of his early *Epistles*: "We are, I suppose, agreed that all things with which our bodily senses acquaint us are incapable of abiding unchanged for a single moment, but, on the contrary, are moving and in perpetual transition, and have no present reality—that is, to use the language of Latin philosophy, do not *exist*. Accordingly, the true and divine philosophy [Platonic philosophy] admonishes us to check and subdue the love of these things as dangerous and disastrous, in order that the mind, even while using the body, may be wholly occupied and warmly interested in those things which are *the same for ever*, and which owe their attractive power to no transient charm." The great passage quoted in the text is plainly influenced by a passage in Plotinus's *Enneads*, V. i. 2, 3, 4.

[2] *Confessions*, p. 124.

[3] *City of God*, Book XXI. chap. xvi.

became a partaker of our own mortality that He might make us partakers of His divinity." Again he says, commenting on Psalm xlix.: "He called men gods *as being deified by His grace*, not as born of His substance."

It will be noted that Augustine, in his mystical passages, is decidedly personal and subjective. He thinks of man as an isolated individual, who may hold high intercourse with God, and who at the highest stage of experience may come into a union of life with God, but he has discovered no social principle; he does not rise to the conception of a mystical corporate life—a living group with many members joined together by one Spirit. "God and the soul," he cries out in his *Soliloquies*, "this and this only!"[1] And this individualism which is characteristic of Augustine continues throughout the whole history of Roman Catholic mysticism, though in both St. Paul and St. John the social and corporate aspect is strongly marked, and will appear again in the groups treated in our later chapters.

It would be interesting, and perhaps profitable, to inquire how far Augustine's doctrine of grace is mystical, but it would lead us through a large and mazy research. One fact, at least, is clear in the doctrine, namely, that something divine comes into man so that he who was before "without merit" has now within himself God's bestowed grace—which is reckoned as merit. The doctrine, however, is not the fruit of personal experience, it is rather a product of historical influence and of logic. It is on a distinctly lower plane than the *personal religion* of St. Augustine, to which this chapter has been largely devoted. It is, of course, a fact that the man cannot be separated from the bishop, his religious experience cannot be sharply divided from his theology, but I believe this mystical side of the great African saint can be emphasized without doing any historical injustice to the Church Father. For the present purpose we may ignore the fact that he taught that God of His own will determines the destiny

[1] See Caird's *Evolution of Theology in Greek Philosophy*, vol. ii. p. 166.

of "everything from angel to worm."[1] Nor are we now concerned with the fact that he formulated the dogma: "No salvation outside the Church."[2] What concerns us is his utterance of the great facts of inward experience, and his personal testimony that the soul is ever on a divine trail, has direct vision of its supreme Goal, and may come into immediate contact and union with That Which Is. The man, with his mighty human experience, is always in evidence. Through the hard crust of cooled theology the warm religious life ever and anon breaks out. Among the arid blocks of logic the flowers of the heart again and again appear. In fact, it is love, not logic, which builds the City of God, though at times the logic seems overworked. "The two cities have been formed by two loves: the earthly by the love of self, even to the contempt of God; the heavenly by the love of God, even to the contempt of self."[3]

[1] *Confessions*, p. 140.
[2] *City of God*, Book V. chap. xviii.
[3] *Ibid.* Book XIV. chap. xxviii.

CHAPTER VI

DIONYSIUS, "THE AREOPAGITE"

AT the end of the chapter on "The Classical Roots of Mysticism," I said that in spite of the attempt to end the reign of Neoplatonic philosophy, it was brought over into the Church and became "spiritual bee-bread" for many centuries. Gregory of Nyssa and St. Augustine were profoundly influenced by the philosophy of this school, as we have seen, and through them many of the loftiest teachings of Plato and Plotinus were translated into Christian thought. The mysticism of the school trickled in through these Fathers, but about a century later it came full flood through an anonymous, mysterious man, whose story and message we must now try to spell out.

At a Council held at Constantinople, in the year 533,[1] the "Severians," a sect of Christians who held that Christ had a single nature, produced in support of their views writings bearing the authorship of Dionysius, who professed to be the convert of Paul in the Areopagus, the first Bishop of Athens, the friend and companion of apostles. The authenticity of the works of the famous Dionysius was at once challenged by the orthodox party. Hypatius, Bishop of Ephesus, pointed out that, if genuine, these works could not have escaped the notice of Cyril and Athanasius, and he declared that no one of the ancients had ever quoted them.[2] But almost from the first these works of Dionysius had a remarkable vogue in

[1] Harnack says that Severus quoted the Dionysian writings at a Council at Tyre, about the year 513, and he is inclined to push their authorship back to a period previous to A.D. 400 (see *Hist. Dog.* vol. iv. p. 282).

[2] This is based on an extant letter written by Innocentius, Bishop of Maronia.

the East. The great Aristotelian physician, Sergius, made a Syriac version of them early in the sixth century, and there were frequent commentaries made upon them by Syrian scholars in the sixth and seventh centuries. They found a great admirer in Maximus "the Confessor" (580-662), who edited them with brief notes and gave them the stamp of his approval. With here and there a notable exception, the writings of Dionysius were, from the time of Maximus, accepted in the Eastern Church as genuine, and their influence became very great, partly because their readers felt through them the genius of a master mind, and partly because they found in them cogent arguments and proofs in favour of existing Church institutions and ecclesiastical authority.[1]

The first extant reference to them in the West is a casual one made by Gregory the Great (in his Homily on Luke xv. 1-10), about the year 600. They are first quoted in a letter of Pope Adrian I., written to Charlemagne.

In 827 a set of the Dionysian writings was sent to Louis I., son of Charlemagne, who turned them over to the Abbey of St. Denis, near Paris. By a confusion, either unconscious or designed, Dionysius the Areopagite was identified with St. Dionysius, or St. Denis, the martyr and patron saint of Paris. This created a great interest in the books, which were not very readable in their peculiarly difficult Greek. Then to cap the climax the arrival of the books was marked by striking miracles—nineteen invalids were suddenly cured of various maladies! This aroused the Abbot, Hilduin, to the duty of preparing a version of the Greek text of the writings, but his scholarship proved too slight for the task.

During the reign of Charles the Bald (843-76), the great Irish scholar, John Scotus Erigena, received a royal command to translate the works of Dionysius into Latin. He not only made the Latin version (which was published, contrary to custom, without the Pope's sanction), but he also wrote an original work which was permeated with

[1] See Frothingham's *Stephen Bar Sudaili*, Leyden, 1886, p. 3.

Dionysian views and which was destined to have a great influence on later generations.

Nearly every great medieval scholar made use of these writings, and the authority of the ancient and venerable convert on Mars Hill came to be almost *final.* A modern writer says that even the *Summa Theologiae* of Thomas Aquinas—the angelic doctor—is but "a hive in whose varied cells he duly stored the honey which he gathered" from the writings of Dionysius, and he became, as we have said, the bee-bread on which all the great mystics fed.[1] Dulac says (*Œuvres de S. Denys l'Aréopagite*): "If the works of Dionysius had been lost, they could be almost reconstructed from the works of Aquinas."

Where did these writings originate? Who was "Dionysius"? Modern scholarship has settled the fact that Dionysius the Areopagite has no historical connection with St. Dionysius of Paris, notwithstanding the miracles worked by the arrival of his books! It has, too, settled the fact that these writings did not come into existence until centuries after Paul's Athenian convert slept the long sleep. The theology and the ecclesiastical system presupposed throughout the writings are unmistakably not of the first or even second century. They are the product of long historical development. The writer in one passage refers to Ignatius, and quotes the words of his epistle: "My own love is crucified."[2] He refers to "Clement the philosopher" (evidently Clement of Alexandria, who died A.D. 220).[3] There is an unmistakable stamp of late Neoplatonic thought everywhere apparent in the Dionysian writings. In fact, it is almost certain that the writer was either a pupil of Proclus or, as is more probable, of Damascius, the second in succession from Proclus, and the last teacher of the Athenian school. It was natural that, when he became a Christian writer, he should assume a name which had sacred memories of

[1] The following is a complete list of the extant Dionysian writings:—I. *On the Celestial Hierarchy*; II. *On the Ecclesiastical Hierarchy*; III. *On the Divine Names*; IV. *On Mystical Theology*; and V. *Ten Letters.*

[2] *Divine Names,* iv. 12.

[3] *Ibid.* v. 9.

Athenian faith, and which was also a link with Greek culture. It is impossible to say whether he intended to deceive his readers, or whether the name was a guileless pseudonym. His letters and books have a slender thread of historical fiction woven into them. They are addressed to "my fellow presbyter Timothy," to "Titus," to "Polycarp," to "John the divine, apostle and evangelist, exiled in Patmos," etc. In the letters to Polycarp, he asks him to remind Apollophanes, a violent opponent of the Christian faith, how when they were fellow students together at Heliopolis, they had beheld the total darkness which covered the world at the time of the crucifixion. In any case, there was as yet no social conscience formed against the assumption of a famous name by an author.

In the book on the *Divine Names*, Dionysius relates how he "with James, the brother of the Lord, and Peter, the chief and noblest head of the inspired apostles," gazed upon the dead body of "her who was the beginning of life and the recipient of God," *i.e.* the Virgin Mary. There are numerous references in the writings to his great mystic master and inspired guide, "Hierotheus." He says that the works of "Hierotheus" were to him "a second Bible." He says in *Divine Names* that his great master, "Hierotheus," has already unfolded the truth, having learned it by an experience in divine things, "and by being made perfect in mystical union." This "Hierotheus" may possibly give us a clue to the locality and date of the Dionysian writings. "Hierotheus" is apparently an assumed name under which a famous Eastern mystic of Edessa named Stephen Bar Sudaili, a scribe and monk, wrote near the close of the fifth century.[1] This Stephen Bar Sudaili held that all Nature is consubstantial with the Divine Essence,

[1] Gregory Bar 'Ebraia, monophysite patriarch of the twelfth century, declared that the work of Stephen Bar Sudaili was entitled the *Book of Hierotheus*, and he supports his assertion on the statement of Kyriakos, patriarch of Antioch (793-817), who says that "the book entitled *Book of Hierotheus* is not by him, but probably by the heretic, Stephen Bar Sudaili." John, Bishop of Dara, a noted mystic, who lived in the eighth and ninth centuries, says positively that the *Book of Hierotheus* was written by Stephen Bar Sudaili, and there was a steady Syriac tradition to this effect (Frothingham, *op. cit.* pp. 63-66).

and that in a final consummation God will become all in all, and all things will be one nature with God. Contemporary accounts connect him with Egyptian influence, where extreme mystical views prevailed among many of the monks. Bar Sudaili claimed for himself direct divine revelations, and believed himself to be an inspired man. He declares that more than once he has attained the highest stage of mystical union with the One—"the Arch-Good," as he calls Him, the goal of all ascent. Already in this *Book of Hierotheus* there appears an account of the *mystical ladder* by which the soul makes its glorious homeward ascent. (1) The soul must unite the spark of Good Nature (*i.e.* the Divine Principle) which belongs to it with the Universal Essence from which it has sprung, by purifying itself of every opposing principle, and by being absorbed in its spiritual goal; then it becomes like a new-born child which passes from darkness into light. (2) It reaches the holy place of the Cross, where it endures a passion and suffers a crucifixion in the same manner that Christ suffered, for unless the soul undergoes all that Christ underwent it cannot be perfected. (3) At a higher stage it receives a baptism of the Spirit and of fire, *without which there is no life*, and thereupon it enters into complete Sonship. (4) There remains a yet higher experience when the soul is utterly and wholly absorbed into its luminous Essence and gets beyond the distinction of self and Other—this is the Ultima Thule of mystical experience. In this stage there is a mysterious silence, a mystical quiet when the soul understands without knowledge and without words.

It is not improbable that this "Hierotheus" is the mystic master of our author, and if so, it is likely that these Dionysian writings first saw the light between A.D. 475 and 525, so that perhaps the ripe seeds of Greek philosophy were being planted in the soil of the Church almost exactly at the time Justinian was banishing the last cultivators of the garden of the Academe.

It has long been the custom of critics to belabour this

monk-philosopher for his "turgid" style, for his hierarchies of "bloodless abstractions," and for his "inscrutable anonymous God," but, after all, there is something genuinely *human* in him, and he was doing his best to "utter himself" in the terms of thought which were the current stock of his time. There is a real throb of heart even under these "turgid" sentences.

There is a fine passage in the eighth *Letter* which reveals a generous, sympathetic spirit, and which indicates that, however he might soar into realms of abstraction, he still knew the tender, loving Christ of the Gospel records. The *Letter* relates how Dionysius had felt it his duty to rebuke a monk for his lack of mercy, and he tells an incident to carry conviction to the stern and unforgiving monk. "I will recount," he says, "a divine vision of a certain holy man, and it is a true story."[1]

"When I was once in Crete, the holy Carpus entertained me—a man, of all others, most fitted, on account of great purity of mind, for Divine Vision. Now, on a certain occasion, an unbeliever had grieved him by leading a Christian astray to Godlessness. And when he ought to have prayed for both, he allowed rancorous enmity and bitterness to sink into his heart. In this evil condition he went to sleep, for it was evening, and at midnight (for he was accustomed at that appointed hour to rise, on his own accord, for the Divine melodies) he arose, not having enjoyed, undisturbed, his slumbers, which were continually broken; and when he stood collected for the Divine Converse, he was guiltily vexed and displeased, saying, that it was not just that godless men, who prevent the straight ways of the Lord, should live. And, whilst saying this, he besought Almighty God, by some stroke of lightning, suddenly, without mercy, to cut short the lives of them both. But, whilst saying this, he declared that he seemed to see suddenly the house in which he stood, first torn asunder, and from the roof divided into two in the midst, a sort of gleaming fire before his eyes (for the place seemed now under the open sky), borne down from the heavenly region close to him; and, the heaven itself given way, and upon the back of the heaven, Jesus, with innumerable angels, in the form of men, standing around Him. This, indeed, he saw above, and himself marvelled; but below, when Carpus had bent down, he affirmed that he saw the very foundation

[1] I have here used the translation of John Parker, London, 1897.

ripped in two, to a sort of yawning and dark chasm, and those very men, upon whom he had invoked a curse, standing before his eyes, within the mouth of the chasm, trembling, pitiful, only just not yet carried down by the mere slipping of their feet; and from below the chasm, serpents creeping up and gliding from underneath around their feet, now contriving to drag them away, and weighing them down and lifting them up, and again inflaming or irritating them with their teeth or their tails, and all the time endeavouring to pull them down into the yawning gulf; and that certain men also were in the midst, co-operating with the serpents against these men, at once tearing and pushing and beating them down. And they seemed to be on the point of falling, partly against their will, partly by their will; almost overcome by the calamity, and at the same time resigned. And Carpus said that he himself was glad, whilst looking below, and that he was forgetful of the things above; further, that he was vexed and made light of it, because they had not already fallen, and that he had often attempted to accomplish the fact, and that, when he did not succeed, he was irritated, and cursed. And, when with difficulty he raised himself, he saw the heaven again, as he saw it before, and Jesus, moved with pity at what was taking place, standing up from His supercelestial throne, and descending to them, and stretching a helping hand, and the angels, co-operating with Him, taking hold of the two men, one from one place and another from another, and the Lord Jesus said to Carpus, whilst His hand was yet extended: 'Strike against Me in future, for I am ready, even again, to suffer for the salvation of men; and this is pleasing to Me, provided that other men do not commit sin. But see whether it is well for thee to exchange the dwelling in the chasm, and with serpents, for that with God, and the good and loving angels.' These are the things which I heard myself, and believe to be true."

It is a bold undertaking to endeavour to put into plain English the difficult mystical system of this Greek monk-philosopher, who speaks in a language quite foreign and unknown to the Protestant Christian of the twentieth century. Peradventure, however, there is enough of the Pentecost spirit in his words for us to hear something in our own tongue. The central point of the whole system is the point common to all classical mysticism, namely, that the Godhead is a Unity, a One, beyond all difference, above all qualities or characters. He is (if a hybrid word may be allowed) "super-everything" which can be named or conceived. The Godhead Himself, from whom the revelation comes, is beyond all revelations that are made or can be made of Him.) Beyond all effects there is the Cause of causes, above all that originates there is a "super-original Origin," behind the created there is an Uncreated or Hidden Deity. To say it finally in Dionysius' most "turgid" fashion: "He is the all-super-Deity!"

(This unrevealed Godhead, the Hidden Dark, is not only "above things manifest"; He is also *above thought*, since thought can deal only with what is differentiated and related.[1])

But though He cannot be *known*, He can, nevertheless, be reached and experienced. There are two ways which lead "yonder"—the affirmative way and the negative way. By the *affirmative way* the seeker follows after the "beneficent progression of God," and gathers up what light he can from the revelations and manifestations, as God unveils Himself by going out of His Hiddenness. The Book on the *Heavenly Hierarchy* tells us of this "progression," down through the ninefold ranks of angelic beings, and the *Ecclesiastical Hierarchy* continues the stages of Divine revelation through the ninefold order of sacred symbols and ministers. "The way down" from the Godhead is a Divine *progression*. "The way up" is a *celestial ladder* which leads back to God. This

[1] Tennyson has beautifully expressed this idea of the Nameless Deity, the Hidden Dark, in his poem *The Ancient Sage*:—

> "If thou wouldst hear the Nameless, and wilt dive
> Into the Temple-cave of thine own self,
> There, brooding by the central altar, thou
> Mayst haply learn the Nameless hath a voice,
> By which thou wilt abide, if thou be wise,
> As if thou knewest, tho' thou canst not know;
> For knowledge is the swallow on the lake
> That sees and stirs the surface-shadow there,
> But never yet hath dipt into the abysm,
> The Abysm of all Abysms, beneath, within
> The blue of sky and sea, the green of earth,
> And in the million-millionth of a grain
> Which cleft and cleft again for evermore,
> And ever vanishing, never vanishes,
> To me, my son, more mystic than myself,
> Or even than the Nameless is to me.
> And when thou sendest thy free soul thro' heaven,
> Nor understandest bound or boundlessness,
> Thou seest the Nameless of the hundred names,
> And if the Nameless should withdraw from all
> Thy frailty counts most real, all thy world
> Might vanish like thy shadow in the dark."

progression is an unveiling of the glory and goodness of God, and shows the steps of return to Him, for salvation is nothing short of being made divine. "To be made divine," he says, in *Ecclesiastical Hierarchy*, i. 3, "is to be made like God, as far as may be, and to be made one with Him."

The first stage of progression from the hiddenness to the light is made through the "Great Intelligences" which are nearest God, namely, the Seraphim, who, though not wholly "like Him" (no being can be like Him), are completely turned toward His Oneness, receive directly His illuminations, imitate Him, and so reflect the Divine Glory.[1] These beings have first-hand illuminations, they "participate in the One Himself, and have the feast of the beatific vision, which makes divine all who strain aloft to behold it"; and the Divine energy which "bubbles forth" from the Godhead is passed on by them to the next rank, and so on down, until "every existing thing participates in the Beautiful," *i.e.* in the Godhead.

The order of ranks of the celestial revealers is as follows:—(1) Seraphim, Cherubim, Thrones; (2) Dominations, Virtues, Powers; (3) Principalities, Archangels, Angels. The highest are at "the vestibule of the Godhead," they have "the unsullied fixity of Godlike identity," and they ray forth the highest manifestation of the Godhead which those below are capable of contemplating.[2]

"It is never lawful," says our author, "to cast to swine the bright, unsullied, beautifying comeliness of intelligible pearls!" or, as he says again, "it is impossible that the beams of the Divine Source can shine upon us, unless they are shrouded in the manifold texture of sacred veils."

Though this descending line of Divine Intelligences is not original with Dionysius, it was his formulation

[1] *Heavenly Hierarchy*, xii. 3.

[2] The *Book of Hierotheus* already contains nine orders of celestial essences which have in graded being emanated from the All-Comprehensive One, so that Dionysius seems not to be the originator of this famous conception. The hierarchy of Great Intelligences, arranged in three triads, is plainly constructed after the triads of Proclus and his followers, though Dionysius has renamed them from Scripture.

of the celestial order which fed the imagination of the Middle Ages, and it was his "taper's radiance" which furnished Dante with "the nature and the ministry angelical." It was here, too, that Spenser got those "trinal triplicities" which

> "About Him wait and on His will depend."

And we get an echo of our monk-philosopher in Tennyson's lines:

> "The Great Intelligences fair
> That range above our mortal state."

The ninefold order of the heavenly hierarchy came to be as much a necessary part of human thought as the pictorial facts of the Gospel were. Nobody presumed to question the reality of this descending chain of heavenly revealers, so that not only the poets and theologians made general use of this Dionysian order of progression from God, but it was, as well, taken up everywhere by the popular mind. The "celestial ladder" leading back to God became, too, the common property of all later mystics, and there is hardly a single mystical writer who does not have somewhere in his book a description of "the upward steps" by which the soul flees from the world and the flesh to an inexpressible union with the One Reality who is above knowledge.

The ninefold order of the ecclesiastical hierarchy continues the transmission of Divine Light downward. Here the "mirrors" are no longer Godlike "Intelligences," but signs and symbols which lead the soul to Christ, Who is at the head of this series, as the Godhead is at the summit of the celestial series. He (Christ), by His incarnation, wrought out a unifying fellowship between us, having supremely united our lowly nature with His most divine nature, in order that we might come into spotless and divine life. He calls the race of man to participation in Himself by union with His divine life, so that we shall truly have fellowship with God.[1]

[1] This is a free interpretation of sections 12 and 13 of the third division of chapter iii. of the *Ecclesiastical Hierarchy*.

The long treatise on the *Divine Names* carries out further the idea that God in His inmost nature is *hidden and nameless*, but that there are partial revelations, through veils and symbols and illuminating names, which manifest Him. The discovery of the truth through manifestations is, as I have said, the affirmative way. It consists in gathering up the holy crumbs which fall from the Divine table. There is a super-abundance of the Godhead, an excess of substance, an overflow of being, and in the *outgoing* of God we can discover the attributes which in the Godhead "at home" are swallowed up in the unity of His perfect self. "He goes forth," says Dionysius, "in an unlessened stream into all things that are, though in things divided He remains undivided."[1] The Scriptures (the "Divine Oracles" he calls them) have given us many names for the "Nameless who is above every name," and each name reveals some truth, some aspect of "the super-essential One," the Deity above attributes. But by this method Dionysius thinks that we are at best in the condition of the person who knows his friend only by the shadow he casts, or by the distant echo of his voice. The *affirmative way* never carries the seeker beyond "reflections" of the ultimate reality.

The affirmative truths of Christianity, the doctrines of the Church, the faiths of the creeds, are, for Dionysius, on a lower level than mystical experience, through which the soul rises into union with the unknowable God. They all give only *relative knowledge*. To arrive at the real goal, "knowledge" must be transcended.

> "We ought to know that our mind has the power for thought, through which it views things intellectual, but that the union through which it is *brought into contact* with things beyond itself surpasses the nature of the mind. We must, then, contemplate things Divine by *union*, not in ourselves, but by going out of ourselves entirely and becoming wholly of God."[2]

He, therefore, prefers the *negative way*, which he

---

[1] *Divine Names*, ii. 11. [2] *Ibid.* chap. vii. sec. 1.

skilfully illustrates by the figure of a sculptor: The Godhead is reached by the negation of all existing things,

> "just as those who make a lifelike statue chip off all the encumbrances, cut away all superfluous material, and bring to light the Beauty hidden within. So we abstract (negate) everything in order that *without* veils we may know that Unknown which is concealed by all the light in existing things."[1]

In another figure he compares mystical theology to "that ladder on which the angels of God ascended and descended." The descending angels stand for the *affirmative way*, and the ascending angels for the *negative way*, which takes the soul up to God. That God, who is super-everything, "dwells in the super-luminous gloom of silence," and must be found with "the eyeless mind."

There is an illuminative passage in Dionysius' address to "dear Timothy," in the opening of *Mystical Theology*, which furnishes the method of mystical progress up into the Divine Dark—dark with excess of Light:

> "O dear Timothy, by thy persistent commerce with mystic visions, leave behind sensible perceptions and intellectual efforts, and all objects of sense and of intelligence, and all things being and not being, and be raised aloft above knowledge to union, as far as is attainable, with Him who is above every essence [or attribute] and knowledge. For by a resistless and absolute ecstasy from thyself and everything, thou wilt be carried up to the super-essential ray of the Divine Dark—when thou hast cast away all and become free from all."[2]

"By laying aside all mental energies," and "by all-pure contemplation," the soul participates "with unimpassioned and immaterial mind" in "that super-essential Light, in which all knowledge pre-exists," and enters into a *union* above thought, above states of consciousness, above knowledge.[3] This is ecstasy, which is the final refuge of all negation mysticism. He describes it thus in *Mystical Theology*: "By ecstasy thou wilt be carried to the

[1] *Mystical Theology*, chap. ii. 1.
[2] *Ibid.* chap. i. 1.
[3] See *Divine Names*, chap. i. 4.

super-essential Ray of divine darkness"; and again, "By the inactivity of all knowledge one is united, *in his better part*, to the altogether Unknown, and by knowing nothing, *knows above mind*."[1]

In one of the most beautiful passages of his writings, Dionysius tells how "pure prayer" draws the soul toward that Divine Union which is the mystic goal. Our prayers elevate us to "the high ascent,"

> "as if a luminous chain were suspended from the celestial heights, and we, by ever clutching this, first with one hand and then with the other, seem to draw it down, but in reality we are ourselves carried upwards to the high splendours of the luminous rays. Or as if, after we have embarked on a ship and are holding on to the cable reaching to some rock, we do not draw the rock to us, but draw, in fact, ourselves and the ship to the rock."[2]

This short, untechnical sketch presents the main features of the famous system of the anonymous Greek. It is far removed from the simplicity of the primitive message. It has few marks of the apostolic word. It is a religion of ripe speculation, and, spite of the abundance of Bible texts throughout the writings, it is, in fact, Neo-platonic philosophy slightly sprinkled with baptismal water from a Christian font. But whatever its origin, it early became the form and type of mystical religion within the Church, and its influence is discernible in every mystical sect of Christendom. We already have in these writings the Christianity of the Cloister. The path upward is a solitary path which the soul travels by itself alone. The goal is beatific gazing, absorption in the Godhead. The world, with its tasks and calls, is left behind and forgotten. Salvation is thoroughly individualistic. We hear enough of "love," but it is no longer the love which fills the primitive message. The "love" of this monk is not a word which means self-sharing and self-giving. It is rather an emotional, sensuous thrill, an exhilaration, intoxication even, which the person experiences from Divine

[1] *Mystical Theology*, chap. i. 1 and 3.

[2] *Divine Names*, iii. 1. This is almost certainly a memory of the beautiful passage in *Clement of Alexandria*.

contact—and it descends easily to unwholesome dreams and pathological states. His first great interpreter in the West, John Scotus Erigena, seized the pantheistical aspect of the system and brought to full emphasis the doctrine of the "progression of God" into all things, and the return of all things into God—a doctrine which brought forth strange fruit when the times were ripe. Even in the system of Dionysius there is no place for genuine *evil.* "All things that exist, so far as they exist, are good; so far as they are deprived of the good, they are not existent."[1] Everything that is, radiates out from God, and therefore evil is nothing but a defect, a negation. The ground of the mysticism is in the faith that the soul itself is Divine, is an outflow of God, and therefore needs only "to come wholly to itself," to come wholly to Him.

One sees at once that we are here far away from the simplicity and concreteness of the Gospels. We are dealing not with the Father whom Christ has revealed, but with the "Absolute One" of metaphysics who is beyond all revelations. We have, too, passed from the Pauline conception of an immanent God in whom men live and move and are, to a mysticism, based on emanations from a hidden centre. The mischief of turning away from the concrete to the abstract, from the God who is known to an unknowable Deity, is fully committed in these writings, and the groping of centuries after a God who hides is the pitiful result.

But in many ways this anonymous monk, who was to teach the foremost Christians for ten centuries to come, served the truth. He kindled in multitudes of souls a pure passion for God, and taught very dark ages that the *one thing* worth seeking with the entire being is God. He iterated and reiterated that God Himself is the ground of the soul, and that there is an inward way to Him open to all men. He insisted on personal experience as the primary thing in religion, and so became the father of a great family of devout and saintly mystics, who advanced true religion in spite of errors of conception. And he

[1] *Divine Names*, iv. 20.

did well in maintaining that there is an experience of Reality which transcends mere head-knowledge—a finding of God in which the whole being, heart, will, and mind, are expanded and satisfied, even though language cannot formulate what is being experienced.

CHAPTER VII

A GREAT LIGHT IN THE DARK AGES

JOHN THE SCOT, CALLED ERIGENA

"THERE are as many unveilings of God (*Theophanies*) as there are saintly souls." Thus wrote John the Scot, often called "Erigena," in the ninth century.[1] It is a great saying. It takes us far away from the formulation of "false decretals," which were stirring the world in those days, and far from the contentions of ecclesiastics, and fixes our thought on the truth that every person may become a revealing place for God, or, as a present-day writer has well put it, "A saintly life makes a man an auditory nerve of the Eternal."[2]

There have been few more luminous illustrations of the truth of his saying than John the Scot himself. Prophets do not come in any age by *observation*, nor is there any astronomy which can calculate the curve of the prophet's movements, but John the Scot is in an unusual degree a surprise. He had to do his work in that gloomy period when European civilization was hard beset by the ravages of the Norsemen, when both England and France were forced to meet that last great inroad of barbarian invaders. Certainly an inauspicious age for philosophy. His coming and his course are as incalculable as the appearance of a meteor. He is a fulfilment of the word, "The Spirit bloweth where He listeth." It is no wonder that his generation did not understand him, or that the

[1] *De Divisione Naturae*, iv. 7.

[2] Brierley in *Ourselves and the Universe*, p. 233.

guardians of orthodoxy failed to find the *shibboleth* in his message, for he was a spiritual alien in the Latin Church of the ninth century—fighting the battles of truth with strange weapons, and using the spiritual coinage of other realms and other dates. It is quite worth our while to get acquainted with him, for he is one of the torch-bearers in the long line of teachers of mystical religion.

The material for the story of his life is very scanty, and the authorities are conflicting. He is variously reputed to have been born in England, Ireland, Scotland, and Wales. It is now, however, fairly well settled that he was a native of Ireland. He was known to his contemporaries as Joannes Scotus, or John the Scot. The term "Scot" at this period would mark him as a native either of Scotland or of Ireland, which was the original Scotland. He designates himself, in his translation of Dionysius, as John Ierugena. This name alternates in early manuscripts with Eriugena,[1] and considerably later becomes fixed as Erigena. It seems to mean "Erin-born," and one of his contemporary opponents, Prudentius of Troyes, says that Hibernia produced him, and speaks of his "Celtic eloquence." Since the sixteenth century he has been generally called John Scotus Erigena, and the unwary have often confused him with the great schoolman of the thirteenth century, John Duns Scotus.

I have called Erigena a *surprise*, and I have said that he came upon his age like a meteor, but, as happens in every case, on close analysis we find that even he was a part of a movement, and when we come to examine his religious environment during the formative years of his life, he turns out to be less meteoric than we first supposed.

Irish Christianity has a history apart from the main lines of the Roman Church, and it has unique and distinct characteristics of its own. The planting of Christianity in Ireland is a beautiful story of missionary effort, even when the halo of legend is removed. Celtic pirates from Ireland

[1] The old name for Ireland was Eriu, of which Erin, the name that has come down to us, is a dative case, and should be spelled Erinn. See article on "Joannes Scotus Erigena," by William Larminie, in *Contemporary Review*, vol. lxxi. p. 559.

carried away with them, from a raid on the coast of Gaul, a boy of sixteen named Patricius, or, in modern form, Patrick.[1] For ten years he was a slave, a keeper of kine, but during these years of servitude he came into possession of a great spiritual experience, which had already begun to dawn in his boyhood home in Gaul. He writes in his *Confessions* that, even in those days of slavery, amidst the frost and snow, he felt no ill, "nor," says he, "was there any sloth within me, because the Spirit was burning within me." After ten years among the flocks he fled from his slavery, and wandered back to his native land, but now there came upon him a call to a service of another sort. In a beautiful passage of the *Confessions* he says:

> "In the dead of night, I saw a man coming to me as if from Ireland, whose name was Victorinus, and who bore countless letters. And he gave me one of them, and I read the beginning of it, which contained the words: 'The voice of the Irish.' And while I was repeating the words of this beginning, I thought I heard the voice of those who were near the wood Foclut, which is nigh to the western sea; and they cried thus: 'We pray thee, holy youth, to come and live among us henceforth.' And I was greatly pricked in heart and could read no more."

The actual facts of his missionary labours are pretty well shrouded in the "dim magnificence of legend," but out of the consecrated work of his life there sprang a very noble form of Christianity, and the missionary passion of its founder was a striking characteristic of the leaders of Irish Christianity.

The Irish Church from the first was organized on a different basis from that of the Roman Catholic Church. The organization of the former was of a primitive and tribal type, suited to a rural and somewhat crude society.[2] It was monastic rather than episcopal, and its emphasis was upon right living rather than upon elaborate theology. An old chronicler of the seventh century says that "Ireland was full of saints." The Irish monastery was in reality a

[1] There was undoubtedly a *planting* of Christianity in Ireland even before the coming of St. Patrick.

[2] See for details, Hodgkin's *Political History of England*, chap. ix.; and Green's *Making of England*, pp. 278-81.

Christian colony, "a holy experiment" for the practice of brotherhood. It had its stern and fanatical aspect, but it had also a very human and practical side. Under the leadership of the noblest of her missionaries, Columba,[1] one of these "Christian colonies" sprang up on the little island of Hy, afterwards called Iona, off the coast of Scotland, and from this centre Celtic Christianity spread across the British Island, transforming the rude inhabitants of Mercia and Northumbria, and producing, in Aidan and Oswald, beautiful flowers of sainthood.

But the missionary zeal of these Celtic Christians was not limited to their group of islands. It has been said that "the Celt yielded not to the Northman in his passion for travel."[2] It was, however, not passion for travel so much as passion for human souls that drove these men from their quiet monasteries to face dangers and difficulties incident to the task of planting Christianity in the neglected spots of the Continent. Three of these Irish travellers, Saint Columban, Saint Gall, and Saint Kilian, stand forth among the most devoted missionaries in the long history of Christian activity. They founded their colonies in the strongholds of barbarism, and made the slender beginnings of a new civilization, a new art, and a new learning.[3] Their passion for learning was as absorbing as their missionary zeal. In fact, it was in the Celtic schools that classical learning was preserved through the Dark Ages. When the narrow spirit of a dogmatic Church was decrying "the idle vanities of secular learning,"[4] and Europe was sinking

[1] Dr. Hodgkin, *op. cit.* p. 150, says of Columba: "A man of somewhat hot temper in his youth, softened and controlled in later life, with a stately beauty of features which seemed to correspond with his princely descent, and with a kind of magnetic power of attracting to himself the devotion of his followers; a lover of animals and beloved by them." "A great open-air preacher, an organizer and a poet, he might perhaps not unfittingly be called the Wesley of the sixth century."

[2] Poole's *Illustrations of the History of Mediæval Thought* (London, 1884), p. 10.

[3] Haddan says (*Remains*, p. 265): "Between the latter years of the sixth and the early ones of the eighth centuries, the missionary work of the Scot stretched along the border of then existing Christendom, from the Orkneys to the Thames, and from the sources of the Rhine and the Danube downwards to the shores of the Channel, from Seine to Scheldt, while at Bobbio, near the River Trebia in Italy, was planted a Catholic Irish colony in the midst of Arian Lombards; and unknown but not less zealous missionaries bore the Gospel northwards, over stormy and icy seas, even to the Faroe Islands and the shores of Iceland."

[4] Letter of Pope Gregory the Great to the Bishop of Vienne.

into ignorance of the very language in which the world's noblest literature was written, Celtic Christians in the monasteries of Ireland were the guardians of classical culture, and they remained untouched by the invasion of barbarism, which well-nigh swamped the rest of Europe. They continued to learn and to teach the Greek language, and to cherish their Greek manuscripts of the New Testament, and they kept aflame a passion for classical literature.[1]

Bede describes a plague which occurred in Ireland in 664, and he says that

"many of the nobility and of the lower ranks of the English nation were there at the time, who in the days of the Bishops Finan and Colman, forsaking their native island retired thither, either for the sake of divine studies, or of a more continent life. Some of them devoted themselves to a monastical life, others chose rather to apply themselves to study, going about from one master's cell to another. The Scots [*i.e.* the Irish] willingly received them all, and took care to supply them with food, as also to furnish them with books to read and their teaching gratis."[2] Bede also tells of the missionary undertakings in Friesland of Wicberht, who was "famous for his contempt of the world *and for his knowledge, for he had lived many years a stranger in Ireland.*"[3]

Wherever these Irish missionaries went their learning went with them, and their centres of culture sprang up like oases in the desert. A monkish chronicler, writing from a cell in the monastery of St. Gall, has left a semi-legendary account of the way in which Irish learning *invaded* the realm of Charlemagne, and, though not to be taken at its face value, the kernel of the story is historically correct. The chronicler says:

"When the illustrious Charles had begun to reign alone in the western parts of the world, and the study of letters was everywhere well-nigh forgotten, in such sort that the worship of the true God declined, it chanced that two Scots from Ireland lighted with the British merchants on the coast of Gaul, men

[1] See A. W. Haddan's *Remains* (Oxford and London, 1876), pp. 271-73; and Poole's *Illustrations of Mediæval History*, pp. 11 *seq.* and p. 57.

[2] Giles' edition of Bede, *Ecclesiastical History of England* (London, 1840), p. 185.

[3] Bede, p. 285.

learned without compare as well in secular as in sacred writings; who, since they showed nothing for sale, kept crying to the crowd that gathered to buy: 'If any man is desirous of wisdom, let him come to us and receive it; for we have it to sell.' Their reason for saying that they had it for sale was that, seeing them inclined to deal in saleable articles and not to take anything gratuitously, they might by this means either rouse them to purchase wisdom like other goods or, as the events following show, turn them by such declaration to wonder and astonishment. At length their cry, being long continued, was brought by certain that wondered at them or deemed them mad, to the ears of Charles the King, who was always a lover and most desirous of wisdom; who, when he had called them with all haste into his presence, inquired if, as he understood by report, they had wisdom verily with them. 'Yea,' said they, 'we have it, and are ready to impart to any that rightly seek it in the name of the Lord.' When, therefore, he had inquired what they would have in return for it, they answered: 'Only proper places and noble souls and such things as we cannot travel without, food and wherewith to clothe ourselves.'"[1]

So great was the *invasion* of Irish scholars that a writer in the reign of Charles the Bald, grandson of Charlemagne, declares that "almost all Ireland, regardless of the barrier of the sea, is flocking to our shores with a troop of philosophers." Of these bearers of learning and devotees of philosophy, John the Scot was easily foremost in original power and in learning. We are in the dark in reference to his early life. We simply find him in the court of Charles the Bald, about 847,[2] without knowing how he came to be there.

His first publication was a tract on "Predestination," written in 851. It was occasioned by the teaching of the monk Gottschalk, who had pushed the Augustinian doctrine of Predestination to such an extreme that there was practically no function left for the Church. The

[1] This account is found in the opening chapter of *Gesta Karoli Magni*. It is published in Pertz' *Monumenta Germaniae Historica*, vol. ii. pp. 731 *seq.*

[2] Prudentius, who was Bishop of Troyes, by the year 847 speaks of a former intimate friendship for John the Scot, a friendship formed in the palace of Charles. In his dedication to the treatise on Predestination, Erigena says: "Amid the waves of the sail-covered sea of the dominion of our lord, the most glorious Charles, even though we have gained the calm of his haven, yet scarce have we been allowed the shortest interval to gaze upon the traces of wisdom," which seems to imply only a short residence in France.

destiny of every individual, by the teaching of Gottschalk, was settled by divine decree—a predestination in two kinds: on the one hand to eternal joy, on the other to eternal woe. There was in the Church no power to change the outcome of these infinite decrees. The monk was declared a heretic at the Council of Chiersey, in 849, and his doctrine was condemned, but the condemnation did not settle the vexing question which had been raised; and Hincmar, Archbishop of Rheims, bethought himself of the Irish scholar in the royal court, and appealed to the philosopher to see if reason could not settle the problem, which would not disappear even before dread anathemas. The Archbishop soon discovered that the man to whom he had appealed was more dangerous than the original heretic. Instead of a plain answer which silenced the advocates of extreme predestination and built up the breach which the enemy had opened, John the Scot started a train of argument with which no churchmen of the period could cope, and dragged into the fold of the Western Church the long-forgotten speculations of the Greek thinkers. If ever a cuckoo's egg was hatched in the theological nest, here certainly was one.

In the front of his tract Erigena announced that true philosophy and true religion are identical, and he asserted that the presentation of the truth is the proper method of combating heresy. His central position is the absolute unity of God, which implies a unity both of will and knowledge. Now, if God predestined to evil, He would of necessity know (*i.e.* foreknow) evil, and that would mean that His nature is a *duality* of good and evil, and not a unity. Therefore, from His very nature God could not predestinate to evil. "The truth is," says this bold follower of Plato, "*evil is merely a negation*, and lies entirely outside the knowledge of God, who only knows and wills the good." Neither sin nor punishment can thus have any ground in the will of God. If evil were predestinated it would mean that there was some power, or fate, above God, *determining* His will. The conclusion is that evil has no ground except in the free choice of human will. Sin is simply perverted individual will. It is always due to absence of God—that is to say, to ignorance of the truth. It is, too, its own damnation, its own Nemesis. God does not punish—the sinner punishes himself. Sin, then, being due to the apparent separation of the individual from God, must vanish when "that which is in part" comes home into the one unity—God. For God, who is the source of all Reality, *evil is not.* It has meaning only in the *sphere of time.* God is not in time, and evil therefore has no place in the eternal order.

This tract on Predestination was twice condemned by Church Councils—at Valence in 855 and at Langres in 859. John was, of course, *refuted* by the theologians of the day. One attack on his tract finds seventy-seven heresies in it, and a later polemic raises the count to one hundred and six! His old friend, Prudentius, Bishop of Troyes, calls his argument the product of a "poison-infected mind" and a "barbarous barking."

John's part in the great contemporary controversy on Transubstantiation is not so easily made out, because no tract—at least none proved to be from his pen—has come down to us. It had long been held that some mystic change was wrought, by priestly consecration, in the "sacred elements." But the specific nature of the change had been left vague. No dogma on this subject had yet been established, and there was no teaching which prevailed *semper et ubique.* The sacred word "Transubstantiation" was not yet adopted. The famous controversy, which finally led to the settlement of the doctrine of Transubstantiation, was opened by the monk Radbertus, who, in the year 844, dedicated to Charles the Bald an edition of his book on the *Sacrament of the Body and Blood of Christ.* Radbertus presented the extreme view that at consecration the Bread is completely transformed into the very Body that was born of the Virgin Mary, and the Wine into the actual Blood of that Body. This view, of course, exalted the priest, and carried with it the necessity for a hierarchy. It was a position which at once found favour with the clergy. It was, however, a view which carried the Church over to a crude materialism, and it was therefore an issue that called for a re-affirmation of the spiritual aspect of religion. The times needed a champion of idealism. There seems little doubt that our Irish philosopher went into the contest on the idealistic side of the issue. In 1050 a book dealing with this subject, and bearing his name, was condemned by the Church.[1] A book was also written by Adrevalt against the errors of John the Scot on the Body and Blood of Christ, and John's name is persistently associated with the anti-materialistic side of this controversy.

Though no special treatise from John the Scot on this subject has survived, we know what he thought of "matter" in general, and he has not left us in doubt as to what position he took in reference to *sacraments.* He says: "There is nothing in the visible and material world which does not signify something immaterial and reasonable,"[2] so that everything is a *symbol*, and has a sacramental significance. *Matter is only a concourse of accidents or qualities, no real being.*[3] It is wholly dependent on thought for its existence, and therefore it would be absurd to say that the "material" Bread and Wine are more than symbols. The *value* of a sacrament for John could only be an inward and spiritual value—a value for faith. There is a striking passage in his Exposition of the Celestial Hierarchy of Dionysius in which he expresses the view, now so familiar among English Protestants, that the sacrament of the bread and wine is an outward and visible sign of an inward and spiritual grace, which grace is a direct participation in spirit with Christ, Whom we taste with our minds and Whom we receive in the inner man for our salvation and spiritual increase, until we come through His presence to an unspeakable deification; this idea of deification being, of course, an inheritance from his Greek masters.[4]

[1] It is now generally held, though the point is not proved, that this particular book was written by Ratramnus.

[2] *De Divisione Naturae*, v. 3.

[3] *Ibid.* i. 62.

[4] The passage reads in the original as follows:—"*Sequitur et Jesu participationis ipsam divinissimae eucharistae assumptionem* [italics in the text]. Intuere,

This position that a sacrament is only an outward sign of an inward event, plainly comes out in what he says on Baptism: "When any faithful persons receive the sacrament of baptism, what happens but the conception and birth *in their hearts* of *God the word, of and through the Holy Ghost*? Thus every day Christ is conceived *in the womb of faith* as in that of a pure mother, and is born and nourished."[1] He says elsewhere: "We who do believe in Him (the Christ), *do in our spirits sacrifice Him and in our minds—not with our teeth—eat of Him*." "The pious mind tastes inwardly the body of Christ, the stream of sacred blood, and the ransom price of the world."[2]

We may safely conclude that though his arguments were powerless to beat back the set of materialistic tendencies, which fastened Transubstantiation on the Church, bringing with it the blight of moral character and the supremacy of the priestly order, there was at least a champion there of the other view of religion. There was —the hostility of officialdom to John shows it—a voice crying in the wilderness that the seat of religion is in the soul of man.

John continued in a very positive way the idea of a progressive revelation, already taught by the Montanists. He marked out in his *Commentary on the Gospel of John* three stages of priesthood. The first stage—that of the priesthood of the Old Testament—was transitory, and it saw the truth only through the thick veils of mysterious types. The second priesthood, that of the New Testament, had a greater light of truth, but still obscured by symbols. The third priesthood, that which is to come, will see God

quam pulchre, quam expresse asserit visibilem hanc eucharistiam ; quam quotidie sacerdotes ecclesiae in altari conficiunt ex sensibili materia panis et vini, quamque confectam et sanctificatam corporaliter accipiunt, typicam esse similitudinem spiritualis participationis Jesu, quem fideliter solo intellectu gustamus, hoc est, intelligimus inque nostrae naturae interiora viscera sumimus, ad nostram salutem, et spirituale incrementum, et ineffabilem deificationem" (Migne, vol. cxxii. p. 140 B).

[1] *De Divisione Naturae*, ii. 33.

[2] The last two quotations are taken from Alice Gardner's valuable book, *Studies in John the Scot*, p. 84. Compare this last quotation with George Fox's testimony: "I saw the blood of Christ how it came into the heart."

face to face. To the first corresponds the law of condemnation, to the second the law of Grace; the third will be the kingdom of God. The first assisted human nature, which was corrupted by sin; the second ennobled it by faith; the third will illumine it with direct contemplation. The Church of the present will be swallowed up by the light of the Church of the future, when souls will actually possess God by direct communion with Him by the Spirit. The Church of the New Testament is only a symbolic image of this Church of the Spirit—the eternal Church, which is to come into existence when the revelation of the Spirit has fully come.[1]

It is for us the most interesting fact in the story of John's life that he made a translation of the writings of Dionysius the Areopagite, a translation which became the great book of devotion for mystical souls for many generations. He undertook the work at the command of Charles the Bald. The translation was a somewhat slavish Latin parallel of the Greek rather than a free translation, but it served its purpose and enabled the Middle Ages to read these mystical books. The Roman Librarian, Anastasius, expressed his amazement at "that barbarian from the ends of the earth having the intellect to grasp and the skill to render such things into another tongue." The Pope, however, was not so well pleased over the triumph of learning. He complained to the King that a copy of the work had not been sent to him for his approval, and he adds significantly that "this Johannes was formerly reported not to have shown true wisdom in some matters." He also translated another profoundly mystical work—*Selections from the writings of the Confessor Maximus.*[2]

It was on this mystical literature that John fed his soul, and out of it he constructed his own world-view; and we must now turn to the book into

[1] *Joannis Scoti Comment. in Evang. sec. Joan.* in Migne's *Patrologiae Cursus Completus*, vol. cxxii. pp. 308-309.

[2] Maximus (580-662), monk and martyr in the Eastern Church; a disciple of Dionysius and of Gregory of Nyssa; author of a commentary on the writings of *Dionysius Areopagita*, and of the *Mystagogia*. *Opera* (Paris Edition), 1675.

which John's life went, the book which marks a philosophical epoch, and which, together with the Dionysian literature, turned the stream of Greek Mysticism into Christian Scholasticism—the book *On the Division of Nature*.[1] The work, composed of five "books," is written in the Platonic dialogue style, the dialogue being between a Master and a Learner. I shall not undertake to give the "system" of Erigena in full. For that I will refer my readers to the valuable essay by Thomas Whittaker in his volume *Apollonius of Tyana*, and other essays. I shall select the aspects of his teaching which have special bearing on subsequent mystical movements. For Erigena the univere is a *divine procession*. In fact, he traces the very word for God (θεός) to the Greek verb *θέω*, which means to *run* or *flow*, *i.e.* to go out. God is both the Alpha and Omega, the cause and the end, the source and the goal, of everything that *is*. In the *procession* there are four stages, or "types," which are the four "divisions of nature"—"nature" meaning here everything that is. The first type, or stage, is, "That which creates and is not created"; the second is, "That which is created and creates"; the third is, "That which is created and does not create"; the fourth is, "That which neither creates nor is created." The first type is God as the ground and principle of all things—the primal, undifferentiated Unity. This takes us back to God before He "goes out" of Himself, and reveals Himself. What God the Alpha—God in Himself—may be, mind can never grasp. In the presence of this mystery intellect is dumb. At this height (or in this depth) there are no attributes, for "attributes" appear only when God "goes out" to reveal Himself—only when He proceeds out of unity into differentiation. God as Principle is "above" all contrasts and distinctions. He is "beyond" all that we can say about Him. Every utterance of ultimate truth about Him must be an "everlasting nay," every road a *via negativa*. God is *not* any finite thing,

[1] It was written in Greek with the title Περὶ φύσεως μερισμοῦ. The title of the Latin translation is *De Divisione Naturae*. The Oxford edition of 1681 was edited by Thomas Gale.

no matter how long the catalogue; nor is He completely known by any finite thing or quality.[1]

But there is a divine "procession" by which God reveals Himself in an unfolding universe. He cannot be "seen" in Himself; He can be "seen" in His creation. The second of the four "divisions"—that which is created and creates—is the immaterial world of Ideas, of prototypes. These perfect patterns of things have their origin in God, they are His thoughts. "God," so Erigena says, "does not know things because they are—they *are because He knows* (*i.e. thinks*) *them*."[2] That which is *real* in any object, what is called the *essence* of the object, is the Divine Idea, which the object manifests, and this Idea, or pattern, *creates* the object, so that our visible world is all only a "copy" of a perfect Divine pattern. These patterns are themselves dynamic—they are Divine *wills*, as well as Divine thoughts; that is to say, when God thinks, things are.

The third "division"—that which is created and does not create—is the visible universe, the world of time and space. This is only an "appearance," or shadow, of the real world of changeless patterns. Creation for Erigena, means only a local and temporal *exhibition of eternal essences*. The visible world is nothing but the *appearance* of invisible primordial Causes. Take away from any object in this visible world all that can be thought about it, *i.e.* its Idea, which constitutes its "primordial cause," and nothing is left. In the last analysis everything turns out to be *immaterial*. "Matter," so-called, is no real being; it is only an aggregation of "qualities." Remove the "qualities" which thought can seize, and *nothing remains*. So that even *now*, and not

[1] Note how a modern poet has expressed this view:

"O Thou that in our bosom's shrine
Dost dwell—unknown because divine;

. . . .

I will not frame one thought of what
Thou mayest either be or not;
I will not prate of *thus* or *so*,
Nor be profane with *yes* or *no*;
Enough that in our soul and heart
Thou, whatsoe'er Thou mayest be, art."

ARTHUR HUGH CLOUGH.

[2] *De Divisione Naturae*, ii. 28, page 84 of Gale's edition.

merely in some remote consummation, the Divine Ideas are all that is. The whole creation is thus a revelation of God. The real nature of things is God, and there is nothing "outside" the nature of things—God is all and in all. Time and space, which change eternal realities to local and temporal appearances, are conditions only of our finite minds. As soon, however, as mind rises from sense to pure thought it finds within itself the eternal prototypes. It leaves behind the world of "broken parts," and sees the immutable whole, "the perfect round" of reality. He gives one curious instance of the way in which the "broken parts" are divinely united. Man was originally a "sexless unity"; by the "fall," *i.e.* by temporal creation, he was divided into two sexes, but in Jesus Christ, by whom God is revealed in a supreme theophany, the unity is restored, for in Him is "neither male nor female"![1]

The fourth "division"—that which is not created and does not create—is God, the Omega, the goal of all that is. When John comes to treat of the consummation, or return, of all things into God, he says that the difficulty of telling it is so great that in comparison all that has gone before is "like plain sailing in an open sea." In reality the primal and the ultimate are identical—God the source and God the goal are *one.* The temporal process, the vast evolutionary scheme, is only a theophany or revelation of God. The web of unity *seems* to be unravelled, but only that its separate threads may be discovered, and then again the threads are woven back into the total seamless piece. As we have seen, the reality of all things even in this visible world is God, and thus the final issue must be upward, until everything ends in Him as it began in Him. "This is the end of all things visible and invisible, when all visible things pass into the intellectual, and the intellectual into God, by a marvellous and unspeakable union." "Everything that is shall return into God as air into light. For God shall be all things in all things, when there shall be nothing but

[1] *De Divisione Naturae*, iv. 20.

God alone."[1] As evil is a negation, an unreality, it has no place or being in the final consummation. Evil will prove to have been nothing but the buffer to try the soul's strength—the stage-setting for the spiritual drama. When the *dénouement* comes, both stage and stage scenery fall away. But it is important to note that John does not teach the re-absorption of the soul into the Absolute. He holds to the permanence of the spiritual self—as he puts it, "without any *confusion or destruction of essence*." "The air," he says, "is still air, though it appears to be absorbed into the light of the sun and to be all light. The voice of man, or of pipe, or of lyre, loses not its quality when several by just proportion *make one harmony* in unity among themselves."[2] He is not in the proper sense of the word a pantheist. He never surrenders personal individuality, and he does not teach that God is merely the totality of things. We know God, he would say, only through the procession of the universe, which is a theophany or Divine revelation; but God, as He truly is, is above all revelation and knowledge, and not to be *confused* with things that appear.

His *mysticism* appears especially in his root conception of man's soul. There is an *ultimate ground of truth* in the depth of personal consciousness. Man is an epitome of the universe, a meeting-place of the above and the below, a point of union for the heavenly and the sensuous. *We* understand the world only because the forms or patterns of it—the Ideas which it expresses—are in our own minds. So that a mind which wholly fathomed itself would thereby fathom everything, and we can rise to Divine contemplation because God is the ground and reality of our soul's being. In very truth the soul is always in God, and by *contemplation* it may rise above the mutable and *become that which it beholds*. In a remarkable passage in the Fourth Book,[3] he says:

"Whoever rises to pure understanding becomes that which he understands. We, while we discuss together, in turn become

[1] *De Divisione Naturae*, v. 8. [2] *Ibid.* v. 8. [3] *Ibid.* iv. 9.

one another. For, if I understand what you understand, I become your understanding, and in a certain unspeakable way I am made into you. And also when you entirely understand what I clearly understand you become my understanding, and from two understandings there arises one."

Man, at the depth (or height) of contemplation, finds God, because in this state God is finding Himself in man. Like knows like, and the soul *is* what it sees. God is found in the deeps of the soul, because the soul at bottom is of God. It is just because of his central faith that the soul is a revelation of God, that he uttered the words with which this chapter began: "There are as many theophanies of God as there are souls of the faithful."

This strange book ends with a beautiful *envoi* to the reader.

"Nothing else," he says, "is to be desired except the joy that comes from truth; nothing is to be shunned except its absence. Take from me Christ: no good will remain to me, and no further torment can affright me. I commit my work to God. Hereafter, when these words of mine come into the hands of those who are truly seeking wisdom, with glad mind they will kiss them as if they were their own kinsmen coming back to them. But if they should fall among those who blame rather than sympathize, I should not much contend with them. Let every one use the light he has until that Light comes which will make darkness out of the light of those who philosophize unworthily, and which will turn the darkness of those who welcome It into light."[1]

The speculations of this bold thinker of the Dark Ages made little stir in the busy world in which he lived. There was a strong current setting in toward materialism in religion, and this Irish scholar was a voice crying in the wilderness. There came another age, however, to which this voice *spoke*, and it awoke movements of vast significance. There can be no question that John's message verged on dangerous ground. He had a mighty *vision* for unity and for the oneness of all Reality, but he dealt feebly with the great facts of sin and evil, change

[1] Taken, with omissions, from the end of the "*Division of Nature.*" *De Divisione Naturae*, v. 40.

and multiplicity. He blurred over the unescapable chasm between the good and the bad, the light and the darkness, and he hurried too easily into a crude monism which was bound to breed, as it did, a crop of pantheistic errors. But there was in him a loftiness of spirit, a boldness of vision, a virile idealism, which were sure to be an inspiration to many noble minds in later ages who were, as he was, consecrated to the service of the Invisible Church.

CHAPTER VIII

THE WALDENSES, AN ANTI-SACERDOTAL SECT

THE Roman Church achieved its world supremacy only to find itself incapable of satisfying the inner, spiritual hunger of vast multitudes of people within its wide fold. The twelfth century, which marked the culmination of the *apparent* power of the Church, also marks the beginning of a revolt against its supremacy which finally ended in the Protestant Reformation four centuries later. The ecclesiastical hierarchy—claiming its authority from Christ Who said: "He that would be first shall be servant of all"—had become the most centralized organization in the world. Every earthly power had to bow before its authority, and every member of its own complex body had to be submissively obedient to the papal head or be ruthlessly cut off. Every member of its mighty priesthood wielded more than royal power, for by his ordination he was believed to be possessed of extraordinary supernatural powers. He could open or shut the celestial gates to the laity. He could work the miracle of the Mass and give or withhold the body and blood of Christ. But the Church had won its apparent supremacy at too great a sacrifice of moral and spiritual power.

Gradually the gap between clergy and laity had become a wide chasm. They used different courts of justice and different standards of ethics. The celibacy of those who were ordained had become, after a long, hard struggle, a settled fact. They neither married nor were given in marriage, but were *supposed* to be like the angels in heaven. They, however, were not. The immorality of the clergy, from the highest rank to the lowest order, was universally recognised. So general was vice and so widespread the scandal that a man making confession to a priest of an illicit amour was forbidden to name the partner of his guilt for fear the priest might be tempted by a knowledge of the woman's frailty.[1] The Church was honeycombed with Simony, which is the ecclesiastical name for what we now call "graft." There were thousands of positions within the gift of the Church which appealed to selfish ambition, and these positions were bought and sold. Men sat in the Bishop's seat and wore the Cardinal's hat not because they bore the marks of the Lord Jesus, but because they had wealth and influence. As fast as Simony spread it ate out the heart and life of the Church, and as worldliness came in, spiritual power went out. "Thou seest," said the Pope to Dominic, as he showed him the papal treasures, "thou seest that the time is past when Peter can say, 'Silver and gold have I none.'" "Yes," said the bold saint, "and the time has gone, too, when Peter can say to the lame man 'rise up and walk.'" The steady growth of supernaturalism had left little place in the Church for moral and rational appeal. Preaching had become well-nigh a lost art, a forgotten function. The priest was not a preacher. He was a mediator between God and man, possessed of supernatural power. He brought cure to sin-sick souls not by revealing the source of spiritual power, but by the exercise of magic rites. He professed to be able to produce before his flock the literal body and blood of the Saviour and to perform anew a sacrifice for their sins. He claimed the power to shorten the period of purgatory by his prayers. He could say, through the magic gift of his ordination, "Son, thy sins are forgiven thee."

It was most natural that such awful claims should be abused. It would have needed Seraphim and Cherubim to exercise such power without abuse, and priests were, in spite of supernatural claims, only frail men. It is no

[1] See Lea's *History of the Inquisition*, vol. i. p. 31.

marvel that the enormous system of salvation by barter crept in. The line of least resistance led straight to the sale of indulgences. The Church had at its disposal all the merits accumulated by Christ's sacrifice and by the extra-merit, the superfluous goodness of the long line of saints. The Church was the sole hydrant through which the stored-up waters of salvation could flow out to humanity, and it could fix at will the conditions upon which this supply of Grace should be applied to individual need. In an evil moment it took the false step and decided that indulgences for sin could be granted in return for money-payments or in return for unusual works and services rendered to the Church in her times of need. For example, the promise of plenary indulgence was made in the first crusade to all who should fall in the service of the Church, and as time went on this extraordinary power was used in capricious ways. Honorius III., at the request of Francis of Assisi, granted a sweeping indulgence which promised to all persons who visited the church of Santa Maria de Portiuncula, between the vespers of August 1st and August 2nd of any year, complete remission of all sins committed since their baptism. The popularity of the indulgence may be judged from the vision which was granted to one of the faithful in which it was revealed to him that this indulgence was depopulating hell.

It could not but work havoc and disaster to put the issues of the soul on such an unethical basis, and by an eternal principle the Institution which thus took the risk of sowing to the wind was bound sooner or later to reap the whirlwind. The prophetic spirits of the time all felt that the Church had largely lost its vision and was unable to minister to the deepest needs of the soul. St. Bernard, the most loyal churchman of the century, cries out in sadness: "Whom can you show me among the prelates who does not seek rather to empty the pockets of his flock than to subdue their vices?" Gilbert of Gamblours says: "The prelates enter the Church not by election, but by the use of money and the favour of princes; not to feed, but to be fed; not to minister, but to be ministered to; not to sow, but to reap; not to labour, but to rest; not to guard the sheep from wolves, but, fiercer than wolves, to tear the sheep."[1]

As soon as the pulsations of the deeper life of humanity became clearer and stronger, there was sure to be a mighty issue between this system and the prophets of the race who voiced the aspirations of the human heart. The rank and file of the hierarchy might settle down at peace with a system which filled their bellies, satisfied their worldly ambitions and gave them magic control of invisible powers, but the Church had sooner or later to reckon with that unstilled hunger and thirst of man for a reality which satisfies his deeper self. Prophets and apostles of the soul's inalienable right to God were sure to come and they were certain to refuse the stone offered for bread, the scorpion for the fish. The gigantic system of mediating supernatural supplies of Grace was hardly organized in its completeness when the hand on the wall began to write "mene." Just when the clouds of superstition seemed covering the sky, the red fingers of a new dawn ran up in the east.

In the twelfth century the church began a battle with "heresy," which has not ended yet. These "heresies," even in their earlier stages, were many-sided, hard to describe in any fixed and general form. They took a variety of shapes according to their local habitat and the peculiar influences of their local leaders, and went under many names and often with strange battle-cries. The spirit of a new age was confronting an old system, and man was slowly winning his right to think and his power to be his own priest. The Waldensian movement was one of the most significant of the many revolts against the worldliness of the Church and one of the most genuine attempts to revive apostolic Christianity.

It was for a long time supposed that the Waldenses, or Vaudois, had an unbroken history down from apostolic

[1] Quoted from Lea's *History of the Inquisition*, vol. i. p. 53.

days. It has often been claimed that in the quiet retreats of their Alpine valleys they preserved the original Gospel uncontaminated and uncorrupted. There are other traditions which hold that there was a band of Christians who protested against the action of Pope Sylvester in receiving temporal possessions from Constantine in the fourth century, and that this band of purer spirits formed an independent sect, withdrew to the Vaudois valleys, and continued, in isolation from Rome, to cherish a Christianity free from secular corruptions. These are, however, only traditions which have had their birth in the common tendency of peoples to push back their origin, and, if possible, to connect it with a sacred person or a momentous event. The belief that they are connected in origin in some way with a "new faith" of the twelfth century, often called Catharism, which had come from the East and had slowly permeated the West, is much more solidly grounded because the Waldensian movement undoubtedly did spread rapidly in sections of Europe where Catharism had flourished.

Catharism was a revised form of Manichaeism.[1] It first showed its appearance in Bulgaria about the middle of the ninth century, where the Eastern and Western Churches were both struggling for converts. It seems to have come into Bulgaria from Armenia, where sects of Paulicians [2] held similar views.

Cathari (the word means "pure men" or "puritans") were certainly widespread in Europe by the middle of the eleventh century, and there were many complaints of

[1] Manichaeism (named from its founder Manes, born about A.D. 216) was a dualistic system with two co-ordinate principles of good and evil, light and darkness, God and Satan, eternally at war with each other, both in the world and within man. It was a union of Mazdean and Gnostic ideas with a sprinkling of ideas from the doctrines of Christianity. St. Augustine was in his younger period a Manichaean.

[2] The Paulicians, probably named from Paul of Samosata, as a separate sect date from the middle of the seventh century. The birthplace of the sect seems to have been Samosata, not far from the ancient "Ur of the Chaldees." The patriarch of the sect was a certain Constantine, who had come under Gnostic and Manichaean influences. He was given a copy of St. Paul's Epistles in which he thought he found his own Gnostical ideas. By allegorical interpretation he harmonized Paul's Christianity with Oriental theosophy and the product was "Paulicianism" in the East and later became "Catharism" in the West.

the prevalence of the "heresy" both from Germany and Italy before the end of the century. It did not appeal much to the subtle minds of the Church. It was seized upon rather by the humble poor folk—those who laboured and were heavy laden and who felt that the Church did not "speak to their condition." They were feeling, however blunderingly, after a reformed and purified Church. The Cathari held, in varying degrees according to locality, that there are two ground principles in the universe—a good God who is the creator of the spiritual world, and an evil god (Satan) who is the creator of the material world. Between these two beings, and between these two worlds, there is truceless antagonism. The battle has been carried even into heaven, and some of the celestial host have been won over to the side of the evil being. This visible world is the sphere of the activity of his forces. The aim of the Cathari was to get deliverance from the power of this evil being, and so from everything belonging to the material world which is *his* world. They were therefore naturally extremely ascetic. They required abstinence from sexual intercourse, from all meats, eggs, cheese, and, in a word, from everything that involves sexual intercourse among animals. They stoutly opposed oaths. They condemned war, and they held that punishment by death was wicked. They contended not only against infant baptism, but against water baptism altogether, even asserting that this rite was introduced by Satan who used John the Baptist as his instrument.[1] They pointed out that in apostolic times those who had received water baptism were still imperfect until they received the Holy Ghost (Acts viii. 15, 16). They carried their opposition to external things to the point of holding that God dwells not in houses made with hands. A house of stone is not a church; a company of good persons only is the Church.

They were divided into two groups—a larger and a smaller, called respectively "believers" and "perfects." The "perfects" were initiated, by the sacrament of laying

[1] See Neander's *History of the Christian Religion*, vol. iv. p. 575.

on of hands (the consolamentum), into the circle of those who were the elect of the Holy Ghost, the group of the "pure." To those "initiated" heaven was assured. There is no question that the Cathari, both in their early stages and in their later period when, especially in France, they are called "Albigenses,"[1] held beliefs which were crude and far removed from the teaching of the Gospel. Their dualism led them to a belief in Satan as only a less powerful being than God—a belief not yet wholly outgrown and suppressed. Their asceticism was largely due to their wild and unsound philosophy, and while revolting from some of the superstitions which prevailed in the Church, they were themselves a prey to other superstitions which made it impossible for their movement to bring a real spiritual deliverance to Europe. They did, however, teach with powerful emphasis the importance of pure, moral living and a severely simple life. They formed rallying-points, wherever they flourished, for those who were grieved over the immorality of the clergy, and who were hostile to the sacerdotalism and secularity of the Church.[2]

It is worth our while to pause for a moment and ask why it was that this formulation of Manichaean doctrines has so persistently appealed to human interest and to human need. What was it in Manichaeism, Paulicianism, Catharism, and Albigensianism that so fascinated the people of so many countries and of so many epochs, and made them, in the strength of these faiths, go bravely to dungeon and to death? It is not quite safe to raise such questions or to try to answer them, for the *outside* view at this safe distance is wholly unlike the *inside* view by which these men lived and died, and the spiritual attitude of those who form a religious movement is so rich and complex as to defy analysis. But the central principle

[1] So named from Albi in France where they flourished.

[2] The Waldenses did not directly spring out of Catharism. It is not possible to trace the *origin* of Waldensianism to the teaching of the Cathari. In fact the Waldenses considered the Cathari to be heretics. But nevertheless there was much in common in the two movements, and it is extremely probable that the anti-sacerdotal spirit and the moral standards of the earlier movement had a weighty influence on the later one.

of this vast movement, which under many names has dominated men, seems to be its simple solution of the mystery of good and evil, which is the mystery that weighs heaviest upon the spirit of man. Manichaeism, in its constantly appearing varieties, seems to us doubtless a crude solution of the mystery, but to multitudes of men it has seemed the *last word of revelation.* Evil is *foreign* to God—it is the work of an enemy who has stolen a march and is making terrible havoc, but God—our God—is incessantly at war with this monster enemy and in the long run will outwit him, and bring His loyal subjects into the fruits of His own victory. It is the exact opposite of the view which appealed so mightily to the mind of the mystic. The latter found his mystery solved and his spirit delivered in the faith that *everything* is Divine. Evil is only a finite illusion, only a temporal dream. Return into God, and the illusion vanishes as the dream does at waking. Both of these views, though diametrically opposed to each other, made their way because they were so transparently simple and adequate to the minds that adopted them. They came as a welcome release to the strain and tension of the perplexed and groping mind. "God is all there is," said the mystic, "enter His allness and be at rest." "God is at war with His enemy and ours, and when He wins the victory and chains the monster of darkness, we shall live in the light, let us join in this battle of Armageddon," said the Cathari. They both felt that they had found a clue to the mystery, that they had a principle by which they could conquer world, flesh, and devil, and in this organizing faith lay their power.

The Waldenses as a separate sect owe their origin to Peter Waldo, a merchant of Lyons, who about 1173 experienced a religious crisis which radically transformed him, and set him forth on a unique spiritual experiment. Waldo, like Melchizedec, is without traceable earthly lineage. His origin and ancestry are unknown. He had come to Lyons about 1155 to make his way in life, and, according to an early chronicle had amassed great wealth as a money-lender, and was everywhere recognized as a successful and prosperous man. The story which has come down to us to account for his spiritual crisis is as follows:[1] He was a man living in the enjoyment of his prosperity and good fortune, when suddenly one day a dear friend fell dead before his eyes. This experience produced a profound impression on him, and this impression was deepened by another experience which followed hard upon the first one. Coming home one day from mass he heard a minstrel singing to a crowd and reciting the story of St. Alexis—a sad tale ending with a complaint of the condition of the Church and the degeneracy of the present compared with the good old times. Waldo took the minstrel home with him, and was so moved by the impression his visitor made upon him that he went next morning, not to his business, but instead to consult a spiritual guide—"a Master of Theology"—whom he knew in the city. He told his guide that he was eager to find the true way to heaven. The guide told him that the surest way was to obey the words of the Master: "If thou wilt be perfect, sell all thou hast and give to the poor and come and follow me." The words struck home, and Waldo took them literally. He settled up all his business affairs, provided for his daughters, and placed them in the Abbey of Fontevraud, fixed a proper share of his worldly goods on his wife, and began at once to use his own part of the property to feed the poor and to spread the truth. Like St. Francis, whom he precedes by a generation, he went to living as the birds do, with no care or anxiety, and going about from house to house, visiting the sick, helping the poor, and reading the Gospels to them.[2] He met with little groups in workshops and at street corners, and showed

[1] There are two early accounts of Waldo's Conversion; one in *Anecdotes historiques, légendes et apologues, tirés du recueil inédit d'Étienne de Bourbon, dominicain du XIIIe siècle*, publiés pour la Société de l'Histoire de France par A. Lecoy de la Marche, Paris, 1877, pp. 290 *seq.*; and the other in the *Chronicon anonymi Canonici Laudunensis* in Bouquet's Recueil, tome xiii. pp. 680-82.

[2] Waldo's wife, when she heard that he was living on the charity of the neighbours, went, with tears, to the Archbishop and claimed her right to feed her husband, and the Archbishop ordered that he should eat with her when he was in Lyons. A quite similar story was related of Raimund Lull, who was born in the

them through the Scriptures the simplicity of the Gospel message and the character of the primitive Church. He employed a translator at his own expense, who put the Gospels and other parts of the Bible into the vernacular Provençal, and he made a collection of extracts from the Fathers, known as "Sentences."[1] The idea which *possessed* Waldo was the necessity of literally following Christ, and the main basis of his movement was the "new law" of Christ which he found in the Gospels. Those who formed the nucleus of his followers were obscure men, mechanics, people "of whom the Church took little count, except to tax when they were orthodox, and burn when heretic." They called themselves "the poor of Christ" or "the poor men of Lyons."[2] They were brave, obedient to their light, and, like the early Franciscans, naive and childlike. They preached the Gospel in the streets, in the fields, and in market-places, and they went from house to house telling their message to everybody in the city. Their simple lay-preaching, backed up by their pure lives and their spirit of kindness, appealed to the people, but it brought them into collision with the officials of the Church. The Archbishop ordered Peter to stop casting his pearls before swine, and to cease usurping the office of preacher which belonged only to the ordained. Waldo appealed to the Gospel for his authority, but made no impression on the Archbishop. The "poor men" thus found themselves forced to choose whether they would obey their clergy or their precious Gospel. In this dilemma Waldo took the apostolic words as his own, and announced as his decision: "We must obey God rather than men." The Archbishop thereupon expelled Waldo and his followers to the number of some thousands from the city, and in doing so expanded the movement from a local affair to continental dimensions.

At the Lateran Council, held in 1179, the "poor men"

island of Majorca in the year 1236. He had, however, come under Franciscan influence, and was undoubtedly taking St. Francis as his model.

[1] According to the other account—that of Etienne de Bourbon—the work of translating the Scriptures was under way *before* the Alexis incident occurred.

[2] They were sometimes called Insabbatati, which means "the Shoed," from the fact that they wore peculiar sandals in imitation of the Apostles.

in person presented a petition to have their vow of poverty confirmed, which was granted. They presented also their translations of the Scriptures, and tried to secure permission to preach as laymen. This permission was granted with a proviso which nullified it, namely that they must first secure the permission of their local clergy, and be under the oversight of a local Bishop. At this Lateran Council,[1] Walter Mapes, the famous Englishman from the court of Henry II., was called in to question the "poor men," and to examine their translations. He found great sport in confusing them with his fine-spun arguments, and he made much fun of their *naïveté* and simplicity.

The anathema of the Church fell upon them with force at the Council of Verona in 1184. The anathema includes the Cathari, the Paterines, those falsely called "the humble," or "the Poor at Lyons," the Passagians, Josephites, Arnaldists—"these are," the decision reads, "eternally anathema, and *we include in the same perpetual anathema all who shall have presumed to preach, either publicly or privately, either being forbidden or not sent, or not having the authority of the Apostolic See or of the Bishop of the diocese.*"[2] This decree further says that "heresies have begun in these modern times to break forth in most parts of the world, so that the power of the Church ought to be aroused." Henceforth the Waldenses were compelled to give up all hope of reforming the Church from within, and to face the hazard of forming a Church separate from "the Church."[3]

About the year 1190 the Waldenses held a public disputation in the Cathedral of Narbonne, and the subjects discussed at this disputation give a very definite idea of their views at this period. The most important points to be combated are the following:—

[1] The Lateran Council of 1179 condemned the Cathari and put them under an anathema.

[2] Decree of Pope Lucius III., in the Council of 1184 (Maitland's *Facts and Documents*, p. 177).

[3] There were, however, many members of the Waldensian group who still retained a nominal membership in the Church. It took a whole century of persistent persecution to shake their loyalty and to drive them into "separation."

1. They refuse obedience to the Pope and prelates.
2. Everybody, even *laymen*, can preach.
3. That according to the Apostles, God is to be obeyed rather than man.
4. That *women may preach.*
5. That masses, prayers, and alms for the dead are of no avail; while some deny that there is any purgatory.
6. That prayer in bed, or even in a stable, is as efficacious as in a church.[1]

Bernard of Fontcaud, who gives us these points under discussion at Narbonne, makes much of the fact that these "poor men" allowed all their members, regardless of age or position, to preach, and, as we have seen, extended the privilege to women.

One of the earliest references to the apostolic preaching of the Waldenses is found in the Edict of King Alfonso of Aragon dated 1192, in which his subjects are forbidden to harbour or shelter Waldenses, Insabbatati ("sandled men"), or Poor Men of Lyons, and they are warned against hearing them *preach*, giving them food, or showing them any kindness.[2]

Further light on their views and practices is shed by a Tract prepared not far from this date at the request of the pope, by Alain de l'Isle, who was called the "universal Doctor." The great doctor finds them a dangerous people, because they hold dangerous doctrines and are determined to *practise their teachings*, and carry them out in daily life. He says that they preach without permission, assuming themselves to be successors of the apostles; that they take women about with them and allow them to preach in public assemblies, and that they support themselves by the work of their hands. He complains that they teach that only ministers who live godly, apostolic lives have the power to loose and bind, that spiritual power is dependent, not on ordination, but on inward life and character, and that the ministration

[1] These points are given in a Tract by Bernard, Abbot of Fontcaud, written about the year 1200.

[2] Müller, *Die Waldenser* (Gotha, 1886), p. 12.

of sinful priests is invalid,—teachings which would woefully cripple the power of the Church. He also finds that they strike another blow at the Church by claiming that confession to a good layman is just as availing as confession to a priest. And finally they reject, as devoid of any efficacy, the whole system of indulgences,—a system against which Luther aimed his first blow three centuries later.[1]

There is a steady testimony, from all our reliable sources, to the purity of the life and the strict moral character of the Waldenses, both in their earlier and in their later periods. They took the Gospel literally, and made a very serious attempt to live it as the law of their daily life. They practised apostolic simplicity, even to the wearing of sandals to be like the apostles. They refused to swear, and the stricter members of the group—"the faithful" or "perfect"—would accept death before they would take an oath. Lea reports the case of an old woman who was given the chance to escape the sentence of death as a heretic if she would take an oath. She refused to save herself on that condition. They opposed war and even judicial homicide, standing literally by the command, "Thou shalt not kill." The passwords of the sect were, "Saint Paul says, 'Lie not'; Saint James says, 'Swear not'; Saint Peter says, 'Do not render evil for evil.'" When one of their members was being "examined" before the Inquisition of Toulouse, he was asked what his religion had taught him. His noble answer was that it had taught him "that he should neither speak nor do evil; that he should do nothing to others that he would not have done to himself; and that he should not lie or swear."

An interesting account of the errors of the Waldenses is given by a contemporary monk of Citeaux, Peter of Vaux-Sernai. He says that:

> "Their errors consisted chiefly in four things, viz. in wearing sandals after the manner of the Apostles; in saying that it is not

[1] See Müller, *op. cit.* p. 14; Lea, *op. cit.* p. 79; Alain de l'Isle died 1202.

lawful on any account to swear; or to kill; and moreover in this —that they asserted that any individual of the sect, in case of necessity, if he only had on sandals, without having received orders from a bishop, could make the body of Christ [perform the miracle of transubstantiation].

When any one went over to the heretics, he who received him said, 'Friend, if you wish to be one of us, it behoves you to renounce the whole faith that is held by the Roman Church,' and he must answer, 'I renounce';—'Then receive the Holy Spirit from good men'—and he breathes seven times in his face. Also he says to him, 'You must renounce the cross made on you in baptism, on your breast, and on your shoulders, and on your head, with oil and chrism.' He must answer, 'I renounce it.' 'Do you believe that water could work your salvation?' He answers, 'I do not believe it.'"[1]

It was not an uncommon thing for persons in the twelfth century to be suspected of heresy when they were discovered to be living lives of extraordinary purity and simplicity. In fact a "heresy hunter" of the period who knew the marks of heresy says:

"Heretics are recognizable by their customs and speech, for they are modest and well regulated. They take no pride in their garments, which are neither costly nor vile. They do not engage in trade, *to avoid lies, and oaths, and frauds*, but live by their labours as mechanics—their teachers are cobblers. They do not accumulate wealth, but are content with necessaries. They are chaste, and temperate in meat and drink. They do not frequent taverns or dances or other vanities. They restrain themselves from anger. They are always at work; they teach and learn and consequently pray but little. They are to be known by their modesty and precision of speech, avoiding scurrility and detraction, light words, lies, and oaths. They do not even say *vere* or *certe*, regarding them as oaths."[2]

One of the most beautiful monuments of the high ethical spirit of the Waldenses is the old Provençal poem, entitled, "La Nobla Leyczon,"—the Noble Lesson. It was long supposed to be a production of about the year 1100, as the poem itself declares that eleven centuries have passed since it was said: "We live in the last

[1] Quoted from Maitland's *Facts and Documents*, pp. 395-96.
[2] Quoted in Lea, *op. cit.* vol. i. p. 85.

times." But scholars are now agreed that these lines have been tampered with and that the poem was written probably by a Waldensian "master" not far from the year 1400. The poem is permeated with the spirit of evangelical Christianity and with the ethical ideas of the Sermon on the Mount. It makes religion consist in following Christ, and in the maintenance of a pure, clean life; and it complains that if a person is found who neither curses, swears, lies, commits adultery, murders, possesses himself of another's goods, nor revenges himself on his enemies, the false shepherds say, "He is a Waldensian."[1]

Their form of organization was very simple and as apostolic as they could make it. They made the smallest possible distinction between clergy and laity. There was a certain number of the members who renounced all property, who devoted all their time to religious teaching and the propagation of the Gospel: these persons were called "majorales" or sometimes the "perfected," and in later times "barbes." They supported themselves by some menial occupation such as cobbling, tinkering, or peddling.[2] Where they devoted their entire time to the Gospel they lived in a simple way on voluntary contributions. Many of the Waldenses, especially their ministers and missionaries, were skilful leeches. They were always ready to use their skill in medicine and surgery to open the door for applying their remedy for the cure of souls. They refused all payment for such service, and silently taught the lesson that "It is more blessed to give than to receive."

They seem not to have had any settled teaching, at least in the earlier stages of the movement, on the doctrine of transubstantiation. At first they took the position that the bread and wine became the Body and Blood of Christ only in the hands of *spiritual* priests, but they gradually came to question, and frequently they

[1] Trench has pointed out in his *Mediæval Church History*, pp. 247 ff., that there is a thinness of quality in all the literature of the Waldenses. He notes too the fact that in the five hundred lines of the Noble Lesson only one line refers to redemption by Christ. It has also often been noted that their Christianity is of the type of St. James rather than of the type of St. Paul.

[2] See Whittier's poem, "The Vaudois Teacher."

even denied, the reality of transubstantiation. There is evidence that some of the inquisitors used transubstantiation as a decisive test when examining those suspected of being Waldenses, and it clearly appears that very often laymen, especially the heads of the families, administered in simple form the communion supper.[1]

In the early part of the fourteenth century we get a fairly full account of the Waldenses of that period from their great persecutor, Bernard Gui, who was inquisitor at Toulouse. This account by the great inquisitor shows that the Waldenses had kept straight on their original lines throughout the century and a half of persecution. He says that they form a society or brotherhood, that they maintain evangelical simplicity and poverty. Those who preach have no property of their own, but go from place to place and are fed and sheltered by those who form the society. They teach that transubstantiation is effected only when the ministrant is a pure and holy person. Supernatural powers are not conferred by *ordination*, but all spiritual powers come directly from Christ to the individual. Transubstantiation may be worked, and absolution may be given by any spiritual person, either man or woman.[2]

Persecution steadily drove them into sharper opposition to the Church, and forced them to realize that the Church could not be reformed from within, so that they finally came to think of themselves as "the true Church," and of the great Church as apostate, or, as they put it, a "house of lies." They organized schools of their own in which their peculiar doctrines and practices were taught. They had their cemeteries set apart for their own dead, and they had a vigorous band of missionaries whose zeal and courage knew no bounds.

[1] See the account from Peter of Vaux-Sernai, quoted above. There was, even in the lifetime of Waldo, a breach between the "poor of Lyons" and the "poor of Lombardy." The latter were much more sharply anti-church in their attitude than the former. The "poor of Lyons" put the great stress on the necessity for those who exercise apostolic functions *to live like the Apostles*. While on the other hand it was the tendency for the Lombard branch of the "poor" to denounce the Roman Church as the whore and to reject its Sacraments.

[2] Gui, *Practica inquisitionis*, publié par Douai (Paris, 1885).

The Waldensian missionary who swam the Ipsis River on a winter night to carry a Gospel message to a Catholic on the mere chance of converting him is only one instance of the spirit which made these "poor men" such an evangelical force in the thirteenth and fourteenth centuries, and each new convert became at once a missionary to others.

The records of the Inquisition show that they existed in large numbers throughout France and Germany—especially Southern Germany. We get a telling proof of their great numbers in Lorraine, even in the twelfth century, for in the year 1192 the Bishop of Toul ordered all Waldensians in his bishopric to be captured and brought to him. His promises to the "hunters" indicate that the "heretics" were numerous. He promises remission of sins to all who perform this service, and he further promises, that *if any are driven from their homes because they engage in this service*, he will provide them with food and clothes. The document now generally known as the Narrative of the "Anonymous of Passau," written about 1260, gives conclusive evidence that in the vast diocese of Passau, the Waldenses existed in great numbers, and they seem almost to have captured the rural districts from the Church. They are here shown to be mostly peasants and simple mechanics, but they are thoroughly familiar with the Scriptures and possess a passion for making converts.

They were not mystics like most of the sects studied in this volume. They were unspeculative, simple Christians, sternly hostile to the corruption and sacerdotalism of the Church, concerned for a return to Gospel simplicity and consecrated to the proclamation of an evangel which the poorest and most illiterate could understand. The most wholesome characteristic of the movement is its social aspect. It had no social *propaganda*, such as characterised many of the later religious uprisings, but it was marked throughout by a genuine feeling of human love and brotherhood. The Waldenses often *called* themselves "Friends," and better still they exhibited the traits of friendship. The spirit of Waldo himself, who sold all he had in order to turn his possessions into channels of love and service, is typical of the entire movement. The Waldensian ministers, under whatever name they are called, were moved by sympathy and love for the poor and the burdened. They would take no salary; they worked for men out of love for them and for Christ. They studied healing arts to relieve pain and suffering, and they resisted successfully the temptation to make their "gifts" a means to wealth and promotion. It was one of their counts against the Church that the Clergy used the terrors of superstition to force money from those who were already poor and hungry. They denounced pilgrimages and the sale of indulgences, because of their moral and social effects. They declared purgatory to be an *invention*, and they taught the people that prayers and offerings to saints were of no avail. In the place of these *expensive superstitions* they called for lives of love and service, and they set the standard themselves by following the Master in going about doing good. It is possible, as Harnack suggests,[1] that if the movement had come a generation later, it might have been taken up into the Church and incorporated with it, as the Franciscan movement actually was. There is no question that Waldo and his Lyonese followers wished to be an organic part of the Catholic Church, and only sought the privilege of living like the apostles. The inherent difficulty was that the Church of the twelfth century had no provision in its system, and no place in its fold, for those who practised Gospel simplicity and lived like the apostles. The Church had not yet awakened to its social duties, and it was deaf to the half articulate cry of its submerged masses. Then further, it had no place in its elaborate machinery for lay ministry. It could not utilize the gifts of the unordained, even though they had discovered how to heal the broken-hearted, and to give the oil of joy for mourning. Still less could it tolerate those who joined to their *unusual activities* teachings which threatened the entire sacerdotal

[1] *History of Dogma*, vol. vi. p. 92.

structure. The very existence of the Church was staked on the theory that transubstantiation and absolution of sins were supernaturally effected, not by the holiness of the ministrant, but by the magical power conferred through ordination. The priest was a supernatural instrument, a channel of divine power, and the miracles of Grace were wrought through him *independently of the manner of his life.* This position the Waldenses boldly challenged and, in doing so, entered upon an irreconcilable contention with the historic Church.

But it would be a mistake to conclude that Europe was at this period ripe for a Reformation, or that the Waldenses had attained to an insight or embodied principles which qualified them to be the bringers of a genuine Reformation. The Great Head of the Church is "the God of all patience," and His world was not yet ready for the larger freedom which the Reformation brought, nor could these "poor men" have led the world into a type of spiritual Christianity such as would have been the fulfilment of the long travail of the ages. In spite of the fact that they represent a movement toward a more ethical type of religion, it cannot be overlooked that we still have in them morality in an infant, negative stage. They did not, and their age probably could not, get beyond a more or less refined *legalism.* Christianity for them was still a new law, and not yet a new life, lived by the inspiration and power of an inward, divine Person.

We may well adopt the words of Sir James Stephen, used by him in reference to the defeat of the Albigenses:

> "The mind of man has not as yet passed through the indispensable preliminary education. The scholastic philosophy, extravagant as it may have been in some of its premises and some of its purposes, had yet a great task to accomplish—the task of training the instructors of the Church in the athletic use of all their mental faculties. Philology, and criticism, and ecclesiastical antiquity were still uncultivated. The Holy Scriptures, in their original tongues, were almost a sealed volume to the scholars of the West. The vernacular languages of Europe were unformed. The arts of printing and paper-making were undiscovered. Such an age could neither have produced

nor appreciated a Wyclif or a Hus; still less could Melancthon, or Luther, or Calvin, or Beza have borne their fruit in such times, if such men had been living. Above all, the world, as it then was, could no more have fostered minds like those of Cranmer, or Ridley, of Jewell or Hooker, than it could have trained up chemists to rival Cavendish, or mechanists to anticipate Watt. If they had succeeded in their designs,—if they had reclaimed the nations from the errors of Rome,—they must infallibly have substituted for her despotism, an anarchy breaking loose from all restraints, divine and human, an anarchy far exceeding, in presumptuous ignorance and audacious self-will, the wildest of the sects which perplexed and disgraced the Reformation of the sixteenth century."[1]

[1] James Stephen's *Lectures on the History of France* (London, 1867), vol. i. p. 252.

CHAPTER IX

ST. FRANCIS AND THE "SPIRITUAL FRANCISCANS"

"ALL religions must be again and again rejuvenated by a return to their original principle. Christianity would have become entirely extinct had not St. Francis and St. Dominic renewed its life and kindled it afresh in the hearts of men by their imitation of Jesus Christ. *They saved religion, but they destroyed the Church.*"

Thus wrote the Florentine Machiavelli in his *Discourse on Livy.*

The attempt to rejuvenate Christianity by a return to its original principle has been made more or less seriously by many Christian prophets through the centuries. All these rejuvenators of Christianity have seized some partial aspect and set it out of balance and proportion with the other equally essential aspects of primitive Christianity. They have all borne unmistakably the temporal quality—the mark of a particular age—while Christ's religion is in a unique sense *eternal.* But I believe that nobody has come so near gaining the feeling, the attitude, the *abandon* to the Divine Father, the spirit of human love and fellowship which characterised the Galilean circle as has Francis of Assisi. Among the prominent reformers of the Church his life is as near an approach to the Divine Model as the world has seen since the apostolic days. Once more there came an apostle who knew nothing save Jesus Christ and Him crucified, and whose great prayer was that he might fill up in his body what was lacking of the sufferings of Christ. "O Lord my Saviour," he prayed at Alverna, "I ask two favours before I die. Let me feel in my soul, in my body even, all the bitter pains which Thou hast felt.

And in my heart let me feel that immeasurable love which made Thee, Son of God, endure such sufferings for us, poor sinners."[1]

There is an account of a night spent in prayer which lets us almost see behind the veil and witness a child face to face with his Father. If one wants an example of the loftiest type of mysticism, he has it here:

> "St. Francis . . . rose up from his bed and set himself to pray, lifting up his hands and eyes unto heaven, and with exceeding great devotion and fervour said, 'My God, my God!' and thus saying and sorely weeping, he abode till morning, always repeating, 'My God, my God' and naught beside."[2]

"He saved religion, he destroyed the Church," Machiavelli tells us. The statement is, of course, an exaggeration, but it aims at a truth. He did carry religion once again into the hearts of the people. He, more than any other medieval prophet, made Christianity once again a lay religion. The Church and the world had lost all hope of heaven, except by works and by purchase. The only key which could open the door to the Kingdom of God was in the hands of the priest. Francis made a fresh discovery of the universal love and Fatherhood of God. He felt again, as men had felt in the days of apostolic faith, that the veil was rent, and that there was free access for even the poorest, meanest soul to go direct to the Father. One day he heard a tender voice, which said: "Francis, there is not a single sinner in the world whom God will not pardon if he comes to Him."

He restored the joy of religion. He prayed out of sheer joy, and not because prayer was enjoined as a duty. In the first rules of his order he put as much emphasis on joy as on chastity and obedience. In an age burdened with its load of gloomy superstitions, an age in which the heavens seemed as brass and the earth as bars of iron, an age when the main hope lay in an apocalyptic catastrophe which should bring a new heaven and a new earth by miracle, Francis came

[1] *Little Flowers*, chap. liv.

[2] *Ibid.* p. 4.

as a holy optimist, throbbing with joyous enthusiasm and with unlimited faith in man and in God. He once said to a novice: "Before me and before thy brothers here, always show a face shining with holy joy. It is not fitting, when one is in God's service, to have a gloomy face or a chilling look."

In no other trait did he come so near the primitive attitude as in his spontaneous uncalculating love for men. He did not in the least have the theologian's attitude, which views man in the abstract—as an offspring of Adam, the inheritor of sin, with a soul to be speculated about—he loved concrete men and gave them his love, shared himself with them in a way that is unparalleled, except in the Galilean. When Francis ate with the leper and kissed him out of pure love for a suffering human fellow, he had discovered the true way to rejuvenate Christianity. It was the beginning of the Reformation, because it was a genuine recognition of a new centre. The Church was no longer the pivot—man himself, with his human hopes and his human needs, was the centre, and religion here began again in earnest to be *life*—a way of living. Francis' first and deepest interest was not in popes or priests, nor in the Church as an entity, it was an elemental interest in man—in common men. One day some robbers broke into one of the retreats of the order, and were forcibly driven away by the guardian of the place. Francis heard of it, and immediately sent to the robbers the bread and wine which had been prepared for his own meal, with such gentle words of kindness that they came and fell down at his feet and asked to be taken into the Order.[1] He reversed the traditional idea that the Church alone could save men's souls, by acting on the belief that the Church itself was to be saved by the faith and work of the common people.

It is a bold, and possibly a rash, undertaking to write a chapter on the Franciscan movement. The story has been told from almost every point of view, it has been a theme which has attracted many noble spirits in our

[1] *Little Flowers*, chap. xxvi.

times, and it is withal a subject which demands an interpreter who has not only mastered the historical facts, but who has so saturated himself with the atmosphere of thirteenth century Italy, and so relived the Franciscan gospel of love and poverty, that it has all become as real to him as the colours of the sky and hills which he sees out of his window. All the material with which the historian of Francis must work is crowded with legend. No man now, be he ever so gifted with critical acumen, can find where to draw the line between cold historical fact and warm poetical imagination. Francis belongs as much to art and poetry as he does to religion, and they have vied with each other in weaving such a veil of fancy about him that the naked personality cannot be discovered, and the only thing to do is to submit and accept the man as art and poetry and religion have transmitted him to us.[1]

Francis, the son of Pietro Bernadone, a rich cloth merchant of Assisi, was born in 1182. "He was," the *Three Companions* say, "merrier than his father and more generous, given unto jests and songs, going around the city of Assisi day and night in company with his like, most free-handed in spending. Even in his clothes he was beyond measure sumptuous. Yet was he by nature courteous, never speaking a harmful or shameful word of any."[2] There was much of the troubadour in him, not only in his youth, but even throughout his life. His friends call him "God's jongleur" as well as "God's little

[1] Sabatier thinks that *The Mirror of Perfection* was written by Brother Leo in 1227. If so, this is the earliest collection of Franciscan stories. Thomas of Celano wrote the earliest life of him. This was written by order of the Pope, three years after the death of Francis—in 1229. Later, after the fall of Brother Elias, a second life (from an entirely different standpoint) was written by Thomas of Celano, and later still a supplement was added to it. In 1247, three of Francis' companions — Leo, Rufino, and Angelo — wrote a *memorabilia*, or Legends of *The Three Companions*, which is singularly free from the miraculous.

In 1263, Bonaventura made a collection of legends, gathered up from the last survivors of the first generation of Franciscans. This was a compromise biography written, deliberately written, to be the official biography, and all other biographies were ordered to be destroyed.

In the fourteenth century the book of *Little Flowers* was anonymously produced. It is a popular, naive, and unrestrained collection of stories about the Franciscan "apostolic age."

[2] *The Three Companions*, chap. i.

poor man," and the former epithet fits him as well as the latter. He possessed in a peculiar degree the temperament of a poet, and it is more than probable that the songs of the wandering troubadours or jongleurs exercised a powerful and refining influence upon him.

The gaiety of his youth was interrupted by a year of captivity as a prisoner of war in Perugia, but even this captivity did not break his jubilant spirit, for he was living on bright dreams of a great future. "You will see one day," he frequently said to his companions, "that I shall be adored by the whole world." [1]

After his return to Assisi, at twenty-two, he plunged again into the gay life of the city. This time his dissipation was interrupted by a serious illness, which left him strangely altered. As he gradually came back to health he found himself met, as so many before him and since have found themselves met, with shifted values of life. Nature no longer gladdened him, there was no appeal in companionship, the emptiness of life oppressed him. The mystery of himself broke in upon him. The inexhaustible resources of his life seemed suddenly shut away and the key lost.

Italy was an eternal battlefield, and Francis joined in an expedition then on foot in the hope that the excitement of battle, under a captain of renown, would give him back his old sense of radiant joy. It was not to be. Something had risen in him which spoiled all his pleasures and made them illusory. All accounts of this period in his life are meagre. There are hints at illness and allusions to dreams and visions; and, acquainted with Francis' psychic nature, as we now are, through the events of his later life, we have no doubt that he was at the time undergoing profound physical and mental disturbances, which made him a puzzle to himself and to everybody else. He suddenly gave up the campaign, tried to resume his old life, but would fall into solitary meditation even in the midst of gaiety. "Francis, what art thou thinking of? Art thou thinking of taking a wife?" his companions

[1] *The Three Companions*, chap. i.

questioned. "In truth I am," he answered, "I am thinking of taking a bride, richer and nobler and fairer than ye have ever seen."

His biographers say that this was his "Lady Poverty," but this interpretation is perhaps too restricted. The bride for whom his perplexed heart yearned was an ideal bride, not yet shaped into concrete form in his mind—something which would unify the life of this dreamy, chivalrous youth, and furnish a powerful motive for his restless will.

It was in the little church of St. Damian, near Assisi, that he had a first revelation of the higher companionship which he was vaguely feeling after. He was praying before the crucifix on the poor little altar, when suddenly he found that he could not take his eyes away from those of Jesus. The holy figure on the cross was, too, becoming alive, and was speaking in the silence with a voice which reached the inmost depth of his being. And this Jesus, who had suddenly become alive again, was asking for his life![1]

This story must not be dismissed as a mere legend. It undoubtedly tells us of an experience which was real and momentous for Francis. He was in a psychic condition in which such an experience could happen without any improbability, and some such crisis seems necessary to account for the new and triumphant Francis who comes before us from this time on. We are dealing here with a person of the most extraordinary mystical nature, with a body capable of being swept from within as a musician sweeps the strings of his instrument, and our psychological laboratories have given us evidence enough that persons of this type may overpass the normal and the ordinary without any necessity of calling in miracle. There are within reach of us all reservoirs of energy if we only knew how to tap them! There are vast stores of power for the higher uses of life if we could only find the key! Happy are those persons who at the crisis of their lives suddenly break through some mysterious wall and find

[1] Bonaventura, chap. i.

the storehouse of energy! The *release of energy* often comes as the result of a great surrender, for not seldom the surrender seems to melt away a middle wall of partition within, which was dividing the life in sunder, and lets the whole of one's power go out in a single direction.

There were many distinct stages in the march of Francis' spirit toward his great surrender, but the final crisis, when all the moorings with the old life were cut, came on the memorable day of his "choice of Father." He had already, in a moment of impulse of human love, kissed a leper.[1] He had made trial of poverty by donning a ragged garb in Rome and standing all day in a line of beggars. He had been chased by the rabble of Assisi and hooted at as a madman. The final test came when his father, whose love had now turned to wrath, demanded that Francis should surrender all claim to inheritance. The "case" was brought before the bishop, and the public of Assisi had come to hear the disinheritance pronounced. Suddenly Francis appeared absolutely naked, with his clothes rolled in a little bundle and with what little money still remained to him; and with words which must have sent a thrill through the throng of listeners, he said: "Until to-day I have called Pietro Bernadone my father, but from henceforth I desire to say nothing else than 'Our Father who art in heaven.'"[2]

It was still somewhat later, while he was at work as a labourer repairing the little church of the Portiuncula ("Church of the little portion") that he received the vision of his career. At the celebration of the Mass on a certain day in the church of St. Nicholas, near the market-place of Assisi, the priest read the passage: "Wherever ye go, preach, saying 'the kingdom of God is at hand.' Heal the sick, cleanse the lepers, cast out devils. Freely ye

[1] Bonaventura tells this incident as follows:—"There came in his way a certaine leper: upon whose sodaine aspect, he conceived in mind an especial horror and loathing. But returning to his already resolved purpose of perfection, and considering that he ought of necessity first to overcome himself, if he would become a soldier of Christ, he presently alighted down from his horse and went to kisse him."

[2] *The Three Companions*, chap. vi.

have received, freely give. Provide neither silver nor gold nor brass in your purses, neither scrip, nor two coats, nor shoes, nor staff, for the labourer is worthy of his meat." The words seemed to him to come, not from the priest, nor from the book, but with Divine authority from that Christ Who had fastened His eyes on him and asked for his whole life in the chapel of St. Damian. With him to see a truth was to practise it, and from this time he took the gospel-call literally and went about the world preaching, as his friend Thomas of Celano says, "in words like fire, penetrating the heart."

There never was a more gentle revolutionist. He did not come with the fire and sword of heresy. He did not flourish the scourge of the ascetic. He did not flay men's sins like the fanatical reformer. He told in powerful words of the Father's love. He asked men to follow the Divine Saviour, and he *practised* the love and tenderness which were the warp and woof of his message. St. Bonaventura says that it seemed as though the Spirit of God was speaking through his mouth. His intimate experience of the heart's need, his manifest sympathy with the poor, his simple, popular language, full of anecdote and parable, his mastery of the springs of laughter and tears, his spontaneous gesture, his absolute *conviction*, made his preaching effective to an extraordinary degree. It was in sharp contrast to the formal, barren services in the churches, where preaching had become a lost art. It is no wonder that legends abound which tell how the multitudes flocked to hear him when he came to hamlet, village, or city, so that vineyards, and fields, and public squares, under the bright Italian skies, were crowded with eager, enthusiastic listeners, who tried to get near enough to touch his rough garments, or to carry away some little relic from the man they loved.[1] It was something new to hear an optimistic gospel in that dark century, and to find that religion was a radiantly joyous affair!

[1] A legend preserves a vision that St. Francis had of crowds coming to his banner: "I saw," he says, "a multitude coming, and lo, the sound of their footsteps still echoes in my ears. I saw them coming from every direction, filling all the roads."

There is a charming story which tells how one Christmas night he invited all the peasants and shepherds of the neighbourhood to come to a stable, and there in the manger, while all knelt, Francis read the story of the Nativity according to Luke, and then preached to his peasant listeners of the Saviour and His Gospel to the poor. No wonder that some of the moved listeners believed that they saw the image of the Child in the manger come to life and open His arms! It was, indeed, something like a real revival of the primitive Gospel.

His directions to the band of missionaries whom he sent out show how completely he had gained the spirit of brotherhood. Even the *rich* are to be treated as brothers. Note, too, the important discovery that it is a great part of a man's business to carry blessing to others rather than to save his own soul: "Go, teach. God in His goodness has called us not alone for our own salvation, but for the salvation of the people. Do not judge nor despise the rich who live at ease and who wear fine clothes, for God is their Saviour as well as ours. We ought to honour them as our *brothers*, for we all have the same Creator. Go, preach peace to men, and preach repentance for the remission of sins. Some will receive you with joy and will gladly hear you; others, evil-minded and full of pride, will denounce you and oppose you. But in little time many nobles and wise men will join you. Be patient in tribulation, fervent in prayer, courageous in labours, modest in speech, grave in demeanour, and grateful for the blessings which come to you. The kingdom of heaven will be your reward."

The little band of men who joined him, at first one by one, steadily grew in numbers, and the plan of the Order of poor little brothers slowly shaped itself in Francis' mind after the model of the Gospels. About 1210, the simple plan, or rule, was allowed by Pope Innocent III., to whom Francis with his companions had submitted it. They simply asked the privilege of leading the apostolic life. The boon was granted, with the reservation that the Church was to be their supreme authority. For the moment, Francis saw in this condition no bond or shackle, and he returned from Rome to his mission with a spirit of joy, which the perilous journey, the fever that laid him low, his half-starved condition, and the rudeness of the lazar barrack which served for his dwelling, could not dampen.

In 1212 the second Order—the Poor Clares, or Clarisses—was founded. Like everything else in the early Franciscan movement, the founding of an Order for women was spontaneous and unplanned. It is an event full of the romantic and the unusual. Francis' preaching had come as a revelation to Clara, the daughter of a prominent citizen of Assisi, when as a girl at the age of sixteen she first heard him in the Cathedral of Assisi. His message and his personality penetrated the depths of her inner being. The transformation wrought in her was like that wrought in Galahad by the pale nun in the "Holy Grail":

> "She sent the deathless passion in her eyes
> Thro' him, and made him hers, and laid her mind
> On him, and he believed in her belief."

The idle, empty, trivial life of a rich lady became henceforth impossible for her. A love had come into her life so wonderful and strange that we almost need a new word to name it. It was a mystical love whose roots were in the invisible and eternal, and which drew both lives not so much to each other as to the one Fountain of love and to their common tasks of love.

According to the later legends, only once did Francis and Clara break bread together, and the story, which throws a mystical cover over the event, must be given:

"When St. Francis was at Assisi, oftentimes he visited St. Clara and gave her holy admonishments. And she, having exceeding great desire once to break bread with him, oft-times besought him thereto; but he was never willing to grant her this consolation: wherefore his companions, beholding the desire of St. Clara, said to St. Francis, 'Father, it doth appear to us that this severity accordeth not with heavenly charity, since thou givest no ear to Sister Clara, a virgin so saintly, so beloved of God—who through thy preaching abandoned the riches and pomps of the world.

And of a truth, had she asked of thee a greater boon than this, thou oughtest so to do unto thy spiritual plant.'

Then spake St. Francis, 'Since it seems good to you, it seems so likewise to me. But that she may be the more consoled, I will that this breaking of bread take place in St. Mary of the Angels, for she has been so long shut up in St. Damian that it will rejoice her to see again the house of St. Mary, where her hair was shorn away and she became the bride of Jesus Christ, and there let us eat together in the name of God.'

When came the day ordained by him, and the hour of breaking bread being come, they sat down together, St. Francis and St. Clara, and one of the companions of St. Francis with the companion of St. Clara, and all the other companions took each his place at the table with all humility. And at the first dish St. Francis began to speak of God so sweetly, so sublimely, and so wondrously, that the fulness of Divine grace came down on them, and they all were rapt in God. And as they were thus rapt, with eyes and hands uplift to heaven, the folk of Assisi and the country round about saw that St. Mary of the Angels, and all the house, and the wood that was hard by the house, were burning brightly, and it seemed as it were a great fire that filled the church and the house and the whole wood together. For which cause the people of Assisi ran thither in great haste to quench the flames—but coming close up to the house and finding no fire at all, they entered within and found St. Francis and St. Clara and all their company in contemplation rapt in God and sitting around that humble board. Whereby of a truth they understood that this had been a heavenly flame, and no earthly one at all, which God had let appear miraculously, for to show and to signify the fire of love divine with which the souls of those holy brothers and holy nuns were all aflame; therefore they got them gone with great consolation in their hearts and with holy edifying."[1]

The later Franciscan chroniclers, with rigid views of asceticism, tried to make their founder an ascetic like themselves, and this legend shows that influence. But whenever we get back to the real person behind the later pictures we find a man dependent upon human sympathy, thriving only in an atmosphere of affection, and enjoying to the full everything in God's world which enlarged his true life, everything which he could use without lessening another's share. The earliest accounts

[1] *Little Flowers*, chap. xv.

tell how the brothers and sisters shared their meals together, and there is no doubt that the refining influence of Clara upon Francis was one of the most wholesome forces which came into his life.

A still more important step was the formation of a third Order for those who wanted to lead a distinctly *religious* life at home. The members of this Order were called *Tertiaries*, or *Brethren of Penitence*. It was an attempt to carry this practical gospel of love and devotion into the home. It was the mission of Francis, as Werner has well said in his *Duns Scotus*, "to awaken in Christian souls everywhere a striving after holiness and perfection; to keep the example of a direct following of Christ before the eyes of the world as a continuous living spectacle; to comfort all the wretched with the consolation of Christian mercy; and, by self-sacrificing devotion, to become all things to the spiritually abandoned and physically destitute."[1]

The third Order, like the second, was forced upon Francis by the situation. It was formed to meet the need of the multitudes which flocked to him as soon as the extraordinary power of his preaching made itself felt. Whole villages crowded about him, and all the inhabitants—men, women, and children—begged to be taken into his Order of Little Brothers. The very crowd of applicants threatened to defeat his purpose. He wanted his Order to be a band of *apostolic men*, living and preaching in the world as the Galilean band had done before, and he never meditated turning the entire world into an Order of Little Brothers. He had no desire to invade the home and despoil it; he wanted rather to penetrate it with a fragrant spirit of love, and to make all Christian hearts channels of love and happiness.

The Order of the Tertiaries was formed to meet the need of the eager multitude; it was a religious brotherhood, open to the devout of both sexes. The members were not asked to give up houses or lands, home or family. It is not possible to decide when the Order actually came

[1] Quoted from Harnack's *History of Dogma*, vol. vi. p. 88.

into being, though Sabatier holds that it was an essential part of the original apostolic mission of Francis.[1]

The rules of the Order were gradually made more ascetic under Roman influence, and the Tertiaries of later history can hardly be called the creation of Francis' genius. The movement, however, grew into a powerful social force. In fact, the founding of this Order has been called "one of the greatest events in the Middle Ages."[2] It brought to Europe a new truce of God; for the members of it were forbidden to bear arms in offensive warfare, and until the rule was altered by Pope Nicholas V., they might not bear arms at all; and they were allowed, though vassals, to refuse military service to their suzerains. The most important feature of the movement was the cultivation of a *group spirit* and the formation of a system of organization among the artizans and working-men, which developed into one of the powerful forces that finally led to the disintegration of the feudal system.

There is a charming legend in the *Little Flowers* which catches the beauty of this group spirit, and which shows how the invisible bonds of brotherhood bound together members, separated most widely by station, into one spirit of fellowship. The story says that once St. Louis, clad as a poor pilgrim, knocked at the door of a Franciscan convent, and asked for brother Giles. A hint from the keeper of the convent, or, as other accounts say, a Divine revelation, gave Giles the secret that his visitor was no less a person than the King of France. Giles ran to meet his guest. They embraced and knelt together in perfect silence. Then, without having broken the silence, Louis arose from his knees and went on his journey. When Giles came back to his cell, all the brothers reproached him for not having said anything to his royal visitor. With fine simplicity Giles answered: "I read his heart, and he read mine."[3]

The real tragedy of Francis' life was his awakening

[1] Sabatier, *Life of St. Francis*, p. 155 and p. 265.

[2] Avède Barine, in the *Revue des deux Mondes* for 1891, p. 782.

[3] *Little Flowers*, chap. xxxiv.

to the fact that his beautiful creation, the child of his soul, his family of brothers—was being transformed, and in measure destroyed, at the hands of those whose thoughts centred in the institution and in outward means and influence rather than in the ideal and its inward transforming power. Ideals of simplicity and poverty were graven on his heart. He had seen his attempt to imitate Christ spread by contagion. He had perfect faith that the inward life and joy which bubbled up so freshly and spontaneously in the first years of the movement would continue for ever. He was a poet, a holy child, a fool in the wisdom of the world. And he had to submit to the authority of cool organizers who looked before and after. He saw visions and dreamed dreams, and far-sighted men with scheming minds wove the visions and dreams into sails for the rigging of the ecclesiastical ship. In his first period, in the days of inspiration, he girded himself and went whither he would; in his later period others girded him and carried him and his movement whither he would not. Francis himself had an instinctive fear of rigid organization, and he had a horror of any system which could occasion a scramble for place or position, or which could give scope for selfish ambition in any direction. He did not want to found an "Order" like the monastic Orders; he wanted to bring back the *apostolic spirit*, and to have it propagate itself unhampered and unrestrained. His ideal was as impossible in the actual world of the thirteenth century as Christ's was impossible in the actual Jerusalem of the year 30. It was an ideal which, with the given environment, involved tragedy, as Christ's involved tragedy twelve hundred years earlier. The Church would not permit a movement which could not be drawn into its scheme, and as the Franciscan brotherhood expanded, the ecclesiastical authorities went cautiously to work to fit it into the architectural plan of the papal Church. It was done with velvet gloves, but Francis felt the cold steel beneath the gloves. The man who changed his simple ideal into an Order of Friars, with a system of fixed rules, was Cardinal Ugolini, afterwards Pope Gregory IX. He was Francis' friend and protector, and he used most *gentle* methods to transform the Franciscan ideals, so gentle that the simple-minded Francis hardly knew that he was losing his ideal until it was gone.

When the poor saint awoke to the fact that his brotherhood was to be forged into an organization under the rule and direction of the papal chair, he retired to pray, and seemed to hear God say to him: "Poor little man! I govern the universe; thinkest thou that I cannot overrule the concerns of thy little Order?"

There can, however, be no doubt that while he adopted as his own "rule" the principle: "He that would save his own life must lose it," and though he was ready to practise his own precept, that "when an inferior sees things that would be better and more useful to his soul than that which his superior commands him, the inferior should offer the sacrifice of his will as to God"—still the sacrifice which he was called upon to make involved an agony which reached the very citadel of his being, and together with profound physical difficulties under which he suffered, prepared the way for his experience of the *Stigmata* in 1224. This is the simple story: For weeks he had been going over in his thoughts the memories of Calvary. His Bible opened of itself to the story of Christ's passion. The love and suffering of Jesus had burned themselves into his heart. He had, too, been fasting for weeks, and the thought of the approaching feast of the Exaltation of the Cross was constantly before his mind. He had spent the entire night—September 14th—in prayer, when a vision came to him with the rising sun.

"A seraph with outspread wings flew towards him from the edge of the horizon, and bathed his soul in raptures unutterable. In the centre of the vision appeared a cross, and the seraph was nailed upon it. When the vision disappeared, he felt sharp sufferings mingled with ecstasy in the first moments. Stirred to the very depths of his being, he was anxiously asking the meaning of it all, when he perceived upon his body the Stigmata of the Crucified."[1]

The entire biography of Francis is full of incidents and accounts, artlessly and naively told, which convince a careful student of them that he was possessed of an extraordinary psychic nature. He was swept by powerful emotions, which sometimes caused automatisms and hallucinations. He possessed telepathic powers, and his influence over others was of a sort which implies hypnotic suggestion and contagion. He also exercised undoubted power over certain forms of disease. They are all traits which are familiar to any one who has worked in a modern psychological laboratory or who has read the literature of psychical research.

Under the power of suggestion, at the opening of his mission, Francis had seen the figure on the crucifix take life, and had felt Christ's piercing gaze upon him and had heard Him speak. It is only another step in the same direction when under the power of auto-suggestion —which may just as well be called a Divine suggestion— under an inward ground-swell of love and sacrifice which swept him as the wind sweeps the aeolian strings, his body received the marks of crucifixion.[2]

The modern interpreter, however, unlike the medieval disciple, finds this event, if it is admitted, a point of weakness rather than a point of strength. Instead of proving to be the marks of a saint, the Stigmata are the marks of emotional and physical abnormality. The "wonder" which moves us in him is the fresh and living fountain of joy and love which Christ opened through him for that age of gloom and superstition; not that he had motor automatisms of this extraordinary sort.

He knew himself where the real *miracle* lay, as one of the most beautiful of the legends shows: Brother

[1] *The Three Companions*, chap. xvii.; *Little Flowers*, chap. liv.; Bonaventura, chap. xiii. For a discussion of the historical evidence—Sabatier, *St. Francis of Assisi*, pp. 433-43.

[2] Those who wish to read an account of a modern case of stigmatization, should read the case of Louise Lateau. It may be found in Myers' *Personality: Human and Divine*, vol. i. pp. 492-3.

Masseo came to him one day with a half-jesting question: "Why after thee? Why after thee? Thou art not a man comely of form, thou art not of much wisdom, thou art not of noble birth. Whence comes it, then, that it is after thee that the whole world doth run?"

> "Hearing this," says the chronicle, "St. Francis, all overjoyed in spirit, knelt him down and rendered thanks and praises unto God; and then with great fervour of spirit turned him to Brother Masseo and said: 'Thou wishest to know why it is I whom men follow? Thou wishest to know? It is because the eyes of the Most High that continually watch the good and the wicked have not found among sinners any smaller man, nor any more insufficient and more sinful, therefore He has chosen me to accomplish His marvellous work. He chose me because He could find no one more worthless, and He wished by me to confound the nobility and grandeur, the strength and beauty and the learning of the world.'"[1]

The finest of all the *Little Flowers* is the conversation with Brother Leo on "perfect joy." They were travelling in the spring, to St. Mary of the Angels, and the day was bitterly cold. For full two miles Francis insisted vehemently that—though the Brothers Minor should give sight to the blind, and cast out devils, and make the deaf to hear, and even raise the dead; though they should know all tongues, all sciences, all scriptures, and reveal things to come; though they should speak with the tongues of angels, and preach so as to win all infidels to the faith of Christ—in none of these achievements would there be "perfect joy." And Brother Leo, having given heed to these sayings, asked, naturally enough, wherein "perfect joy" did consist. And St. Francis thus made answer:

> "When we come to St. Mary of the Angels, all soaked as we are with rain and numbed with cold and besmeared with mud and tormented with hunger, and the porter comes in anger and says, 'Who are ye?' and we say, 'We are two of your brethren,' and he says, 'Ye be no true men; nay, ye be two rogues that gad about deceiving the world and robbing the alms of the poor;

[1] *Little Flowers*, chap. x.

get ye gone,' and thereat he shuts the door, and makes us stand without in the snow and the rain, cold and hungered, till nightfall; if there withal we patiently endure such wrong and such cruelty, without being disquieted, and with patience and charity—Oh, Brother Leo, write that herein is perfect joy. And if we, still constrained by hunger, cold, and night, knock yet again—and pray him with much weeping for the love of God that he will open and let us in, and he yet more enraged should say: 'These be importunate knaves, I will pay them well as they deserve,' and should rush out with a knotty stick and throw us upon the ground, and beat us with all the knots of that stick, if with patience and gladness we suffer all these things, thinking on the pains of the blessed Christ—Oh, Brother Leo, write that herein is perfect joy!—Above all graces and gifts that Christ giveth to His beloved, is the grace and gift willingly for His love to endure pains and insults and shame and want; insomuch as in all other gifts of God we may not glory, since they are not ours but God's, but in the cross of tribulation and affliction we may boast since this is ours; and therefore saith the apostle, I would not that I should glory save in the cross of our Lord Jesus Christ."[1]

Here we come in sight of the "secret" of Francis' life and power. He discovered again the meaning of love, and he made his life a continuous exhibition of it. "Art thou Brother Francis of Assisi?" said a peasant to the saint one day. "Yes," replied Francis. "Then, try to be as good as all people think thee to be, because many have faith in thee, and therefore I admonish thee to be nothing less than people hope of thee." Francis immediately kneeled and thanked the peasant.[2] What an inimitable story! It perfectly fits the life of this childlike lover of men. In him we have once again religion of the first-hand type. Fellowship with God, the imitation of Christ, enthusiasm and love and joy springing out of the life because God has come into it—these things take the place of rites and ceremonies, which drop to a place of subordinate importance.

But the beautiful Franciscan ideal was short-lived It had to take its chances in a very harsh and stubborn

[1] *Little Flowers*, chap. viii. [2] *Ibid.* chap. liv.

world. One glimpse into the kind of world which existed in the second half of the thirteenth century will suffice. It is from the powerful pen of Brother Salimbene, a Franciscan friar of the next generation after Francis:[1]

> "Near the towns armed soldiers guarded the labourers all day long; this was necessary on account of the bandits, who had increased beyond measure. For they would take men and carry them off to their dungeons; and those who did not redeem themselves with money, them they would hang up by their feet or by the hands, or pull out their teeth. For they were more cruel than devils; and he that went by the way would as lief meet the devil as meet his fellow-man. For one ever had suspicion of another, lest he might purpose to carry him off to prison; and the land became a desert, wherein was neither husbandman nor wayfarer. And evil was multiplied upon the earth; and the birds and the beasts of the field increased beyond measure, for they found no household beasts in the villages to eat according to their wont, since the villages were altogether burnt. Wherefore wolves came thronging thick together round the city moats, howling horribly for intolerable anguish of hunger; and they crept by night into the cities, and ate men, women, or children that slept under the porticoes or in wagons; nay, at times they even broke through the walls of houses and throttled babes in their very cradles. No man could believe, but if he had seen it with his own eyes, as I did, the terrible deeds that were done at that time, both by men and by divers kinds of beasts."

This fearful picture of social conditions is hardly more sombre than the dark pictures of the moral condition of the clergy, high and low, which are found everywhere in this chronicle, that covers a period of more than seventy years.[2] Francis was hardly in his grave before the powerful influences of a society like that and the influences of a degenerate Church began to work degeneration in the Order. One does not need to go to Chaucer or Langland or Erasmus for evidence of the decay of the Order and of the corruption of the friars. It appears already in the writings of those who loved the Order as they did

[1] Brother Salimbene di Adamo was born of a noble family of Parma in 1221.

[2] It has been condensed and edited by G. G. Coulton, under the title *From St. Francis to Dante*. The above quotation is taken from this book, p. 56.

their very lives. St. Bonaventura, himself minister-general of the Order and official biographer of St. Francis, tells how the friars have already, by the year 1260, become "legacy hunters"; extravagant alike in public buildings and in private expenses; "contemptible in divers parts of the world" on account of their familiarity with women, and feared by the wayfarer, as armed robbers were feared. He cries out: "I would willingly be ground to powder, if so the brethren might come to the purity of St. Francis and his companions, and to that which he prescribed for his Order." "Francis himself," he says, "cries aloud for reform."

Matthew Paris, a witness from the same period, gives the same testimony. He says:

> "It is horrible, it is an awful presage, that in three or four hundred years, even in more, the old monastic Orders have not so entirely degenerated as these fraternities. The friars, who have been founded hardly twenty-four years, have built, even in the present day in England, residences as lofty as the palaces of our kings. These are they who, enlarging day by day their sumptuous edifices, encircling them with lofty walls, lay up within them incalculable treasures, imprudently transgressing the bounds of poverty, and violating, according to the prophecy of the German Hildegard, the very fundamental rules of their profession. These are they who, impelled by the love of gain, force themselves upon the last hours of the lords, and of the rich whom they know to be overflowing with wealth, and these, despising all rights, supplanting the ordinary pastors, extort confessions and secret testaments, boasting of themselves and of their Order, and asserting their vast superiority over all others. So that no one of the faithful now believes that he can be saved unless guided and directed by the preachers or Minor Friars. Eager to obtain certain privileges, they dwell in the courts of kings and nobles, as counsellors, chamberlains, treasurers, bridesmen, or notaries of marriages; they are the executioners of the papal extortions."[1]

There was, however, an unbroken succession of spiritual sons of St. Francis who fought manfully to stem the degeneracy of the Order and to preserve the

[1] Matthew Paris' *Chronicle from the Years 1235 to 1273*. Translated from the Latin by the Rev. J. A. Giles, London, 1852, vol. i. p. 475. There are many other passages in the *Chronicle* which show the imperfections of the Friars.

ideal of the founder. The Church had begun, even before Francis' death, as we have seen, to remould the Order to fit ecclesiastical schemes, and, as soon as he was in his grave, it went to work to construct a traditional, conventional "St. Francis." By a decree of 1266, all the early legends of St. Francis, which did not fit the portrait of him made by Bonaventura in 1263, were suppressed as far as possible, and everything was done to embarrass and defeat the "spiritual Franciscans," who clung tenaciously to the simple life and the ideal of poverty. Two parties appeared in the Order, even from the time of Francis' death. One party admitted that the Franciscan ideal was beyond the reach of mortal powers, and would require superhuman beings to realise it. This party favoured loose construction of the Rule of Francis, or the softening of it by papal dispensation. The head of this party and the master-mind in its councils in the first period after Francis' death was Brother Elias of Cortona. The other party, which finally developed into open schism under various names, believed that the ideal of poverty was a new revelation of God, a new stage in the spiritual life of the race. In their thought Francis was a divinely endowed being, the founder of a new epoch, whose rule was at least of equal authority with the Gospel. Brother Leo was the head of this party, which came later to be known as the party of the "Spirituals." This party, whose members stood for the strict observance of the rule of poverty and simplicity, always endeavoured to show that they were the true, "original" Franciscans, and that there was no break in the spiritual succession between them and their founder. The *Mirror of Perfection* was written to show this spiritual succession.[1] The "Spirituals" had a short period of triumph under the minister-generalate of John of Parma from 1247 to 1257. He was sincerely devoted to the task of "restoring" the Order to its primal purity

[1] Sabatier, in the face of much opposition, has made a very strong case for the view that the *Mirror of Perfection* was written in 1227, probably by Brother Leo. *Speculum Perfectionis seu S. Francisci Assisiensis Legenda Antiquissima*, Auctore Fratre Leone, edited by Paul Sabatier, Paris, 1898.

and simplicity. Salimbene, who knew him like a brother, says that "his face was as an angel's face, gracious and ever bright of cheer. . . . He was full of power and wisdom, and God's grace was with him. . . . He was a mirror and an example to all that beheld him, for his whole life was full of honour and saintliness, and good and perfect manners, gracious both to God and man."[1] The old friends of Francis were full of joy over the election of John of Parma. "It is well," cried Brother Egidis; "thy coming is happy, but thou comest very late." He was, however, forced from office in 1257. From that time on the "Spirituals" became more and more a party of opposition, pushed evermore in the direction of separation and revolt from the dominant and governing part of the Order, and were subjected to a steadily increasing persecution. "It was," writes D. S. Muzzey, in his illuminating monograph,[2] "a prolonged moral struggle for supremacy between the party of accommodation to prevailing ecclesiastical standards and the party of uncompromising fidelity to the lofty ideal of self-abandonment and self-emptying which was set up by the Poverello. The party of accommodation won when they overthrew John of Parma."

It was during the generalate of John of Parma that a movement of extraordinary interest and significance broke forth under the name of "the Eternal Gospel," and which played an important rôle in the history of the "Spiritual Franciscans." "The Eternal Gospel" was the creation of a little group of "Spirituals" who held to the ideal of Francis. The book itself, in which the new Gospel is set forth, came to the light in 1254, and in its final form was the work of a young friar named Gerard de Borgo San Donnino, but the ideas embodied in it had a long history of development, and for their real origin go back to a predecessor of Francis—Joachim of Floris. Joachim was the founder of a new Order of monks, stricter and more ascetic even than the Cistercians, living in strict chastity and extreme poverty. The mother-house of the

[1] *Op. cit.* p. 101. [2] *The Spiritual Franciscans*, New York, 1907, p. 14.

Order, an Order never very widespread, was at Fiori, or Floris, in Calabria, and there Joachim died about 1202.

As a child he had been of a solitary and meditative type; as a young man he journeyed through the East and visited the scenes in the life of the Saviour, dreaming even then of a revived and transformed Christianity. As he grew to manhood he felt a prophetic mission laid upon him. He devoted himself to the study of the Scriptures and gradually drew from them his message of relief—a vision of a new Church and a new age. He profoundly felt that his times were out of joint, and that the Church was being wrecked by worldliness. He took refuge from the hard present in the apocalyptic visions of the Old and New Testament, and he left behind him three books in Latin:[1] (1) *A Harmony of the Old and New Testament*, (2) *A Commentary on the Apocalypse*, and (3) *The Psaltery of Ten Strings*. He was always on the watch for parallelisms between the "old dispensation" and the "new," and by a strained exegesis he hit upon a scheme of "three ages"—two already past, and the third, or age of the Holy Ghost, just about to dawn. The first age is the age of the Father, beginning with Adam, coming to its *clarescence* in Abraham, and ending with Zacharias. The second stage, the Church of the Son, dawned before the first age ended, had its *clarescence* in Christ, and was now about to end, and the third stage, that of the Holy Spirit, to begin. The Church of the Father was a stage of law. The Church of the Son is still an imperfect stage, with priests and sacraments, a stage typified by Hagar, who neglects her children! The third stage is typified by Sarah, the true mother, an era without priests or sacraments, without altar or sacrifice, an era of direct contemplation or perfect liberty. The first age was the age of slaves, the second of sons, the third will be of friends;

[1] There is a legend that, while in the Holy Land, Joachim was overcome with thirst in a trackless desert. In his dire strait, he had a vision of a man standing by a river of oil, and saying to him: "Drink of this stream." At once he drank to his full satisfaction, and when he awoke he found that he had a complete knowledge of Scripture, though previously he had been illiterate!

the first period was an age of fear, the second of faith, the third will be one of love. The first was an age of starlight, the second of dawn, the third will be full day. The first was winter, the second spring, the third will be glorious summer. The first bore nettles, the second roses, the third will bear lilies! It will be a time of peace and truth over the whole earth.

The new era, which Joachim calculated would begin in 1260,[1] would, he believed, witness a sudden spiritual expansion—there would come a new order of men who would possess a mystical consciousness and know within themselves the mind and will of the Spirit. They would be no longer slaves to the letter of Scripture, because they would see face to face, and have unbroken communion with God. The machinery of the Church would be unnecessary, for all men "from sea to sea" would then have direct access to God by the Spirit. This new religion of liberty, of contemplation, of direct revelation, Joachim called the "spiritual Gospel of Christ," or sometimes the "Gospel of the kingdom," and, in a famous passage commenting on the Apocalypse, he uses the phrase, which was later revived with far-reaching significance, the "Eternal Gospel."

> "I saw the angel of God, who flew into the middle of heaven, having the eternal Gospel. This gospel is called eternal by John because that which Christ and the apostles have given us is temporal and transitory so far as concerns the form of the sacraments, but eternal in respect to the truths which these signify."[2]

Still more important than the books he wrote was the little group of disciples whom he left behind him. They believed that their abbot had been a supernaturally inspired prophet, they piously cherished his ideals of simplicity and holiness, they produced a number of prophetical books, written in the style and spirit of their master and in his name, and which contained vivid

[1] He counted between Adam and Christ forty-two generations of thirty years each, which gave him 1260 years, and he assumed that the age of the Son would be of the same length.

[2] Gebhart's *L'Italie mystique* (fifth ed., Paris, 1906), p. 72.

descriptions of events then transpiring, as though foreseen and foretold by Joachim. In 1240 an old abbot of Floris, fearing that his convent would be pillaged by the soldiers of Frederick II., who was regarded as the arch-enemy of the Church, carried away to Pisa the Joachim writings of his convent, and begged the Friars of Pisa to guard them safely. The Friars of Pisa began to read these precious books, and lo, they found in them exact and striking "prophecies" of events which were happening before their eyes.[1] The astonished readers, supposing that they were all genuine books by Joachim, believed that he was a prophet of the first order—the beginner of a new epoch. Under his inspiration, or rather under the inspiration of the "Joachim writings," there sprang up a small "school of prophets" within the Franciscan circle. They carried the idea of the three ages to its full development, and gave vivid and concrete pictures of the glory of the new age, just breaking. Joachim had drawn a parallel between Abraham, Isaac, and Jacob, with his twelve sons, and Zachariah, John the Baptist, and Christ with His twelve disciples. The Joachimite prophets of the thirteenth century carried this idea farther, and pictured the third and final stage—the dispensation of the "Eternal Gospel," or religion of the Spirit—with Joachim, Dominic, and Francis, and with the twelve apostles of Francis as the divine initiators of it.

This system was fully developed and given to the world by Gerard of San Donnino, who was studying in the University of Paris, and had gathered about him a Joachimite circle, in which apocalyptic ideas and expectations flourished, and in 1254 he put forth the famous book on the "Eternal Gospel." It was a composite work, made up of extracts from the genuine works of Joachim, with an Introduction (which contained the "Eternal Gospel" proper) and Notes on the collected extracts from Joachim, both the Introduction and Notes

[1] The "Joachim Writings" include commentaries on Jeremiah, on Isaiah, on Ezekiel, Daniel, and the Minor Prophets. All these are spurious, *i.e.* they were written after Joachim's death, and the exact "prophecies" of events were in fact written after the events had transpired.

being by Gerard.[1] The Introduction and Notes show intense hostility to the papacy, a similar hostility to the corrupt and wealthy clergy, a loss of faith in the existing Church, and a vivid expectation of the end of the age in 1260, which was to usher in the new age of the *Eternal Gospel.* The "new age" is to be far superior to all ages that have preceded it. The New Testament is to be superseded as the Old Testament had been. Monks who are *saintly and go barefooted* are to take the place of easy-living priests; the entire sacerdotal system of the imperfect Church is to be swept away and the religion of the Spirit will take its place.

Few more startling books have ever appeared to disturb the peace of an infallible Church, and a papal commission consisting of three Cardinals was summoned to deal with it. The commission sat at Anagni, in 1255, and condemned the *Eternal Gospel* as "heretical," and ordered it burned. John of Parma was forced from office, and the Joachimites were everywhere suspected and pursued with persecution, though the idea of a new age and a coming religion of the Spirit was never killed out. Whenever the "Spirituals" were pushed to the verge of despair by the fury of their persecutors they continually revived these "visions of relief," these apocalyptic hopes, and as the issue grew sharper between the "Spirituals" and the party of accommodation, the former came to regard the Church as apostate, and to consider themselves as the Divine "Remnant," the only true Church.

There formed, in succession, out of this "left wing" of the Franciscans, a host of tiny sects, which, like an army of gnats, continually annoyed and disturbed the peace of the Church. As the gap widened between themselves and the persecuting Church, these groups more and more came to claim direct revelation, and to believe themselves special organs of the Spirit. They came to assume that they were the only true followers of Christ and imitators of St. Francis, who for many

[1] See Renan's valuable monograph, *Joachim de Flore et l'évangile éternel.* The same conclusion is reached by Denifle in *Archiv für Literatur und Kirchengeschichte,* vol. i. 1885.

of these "Spirituals" was on a level with Christ Himself.[1]

The most important of the many groups of *Zealots* were those who received the name of "Fraticelli," or "Little Brothers." The name was first used in an opprobrious sense for the "Spirituals" of Tuscany, who, separated entirely from the larger Franciscan community, elected their own officers, as the true Franciscan "Remnant," and practically defied the Church. The term, however, was soon extended to cover any Italian groups of "Spiritual" Franciscans in revolt from the authority of the Church.[2] Like the Beghards and Beguines of Germany, with whom they had many points in common, they practised poverty outside the convent, and became more or less infected with the popular mysticism of the time—a widespread belief in man as an incarnation of the Holy Spirit.[3]

Like many other spiritual revivals, the Franciscan movement both succeeded and failed. It failed to produce an organization which adequately embodied the ideal of the saint of Assisi. He himself was incapable of organizing a permanent society. He was a mystic, a poet, a prophet; he could inspire, kindle, quicken. He could fuse men into a spiritual group by the personal power of his own vision and ideal, and send them into

[1] Angelo Clareno writes: "The blessed Francis was in the world under the form of Christ crucified. He humiliated himself, therefore Christ has exalted him." Brother Angelo Clareno, who died at an advanced age in 1337, and who had endured sixty years of persecution, was one of the great leaders of the "spiritual group"; and he developed in his *History of the Seven Tribulations of the Church*, and in his extraordinary *Epistles*, the view that the true followers of St. Francis form the Church within the Church—"the only true Church." He did not hesitate to put the papal Church on a lower level than this Church of the Spiritual Franciscans. "Seek," he writes to the spiritual flock, "the things above; desire spiritual things; scorn earthly things; follow those things which are before; forget those things which are behind. It is our vow to imitate Christ, the pledge of our immortality; to observe the rule [of St. Francis] perfectly, against which neither law nor decree can prevail, and to which every authority and power should give way. . . . If a king or a pope orders us to do anything contrary to this faith, we must obey God rather than men." "Let us pray from repentant hearts that Grace may cleanse us of our sins, and we shall have a remission and inward absolution greater than those who would absolve us could understand. All fear will be expelled from our hearts, and we shall have the witness of the Spirit within us" (*L'Italie mystique*, pp. 189 and 191).

[2] See Muzzey, *op. cit.* pp. 41-47.

[3] See chapter xi. on Brotherhood Groups in the Thirteenth Century.

world-wide missionary activity. But he could not construct a system. The Franciscan Order, as we know it in history, is not his creation. It is a mongrel offspring. It is the bungling attempt of the Church to catch and use for its purposes the extraordinary energy developed by this band of men who rediscovered the apostolic idea. The "Order" was, from the nature of things, doomed to failure, and it failed.

The movement itself, however, was a mighty spiritual force, which influenced thousands of lives, and has not spent itself yet. Its supreme saint bore, in a very dark age, a real likeness to his Divine Master. He entered deeply into the meaning of redeeming love, felt its unparalleled power, and was himself melted into radiant love by its warmth. He exhibited religion with selfishness washed out of it, and he revealed, by its contrast with his own pure life, the spiritual poverty and nakedness of the Church. The inspiration of his life and holiness produced a literature of sainthood which is unsurpassed, and it produced an influence on art second only to that of the inspiration of Christ Himself. Again and again kindred souls have gone back to this "little poor man" of Assisi for their model; they have caught again from his story the passion of humanity; they have "believed in his belief," have seen his vision, and have felt the same fountain of love open in their hearts—and so he has succeeded.

CHAPTER X

A GROUP OF PANTHEISTICAL MYSTICS[1]

WE have seen how John Scotus Erigena brought to light in the ninth century a conception of God and of man, based upon the philosophy of the Platonic School and the mystical teaching of Dionysius, a conception which fitted very badly with the dominant theology of the Western Church. The Church authorities were puzzled over his profound expositions, but the Church of that century had forged no weapons for fighting such daring speculations. Their attempted refutations of the solitary scholar are ridiculous. There was, however, little need of refuting him. The age which followed him could not understand him, and his works fell into an innocuous oblivion. A dim halo of fame hung about his name, and legend made him the founder of two universities—the University of Paris and that of Oxford,—associated him with the great Alfred, and wove a tragic tale of his death in the school of Malmesbury, where he is said to have been stabbed by the pens of his scholars. For three centuries he appears to have been well-nigh forgotten. The battles which he fought seemed all settled, and settled adversely to his positions. An occasional theologian or schoolman cites his writings,[2] but he was in no sense an influence to be reckoned with.

[1] I am indebted in the preparation of this chapter to Hauréau's *De la philosophie scolastique*; Jourdain's *Mémoire sur les sources philosophiques des hérésies d'Amaury de Chartres et de David de Dinan*; Delacroix' *Essai sur le mysticisme spéculatif en Allemagne au xiv. siècle*; and Jundt's *Histoire du panthéisme populaire.*

[2] Wibald, the abbot of the Monastery of Corvey, writing to Manegold of Paderborn about the middle of the twelfth century, speaks of Erigena as closing

Suddenly, toward the end of the twelfth century, this submerged influence broke out in a widespread popular movement which startled the ecclesiastical authorities. The first sign of trouble was the discovery that a celebrated master in the University of Paris was teaching "that every man ought to believe, as an article of his faith without which there is no salvation, *that each one of us is a member of the Christ.*"[1] To the theologians of the day that "article of faith" had a dangerous ring to it—it was "new theology" to them, and they set vigorously to work to silence the teaching.

The man who thus drew the suspicious attention of the Church upon himself was Amaury (often given in its Latin form, Amalrich). He was a native of Bene, a small village in the diocese of Chartres. He had studied theology in Paris, and at length became a master in the university and a person of wide and commanding influence. At about the opening of the thirteenth century his methods and his views came under the suspicion of the University authorities, and he was by them condemned in 1204. He appealed, however, to the Pope, Innocent III., who also condemned his teaching in 1205. He died soon after this decision, his death being hastened by his grief over his condemnation. But like many another teacher he had scattered far and wide the seeds of his doctrine, and these seeds went on germinating in spite of the master's condemnation and death. A few years after his voice was hushed the Archbishop of Paris got a clue, which led to the revelation that there was in and about Paris a vigorous "society" propagating the views of the dead master, and threatening the very foundations of orthodoxy. The central idea which this "society" expressed was the actual reign of the Holy Spirit *now* in the hearts of men. Those who formed the group of new disciples—apparently following the teaching of Amaury

the line of great masters which began with Venerable Bede—"Men," he says, "most learned, who by writing and reasoning left in the Church of God illustrious monuments of their genius" (see Poole, *op. cit.* p. 78).

[1] *Gesta Philippi Augusti* by Guillaume le Breton in Bouquet's *Recueil des historiens*, tome xvii. p. 83.

—insisted that God is not far off in the sky, but lives and moves and has His real being in the lives of those who open themselves to Him. And as soon as He becomes a present life within any person that person is at once raised above rules and forms and rites, which have a use only for those who are on a lower spiritual level. The supreme attainment in religious experience, they held, is the joy of finding oneself free in God, and of feeling His life palpitate within one's own being. In order to arrive at this culminating experience the members of this society encouraged silence and cultivated the appreciation of the inward Presence. This is the way the sect was discovered:[1]

A certain William, a goldsmith—one of the leaders of the new society, called in the Chronicle one of their *prophets*—went to Raoul of Namours and told him that he had been sent by God to instruct him, and then revealed to him the views of his society, which were as follows: "That God the Father had acted in Old Testament times under forms of *law*; that God the Son had worked through certain forms, such as the sacrament of the altar and baptism, but that as the coming of the Son had ended the legal system, so, too, all the forms through which Christ had worked were now to cease and the Person of the Holy Spirit was to manifest Himself in those in whom He was incarnating Himself," namely in the members of the new society. Raoul was quick to scent the heresy lurking in what he heard, but he was cool-headed enough to see the importance of gathering within his net as many of the dangerous group as possible. He therefore made use of a stratagem too often used to save the Ark. He said to the unsuspicious William, "I have been informed by the Holy Ghost that a certain priest and I ought to preach this new doctrine," and he asked to be taken into the group. As soon as he had left William, he ran at once to the ecclesiastical authorities and told them of his

[1] The following account is taken from the Chronicle of Caesar of Heisterbach. (*Illustrium miraculorum et hist. memor. a Caesario Heisterbachensi* (1591), Book V. chap. xxii.)

discovery. They planned an elaborate scheme for capturing the entire group. Raoul and his companion-priest joined themselves with the members of the "society," and lived among them for three months, going through all the four dioceses where there were members of the sect. Raoul proved an adept at deceiving the "elect." He would pretend to fall into ecstasy, with his rapt face turned toward heaven, and then, recovering consciousness, would impart to the group the visions which had been granted to him, which means, of course, that the new "society" was trying to revive a prophetic type of ministry.

When Raoul had gathered all the information needed, he returned to Paris and helped the Bishop cast his ecclesiastical net over the leaders of the movement. They were seized, thrown into the episcopal prison, and put through a rigorous examination, a provincial council having been called for the purpose. They were found guilty of heresy, were stripped of their clerical robes before the multitude, and, in due time, those who remained "obstinate" were put to the stake, "without showing any sign of repentance." The chronicler's account of the execution is such a characteristic picture of the times that I give it here:—

> "When the victims were led to their punishment, a furious wind arose, provoked, no doubt, by the spirits of hell who, being the authors of the error of these men, were also the authors of their tragic end. And, during the following night, the leader of the heretical group came, and knocked at the cell of a recluse, and bitterly confessed his error, saying that he had been received in hell as a person of importance and was condemned to the eternal fires."

A peculiarly interesting item comes out in the ancient chronicle from which I am quoting, namely that many of the members of the little society of these disciples of the Holy Spirit were prominent persons in the Church. It was not a group of the Paris rabble, but a serious company of highly-trained and enlightened men, undoubtedly with a large nucleus of university students.

Some are called in the report "naive and credulous." There were also some women members seized, but they were pardoned on the ground that they had been led astray by their simple credulity.

The Council, which was held in Paris in 1209, was not content with burning the living alone. They ordered the bones of Amaury of Bene to be dug up and thrown into unconsecrated ground, or even burned as some accounts would have it, and then they struck at those longer dead who were believed to be the source of the new and dangerous thought. The Council condemned the works of Aristotle *On Physics* and the commentaries upon them, forbidding the reading of those works, and, according to the Chronicle of Martin of Pologne, it condemned a book called *Periphysion* (Greek for *De Natura*). This last-named work is evidently the book on the *Division of Nature* by our philosopher, John the Scot. This old chronicler, Martin of Pologne, did not know apparently who wrote the "wicked book," *Periphysion*, but his account, written in shocking Latin, shows what was thought of the sect in 1271. He is reporting the papal condemnation:—

> "We condemn Amaury who has declared that the ideas which are in the Divine Mind create and are created. He has declared also that God is called the End of all things, because all things are to return into Him and to remain unchangeable in Him. Just as the *nature* of Abraham is not different from the *nature* of Isaac, but the same *nature* is common to both, so, according to Amaury, all beings are at bottom one being and all beings are God. He holds that God is the essence of every creature, and the ultimate reality of everything that is. He also teaches that as the light cannot be perceived in itself, but in and by means of the air, so God cannot be seen in Himself, either by angel or by man. He can be seen only in His creatures. It is further one of the views of Amaury that, if it had not been for sin, there would have been no distinction of sexes, but men would have multiplied without the process of generation, after the manner of the angels; and that after the resurrection, the two sexes will be reunited, as they were at creation."[1]

[1] Chronicle of Martinus Polonus (Antwerp, 1574), p. 393.

Every one of these views is distinctly and definitely taught by John the Scot. Cardinal Henry of Ostia in his account carries the "heresy" back to its true source. He says: "The doctrine of the wicked Amaury is comprised in the book of the Master John the Scot, which is called *Periphysion*, which the said Amaury followed,"[1] and he repeats the charges already made.

It would seem that Amaury, in the pursuit of his philosophical studies, had unearthed a forgotten book, and had interpreted it to his university classes with oral comment, as other scholars were doing with Aristotle. The passages selected for condemnation, as noted above, are evidently not so much the views of Amaury as passages which he had selected from *De Divisione Naturae* for comment in his classes. It is doubtful whether he would have been disturbed in his teaching if no one had drawn any practical conclusions from the doctrine. But the moment these ideas came down from the realm of pure metaphysics, and began to receive practical application, as they did in the spiritual "society" discovered in Paris, the storm broke. A few years later, in 1225, the pope, Honorius III., issued a bull of final condemnation on the writings of John the Scot, having heard from the Archbishop of Paris that "the worms of this abominable heresy" had wriggled out of the said *Periphysion*.

One reason that the authorities of the Church showed such vigour in their attack on the author of the *Division of Nature* apparently is to be found in the fact that numerous copies of his book were found among the Albigenses in the south of France, who at this particular epoch were occupying the focal point in the attention of the Church.

"Since as we have heard," the bull runs, "that this book is to be found in various monasteries, and other places, and several monastic and scholastic persons, being unduly attracted by novelty, give themselves eagerly to the study of the said book, thinking it

[1] This is found in *Lectura sive apparatus domini Hostiensis super quinque libris decretalium*. I have taken this citation from Preger's *Geschichte der deutschen Mystik*, vol. i. p. 166.

a fine thing to utter strange opinions—though the apostle warns us to avoid profane novelties—we, in accordance with our pastoral duty, endeavouring to oppose the power of corruption which a book of this kind might exercise, command you all and several, straightly enjoining you in the Holy Ghost, that you make diligent search for that book, and wherever you succeed in finding the same, or any portion thereof, that you send it, if it may be done with safety, without delay to us to be solemnly burned; or if this is impossible that you do yourselves publicly burn the same."[1]

Before entering upon our study of the character and significance of the sect which sprang from Amaury's teaching, and which seemed so dangerous to the officials in the thirteenth century, we must say a few words in reference to the strange condemnation of the works of Aristotle coupled with this condemnation of Amaury and John the Scot. There is no indication that Amaury had sucked any poison from Aristotle. But a certain David of Dinant, of equal fame with Amaury, was denounced by this same Council of 1209, and his books burned. According to Albert the Great, who was a contemporary,

"David of Dinant held that God, intelligence, and matter are identical in essence, and unite in a single substance, that consequently everything in nature is one—that consequently individual qualities which distinguish beings are only *appearances* due to an illusion of sense."

Saint Thomas Aquinas, who was a disciple of Albert the Great, gives this further account of David's doctrine:

"David of Dinant divided the beings of the universe into three classes—bodies, souls, and eternal substances. He said that matter is the first and indivisible element which constitutes bodies, that intelligence (*nous*) is the first and indivisible element which constitutes souls, and that God is the first and indivisible element which constitutes eternal substances; and finally that these three—God, intelligence, and matter—are *a single thing, one and the same.* From which it follows that everything in the universe is essentially one."

Here, then, was another teacher of extreme pantheism, who also had a following. He, too, as we know, had been reading John the Scot, but he had also been reading the

[1] Quoted from Alice Gardner's *Studies in John the Scot*, pp. 139-40.

works of Aristotle, which had just freshly come to light in Europe. Until the middle of the twelfth century Europe possessed of Aristotle's writings only a part of the Logic, in a Latin translation ascribed to Boethius. The other works of the great Greek master came first to the knowledge of the Christian scholars through the Arabians, who for more than three centuries had produced a succession of interpreters and commentators of his writings. The earliest collection of Aristotle's physical and metaphysical works which came into the hands of Christian readers, was a Latin translation made from Arabic. Bound up with this collection there were also books and commentaries by the foremost Arabian philosophers, and some of these commentaries were at first believed to be works by Aristotle himself. There was a very strong tinge of Neoplatonic mysticism in the Arabian interpretation, and it is well-nigh certain that in this Aristotelian collection there was some particular book on physics which gave a basis for David's doctrine.[1] It is probable that one of the *sources* of the teaching both of David and Amaury, and through them of the mysticism which followed, was the writings of Alexander of Aphrodisias, the great commentator of Aristotle in the second century. Alexander taught that the *active reason* in man is Divine, and all the *ideas* which are the prototypes of the universe have their origin in this "active reason," and thus have their origin in God, so that everything *real* is Divine. Caesar of Heisterbach, in his account, says that the Council of 1209 forbade the reading of Aristotle for *three years*. But it is certain that the Lateran Council, held in 1215, repeated the ban on the Aristotelian books, and Pope Gregory the Ninth, in a bull of the year 1231, declared that the books of Aristotle *On Nature*, "the reading of which has already been forbidden by a provincial Council, shall not be read until they have been examined and purged of every suspicion of error." This interdict on the physical

[1] For an extended discussion of the subject the reader is referred to Hauréau, *Philosophie scolastique*, and Jourdain, *Excursions historiques et philosophiques*.

writings of the great philosopher fell quickly into oblivion, for as soon as the leading scholars of the time succeeded in discovering the real Aristotle, purged of Arabian colouring, he was found to be the greatest buttress of the faith of the Church; and before the end of the thirteenth century he was settled in his place as the "official philosopher," whose *ipse dixit* could not be contradicted without accusation of heresy.

The facts warrant us in concluding that as the first effect of the revival of the teaching of John the Scot, coupled with the study of the Aristotle of the Arabs, there appeared in Paris two powerful teachers who had arrived at the conviction that everything in the universe, in the last analysis, is God. The point in common in their teaching is the negation of any principle of distinction—*everything is one because everything is God.* It is easy now to see why the authorities found so much danger in the words of Amaury, words that sound to us so apostolic: "Every man ought to believe as an article of his faith that each one of us is a member of the Christ," for he evidently used the words in a pantheistical sense.

The teaching found ready listeners, and could not be suppressed by papal bulls, by martyr fires, or by pious stories relating how the chief heretics were faring in hell. This type of religious thought has a fascination for many minds, primarily because there is an elemental tendency in us to arrive at an all-embracing Unity, and it has played a mighty rôle in man's spiritual history. It cannot be dismissed by the easy method of tagging the opprobrious nickname of "pantheism" upon it. We have here the outbreaking of a mystical movement which had momentous possibilities for good and for evil, and which can give us much instruction as to where the danger in mysticism lies, and where its safeguards are to be sought.

There was already by 1209 a widespread "society" in and about Paris, evidently loosely held together, and yet showing some indications of internal organization. We learn of specific ministry through "prophets," and we find an important stress put upon ecstasy and inspirational speaking. The members of the sect rejected, as suited only to the condition of the ignorant and unspiritual, the traditional formulae, rites, and ceremonies of the Church. They denounced as superstition the worship of saints and the veneration of relics. Goodwill and spiritual insight, they held, are more efficacious than the sacraments.

"They denied," says the Chronicler Caesar of Heisterbach,[1] "the resurrection of the body. They taught that there is neither heaven nor hell, as places, but *that he who knows God possesses heaven*, and he who commits a mortal sin carries hell within himself just as a man carries a decayed tooth in his mouth. They treated as idolatry the custom of setting up statues to saints, and of burning incense to images. They laughed at those who kissed the bones of martyrs."

The movement was marked by a bold freedom of spirit toward traditional religion. In fact, the disciples of Amaury believed that they were inaugurating a new era of spiritual experience and a new epoch of revelation. They taught, as we have already seen, that there are three distinct dispensations. In the earliest the Father worked alone, without the Son and without the Holy Spirit, until the incarnation of the Son. The Father, they taught, was incarnated in Abraham; the Son in the child of Mary's womb; and *the Holy Spirit has become incarnated in them.*[2] The dispensation of the Son lasted until the time then present, and the dispensation of the Holy Spirit was beginning *then.* The reign of the Father was a reign of law, and was stern and severe. The reign of the Son was milder and gentler, for he was born of a woman. He abolished the law, destroyed the temple, and gathered about Himself those of goodwill. But the "new law" of the Son was also a burden to be borne, and it had its limitations. The reign of the Holy Spirit frees humanity

[1] Book V. chap. xxii. p. 386.

[2] There is in these teachings an unmistakable likeness to the prophetic ideal of Joachim of Floris, and there was possibly a direct influence of the Calabrian prophet on the followers of Amaury, though such a conclusion is not necessary. The idea of three "dispensations" was very ancient, certainly as old as the Montanists, and there are furthermore very marked differences between the two conceptions of the "Dispensation of the Holy Spirit," as held respectively by Joachim and by the followers of Amaury.

from all burdens and servitude. In Him all laws and commandments are at an end. There is no more need of confession, of baptism, of the eucharist. There is no place for sacrifices to win over God, and there is no need of a mediator between God and man. *The direct inward work of the Holy Spirit brings salvation, without any exterior act or ceremony.* They believed that every man is a temporal manifestation of Divinity, that there is something in man which the fall and sin have not destroyed; that the Spirit is everywhere and in everything, but that He is especially incarnate in the members of their sect. Their faith in the eternal and indestructible Divine Life within themselves made them scorn persecution and misery. One of the members even declared that he could not be burnt, because there was something of God in him. They held that children born of parents belonging to the sect had no need of baptism, for there was no original sin in such a child. Already the spring flowers of the kingdom of the Holy Spirit were appearing, and of the increase of holiness and goodness there was to be no end. *The final achievement of God is the manifestation of Himself in the hearts of men, and the highest achievement of man is the inner consciousness of God.*[1]

Gerson (1363-1429), who was Chancellor of the University of Paris and himself a mystic, reports that Amaury taught that "the creature is changed into God, and that each person finds in Him his own peculiar being and ideal." He says that Amaury's disciples believed with him that "the soul, when it has risen to God by means of love, sloughs off its own particular nature, and finds in God its eternal and immutable essence. Such a soul loses its own being, and receives the being of God, so that it is no longer a 'creature,' it no longer sees and loves God (as a foreign object), but it becomes God Himself, the object of all contemplation and love."[2]

These doctrines — that the universe is a Divine

[1] The data on the views of the sect are: Martène et Durand, *Thesaurus Novus Anecdotorum*; Caesar of Heisterbach, *Hist. Memor.*; Guillaume le Breton, *De Gestis Phil. Aug.*

[2] Quoted from Jundt's *Histoire du panthéisme populaire*, pp. 25-26.

Emanation, that God is being incarnated in man, that each person may rise to a substantial union with God, that external law is abolished and ceremonial practices outdated, that the final revelation of God is being made through man himself—these doctrines are loaded with dangerous possibilities as soon as they receive popular interpretation.

It is wellnigh certain that Amaury, and David as well, were led on by purely philosophical interests, and there are no reliable charges against them except charges of error in doctrine. The case is not so plain in reference to their disciples. There is no lack of charges of immorality in our original accounts of the sect. On this point Caesar of Heisterbach reports: "They said that if any one possessing the Holy Spirit commits the sin of fornication, or defiles himself in any other manner, his act is not imputed to him as sin, because he has written within him the Holy Spirit who is God, and because everything in us is done by the Holy Spirit."[1] In the same line Guillaume le Breton says: "They used the virtue of charity in such a broad sense that they claimed that an act usually considered sin was no longer sin if done in the virtue of charity. Thus in the name of charity they committed the grossest sins. They held out to those who did sin complete forgiveness on the ground that God is goodness and not justice."[2] We must remember, however, that this is hostile testimony, written by men who have a horror of heresy, and who easily catch up any damaging charge that happens to be afloat.

It is true that the principles enunciated by this sect are open to an immoral practical application. If the law is abolished, if the believer holds that God does through him whatever he does, if he has lost all standards of distinction, so that he asserts that "God spoke through Ovid as much as through Augustine," as one chronicler says they taught, the step down into an immoral life is very easy. But there is no proof that the disciples of Amaury actually

[1] Caesar of Heisterbach, *op. cit.* p. 386.
[2] Guillaume le Breton, *op. cit.* p. 83.

took this step. There is no such charge in the earliest account of the sect, and the charges increase in virulence as the writers are more remote in time from the facts which they record. In the first stage of the movement the lofty, serious purpose of the sect would keep the members from drawing practical consequences, into which a lower type of members might easily fall in the second and third generation. The doctrine of spiritual freedom and of Divine Immanence does not necessarily involve the reign of caprice and immorality,[1] and we need more proof before we conclude that the members of this mystical group turned their freedom into licence and used their new faith in the presence and goodness of God as an excuse for taking the path of least resistance. The aim and purpose of Amaury seem to have been to raise men to such a spiritual height that sin would no longer be possible to them.

The martyrdom of the leaders in 1209 did not stop the movement, which had already spread through four dioceses about Paris. Persecution that made it difficult for the members of the society to live in Paris drove them abroad into regions where the authorities were less on their guard. Two years later, in 1211, one of the leaders of the sect of Amaurians named Godin, was found in Amiens, and was burned at the stake there. A heretic was burned at Troyes in 1220 on the charge that he claimed to be an incarnation of the Holy Spirit, and St. Thomas Aquinas speaks of a knight of this period who, when asked to do penance for his sins, replied: "If St. Peter was saved I shall be, for the same Spirit dwells in me that dwelt in him."[2] Before this period there is little trace of mystical sects in Strasbourg and the cities of the Rhine. From this time on they are continually in evidence, and they all bear the family marks which are characteristic of this Paris "society" founded by Amaury. There is no *documentary* evidence which indisputably fixes a direct connection between Amaury and the mystical sects of

[1] See for a good statement of this position Delacroix, *Essai sur le mysticisme spéculatif*, p. 37.

[2] Jundt, *op. cit.* p. 31.

Strasbourg and the Rhine countries, or the similar groups in Southern France and Italy, but there is an overwhelming probability that, however submerged the stream of influence, there *was* a connection. We get a graphic account from a famous inquisitor—Stephen of Borbone—of a sect in Lyons which looks like a union of the disciples of Amaury with the Waldenses. The sect exhibits the strict morality of the latter, and the pantheistic metaphysics of the former. Stephen of Borbone made his investigation between 1223 and 1235. He describes the sect as follows:

"They absolutely refuse obedience to the Roman Church, which they call the unholy Babylon of the Apocalypse. They hold that all good persons, according to some, even women, are priests, having received direct ordination from God, while ecclesiastics receive it only from men. All good persons, even women, can pronounce absolution, and can consecrate the bread. They teach that it is sufficient to confess sins to God, and that God alone is able to excommunicate."

Then follows an account of moral and anti-sacerdotal teaching characteristic of the Waldenses,[1] and the account continues with a description of an extreme form of mysticism:

"They pretend that every man is a Son of God in the same manner that Christ was. Christ had God or the Holy Spirit for soul, and they say that other men also have. They believe in the incarnation, the birth, the passion, and the resurrection of Christ, but they mean by it the Spiritual conception, Spiritual birth, Spiritual resurrection of the perfect man. For them the true passion of Jesus is the martyrdom of a holy man, and the true sacrament is the conversion of a man, for in such a conversion the body of Christ is formed. In the doctrine of the Trinity, the Father is he who converts a stranger to their doctrine. The Son is he who is converted, and the Holy Spirit is the truth by means of which the conversion is accomplished. This is what they mean when they say that they believe in the Father and the Son and the Holy Ghost. They declare that the soul of all men since Adam is the Holy Spirit. . . . It is because God thus dwells in them that all good men are priests. It is God who works through them and gives them power to loose and bind."[2]

---

[1] See chapter on the Waldenses.

[2] Jundt, *Histoire du panthéisme populaire*, pp. 31-32.

Only a few years after the death of Amaury a powerful sect came to light, with mystical and pantheistical ideas which seem like a propagation and expansion of the views of this group that we have been studying. It was called in its earlier stages the "Sect of the New Spirit," though this name was soon superseded by the name Brethren of the Free Spirit. The sect appears to have sprung up in the city of Strasbourg, and to have owed its origin to a man named Ortlieb, who was almost certainly an Amaurian. Among the eighty "heretics" burned at Strasbourg in 1215 there were a few who held the views of the Amaurian sect, and a Swiss chronicler of the time says that this heresy already had advocates both in Alsace and in Switzerland.[1] About all we know of Ortlieb is the fact that he lived in Strasbourg, and was condemned by Pope Innocent III. for having taught that "*A man ought to give up all externals and follow the leadings of the Spirit within himself*."[2] There are various spellings of the name, such as "Ordevus," "Orclenus," "Ortlevus," and "Ortlibus," but the manuscript of Mayence (see note) gives the name "Ortlibus," *i.e.* Ortlieb, and says definitely that he was the founder of the "Sect of the New Spirit.' The sect is often mentioned under the name *Ortlibenses* or *Ordibarii*, *i.e.* "Ortliebiens," though the founder's name was soon forgotten. The document by the "Anonymous of Passau" contains ninety-seven propositions setting forth the docrines of the Sect of the New Spirit.[3] These propositions indicate that there were grades and degrees of perfection, and that the teaching of the sect was tempered to fit the degree of spiritual illumination attained by the members. The newly initiated were not expected to

[1] Nauclerus' *Chronica*, p. 912 (cited in Jundt, *op. cit.* p. 40).

[2] The main document for the study of this movement is a compilation of the history of the religious sects of the period. It is by an unknown author. It was formerly supposed to have been written by Reiner Sacchoni, who wrote *Summa de Catharis et Leonistis*, and who died in 1259. The writer of it is now generally called the Anonymous of Passau. There are two MSS. of it in the Library of Munich, and also a MS. in the Library of Mayence. Preger publishes this compilation in his *Geschichte der deutschen Mystik im Mittelalter*, vol. i. pp. 461-71.

[3] These ninety-seven propositions have been traced back to Albert the Great, and were evidently in their earliest form drawn up by him. See Preger, *op. cit.* vol. i. pp. 168-73, and Delacroix, *op. cit.* pp. 55-57.

break at once with the traditions and customs of their former religion as members of the Roman Church. They were rather led by slow steps into a *life of freedom*, in which they could finally dispense entirely with the practices of the Church. Like most of the sects of a similar character they had a lower and a higher state—a religion for the ignorant and a vastly higher type for the *perfect*. For the former, traditions, sacraments, symbols, and forms had a place. *For the perfect, these things had no place at all.* They evidently had books and tracts in the language of the people through which the doctrines of "the New Spirit" were propagated; but these popular books, if they ever existed, are all lost, and we are forced to form our notions as best we can from the reports of their bitter enemies and persecutors.

According to the propositions preserved by the Anonymous of Passau, they pushed the doctine of Divine Immanence to its limits. Every man is of the same substance as God, and therefore every man is capable of becoming Divine. There is nothing that can hinder a person from rising to union with God *if he puts forth the will to rise.* As soon as he reaches this state of union he attains a glorious freedom. He may then reject all externals, and follow the promptings of the Spirit within himself. Rules and commandments drop away. Supplications, fasts, sacrifices of every sort are seen to be useless. It is possible even to pass in holiness all who have been counted saints in earlier dispensations, not excepting her who by the Church has been called the Mother of God. Nay, even he who acts like Christ can become equal to Him. Man in his own nature—man as man—is capable of becoming Divine. But at whatever height he reaches he is still man, for God works in him in human form. Man can take on the Divine quality without in the least losing his humanity. They denied the doctrine of the resurrection as the Church taught it, because they said that the free man who possesses the Spirit has already experienced the resurrection. In this state of perfection there is no law. What the vulgar call sin is now impossible. The Holy Spirit circulates within and carries holiness through the life so that there can be no sin. Sin is the will to offend God, and he whose will has become God's will cannot offend God. His will is God's will, and God's will is his will. A man may become so completely Divine that his very body is sanctified, and then what it does is a Divine act. In this state the instincts and impulses of the body take on a holy significance. In fact a powerful instinct, an insatiable energy, was believed, for the very reason that it was irresistible, to be of spontaneous, Divine origin.

These views would easily lead to a scandalous life as soon as they were carried out in practice by persons of weak moral power. The members of the sect were charged—though the charge has the look of a hostile *inference* from their central principle—with holding that, as the earth is the Lord's, any man who has the Spirit of the Lord in him may take anything he wants, wherever he finds it. The charges of immoral practice, which run through these propositions, must be taken with much caution. They are probably hostile inferences from the principles rather than actual reports of practices,[1] though it would not be long before persons of looser life and weaker control would seize upon the principles as a cover for vice. Even this hostile report implies that they allowed nothing which in its results would have bad social effects.

In the primitive stage of the movement—in the lifetime of Ortlieb at least—it was almost certainly not a religion of licence, but a serious effort to reach a religion of the Spirit. The real offence was that the members of the sect put their inward experience of God in the place of all the so-called external means of grace which the Church supplied. It seems probable from the scanty data at hand that the general movement which we are here studying—pantheistical mysticism in the thirteenth century—gradually divided into two wings; on the one hand a wing with marked ascetic tendencies; on the

[1] The earliest accounts of the sect do not contain definite charges of immoral practice.

other hand a wing with a dangerous tendency toward licence. Wherever groups of these mystics came under Waldensian influence they would feel the stricter, moralizing influences of that sect, and where the seeds of the doctrine fell into bad soil they produced a corresponding crop of weeds. The principles of the doctrine are capable of being put to the highest conceivable moral ends, as they are unfortunately capable of being dragged down to serve as an excuse for a life which is at the mercy of natural instincts. The principles undoubtedly developed in both directions, and we shall see when we come back, in a later chapter, to study the Brethren of the Free Spirit in their maturer stage, that there was a harvest of weeds as well as of wheat. My conclusion, however, is that the Amaurians in Paris and the Ortliebiens in Alsace in the early half of the thirteenth century were children of the Spirit. They were endeavouring, with the dim light at their command, to find the spiritual trail to the Father's house. "Every man ought to be a member of the Christ," is the gospel of the leader, Amaury. "Every man ought to follow the Divine Spirit within himself" is the gospel of the disciple, Ortlieb. For both, the true earthly life is a personal manifestation in the flesh of the Divine life—a finite personalization of God. They, and the groups that gathered about them, undervalued the external, the historic, the social embodiments of truth and of Divine revelation. They were excessively individual, gave too much chance for caprice, and launched, without sufficient store of charts and compasses, on the dangerous sea of Spiritual Freedom. But they do not deserve to be forgotten, for they belong to the brave list of those who have grandly trusted the soul and who have helped, even at great risk and cost, to set it free.

CHAPTER XI

BROTHERHOOD GROUPS IN THE THIRTEENTH CENTURY

WITH the thirteenth century there came a strange period of incubation. Europe had not yet come to full self-consciousness, but already the long period of infancy and of instinct was drawing to a close. Man was beginning to discover himself and to assert himself. In every phase of life during this century there are signs of the coming of a new epoch. The spirit of democracy is apparent in almost all the movements of the time. The *people* are no longer dumb and obedient; they are restless, and on occasion clamorous for rights and privileges. There is at work, at first silently and then vocally, a spirit of revolt from authority and a growing consciousness that the personal soul ought to work out its own salvation. A hidden leaven seems to be fermenting beneath the surface, for there break out, almost simultaneously in widely sundered places, movements which are strangely alike. Once more the Pentecost Spirit is abroad, and the Rhine dweller, the Italian peasant, the French weaver all speak the same spiritual tongue.

The most characteristic religious note of the popular movement was the call to *follow Christ.* It occurred to multitudes, as it did to St. Francis, that traditional Christianity had lost the *way* the Master made for it, and was on a bypath. Throughout all Christendom prophetic spirits were striving to restore apostolic and evangelical piety and to discover how to bring religion vitally into the lives of the people. It was a time of vast upheaval and ferment, like that which appeared four centuries later in the English commonwealth, and the swarms of sectaries which fill the period is, to say the least, confusing. Cathari and Waldenses are already numerous. The Franciscan and Dominican movements are the most powerful expressions of the profound desire for a return to the religion of the Galilean. Simultaneously with the rise of these two great popular orders, there sprung up another type of religious society hardly less remarkable, or less influential historically, than the Franciscan movement itself,—the sisterhoods of *Beguines* and brotherhoods of *Beghards.*

The sisterhoods came first in the order of time. The Crusades, and incessant wars, had left the women of Europe in pitiable plight. There were orphans and widows everywhere, who had no protectors, and who had no means of livelihood. There was no choice for these women except between beggary and shame or the convent. The result was that every city had its hordes of ragged women who thronged the market-place and uttered their mournful cry: "Bread, for God's sake" (Brod durch Gott); "Give us bread." This serious social and economic situation gave rise to the new type of sisterhood, quite unlike that of the convent.

The man whose insight first formulated the plan and put it into operation was a certain pious priest of Flanders, of the city of Liége, named Lambert.[1] An annal of the year 1180, quoted by Du Cange,[2] says: "God stirred up the spirit of a certain holy priest, a man of religion, who was called Lambert le Bègue (because he was a 'stammerer') of St. Christopher in Liége, from whose surname women and girls, who propose to live chastely, are called Beguines, because he was the first to arise and preach to them by word and example the reward of chastity."

[1] Lea in his *History of the Inquisition*, vol. ii. p. 351, says that there is a charter extant for a convent of the Beguine type at Vilvorde near Brussels that dates from 1065. Very much has been made of this document, especially by the adherents of St. Begga (daughter of Pepin von Landen), who wish to regard her as the foundress of the Beguines. But the Vilvorde document is almost certainly spurious.

[2] Du Cange, *Glossarium mediae et infimae Latinitatis*, under the word "Beguine." This annal is given also in Gieseler's *Ecc. Hist.* vol. iii. p. 264.

The names "Beguine" and "Beghard" have given rise to much discussion, and lively etymological battles have been waged over them The view maintained by Mosheim and Jundt that these names were derived from a Flemish verb *beggen* to beg, has been repeated with approval by many writers. Some have construed the begging literally, others metaphorically, and one is often told that the Beghards were so named because they were powerfully prevailing in prayer,—they were men who "begged hard" of God.[1] This view is, however, entirely constructed out of imagination. The overwhelming objection to it is the fact that no such Flemish verb as *beggen* ever existed. It is much more likely that the verb "to beg" is derived from "Beguine" than that "Beguine" is derived from some continental word meaning to beg.[2] It is in fact now established, practically beyond dispute, that the name "Beguine" is derived from Lambert's nickname "le Bègue" which means "the stammerer." Beghard is only a masculine variant from Beguine. What Lambert did was to gather the needy but pious women of his region, both virgins and widows, into an association, half religious, half secular—a society of demi-nuns—and to settle them in a common living-place under religious oversight. The common living-place was in Lambert's day an ordinary house, somewhat enlarged and adapted. But as the movement grew, the living-place expanded into a *Béguinage*, which was a sort of present-day "model village." It consisted of a group of little houses built around a church. Generally there would be, too, near the centre of the "village" a hospital for the sick and aged, and near by a little cemetery where the sisters laid away their dead.

They had all the advantages of the monastery without

[1] Mosheim says Beghard "signifies to beg for anything earnestly and heartily. The syllable 'hard,' which is a frequent termination of German words, subjoined to the verb *beggen*, produces the name Beggehard which denotes a person who begs often and importunely" (Mosheim, *Ecc. Hist.* p. 461). Mosheim in his monograph on the Beghards and Beguines (*De Beghardis et Beguinabus Commentarius*, Leipzig, 1790), which is one of the most valuable sources in existence, discusses the origin of the word, pp. 96-98.

[2] For a detailed etymological discussion see the *Oxford Dictionary*.

its disadvantages. They had protection and support; they had leisure for meditation and prayer; they had great opportunities for society and fellowship, the heightening of their religious experience through the *group-feeling*; and they had common tasks and occupations provided for them. On the other hand they were not actually cut off from the world. They did not renounce all property; they could leave the Beguinage if they wished, and go back to their old life again; they were not asked to take a vow against marriage. They were, in short, groups of pious, virtuous women, who devoted themselves to charity and religion, and divided their time between religious practices, works of industry, and deeds of mercy.

This movement, thus inaugurated in 1180, spread, as so many other things did in this century, like contagion. Matthew Paris, a half century later, says that the rapid progress of the movement is one of the wonders of his age. By the middle of the thirteenth century there were societies of Beguines in almost every large city, and already the example set by the women was everywhere being imitated by the men.

The Beghards, who were often called "apostolic men," sometimes also "poor men," were first organized in Louvain in 1220.[1] They were bands, or brotherhoods, of pious laymen who, without entering monasteries, devoted themselves to religion. They went about the country performing deeds of mercy, preaching in the vulgar tongue, and performing any kind of service which their hands found to do. In Frankfort, for instance, they took care of the sick without pay, they carried the dead to their graves, and they administered spiritual comfort to condemned persons who were to be executed.[2] In some cities they took care of the insane. They lived on charity, and formed an order of religious individuals who were sort of half monks. They were distinctly more secular than the friars, as they might at any time marry and take up the secular life, and, even while they were living as

[1] Gieseler, *Ecc. Hist.* vol. iii. p. 266.

[2] Delacroix, *Essai sur le mysticisme spéculatif en Allemagne*, p. 83.

Beghards, they often spent part of their time in secular occupations. Then, furthermore, these associations, both of brothers and sisters, in their early stages, were not under rigid ecclesiastical rule and control as the orders of friars were. Both the Beguines and Beghards lived partly by labour and partly by begging.

Delacroix[1] has pointed out that there were three well-defined classes of Beguines. There was (1) a class of rich women who went into the Beguinage to live the simple life, *i.e.* to get free from the cares and burdens of the world. These women did not beg, but contributed of their means to the support of the Beguinage to which they belonged. Then (2) there were Beguinages founded and maintained by rich patrons, which were homes for poor women who, like the first class, lived without begging. There was everywhere in Europe at this period an extraordinary *cult of poverty*. Those who did not actually practise poverty were eager to assist those who did practise it. There was an almost hypnotic spell on men's minds as to the peculiar *merits* of poverty, and many a rich man quieted his conscience, and hoped he was smoothing the road to heaven by contributing liberally to homes for sisterhoods. The Counts of Flanders were lavish in their gifts to maintain Beguinages in their region, and seemed never weary of putting money into this charity.[2] The Beguinage of the thirteenth century appealed to the sympathies of the pious rich much as the colleges and universities of the twentieth century appeal to the charitable instincts of present-day money kings.

There was finally (3) a third class of Beguinages which were retreats for poor women who lived solely by work and begging, with the emphasis on the latter occupation. These women came from the great lower class—women who did not "take up" poverty as a cult, but who had it thrust upon them. Even *they* suddenly found that there was a religious career open for them. They had very simple rules, and they lived a somewhat free and unrestrained life. During the early period while

[1] *Op. cit.* pp. 81-82. [2] See Lea, *History of the Inquisition*, vol. ii. p. 352.

poverty and begging were in high favour, and Beguinism had not yet developed any heretical tendencies, the movement seemed to have solved one of the most difficult social problems of the age. Instead of hordes of ragged women, crying up and down the streets, "For the love of God give us bread," each city now had its band of well-housed sisters, dressed in "simple smock and great veil-like mantle," living in an atmosphere of religion, doing the pastoral work of the neighbourhood, and taking up the tasks which were unsuitable for the priests. When they begged they begged in an orderly fashion, which suited the dignity of their sisterhood, and their poverty took on a sacramental touch.[1]

But these fellowships of men and women, organized for the cultivation of personal piety and for the practice of social religion, soon degenerated. In the first place it was extremely difficult, in that age of loose morals, to guard the purity of the life of the Beguines. They were exposed in numerous ways to temptations, and the moral dangers which beset the lives of these women were not sufficiently foreseen and forestalled when the system was framed. We find the authorities busy in almost every section devising rules to meet this moral situation. Even as early as 1244 the Archbishop of Mayence forbade any Beguine association to admit a woman under forty years of age. Before the end of the thirteenth century the ecclesiastical authorities were everywhere at work bringing these associations under the care of the Franciscans or the Dominicans. The Council of Vienne in 1311 discovered that the Beguines were *following the religious life* without having promised obedience, and without having adopted any approved *rule*. They had a special garb, and they had *self-chosen* superiors. They were actually preaching on such subjects as the Trinity and Divine Guidance, and the report adds that they were endangering the faith of many, and hazarding their eternal salvation. These associations naturally provoked clerical hostility and

[1] This was the ideal, and was not always realized, and in most communities begging soon became a public nuisance. In Mayence the Beguines were forbidden to beg by Act of Council in 1310.

jealousy. They cut into the Orders of Friars both in membership and donations, because being less strict they were extremely popular. They were a disadvantage to the local clergy in their neighbourhoods, because the burials and masses of the Beguines were conducted independently of the local priest, and he missed the fees. They were thus almost ceaselessly worried, harried, and persecuted, so that even in 1261 Pope Urban IV. wrote to an authority in Louvain to protect the Beguines against "rash persons who afflict them," and he urges him "not to allow any one to injure them, either in person or in goods."[1]

And, secondly, the associations were rapidly permeated by the "new thought" of that age, which quickly made them centres of "heresy" and brought them under general suspicion. What I have here called "new thought" was really the popular product of the speculations, studied in earlier chapters of this book. The somewhat abstract doctrines of Dionysius, Erigena, and Amaury had now filtered down into the common mind, and were being changed from academic truths to practical truths. They began to be translated from their safe place in books into the dangerous stuff of human life. So long as the teaching of the Allness of God and the possibility of every person being an expression of His nature was wrapped away in the difficult verbiage of a philosophical treatise, matters went on as though the book had never been written, but the situation was mightily altered when those views spread through the world and became a *popular doctrine*, as they now did. Amaury and Ortlieb began the dangerous business of making these views popular, but the movement begun on this small scale gathered volume, and soon became the *spirit of the epoch*. It worked like leaven through every rank of society, and affected every sect and party. The movement had many aspects and variations as it ran its course, and no simple phrase covers all its forms; but I shall for the present deal with the spread of the doctrine among groups of men and women who were called the "Brethren of the Free Spirit."

[1] Mosheim, *De Beghardis et Beguinabus*, p. 141.

The societies of Beguines and Beghards offered splendid opportunity for the spread of the leaven of "Free Spirit," as the popular doctrines evolved from the teachings of Amaury and Ortlieb were called. There were among these Beghard and Beguine groups many persons of intelligence, who devoted much time to reading and thought, and they became influential instructors of the rest. There was always in these societies a spirit of independence; they were not under strict watch and guard; there was much leisure for meditation; the group spirit was attained to a high degree, so that any powerful movement which affected the leaders was sure to become contagious. Pantheism and mysticism had been brought, as I have said, from abstruse treatises into popular books and sermons. Such ideas admirably fitted the psychological temper and climate of the age. Here was a situation which was most favourable to the spread of the leaven, and before the authorities were aware of it, the societies of Beghards and Beguines were being transformed into "Brethren of the Free Spirit." The Church suddenly awoke to the danger it was facing, and by the opening of the fourteenth century the authorities use the words "pest" and "heresy" with great frequency as a description of these brotherhood movements.

Unfortunately we are compelled to study the doctrine of the "Free Spirit" wholly through the reports of its enemies. It was an anti-ecclesiastical movement; it was a popular uprising for larger liberty; it was a powerful exhibition of lay religion, and from the nature of the case we cannot look for a calm, impartial, judicial account of the "pest" from the ecclesiastics who investigated it. The lurid colours in these descriptions must be taken with much caution.

Albert the Great had already, in 1250, written such dreadful details of the beliefs and doings of "heretical" Beghards that a later author, who has Albert's *Manual* before him, declines to write out the description.[1] But it was not until the early years of the fourteenth century

[1] Jundt, *Panthéisme populaire*, p. 48.

that this "pestiferous liberty of spirit" was discovered to be widespread, and to have permeated the brotherhoods and sisterhoods. In 1306 the Archbishop of Cologne, Henry of Virnebourg, issued an edict against "heretical" Beghards and Beguines. He describes them as "people practising a new kind of life under the pretext of poverty"; they "beg instead of working," to the injury of "Christianity," *i.e.* to the detriment of the begging friars; they "preach publicly though they are only lay-people"; they "wear long tabards, tunics, and cowls," and they teach the following "heresies": "Those who are led by the Spirit of God are no longer under law, for the law is not imposed on the good, on those who live without sin"; "He who follows me (*i.e.* becomes a member of this sect), they say, can be saved, for I do not commit sin"; "These truths have been given to them, they say, by divine revelation."[1]

The threats of excommunication and persecution which the Archbishop levelled against them did not accomplish anything. On the contrary they grew in numbers and power to such an extent that the regular "Orders" materially decreased, and it was decided to see what argument and persuasion would do. The greatest theologian of the age, Duns Scotus, was brought to Cologne to confound them, but his untimely death in 1308 removed the great schoolman from his difficult task, leaving it unaccomplished. We hear a little later that "almost the entire city is infected with heresy." The Council of Trèves in 1310 gives an interesting picture of the Beghards, though it throws little or no light on the prevailing *ideas* of the movement:

> "In the diocese of Trèves there are a number of lay-people called Beghards. They appear in public clothed in long tunics and with cowls, and they avoid all manual labour. At certain times *they hold meetings, in which they give, in the presence of their believing members, the appearance of being profound interpreters of Holy Scripture.* We disapprove of their society as foreign to every type of congregation recognized by the Church."[2]

[1] See Jundt, *op. cit.* p. 49, and Lea, *History of the Inquisition*, vol. ii. pp. 367-68.

[2] Mosheim, *De Beghardis et Beguinabus*, p. 235.

The "heresy of the Free Spirit" was the absorbing question before the Council of Vienne in 1311. Pope Clement IV. had become greatly disturbed over the spread of the Free Spirit, and under his direction the famous Council of Vienne set itself to the task of finding out the character of the "heresy" and of exterminating it. The decrees of this Council are called *Clementines*, and they give us a very full description of the "errors."

"We have learned," says the first *Clementine* decree, "that there are many Beguines, smitten apparently with madness, who give discussions and sermons on the Trinity and on the Divine Essence, and who are heterodox on the articles of faith and the sacraments of the Church. They lead many simple, credulous persons into error, and under the veil of sanctity they do many things which endanger the soul."[1]

All this is indefinite enough, but the second decree is more precise. We read that "these perverted men and faithless women, vulgarly called Beghards and Beguines," hold the following views:

"This is the dispensation of the Holy Spirit, a dispensation of liberty for one to do whatever he pleases. . . . Man can arrive here in the present life to the fulness of divine blessedness. . . . Every intellectual being possesses within himself by his very nature perfect blessedness. . . . The soul has no need of Divine Light (*i.e.* beyond what he has within himself) to rise to a contemplation of God. . . . Man can attain in this life such a degree of perfection that he will become incapable of sinning, and that he can make no further progress in divine grace, for if he were able to progress further he might attain a greater perfection than that of Jesus Christ. . . . When a person has attained the highest degree of perfection there is no more need of fasting or praying, for the senses are now so completely subject to reason that the body may be given absolute liberty. . . . Those who live in this state of perfection, and are moved by the Spirit of God, are no longer under any law or ecclesiastical regulation, for where the Spirit of God is there is liberty. . . . He who must still practise virtues is an imperfect person. The perfect soul has got beyond virtues. . . . When the body of Christ is presented in divine service it is not necessary to rise or to show any respect for the host, for it would be a sign of imperfection to come down from

[1] Mosheim, p. 245.

the heights of pure contemplation to dwell on thoughts of the sacrament or the passion of the Saviour."[1]

The metaphysics of this movement are quite plain and simple, for every time we get a glimpse of the doctrine the *central idea* is the same. God is all. He goes out of His unity into plurality and differentiation. In this universe of multiplicity everything *real* is divine. The end of all things is a return to the *divine unity.* Man has within himself the possibility of return — he can become like Christ, like God. He can even become God. In man's state of perfection God does all in him that he does. The Church therefore is unnecessary. Man himself is a revelation of God. Heaven and hell are allegories. God is in man and in all things as much as in the consecrated bread and wine.[2]

The question of the moral outcome of the doctrine and its extravagancies will be discussed later. The urgent *issue* to the Church was its own supremacy. This doctrine made the Church unnecessary, made ecclesiastical supremacy a mere assumption. It was a life and death issue on which there could be no compromise. The Council of Vienne called for the entire suppression of the Beguinages. It decreed the abolition of the "Orders" of Beghards and Beguines. These decrees, however, though passed in 1311, were not actually published until 1317, under the new Pope John XXII. The reason for the delay apparently was that many of the groups of Beghards and Beguines were free from taint of heresy, and were orthodox and loyal Catholics. It seemed a shame to smite all alike, while on the other hand it was a hopeless task to separate the sheep from the goats. It was easy to describe the "heresy" on *paper*; it was extremely difficult to mark the distinction of orthodox and heterodox in dealing with *persons.*

Wherever the edicts of Vienne were actually executed the results were pitiable. The Beghards, being men, could shift for themselves, and flee from persecution to some safer part of the world. The women, who were

[1] Jundt, *op. cit.* pp. 50-51.

[2] See Jundt, *op. cit.* p. 55.

deprived of their Beguinage and turned adrift without means of support, and forbidden to beg, were compelled to die of want, or to find husbands, or to sink to a life of prostitution. The tragedy of this situation deeply impressed the popular mind, and it became current report that on his death-bed Pope Clement had bitterly repented of his attack on the Beguines.[1]

The most precious document for gaining a knowledge of the principles of the "Free Spirit" is a letter written in 1317 by the Bishop of Strasbourg, and addressed to his subordinates. His facts were gathered through an inquisitorial commission which had carried its investigation through the diocese.[2] The letter reads:

"There are found in this city and in this diocese many sectaries who are popularly called 'Beghards' and 'begging sisters' (Schwestrones Brod durch Gott), and who call themselves 'the Sect of the Free Spirit,' and 'brothers and sisters of poverty.' Among their number, we are sorry to say, there are monks and priests, and many married persons. *We condemn all the doctrines and ceremonies of the sect.* We order that these heretics be driven from their abodes, and that the houses used for their meeting-places be sold for the benefit of the Church. The books which contain their doctrines are to be turned over to the priests within fifteen days and burnt.[3] All who do not repent and give up their garb within three days will be excommunicated, and those who give them charity will be dealt with likewise. Exception will be made of Beghards who accept the Third Order of the Franciscan rule, or who come under some Order approved by the Church. Exception is also made of Beguines who lead a pure and pious life."

Here follows the statement of doctrine:

"God is in form everything that is.[4] They claim to be divine by nature, and they make no distinction between God and themselves. Man can be so united to God that man's will, power, activity, become God's will, power, and activity. Every

[1] It was, however, as we have seen, under John XXII. that the edicts were published and executed.

[2] Mosheim and Jundt say that this letter was written by John of Ochsenstein, who, they suppose, was Bishop of Strasbourg. It has, however, been settled that John of Durbheim was bishop at the time and author of this letter (see Delacroix, *op. cit.* p. 92). Mosheim gives the text of the letter, pp. 253-61.

[3] Not a copy has escaped, more's the pity.

[4] This means that the *essence* or *idea* in everything is a *thought of God's.*

man, they say, can by virtue of his nature become as perfect as Christ, and can acquire even greater merit than Christ. Many of them say that they are more perfect in the three virtues than St. Paul or the Virgin. All divine perfections are joined in them; they claim that they have eternity in the depths of their own souls, and are living in eternity here below. The Catholic Church is folly and vanity. The perfect man is under no obligation to obey commandments, not even that which imposes respect for parents. In virtue of their liberty they nullify the teaching of the clergy and the statutes of the Church. They show no respect for the body of Christ in the sacrament, and say blasphemously that *the body of the Saviour is found equally in all bread as in the consecrated wafer.* They say that any pure layman can consecrate the elements as well as the priest, that it is not necessary for salvation to *confess* to priests, that the acceptance of a consecrated wafer from the hands of a layman brings deliverance to a departed soul as much as priestly mass does.[1] There is neither hell nor purgatory as a place. There is no last judgment; man is judged at the moment of death. The Spirit will then return to God and become so completely united with Him that He alone will remain as He was from eternity. Nobody will be lost, not even Jews or Saracens, because their spirits will return to God. Scripture contains many poetical passages which are not to be taken as literal truth. If all the books of the Catholic Faith were destroyed, the members of this sect could compose better ones. For this reason more faith should be given to the things which come from the human heart than to the gospels; the soul's Inward Voice is safer than the truths preached in the Church. Many among them have attained such a degree of perfection they say that they cannot sin. They pretend that all things are the common property of all, and that any one may take what he likes. They say that one should have no creaturely desires, not even the desire for the kingdom of heaven. They hold themselves immovable on the summit of the ninth rock,[2] and neither rejoice nor lament; and if they could by a single word banish all mortal woes, they would not speak the word."

The most impartial testimony which we have of the views, teaching, and practices of those who professed these

[1] This is in every respect like the teaching of the Waldenses. No sharp line can be drawn between these various sects.

[2] This is a mystical symbol for the highest degree of union with God, of which union there were nine stages. *The Book of the Nine Rocks* will be discussed in the chapter on the "Friends of God." There seem to have been other books besides this famous one, and evidently the conception of the "Nine Rocks" was gradually developed by the mystics of the time.

extreme principles of "divine unity" and "freedom" is from the great mystic preacher, John Tauler. In one of his sermons he contrasts *spurious spiritual freedom* with *sound spiritual freedom*, and gives a description of the type of "Free Spirit" which we are studying. He says:

"They stand exempt from all subjection, without any activity upward or downward, just as a tool is passive and waits until its master wishes to use it, for it seems to them that if they do anything then God will be hindered in His work; therefore they count themselves above all virtues. They wish to be so free that they do not think, nor praise God, nor have anything, nor know anything, nor love nor ask nor desire anything; for all that they might wish to ask they have (according to their notion). And they also think that they are poor in spirit because they are *without any will of their own* and have renounced all possessions. They also wish to be free of all practice of virtue, obedient to no one, whether pope, or bishop, or priest. They wish to be free of everything with which the Church has to do. They say publicly that so long as a man strives after virtues, so long is he imperfect and knows nothing of spiritual poverty, nor of this spiritual freedom.

They consider themselves to be higher than the Angels and above the stage of human merit and human faith, so that they cannot increase in virtue nor yet commit sin. Whatever nature desires, according to their notion, they can do freely without sin because they have reached the highest innocence, and no law or commandment is put upon them. *Whenever their nature urges them in any direction they follow the impulse*, so that the freedom of the spirit may be unhindered."[1]

As time went on the rigours of persecution steadily increased, and the Church resolved on the annihilation of all begging sects not affiliated with the established Orders, and on the extermination of all pantheistical heresies. The final blow of extermination of these associations, which fell early in the fifteenth century, was largely due, as the persecution throughout had been, to the influence of the established Orders — especially the Dominican Order. All the powers of the Inquisition had for a half century been let loose on these suspected religious sects,

[1] Preger, *Geschichte der deutschen Mystik im Mittelalter*, vol. iii. p. 133.

and the wonder is that they existed at all through the pitiless storm of persecution. In many places the "houses" of the Beghards were turned into prisons for "heretics," and, by a shameful stretch of persecuting fanaticism, the inquisitors were authorized in 1369, both by the Emperor Charles IV. and Pope Gregory XI., *to burn all books, tracts, and sermons written in the vulgar tongue.* This outrageous edict swept away a precious mass of popular literature. Anything popular was apparently dangerous.

Among the many Beghard martyrs there is one name which has had a great place in the history of "the Friends of God"—that of Nicholas of Basle. He was long believed to be "the Friend of God from the Oberland," who is in history intimately associated with the life of John Tauler. This belief is wholly without historical foundation. Nicholas of Basle was a prominent Beghard, who travelled widely as a missionary, and propagated the teachings of the sect. For many years he succeeded in escaping the Inquisition, though he was vigorously sought after. He was finally seized in Vienna about 1397, and was there burned at the stake with two of his "disciples," John and James.

We now come to the difficult task of estimating the significance and value of this movement. The societies of Beghards and Beguines, in their primitive stage, were an expression of the spirit of the epoch, a form of that hypnotic spell which carried men and women in all Christian lands into an unreasoned exaltation of poverty, an obsession of renunciation. The peculiarity which marks off these associations from the other groups which practised the cult of poverty is the tendency toward pantheistical ideas and mystical views which prevailed among them.[1] There were throughout their history many "ortho-

[1] It is true, as we have implied throughout this chapter, that it is often difficult to distinguish Beghards from Waldenses. They mutually influenced each other, and with our scanty historical material are easily confused. For example, the inquisitor Garin, who, with the Bishop of Metz, "investigated" the Beghards in 1334, has given a description which reveals many Waldensian traits. He says: "These impious men call themselves brothers of poverty, and they claim that they imitate Christ and follow the gospel. They say that they do not even own their clothes and the other things which they use, but that God is the Master of all their goods." He says that *their meetings are held at the moving of the*

dox" Beghards and many societies even which continued to be "untainted" by the doctrine of "Free Spirit," but there was a very great element in the groups, throughout the fourteenth century, which held a pantheistical form of mysticism. The doctrine was based, as I have already said, on the fundamental idea that God is all, and that man may become a revelation of Him. These popular mystics differed from Dionysius and Erigena only in their crudeness and in the boldness of the application of their doctrine.

The fatal weakness of this entire mystical movement, all the way back from its popular form in the fourteenth century to its lofty formulation in Plotinus and Plato, is the negative and abstract feature of it. God, the Divine Reality, is reached by a process of negation. He is everything that finite things are *not*. He is Absolute—but without any qualities or characteristics by which we can *know* Him. He is an *indeterminate* Absolute. He is an abstract Universal in which all finite particulars are swallowed up and lost, not a self-revealing Spirit who explains all finite particulars. All roads lead to Him, but no one comes back with any light which explains the finite, or which gives illumination for the daily tasks of a concrete life. When the "Beghard," with the "Free Spirit" ideas, believed that he was "Divine," he had no way of thinking out what it meant to be "Divine." God was an indefinite All, which had swallowed him up and merged him into His Allness. He had no will of his own any more. He, too, like God, became *indeterminate*, with his finite likes and dislikes, his particular choices,

Holy Spirit. They claim a state of perfection which puts them above the pope and the clergy—and above excommunication. He does not charge them with impure life, but says that they deny the right to any one to inflict capital punishment, and *they refuse to swear*. He says they refuse to "confess," claiming that they have not committed sin. Even in the death hour they refuse to call upon the Virgin or the saints, "which proves that they continue in their malicious errors" (see Delacroix, *op. cit.* pp. 115-16). Wasmod of Hamburg, Inquisitor of Mayence, in his tract written at the very end of the fourteenth century, gives similar traits. He says the Beghards *reduce the Church to their own circle*: they say that the clergy have no power to pardon sins, because they are in a state of sin themselves; they say that the priest, who is in a state of mortal sin, cannot consecrate the sacrament, and that one may perform priestly functions without consecration.

desires, and volitions annulled. He would now do nothing except what the Allness did through him. But how could he know what a God of this Absolute sort would do? Eckhart, in one of his sermons, has a keen analysis of this *negative freedom* which comes from making God indeterminate.

"There are persons who say, 'I have God and His love, I can do what I wish.' This view shows an ignorance of true liberty. When thou wishest to do a thing contrary to the will of God and His law, thou hast not the love of God, even though thou endeavourest to make the world believe that thou hast. That man who has established himself in the will of God and in the love of God does what God loves and leaves undone what He forbids. It is as impossible for him to do what God does not will as it is not to do what He wills. The man whose feet are bound cannot walk, and the man who lives in the will of God cannot sin."[1]

With no positive vision of the Divine Character, with a conception of liberty which meant freedom to do anything, the mystic of the "Free Spirit" type was at the mercy of his strongest impulses. Whatever pressed upon him urgently and powerfully would be taken as the leading of the Absolute with which he was united. He believed himself absolutely *free*, because he believed that his will had become God's will, but when he *came to select a particular thing to do*, the selection would always be due to some prepotent, some dominating impulse or idea. By surrendering his will to an *indeterminate Absolute* he thus opened wide the door for caprice and vagary.

There were two quite distinct tendencies which flowed out of this abstract pantheism, this negative mysticism, both of them the natural outcome of the psychological situation just outlined. They were (1) a tendency to asceticism and (2) a tendency to libertinism. We find among these brotherhood and sisterhood associations groups of both types. It is a natural inference from the Allness of God to conclude that the finite is vain and illusory. On this inference the "perfect man" will with-

[1] Pfeiffer, *Meister Eckhart*, p. 232.

draw as far as he can from all finite satisfactions and from all dependence on illusory joys. He will *mortify* his body, and kill out his vain desires. He will approximate to his ideal of a life unmoved and undisturbed—a passive, indeterminate life in which *will is annulled.* Where the Brethren of the "Free Spirit" came under Waldensian influences they swung toward this ascetic extreme. Ruysbroek has given a good account of this extreme Asceticism of one branch of the Brethren of the Free Spirit:

> "We are," they say, "sent into the world to live the contemplative life, which is superior to the active life of Christ. By withdrawing into ourselves, and by separating ourselves from all forms, all images, all particular qualities, we feel within ourselves the eternal wisdom of God. If the Saviour had lived longer He would have reached the same height of the contemplative life to which we have attained."[1]

The other easy inference from this central doctrine was the conclusion that any urgent impulse was Divine. This led to *Libertinism.* The only basis of right and of truth, they held, is the immediate revelation within. Whenever an impulse to act surges up within, it is a revelation of the Divine will. God, they believed, is no more revealed in the moral system of Sinai than in the present prompting of man's heart, for this, too, is Divine. God is no more revealed in the teachings of the Mountain Sermon than in a present urgent impulse which springs out of man's nature, for this, too, is Divine. This view, when pushed to its extreme consequences, left no moral standards and no moral distinctions. Right and wrong, high and low, were blurred. Whatever a person in his "perfect state" wanted to do was as *right* as anything else.

It is by no means certain that the members of these societies actually carried out their dangerous doctrines into their practical consequences, though the testimony pointing toward immorality is too steady and universal to

[1] Quoted from Jundt, *op. cit.* p. 99.

be ignored.[1] There would at any rate be some persons who would take advantage of views which gave *carte blanche* to the weakness of the flesh, while the religious emotions which go with this highly-wrought type of religion would tend, as we now know, to produce a lax control over sexual passion. The moral standards of the period were, too, extremely low. Some of the most famous churchmen of the time were living lives of shocking immorality, and it is more than likely that there were *orgies of immorality* in some groups which were affected with "Free Spirit" ideas. The particular stories, however, which the inquisitors tell are decidedly open to suspicion, and it is a noteworthy fact that the Beghards and Beguines generally had the sympathy and support of the common people.

The stories which tell how the members of these sects, both men and women, met by night in a cave called "Paradise," and gave rein to their passions, are thoroughly unreliable. They are without local details, and they are built on the traditional model which has been used in every epoch when men wished to besmirch and disgrace a hated religious sect. The famous "confession" of John de Brunn is wholly worthless as evidence against the moral character of the Beghards. This John claimed that he had lived the Beghard life for twenty-eight years. At first he was put through a very stern training, under strict discipline, until he attained "the liberty of the Spirit," when "God was totally formed in him, and all his movements became Divine." He now gave himself up to "a practice of liberty" of the most disgusting sort. At the end of twenty-eight years he was smitten with repentance, and joined the Dominican Friars. They imposed as a penance upon him that he should tell all the secrets of the association to which he had belonged. His "confession," which is collaborated by the Inquisitor, is lurid with revelations of depravity. The "confession" bears

[1] The most damaging testimony to the erratic character and the lax life of these sectaries is found scattered through the pages of Eckhart, Tauler, Suso, and Ruysbroek, who were themselves profoundly mystical, but who were solidly anchored in the reality of moral distinctions.

all the marks of being the work of a "degenerate." It is no more reliable than the testimony of a condemned witch to the existence of witchcraft in the community. There is a strange fascination for such persons in telling a morbid tale, and this John knew that his own standing with the Dominicans would be improved by his ability to make out a powerfully damaging case against their enemies the Beghards.[1] The very methods by which the "perfect state" was to be attained tended to produce the degenerate type, and the "revelations" which, under pressure, were drawn out of this man of abnormal traits, seem to me of no more value than the account of a highly wrought man who has been to a *séance*. The specific incidents which the Inquisition furnishes are not convincing, but our study of the movement itself leaves us with a serious impression of its moral dangers.

There is perhaps no greater religious task to be worked out in the history of the race than the achievement of true spiritual liberty. It is manifestly not enough to destroy tradition and law and authority. Be they ever so heavy a weight on the spirit, they are better than *sheer liberty*, which is not grounded in the vision of a concrete moral goal. "Love God and then do what thou wilt," is St. Augustine's famous declaration of spiritual emancipation. It is sound and wise, if only one puts enough meaning into the two words "love God," but just there is the crux. If God is for thought only an Infinite-Nothing-in-particular, if He is as much one thing as another thing, if He is vague, empty, and characterless, "love for Him" will easily focus into "love for what I myself like," and "liberty" will degenerate into meaning "liberty to do what I with my impulses please." The great achievements of the soul do not come along the easy negative paths. The spirit of man is never *free* until the man himself is a good man, and the supreme task of spiritual religion is this positive task of discovering how a man like one of us can go up into a vision of God and come back with

[1] The Confession will be found in Wattenbach, "Ueber die Sekte der Brüder vom freien Geiste" (*Besitzungsberichte der k. Akademie zu Berlin*, 1887), pp. 523-37.

power for the transformation of his human desires, his finite will, and his daily activities. The true freedom that goes with complete love of God is a freedom that has been *won* through the discipline of the spirit by habitual conformity to the will of God, as revealed in Christ; in the moral message of the Scriptures; and in the socially tested morality of the race. It is no empty will-lessness that is to be sought, no capricious freedom "to do anything we like," but the "liberty of the sons of God," who have been *made free by the perfect Son*—"Ye shall know the truth, and the truth shall make you free."

CHAPTER XII

MEISTER ECKHART

ONE soon finds that he cannot even touch the surface of fourteenth century mysticism in Germany without making up accounts with Eckhart. He is one of those great watershed personalities, to be found in epoch periods, who gathers up into himself the influences of preceding centuries, and gives new direction to the spiritual currents of succeeding generations. By temperament and by intellectual training he was able to absorb the mystical teaching of his great predecessors, Augustine, Dionysius, Erigena, Albertus Magnus, and Thomas Aquinas, and by his real endowment of genius and his fertility of mind he was able to become the interpreter of this mystical message to the people. He is a remarkable example of the union of a profoundly speculative mind and a simple childlike spirit. No mystic has ever dropped his plummet deeper into the mysteries of the Godhead, nor has there ever been a bolder interpreter of those mysteries in the language of the common people. He was at the storm centre of heretical mysticism—the mysticism of the "Free Spirit"; he pushed his speculations up to the perilous edge, "beyond the flaming bounds of time and space," and for an entire generation, with the boldest of freedom, he preached to the multitudes in the German tongue on topics bristling with difficulties for the orthodox faith.

The wonder is, not that the Church, after he was dead, found twenty-eight questionable "items" in his sermons, but rather that he was allowed all those years to preach unhindered; and even greater still is the wonder that the common people of Germany in the fourteenth century should have crowded to hear these sermons of Eckhart—sermons which would be beyond the depth of the vast majority of those who go to hear sermons to-day! There has in recent years been much excellent work done on Eckhart, especially by German and French scholars.[1] These scholarly researches have helped to rediscover this great mystical teacher, and though they present a variety of possible interpretations, as is bound to be the case with a message like Eckhart's, they have brought him out of the dark[2] and have made him once more a living personality, shaping the spiritual attitude of his contemporaries. Even yet, however, we are compelled to use the words "probably" and "about" quite frequently in telling the story of his life.

Heinrich Eckhart was born probably at Hochheim in Thuringia, somewhat before the year 1260.[3] He entered, not earlier than his fifteenth year, a Dominican convent, most likely in Erfurt. The course of studies for a Dominican priest was arranged in ascending order, with dogmatics at the top, and required at least nine years. Eckhart's earlier studies were pursued at Erfurt, his higher studies were probably carried on in the "High School" at Cologne, where Albert the Great (1193-1280) had

[1] The best of the works referred to are: Lasson, *Meister Eckhart, der Mystiker*, Berlin, 1868; Preger, *Geschichte der deutschen Mystik im Mittelalter*, vol. i., Leipzig, 1874; Pfeiffer, *Meister Eckhart*, Leipzig, 1857; Denifle, *Archiv für Literatur und Kirchengeschichte des Mittelalters*, Berlin, 1885. It was Denifle who made the discovery of Eckhart's Latin writings, which were practically unknown until 1880. Büttner, *Meister Eckeharts Schriften und Predigten, aus dem Mittelhochdeutschen übersetzt und herausgegeben*, erster Band (Leipzig, 1903). Jundt, *Essai sur le mysticisme spéculatif de Maître Eckhart*, Strasbourg, 1871; and *Panthéisme populaire* by the same author, Paris, 1875; Delacroix, *Essai sur le mysticisme spéculatif*, Paris, 1900. In English the best contributions are those by Karl Pearson, "Meister Eckhart the Mystic," in *Mind*, vol. xi. p. 20; and by Josiah Royce, "Meister Eckhart," in *Studies of Good and Evil*, New York, 1898.

[2] As late as 1829 Görres, in his Introduction to the works of Suso, calls Eckhart "a wonderful figure, half veiled in the mist, and almost mythical."

[3] The questions of date and birthplace are argued at length in Jundt, Preger, and Delacroix. Jundt strenuously holds to the position that Eckhart was born in Strasbourg. Delacroix presents the most recently discovered data, and decides, rightly, I think, for Hochheim. Denifle discovered a sermon in Latin preached in Paris, which ends with this note, also in Latin: "This sermon was reported from the lips of Eckhart of Hochheim."

just before this period been the most renowned teacher of the age, where his influence was still paramount, and where his great pupil Thomas Aquinas (1225-1274), by his writings, was beginning his rule over the minds of men. Albertus, the one scholar of the Middle Ages who received the title "Magnus," generally reserved for great warriors, was himself a mystic and a prolific fountain of mysticism in the generation following. He begins his treatise *De Adhaerendo Deo* with these words:

"When St. John says that God is a Spirit, and that He must be worshipped in spirit, he means that the mind must be cleared of all images. When thou prayest, shut thy door—that is, the doors of thy senses. Keep them barred and bolted against all phantasms and images. Nothing pleases God more than a mind free from all occupations and distractions. Such a mind is in a manner transformed into God, for it can think of nothing, and love nothing, except God; other creatures and itself it only sees in God. He who penetrates into himself, and so transcends himself, ascends truly to God. He whom I love and desire is above all that is sensible, and all that is intelligible; sense and imagination cannot bring us to Him, but only the desire of a pure heart. This brings us unto the darkness of the mind, whereby we can ascend to the contemplation even of the mystery of the Trinity. Do not think about the world, nor about thy friends, nor about the past, present, or future; but consider thyself to be outside of the world and alone with God, as if thy soul were already separated from the body and had no longer any interest in peace or war, or the state of the world. Leave thy body and fix thy gaze on the uncreated Light. *Let nothing come between thee and God.* The soul in contemplation views the world from afar off, just as, when we proceed to God by the way of abstraction, we deny to Him, first of all, bodily and sensible attributes, then intelligible qualities, and, lastly, that being (*esse*) which would keep Him among created things."

This is mysticism of the extreme negative type, and it was teaching which profoundly influenced Eckhart and his group of followers.

Eckhart was certainly a student in the great school of theology in Paris in 1302.[1] But already, before the

[1] He is enrolled as "Brother Aychardus, a German" (Teutonicus).

period of study in Paris, he had been elected Prior of the Dominican convent at Erfurt and Vicar for the district of Thuringia. It is believed by many that his famous *Treatise on Distinction* was written during the Erfurt period. If so, it is the earliest work we have from him, and the first glimpse we get of his inner life. It deals with the distinctions between the essential and the unessential. The treatise lays great emphasis on the fact that the essential thing which characterises a man's will is the *spirit* of it rather than the overt deed which the man does. There is no virtue in the mere act of fasting nor in the fact that one has a heavenly rapture. "Even if," he says, "one were in a rapture, like Paul's, and there were a sick man who needed help, I think it would be far better to come out of the rapture and show love by serving the needy one." There is already here in this early venture of his spirit that "sincere tone of personal experience" which characterises him to the end of his life, joined with that profound penetration of mind which is so evident in the work of his mature years.

The years of study in Paris brought him the title, by which he has ever since been called, "Meister," but he does not appear to have been at all impressed with the art of threshing theological straw, in which too many schoolmen indulged, or with the value of mere head learning. There are scanty references in the sermons to events in his own life, but there are at least three passages that give a clue to his estimates of scholastic learning. He says in one place: "I was asked in the school at Paris how one can completely fulfil the Scripture, then I answered, 'He who would fulfil the Scriptures must see to it that he does not miss God in his own soul.'"[1] And again in another sermon, which was almost certainly an early one, he says: "There are many masters among us who have used the Bible for thirty years or more and who understand it now in its unity as little as a cow or a horse would."[2] There is a third passage preserved among the "sayings" of Eckhart,

[1] Pfeiffer, *op. cit.* p. 352, line 27.

[2] Preger, *op. cit.* p. 335.

which runs: "If I were looking for a master of the Scriptures, I should seek him in Paris in the schools, but if I wished to learn about the perfect life, he could not teach me about that."[1] On leaving Paris, probably in 1303, he was chosen Provincial-Prior of the Dominican Order for Saxony. His territory stretched from Thuringia to the North Sea, and from Utrecht to Dorpat in Livonia, and included fifty-one monasteries and nine nunneries. In 1307 he was chosen Vicar-General for Bohemia, and also re-elected Provincial-Prior for Saxony. In 1311 he returned to his studies in Paris, and now, with his fully developed powers, he seems to have devoted himself to mastering the men of earlier times who were kindred in spirit to him. At least when he left Paris for his great career as a preacher in Strasbourg, he certainly carried away with him as a part of himself the mystical world-view of Dionysius and Erigena which he was to translate in scores of sermons to the people of Strasbourg. This city was at this period the foremost religious centre in Germany. Every type of Christian society and every form of piety was to be found in Strasbourg. There were seven Dominican convents in the city. Scholars had gathered there, and so, too, had the heretical sects which were disturbing the peace of the Church. It was a rule of the Dominican Order that the intellectual and spiritual training of the sisters of the Order should be in the care of "highly learned brothers," and it is probable that Eckhart would be one of these "highly learned brothers" who would teach and instruct and counsel the "sisters" of the Strasbourg convents. There is a curious poem, written by a Dominican nun of this period, which tells how "wise Master Eckhart speaks to us about Nothingness. He who does not understand that, in him has never shone the light Divine."[2] This poem is only one indication among many that Eckhart preached much to the convent women of the city, and we know that there was at this period a predisposition in the convents for mystical teaching, which would make Eckhart a favourite preacher.

[1] Pfeiffer, p. 599.

[2] Preger, vol. ii. p. 138.

There is a very famous account of "Swester Katrei"—Sister Katharine—called in the narrative "Eckhart's Strasbourg Daughter." This narrative is published by Pfeiffer (p. 448) among Eckhart's writings. It is an extreme example of morbid quietistic mysticism, running over the line of safety into pathological states. This spiritual "daughter," who is instructed by her confessor in the difficult mystical path to perfection, finally outstrips the confessor himself, attains to the goal of perfection, and then in her turn becomes instructor to her former spiritual "father." She makes the attainment of spiritual *indifference* the mark of perfection. She says that "not even desire of heaven should tempt a good man toward activity." On one occasion she became cataleptic, and was being carried to burial for dead. Her confessor, just in time, discovered that it was trance instead of death, and awoke her. Katharine exclaimed: "Now I am satisfied, for I have been dead all through."

It seems, however, improbable that "Sister Katharine" is a real person, or that this account is to be taken for biographical history. The "story," is most likely one of many similar pieces of "tendency" fiction, written to show how the priest or confessor needs to learn perfection from a spiritual *lay-person.* This was a favourite idea with the "Friends of God," as we shall see, and they produced many stories of this type. It is probably written later than Eckhart's time, though it is possible that there was some actual experience in Eckhart's life which furnished the nucleus of the story, and it may throw some light on his convent work, but it must not be taken as an exposition of his mystical teaching.[1]

The Beghards and Beguines of Strasbourg were at this time "suspected," and under the watch and guard of the officials of the Church. It would be extremely interesting to know what attitude Eckhart took toward his fellow mystics, but unfortunately we are largely in the dark on the subject. Karl Schmidt has endeavoured to show that the great mystical preacher had close

[1] See Delacroix, *op. cit.* p. 145.

relations with the Beghards, but there are few historical facts to support his claim.[1] The assertions made by Preger to prove that Eckhart's sympathy with these mystical heretics brought upon him the stern displeasure of the bishop are equally without foundation.[2] It is quite possible that Eckhart's views underwent a change as his experience enlarged and as he saw the moral danger involved in the teaching of the sects, and that, as he matured, he pushed down to a more solid moral foundation. There is a passage in one of his Strasbourg sermons[3] which is in hearty sympathy with some religious people, who seem to have views much like the Brethren of the Free Spirit. It is as follows:—

"That person who has renounced all visible creatures and in whom God performs His will completely—that person is both God and man. His body is so completely penetrated with Divine light and with the soul essence which is of God that he can properly be called a Divine man. For this reason, my children, be kind to *these men*, for they are strangers and aliens in the world. Those who wish to come to God have only to model their lives after these men; no one can know them unless he has within him the same light, the light of truth. Those who are on the way to the same God and have not yet arrived will do well to become acquainted with these people who have attained."

In a later sermon, however, we have this beautiful passage which shows that Eckhart has grasped the distinction between false liberty and true liberty:

"The perfect spirit cannot will anything except what God wills, and that is not slavery but true freedom. There are people who say, if I have God and His love, I may do what I like. That is a false idea of liberty. When thou wishest a thing contrary to God and His law thou hast not the love of God in thee."[4]

He says again:

"There are those who do not consider sin as sin, who do not practise Christian virtues, who do not know Christ in the

---

[1] See Schmidt, *Theol. Studien und Kritiken*, pp. 666-738.

[2] Preger has confounded our Meister with another brother Eckhart (see Delacroix, *op. cit.* p. 140).

[3] Pfeiffer, p. 127, line 38 ff.

[4] *Ibid.* p. 232, line 25 ff.

nobility of His nature, and who prate of intimate life in the bosom of God although in fact that life is foreign to them."[1]

Here is a splendid passage which has the right moral ring, and in which Eckhart shows himself to be wholly out of the bog of Antinomianism:

> "It is necessary to be on the guard against false wisdom, against believing that one can sin without any fear of consequences. *One is never free of consequences until he is free of sin.* When one is free of sin, then only do the consequences of sin disappear. As long as one is able to sin, the distinction of right and wrong must be scrupulously maintained."[2]

Eckhart had a second great period of influence in Cologne, whither he went, perhaps, about 1320. The immediate intellectual and spiritual stimulus of his teaching in Cologne was very marked. There gathered about him here a group of disciples who caught his spirit, and who taught in his "manner" to such an extent that we cannot always be sure, with a given sermon, whether it is from the Master himself or from one of his disciples. I shall speak of Eckhart's final collision with the guardians of orthodoxy and of the close of his life after I have presented an outline of his teaching.

One of the old scribes has given us a couplet which reads:

> "This is Meister Eckhart
> From whom God kept nothing hid."

He was the profoundest of all German mystics, and is much the most difficult to interpret, but we shall find him in the main following the lines of thought which are now familiar to us in the great systems of Plotinus, Dionysius, and Erigena. In his profoundly original style of speech we shall hear again of the *undifferentiated Godhead, the Divine Procession, and of the soul's return home.*

The first point which must be grasped is the distinction between "God" and the "Godhead." There is —and this is the core of Eckhart's entire doctrine—

[1] Jundt, *op. cit.* (Appendix, *Eckhart's Sermons*, p. 255).
[2] Pfeiffer, p. 664, line 6.

there is a central mystery which for ever lies beyond the range of knowledge. He whom we call "God" is the Divine Nature manifested and revealed in personal character, but behind this Revelation there must be a Revealer—One who *makes* the revelation and is the Ground of it, just as behind ourself-as-known there must be a self-as-knower—a deeper *ego* which knows the *me* and its processes. Now the Ground out of which the revelation proceeds is the central mystery—is the Godhead. It cannot be revealed because it is the Ground of every revelation, just as the self-as-knower cannot be known because it is precisely that which *does the knowing*, and this cannot itself be caught as object.

This unrevealable Godhead is the Source and Fount of all that is, and at the same time the consummation of all reality, but it is above all contrasts and distinctions. It is neither *this* nor *that*, for, says Eckhart, in the Godhead, "all things are *one* thing"—all the fulness of the creatures (*i.e.* created things) can as little express the Godhead as a drop of water can express the sea.[1]

> "All that is in the Godhead is *one.* Therefore we can say nothing. He is above all names, above all nature. *God works; so doth not the Godhead.* Therein they are distinguished—in working and not working. The end of all things is the hidden Darkness of the eternal Godhead, unknown and never to be known."

Nobody has gone farther than Eckhart in the direction of removing all anthropomorphic traits from God, *i.e.* the Godhead, but the result is that He is left with *no thinkable characteristics.* He is not an "object" for human understanding. He utterly transcends knowledge, and everything one says of Him is untrue. "Be still," he says in a sermon,[2] "and prate not of God (*i.e.* the Godhead), for whatever you prate in words about Him is a lie and is sinful." "If I say God is good, it is not true; for what is good can grow better; what can grow better

[1] Pfeiffer, p. 173. This shows that Eckhart is not properly called a pantheist, for he never holds that the sum of all things is God; in fact in the above passage he says precisely the opposite of that.

[2] Pfeiffer, p. 319.

can grow best. Now these three things (good, better, best) are far from God, for He is above all," *i.e.* all such distinctions. No word that voices distinctions or characteristics, then, may be spoken of the Godhead. Eckhart's favourite names are: "the Wordless Godhead"; "the Nameless Nothing"; "the Naked Godhead"; "the Immovable Rest"; "the Still Wilderness, where no one is at home." All mystics have insisted that God in His essence is beyond "knowledge," for "knowledge" must deal with a finite "this," or a finite "that," while God in His absolute reality must be above any "this" or any "that." Eckhart's "nameless Nothing" is only a bold way of saying that the Godhead must be above everything that limits or defines—above everything that can be "thought," or envisaged. As he himself says: "In the Naked Godhead there is never form nor idea," *i.e.* there is nothing thought can seize. "He is an absolute, pure, clear *One*"—"the impenetrable Darkness of the eternal Godhead." The unoriginated Being, the Ground of all that is, is the central mystery, and he who would fathom this mystery must transcend knowledge, must have recourse to some other form of experience than that which defines and differentiates as the knowing process does.

The reader who finds himself somewhat dazed in this height of speculation would run up into the same difficulty himself, if he should undertake strenuously to think out what is involved in the word *Infinite* which he, without giving it much thought, applies to God. He supposes that he glorifies God by calling Him "infinite" or "absolute," but in doing it he has, whether he realizes it or not, raised Him above "knowledge" and has "reduced" Him to an empty indeterminate abstraction which for thought is as truly "nothing" as it is "everything." "Infinite Being" is the *emptiest* of all conceptions. It is, however, a method of thought by no means confined to ancient mystics. Few of us, like Eckhart, have either the desire or the intellectual power to *think our thoughts through to the bottom.* We avoid many difficulties because we do not feel the necessity of universalizing our concepts. We rest satisfied with the bare words, and save ourselves a deal of trouble by not asking the further questions which are involved in our words about God!

To return to Eckhart, God—the personal God—is the self realization, or revelation, of the Godhead, the forthcoming of the Godhead into personalization and manifestation. The Godhead is the "*unnatured Nature*," *i.e.* the unoriginated Reality, the Ground of all revelation; God is the "*natured Nature*," *i.e.* the Divine expressed in Personal Form. The Godhead is the *Wordless One*; God is the *uttered Word*. The procession of God, in Eckhart's system, is by no means the same thing as the Divine Emanations in the system of Plotinus and his followers. For Eckhart there is no mere "overflow" of the Godhead—his idea is much subtler than that. The forthcoming of God is in this wise. The Godhead, "the unnatured Nature," in an "Eternal Now," beholds, Himself, *i.e.* becomes an object of consciousness to Himself, and thus He becomes revealed to Himself. This is the beginning of the process of revelation. This is called "the begetting of the Son," the uttering of the Divine "Word." When God becomes conscious of Himself, there is differentiation into subject and object, or, as Eckhart says, into Father and Son. But we must not suppose that it *happened* at a temporal moment, before which the Son was unborn and God was not yet God. That view is too crude. Eckhart insists that the Son is eternally begotten; "He beholds himself in an Eternal Now"; "God is ever working in one Eternal Now, and His working is a giving birth to His Son. He bears Him at every instant."[1]

The divine differentiation into personality and self-expression is thus no accident, no capricious overflow. It belongs to the very constitution of the Godhead to become self-conscious, *i.e.* to be a Father with a Son.[2] This is the genesis of the personal God, for there can be

[1] Pfeiffer, p. 254.

[2] It is only another way of saying that God is Love, for if He is Love He must eternally beget a Son—there must be a real "Other" for Love to be real.

no personality until there is differentiation into subject and object, until there is a sundering into "Self" and "Other." Instead of "the Wilderness, where no one is at home," we now have Father and Son united in the bond of love, which is personalized as the Holy Spirit. The Trinity is thus the eternal process of the Divine Self-consciousness. So also is the *World* an eternal process. Creation is not a temporal act any more than the procession of the Trinity is. As soon as God beholds Himself in that Eternal Now, He beholds within Himself the forms or Ideas of the entire universe — all that has essential reality in the universe. In fact for Eckhart, the Son, the Word, stands for the total unity of the Divine Thought, the forthcoming of God into expression, the utterance of Himself, so that he often calls God's thinking the archetypal forms, or Ideas, "the begetting of the Son." These archetypal forms, the expressions of God's thought, are "the natured Nature," and these forms, projected into space and time, are our world of nature—the "world of creatures." God is like a perfect architect who *thinks* his structure and it is done. There are no stages in it, no before and after. God thinks and Creation *is*. The world which is thus uttered into being has two faces, one turned out toward differentiation and multiplicity and the other turned in toward God and unity—in very fact all reality is in God, and "if God drew back His own into Himself, all the creatures would become nothing at all."[1] The real world is the world of archetypes—divine Ideas—and that world is not created, it always *is*. "God," he says, "creates the world and all things in an ever-present now" (*Got schöpfet die welt und elliu Dinc in eine gegenwurtigen Nun*). So that by a temporal regress we should never get back to a *time* when God existed alone as a naked Godhead, for without the Word, *i.e.* without the Son, without the expression of Himself, God would not be God. This Divine procession is therefore not an "event" in time, and this temporal world, characterized by multiplicity and change, this world,

[1] Pfeiffer, p. 51.

in sundered heres and nows, is only a show world, a shadow of the Real—the Real read through the goggles of space and time.[1] "In the Godhead," he says, "there is no number for He is One, but in time and space there are divisions—parts. If my face were eternal, and I held it before a time-mirror, it would be received by the mirror in time, yet it would in itself be eternal." So, too, the real world is an eternal unity in God; the temporal world is a show or reflection, but a reflection of an eternal reality.

We have found that Eckhart starts out with the assumption of an unnatured Nature in God—His Ground and Essence. So also, when he turns from God to man, he starts out with the assumption that there is in *us* an unnatured nature—the essence and ground of the soul. "There is in the soul something which is above the soul, divine, simple, rather unnamed than named." This unoriginated essence Eckhart calls by various names, though he insists that names are of little value. He calls it "Fünklein," *i.e.* "Spark"; "Kleine Ganster," or "Little Glimmer of the Soul"; "The Soul's Eye"; "The Inmost Man"; "the Ground of the Soul"; "*Synteresis*," *i.e.* Moral Conscience, and "Active Reason." But, as Eckhart tells us, names help us very little; we must try to grasp what he has to teach us of the real nature of the soul, for it is Eckhart's main contribution to mysticism. In his *lower* consciousness (*i.e.* passive reason) man is dependent on the experience of the senses. His knowledge is mediated by images, and is always marked by a *here* and a *now*. It is necessarily "in part," in "sundered portions, and in divers manners." If one thought is present, any other thought must stay out and wait its turn. This lower consciousness is able to deal only with the particular and finite—its sphere is the show world, where experience never gets beyond the *this* and *that*. It is this lower consciousness of ours which ties us down to a stage of mutability, a welter and flux of

[1] Karl Pearson has pointed out that there are many points in which Eckhart's system resembles Kant's. For both, the real world is not in time or space, the world of appearance is a show world.

"images." The life in this lower stage is always restless and unsatisfied, for it is endeavouring to anchor upon fleeting, vanishing things. "If I had everything that I could desire, and my finger ached, I should not have everything, for I should have a pain in my finger and, as long as that remained, I should not enjoy full comfort. Bread is comfortable for men when they are hungry; but when they are thirsty they find no more comfort in bread than a stone. So it is with clothes; they are welcome to men when they are cold, but when they are too hot clothes give them no comfort. And so it is with all the creatures (*i.e.* things in the show world). The comfort which they promise is only on the surface, like froth, and it always carries with it a want."[1]

The "way" to peace, to reality, to God is complete renunciation of this world of finite objects, this temporal experience through images of the *now* and *here.* The soul must *die* to "creature knowledge" before it can be born to the blessedness of mystical contemplation. Nobody ever took the beatitude of "the poor in spirit" more seriously than Eckhart.

> "A man shall become as truly poor," he says, "and as free from his creature will as he was when he was born. And I say to you, by the eternal truth, that as long as ye desire to fulfil the will of God, and have any desire after eternity and God, so long are ye not truly poor. He alone hath true spiritual poverty who wills nothing, knows nothing, desires nothing."

The soul must withdraw not only from possessions and "works," but it must also withdraw from all sense experience, from everything in time and space, from every image of memory, every idea of the understanding into an experience above this lower form of consciousness—an experience in which "all things are present in one unified now and here."[2]

Such an experience is possible, he believes, because the soul possesses inalienably a faculty of *higher* consciousness.

[1] Pfeiffer, p. 300. I have used the translation made by W. R. Inge, in *Light, Life, and Love.*

[2] Alle miteinander in eime Blicke und in eime Punte" (Pfeiffer, p. 20).

This higher consciousness is the Active or Creative Reason. There are running through Eckhart's writings two views which are never quite reconciled by him. Sometimes the Divine "Spark," by which the soul rises to "new birth" and to contemplation, in "an Eternal Now," is thought of as the unoriginated essence, or ground, of the soul. It *remains* in the Godhead, it has never "come out" from God; it is the point in common between the soul and its Divine Ground. Eckhart says in a bold passage: "The eye with which I see God is the *same* eye with which He sees me." At other times he speaks as though the soul's "Spark" were a *created faculty*, above all the other faculties of man. It has come from God, to be sure, but it is not the identical essence of God—it is the centre of a separate personality, and will remain separate for ever. In a famous sermon, which he says he must have preached, even though nobody had been present, and he had had only a stick for hearer, he uses a fine illustration of the reflection of a mirror to show how "God goes out of Himself into Himself." He says:

> "I take a vessel of water and put a mirror in it and place it in the sunlight. The sun sends out its light without losing any of its substance, and the reflection of the mirror sends back sunlight. Sun and reflection are the same thing. So it is with God. God with His own nature, His essence, His Godhead is in the soul, and yet He is not the soul (*i.e.* He is infinitely more than the soul). The soul sends back a divine reflection to God, so that they both are the same light. The Word or expression of God becomes God."[1]

He apparently taught in his *earlier period* that the Active Reason, or Soul's Eye, is a God-given Light, a spark which has come from God, and by which the soul can return to God, a faculty which brings man face to face with God. It is so near to God that it makes with Him "an inseparably unified one." At this period of his teaching the "Spark" is still Reason, it is that in the soul into which God shines and which reflects Him back to Himself. In his later teaching the "Spark" is a

[1] Pfeiffer, p. 180-81.

hidden higher Ground of the soul, above Reason (for Reason knows before and after). It is thought of as an unoriginated essence, beyond all distinctions of before and after, a naked, nameless entity, stripped of change, bare of qualities, freed of all desire, transcending Reason and will. "It is," he says, "higher than knowledge, higher than love, higher than grace, for in all these there is distinction." This peak of the soul is *one with the Godhead*, and would remain unlost, even if the soul were in hell. We need not, however, make much of the difference between the earlier and the later teaching. In any case Eckhart holds that at bottom (or at top) the soul and God belong together. "The Father," he says, "knows no difference between thee and Himself"—"The Father makes me Himself and Himself me."[1] The return of the soul to its Divine centre, to its "Spark," is blessedness—is salvation. Eckhart calls it "the begetting of the Son" in man.[2] It is the process by which the soul gets free of sense and *lower* consciousness and rises to an immediate experience of God. This experience comes as soon as the soul withdraws into its Ground, for there God and the soul are one. He who would enter into the inmost essence of the Godhead, and come into union with That which is above changes and determinations, must of necessity rise above "knowledge." So long as the soul dwells at the level of finite distinctions it has not come into its own highest region nor to the point where it could find the undifferentiated nameless Godhead. But by a Divine birth the soul may rise to a mystical insight, which is above knowledge and which is *union*—an experience beyond subject-object. So only does the soul escape from the show-and-shadow world. He only can arrive at reality who can rise to the *Ever-present Now* in which all things are together. "All the truth which any master ever taught with his own reason and understanding,

[1] Pfeiffer, pp. 291 and 205.

[2] There is a double "begetting of the Son" in Eckhart. He uses the expression for the process by which God goes out of Himself into a natured nature, and for the process by which the soul rises into union with God. It is thus a circular process.

or ever can teach to the last day, will not in the least explain *this knowledge*."[1]

Again and again he says that, when the soul rises into its own Ground, it becomes one with the Godhead in an Eternal Now. The twain become a single One. He even says that then—in this union—God *brings to birth His Son in Himself and in me*! "I am so one with Him that He makes me as though I were not parted from Himself, and the Holy Ghost takes his origin from me as from God since I am in God. If He did not take His birth from me, He would not take it from God, for God makes me as though in no wise separate from Him."[2] In another sermon he says: "When I attain this blessedness of union, then all things are in me and in God, and where I am there God is, and where God is there am I."[3] But he still does not go over into sheer pantheism—the soul's identity is not *lost* in God. "I might ask," he says, "how it stands with the soul that is lost in God? Does the soul find itself or not? To this I will answer as it appears to me, *that the soul finds itself* at the point where every rational being understands himself with himself. Although he sinks and sinks in the eternity of the Divine essence, yet he can never reach the ground (*i.e.* bottom). Therefore God has left a little point wherein the soul turns back upon itself and knows itself to be a creature."[4]

It is true, as various critics have pointed out, that Eckhart does not clear himself sufficiently from the charge of pantheism, but he does not quite fall into pantheism. He makes personality inherent in the very nature of God, and equally inherent in the nature of man—it belongs to the very nature of the soul "to reflect itself and to call itself a Person."[5] Eckhart says that when Paul was caught up into the third heaven all his "faculties" were absorbed and abolished, so that he knew God with the essence of his soul, *i.e.* with his inmost nature, or *spark* of being—"it was not a temporal consciousness." When he came back to the world again nothing was forgotten, but

[1] Pfeiffer, p. 10. [2] *Ibid.* p. 55. [3] *Ibid.* p. 32.
[4] *Ibid.* p. 387. [5] See Preger, pp. 419-20.

the entire experience was so deep within the ground of the soul that reason, or the "faculties," could not reach it and draw it forth. To get it he had to retire back into himself, but the experience had eternally become a part of himself, therefore he says neither death nor any other thing can separate me from what I have experienced *in myself*.[1] Personality is *real* from all eternity, and even at the highest point of the soul's "union" with God, personality remains unlost—"the soul still finds itself." This is not fairly called pantheism.[2]

His treatment of sin, in similar fashion, is up near the perilous edge of pantheism, but he still keeps on the hither side of it. There are passages in his Sermons in which distinctions are lost, and God is in everything "from angel to spider," and yet there are other passages which imply that sin is a *positive* fact. In his positive view sin is self-will. It is the setting of the individual will against the Divine will. The "disease of sin," "the blindness of sin," he says, comes from "self-love"; "all love of the world springs out of self-love." Sin is not merely an affair of the *flesh*; it is an attitude of will, for even Lucifer, who was pure spirit, fell and is eternally fallen. Everything turns on the attitude of the will. Here are some of the scattered sayings: "If your will is right, you cannot go wrong"; "With the will I can do everything"; "There is nothing evil but the evil will"; "Love resides in the will—the more will, the more love."[3] This attitude of the will, which is the ground of sin, has its origin in the lower consciousness, but it may spread and *become* the death of the soul by separating the soul from God.[4] The reality of moral distinction persists

[1] Pfeiffer, p. 8 (see also Preger, p. 421).

[2] It must, however, be said that Eckhart saves himself from pantheism by shying away from the logic of his system. There are many passages which go fearlessly on to the conclusion that everything in the universe is a differentiation of the Godhead and has no reality "out of" the Godhead, but he occasionally tempers his doctrine and introduces distinctions which are not involved in his premises. There are throughout his system two strands which are never quite woven together. His intellect carries him straight on to a monistic system in which God is all; his heart keeps him in sympathy with the beliefs of the Christian Church.

[3] Quoted from Inge, *Christian Mysticism*, p. 161.

[4] Pfeiffer, p. 215.

eternally. There is a "last judgment," though it is not as people imagine it: "Every man pronounces his own sentence, as he shows himself here in his essence so will he remain everlastingly."[1] Sin, he says, strips away from the soul all its graces, so that when a deadly sin takes place "a man becomes bare of all grace." I have already quoted a passage in which Eckhart insists that there is no freedom possible for the soul so long as sin is there—"One never becomes free until he is free from sin, for as long as one is capable of sinning the distinction between good and evil must be rigorously maintained."[2]

Like all mystics of this type, Eckhart does not find it easy to make the historical plan of salvation fit organically into the mystical process, by which the soul comes into immediate union with God by "bringing forth the Son" within itself. He, however, insists on the reality of the incarnation, and declares that the expression of God in the Son was an eternal necessity of the Divine Nature, and this self-revelation of God would have been made even if Adam had never sinned. This view, so far, fits his whole conception of the procession of God. When, however, he comes to deal with the atonement he "adopts" the language of evangelical theology, but does not try to square it with his mystical process. One of his great atonement passages will be found in his sermon on John vi. 44: "No one can come unto Me except My Father draw him."[3] He says Christ speaks to God and says:

> "Heart-dear Father, when Thou couldst not forgive the sin of the world through the sacrifices that were offered to Thee under the old covenant, then said I, 'My Father, I, the only begotten Son of Thy heart, who in all things am like Thee in Godhead, in whom Thou hast hid all the treasures and riches of Divine love, I go to the cross, in order that I may become a living sacrifice in Thy Divine sight, that Thou mayst turn the eyes of Thy fatherly pity, and see me, Thy only begotten Son, and behold my Blood flowing from my wounds, and sheathe that fiery sword by which in the hand of the Cherubim Thou hast closed the way to Paradise, so that all who repent and make

---

[1] Pfeiffer, p. 471. [2] *Ibid.* p. 664 (see Jundt, *op. cit.* p. 96).
[3] *Ibid.* pp. 216-20 (see especially p. 219).

atonement for their sins in me may go in there in perfect freedom.'"

Eckhart also speaks of Christ—and this view fits well in with his mysticism—as the representative of Collective humanity—the ideal *Man*, in Whom all *men* have their unity and reality, so that when a person rises to the ground and reality of his essential being he partakes of Christ and becomes one with Him and so one with God: "All creatures that have flowed out from God must become united into one Man, who comes again into the unity Adam was in before he fell. This is accomplished in Christ. According to this truth all creatures are One Man, and this Adam is God (Christ the Son of God)."[1] However profound and complicated Eckhart's metaphysics may appear, his practical religion is as simple and straightforward as that of the popular saints. One would expect, as he toils through the tangled passages which tell about the "nameless Nothing" of the Godhead, and which call for an *Abgeschiedenheit* or separation of soul from everything sensible, imaginable, or conceivable, that the outcome would be a quietism amounting to absolute self-death; one would suppose, as he follows the great mystic in his cry of "vanity" toward all things temporal and mutable until not a rag of human merit is left in heart, mind, or will, so that nothing "good" can come in man unless God becomes the centre of his being, and wills through him, in place of his own will, that this finite life would be rendered wholly abortive in "a fascinated gazing" toward the blank of Reality "yonder." Quite the contrary is the fact. Eckhart was a highly practical man, who did his day's work with fidelity and with telling effect. He eminently preserved his *balance*, and he kept his spiritual perspective healthy. While insisting that no temporal thing may be put in the place of the soul's own goal, he does not neglect to make proper use of the things that are now and here. The world of "creatures" is, after all, a Divine expression of the Word of God, but we need to remember that God "has given every gift, which He has

[1] Preger, vol. i. p. 427.

given in heaven or in earth, in order that He may be able to give us *the one gift*—Himself." [1]

He attaches little importance to forms, rites, or ceremonies. There is only one way to a spiritual height—to a spiritual victory—the soul itself must rise to it and achieve it. Nobody has more strongly insisted that spiritual results come by spiritual processes—not by magic, not by easy requests: "I will never pray to God to give Himself to me. I will pray Him to make me purer. If I were purer, God must give Himself to me of His own nature and sink into me." [2]

> "Some people," he says, "are for seeing God with their eyes, as they can see a cow (which thou lovest for the milk, and for the cheese, and for thine own profit). Thus do all those who love God for the sake of outward riches or of inward comfort; they do not love aright, but seek only themselves and their own advantage."

The whole value of the sacrament depends not on the use of bread and wine but on the attitude of the soul. The partaking of something physical can effect nothing. If a spiritual condition is to be attained the soul must *go beyond* the sacrament: "*When I rise above the sacrament I experience God, and become actually changed into that which I experience.*" [3] Even the historical Christ is thought of only as a symbol of the divine humanity to which our souls should rise: "When the soul brings forth the Son, it is happier than Mary." [4]

But the very fact that events in time and space are symbolic, and point the soul toward the reality which they symbolize, keeps Eckhart from being over-ascetic. He will not stop short of God in His absolute wholeness, but he will use "broken manifestations" of Him as far as they will carry him. The goal is union in the Godhead, but everything on the way may be made a help toward the final attainment. He has a human interest in the people about him; he feels their sorrows and needs, and is *active* in his sympathies. He lays down a noble principle,

[1] Pfeiffer, p. 569.
[2] *Ibid.* p. 290.
[3] *Ibid.* p. 592.
[4] *Ibid.* p. 290.

which he himself also practised: "What a man takes in by contemplation he must pour out in love." In the same practical fashion he puts Martha above Mary, *i.e.* activity above contemplation. "Mary hath chosen the good part, that is, she is striving to be as holy as her sister. Mary is still at school: Martha hath learnt her lesson. It is better to feed the hungry than to see even such visions as St. Paul saw."[1] The same practical truth is set forth in a fragment of a sermon in Pfeiffer's collection (p. 553):

> "If a man were in rapture such as Paul experienced, and if he knew of a person who needed something of him, I think it would be far better out of love to leave the rapture and serve the needy man."

He puts great value on the discipline of sorrow, and finds in suffering a revelation of Divine reality:

> "I say that after God there was never anything that is nobler than sorrow, then surely the Father from heaven would have granted that nobler gift to His Son Jesus Christ. But we find that, except for His humanity, there was nothing of which Christ had so much as sorrow. . . . Yes, I say, were there anything nobler than sorrow, then therewith would God have redeemed man. . . . But we do not find that Christ was ever an hour upon earth without sorrow; therefore sorrow must be above all things."[2]

The true victory of the soul is not won by withdrawal from the struggles incident to life, but by the cultivation of patience and endurance in the struggle—an overcoming of the world by living through it:

> "That a man has a restful and peaceful life in God is good. That a man endures a painful life in patience, that is better; but that a man has his rest in the midst of a painful life, that is best of all."[3]

He urges his friends not to divide life into two compartments—the sacred and the secular—but to maintain the same disposition in the crowd, amid the unrest and

[1] Quoted from Inge, *Christian Mysticism*, p. 161.

[2] Pfeiffer, p. 357; Royce's translation in *Studies of Good and Evil*, p. 286.

[3] Pfeiffer, p. 221.

manifoldness of the world, which they have in church or in their cells,[1] and to realize that it is just as important to practise faithfully a small duty as one which the people call great. Those among his hearers who missed the meaning of his lofty flights of speculation must have listened with their heart as he told them that God was not only Father but Mother too, and as he repeated in fourteenth century language the gospel of Christ to the poor:

> "Look you, the most ignorant and the lowest of you all can obtain God's grace, in ever richer fulness, till he comes to perfection—he can obtain it before he leaves this church, yea, before I finish this sermon, as sure as God lives and I am a man."[2]

In a tumultuous age, revolting from dry formalism and empty orthodoxy, it was a great thing to have a man tell his hearers that the God Whom they missed in the Church they could find in their own souls.

The doctrines which he preached in German to the common people he also taught in Latin to scholars and theologians, and it seems extraordinary that he should have taught so many years unmolested. It indicates that there was a freedom of thought allowed in the fourteenth century which many historians of the Church have hardly suspected. There is no indication that Eckhart's "soundness" came under suspicion before the year 1326.[3] The first complaint against him was brought by the Archbishop of Cologne in the year just given. The complaint was taken up by Nicholas of Strasbourg, who was friendly to Eckhart. Nicholas was Vicar-General to the Dominican Order and "Visitor" for his province, having been entrusted by the Pope in 1323 with the oversight of the convents of Germany. Early in 1327 he took up the complaint against Eckhart, deciding that the archbishop had no jurisdiction over Dominican preachers, and carrying the whole matter by

[1] Pfeiffer, p. 547. [2] *Ibid.* p. 187.

[3] The "brother Eckhart," Prior of Frankfort, suspected of heresy in 1306, cannot be identified with our Meister Eckhart.

appeal to the papal chair. Eckhart, in his own name, took a similar course, denying the right of the archbishop to interfere with his teaching, and asking for a papal decision. On the 13th of February of the same year he preached to the people of Cologne, affirming in his sermon the purity and soundness of his faith, expressing his horror of all heresy and immorality and offering to retract everything he had ever said that conflicted with the doctrine of the Church. We learn from this sermon that the two charges formulated against him were: (1) that "his little finger has created everything," and (2) that "there is something uncreated in the soul." The first statement in its literal meaning is of course absurd and paradoxical, but Eckhart did make free use of such paradoxical language, and it is an over-bold and vigorous way of stating the unity of God and man in creative activity which in many passages he affirms. The truth of the second charge is proved by scores of passages in Eckhart's writings. His sermon is a lame attempt to explain away the difficulty by putting an allegorical meaning on the words and by endeavouring to show how they square with popular orthodoxy. He reveals at this crisis a very submissive, almost naive, spirit. But I see no reason for calling him cowardly, or for supposing that he had no *convictions*. He never explicitly realized that there was inconsistency between his mysticism and Church doctrine, and he had not remotely conceived it a part of his mission to set himself against the authority of the Church. We may regret that Eckhart did not show the heroic spirit of a reformer and stand unflinchingly for the right to think freely, but it is unhistorical to expect it of him. He must be judged in the light of his age. There had always been an evangelical and popular side to his teaching, and now in his defence he simply goes further than the case would warrant in showing that his pantheistical utterances were open to a harmless interpretation. I am inclined to think that he is here naive rather than disingenuous.

Before his case was settled at the papal court Eckhart had finished the term of his life—dying in this very year 1327. By a papal Bull of 1329, twenty-eight propositions, found in Eckhart's writings, were condemned—seventeen were pronounced heretical, and the rest were called rash and *suspect.* "He has wished to know more than he should!" is the curious verdict of the Pope. Yes, it is true that he "wished to know" things about which the Church could give him no light; that he fearlessly pushed his speculation into realms which were uncharted in the books of dogma. "We are transformed totally into God, even as in the sacrament the bread is converted into the body of Christ," is one of the twenty-eight "items," and one of the seventeen propositions found "heretical." It is a fair statement of Eckhart's teaching, and well sums up his message—Man through the Divine Spark within his soul may rise into union with the Godhead in an Eternal Now. It has "an ill sound" and is "very rash," says the Pope's Bull. Such teaching—if it were found that experience verified it—would surely make popes unnecessary, and would render the elaborate Church machinery of the fourteenth century as useless as medieval armour is to a citizen of the modern world. The Pope's Bull unfortunately neglects to settle for us the question whether Eckhart's message of Divine Union fits the eternal nature of things or not, it only decides that it does not fit dogma.

CHAPTER XIII

THE FRIENDS OF GOD

I

ONE of the most important and remarkable expressions of mystical religion in the history of the Christian Church is that which flowered out in Germany in the fourteenth century, and whose exponents are known under the name of "Friends of God." The title does not cover a sect, nor even a "Society," in the strict sense of the word. It, rather, names a fairly definite type of Christianity, which found its best expression in persons of the prophet-class in that century, both men and women, who powerfully moved large groups of Christians by their preaching, their writings, and their extraordinary lives. All the leaders of the movement were profoundly influenced by the teaching of that luminous figure of German mysticism, Meister Eckhart, but they were hardly less definitely influenced by the apocalyptic writings of the great German "prophetesses" of the two preceding centuries—St. Hildegarde, St. Elizabeth of Schoenau, and St. Matilda of Magdeburg. The writings of these famous women are full of incidents, phrases, and images which formed "suggestion material" for the experiences and ideas of the Friends of God. In fact, they have very similar conceptions of the Church and the world, and of the impending catastrophes that are about to break upon both the world and the Church. I shall give illustrations of this influence later.

The period covered by the movement which we are now studying was one of the most troublous epochs in medieval history. Woes and disasters came thickly one after the other, and they produced a "psychological climate," which partly accounts for the morbid features which characterize the movement, and which partly explains the abnormal occurrences in the lives of many of the "Friends of God." Every sensitive person was overwrought and strained. There was a widespread expectation that apocalyptic prophecies were soon to be fulfilled; this visible world was believed to be the sport of supernatural powers, both good and bad, and men and women everywhere were in "hair-trigger condition" of response to any captivating suggestion, as the terrible outbreak of flagellation which swept many of the Rhine cities plainly indicates. A few of the events which helped to produce this "mental climate" may be mentioned here. From 1309 to 1377 occurred the so-called "Babylonish Captivity" of the Church, when the papal seat was changed to Avignon, and when the popes were more or less puppets of France. To many of the faithful this "captivity" was a supreme woe—the reward and result of sin and apostasy. A still greater misfortune followed hard after the period of "captivity." Upon the death of Gregory XI., in 1378, there occurred a double election, resulting in two rival popes, and during the next forty years the Church was torn and almost wrecked by what is known as the "Great Schism," which lasted from 1378 to 1417.

More important for our distinct period, and carrying with it more serious practical consequences for the common people of the German cities, was the "Great Civil War," which resulted from a double election of emperors. Louis of Bavaria was chosen Emperor in 1314, by one party of electors, and Frederick of Austria by another party. The Pope took sides against Louis, excommunicated him, and laid an interdict upon all cities which supported him. By the interdict, all public religious services were prohibited, and all consolation of religion suspended, through the section of the country covered by the interdict. Infants were unbaptized, the Mass was not celebrated, the sacred offices for the dead ceased. In many cities of Germany where the citizens were loyal to Louis, the priests were forced to go on with their religious functions in spite of the interdict, or to go into banishment.

While Europe was thus suffering through the wrath of man, a veritable scourge, which in that age seemed traceable directly to the wrath of God, fell upon the German cities. It was a pestilence known in history as the "Black Death." It first struck the west of Europe in 1347, and raged for two years, returning again in less virulent form in 1358 and in 1363. In some places the mortality was so great that it is estimated that only one-tenth of the population survived. There were, too, many earthquakes through the Rhine valley about the middle of the century, one of which, "the great earthquake," left the city of Basle a heap of ruins, and wrought similar havoc in many small towns.

The Friends of God formed small groups, or local societies, gathered about some spiritual leader or counsellor. There was little or no organization. The type of each particular group was largely determined by the personality of the "leader," while the whole movement was unified and moulded by the work of itinerant "prophets," and by the production of a very remarkable literature. These mystic circles, or groups, were widespread, and were formed in far-sundered places, stretching from Bavaria, possibly from Bohemia, to the low countries, with the most important groups in Strasbourg, Cologne, and Basle.[2]

There was a voluminous exchange of letters among the leaders, and frequent personal visits. The visits and the itinerant missions were generally prompted by some

[1] Speaking of the "society" in Cologne, Henry of Nördlingen says in a sermon: "I do not know in the whole universe, from one end to another, any place where the word of God has spread so widely, and has manifested itself so richly and purely, during the last sixty years, or where it is announced to-day by so many illuminated doctors, or so many Friends of God as in the city of Cologne."

[2] Lady Frick, a close friend of Henry of Nördlingen, on her return to Basle after an absence, writes that she is "filled with joy to be again in the holy and spiritual society at Basle," which she says is "large," and she feels as though she had come from purgatory to paradise. She declares that she would not change her home in Basle for any other, unless it were for one in Medingen, in Bavaria, where there was a group of Friends of God, with Margaret Ebner as its head.

direct revelation. In fact, the whole plan and direction of the movement, as well as the preparation of the most important pieces of their religious literature, are ascribed to direct revelation granted to the leaders.

Some of the societies had retreats in which the members lived—"quiet nests" Tauler calls them. They were "brotherhood houses," modelled on the plan of the Beghards. In many respects the Friends of God were like the Beghards—there is no sharp line of differentiation between them, though the former are always radically opposed to the loose and antinomian tendencies which affected many groups of Beghards and Beguines. The Friends of God were inclined, rather, to err in the opposite direction. Their failing lies in the direction of extreme asceticism and self-renunciation. All the leading Friends of God, both in sermons and in writings, speak vigorously against the negative freedom and licence of the "Brethren of Free Spirit."

The leading figures of the group are Rulman Merswin of Strasbourg; his friend and secretary, Nikolaus von Löwen; John Tauler; Henry Suso; Jan Ruysbroek; Margaret and Christina Ebner; Henry of Nördlingen, and the great unknown, who wrote the little book called *German Theology*. The most important literature for the purposes of this study are the writings attributed to Rulman Merswin and to "The Friend of God of the Oberland"; the sermons of Tauler; the writings of Suso and Ruysbroek; the *German Theology*, and the correspondence between Margaret Ebner and her friends.[1]

As I shall often refer in this chapter to Rulman Merswin and his "double," the so-called "Friend of God from the Oberland," it will be well to consider here who they were. There is no more difficult problem in the history and literature of mysticism than that of the identity and personality of this "Friend of God"—everywhere treated as a somewhat supernatural "character"—who figures so prominently in the great collection of

[1] The letters are published in Heumann's *Opuscula* (Nürnberg, 1747), pp. 331-404.

mystical literature ascribed to him and to Rulman Merswin.[1]

It was assumed in the fifteenth century that this mysterious "Friend of God from the Oberland" was a certain Nicholas of Basle,[2] and this tradition came down with little challenge until recent times. It was adopted and given wide currency by the valuable publications of

[1] The great religious books, or treatises, which have been in part or in whole ascribed to "The Friend of God from the Oberland" or to Rulman Merswin, are as follows: First a collection of sixteen treatises which are preserved in the "Great German Memorial" (Das grosse deutsche Memorial). They are:

(1) *Two Fifteen-year-old Boys.*
(2) *The Imprisoned Knight.*
(3) *The Story of Ursula and Adelaide.*
(4) *Two Holy Nuns in Bavaria.*
(5) *The Spiritual Stairway.*
(6) *The Spiritual Ladder.*
(7) *The Spark* (Fünklein) *in the Soul.*
(8) *A Lesson for a Young Brother of the Order.*
(9) *Story of a Man Endowed with Worldly Wisdom.*
(10) *A Revelation given to "the Friend of God" on Christmas Night.*
(11) *A Young Man of the World.*
(12) *Warnings which "the Friend of God" sent to the People.*
(13) *The Book of the Banner of Christ.*
(14) *The Three Halting-places* (Durchbrüche).
(15) *The Seven Works of Mercy.*
(16) *Book on Prevenient Grace.*

The MS. of *Das grosse deutsche Memorial* is in the Universitäts- und Landes-bibliothek at Strasbourg. The Treatises numbered 1, 2, 10, and 12 have been published in Karl Schmidt's *Nikolaus von Basel* (Wien, 1866). Those numbered 5 and 6 have been printed in Jundt's *Rulman Merswin* (Paris, 1890). In the collection known as *Pflegermemorial* the following Treatises are preserved:—

The Book of the First Four Years of Rulman Merswin's New Life, and the *Book of the Five Men*, which is the story of "the Friend of God" and his companions. There is a fifteenth-century manuscript of this in the Bezirksarchiv of Strasbourg. "The Book of the Five Men" is published in Schmidt's *Nikolaus von Basel.*

Besides these the most important Treatises for the Religious ideas of the Friends of God are the *Book of the Master of Holy Scripture*, the *Book of the Two Men*, and the *Book of the Nine Rocks.* "The Book of the Two Men" is published in Schmidt's *Nikolaus von Basel*, and it has also been edited and published by Lauchert, *Des Gottesfreundes in Oberland* [= *Rulman Merswin*], *Buch von den Zwei Mannen* (Bonn, 1896).

There is an autograph MS. of the *Nine Rocks* in the Universitäts- und Landes-bibliothek at Strasbourg [L. germ 665; Neun Felsen: Rulmanni Merschwin, Fundatoris domus St. Johannis de 9 Rupibus autographus]. This was edited and published by Schmidt, *Das Buch von den Neun Felsen* (Leipzig, 1859). *Das Meisterbuch* [Book of the Master of Holy Scripture] is in the collection known as *Das erste übriggebliebene Lateinbuch.* It has been published by Schmidt under the title: *Nikolaus von Basel, Bericht von der Bekehrung Taulers* (Strasbourg, 1875).

There is also an important collection of Letters (*Briefbuch*) professing to be Letters to and from the "Friend of God." There is a MS. of this *Briefbuch* in the Bezirksarchiv [H 2185]. The Letters are printed in Karl Schmidt's *Nikolaus von Basel.*

[2] This Nicholas of Basle was a Beghard, and was burned at the stake in Vienna, as a heretic.

the famous Strasbourg historian, Karl Schmidt. It is a view, however, now everywhere discredited by scholars. Preger believes that he was a great unknown who lived in or near the city of Chur (Coire), in Switzerland, and Jundt held this view when he wrote his valuable book, *Les Amis de Dieu* (1879). But since Denifle's important studies in the mystical literature of the fourteenth century, the belief has been growing that the "Friend of God of the Oberland" is not an historical personage at all.[1] All his movements are wrapped in profound mystery. There is no historical evidence of his existence outside the evidence furnished by this collection of literature, ascribed to him and Merswin. The accounts of his life say that sometime about 1343 he was forbidden to reveal his identity to any one whatever, except to Rulman Merswin. In the correspondence, supposedly between the "Friend of God" and John of Schaftholsheim, a prominent Church official at Strasbourg, the latter, writing about 1363, urges his unknown correspondent to reveal himself to him. The answer comes back that he cannot do it: "I should like to grant your request, but it is impossible. Cease to ask it, for the love of God. More than twenty years ago God forbade me to reveal myself to any man except one." Every effort is made to destroy all traces of his personal identity, and there is an evident purpose, both in the correspondence and the books ascribed to him, to leave the impression that whatever he does is done by the Holy Spirit. The human medium is, for this very purpose, made as mysterious and shadowy as possible. This entire collection of writings betrays the marks of a single hand. There is a striking similarity in the experiences which occur both to Merswin and the "Friend of God," though there is a boldness of tone and a sureness of direction in the utterances ascribed to the latter which are missing in the former. The same expressions and the same phrases appear and reappear in the writings ascribed to both

Before, however, undertaking to account for his

[1] See especially Denifle's *Der Gottesfreund im Oberlande und Nikolaus von Basel* (1870).

mysterious "double," we must endeavour from the literature at hand to get some biographical details concerning Rulman Merswin. He was born in Strasbourg in 1307. As a young man he became a banker, and amassed a large fortune. He was "a man of watchful conscience and of great fear of God," and he belonged to a very important family of the city. When he was forty years of age he gave up business, "took leave of the world," and devoted himself entirely to divine things, after the manner of the Franciscan Tertiaries, or the Waldensian brothers. He, however, did not give away his money; he kept it "to use for God," as He might direct from time to time. His wife, Gertrude of Bietenheim, though a pious woman, had not yet attained what the Friends of God call "the light of grace." With Waldensian rigour he resolved to live henceforth as celibate.

His first experience of ecstasy came to him at the time of his resolve to devote all his money to the service of God—as the first step in his "new life." Suddenly he felt himself raised from the earth and carried through the air all about the garden. At the same time he felt unutterable joy and spiritual illumination unknown before. He passed through the usual "stages of spiritual experience" that were expected at this epoch. He had terrible inward temptations and struggles; he endeavoured to conquer his evil nature and his "hated body" by extreme ascetic practices. John Tauler became his confessor in 1348, and he wisely told him to stop his macerations. Merswin was next called to pass through an absolutely joyless period when he felt himself destined to burn in hell for ever; then, at length, all sufferings left him, and he came into "the joy and peace of the Holy Spirit." [1]

The Story of the First Four Years of a New Life,

[1] During the years of his "commencement," as they termed the period of preparation, he underwent, according to the accounts, almost unbelievable transformations and psychic experiences. For example, whenever he saw blood, as, for instance, when he was bled by the physicians, the thought of the sacrifice of Christ would so fill his mind that he would swoon away into an ecstasy. He was the frequent recipient of "Divine voices," and many important situations were revealed to him.

which is a remarkable piece of biographical literature, was, according to Merswin's friend, Nikolaus von Löwen, found after his death in a sealed cupboard. This document gives an account of the first appearance of the mysterious "Friend of God." Merswin says:

"Of all the wonderful works which God had wrought in me I was not allowed to tell a single word to anybody *until the time when it should please God to reveal to a man in the Oberland to come to me.* When he came to me, God gave me the power to tell him everything. He became my intimate friend; I submitted myself to him in the place of God, and I told him all the secrets of those four years as God inspired me to do. Then he said: 'My dear, beloved friend, take this book;[1] thou wilt find in it the story of the five years of *my* conversion, and now give me in writing the story of thy four years of conversion.'"

Merswin stoutly resisted the request to write his experiences, but finally the unnamed friend "commanded me to write, in the name of the obedience which I had promised him, and I was compelled to submit. He knew very well that my refusal came entirely from my humility."

The sentence above in italics, which intimates that Merswin had a subjective idea of the "Friend of God" sometime before he had ever seen him or even heard of him, is certainly suspicious, and would, on the face of it, make us inclined to question the historicity of the narrative. Even more suspicious is the account given of the most important event in Merswin's life—the purchase of Grünenwörth, or the "Convent of the Green Isle." This was purchased, according to the narrative, by Merswin, and fitted up as a quiet retreat—"a mystic nest"—for the Strasbourg circle of the Friends of God, a sort of "school of prophets" for which the most important books of this mystical collection were written. Merswin himself is *supposed* to be the author of the account of the founding of the retreat. He brings in his mysterious "Friend," and gives the entire transaction a miraculous colouring. He says that during the night of October 9, 1364,

[1] *The Book of the Two Men*, containing the story of the conversion of the "Friend of God."

the "Friend of God," in his Oberland home—"six days' journey" from Strasbourg—dreamed that he was ordered by God to go to his friend Rulman Merswin, and help him to found a "nest" in Strasbourg for the Friends of God. The same night, in a dream, Rulman Merswin himself had a revelation that *he* ought to found such a retreat in Strasbourg!

Both men were opposed to the idea of founding such a retreat, and they refused to follow the suggestion made in their dreams. The night of the following Christmas they both simultaneously in their respective homes fell seriously ill at midnight; the illness increased until they were at the point of death; suddenly, at precisely the same time, they were told in indescribable visions to found the retreat! The "joint" illness lasted for nearly two years, when a general paralysis of their limbs rendered them both helpless! They were now told that this condition would last until they followed the will of God. At length they yielded, and immediately they were both restored to health! Confirmed by such miraculous signs, the two friends now set to work to carry out the plan which had been revealed to them.[1]

The later accounts, which describe the last years of Merswin and the "Friend of God," throw even more suspicion on the historicity of the narratives, and force us to question the existence of this mysterious "Friend of God." Shortly before his death, which occurred in 1382, Merswin and the "Friend of God," with eleven other Friends of God, met miraculously for a "divine diet" to intercede for Christianity. On Good Friday, 1380, as they were praying, a letter fell from the sky in

[1] Merswin bought the Isle with its ruined convent in the autumn of 1366, and put it in complete condition for a retreat of peace and calm, suited to the mystical life. As the result of another "joint revelation," the retreat was turned over to the Order of Saint John in 1371. The important documents for the story of Merswin's connection with Grünenwörth, or "the Convent of the Green Isle," are the collections known as *Das grosse deutsche Memorial*, *Erstes lateinische Memorial und Pflegermemorial*, and *Johanniter Chronik*, all of which are in the Universitäts- und Landesbibliothek; and the collection known as *Das Pflegermemorial* and *Erweitertes Pflegermemorial* and *Das Briefbuch* in the Bezirksarchiv. The reader who wishes to study the actual *history* of Grünenwörth, freed from the colouring of fiction, should read Karl Rieder's *Der Gottesfreund vom Oberland* (Innsbrück, 1905).

their midst, and an angel told them that God had granted to Christianity a reprieve of Judgment for three years, on condition that they—these thirteen Friends of God—would, according to the contents of the Divine letter, become "the captives of the Lord," *i.e.* die absolutely to self and the world, giving their lives "as a continual sacrifice for the salvation of Christianity"—and so they did! The last word that came from the "Friend of God," now grown even more mysterious than ever, was an *instruction* on how to begin and end the day with prayer, during the pestilence of 1381, and Rulman Merswin, still "the captive of the Lord," died in 1382.

Everybody who has worked over this collection of Friends of God literature has been impressed with the difficulties of the problems involved in it. It seems well-nigh certain that "the Friend of God from the Oberland" was not a historical person, but, if not, who "created" him?

It has been assumed, especially by Denifle, that "the Friend of God" is a literary creation of Rulman Merswin. This entire collection of mystical treatises, it is assumed, was written by Merswin, with the assistance, perhaps, of a school of prophets, and it is all *tendency-literature*, composed to express and develop the ideals of the great religious movement to which Merswin's life was devoted.

The "great unknown" from the Oberland is the ideal character—the "Christian" of a fourteenth-century *Pilgrim's Progress*—who illustrates how God does His work for the world and for the Church through a divinely-trained and spiritually-illuminated layman. On this hypothesis Rulman Merswin as the creator of this ideal Christian of the fourteenth century, as the author of this remarkable autobiographical literature, and as the writer of the great *Book of the Nine Rocks*, would take rank as a genius of uncommon order and as one of the foremost exponents of mysticism in any age, though, as Denifle points out, he would have to be regarded as an arch-deceiver who wilfully misled all his associates and befooled all his readers for four centuries.

In order to clear Merswin from the charge of deceit, Auguste Jundt has proposed a very bold and ingenious hypothesis to solve the mystery. He suggests that Rulman Merswin was a "double personality," of a pathological type now well known to all students of psychology.[1] In his *primary state* he wrote the books ascribed to him and experienced the events recorded in his autobiography; while in his *secondary state* he became the person known as "the Friend of God from the Oberland," and in this state he wrote the books, treatises, and letters ascribed to "the Friend of God." This view, if proved sound, would surely make Rulman Merswin one of the most interesting psychological "subjects" in the entire range of history.

There is a third hypothesis which rests on solider ground than either of the two preceding views. It is presented with sound learning and minute and accurate scholarship by Karl Rieder.[2] He holds that Rulman Merswin is neither a deceiver nor "a double personality," and, with the iconoclasm characteristic of modern German scholarship, he concludes that Merswin is not the author of any of these mystical treatises, and that none of them furnish reliable biographical facts bearing on Merswin's life.

What he finds is that this entire collection of literature has gone through the hands of Nikolaus of Löwen and been transformed by him. Nikolaus was a friend and trusted secretary of Rulman Merswin, his associate in the foundation and development of the Religious House of Grünenwörth, afterwards the House of St. John, and the first local head of the House of St. John during the lifetime and after the death of Merswin.

There came into the hands of Nikolaus, possibly as part of the library of Grünenwörth, a rich collection of mystical treatises, the creation of different members of the group of Friends of God, but with no definite authorship

[1] A. Jundt, *Rulman Merswin et l'Ami de Dieu* (Paris, 1890). It is a very interesting piece of work, and the theory is ably presented.

[2] *Der Gottesfreund vom Oberland: eine Erfindung des Strassburger Johanniterbruders Nikolaus von Löwen*, von Karl Rieder (Innsbrück, 1905).

attached to them or ascribed to them.[1] In order to glorify the Religious House to which he belonged, and to give a weighty influence and authority to its founder, Nikolaus attached Merswin's name to some of these anonymous treatises, and finally created out of his own imagination the mysterious and somewhat supernatural adviser, "the Friend of God from the Oberland," to whom he ascribed the origin of most of the remaining mystical treatises. As the plan grew, Nikolaus expanded the anonymous narratives relating extraordinary experiences, and inserted the names of Merswin and "the Friend of God," and passed them off as autobiographical, inventing a concrete setting for narratives which in their original form had been purely fictitious, and written to illustrate principles which were dear to the Friends of God. The arch-deceiver, therefore, was Nikolaus von Löwen, and his was the genius that created "the Friend of God from the Oberland."

Rieder's main contention that this mystical literature has received a transformation and a local setting at the hands of Nikolaus von Löwen, and that he has woven in much fictitious material to glorify the House of St. John, and its founder, Merswin, seems to me sound; but I see, however, no good reason for the conclusion that Rulman Merswin is not the author of any of these mystical treatises. It now becomes difficult, if not impossible, to *prove* that he wrote, for example, *The Banner of Christ* and *The Book of the Nine Rocks*, but if he were known to Nikolaus and to others of the religious circle to be the actual author of some of these important treatises, it makes it much easier to understand how Nikolaus could have conceived his bold scheme of enlarging the scope of his friend's activity, and how he was able to deceive so successfully his contemporaries.

We shall, however, in any case be compelled to give up using any of this collection of mystical literature as genuine biographical and historical material. It is all

[1] This modesty of authorship appears to be a characteristic of many writers among the Friends of God.

tendency-literature, full of fictitious situations, and, until more light is thrown upon it, it must be treated as anonymous. It does, nevertheless, furnish us material for discovering the prevailing ideas and ideals of these mystical groups of the period, known to us as Friends of God, and I shall now endeavour to gather up the trend and characteristics of the movement.

Their religion was extremely simple and practical. They humbly claim that they "have drunk at the heavenly fountain," and have had their "inner eyes opened." They were not primarily speculative, like Eckhart, but were rather concerned with the concrete matters of actual life, though they evidently put undue emphasis on "experiences" and on visions, and they shared the tendency of the times to drift into exuberant apocalyptic fancies. But, however deep and intense their piety was, it always conformed to the medieval type rather than to the spirit of the Reformation period. Some writers have tried to find in these Friends of God Protestants before the Reformation, but a careful historical study gives little ground for such a view. Even the most spiritual of them were scrupulous in their obedience to the rules of the Church; they were the children of their age, and they were loyal to Roman Catholic ideals. Even during the terrible period of the interdict there is little indication of a revolt, though some of the Friends of God rose to the discovery that it is possible to have spiritual life without the mediation of the Church.

It was distinctly a *laymen's* movement, and there is an evident purpose in the literature of the Friends of God to exalt the ordinary lay Christian, and to show how the Church can be saved and the ministry purified by unordained persons; but these men do not show any spirit of revolt from the ancient system, they have not gained the Protestant temper, and they never dreamed of dispensing with the mediation of the Church, though they occasionally admit that spiritual life is possible without such mediation. The nearest approach to a religion purely of the Spirit is found in *The Book of the Nine*

Rocks, where it is said that even Jews and pious pagans, who are hampered only by *ignorance*, will be saved at the moment of death by ways known only to the Holy Spirit. Here is the passage:

"If a Jew or Mohammedan fears God from the depth of his heart, and leads a good and simple life; if he does not know any better religion than the one in which he was born; if he is ready to obey God in case He reveals to him a better faith than his own, why should not such a man be dearer to God than wicked and impious 'Christians' who, though having received baptism, wilfully disobey the commands of God? When God finds a good Jew or Mohammedan of pure life He feels a thrill of love and infinite pity for him, no matter in what part of the earth he lives, and *God will find some way of saving him unknown to us*!" "If baptism cannot be conferred upon him, though he has a desire for it, *God can baptize him in the holy desire of his will*, and there are in the eternal world many good pagans who have been received in this way."[1]

One of the utterances which sounds most like a spirit of revolt came from Christina Ebner, who, beholding the miseries of the unshepherded people, cried out: "The actions of the Pope toward the clergy make groans and cries rise to heaven."

It is not possible to decide whether Tauler obeyed the interdict or not, but it is at least certain that he said in one of his powerful sermons: "While the Holy Church is able to take from us the external Sacrament, no one can take from us the spiritual joy which comes from union with God, *i.e.* inward joy from the free partaking of the body and blood of Christ."[2]

During the period of the interdict and the "Black Death," when the religious services were suspended in Strasbourg, a plan of life, ascribed to Rulman Merswin, was drawn up by which a Christian layman could dispense with the services of the priest. This proved so valuable that it was copied and spread broadcast, not only throughout the city of Strasbourg, but far beyond its limits. This "Advice" well illustrates the simple, practical, spiritual religion of the "Society." It reads as follows:—

[1] *Book of the Nine Rocks.*

[2] Tauler, Sermon No. LXXI.

"All those in whom the love of God, or the terror created by the terrible calamities of the present, arouses a desire to begin a new and spiritual life, will find great profit in a withdrawal into themselves every morning when they rise, to consider what they will undertake during the day. If they find in themselves any evil thought, any intention contrary to the Divine will, let them renounce it for the glory of God. Likewise, in the evening, on going to bed, let them collect themselves and consider how they have spent the day; what acts they have done, and in what spirit they have done them. If they find that they have done any good, let them thank God and give Him the glory. If they find they have committed any sin, let them attribute the fault of it to themselves, and to nobody else, and let them show to God a deep repentance, saying to Him:

'Oh! Lord, be merciful to me—poor, unworthy sinner, and forgive me all the sins of this day, for I seriously repent, and I have a firm purpose henceforth with Thy help to avoid sinning.'"

But, notwithstanding the fact that they often caught a glimpse of a spiritual religion far in advance of the prevailing ideals of their time, they shared for the most part the theology of their age, and in some instances they were grossly superstitious, like their unmystical countrymen.

They had not yet outgrown a naive faith in the efficacy of "holy relics." Henry of Nördlingen is one of the leading "experts" of his time in the efficacious *values* of different relics, and we frequently hear of him in some remote region, searching for the holy bone of a saint which is to work wonders among the faithful. He carries his superstitious worship to such an extreme that he even believes that there is a supernatural power in objects which have touched the body of his saintly friend, Margaret Ebner, the Friend of God, who was head of the "circle" at Medingen in Bavaria.

There is, too, an excessive love of supernatural manifestations apparent in all the literature of the movement. In the earlier stages of what they called their "commencement," the Friends of God subjected themselves to terrible bodily tortures, self-inflicted, often of the most ingenious sort, and they generally emerged from this aberration with enfeebled constitutions and wrecked nervous systems. Certain typical "experiences" were expected, and sooner or later they generally occurred. The stress and strain of the troublous epoch produced a mental type of person easily affected by suggestion, and thus the ideas and experiences of the leaders spread in this responsive material. We find in the literature of the movement accounts of almost every known form of *psychic experience.* There are accounts of hallucinations of every sense—sight, touch, smell, taste, and hearing. I give one instance from the *Imprisoned Knight.* This knight had been taken prisoner, and was thrust into a dungeon under a tower, where, loaded with chains, he had passed six months. Feeling himself about to die, he wished to take communion, but his request was harshly denied. At midnight he saw a "radiant light," and heard a voice saying that the mother of God had come to his aid. "She has prayed her Son," the voice continued, "to divide between the chaplain of the castle and thee the wafer which will be used to-morrow in the consecration of the Mass. The wafer will be divided into two parts, but the Lord will be entirely present without division in both parts." The next morning the knight *saw,* surrounded with a dazzling light, a half wafer enter his prison! It went directly into his mouth, and at once revived his strength, so that for the entire day he took none of the food which was brought to him. This miracle was repeated for six consecutive days, and after the first day the jailer also saw both the light and the wafer.[1] Reports of collective hallucination are frequent in the literature of the "Society." Christina Ebner, head of the circle at Engelthal, in Bavaria, many times heard the Divine Voice say that Tauler was of all men the one whom God most loved. She also was *told* that there were two names written in heaven—those of John Tauler and Henry of Nördlingen. The voice said that God dwelt in Tauler like melodious music. The members

[1] It is true that this narration is fictitious, but the writer is not creating *mere fiction.* He is writing for edification, and he gives what he believes is *possible* experience for the group.

of the group were *telepathic* and often felt what was happening to some other Friend of God far away.

They all looked upon the state of ecstasy as a supreme divine favour. In these moments of "unspeakable ecstasy" they believed that God was talking with them face to face, and the uprushes of intimation which came at such times were counted as veritable "revelations" from the Holy Spirit. These revelations were considered by them as authoritative as the Holy Scriptures. Henry of Nördlingen calls the revelations which come through Margaret Ebner "a holy scripture." He allows the Friends of God in Basle to have communion during the interdict, and he explains in a letter that he granted the privilege to the *spiritual circle* on the strength of a personal revelation given to Margaret Ebner. In an ecstasy, Margaret was called into the presence of the Saviour Himself, and in tender love He invited her to take His holy body, and Henry adds: "I dare not oppose myself to Thee." In the *Book of the Master of Holy Scripture*, "the Friend of God," speaking as an oracle of the Holy Spirit, says to the Master: "If you are to receive the words I speak as though they come from *me*, I shall say no more to you." Their writings everywhere imply or assert that God speaks through them in the same way that He spoke through "His Friends in the Old and New Testament"; in both dispensations the "counsel" of a Friend of God is "the counsel of God Himself."

They never question the authority of the Scriptures, nor undervalue their teaching; in fact, they were in no other respect so like the Protestants of the sixteenth century as in their devotion to the Bible—but at the same time they insisted on the reality of present inspiration and continuous revelation. Those who receive "the luminous grace of the Holy Spirit" are granted immediate revelations bearing upon both inner experience and outer events. They talk of two stages of truth. To the *lower stage* belong the interpretations of Scripture which the learned doctors of the Church give. It is their function to tell what has been revealed in past ages.

The higher stage is the truth of immediate revelation. "God has a few whom He whispers in the ear!" They have the privilege of being the bearers of a first-hand word from Him. "They hear," as one of them says, "in their own souls what they are to speak." This stage they call "the upper school of the Holy Spirit." This distinction between the "lower school" of those who have only "knowledge about" and the "higher school" of those who have also "knowledge of experience" is well illustrated by a passage from the *Book of the Two Men.*

"If two men gave thee a description of the city of Rome, one by mere hearsay, and the other by experience after he had been there, thou wouldst give thy attention mainly to the second. So also, if a man who has been touched inwardly by divine grace hears the preaching of a doctor who still loves himself, he feels that the preaching of such a doctor does not come from pure and unadulterated love of God. The soul that is filled with divine love is not touched by such a sermon. Such a preacher is speaking only by hearsay of the heavenly Rome, and of the roads which lead to it. He knows only what he has learned from Scripture. But if the same man hears the preaching of a master who knows both from Scripture and through his own spiritual experience, a master who has renounced all self-love and self-advantage, who knows the heavenly Rome, not only by hearsay, but because he has travelled the road to it, and because he has seen the form of its buildings, he rejoices to hear his message, because it proceeds from the Divine Love itself."

Those who have had this first-hand experience, and belong to this "upper school of the Holy Spirit," are the true teachers and guides of the rest.[1] For this reason the Friends of God insisted, as a matter of first importance, that all who were in the stage of "preparation" should submit themselves entirely to the counsel and direction of some holy man of the "Society."

By far the most famous account of submission and direction is that recorded in the *Book of the Master.* This book relates that in 1346 there was "a great doctor, a master of Holy Scripture," who preached in a certain city, and multitudes flocked to hear him—"his preaching

[1] This phrase, "upper school of the Holy Spirit," had already been used by Matilda of Magdeburg.

was talked about for miles around." "A certain *layman*, a man full of divine grace, the beloved Friend of God from the Oberland, came by command of God" ten days' journey, and heard five sermons by the master. He perceived that the "master," though "a man of good heart," was "still in the dark and without the full light of grace." At the end of the fifth sermon the "Friend of God" asked "the doctor" if he would preach a sermon on "The way to attain the highest degree of spiritual life." The preacher demurred for a time on the ground that the layman could not understand it if he should preach it, as it would be beyond his experience and comprehension. He, however, finally assented and preached the sermon. In this sermon the great preacher pointed out, in mystical fashion, that the highest state of spiritual life is found in an experience beyond "intellectual comprehension," beyond ideas and images. Quoting from Dionysius, he says that the light of faith takes man above the sphere of intellectual conceptions. The perfect man must rise above everything sensible and intellectual, must empty himself of all content, and then God will come in and dwell in him. He must absolutely renounce self, self-will, self-love, and the pursuit of all personal advantage either in this world or in the next.

After a day of consideration the "Friend of God" came back to the preacher and passed severe criticism on the sermon and on the preacher himself. He told him that he was preaching what he had not yet experienced, and even went to the length of calling "the doctor" a Pharisee, and an imitator of the work of the Pharisees. The preacher showed great offence at this freedom on the part of a mere layman, but as the layman went on to reveal the height and depth of his own spiritual experience, the master of Holy Scripture perceived that he was in the presence of one who had attained something which he himself had not at all reached, and in great humility he asked the layman how he had gained such a degree of spiritual experience. The layman answered that God had brought him into complete humility and abandonment of self, and so had taught him directly by the Holy Spirit. "The Holy Spirit," he says, "has the same power to-day as ever. He is as able to speak through me, a poor sinner, as He did through the mouth of the sinner Caiaphas. In truth, if you think that these words which I speak come through me, I will not speak another word to you."

Under this criticism and instruction, the preacher, seeing his own inner poverty revealed, asks how he can begin for himself a new course of life so as to attain to the highest degree of spiritual life, saying that even if he must die for it he will follow "the counsel." Thereupon, the layman gives him first of all the A B C of religion to study, which was a series of twenty-three sentences bearing upon the rudiments of religious experience. At the end of six weeks he set before "the great doctor" the conditions upon which he can advance to a higher life. He is to go into his cell, and separate himself from all his old life and occupations. He is to say Mass every day, and spend the rest of the day in solitary meditation, comparing his life with that of the Saviour, and thinking of what he has lost by self-love, until he shall arrive to complete humility. He is told that he will be called a fool, will lose his best friends, and will be the laughing-stock of all his companions, but this will be to him a blessing, for it will bring him to the point of having confidence in none but God Himself.

For two years "the doctor" underwent a life of this rigid regime, exposed to ridicule and scorn, and then there came upon him a wonderful experience. He lost all consciousness, and was carried he knew not whither. When at last he awoke and came to himself, he felt new forces throughout his whole being, and immeasurable joy filled him, such as he had never known before. His mind was illuminated with a light from above.

On hearing of this experience the layman said to him: "Thou hast been touched by God with spiritual knowledge, in the very highest part of thy soul, and now," he adds, "thou wilt have the Holy Spirit added to thy knowledge of Scripture, and one of thy sermons will do more good than a hundred of thy former discourses did."

Before leaving him the "Friend of God" told him that henceforth he must live in the Spirit, and not in the letter which kills. Instead of wasting his time in the study of the letter of holy books and writings of great doctors, he should penetrate to the spirit and the wisdom which the books contain. Many of the passages, he says, which formerly seemed obscure and contradictory, will now become clear. "You will discover that all Scripture is one, and now you may commence again to preach and instruct your fellows; henceforth your words will come from a pure vessel, and will be received with joy by all who love the Lord. I shall give you no more instruction. It is now for you to instruct me, and I shall stay until I have heard many of your sermons. As much as you have been scorned, so much you will now be esteemed by those about you. Continue in humility, and do not lose what you have gained."

The master announced that in three days he would preach to the people. A crowd gathered, and he began his sermon, but was overcome with emotion, and found it impossible to speak. The news spread rapidly that the master had failed to meet their expectation, and more than ever he was the laughing-stock of the people, and it was even believed that he had lost his mind. Once again he gained permission to attempt a sermon, and this time he preached with great power on the text, "Behold the Bridegroom cometh, go ye out to meet Him." With extraordinary power he worked out the allegory of the Lord coming to meet His bride. Suddenly one of the listeners cried: "It is true," and fell to the ground in a swoon. When the sermon was over, fully forty persons lay on the floor incapable of movement. From this time to his death, nine years later, "the master" increased in power and reputation. He fearlessly attacked the evils and corruptions of the Church, leaving no class of the clergy untouched by his vigorous criticism, and though the offended monks made a strenuous effort to stop him from preaching, the common people of the city implicitly trusted him and obeyed him, so that he enjoyed almost unlimited influence, and was consulted on all the affairs of Church and city.

This book has for centuries been taken as actual history, and "the master of Holy Scripture" has generally been identified with John Tauler. The identification with Tauler, however, rests wholly on tradition. In his searching critical study of this episode, Denifle first showed what slender historical basis there is for the Tauler tradition.[1] The question has been hotly debated since the appearance of Denifle's investigation, and good scholars like Karl Schmidt and Preger and Jundt continued to stand by the historicity of the *Book of the Master of Holy Scripture*, and to see in it an important chapter in the life of the famous Strasbourg preacher.[2] The historical view has, however, lost ground, and is untenable.

The *Book of the Master of Holy Scripture* is in the main fictitious—a piece of tendency-literature, written to set forth a special religious truth. The central idea embodied in the book is the extraordinary influence of a holy layman when he has been illuminated by the Divine Spirit. He is able to become the infallible counsellor to the greatest preacher in the country, and his instruction is sufficient to bring "the master" from his stage of mere head-knowledge to the stage of first-hand spiritual experience, so that he can rise to a wholly new level of power. It is a telling, concrete illustration of the ruling idea of the Friends of God that a divinely-instructed layman, who has attained the highest stage of mystical experience, "speaks in the place of God," and has an apostolic authority which puts him above any priest or doctor who has only the authority of ordination or of scholarship. For a comprehension of the views of the Friends of God this book is most important, but it must not be treated as furnishing the account of an historical event in the life of Tauler.

[1] Denifle, *Taulers Bekehrung*, Strasbourg, 1879.

[2] See Preger, *Geschichte der deutschen Mystik* (Leipzig, 1893), vol. iii. pp. 116-139. Jundt, *Les Amis de Dieu.*

II

There is a powerful apocalyptic strain in all the literature of the Friends of God. In this particular they show a close affiliation and relationship with the German prophetesses, St. Hildegarde, St. Elizabeth of Schoenau, and St. Matilda of Magdeburg, who were granted "visions" of the corrupt condition of Christianity and of the speedy judgments of God.

"The Church has lost its state of purity," cries St. Hildegarde; "its crown is tarnished by schism and heresy. Its servants, its priests, who ought to make its face shine like the morning and its garment like the light, have by their simony, their avarice, their dissolute morals, covered its face with dirt and soiled and rent its garments. Their wickedness is as habitual as if it were commanded; they enjoy sin as the worm does earth. Deaf and dumb, they no longer hear the Scriptures, and they no longer teach others. All classes of Christianity are corrupt. The Church no longer has any staff to sustain it. All its commandments are ready to disappear; each one takes his own will for rule."

St. Elizabeth of Schoenau speaks with the boldness of a Hebrew prophet:

"Cry with a loud voice! cry to all the nations! Woe, for the whole world is covered with darkness. The vineyard of the Lord has perished; there is no one to cultivate it. The Lord has sent labourers into it, but they have all proved idle. The head of the Church is sick, and its members are dead. Each one wishes to govern himself, and to live according to his own caprice. Very rare are those in the Church who follow the commands of the Lord. But I swear by My right hand and by My throne, says the Eternal One, this condition shall not continue. To all you who are in authority on the earth—kings, princes, bishops, abbots, priests—I order you to purify My Church, otherwise you will be smitten with the sword of My mouth. Miserable hypocrites, you appear religious and innocent in the eyes of men, but inwardly you are full of the spirit of wickedness. Shepherds of My Church, you are asleep, but I will wake you."

In similar strain, Matilda of Magdeburg takes up her prophecy:

"Oh, holy Christianity, glorious crown, how thy splendour has vanished! Thy precious stones are fallen, thy gold is tarnished by impurities. Oh, bride of God, thy face once so pure and chaste is blackened by the fire of guilty passions; on thy lips are lies and hypocrisy; the flowers of thy virtues are faded! Oh, holy clergy, shining crown, how thy glory is dimmed; thy beauty is gone; thy strength is weakened; thy ruin comes on! He who is ignorant of the road to hell has only to watch the debauched and corrupted clergy! The road they follow leads straight into it! Therefore God has decided to humiliate them. His vengeance will break upon them in a day when they do not expect it."[1]

The fallen condition of Christianity is constantly on the lips of the prophets of the movement we are now studying, and they paint its future in very sombre colours. The apocalyptic element is not wild and excessive, but they all announce that the Church is far out of the way, that Christianity is sadly sunk in the ways of the world, and that Divine judgment is fast approaching. As the woes and disturbances of the period increased, especially in the middle decade of the fourteenth century, the sombre tone of apocalyptic prophecy increased in the writings of the Friends of God. They have "revelations" that the evil condition is to go on from bad to worse, until God will be compelled to chastise Christendom with pestilence, earthquake, famine, divisions, wars, and heresies, and that many will lose both body and soul in this time of testing.

In 1356 a catastrophic earthquake, already mentioned, occurred throughout the Rhine valley, with its most disastrous central point at Basle; the city was turned into a heap of ruins, and a terrible fear struck all hearts, the echo of which appears in all the mystical writings of the time. The mystical prophets saw in this awful catastrophe warning signs of the approaching end of the world, and of a reconstruction of the universe.[2] "God," they say, "is about to winnow the whole of Christendom, and those only who bear the seal of God on their foreheads will be preserved through these calamities."[3]

[1] These passages are translated from Jundt, *Rulman Merswin*, pp. 4-6.

[2] The "Black Death," it will be remembered, fell upon Germany in 1347, and returned again in 1358 and in 1363.

[3] These "sealed ones" are evidently the Friends of God.

Through the tribulations of the present age they see signs of the coming of new heavens and new earth, and they declare that out of the "saints of the earth" God will select for blessedness an equal number with that of the fallen angels, so that the population of the new heaven will be the same as the population of the primitive celestial city before there was a fall!

Even Tauler, in the sermons of this period, occasionally speaks in apocalyptic imagery. In one of his sermons he says:

> "It is written in the Apocalypse that calamities, hardly less terrible than the last judgment, will come upon the earth. The time which, according to the prophecy, is to pass before these calamities, is now fulfilled. We expect their appearance every year, every day, every moment, and nobody who is not sealed with the Divine seal can come through them and endure."

The writings ascribed to Rulman Merswin and to "the Friend of God from the Oberland" tell how they, after having passed through terrible suffering and temptations in the various stages of their conversion, are promised that henceforth they will have "*no other trials to pass through, except to see the evil state of Christianity—that will be their cross.*" In the book entitled *Revelation Addressed to the Friend of God from the Oberland during Christmas Night, at the time when great and terrible earthquakes occurred,*[1] the writer sees the end drawing near, and he tells how he experiences in his own body the sufferings which are due for the sins of the Church. He hears Divine Mercy tell Divine Wisdom to forbid the Friends of God to intercede any longer for the wicked world, and thereupon he addresses *a last warning.* As has happened so often before and since, the event miscarried, and the Divine judgment was postponed! But, as new "signs" appeared (desolations of war in 1375; the papal schism in 1378; Christianity divided into hostile camps), again the fatal moment seemed near, and there were new prophecies of

[1] This book contains the famous "Epistle to Christianity"; or "The Lament of a German Layman of the Fourteenth Century on the Decline of Christianity," printed by Karl Schmidt, in his *Nikolaus von Basel.*

impending doom uttered. The Friends of God, under the inspiration of Merswin, again intercede for the world, and as "God could not remain deaf to the prayers of His Friends," a "suspension" of judgment was granted. This extraordinary spiritual drama, with God, on the one hand, holding the doom of the world in His hand, and the Friends of God keeping back the phials of wrath by their prayers, goes on for years, until there comes a final command to pray no more for Christianity.[1]

One of the greatest mystical apocalypses of the middle ages is the *Book of the Nine Rocks*—and it may, I think, be called the greatest literary creation of the Friends of God. It is the best illustration there is of the ideas current among these mystical Christians on the state of Christianity and on the expected "tempest of God," and it is also the best account we have of the "stages" of spiritual experience by which the soul rises to its goal. The book contains a series of "visions" which the author of it *saw* about 1351. He was commanded to write them down. He long resisted the command, saying: "Are there not books enough by great doctors, who can write much better than I can?" and protesting that his book "will carry no conviction, because it is not proved by the Scriptures." The Divine Voice answered: "Without doubt the Scriptures came from the Holy Spirit, but why cannot God still write such a book? Thou art not the first person through whom the waters of Divine Grace have come. Is not the power of God the same as in Scripture times? Whoever does not believe that God can work His wonderful works through His 'Friends' to-day, as He did in the times of the Old and New Testament, *that man is not a Christian, for he does not believe that the Divine power remains the same throughout the centuries.*" "I will obey," cries the author; "thou hast uttered the truth

[1] There is a curious account which relates how, in the year 1379, eight Friends of God from different countries met in a "Divine Diet," on a mountain top, to pray God to postpone His judgment. On the eighth day they were surrounded by darkness, assailed by demons, and heard groans coming from the forest. Suddenly the darkness disappeared, a radiant light broke forth, and an angel stood before them and announced that *judgment was delayed for one year*, but they must not pray for any further postponement, for Christianity must be chastised.

through Caiaphas; speak as thou wilt through me, poor sinner."[1]

The theme of the early part of the book is the terrible decadence of Christianity as compared with the pristine glory of the primitive Church. In a series of stern judgments the various orders of Christianity are passed in review and condemned. For example, here is the "vision" of the state of the papacy:

> "Open thy eyes and see how popes live to-day! All respect for the commandments of religion is extinct in them. They are ambitious for worldly goods; more zealous for their own honour than for that of God; they think only of *places* for their relatives and friends. Once popes chose awful deaths before they would swerve for an instant from the will of God. Now no pope for a long time has been sainted."

After seeing doleful "visions" of the ecclesiastics of the Church from the top down, he is told that "God has now conferred His grace on *other men* [these are, of course, Friends of God], whom He has richly endowed with spiritual gifts. These men are, alas! few in number, but if they wholly disappeared from the world, Christianity would utterly come to an end."[2]

In the second part of the book is described the *vision* of the nine rocks. The writer *sees* an immense net which covers the entire earth, except one mountain in which nine great platforms in ascending stages are cut in rock. These nine platform-ledges rise like the stages of Dante's Purgatory from the level plain, where stands a terrible figure, stretching his net over men and catching them in it. The seer opens his eyes and sees men running away from the net and beginning to climb the mountain. Those on the *first rock* receive the colour of health, and, by sincere confession, are delivered from the mortal sins with which their hearts were stained. But, unfortunately, persons keep falling off this rock back into the net again.

On the *second rock* are those who have made a solid

[1] This resistance against the command to put revelations into writing is almost universal with mystics. It appears in quite similar form in the writings of Hildegarde, Elizabeth of Schoenau, and Matilda of Magdeburg

[2] They thus devoutly believed that they were the true Church.

resolution to give up their own will, and to submit to an illuminated Friend of God, who shall be their guide and counsellor in the place of God. The *third rock* is the abode of those who are practising severe mortifications of the body, and are doing it for the purpose of gaining heaven. They are still in the state of a religion of self-interest. Those on the *fourth rock* are still practising self-mortification, but have the purpose of doing it solely to please and glorify God. Unfortunately, they are still animated by self-will, and have themselves chosen mortification without discovering the Divine will for them. The dwellers on the *fifth rock* have entered upon the sacrifice of their own will, though they have not yet attained to a complete and final *death* to self-will and self-pleasing. Those on the *sixth rock* have completed the sacrifice begun on the rock below. They have burned their bridges, and have entirely abandoned themselves to their Lord. Their only imperfection is that they desire the supernatural revelations which they see others enjoy. Those who have reached the *seventh rock* have got beyond this desire for supernatural revelations, but they take an excessive joy in such revelations when they are granted to them. Those on the *eighth rock* have nearly conquered the enjoyment of anything that concerns self. They have renounced earthly possessions except to use them for God; they have given up counting on heaven. They are ready to accept what God gives them, both in time and in eternity. Their only imperfection is that they have not attained the state where they can have perfect peace, even when God hides His face from them and leaves them no tokens of His grace.

The *ninth rock* is the top of the mountain. The number of the denizens on each rock decreases as the stages go up, until finally on this summit there are only three dwellers to be seen. In them, all personal desire is destroyed. They are crucified to the world, and the world to them. They enjoy whatever God does. They have attained an absolutely disinterested state. They seek no "signs"; they wish for no "manifestations." They have lost all fear. They have arrived at the full stature of a man, and they love all men in God with an equal love. Here on the top is granted the supreme experience, dimly felt sometimes on the lower levels, *the experience of beholding the Divine Origin.* "The man," the voice says, "who beholds the Divine Origin, loses his own name and no longer bears an earthly name. He has now become God by grace, as God is God by nature!"

There comes at last to the writer of the book himself this supreme vision of the Divine Origin, and when the indescribable glory passes he hears a voice saying: "Thou hast been in the upper school where the Holy Spirit teaches directly within the man himself. This august Master of the school has taken thy soul and filled it with such an overflowing love that it has flooded even thy body and transfigured it." "My beloved!" cries the man in a transport of Divine love, "thou hast become so dear to me that with all thy power thou couldst not do anything that would be disagreeable to me. Do toward me whatever thou wilt; whatever thou givest, whatever thou takest away, I shall rejoice in it."

Here we have drawn for us by a leader of the movement the ideal Friend of God.

It has already become apparent that the Friends of God put a heavy stress on *renunciation.* They often pushed it to the extreme of annihilation of will altogether. "The true Christian who wishes to follow the mystical life," says the "Friend of God," in the *Book of the Two Men,* "must renounce all self-pleasure and all self-will; he must destroy all will that aims at anything for self; he must give up all selfish joys and *all self-imposed sufferings.* He must be wholly directed by God, ready to receive from Him with equal submission either pain or joy, temptation or ecstasy, sickness or health."

There is an extraordinary case of a Friend of God who got to the indifference-point to such a degree that he, "through the power of love, became without love," and in this state of perfect surrender, he heard a voice say to him: "Permit Me, My beloved child, to share in thee and with thee all the riches of My divinity;

all the passionate love of My humanity; all the joys of the Holy Spirit," and the "Friend of God" replied: "Yes, Lord, I permit Thee, on condition that Thou alone shalt enjoy it, and not I!"

There is also the case of Ellina of Crevelsheim, called the "Holy child of God," who, in an ecstasy of the marvellous love of God, remains seven years without uttering a word, and at the end of this period God touched her with His hand, so that she fell into an ecstasy which lasted five days, and in this ecstasy the *pure truth* was revealed to her, and she was given the privilege of entering the holy interior of the Father's heart. She was raised to an experience of God and the Supreme Unity; she was bound with the chains of love; enveloped in light; filled with peace and joy; her soul carried above all earthly sufferings; and she attained a complete submission to the will of Christ, whatever it might be.[1]

Throughout this literature the ideal Friend of God endeavours to hide his life, to be anonymous, to efface himself by becoming "a captive of the Lord," "a hidden child of God." There was in this tendency much that was morbid and misdirected. It was often a waste of noble powers, and often a mock humility. The strained introspection of inward spiritual states; the constant analysis of themselves to see whether they had "a disinterested love of God"; whether they were "ready to go through the eternal sufferings and pains of hell for the love of God"; whether they had reached a complete annihilation of will—all this is unhealthy enough, as we now know. But we must judge men in the light of their age, and when we do that we must pronounce these Friends of God the noblest representatives of popular mystical religion in the middle ages. The best of them attained to an *unconscious* holiness, "*shining within like angels of light, without knowing that they were shining.*" "Dost thou not know," says the heavenly voice to one of these Friends of God, "that thy earthly marrow and

[1] Jundt, *Les Amis de Dieu*, p. 59.

blood have been consumed, and that thou hast received a new blood of perfect purity?" "No, I know nothing of it," answers the unconscious saint. "That is precisely it," replied the heavenly voice; "thou hast forgotten it, and it is just this forgetfulness of self that makes the willing, glowing, Divine love come to birth in thee and possess thee!"[1]

Then, when we remember that these men bore their sufferings and strove to annihilate self-will, and even accepted the hiding of all self "as captives of God," in order to be vicarious offerings on behalf of the corrupt Christianity of their time, we find a touch of real sublimity in their saintly lives which does much to atone for their errors of judgment.

Tauler gives this touching incident in one of his sermons:

> "One day the Lord offered to kiss a Friend of God with a kiss of divine love. The Friend replied: 'I do not want to have it, for the joy of it would flood my heart so that I should lose consciousness, and *then I could no longer serve thee*!'"[2]

They succeeded as well as any mystics have done in avoiding the *pitfalls* of perfectionism. They taught, no doubt, that a man may attain even here below to a life with God, may even become through grace what God is by nature, may achieve perfect peace, may come into the very presence of the Divine Origin. Tauler says that "the Divine and heavenly man enters by God's grace even in this present life into life eternal. He already has one foot in Heaven. He lives attached to his Origin, and God can no more abandon him than He can abandon Himself. The heavenly life has begun in such a man, and will go on for ever." But they held that, with all his attainments, it always remains possible for a man to fall away into sin. Until the end he may never intermit his vigils and watchfulness. Tauler says that the evil basis of our human nature is never completely annihilated in this earthly life. To the very end—on the highest

[1] *Book of the Nine Rocks.*

[2] Sermon XXXIV. (Frankfort edition, 1825).

heights of spiritual experience—these Friends of God are examples of humility; they still speak of themselves as "poor sinners"—"poor unworthy creatures." The "Friend of God from the Oberland" teaches his friends these prayers, which are good for all stages and steps of the spiritual ladder:

"In the morning say, 'Oh Lord, I wish, for the love of Thee, to keep from all sin to-day. Help me this day to do all I do to Thy glory and according to Thy dear will, whether my *nature* likes it or not'; and in the evening say, 'Oh Lord, I am a great sinner, a poor and unworthy creature. Be merciful to me and forgive me to-day all my sins, for I repent of them, and sincerely wish by Thy help to commit no more.'"

They do not teach a fixed and final *state* of perfection. There is no "Olympian calm" where progress ends. To *stop* on the "road of perfection" is to *go back*, as one of their wise men says. The "spiritual ladder" in reality has no last round on which the completed saint may sit in moveless felicity! *The Book of the Five Men* urges its readers to expect no gifts of grace from the Holy Spirit if they are living in the "holy inactivity" of absolute quietism.

There can be no question that these Friends of God took themselves very seriously, and thought themselves to be the spiritual "remnant" that was to save Christianity from the utter wreck into which they believed it to be drifting—they were in their own estimation the true Church of God within the visible Church. "If a Friend of God," says the *Book of the Nine Rocks*, "were put at the head of Christianity, he could transform it, because he would have the counsel of the Holy Spirit. If any city in the world would submit to the direction of a holy Friend of God, it would be saved from the woes and plagues that are falling on the world." John Tauler fully shared this view, and in many of his sermons he puts the highest estimate on their spiritual service. Here are a few examples:

"Those whom God has drawn into the unity of the Godhead are the persons on whom the Church rests. They are divine, supernatural men, and they hold up the world and the pillars of it: *If they were not in Christendom it would not last an hour.*"[1]

"Without the help of the Friends of God, God could give no blessing to sinners, for His justice demands satisfaction, and here is precisely the service of the Friends of God—they intercede in favour of Christendom, and their prayer is heard."[2]

"In case of need, these men (the Friends of God) could govern the country, by the help of the Divine gift and the light of eternal wisdom with which their souls are filled."[3]

"Get the Friends of God to help you return into the Divine Origin, where the true light shines. Attach yourself to those who are attached to God—for they can take you with them to Him."[4]

"If it were not for the Friends of God—who are in the world—we should indeed be badly off."[5]

III

I have already referred often to John Tauler, and have frequently quoted from his sermons to illustrate principles and tendencies of the Friends of God. I must now bring together the most important characteristics of his teaching, for he was one of the purest and noblest leaders of this religious movement, and, with all his imperfections, one of the best exponents of spiritual religion in his century. He was undoubtedly regarded by the Friends of God themselves as their greatest man, and he was best loved by the people because his sermons helped them most to find the door of hope and comfort and joy. Tauler "is passing through deep suffering," writes Henry of Nördlingen in 1347, "because he is teaching *the whole truth* as nobody else teaches it, and furthermore his whole life conforms to it."[6]

There is very little to tell of his outward life. He was born in Strasbourg, about 1300. In his early youth he entered a Dominican convent, and after the proper steps of training he was ordained a priest in that Order. He had already come under the powerful influence of Meister Eckhart, and was deeply versed in the writings of

[1] Sermon LXI.
[2] Sermon XXXIV.
[3] Sermon LXIX.
[4] Sermon XLIV.
[5] Sermon XLIII
[6] Jundt, *Les Amis de Dieu*, p. 53.

the great Christian mystics, who were always his most intimate outward guides. In 1338-39 he was in the city of Basle, where he was the central figure of a mystical group of Friends of God. His friend, Henry of Nördlingen, writes that "God is daily working a great and marvellous work, through Tauler, in the hearts of men at Basle."

It is a much-debated question whether Tauler obeyed the interdict, or whether he continued in defiance of it to perform religious services for the people. It has been the delight of Protestant writers to show Tauler as a fearless reformer before the Reformation, defying the Pope, claiming a direct authority from the Holy Spirit, and to represent him as speaking words which have the ring of Luther's spirit in them.[1] There are, however, no *well-authenticated facts* to support this position. It is more than probable that he obeyed the interdict. These words, from one of his sermons, at least do not indicate that he would be likely to lead a revolt from the authority of his Church:

"I received the privilege of belonging to my Order from the grace of God and from the holy Church. It is from both that I have this hat, this coat, my dignity as priest, my right to preach and to hear confession. If the Pope and the holy Church, from whom I have received these privileges, wish to take them from me, I ought to obey them without reply; to put on another coat if I have one; leave the convent; cease to be a priest, and stop preaching and hearing confession. I should have no right to ask the wherefore of such a decision. . . . If the holy Church wishes to deprive us of the external sacrament, we must submit. *But nobody can take from us the privilege of taking the sacrament spiritually* (*Aber geistlich zuo nemende, das mag uns nieman genemmen*), although everything which the Church has given us it can take from us, and we ought to obey without a murmur."[2]

---

[1] There is no historical evidence to establish as genuine the following words, frequently quoted as though spoken by Tauler: "Those who hold the true Christian faith and sin only against the person of the Pope, are no heretics. Those, rather, are real heretics who refuse to repent and forsake their sins; for let a man have been what he may, if he will do so, he cannot be cast out of the Church."

[2] Tauler, Sermon No. LXXI.

If he *did* obey the order of the Pope as a faithful churchman of his time, he rose far above a merely external religion which could be given or taken away at the caprice of a pope, and he found the secret of eternal religion in a direct spiritual intercourse with the Saviour; and, moved with tender sympathy for the common people, he tried to turn them to spiritual religion. The importance of this inwardness and directness of religion comes out again in another sermon, where he says: "Great doctors of Paris read ponderous books and turn over many pages. *The Friends of God read the living Book where everything is life*"[1]; and he tells us that one of the greatest Friends of God he had ever known was a simple day labourer, a cobbler, who had no magic of ordination and no wisdom of scholarship.

I have already discussed the question of the historicity of the narrative which records the conversion and discipline of "the master of Holy Scripture," by "the Friend of God from the Oberland." I am convinced that this cannot be used as material for the life of Tauler. This conclusion takes away a most dramatic incident from his biography, and we are left with very little material indeed with which to draw the figure of the popular preacher of Strasbourg, who did a great work there six hundred years ago. We only know that from 1340, until his death in 1361, he comforted multitudes of souls with as pure an evangel as his century heard, and he showed many devout spirits the inward, secret way to the Father of Light and Love.

Tauler, like all true mystics, insists on the fact of an *inner Light*—the master light of all the soul's seeing. He says that the Friends of God have "an inward, divine knowledge, a Divine Light which illuminates them and raises them into union with God." "God illumines His true Friends," again he says, "and shines within them with power, purity, and truth, so that such men become divine and supernatural persons."[2] Again: "This Light gives man *all truth* (*alle warheit*)—a wonderful discernment, more perfect than can be gained in any other

[1] Sermon LIX. [2] Sermon VII.

manner here below." "These divine men" [the Friends of God], Tauler says in another sermon, "enjoy an enlightened understanding."[1] When they have been disciplined by temptations, they possess the gift of discerning spirits; by merely looking at their neighbour they can tell his inward state; they know whether he belongs to God or not, and what hinders him from spiritual progress.[2] "The vision of the eternal Light makes their souls so luminous that they could teach all men if the occasion for it came."[3] "They become endowed [by this Divine Light] with a perfect conscience in respect to what they ought to do and what leave undone."[4] "They gain [from their inner illumination] an inward peace and joy in the Holy Spirit."[5] "The Divine illumination gives a man a marvellous discernment, more perfect than he is able to acquire on earth in any other manner."[6] In his sermon "On the Feast of St. Mary Magdalene," he says: "In one short hour you can learn more from the inward voice than you could learn from man in a thousand years."

None of these passages indicate that Tauler believed that this illumination belonged to man as man—he is here speaking of the "gifts" which belong to a special class of men, whom he calls "divine and supernatural men."[7] He does, however, sometimes speak in his sermons of "the uncreated ground of the soul"; "the apex of the soul"; "the kingdom of God in the innermost recesses of the spirit"; "the unseen depths of the spirit, where lies the image of God," as though there were something of God in the very structure of the soul, unlost by the fall, or the sin, or the stupidity of man. This is vigorously said in a striking sentence from Tauler: "As a sculptor is said to have exclaimed on seeing a rude block of marble, 'What a godlike beauty thou hidest!' so God looks upon man *in whom His own* image is hidden." But this "Divine soul

[1] Sermon XLVI.
[2] Sermon XLVIII.
[3] Sermon LXXXI.
[4] Sermon LXXXIV.
[5] Sermon LII.
[6] Sermon XV.
[7] In his sermon "On the Conception of Our Lady," he says: "There is nothing so near the inmost heart as God. He who will seek there shall find Him. Thus, every day we find Him in the Blessed Sacrament and *in all the Friends of God.*"

centre" does not become an operative power, *a dynamic possession*, until "the outward man is converted into this inward, reasonable [intelligible] man, and the two are gathered up into the very centre of the man's being—the unseen depths of his spirit, where the image of God dwelleth—and thus he flings himself into the Divine Abyss in which he dwelt eternally before he was created; then when God finds the man thus solidly grounded and turned towards Him, the Godhead bends and nakedly descends into the depths of the pure, waiting soul, drawing it up into the uncreated essence, so that the spirit becomes one with Him."[1]

He is much less speculative than his master, Eckhart. In the language of simple experience he tells his listeners that "there is nothing so near the inmost heart of man as God," but he can also on occasion use the language of speculation, and talk with his great mystical teacher of "the Hidden God"—"the calm waste of the Godhead"; "the necessity of withdrawing into the bosom of the Divine Dark." There are passages in his sermons where, by the road of negation, he takes us up to the same empty abstraction which we have so often found in speculative mysticism.

> "God is," he says in his *Third Instruction*, "a pure Being [that is, a Being with no attributes], a waste of calm seclusion—as Isaiah says, He is a hidden God—He is much nearer than anything is to itself in the depth of the heart, but He is hidden from all our senses. He is far above every outward thing and every thought, and is found only *where thou hidest thyself in the secret place of thy heart*, in the quiet solitude where no word is spoken, where is neither creature nor image nor fancy. This is the quiet Desert of the Godhead, the Divine Darkness—dark from His own surpassing brightness, as the shining of the sun is darkness to weak eyes, for in the presence of its brightness our eyes are like the eyes of the swallow in the bright sunlight—this Abyss is our salvation!"

In harmony with this conception of a God *above* all attributes and distinctions, he makes much of the *negative*

[1] Tauler's "Sermon for the Fifteenth Sunday after Trinity," Hutton's *The Inner Way, being Tauler's Sermons for Festivals.*

road to Him, *i.e.* the way of self-dying and renunciation. There are three stages of self-dying.[1]

The first stage is found in those who practise acts of self-denial through fear of hell and for the hope of heaven. At this "half-way stage" they believe that what is painful to the flesh is highly prized by God. The person at this stage is self-centred, unloving, harsh in judgment; what he does is from constraint of fear rather than from love.

The second stage of self-death is found in the person who endures insult, contempt, and such-like depths; who learns in humility and patience to pass through spiritual destitution, and to be bereft even of the gracious sense of the Divine Presence. These "barren seasons" are for discipline to bring the man by inward poverty to a dissatisfaction with himself and to carry him to a state where he shall cease to be occupied with himself. The third stage is one of perfect union of the human will with the Divine will—entire resignation and perfect denial of self and self-love. All delight in having one's own will is overmastered and quenched, because the Holy Spirit has supplanted the man's will and love, and he wills nothing on his own account—though he cannot fathom the Abyss of God, he feels perfect joy in the *experience of God.*

In another sermon,[2] Tauler says that those who wish to be Friends of God *must rid themselves of all that pertains to the "creature"*; must especially free themselves from all that is called "necessary"; must avoid being blinded by "transitory things," and look alone to the source and Origin. "Divine Love can brook no rival," therefore all unnecessary conversation, all outward delight in human beings, all images external and internal that merely please the natural man, must be cut off so that God can work His work freely—even external works of love may blind us and prevent us from perceiving the Divine Voice. "We shall never find God anywhere so perfectly, so fruitfully, and so truly as in retirement and in the wilderness." In a beautiful sermon on the temple

[1] See Sermon IV., "On the Feast of St. Stephen," *The Inner Way.*
[2] Sermon XV., "On the Feast of St. Mary Magdalene," *The Inner Way.*

within man,[1] he points out that as man is meant to be a temple—"a clean, pure house of prayer"—he must first drive out all "traders," *i.e.* all human fancies and imaginations; all delight in the creature and all self-willing thoughts of pleasure, aims at self-gratification, ideas of temporal things. These are the "traders" that keep God out of His house.

But Tauler does not stop with negations, and he does not make the attainment of a state of "barren wilderness" his spiritual terminus. In this same sermon he goes on to say that after the inner mind has become "free of traders," there must come a *positive devotion* of spirit, an inner *consecration* of self toward the attainment of union and communion of the man with God; and finally there comes the experience—again a positive experience—that the soul in its inmost deeps actually is a temple where God eternally reveals "His Father Heart" and begets His Son, "a temple where is the true, pure presence of God, in whom all things live and move, and where all suffering is done away!" But even this life in the inner temple is not wholly an end in itself. We cannot expect a devout Catholic of the fourteenth century to enter fully into the spirit of service, which is the very breath of our best modern Christianity, but Tauler often rises to an insight which carries him far beyond contemplation and joy in inward states, however exalted. "Works of love," he says, "are more acceptable than contemplation"; "spiritual enjoyments are the food of the soul, but they are to be taken only for nourishment and support *to help us in our active work*"; "sloth often makes men eager to get free from work and set to contemplation, but *no virtue is to be trusted until it has been put into practice.*"[2] One of the finest passages in his sermons—in fact, one of the finest words that any mystic has given us—is the well-known and often-quoted passage, which has the true note of social service:

[1] Sermon XXXVI., "Second Sermon at the Dedication of a Church," *The Inner Way.*

[2] Those three passages are taken from Inge, *Christian Mysticism*, p. 188.

"One man can spin, another can make shoes, and *all these are gifts of the Holy Ghost.* I tell you, if I were not a priest, I should esteem it a great gift that I was able to make shoes, and I would try to make them so well as to be a pattern to all."

The most important feature of Tauler's teaching—a feature which allies him with all the great prophets of the soul—is his constant insistence on *a religion of experience.* There are long passages in his sermons which are too scholastic to be of any permanent value; there are other passages which are too much bound up with the conceptions of the medieval Church to touch our lives to-day; there are still other passages—even whole sermons—which are commonplace and devoid of inspiration, but again and again the reader finds in the writings of this pre-Reformation prophet words which are laden with a living message, good for all men, and quick and powerful for any century. "The man who truly experiences the pure presence of God in his own soul," he tells his "dear children,"[1] "knows well that there can be no doubt about it"—by "devout prayer and the uplifting of the mind to God" there is "an entrance into union of the created spirit with the uncreated Spirit of God," so that all the human is "poured forth into God and becomes *one spirit* with Him." But this knowledge is not something to be learned from "the Masters of Paris"; it can come only through *experience* of "entering in and dwelling in the Inner Kingdom of God, where pure truth and the sweetness of God are found." "What this is and how it comes to pass is easier to experience than to describe. *All that I have said of it is as poor and unlike it as a point of a needle is to the heavens above us!*"

IV

The other member of this spiritual society whom I shall consider in this chapter is Henry Suso, for I shall postpone the treatment of John Ruysbroek to the next chapter. Suso was plainly a disciple of the great mystic,

[1] Sermon XXXVI., "Second Sermon at the Dedication of a Church."

Eckhart. In one of the most important spiritual crises of his life he went to Eckhart for comfort, and he tells us that the latter "set him free from a hell which he had long been enduring." He also refers to Eckhart with deep veneration, and, though utterly different from him in temperament and in style, he holds the same fundamental conceptions as his master.

He has all the characteristic marks of the other well-known "Friends of God." He is subject to spiritual visions; he passes through great soul-crises; he practises austerities; he experiences ecstasies, and he is profoundly conscious of the immediate presence of God.

He was born about 1300, of a noble Swabian family. The influences of his home were of a very mixed sort. His father was "full of the world," unconcerned about things of the Spirit, and through this unconcern he caused Suso's mother much suffering. The mother was a woman "full of God, and one who would fain live in a godly manner." She was deeply concerned to bring her boy into this "godly manner of life." [1]

While he was still a boy at school in Cologne, his mother died, but at the hour of death she appeared to him, bade him love God, told him that though gone from the world she was not really dead; she then "kissed him on the mouth, blessed him, and vanished." This is the first of Suso's recorded psychic experiences, and it is interesting as indicating his peculiar constitution and temperament.

At the age of thirteen he entered the Dominican monastery at Constance, where he spent five years in study. Through this period he frequently experienced "spiritual visions," though he had not yet gone through a "conversion-experience." At about the age of eighteen he underwent a great spiritual awakening—a time of marked crisis, and under what he calls "the direct Divine work upon his soul," he experienced his "commencement." He says that "the hidden drawing of God turned him

[1] The data for Suso's life and experiences are found in his autobiography, *The Life of the Blessed Henry Suso*, by himself.

away from *creatures* and called him to the inward hidden life." "I turned wholly from *things*."

In this period, like the great mystic of the Commonwealth, George Fox, he went through a period of extreme loneliness, when he tried, all in vain, through human friendship and earthly love, "to lighten his spirit." The more he endeavoured to lighten his heart, the sadder he grew. In this condition of inward loneliness and of spiritual suffering, he was the recipient of many marvellous visions, and "whether in the body or out of the body," he often had "the powers of his soul filled with the sweet taste of heaven."

I give his account of one of these ecstatic experiences:

"He was alone after his midday meal, undergoing a severe suffering. Of a sudden he saw and heard what no tongue can express. What he saw was without definite form or shape, and yet had in itself the beauty of all forms and all shapes. It was at once the climax of his desires and the realisation of his hopes, in a forgetfulness of everything and of self in a blessed state. He felt the sweetness of eternal life in calm and silence. This experience lasted an hour or less, and when he came to himself again he felt that he had come back from another world, and he was still full of divine joy, and felt himself as light as if he were soaring in the air."

In this early stage of his experience, in order to help him turn away wholly from "creatures," he decided to mark out for himself, in thought, three circles, within which he shut himself up as in "a spiritual entrenchment."

"The first circle was his cell, his chapel, and the choir. When he was within this circle he seemed to himself in complete security. The second circle was the whole monastery, as far as the outer gate. The third and outermost circle was the gate itself, and here it was necessary for him to stand well upon his guard. When he went outside these circles it seemed to him that he was in the plight of some wild animal which is outside its hole and surrounded by the hunt, and therefore in need of all its cunning and watchfulness." [1]

[1] *Life of the Blessed Henry Suso*, by himself, translated by T. F. Knox, London, 1865, p. 168.

He came into a dangerously morbid condition, and began the practice of such awful austerities, that his case stands almost in a class by itself in mystical literature.[1]

He gives two reasons for the practice of these austerities:

(1) That "he might conquer the lively nature of his youth"!

(2) His great love for Jesus Christ, Whose suffering he wished to imitate.

The following passage, describing his self-tortures, is taken from his Autobiography, which is written in the third person:—

"He was in his youth of a temperament full of fire and life, and when this began to make itself felt, it was very grievous to him, and he sought in many devices how he might bring his body into subjection. He wore for a long time a hair shirt and an iron chain, until the blood ran from him, so that he was obliged to leave them off. He secretly caused an under-garment to be made for him, and in the under-garment he had strips of leather fixed, into which a hundred and fifty brass nails, pointed and filed sharp, were driven, and the points of the nails were always turned towards the flesh. He had this garment made very tight, and so arranged to go round him and fasten in front, in order that it might fit closer to his body, and the pointed nails might be driven into his flesh; and it was high enough to reach upwards to his navel. In this he used to sleep at night.

Now in summer, when it was hot, and he was very tired and ill from his journeyings, or when he held the office of lecturer, he would sometimes, as he lay thus in bonds, and oppressed with toil, and tormented also by noxious insects, cry aloud and give way to fretfulness, and twist round and round in agony, as a worm does when run through with a pointed needle. It often seemed to him as if he were lying upon an ant-hill, from the torture caused by the insects; for if he wished to sleep, or when he had fallen asleep, they vied with one another. Sometimes he cried to Almighty God in the fulness of his heart: Alas! Gentle God, what a dying is this! When a man is killed

[1] This extraordinary practice of asceticism is baffling to the ordinary healthy person who revels in the joy of living, but there must be in asceticism a powerful psychological effect which accounts for the great rôle it has played in man's spiritual history. It was felt by the mystic, no doubt, to minister toward the supreme end in view, namely beatific vision, and there almost certainly came to those who practised asceticism states of intoxication, or swoon, in which there was a sense of the fulness of life.

by murderers or strong beasts of prey it is soon over; but I lie dying here under the cruel insects, and yet cannot die. The nights in winter were never so long, nor was the summer so hot, as to make him leave off this exercise. On the contrary, he devised something further—two leathern hoops into which he put his hands, and fastened one on each side of his throat, and made the fastenings so secure that even if his cell had been on fire about him, he could not have helped himself. This he continued until his hands and arms had become almost tremulous with the strain, and then he devised something else: two leather gloves, and he caused a brazier to fit them all over with sharp-pointed brass tacks, and he used to put them on at night, in order that if he should try while asleep to throw off the hair under-garment, or relieve himself from the gnawings of the vile insects, the tacks might then stick into his body. And so it came to pass. If ever he sought to help himself with his hands in his sleep, he drove the sharp tacks into his breast, and tore himself, so that his flesh festered. When, after many weeks, the wounds had healed, he tore himself again and made fresh wounds.

He continued this tormenting exercise for about sixteen years. At the end of this time, when his blood was now chilled and the fire of his temperament destroyed, there appeared to him in a vision on Whit-Sunday, a messenger from heaven, who told him that God required this of him no longer. Whereupon he discontinued it, and threw all these things away into a running stream."

Unfortunately, he had not yet learned his lesson, and he next tells how, to emulate the sorrows of his crucified Lord, he made himself a cross with thirty protruding iron needles and nails. This he bore on his back between his shoulders day and night.

"The first time that he stretched out this cross upon his back his tender frame was struck with terror at it, and he blunted the sharp nails slightly against a stone. But soon, repenting of this womanly cowardice, he pointed them all again with a file, and placed once more the cross upon him. It made his back, where the bones are, bloody and seared. Whenever he sat down or stood up, it was as if a hedgehog skin were on him. If any one touched him unawares, or pushed against his clothes, it tore him."

Suso next tells of his penitences by means of striking this cross and forcing the nails deeper into the flesh, and likewise of his self-scourgings—a dreadful story—and then goes on as follows :—

"At this same period, the Servitor[1] procured an old cast-away door, and he used to lie upon it at night without any bedclothes to make him comfortable, except that he took off his shoes and wrapped a thick cloak round him. He thus secured for himself a most miserable bed; for hard pea-stalks lay in humps under his head, the cross with the sharp nails stuck into his back, his arms were locked fast in bonds, the horse-hair under-garment was round his loins, and the cloak, too, was heavy and the door hard. Thus he lay in wretchedness, afraid to stir, just like a log, and he would send up many a sigh to God.

In winter he suffered very much from the frost. If he stretched out his feet they lay bare on the floor and froze; if he gathered them up the blood became all on fire in his legs, and this was great pain. His feet were full of sores, his legs dropsical, his knees bloody and seared, his loins covered with scars from the horsehair, his body wasted, his mouth parched with intense thirst, and his hands tremulous from weakness. Amid these torments he spent his nights and days; and he endured them all out of the greatness of the love which he bore in his heart to the Divine and Eternal Wisdom, our Lord Jesus Christ, whose agonising sufferings he sought to imitate. After a time he gave up this penitential exercise of the door, and instead of it he took up his abode in a very small cell, and used the bench, which was so narrow and short that he could not stretch himself upon it, as his bed. In this hole, or upon the door, he lay at night in his usual bonds, for about eight years. It was also his custom, during the space of twenty-five years, provided he was staying in the convent, never to go after compline in winter into any warm room, or to the convent stove to warm himself, no matter how cold it might be, unless he was obliged to do so for other reasons. Throughout all these years he never took a bath, either a water or a sweating bath; and this he did in order to mortify his comfort-seeking body. He practised during a long time such rigid poverty that he would neither receive nor touch a penny, either with leave or without it. For a considerable time he strove to attain such a high degree of purity that he would neither scratch nor touch any part of his body, save only his hands and feet." At length "God made him sure that the time was come when he might be released from these sufferings."[2]

---

[1] He calls himself "the Servitor" of "Eternal Wisdom."

[2] *The Life of the Blessed Henry Suso*, pp. 56-80, abridged.

He was subject, not only during this long period of austerities, but throughout his life, to "visions." His world was no longer this world of sense-objects, it was a world beyond time and space—a world of celestial denizens, angels, saints, the Virgin, with their scenery and circumstance. He saw the scenes of this other world as vividly, and with as much sense of their objectivity, as we see the things of space and time. He was a person of extraordinary visualizing power, and could actually see anything which he had heard described. His "other world sights" were plainly formed out of "suggestion-material," and they came to him often when he was exhausted by the chastisements of his body, and when the control and guidance of the will were weak, so that they correspond to the vivid flights of the mind in the borderland state between sleeping and waking.

In one of these visions he was granted a sight of "how God dwells in the soul."

> "He was told to look into himself, and there he saw as through a crystal in the midst of his heart the Eternal Wisdom in lovely form, and beside Him his own soul leaning lovingly to God's side, and embraced in His arms and pressed to His Divine heart, and lying entranced and drowned in the arms of the God he loved."

One of his most striking visions was the one granted to him at another spiritual crisis in his life, when he gave himself in spiritual espousal to Eternal Wisdom as his heavenly bride.

> "It happened to him often," he tells us, "as when a mother has her sucking child pressed in her arms lying on her bosom, and the child lifts itself with its head and with the movement of its body towards its tender mother, and by its lovely bearing shows forth its joy of heart, so often did his heart within his body, turning towards the presence of the Eternal Wisdom, overflow with tenderness."

Once the Virgin granted him the privilege of *holding the Holy Child.*

> "He contemplated its beautiful little eyes, he kissed its tender little mouth, and gazed again and again at the infant members

of the heavenly treasure. Then, lifting up his eyes, he uttered a cry of amazement that He who bears up the heavens is so small, so beautiful in heaven, and so childlike on earth! "

We get another vivid picture of his power of visual imagination when he tells us that "the food which he did not like he dipped in the wounded heart of his Beloved," and then ate it with joy. And in a beautiful poetical passage, which seems like Walt Whitman baptized with spiritual fervour, he tells us how he sees the whole world praising God:

"I set before the eyes of my soul myself, all that I am, with body, soul, and all my powers, and set around me all creatures which God ever created in heaven, in earth, and in all the elements, each with its name, were it birds of the air, beasts of the forest, fish of the waters, leaf and grass of the earth, and all the unnumbered sand of the sea, and therewith all the little motes which shine in the sunbeam, and all the little drops of water, of dew, and snow, and rain, which ever fell or have fallen, and wished that each of them had a sweet instrument of music made ready out of my heart's innermost chords, and thus forth-sounding from first to last, should bring to the beloved, tender God new and glorious praise."

After years of self-inflicted pain, and experiences which one would have thought would have shattered his sanity, he came upon the discovery that what he had been enduring had been prompted by his own reason; that thus far he had been only "in the lower school," and that he was still far from "the highest knowledge."

At this stage he experienced, as did most of the other mystics of his group, a time of deep inward testing. He passed through the desolation of feeling utterly forsaken by God. "It seemed to him that his soul would never be saved, but would be eternally damned, whatever he might do or suffer"; and at the same time he found himself separated from his closest friends, misunderstood and falsely accused, charged with heresy, taken for a charlatan, and called "a fool always gaping towards heaven."

During these hard years—altogether nine years—"with crying heart and weeping eyes" he passed through dark perplexities over questions of faith, but he came through into the light and *found* the God he sought.

As a relief to this morbid occupation with his own troubled spirit, there is a touching story of the way he rescued his sister, a nun, who had fallen into mortal sin, and had run away from the convent. When Suso heard of her sin, straight he became "like a stone for sorrow, and his heart died," and the resolve rose up in him to "spring after her into the deep pit and lift her out." After a long, desperate search, being himself half-dead from a fall into the river, he hit upon the little hut where his sister was hiding. He fell fainting and helpless on the bench at her side, clasped her in his arms, and cried: "Alas! my sister, what have I endured for thee!" and fainted. "Then his sister rose and fell at his feet with great bitter tears, and said mournfully: 'Ah, Lord and Father, what a sad day was that which brought me into the world, for I have lost God and have given to thee such pain.'" At length he had the great joy of seeing his sister restored and "brought back in his own arms to the kind God."

Not only in this touching incident, but in all his teaching, he insists on the value of practical love, and, though he is excessively concerned with his own inward states, and lays down the maxim: "Live as if there were no creature in the world but thyself," he shares with Eckhart, and his other fellow-mystics, in the *practice* of love in the ordinary duties of life.

The ultimate reality for Suso, as for Eckhart, is "the eternal, uncreated truth." "Here in this eternal, uncreated truth," he says, "all things have their Source and Eternal Beginning." "Here the devout man has his beginning and his end." Whatever flows out from this *Source*, the Godhead, can turn back again into its Source, and so come to reality and to bliss, and even while he is living on the earth "a man may be in eternity."

There is "an image of God in the soul" which can rise to the Divine Essence, or Source, and which, "unhindered by the clouds and veils of created things, may contemplate, in silent darkness, in absolute repose, the marvels of Divinity." Suso pushes quite too far his "silent darkness and absolute repose," and though his religious *instincts* carry him out into a life of loving and unselfish service, his *speculations* too often carry him into barren wildernesses where "something and nothing are the same." His account of "union with God" outdoes even Eckhart, and may be taken as the extreme doctrine of ultimate Divine and human *oneness*. This highest state of union, he teaches, is an indescribable experience in which all idea of images and forms and differences has vanished. All consciousness of self and of all things has gone, and the soul is plunged into the abyss of the Godhead, and the spirit has become one with God, as in the experience of Paul when he said: "I live, yet no longer I; it is Christ that liveth in me." In this highest state God becomes the inner essence, the life and activity within, so that whatever the person does, it does as an *instrument*.

> "Like a being," he says, "which loses itself in an indescribable intoxication, the [human] spirit ceases to be itself, divests itself of itself, passes into God, and becomes wholly one with Him, as a drop of water mingled with a cask of wine. As the drop of water loses its identity, and takes on the taste and colour of the wine, so it is with those who are in full possession of bliss; human desires influence them no longer; divested of self they are absorbed in the Divine Will, mingle with the Divine Nature, and become one with it."[1]

Poor soul! was it to gain such annihilation of identity and personality that he suffered the terrible tortures of those sixteen years? was it for this he wore the crucifix with its lacerating nails in his flesh? We must not, however, make too much of his over-emphasis of a line of teaching, and of pathological experiences, which had by this time become second nature in all mystical circles. The spirit of kindly love, the passion for the redemption

[1] As an orthodox Christian, Suso tries to save himself from the logical outcome of this complete absorption. He says that there is no temporal moment when the identification of the human with the Divine is *complete*. The personal *I* is never destroyed, though, while the theopathic state lasts, there is no personal consciousness of it. This theopathic state is set forth in his *Book of the Truth*.

of sinners, the utter loss of selfish interest, the sweet consciousness of Divine love, and the complete obedience of will to the heavenly leading which mark this Friend of God, must cover for us the blindness and error which were mainly due to his intellectual environment and to the subtle influences of suggestion.

V

The literary gem of this religious movement is a little book which bears the name *Theologica Germanica.* It lacks the robustness of *The Nine Rocks*, but its beauty of style and its depth of inner experience give it the right to be entered among the classic books of mystical literature. Inge goes so far in praise of it as to say that "in some ways it is superior to the famous treatise of à Kempis on the *Imitation of Christ.*" It was put by Luther in the highest company: "Next to the Bible and St. Augustine," he says, "no book hath ever come into my hands from which I have learned more of what God and Christ and man and all things are!"

Its author is unknown, for the very reason that he strictly practised what he taught—namely, the hiding of the "creature," that no glory might accrue to him who held the pen. The unknown author's great prayer: "I would fain be to the Eternal Goodness what his own hand is to a man"[1]—is beautifully fulfilled in this book. The passive writer "lent his hand" to the Eternal Goodness, and he had no concern to sign his human name at the end of his book. The preface, which appears in the earliest extant MS., says:[2]

> "This little book hath the Almighty and Eternal God spoken by the mouth of a wise, understanding, faithful, righteous man, *His Friend*, who aforetime was of the Teutonic Order, a priest and a warden in the house of the Teutonic Order in Frankfort; and it giveth much precious insight into divine truth, and

[1] The quotations will be made from Susanna Winkworth's translation, London, 1874. This quotation is from p. 30.

[2] This MS. was found in the library of Wurzburg University in 1850. It dates from 1497. It has been published verbatim by Pfeiffer.

especially teacheth how and whereby we may discern the true and upright *Friends of God* from those unrighteous and false free-thinkers, who are most hurtful to the holy Church."

The writer is plainly influenced by Eckhart, and shows the "family characteristics" of the Friends of God. He quotes from Tauler, and he holds much the same ideas which appear and reappear in Tauler's sermons.

The fundamental conception of the writer is the view, made familiar enough in these studies, that the finite, the temporal—everything which can be called "the creature," everything which can be conceived as severed from the wholeness of God—must be transcended before the soul can come upon Divine Reality. The supreme error, therefore, in the mind of this unknown mystic is having a will which aims at getting some particular thing for self. "So long," he says, "as a man taketh account of *anything which is this or that*, whether it be himself or any other creature; or doeth anything; or frameth a purpose for the sake of his own likings, or desires, or opinions, or ends; he cometh not unto the life of Christ."[1] "So long as a man seeketh his own will and his own highest good, because it is *his* and for his own sake, he will never find it. For so long as he doeth this, he is seeking himself and dreameth that he is himself the highest Good. But whoever seeketh, loveth, and pursueth Goodness (*i.e.* the Good *per se*), and for the sake of Goodness, and maketh *that* his end, for nothing but the love of Goodness: not for the love of I, me, mine, self, and the like, he will find the highest Good, for he seeketh it aright."[2] The very mark and brand of the "natural man," as distinguished from "the divine and spiritual man," is found here in the *aim of the will*: "To the creature—the self according to Nature—it belongeth to be somewhat—to be this or that —*and not simply what is good without any wherefore*!" But "he who is made a partaker of the Divine nature neither willeth nor desireth nor seeketh anything save Goodness as Goodness for the sake of Goodness."[3] Nay, more, in this *aim of the will* is manifested the very "secret"

[1] P. 61. [2] P. 168. [3] P. 135.

of heaven and hell: "No thing burneth in hell but self-will [the aim at some particular thing for self], and therefore it hath been said, put off thine own will and there will be no hell!"[1] "Were there no self-will there would be no ownership, and in heaven there is no ownership. If any one in heaven took upon himself to call anything his own, he would straightway be thrust out into hell. If there were any person in hell who should get quit of his self-will, and call nothing his own, he would come out of hell into heaven."[2] Again: "If there were no self-will there would be no devil and no hell; and by self-will we mean willing otherwise than as the One and Eternal Will of God willeth."[3] He tells us over and over what he means by the way in which "the One and Eternal Will of God willeth": "With God there is no willing, nor working, nor desiring"; "It is the property of God to be without *this* and *that*, without self and me."[4] The result of this view is a corresponding emphasis on renunciation, self-abandonment, and annihilation of will. God cannot come in until the man goes out: "Whenever a man forsaketh and cometh out of himself, then God entereth."[5] It is a view which is gloriously true in one aspect, and pitiably false in another aspect. In the negative aspect in which our unknown mystic uses it, it leads to emptiness and quietism. Its goal is a person who wills nothing—which is a blank contradiction, for the central feature of personality is will-activity. A being "taking no account of anything which is this or that," a being that "neither willeth nor worketh nor desireth," is not a person—in fact, is in the very lowest scale of life, not in the highest. The root of the difficulty lies in the false conception, common to all medieval speculation, that the One, the Perfect, is a Being without attributes or distinction. As our author puts it: "To God, as Godhead, appertains neither will, nor knowledge, nor manifestation, *nor anything that we can name, or say, or conceive.*" He is an Infinite beyond all that is finite, an Absolute beyond all that is relative, a Perfect beyond all that is imperfect, an abstract Being

[1] P. 115. [2] Pp. 192-93. [3] P. 180. [4] Pp. 77 and 90. [5] P. 78.

beyond all that is concrete and particular; and therefore to rise to Him and become joined to Him involves the negating of everything that is "this" or "that"; in short, the annihilation of will to the extent that "something and nothing have become alike."[1]

The time was not yet ripe, when our author lived and wrote, for the truer, positive view of immanence, the view which finds the Infinite in the finite, the Absolute in the relative, the Perfect in the imperfect, the Universal in the particular; and so, too, the time was not ripe for the truer view of self-surrender, the view that all genuine self-surrender is the affirmation of a higher self, that all genuine self-sacrifice is consecration to the realization of a wider self. There must be annihilation of aims that end in the isolated self, "the I, me, and mine," but that does not mean annihilation of will, or the destruction of desire—it only means that desire is to be heightened by a vision of service to God and man, and that our will is to become consecrated to the tasks which God is working out in the world of which we are a part. But to the end, however far one may travel on the path of holiness, the aim must be *concrete*, and it must be motived by a concrete motive, for a desireless, will-less man can be called neither good nor bad. A person is not good until his own will wills the good deed, because he sees that it is good, and chooses to put his life into it.

Some hints of this *affirmative* spirituality appear here and there in this little book, and even where the fundamental *conception* of it seems to us wrong, there is a constant feeling that the writer's *heart is right*. He did his *thinking*, as we all do, in the terms and ideas of his time, but he attained a religious mood, a spiritual attitude, which has a timeless aspect about it. What noble words these are:

> "A true lover of God loveth Him alike in having or in not having, in sweetness or in bitterness, in good report or in evil report. And therefore he standeth alike unshaken in all things, at all seasons."[2]

---

[1] P. 173.

[2] P. 32.

And where can one find a finer note of positive consecration to service than in those words already quoted? "I would fain be to the Eternal Goodness what his own hand is to a man." His words on the union of the human and Divine are well balanced, and are as favourable to a practical life as to a life of quietism:

"God and man should be wholly united, so that it can be said of a truth that God and man are one. This cometh to pass on this wise: where the truth always reigneth, so that true perfect God and true perfect man are at one, and man so giveth place to God, that God Himself is there, and this same unity worketh continually, and doeth or leaveth undone, without any I or me or mine—behold *there* is Christ, and nowhere else."

His view of Christ's suffering over sin is very modern, and has no mark of the traditional or dogmatic temper. It shows how penetrating a spirit he was, and how profoundly he was influenced by *experience.* Wherever God reveals Himself personally—or to use the author's own words, "wherever God is made man or dwelleth in a truly godlike man"—He always reveals His sorrow over sin. Christ is the supreme instance of the Perfect God flowing forth into a person and bringing forth His Son in a person. As a man rises in the spiritual scale and partakes of God he grows more sensitive to sin, and his sorrow over it increases; and this sorrow over sin comes from the fact that God is in the man, for it is the nature of God Himself to grieve over sin, and such grief is always a sign of God's presence. This is the cause of that unutterable anguish and grief of Christ, who is God made man in fullest measure. *He* has shown to us that sin is so hateful to God and grieves Him so sore that He would willingly suffer agony and death, if even one man's sins might be washed out thereby; and wherever God finds this grief for sin, He loveth and esteemeth it more than aught else.[1]

Like all the other members of this group, our author

[1] See especially chap. xxxvii. It is interesting in this connection to note that the author's great *test* of an act or an attitude is whether such act or attitude would be *seemly* for God if He were made man (pp. 196-97).

makes much of first-hand experience, and much less of "knowledge-about." He says:

> "Although it be good and profitable that we should ask and learn and know what good and holy men have wrought and suffered, and how God hath dealt with them, and what He hath done in and through them, *yet it is a thousand times better that we should in ourselves learn and perceive and understand who we are, how and what our life is, what God is and is doing in us, what He will have from us, and to what ends He will or will not use us*."[1]

In another fine passage he asks "in what Blessedness lieth," and he answers that it is not in anything whatever *outside us*—"not in any works or wonders that God hath wrought, or ever shall work, so far as these things exist or are done outside." "*These things can make me blessed only in so far as they exist or are done and loved, known, tasted, and felt within me*."[2] In this connection it is interesting to note that this Friend of God in the fourteenth century used the term "Light" almost precisely as the Friends of the seventeenth century did. There is, he says, a true Light within the soul which gives us our sense of sin; it leads us to frame and build our lives after His life. In a single golden sentence he says: "The true Light is God's seed, and it bringeth forth the fruits of God."[3] There are two persons who have no sense of sin—Christ and Satan, and the sense of sin in a man decreases as he moves up or down toward either of these divergent goals. Those who are losing their sense of sin by following the Light toward Christ have always this sign and seal, that they are "inflamed and consumed with love": "The Light is worth nothing without love"; "to be a partaker of the Divine Nature, that is, to be a God-like man, means to be illuminated by the Divine Light, and to be inflamed and consumed with Divine Love."[4]

In spite of his dread of being tangled in the finite and temporal, and his tendency to reduce all that is seen to

[1] P. 26.
[2] Pp. 28-29.
[3] This is iterated and re-iterated throughout the writings of Isaac Penington (*Works*, London, 1681).
[4] See especially chapters xl. and xli.

zero in order to exalt the unseen and eternal to infinity, he nevertheless calls the world that now is "an outer court of the Eternal," and he says that temporal things "manifest and remind us of God," so that things which are made—"creatures"—are "a guide and a path unto God and Eternity."[1] And the supreme thing about an earthly life is that it can become a revealing place for God:

> "Thanks be unto the man, and everlasting reward and blessing, who is fit and ready to be a tabernacle of the Eternal Goodness and Godhead, wherein God may exert His power and will, and work without hindrance."[2]

It remains to point out that our author, like the other members of his group, has "a spiritual ladder" for the soul's upward path. His ladder has three stages, each of which has three sub-stages. The first upward step of the soul is "Purification." The first degree of Purification is (*a*) sorrow for sin; the second (*b*), full confession of sin; and the third is (*c*) hearty amendment of life. The second stage of the soul is "Enlightenment," with its three degrees of advance: (*a*) Eschewal of sin, (*b*) practice of virtue and good works, and (*c*) endurance of trial and temptation. The third stage is "Union," which ends upward in the perfect life. Its three degrees are (*a*) pureness and singleness of heart, (*b*) love, and (*c*) contemplation of God.[3] But at every *stage* on the spiritual ladder, the soul that is progressing toward the Light and Love and Vision of God "must live by God as the body liveth by the soul."[4]

[1] P. 181. [2] P. 57. [3] See chap. xiv. [4] P. 211.

CHAPTER XIV

THE BRETHREN OF THE COMMON LIFE

THE mysticism of all these societies and groups in the fourteenth century, which we have so far studied, was weakened by its heavy load of scholastic speculation. There was at the heart of it a deep, sincere craving for God, its exponents were trying to utter the unstilled hunger of the soul; but it was always at the mercy of prevailing intellectual currents, which swept it now into the dangers of an unmoral, or even immoral, pantheism, and now into a *via negativa*, ending in a blind alley of Quietism. It was always too subtle for the common people, too far removed from the warm pulses of actual human life. It was, furthermore, too much absorbed in the introspection of inward states, in the cataloguing of stages of "experience," to become a social gospel, a spiritualizing power for the age. The times called loudly for a religion of experience, an intimate life with God, but at the same time for a religion more simple, practical, social—in a word, more Christlike, than any of these spiritual movements. The New Learning was already working its noiseless revolution. Unsuspected transformations were commencing to remould the mind of Europe, and with the new intellectual dawning there also began to spread, unconsciously and without observation, *a new mysticism*, born out of the old, but more practical and social than it; more eager to minister to the whole man, and with wider interest in the entire spiritual mission of Christianity.

The visible Church was sick with an astonishing complication of diseases, which none of its doctors, "greedy for quick returns of profit," could cure. Its spiritual power had waned; its hierarchy was honeycombed with corruption; its oracles were dumb; it had no word of authority for the sin-burdened multitude that "looked up and were not fed." The great Church that had conquered the Empire and led captive the barbarian conquerors, and had turned the tribes of Gaul and Germany and Britain into men of faith, was sinking into a temporal corporation for dispensing wealth and patronage and power. But in the dark days at the end of the fourteenth century even its temporal power and prestige, which had been slowly built up by the cunning statesmanship of popes, was crumbling. The seventy years of "Babylonish Captivity" had put a deep stain on the glory of the official Church, had weakened its world-authority, had brought to light its insincerity, and had been a terrible witness to its corruption and rottenness. But the "great schism" that followed the return to Rome wrought still greater havoc. The unity of Christendom was shattered. There was no longer any pretence of a single spiritual head to the official Church. Each country followed its own interests in deciding which papal head to acknowledge; and the mystic order, the seamless robe, was rent in twain—and finally into three parts.

"The body of Christianity," writes Gerson, at the end of the fourteenth century, "is covered with sores from head to foot. Everything is rushing from bad to worse, and every one must take his part in the sum of evils." There was no hope of a spiritual regeneration from the official Church. It was busy bartering and trafficking in the temple, busy with world politics and temporal schemes. Even when the rent in the mystic order was patched up at Constance, the next concern was to burn the man who was most keenly diagnosing the moral and spiritual diseases from which the Church was suffering. If *the religion of Christ* was to be revived in power and supplant the caricature of it, the age had to produce prophets of the invisible Church—voices of the Eternal Christ to cry in the ears of men—who could exhibit in powerful fashion new and compelling ideals of spiritual religion.

Such prophets, in fact, did appear, and helped to turn the battle from defeat to victory. The work of the mystics of the thirteenth and fourteenth centuries was not lost. Their teaching burned in the hearts of the high-minded men and women who heard them; their books and sermons were like torches passed on by dying hands to living successors, and the dark period of schism and spiritual incapacity in the visible Church was relieved by the appearance of many worthy representatives of that invisible Church which never dies, which must always be reckoned with by official hierarchies and traditional systems, and which is still the hope and promise of that kingdom of God for which Christ lived and died.

The "new mysticism" of the late fourteenth and early fifteenth centuries was more emancipated from scholasticism than the mystics of the early fourteenth century had been. The influence of Dionysius and Erigena was weakening, and the influence of Christ and of the primitive ideals was growing. There was still an air of the recluse about it, a smell of the cloister was upon it, and the old tendency to be over-occupied in the cultivation of inward states was not conquered, but there appeared now a new passion for service, a consecration, not so much to the attainment of the "Divine Origin" for the individual as a consecration to the task of building the spiritual Zion, the invisible Church for humanity. The great mystics of this period at the turning of the century were concerned to revitalise Christianity, and to restore the Church to its apostolic power, not by miracle and cataclysm, but by a positive *imitation of Christ*, by the cultivation of brotherhood, by the religious education of little children, and by most strenuous efforts to heal the diseases of the Church and to bring its official guides to the Light of Christ. These champions of inward religion were confined to no locality and to no one nation. Nearly every Christian country had its leader, or leaders, of this new mysticism, which was forcing the attention of the most serious minds at the very time when the New Learning was beginning to attract the interest of little groups of men in widely-sundered centres. France had her Gerson; Italy her Catharine of Siena; Sweden her Bridget; England her Walter Hilton and Lady Julian; Holland was the home of a great mystical brotherhood—the successor of the Friends of God—"the New Devotion" or "Brethren of the Common Life," out of which came the most influential piece of mystical literature the world has seen—*The Imitation of Christ.*

I

Catharine's life covers the years from 1347 to 1380.[1] She was a charming, joyous child, but given to visions, and filled with longing to imitate the desert hermits, even at the age of six. Already at this childish age she had her first ecstasy, and became so absorbed with the vision of Christ that her little brother had to pull her by the hand to bring her back to earth, and she took the vow of virginity when she was seven! At fourteen she put on the black and white garb of St. Dominic, and became a Dominican tertiary. When her father endeavoured to compel her to marry, and deprived her of solitary contemplation to force her into the worldly life, "the Holy Ghost taught her how to make for herself a solitude in her heart, where amid all her occupations she could be as though alone with God, to whose Presence she kept herself no less attentive than if she had no exterior employment to distract her."

In 1370 she underwent a mystical death and returned to life under the Divine command to go abroad to save souls and to minister to the needy world. She experienced, she tells us, "the sweetness of serving God, not for her own joy; and of serving her neighbour, not for her own will or profit, but from pure love."[2] And this love of hers, burning with intense desire, was kindled in her

[1] She was the youngest of the twenty-five children of Jacopo Benincasa, of Siena.

[2] See *Letters of St. Catharine of Siena*, by Vida D. Scudder, 1905, p. 63.

heart by a clear perception of the love of God as the supreme reality of the universe, which breaks out in that great sentence of hers: "For nails would not have held the God-man fast to the cross had not love held Him there."[1]

The corruptions of the Church and the evils of the times oppressed her with a weight heavy almost as death, and brought her under a severe mental strain and an intense passion for Christ. In an extraordinary ecstasy she experienced an espousal to Christ, and she felt herself to be ever after the espoused bride of the King of Heaven, pledged "to do manfully and without hesitation" whatever she might be called to do. Even more extraordinary was a later ecstasy, in which, like St. Francis, she experienced the imprint of the five wounds of Christ—the *stigmata.* She felt a torrent of blood and fire poured out upon herself, and was conscious of a mystical cleansing wrought by this torrent, so that she was "changed into another person." In the ardour of this experience she prayed for a sign, and suddenly felt her outstretched palm pierced through by an invisible nail. The final imprint of the stigmata came somewhat later. Her own description of this experience is as follows:—

> "I saw the crucified Lord coming down to me in a great light. . . . Then from the marks of His most sacred wounds I saw five blood-red rays coming down upon me, which were directed towards the hands and feet and heart of my body. Wherefore, perceiving the mystery, I straightway exclaimed, 'Ah! Lord, my God, I beseech Thee, let not the marks appear outwardly on the body.' Then, while I was speaking, before the rays reached me, they changed their blood-red colour to splendour, and in the semblance of pure light they came to the five places of my body, that is, to the hands, the feet, and the heart. So great is the pain that I endure sensibly in all those five places, but especially within my heart, that unless the Lord works a new miracle, it seems not possible to me that the life of my body can stay with such agony."[2]

By a later experience the "new miracle" was granted,

[1] *Letters of St. Catharine of Siena*, p. 8.
[2] Gardner's *St. Catharine of Siena*, p. 134.

so that the wounds not only ceased to afflict the body, but even fortified it.[1]

The next year, after these experiences (1376), she threw herself into the task of restoring the spiritual power of the Church. She had poor material at hand with which to build a kingdom of God in those years, but one feels a sense of awe as he sees this woman, girt about with no forces but the invisible might of God, going to work to bring the head of the Church back to Rome and to his ancient dignity. She finds abject superstition in the court of Avignon; vacillation and cowardice in the heart of her Pope, but she rises to a full sense of her spiritual mission, and speaks with the authority of one inwardly conscious of a Divine commission.

> "When I told you that you should toil for Holy Church," she wrote to the Papal Legate, "I was not thinking only of the labours you should assume about temporal things, but chiefly that you and the Holy Father ought to toil and do what you can to get rid of the wolfish shepherds who care for nothing but eating and fine palaces and big horses. Oh me, that which Christ won upon the wood of the Cross is spent with harlots! I beg that if you were to die for it, you tell the Holy Father to put an end to such iniquities. And when the time comes to make priests or cardinals, let them not be chosen through flatteries or moneys or simony; but beg him, as far as you can, that he notice well if virtue and a good and holy fame are found in the men."[2]

That has the ring of the prophet, but it is only the prelude. The same year she writes to the Pope himself, Gregory XI. With the licence of a little child, she calls him "sweetest 'Babbo' mine!" but she tells him the plain facts that the "blind shepherd-physicians" are leading the Church straight into the ditch; and rising to the very limit of daring, she says:

> "I hope by the goodness of God, venerable father mine, that you will quench this perverse and perilous self-love in yourself, and will not love yourself for yourself, nor your neighbour for yourself, *nor God*; but will love Him because He is highest and

[1] There are few pieces of autobiographical description which better show the power of auto-suggestion than this.

[2] *Letters*, p. 115.

Eternal Goodness, and worthy of being loved; and yourself and your neighbour you will love to the honour and the glory of the Sweet Name of Jesus. I will, then, that you be so true and good a shepherd that if you had a hundred thousand lives you would be ready to give them all for the honour of God and the salvation of men. . . . Let no more note be given to friends or relatives or to one's temporal needs, but only to virtue and the exaltation of things spiritual. *For temporal things are failing you from no other cause than from your neglect of the spiritual.*" . . . "I wish and pray that the moment of time that remains [for you] be dealt with manfully, following Christ, whose vicar you are, like a strong man."[1]

Again, writing to Gregory as his "unworthy daughter Catharine, servant and slave of the servants of Jesus Christ, in His precious blood," she urges that

"Holy Church *should return to her first condition*, poor, humble, and meek, as she was in that holy time when men took note of nothing but the honour of God and the salvation of souls, caring for spiritual things, not for temporal. For ever since the Church has aimed more at temporal than at spiritual things it has gone from bad to worse."[2]

There is something sublime in a message such as the following from the daughter of a dyer of Siena to the sovereign Pontiff of the world :—

"The sick man is blind, for he knows not his own need; and the pastor, who is the physician, is blind, for he considers nothing save his own pleasure and advantage, and, in order not to lose that, does not employ the knife of justice or the fire of most ardent charity. *Such a one is truly an hireling shepherd* . . . and does not follow sweet Jesus, the true Shepherd, who has given His life for the sheep. Oh, Babbo mine, sweet Christ on earth, follow that sweet Gregory [Gregory the Great], for *it will be as possible for you to quench self-love as it was for him.*"[3]

Finally, she went in person to Avignon, and, as the messenger of Christ, persuaded the wavering Pope to return to Rome, triumphed over all obstacles, and induced him to "fulfil what he had promised God."[4] Another

[1] *Letters*, p. 131. [2] *Ibid.* pp. 119-21. [3] Gardner, p. 154.

[4] There is an account, undoubtedly fictitious, in the *Book of the Five Men*, attributed to "The Friend of God from the Oberland," of how he received an order from God

trait in this great woman, no less wonderful than her statesmanlike grasp and her penetrating insight into public affairs, was her power of seeing the hidden possibilities within the persons who came in contact with her, a certain creative power which all the greatest mystics show. She tells in one of her letters how one in close unity with God can help bring a friend, a fellow-man to his full possibility:

"Nay, there grows within one a love made of great and true compassion, and with desire he brings his friend to the birth, with tears and sighs and continual prayers in the sweet presence of God. . . . There is no spirit of criticism in it nor displeasure because it loves the friend not for himself, but for God."[1]

Her later life was devoted in the same fearless strain to the discouraging task of rousing spiritual passion in the hearts of officials who were immersed in material concerns. Her noble life admirably illustrates her lofty confession: "*I would rather exert myself for Christ crucified, feeling pain, gloom, and inward conflict, than not exert myself and feel repose.*"[2] She knew in her own experience of having entered "that sea of peace where thou shalt never have any fear of being separated from God."[3] She gave her testimony to the fact that the soul "bears ever within it the place where God lives by grace—the house of our soul wherein holy desire prays constantly,"[4] and, in words of lofty spiritual import, she wrote: "I desire to see you seek God in truth, *without anything between.*"[5]

II

It was a saint and mystic, Catharine, who was the chief instrument in bringing the "Babylonish Captivity" of the Church to an end; so, too, it was a mystic and politician,

to go to the Pope, Gregory XI., upon his return to Rome, to warn him of the woes which were coming, and to call upon him in the name of the Holy Spirit to reform the Church. At first the Pope was angry at the freedom with which he, a layman, spoke of the sins of the Pope and of Christendom, but as he saw the proofs of the layman's divine mission, the Pope promised to obey him in everything. St. Bridget of Sweden had already, in 1366, under a Divine intimation, paid a visit to Avignon, to urge Pope Urban V. to return to Rome.

[1] *Letters*, p. 250. [2] *Ibid.* p. 160. [3] *Ibid.* p. 96.
[4] *Ibid.* p. 151. [5] *Ibid.* p. 89.

Jean le Charlier de Gerson (1363-1429), who was the chief instrument in ending the "great schism." He won for himself the title "Most Christian Doctor," he held the foremost scholastic position in Europe, Chancellor of the University of Paris, and he was the controlling power in the great Council of Constance. It was the deepest purpose of his life to build up again the invisible Church within the visible, but he was a politician, a reconciler—a man who was ready to put unity above truth, and the result was that in doing much good he also did some evil, and that while toiling with valiant spirit to realize the kingdom of Christ, he also furnished some material for the kingdom of Anti-Christ. With a boldness and frankness which reminds one of Catharine speaking to her "sweet Babbo," Gerson in a powerful sermon in 1405 told the King of France the pitiable condition of his people, robbed by princes and plundered by soldiers, and called him to his duty to relieve the sufferings of these people, and to give them their rights as men. A still greater service he rendered to the people by teaching in person the children of the poor, declaring that they were the children of God, inheritors of the kingdom of heaven, and that it was as great an honour to teach them as to teach princes. In behalf of these little children he powerfully attacked the superstitions which were fed to them in place of truth, and to train their innocent spirits he wrote an *A B C for Little People*, telling them about the Divine Father and His holy will. Higher than his title of "Most Christian Doctor" was the other title he gained, "Doctor of the people and Doctor of little children."[1]

His mysticism is worked out in a series of very dry books, which show much more subtilty than originality and more learning than personal experience. He was the stern foe of any mysticism which leaned toward pantheism or which ended in a Divine Dark, but he was not very successful at the task of blazing the way to a positive mysticism which could ground the active life in an inner consciousness of God. His psychological studies

[1] See De Montmorency, *Thomas à Kempis*, p. 22.

of mystical processes are formal and scholastic rather than genuine analyses of experience itself, and have little value to-day. The main point of interest is his conclusion, in his *Mystica Theologia*,[1] that the soul has an intuitive faculty above the reasoning faculty—a *synderesis* or power of mind, for receiving truth immediately from God; that all genuine mystical exercises are exercises of *love* rather than of *thought*; that it is in contemplation of Divine Love that the soul experiences its love-union with God, and so finds its own true activities, and that only a few souls attain the mystical experience, since it is a rare grace or achievement, and most men stop at lower levels.

It was, however, significant that the foremost scholar of the time was looking for God within the soul rather than above the dome of the sky or in the bread and wine of the altar, and it meant much for such a man to point out that God and man discover their oneness through love. His good and his evil work at the Council of Constance cannot be told here. He cured the schism by formulating the great principle that Councils are above popes, and can unmake and make them. He stood by the mystical movement in Holland, and saved "the Brothers of the Common Life" from their ecclesiastical enemies; but he, though in intention a member of the Invisible Church, helped to destroy its noblest living stone by consenting to and even urging the death of John Hus.

Forced into exile at the very height of his glory, because he dared in the Council to stand for righteousness in a cause which called upon him the hate of the Duke of Burgundy, he ended his public service as he began it—teaching little children. The world may forget the mystic commentary on the Song of Songs which he wrote in his years of exile at Lyons, but it cannot well forget the beautiful picture of this great scholar, unifier of the Church, and mystic, surrounded by a band of poor children listening to his words of life, and crowding around, as he lay dying, to pray for "our dear father, Jean Gerson."

[1] *Doctrina Johannis Gersoni de Theologia Mystica*, Paris, 1838.

III

But this chapter must be mainly devoted to the quiet work for the realization of the invisible Church performed in the mystical groups of "the Brethren of the Common Life"—a movement often called by its own members the "New Devotion," which gives us the ripest fruit of mysticism before the Reformation. The actual founder and spiritual guide of the movement was Gerard Groote, at the same time the bearer of a new evangelism, a new education, and a new mysticism. But Gerard owed so much to his spiritual father, John Ruysbroek, the Flemish mystic, that I shall introduce him here as a vital part of "the New Devotion." Ruysbroek is the link that joins the two movements—the Friends of God and the Brothers of the Common Life—together, and the spirit of both groups is found in him. He was the intimate friend, on the one hand, of Tauler and Suso, and, on the other, of Gerard and his companions.

He was born, probably of German parents, in the year 1293, in the little village of Ruysbroek, on the Senne, between Brussels and Hal, and now his "village name" is the only name for him we know. He was not, like his friends Tauler and Groote, a scholar. "He had," says Denis the Carthusian, "no teacher but the Holy Ghost. He was ignorant and illiterate. Peter and John were the same. His authority I believe to be that of a man to whom the Holy Ghost has revealed secrets." With considerable exaggeration his great admirer, Maeterlink, comments thus on his ignorance and astonishing wisdom:

> "This monk possessed one of the wisest, most exact, and most subtle philosophic brains which have ever existed (!). He lived in his hut at Grönendal (Green Valley), in the midst of the forest of Soignes. He knew no Greek, and perhaps no Latin. He was alone and poor; and yet in the depths of this obscure forest of Brabant his mind, ignorant and simple as it was, receives all unconsciously dazzling sunbeams from all the lonely, mysterious peaks of human thought. He knows, though he is unaware of it, the Platonism of Greece, the Sufism of Persia, the Brahmanism of India, and the Buddhism of Tibet; and his marvellous

ignorance rediscovers the wisdom of buried centuries, and foresees the knowledge of centuries yet unborn."[1]

He at least knew Latin enough to receive priest's orders, which he took in his twenty-fourth year, and became vicar of the Church of St. Gudule, in Brussels. He performed the duties of his priesthood with zeal and fidelity until his sixtieth year, when he retired with a little band of companions to the monastery of Grönendal, where in the solitude of the forest he devoted himself to meditation and to the composition of his mystical books. He devoutly believed that he was the recipient of immediate revelation, and he told Gerard Groote that he was firmly convinced that he had not written a word except under the impulse of the Holy Spirit. He wrote in the tongue of his own people, but he travelled so far up "within the polar circle of the mind" that it is desperately hard to follow him, and, as Maeterlink says, his words and phrases are but "poor double horn-panes," through which the light of his mind comes to us. His reputation for saintliness spread widely abroad, and drew many visitors to his retreat—some seriously seeking the wise man's counsel, and some coming to satisfy their curiosity. Among the many legends which his fame and holiness inspired there is one which ought to be true, whether it actually is or not. Some priests from Paris presented themselves to him one day, desiring to consult him on the state of their souls, but his only answer was, "You are as holy as you desire to be." They were naturally nettled and annoyed at such an answer, for they missed its profound meaning. "My very dear children," continued the spiritual counsellor, "I said that your holiness was that which you desired it to be; in other words, it is in proportion to your goodwill. Enter into yourselves, examine your goodwill, and you will have the measure of your state."[2]

One touches in those words the very *secret* of mysticism, that in the inward life itself, not in outside props, lies the

[1] Maeterlink, *Ruysbroek and the Mystics*, translated by Jane T. Stoddart, London, 1894, p. 12.

[2] Bailie, *Reflections from the Mirror of a Mystic*, London, 1905, p. 13.

man's salvation and power. The legend writers miss just this *secret* when, to glorify him, they tell how once Ruysbroek was lost in the forest, and the brethren sought in all directions for him. At length one of his most intimate friends saw a distant tree wrapped in light, and, when he drew near, he found it enveloped in flames, while under it sat the master in an ecstasy of meditation! He died at a ripe old age in 1381.

It is a primary principle of his teaching that "the soul finds God in its own depths": "God suffices for all, and every spirit, according to the measure of its love, has a manner more or less profound of seeking God in its own depths."[1] The deepest root and very essence of the soul in every man is *the eternal image of God* there—there without any agency of our own, there before our personal creation, and there for ever. In the *mirror of the Son* God sees, and we too may see, the types or patterns of all reality; and the way to find ourselves and God and all that Is, is to stretch forth our arms toward the Divine pattern which is ours: "Flying from brightness to brightness, the spirit aspires with outstretched arms to reach this immortal pattern according to which it was created."

The "spiritual ladder," by which the created spirit climbs up "that mountain without summit," has, according to Ruysbroek, three steps or stages. The first stage is the *active life*. This is a stage of religion which consists of outward acts, such as abstinence from things harmful, deeds of penance, acts of self-denial, the performance of virtuous deeds—in short, the living of a morally good life, in accordance with the laws and commandments of God. To look upon outwardly, this life appears to conform to its pattern; the thing, however, which spoils it, and puts the trail of imperfection on all its deeds, is its *intention*. It is a stage of self-love and self-concern. The soul does what it does for reward and gain. It is moved by fear of hell or desire for the joys of heaven. It is a religion of legalism, and those who are in this stage can be called by no higher name than "Servants of God."

[1] Bailie, *op. cit.* pp. 22 and 23.

The second stage is the *Inward Life*. Deeds of goodness and outward acts are not left behind as the soul comes up to this higher level. The ascent is rather marked by change of *intention*. What is done now is done from sheer love. The heart, by love, has come into a oneness of purpose with God, so that its deeds are no longer from calculation and outward constraint; they are the natural fruit of the transformed soul, which burns with pure love and devotion. The soul surpasses in aspiration all that it does or can do. In a beautiful passage Ruysbroek says:

"The pure soul feels a constant fire of love, which desires above all things to be one with God, and the more the soul obeys the attraction of God the more it feels it, and the more it feels it the more it desires to be one with God."[1]

Again he says:

"We follow the splendour of God on toward the source from which it flows, and there we feel that our spirits are stripped of all things and bathed beyond all thought of rising in the pure and infinite ocean of love. This *immersion in love* becomes the habit of our being, and so takes place while we sleep and while we wake, whether we know it or whether we know it not. . . . It is simply an eternal going forth out of ourselves into a transformed state."[2]

And in his *Ladder of Love* he reiterates the rapturous cry:

"Love the love which loves you everlastingly—for the more you love the more you desire to love," and "when we spirits hold fast by love, He by His Spirit remakes us, then joy is ours. The Spirit of God breathes us out toward love and good works, and it breathes us into rest and joy; and that is eternal life, just as in our mortal life we breathe out the air which is in us and breathe in fresh air."

Perhaps we can get a sense of the selflessness and spontaneity of this stage of the *inward life* best of all from the personal testimony of Ruysbroek: "Lord, I am Thine, and I should be Thine as gladly in hell as in

[1] From *The Book of the Sparkling Stone*. In the following passages from Ruysbroek, I have used Jane T. Stoddart's translation.

[2] *Ibid.*

heaven, if in that way I could advance Thy glory!" and this attainment he tells us is wrought "when Christ the Eternal Sun rises in our hearts and sends His light and fire into our wills, and draws the heart from the multitude of 'things,' and creates unity and close fellowship, and makes the heart grow and become green through inward love, and bear flowers of loving devotion."[1] Those who come upon this level of the spiritual life are called no longer Servants, but "Friends of God."

But there is still a third stage—*the contemplative life*—to which only a few attain, and which is an experience for pinnacle moments rather than a plateau where the soul normally tabernacles. "Those," he says, "who have raised themselves into the absolute purity of their spirit by love stand in God's presence with open and unveiled faces," and then, "by the Light and Splendour which radiate from God they behold the very substance of God above reason and beyond distinction." In other words, it is a kind of knowledge, or rather of *seeing*, in which there are no modes or distinctions. There is no power of description, because what is seen is above all *this*, or *that*. In Ruysbroek's own words:

> "It is as when you stand in the dazzling radiance of the sun, and turning away your eyes from all colour, from attending to distinguishing all the various 'things' which the sun illuminates, you simply follow with your eyes the brightness of the rays, and so are led up into the sun's very essence."[2]

In this sublime experience—of seeing God—the human spirit becomes what it sees, is one with the very light by which it beholds the object of its vision. In the beautiful words of our mystic: "What we are, that we behold; and what we behold, that we are; for in this pure vision we are one life and one spirit with God."[3] In this experience, when the soul is burning and consumed in the fire of love, "God possesses us and we Him in unity, and we enjoy God and rest in blessedness." Those

[1] From *The Book of the Adornment of Spiritual Marriage.*

[2] From *The Book on True Contemplation.*

[3] From *The Book of the Sparkling Stone.*

who come to this round of the ladder are more than Friends of God, they are Sons of God.

But it must be noted that Ruysbroek never taught the *fusion* of the self in God. On the highest height of the ascent the soul never loses its identity—the creature is to the end creature, and God is God. The union is one of likeness in love and in spirit, not oneness of being. When we live wholly in God, then for the first time we live wholly in ourselves. "In this," he says, "consists the nobility of our nature, now and everlastingly, that it is impossible for us to *become God* and lose our created essence," but "overwhelmed in love we are one with God."[1]

One who read only the passages on the contemplative life would doubtless conclude that the "ecstatic doctor" of Grönendal, like many others of the mystic order, was too far removed from actual human life, was straining after a spiritual vacuum, or at least that his words are "double horn-panes" to our intelligence, but I believe that, taken in the whole of his life and message, he is one of the rarest souls in the goodly fellowship of mystical teachers. One comes away from a study of him feeling a sort of reverent awe at being so long in the company of a man who had "entirely enveloped and saturated the kingdom of his soul" in love. He was certainly a pillar in the Invisible Church of God, and by the contagion of his life he built many other souls into the same kingdom to which he belonged. In words that burn across the five centuries that intervene he pictures the rottenness and corruption of the visible Church—"priests and doctors live such a life that they are incapable of receiving divine wisdom." Prelates and even popes "seek their own honour, and live for the world"—but his own peculiar service was his life-long exhibition of the presence of God in the holy temple of a human soul. Nor was he a mere recluse withdrawing from actual life to indulge in the luxury of beatific vision. He says, with fine balance—and his life was behind the words—that "the act of life must drive

[1] *Book of the Sparkling Stone.*

man outwardly to practise virtue; the act of death must drive him into God, in the depth of his own being. These are the two movements of the perfect life, united as matter and form, as soul and body."[1] He has little patience with those who sit idly, "with introverted eyes," waiting for a formless vision. The thing which most impressed Gerard Groote at the time of his visit to Ruysbroek was the *practical* side of his life. It seemed to him that the religious life of the little society at Grönendal, of which Ruysbroek was the central figure, realized the idea of a true brotherhood upon the highest Christian principles. A genuine family spirit reigned among the brethren which put them all on the same social level. Ruysbroek himself, though prior, performed the lowliest tasks, while the humblest servants, down to John the cook, were treated as friends, and were taken into counsel on spiritual affairs of high moment.[2]

IV

I shall turn now to his most famous disciple—using the word disciple in a somewhat loose sense—Gerard Groote, called by one of the brothers,[3] "the first father of our Reformation," and "founder of all our modern devotion." Gerard was born at Deventer, the chief city of Overyssel, about sixty miles from Amsterdam, in 1340. He was the son of wealthy and distinguished parents, who planned a great career for him. He was sent to the University of Paris at the age of fifteen, and in three years received the degree of Master. His keen, well-equipped mind and his prominent family connections promised him a brilliant future, though, as Thomas à Kempis, his loving

[1] Bailie, *op. cit.* p. 32.

[2] The account of the visit is given in Thomas à Kempis's *Vita Gerardi*. Neale, in his *Jansenist Church in Holland*, p. 68, says: "What his influence (that is Ruysbroek's) must have been is gathered from the tone taken at once by all his scholars—that intense love to God, that overwhelming devotion to the Passion, which characterized the mystic school of Holland from Ruysbroek himself to De Neercassel."

[3] This was John Buschius, a contemporary of Thomas à Kempis. He wrote the *Chronicles of Windesheim*, which with Thomas à Kempis's *Vita Gerardi* are the main sources of information on the early history of "The Brethren of the Common Life" (*Chronicon Canonicorum Regularium Ordinis S. Augustini, Capituli Windesemensis*, Antwerp, 1621).

biographer, says: "He was not yet seeking the glory of Christ, but in the broad ways of the world was following the shadow of a great name." He obtained a professorship in Cologne, was the recipient of important ecclesiastical positions, lived in the public eye, and had the admiration of a distinguished circle in the University and in the Church. He was apparently satisfied with a comfortable place in the visible Church, where all his worldly tastes were met, and where he "dabbled in magic and astrology." But, unexpectedly to himself, by a series of events, he was slowly prepared for a place in the invisible Church.

The first incident which turned his mind inward occurred while he was watching a public game in Cologne. A stranger, with a devout face, an unnamed "Friend of God," clothed in very simple garb, sad at seeing Gerard wasting his rare powers of mind and spirit, came softly to his side and said: "Why standest thou here?—thou oughtst to become *another man*."[1] The stranger remains unknown to us, but he belonged also to God's invisible Church, and was building better than he knew, when he followed his inner impulse on that day at the game. At the moment the effect of the word dropped into Gerard's mind seemed slight, but it went on working. Some time after he fell dangerously ill, and was brought face to face with the deeper issues of life and death. This illness marked a distinct turning-point, but his definite devotion to spiritual religion was, humanly speaking, brought about through the personal influence of his old Paris friend, his teacher in the University days, Henry de Kalkar, a devout Carthusian, who had become prior of a monastery not far away from Deventer, and who came to visit Gerard for the definite purpose of calling his young friend to a new life. Human instrumentality was used to help him find the path, but Gerard himself always attributed the great change in his life to the direct work of the Divine Spirit. Thomas à Kempis reports Gerard's cry of joy:

[1] This phrase is twice used by Thomas à Kempis.

"Oh the power and grace of the ineffable Spirit, who can so easily change the heart of a man whom he inwardly visits and illumines! This is the mighty power of God alone. He has turned the lion into a lamb, predestinating him who was before in the world to be incorporated into Himself."

After a period of retirement and preparation, he set out to preach the Gospel as a lay-evangelist. The "preparation" which he underwent was mainly preparation of heart; communion with the spirits past and present who could interpret the devout life to him, among whom the influence of Ruysbroek was greatest. "I never loved or honoured any mortal man so warmly," he wrote to the brothers at Grönendal. His university studies had carried him into the practice of magic, and had overtrained him in subtilties which led to nothing; and with his entrance upon the new devotion he revolted from the higher learning of his time, and became henceforth the advocate of a more simple but, at the same time, more practical culture, a culture which aimed primarily at the development of a good life; while his observation of the priesthood of his day inclined him to prefer the life and service of a layman, and to the end of his days he refused to be ordained.[1]

In 1379, with a spirit aflame and with an anointing from on high, Gerard went forth, like George Fox in the English Commonwealth, like Wesley in the spiritual drought of the eighteenth century, to preach to the people and to call them to a religion of following Christ.[2] He was granted a permit by the Bishop of Utrecht to preach anywhere within that diocese. He was dressed in the utmost simplicity, and in every way he showed his nearness to the people and his sympathy with them. His gospel, like his garb, was very simple. Scholastic subtilties seemed to him stones instead of bread. Ruys-

[1] His refusal to be ordained came partly at least from the fact that his ideal of a genuine priest seemed unattainable in the world as it then was.

[2] "He was seen, as of old Peter de Bruys and Henry of Lausanne, as afterward St. Norbert, and as in still more recent times George Fox, William Penn, and others, in mean attire, travelling through towns and villages, and everywhere exhorting the people to repentance and amendment of life, with overpowering eloquence" (Ullmann, *Reformers before the Reformation*, vol. ii. p. 64).

broek had taught him to rise above appeal to rewards and punishments. He broke completely with the traditions of the time, and his message formed the strongest contrast to the puerilities of the mendicant monks. The central note in his preaching was the love of God, the Divine search, the great salvation, the possibilities of life with God. He possessed a powerful eloquence, though the secret even of his eloquence was simplicity, directness. It was intensity of spirit, absolute conviction; as Thomas à Kempis well noted, it was the powerful appeal of personal *experience*. He preached out of his own life—what *he knew*. Another secret of his power was the novelty of preaching in the popular dialect. The Latin droned in church had no more dynamic effect than a "dead wire"; Gerard's words were quick and powerful, with a live faith and a burning passion for souls.

Then, too, it was an element of the first importance that he took no pay. Every vestige of selfishness was removed. Here was a preacher who came to the people for the sole reason that he loved them, who had none of the marks of a "professional" about him, and whose life rang true to every test.[1] He was like the later Reformers and the Evangelists of the Protestant era in that he turned back to the Scriptures for his material, and to the Gospels for his model. He thoroughly understood men, and one of the old chroniclers has taken pains to tell us that Gerard had a way of taking in his audience with a quick survey of eye, in which he read their mood and their needs, and which enabled him "to speak to their condition." His message was decidedly a *new Evangelism*, and it worked powerfully. The people flocked to hear as they had not done since the days of the great preacher of Assisi. Whole towns left their occupations and came to listen to Gerard's message. Every class and rank of society yielded to his spell, even meals were neglected! Where the local church was too small for the multitude the meetings were held in the open, frequently in the

[1] Thomas à Kempis has preserved an epitaph on Gerard, which runs thus: "He did what he said, and what he taught *that* he also lived."

churchyard, and the sermon sometimes lasted two or three hours. But more important than enthusiasm and neglect of meals was the moral and spiritual amendment of life wrought by the preaching. It set men and women to living on a new moral level. They gave up vanities and vulgar pursuits, and began to live in more Christlike fashion. Men who had been living in sin and wickedness turned straight about in spirit and in practice. Gerard had a way of diagnosing the diseases of the visible Church—he drew the picture of apostolic holiness and zeal, and over against it he set the actual conditions which all the hearers saw day by day, and he asked his listeners to "look on this picture and then on that, the counterfeit presentment." Many of the clergy were brought to shame and conviction by his preaching, and dedicated themselves to a holy life and a pure service. With good right his admiring biographer cries out: "Blessed be God who raised up such a preacher among us and gave us such preaching, that through it the light of the heavenly life might shine upon us in this uncertain world!"

But it is serious business in any age to let "the light of the heavenly life shine upon this uncertain world." There are always Golgothas for genuine light-bringers, and Gerard soon found that the representatives of the visible order, living at their ease under the old system, would not tolerate a new revealer of the living Christ.

There was little hope of easy paths for a man in the fourteenth century who dared to say these words:

> "The decadence of the Church is visible in everything. The ruin of the whole body of the Church has been a long time threatened. What do I say? It is already falling in ruins. We suffer especially in the head—the Pope; for following the doctrine of the physicians, the disorder of the head is the symptom of a grave malady, and the effect of a fever which ravages the whole organism. We are like inexperienced physicians; we see the actual symptoms of the evil without taking note of older symptoms, which are not less important. I hold it as certain that the candlesticks of the Church are to be removed because of the cupidity and luxury of the ecclesiastics.

This schism will not be cured without leaving a large scar, and I, who desire the return of the Church to unity, I could wish that the two rival Popes were in heaven to sing the *Gloria in excelsis*, and that a veritable Eliakim would descend upon the earth to establish peace, if only he be not of this race of vipers."[1]

The contrast between the spiritual ideal and the actual Church had been made too plain to go unchallenged, and Gerard found one day that his permit to preach was revoked. He quietly yielded to authority, declined to make a scandal, or to turn upon those who sought his hurt. "Let love be inflamed within us," he wrote, and "let us be patterns."

This brought to an end his career as an evangelist, but it only opened the door for another type of service hardly less important—the formation of a new brotherhood. His five years of preaching had awakened in many young men a pure desire for a spiritual life. There were groups of these aspirants in all the centres where he had laboured. They were eager for some movement which would give them scope for their new zeal. Gerard himself had always loved young men, had gathered them about him, and had done much to promote their education. He had a passion for good books—as his biographer puts it: "He was more than avaricious for good books,"—and it occurred to him to gather bands of these young men together and give them copying work to do to earn money for their education. This plan accomplished a number of ends: it enabled him to multiply his beloved manuscripts, to forward his educational aims, to influence his young friends toward a holy life, and, incidentally, to use his means for the glory of God. It was his dear friend Florentius Radewin (or Radewyn), the statesman of the movement, who first suggested the idea of a community-life—that all those engaged in copying and beautifying manuscripts should put their earnings into a common purse and share equally in

[1] This is a letter written to Guillaume de Salvavarilla, Archdeacon of Liége. I have translated it from Bonet-Maury's *Gerard Groot un précurseur de la Réforme*, Paris, 1878, pp. 38-39.

common. The idea impressed Gerard, and he worked it out, largely on the model of the primitive Church as recorded in Acts. The first community was formed at Deventer, with Florentius at its head, and the movement spread rapidly through the towns of Holland and Germany. *Brother-houses*—in some instances, *sister-houses*—were provided. The members took no permanent vows, they mingled freely in the world for purposes of service, and lived from their manual labour without any resort to begging. They wore a simple grey garb, and followed a very simple manner of life—it was an effort to make daily life spiritual. Their emphasis was on *practice* rather than on contemplation. The most visible social service which came from the movement was the impetus it gave to practical education, in which direction Gerard was the prime mover. Through his brotherhoods he provided not only copies of the Scriptures and other holy books for the people, but what was still more important, he provided for the instruction of the common people, especially the children. His brothers gave free teaching in their communities to the poorer people, teaching them to read and write, and creating in their minds an appreciation of the real meaning of their religion. His aim in education, as in everything else, was practical. He wanted his young friends to be *not more learned, but imbued with better learning.* He had come to feel that the higher learning of his time was unprofitable, that it was more or less in league with astrology and magic, and over fond of the subtilties of logic and useless disputation. His plans for the new education bore entirely on moral and spiritual improvement. His one concern was the formation of good lives. He discounted degrees and all the show-aspects of education. He did nothing to encourage training for lucrative professions.[1] His aim may be summed up in his own

[1] His attitude toward theological degrees anticipates George Fox. He says: "Thou shalt never study to take a degree in Theology, for it is not right to make gain thereby, while knowledge and fame can as well be got without a degree. The degree appeals to the flesh, and is the aim of those who are wise according to the flesh." And finally, to get a degree one must attend "many vain lectures"!

words: "Let the root of thy studies and the mirror of thy life be first of all the Gospel." It was, one sees, a narrow plan of guarded education with a single aim, to cultivate devotion and to fashion holy lives among the people. It must be judged by its fruits, which were groups of devout and saintly men and women scattered through Holland and Germany, raising the spiritual level of religion among the people; and in the second generation the production of a book which has influenced Christendom next to the Bible itself—*The Imitation of Christ*.[1]

His mysticism is of a mild and practical sort. It was simply a religion of inward, personal experience, and a positive experiment at re-living Christ. Thomas à Kempis has preserved for us Gerard's testimony that "the Holy Spirit inwardly visits, illumines, and changes the heart of a man," and that finally "He incorporates the man into Himself." He dwelt, in his preaching, on the spiritual truth that the kingdom of God is within man, and is righteousness, peace, and joy in God. He insisted throughout on grounding religion in experience, and on making it an affair of life. He said to some anxious youths, who were smitten with the plague: "*If you have a goodwill to serve God*, you may die in peace."[2] We have only scraps of sayings from him,[3] but enough is preserved to show that he is the true spiritual father of the author of the *Imitation*. The same note is struck in these sayings that reverberates throughout the great treatises of the disciple: Conquer thyself; turn thy heart from creatures; point thy mind continually to God, do not for anything suffer thy mind to be discomposed; practise obedience; accept things that are difficult and irksome; exercise thyself always in humility; continually observe the principle of moderation, and above all and

[1] Neale says that this movement was the commencement of Holland's reputation for learning. "The universities of Leyden, Utrecht, and Groningen, all owe their name and fame to the impulse given by the scholar-monk of Deventer" (Neale, *Jansenist Church of Holland*, p. 79).

[2] The brothers were often called "Brothers of Goodwill."

[3] These are preserved in a sort of appendix chapter to Thomas à Kempis's *Vita Gerardi*, from which I have taken them.

first of all, let Christ be the root of thy studies and the mirror of thy life. There are three or four of these sayings which will do for permanent spiritual principles: for instance—"The farther a man knows himself to be from perfection, so much the nearer he is to it"; "The greatest temptation is not to be tempted at all"; "Never breathe a word to show yourself off as very religious or very learned"; "Nothing is a better test of a man than hearing himself praised."

The spirit of love, which was a dominating feature of his life, found beautiful fulfilment in his death. He had for some time been meditating a further step in the New Devotion—the foundation of a higher grade, or order, of Brotherhood, made up of the brothers who wished to go on and take vows and devote themselves wholly and irrevocably to the service of God. But Gerard's fortune had been already exhausted in his works of love, and no money was at hand to build the house needed for the new movement. While he was waiting for means to accomplish his plan, a fearful visitation of the plague came upon Deventer. One of his friends was stricken with it, and Gerard at once went to him to render what help he could. He was unable to save his friend, but as the latter was dying he left a large sum of money for the realization of Gerard's hope. He was, however, not to see its fulfilment, for in his ministrations of love he contracted the dread disease, and died of it. His most intimate disciple, Florentius Radewin, had already imbibed his spirit, and was in all respects his spiritual successor. As he was dying, Gerard said to his band of scholars: "Here is Florentius, the beloved disciple, in whom of a truth the Holy Ghost rests: he shall be your father and ruler. Hold him in my place." Under the direction of Florentius the spiritual brotherhood developed, the life of devotion and simplicity was cultivated,[1] and the new

[1] Florentius sometimes pushed the "simple-life" idea to extremes. In his desire for simple clothes he is said to have asked a tailor if he could *make* him an *old* coat! It was his great disciple, à Kempis, who wrote, "Blessed is the simplicity which leaves the difficult ways of dispute."

order, the *Canons Regular*, as they were called, was founded —their first monastery being that of Windesheim, and their most famous one that of Mount St. Agnes, made immortal by the life and work of its foremost brother, Thomas à Kempis.[1]

V

There is, fortunately, no need now for an elaborate discussion of the real authorship of the *Imitation of Christ*, nor for the re-telling of the life of the man who wrote it. One does not often have the satisfaction of reading a piece of work more adequate for its purpose than De Montmorency's *Thomas à Kempis: His Age and Book* (London, 1906), and everybody who cares for light on this great spiritual movement in Holland is under obligation to the Rev. S. Kettlewell for his two volumes on *Thomas à Kempis* (London, 1882). There are three names intimately associated with the *Imitation* as possible authors of it: Thomas à Kempis, Chancellor Gerson, and Walter Hilton. It cannot be said that the claims for Thomas à Kempis are *absolutely proved* as against the claims for Walter Hilton, but the circumstantial evidence is so overwhelming that the "case" for the Canon of Mount St. Agnes is as good as settled.

I shall only attempt in this chapter to indicate the type of religion exhibited in this extraordinary book; how it took men away from creeds and systems to the eternal idea of Christianity; how it ministered to an inward, first-hand spiritual life—in a word, how this quiet, unassuming, self-forgetting brother in his cloister at Mount St. Agnes builded, all unconsciously perhaps, at the invisible Church of the ages.

Thomas' real name was Haemerlein. He was born in 1379 or 1380, in the village of Kempen (about forty miles from Cologne), hence his name *à Kempis*. In 1392

[1] Charles Bigg says that "within thirty-six years the mother-house of Windesheim had given birth to forty-five daughter convents, of which eight were for women and thirty-seven for men" (Bigg, *Imitation of Christ*, Introduction, p. xxii.).

he went to Deventer, in Holland, to get his education in the schools of the Brethren of the Common Life, where his older brother John was already settled. Florentius was his teacher, his adviser and his friend—"My good father and sweet master," he calls him. He has left a most charming picture of this "sweet master."

"As often as I saw my superior, Florentius," he writes, "standing in the choir, the mere presence of so holy a man inspired me with such awe that I dared not speak when he looked up from his book. On one occasion it happened that I was standing near him in the choir, and he turned to the book we had and sang with us. And, standing close behind me, he supported himself by placing both his hands on my shoulders; and I stood quite still, scarcely daring to move, so astonished was I at the honour he had done me."

Thomas entered the Community at Mount St. Agnes in 1400, and spent there seventy years, dying in 1471. De Montmorency gives this description of the life in this Community:

"It knew nothing of ambition, nothing of controversy, nothing even of the great spiritual movements of which it was the heart. It was the silent, motionless centre of a whirling and incomprehensible world. . . . The poor little monastery was composed of a tiny group of men who thought only of Christ and strove to imitate Him; whose sins were minute fallings away from their ideal of the Man of Nazareth—sins wept over and watched; whose hope lay on the other side of the grave that offered them no terror; whose faith came so near to the faith of the first Christians that the days of Christ seemed to have returned. Mount St. Agnes was the Little Gidding of the fifteenth century. It represented the noblest form of Christianity that that or perhaps any age could produce. The rule of the Community inculcated the fundamental law of love towards God and man; the lessons of humility as taught by Christ; the preparation of body and soul for orderly prayer, by proper and simple attention to both body and mind. Nothing in excess was the ideal of the Community. *The body was to be made absolutely efficient for the purposes of the soul*, and the duty of man to his neighbour was to shadow forth the duty of man to his God. Perfect simplicity in dress and manners, food and drink, work and play, was the ideal for the body; perfect charity to all men, to the young, to the sick, to the sinful, was the ideal for the mind; and the love of God which passeth all understanding was the ideal for the soul."[1]

Here in this atmosphere of spiritual strivings and holy aspirations, probably sometime between 1400 and 1425, Thomas à Kempis wrote his book—a book which, next to Dante's "miracle of song," is the most perfect flower of medieval Christianity, and which comes nearest of any voice that was raised to being "an answer to the sighing of Christian Europe for a light from heaven."

"This small, old-fashioned book, for which you need pay only sixpence at a bookstall, *works miracles to this day*, turning bitter waters into sweetness; while expensive sermons and treatises, newly issued, leave all things as they were before. It was written down by a hand that waited for the heart's prompting; it is the chronicle of a solitary, hidden anguish, struggle, trust, and triumph—not written on velvet cushions to teach endurance to those who are treading with bleeding feet on the stones. And so it remains to all time a lasting record of human needs and human consolations; the voice of a brother who, ages ago, felt, suffered and renounced . . . with a fashion of speech different from ours, but under the same silent, far-off heavens, the same strivings, the same failures, the same weariness."[2]

No other piece of literature presents greater psychological puzzles. Nobody has ever said worse things about this world of ours than the author of the *Imitation*; nobody has painted a darker picture of man, the poor worm of the dust; nobody has struck a deeper note of pessimism. We are living in a mutability where nothing is of worth—all is but "vain vision," "deceitful shadows." We are "exiles from our native home," "strangers and pilgrims with no real concern for the business, the cares, or the pleasures of this wretched world." The trail of vanity and evil is over everything, and "death, that awful event," is dogging the steps of us all!

And yet this book has "worked miracles" in every generation since it was written: it has been like fresh water to shipwrecked men; it has helped thousands to turn defeat to victory and despair into optimism. No

[1] *Op. cit.* pp. 89-90.

[2] *Mill on the Floss*, Book IV. chap. iii.

other book except the Bible has been a more permanent source of joy and comfort and hope. It is a standing paradox, a baffling contradiction. The politics and world-ambitions of fourteenth century popes are things of little interest to us now, but this poor monk's vision of eternal reality, his message of the inward way to the kingdom of the Spirit, his discovery of the invisible realm whose excelling glory makes the soul forget its temporal miseries, have persistently attracted the attention of men, and will continue to attract it as long as the heart pants for the living God.

There is, let us admit at once, a *negative* side to the *Imitation*, as to much other mystical literature, which is false in emphasis and, more than that, false to the facts of experience and reality. This picture of the worthlessness of the finite, the vanity of all that is, is untrue and impossible. Taken consistently, it cuts the nerve of spiritual effort, and destroys all faith in the significance of earthly life with its myriad moral issues. It turns the gaze away from the very stuff out of which moral and spiritual fibre is to be woven. It is an attempt to climb up by first destroying the ladder which has been given to us. "A man ought to rise above all creatures (finite things), and perfectly forsake himself and stand in ecstasy of mind and see that Thou God art in no respect like creatures" (Book III. chap. xxxi.). "Few attain to the blessed privilege of contemplating the infinite, because few totally abandon that which is finite" (Book III. chap. xxii.). "Abandon all, and thou shalt possess all; relinquish all desire, and thou shalt find rest" (Book III. chap. xxiv.). "Learn for the love of the Creator to subdue earth-born love for any creature, since God suffers no rival to His love."[1] "The more nature is subdued, the more Grace is infused." This two-world scheme, this stubborn dualism, which sets the eternal wholly over against the temporal, and *negates* all that experience gives us, in order to glorify the unseen and unexperienced, mars the book for us and tempts us in our haste to say with Thackeray:

[1] The substance of Book III. chap. xxxii. rather than a literal quotation.

"The scheme of that book (*The Imitation*) carried out would make the world the most wretched, useless, dreary, doting place of sojourn. There would be no manhood, no love, no tender ties of mother and child, no use of intellect, no trade or science —a set of selfish beings, crawling about, avoiding one another, and howling a perpetual Miserere!"[1]

But this is certainly a hasty and superficial conclusion. Thomas à Kempis has "crystallized into perfect literary form the Godward yearnings of humanity through fourteen centuries of time,"[2] and his message is bound to bear the marks of the intellectual climate in which it grew. If one wants doctrines of evolution he will not go to Dante for them, and if he is seeking for a monistic view that does full justice to the concrete facts of experience he will not go to à Kempis for it. But if he wants the *voice* that utters the passion of the mightiest spirits of the medieval world; if he wants to see how a great spiritual soul, conscious of a divine mission, builds a permanent refuge against the defeats of the present; if he wants a seer who can project into this finite world the reality of worlds not yet realized, then let him go to Dante and à Kempis. We must not be too much disturbed over the temporal aspects, which get outdated with the flow of time, to see and appreciate the eternal message of this sincere and genuine book. Let us try to find the *positive* and permanent notes which have given this medieval book its power over men and women of all religious types and of all intellectual stages.

The eternal thing in the book is its calm and compelling revelation of the reality of the spiritual kingdom, and its complete sufficiency for the soul. All is well the moment the soul changes its centre of gravity from the world of vain and fleeting things to the world of unchanging reality where God is all. Its real remedy for misery is not the stoic one of lopping off desires, but of getting a new set of desires. It would raise the value of life not by decreasing the denominator, but by increasing the numerator. The passion of love, which shifts the

[1] *Letters of W. M. Thackeray*, p. 96. [2] De Montmorency, p. 172.

values of life, is the key to peace and to the victory that overcometh the world.

"The saints of God," this is the message which Thomas à Kempis gathers out of the past, "ravished above self and drawn out of love of self, *plunged wholly into love of Me* (Christ): in whom also they rest in fruition. Nothing can turn them back or hold them down, for being full of eternal truth, *they burn with the fire of unquenchable love*" (Book III. chap. lviii.). "The saints of God, and all the devoted friends and followers of Christ, regarded not the things that gratified the appetites of the flesh, nor those that were the object of popular esteem and pursuit; but their hope and desire *panted* for the purity and glory of the celestial kingdom: their whole soul was continually elevated to the eternal and invisible" (Book I. chap. xxii.). "*Love panteth* after its original and native freedom. . . . Nothing is sweeter than love, nothing stronger, nothing loftier, nothing broader, nothing pleasanter, nothing fuller or better in heaven or in earth; for love is born of God, and cannot rest save in God from whom it is derived. He who loveth flyeth, runneth, and is glad; he is free and not hindered; he giveth all for All and possesseth all in All, because he hath the One from whom all good proceeds. He looketh not for gifts, but turneth to the Giver above all gifts. Love knoweth no limits, feeleth no burden, considereth no labour. . . . Expand my heart with love that I may be dissolved in its holy fire. . . . Let me love Thee more than myself, let me love myself only for Thy sake, and in Thee love all others . . . for that which seeketh itself falls immediately from love" (Book III. chap. iv.).

When the soul has thus found its centre, nothing can disturb it; when it has "plunged wholly into love," it has pulled the sting from every earthly woe. It can calmly say:

"If Thou pourest Thy light upon me, and turnest my night into day, blessed be Thy name; and if Thou leavest me in darkness, blessed be Thy name. I will take alike from Thee sweet and bitter, joy and sorrow, good and evil: for all that befalleth me I will thank the love that prompts the gift" (Book III. chap. xii.).

The real problem for Thomas is not how to find a different and more comfortable world, it is how to get a *different self*:

"Acquisition and increase of goods cannot help thee to peace. Neither can change of place avail. Thou mayest change thy situation, but thou canst not get away from the real evil, which is *thy own selfish will*" (Book III. chap. xx.). "Thy peace can depend on nothing that makes no alteration in thy real character" (Book III. chap. xxi.). "He that purely and simply intends and desires only the re-union of his soul with God, will not easily be moved by what he see or hears" (Book II. chap. v.). "*If thy heart were right, then every creature would be a mirror of life and a book of holy doctrine to thee.*"

This is the very core of Thomas' message. Poverty in itself is no sovereign remedy. Mere abandonment of earthly goods will not bring us to any goal. Self-mortification, even self-crucifixion, alone does not carry the soul anywhere. The soul must be kindled and burn with a holy passion of love which carries it above all dependence on and attachment to the fleeting, failing things of the world, and be "inwardly united" to the Divine Fountain from whom all good flows—then, in this union with God, everything becomes a mirror of life. But this "condition" of heart is not *natural*; it does not form itself in us while we sleep and play. The Church cannot bestow it. It cannot be bought as an "indulgence" can be. It is the business of life to conquer and win it:

"If thou desirest to obtain victory, make ready for the battle. The crown of patience cannot be received where there has been no suffering. If thou wishest to be crowned, thou must fight manfully and suffer patiently: without labour none can obtain rest, and without contending there can be no conquest" (Book III. chap. xiii.).

Nobody has exalted *Grace* more than has à Kempis—Grace as a "supernatural and special gift of God operating on the soul"; nobody has put a firmer emphasis on the work of the Cross for human redemption, but he has seen, as all true mystics see, that in the last resort salvation, deliverance, victory, depend on *the act of the soul.* "He who will have a hearty sense of what Christ suffered on the Cross *must suffer the like himself*" is his great word to men:

"Turn thyself upwards, turn thyself downwards, turn thyself outwards, turn thyself inwards; everywhere thou shalt find the Cross; and everywhere thou must needs keep patience, if thou wilt have inward peace and earn an everlasting crown" (Book II. chap. xii.).

Thomas says less than the earlier mystics of the Divine in man, because his gaze is turned more than theirs was to Christ and His revelation of God, but the direct, inward revelation in the soul is by no means ignored. "The outward word," he says, in a passage which might have come from Fox's *Journal*, "the outward word, even of Moses and the prophets, is only *letter*; it cannot impart the Spirit. Speak Thou, God, Eternal Truth, speak to my soul" (Book III. chap. ii.), and he goes on to say that the same Spirit that taught prophets and holy men of old now teaches us.

"Some," again he says, "place their religion in books, some in images, some in the pomp and splendour of external worship, but some with illuminated understandings hear what the Holy Spirit speaketh in their hearts" (Book III. chap. iii.). "The Holy Scriptures must be read with the same Spirit by which they were written" (Book I. chap. v.).

Like all men of his type, he insists on *life* as more important than doctrine:

"Of what benefit are thy most subtle disquisitions on the blessed Trinity, if thou art destitute of humility? It is not profound speculations, but a holy life that makes a man right and good and dear to God. *I had rather feel compunction than be able to give the most accurate definition of it.* . . . It is vanity to wish that life may be long and to have no concern whether it be good" (Book I. chap. i.).

In another fine passage, that sounds like the text on which Kipling's *Tomlinson* was written, he says:

"In the day of universal judgment, it will not be asked what we have read, but what we have done; not how eloquently we have spoken, but how holily we have lived!" (Book I. chap. iii).

Some have tried to show that the religion of the *Imitation* is a religion of slavish copying of a model.

But that view is superficial, for it never stops with a *copy* of the outward life of Christ. It calls rather for a deep inward, mystical appreciation of the Spirit of Christ and life in that Spirit—"only he who endeavours to get the Spirit of Christ can imitate Christ" (Book I. chap. i.).

It has, too, been condemned as Quietism, but Thomas is not a Quietist. An act of helpfulness to a brother is better than the performance of a "religious exercise," and he calls his readers to have their "loins girt like valiant men."

> "Never be idle or vacant," he says, "be always reading or writing, or praying, or meditating, *or employed in some useful labour for the common good*" (Book I. chap. xix.).

It has also been condemned as a religion of refined selfishness—"A spiritual hedonism." "*The Imitation of Christ* begins in self and terminates in self," wrote Dean Milman.[1] It is true that the book is full of that passion for a holier self which is a spring of all pure religion, and which cannot be washed out without destroying religion itself, but it is not true that the aim of the *Imitation* is selfish. The constant prayer of its author is to "conquer self utterly," to "retain not the least leaven of self-love." He had not discovered, it was not possible for his age to discover, the true scope of the social, altruistic spirit, but he has the attitude of uncalculating love, and he announces that "*he* does much that loves much; and *he does well that serves the community rather than his own will*" (Book I. chap. v.). And he has found and left for us a great spiritual law in the principle: "If thou wilt be carried, carry another thyself" (Book II. chap. iii).

The Imitation of Christ is by no means the last word of Christianity. It is not a *full* account of the Gospel of Jesus Christ. It is not a type of Christianity that stirs profoundly the mass of men in these strenuous, virile times, but the heart of it is sound and genuine. It is not concerned to find some easy way to a heaven

[1] *History of Latin Christianity*, Book XIV. chap. iii.

beyond the stars. It tells how the soul comes to its own kingdom—a kingdom which is one with Eternal Reality—and thus joins the invisible Church—and every age needs this message.[1]

[1] One of the greatest "disciples" of Thomas was John Wesel Gansfoort (1419-1489). He was educated in the School of the Brothers of the Common Life at Zwolle. He travelled widely, and studied in the Universities of Cologne, Heidelberg, and Louvain, and made himself one of the most famous scholars of his time. "Through truth alone," he said, "lies the way to life." He also, like his master, wrote books of meditation, and taught his contemporaries the art of contemplation, but his greatest service was his work toward a genuine spiritual reformation of the Church. He put the authority of the Scriptures above that of the Church: he powerfully attacked confession, excommunication, transubstantiation and absolution. Luther himself said: "If I had read Wesel sooner, my adversaries would have presumed to say that I had borrowed my whole doctrine from him; our minds are so consonant with each other."

CHAPTER XV

THE PRE-REFORMATION IN ENGLAND

WYCLIF AND THE LOLLARDS

WHILE the forces of the invisible Church were thus silently gathering intensity and volume on the continent, and the religion of the Spirit was working like hidden leaven in the mass of the visible Church, a still mightier spiritual movement was spreading in England—in a very real sense the dawn—"the morning star"—of a new spiritual day. Wyclif is England's greatest religious prophet—in fact he ranks among the foremost prophets of the Christian Church.

But Wyclif is by no means a lone figure, a solitary path-breaker, the sudden initiator of a fresh movement. He is rather a part—to be sure *magna pars*—of a great national movement which was well under way when he appeared, and of which he was the mightiest voice.

One of his great forerunners was Robert Grossetête, Bishop of Lincoln and Chancellor of Oxford (born about 1175, died 1253). He was the foremost English scholar of his time.[1] It was under his direction and oversight that the first translation of Aristotle's Ethics from the Greek was made; he wrote Commentaries on Aristotle's Logic and Physics; and he was one of the founders of the new scholasticism under the sway of Aristotle. Great scholar as he was, and bishop of inflexible authority, his spirit was gentle and childlike. He was a man of the

[1] Roger Bacon calls Grossetête and Adam Marsh "the greatest clerks (scholars) in the world, perfect in divine and human wisdom!"

mystical type, and by his translation of the writings of Dionysius the Areopagite, he started the wave of interest in mystical religion which became a distinct feature of the religious literature of the fourteenth century in England.[1] He taught that the soul has an eye as well as the body, and this eye is Love: "Love," he says, "absorbs all the acts of the soul. One day we shall know God face to face, as even now some choice spirits know Him, by Love." He, like Wyclif, made the Scriptures the foundation of all true learning, and he infused into the students of his generation a new spirit of devotion to the Bible. The supreme passion of his soul was the spiritual shepherding of the flock.[2]

Oxford was, in the fourteenth century, the centre of an intellectual and spiritual movement in England, as extraordinary as any that has ever come from that famous seat of learning. Duns Scotus, the century before (died 1308), had been the leader of a new scholasticism—the last stage and culmination of scholasticism. William of Occam, the flower of Oxford, in the early part of the fourteenth century (died 1346), had taken the step which destroyed scholasticism, sundered science and theology, and prepared the way for the method of experience and induction. In its next period Oxford was to furnish the leaders of English mysticism, the creators of English literature, and the spiritual reformers of the English Church.

The first of the English mystics of the period was Richard Rolle—generally called Richard Rolle of Hampole—who was born in Yorkshire, near Pickering, about

[1] His edition of Dionysius the Areopagite was printed in Strasbourg in 1502.

[2] It has generally been supposed that the great bishop was a protestant before his time, and that he wrote in burning words of remonstrance to the Pope: "He who commits the care of a flock to a man in order that he may get *the milk and the wool*, is a persecutor of Christ in His members." "The cure of souls consists not in the dispensation of sacraments, in the singing of hours, and the reading of masses, but *in the true teaching of the word of life, in rebuking and correcting vice, in deeds of charity, and in the instruction of the people in the holy exercises of active life*," and that in old age, when he was brought face to face with the reckless power of the corrupt Church, he rose to the height of an ancient prophet, and called upon the head of the Church to "fulfil its office for the eternal salvation of the sheep of Christ." But these famous letters are almost certainly spurious (see Charles Jourdain's *Excursions historiques et philosophiques à travers le moyen âge* (Paris, 1888), pp. 149-71).

1300.[1] He went to Oxford with a passion for learning, but whether by a revolt from the dry and subtle scholasticism of the time, or through the influence of his studies of the continental mystics, he suddenly abandoned his University career, withdrew wholly from the world, and devoted himself to the mystic ideal of contemplative life. Everybody thought him mad, and he evidently underwent in the early period of his "new life" profound psychic changes,[2] but after passing through the three mystic stages of *purification*, *illumination* and *contemplation*, he came into an experience of pure and holy *love* which brought him great inward calm, more stable nervous conditions, and finally gave him a rare creative power. He sometimes felt the promptings of an inward voice, which drove him from his solitary contemplation, and turned him into a powerful preacher of the life of love. Unordained, and with no commission but that of the voice of God in his soul, he stood up in church on one occasion and spoke with such resistless power that the entire congregation broke into tears. His life, however marred by its excessive emphasis on withdrawal from the world and on the joys of indulgence in contemplation, was a striking exhibition of a new type of religion. He was absolutely free from the ecclesiastical *system* of his age. He made no use of the machinery of the Church. He owned no head but Christ, he had no creed but *love*, he was in his own right a king and priest unto God, and he flung his passionate soul into lyrics of great fervour and beauty. He was one of the first, after the Norman Conquest, to use his mother-tongue in the service of religion. He turned the psalms into English, and was thus the beginner of the great work which Wyclif helped to complete. His writings, edited by C. Horstman, fill two ponderous volumes, and they must have played a great part in the spread of a freer religion of the heart. "He is," says Horstman, "the head and parent of the

[1] He died at Hampole in 1349.

[2] "He was sitting one day in a church, rapt in meditation, when he felt in his breast a strange and pleasant heat, as of a real sensible fire, so that he kept feeling of his breast to see if the heat was caused by some exterior cause. He often *heard* heavenly music" (see Horstman, *Richard Rolle of Hampole*, vol. ii. p. vii.).

great mystic and religious writers of the fourteenth century."[1]

Sometime during this century there appeared the first English translation or paraphrase of the *Mystical Theology* of "Dionysius," under the title *Dionise Hid Divinite*, that is, "The Hid Divinity of Dionysius."[2] There appears to have been a school of mystics gathered about the writer of the "Hid Divinity," and once again the anonymous Greek of the fifth century had a large spiritual progeny. There still exist in manuscript a number of mystical treatises which came from this group.[3] The important treatises are (besides *Dionise Hid Divinity*) *The Cloud of Unknowing*, *A Pistle of Private Cowncelle*, *A Pistle of Praier*, *A Tretyse of Discrecion in Knowyng of Spirites*, and *A Pistle of Discrecion in Styrryngs*. The great mystical strain which runs through these early English writings is that God is beyond the reach of "bodily wits, as hearing, seeing, smelling, tasting, and touching," and also beyond the reach of "ghostly wits," *i.e.* the powers of the understanding, and to be found only when the soul has "learned to know beyond 'knowing,'" and has entered "the cloud of *un*knowing," that is, has attained to an experience in which "self" and "other" are undifferentiated. No mystic of this type has come nearer giving an adequate account of the "experience" than has the writer of *The Cloud of Unknowing*. He says: "It is a swift, piercing *act, an act of direction, a naked intent of the will fastening itself upon God.* For the substance of all perfection is naught else but a *good will*," and "this work of perfection is the shortest work of all that man can imagine; it is neither longer nor shorter than is an atom." But the mystical experience is more than will, as it is also

[1] *Op. cit.* vol. ii. Introduction, p. xxxv.

[2] My attention was first called to this "Hid Divinity" in an article with the title, "The Cloud of Unknowing," by David M. M'Intyre, in the *Expositor* for October 1907. He incorrectly says, in the above article, that a Cistercian monk, named Ambrose, in Fountains Abbey, translated the *Mystical Theology* of Dionysius into Latin in 1346. The MS. to which he refers was made by a monk named Ambrose, but in *1436*, and in the Monastery of *Bonne Fontaine* on the continent (see MSS. Linc. Col. Ox. 49).

[3] The two collections I have examined are MSS. Univ. Col. Ox. 14, and MSS. Harl. 674 (in British Museum).

more than knowing. "It is a sharp dart of longing love directed to God, and in this great joy of loving Him there is taken away from the man all knowing or feeling of his own."

The writer is evidently endeavouring to suggest an experience which includes and embraces all the powers of the inward being, functioning in an undifferentiated activity, like that of primitive experience in the child, though informed and heightened by all the gains of a lifetime and by all the suggestions of the social environment. He calls this "the cloud of unknowing."

> "It is needful for thee to bury in a cloud of forgetting all creatures [all differentiated objects] that ever God made, that thou mayest direct thine intent to God Himself." "Therefore lift up thine heart unto God with a meek striving of love, and be thou loth to think on aught but Himself; so that naught work in thy wit nor in thy will, but only Himself. When thou dost next begin in this work thou wilt find but a darkness—a cloud of unknowing—between thee and thy Lord, so that thou art able neither to see Him clearly by light of understanding in thy reason, nor feel Him in sweetness of love in thine affection. Yet if ever thou shalt see Him or feel Him—in the measure in which it is possible in this life to do—it behoveth thee always to abide in this cloud and darkness. When thou enterest this cloud, peradventure thou feelest far from God, but thou art nearer Him than formerly; He hath set a darkness between thee and all creatures that ever He made. If any thought, therefore, should come between thee and thy God, then (even though it seem to thee most holy) tread it down with a stirring of love, and say, 'It is God whom I covet, whom I seek.' Take thee a sharp, strong word of prayer; with this word thou shalt beat down all thoughts under thee. Even to think of God's kindness or worthiness would hinder thee in this work. For though it be good to muse on the perfections of God, and to praise Him therefor, it is far better to think on the native substance of Him, and to love and praise Him for Himself. But now thou askest me, 'How should I think on Himself, and what is He?' Unto this I cannot answer thee. I wot now that thou has brought me into the same cloud of unknowing that I would thou wert in thyself. But this will I say: 'By love He may be gotten and holden, but by thought never.'"

In the *Pistle of Private Cowncelle* the writer insists

still further on "the naked *intent* stretched toward God," and on a life "fully meekened in noughting itself." "Thou shalt make spoil and utterly unclothe thyself of all manner of feeling of thyself; so shalt thou be clothed with the gracious feeling of God Himself. . . . Yet this is not to *unbe*—that were madness, but it is to forego the witting and the feeling of thy own being."

These treatises, produced under the influence of the Dionysian writings, had a wide circulation, and, in the words of an old writer,[1] "walked up and down (England) at deer rates."

Walter Hilton is the best known of the popular writers of mystical literature in England in the fourteenth century. He was, as was Rolle, an Oxford scholar and a contemporary of Wyclif—the probable date of his death being 1395. He was a man of rare and saintly life, "travailing busily with all the powers of his soul to fulfil the truth of good life." A very strong case has been made out for settling upon him the authorship of the *Imitation of Christ*, and, though it is practically certain that he did not write it, it is high praise to say, what critics generally admit, that he *might have written it*.[2] What he did write is the profoundly mystical book called *The Ladder of Perfection*, in which he tells his age how the soul can learn, not through priests and ecclesiastical systems, but in direct intercourse with God, to "*see and know* spiritual things." He is not concerned, like his greater contemporary Wyclif, with the task of making a new England. His problem is to tell man how to "enter into himself, and know his own soul and the powers of it," "to see by inward sight the nobility and dignity that belong to the soul."[3]

"The Divine treasure," he says, "lies hidden in thy

[1] Quoted by D. M. M'Intyre, from whose article the passages quoted above are taken.

[2] Hilton wrote both in English and in Latin. It is still an unsettled question whether he wrote his books originally in English or Latin, though De Montmorency thinks that the evidence is in favour of English. It is well known that he translated Latin writings into English, among others Bonaventura's *Stimulus Amoris*.

[3] *The Scale of Perfection* (London, 1870), p. 49.

own soul." "The piece of money—the groat—is lost in thy own house."[1]

"Behind this dark and formless shape of evil is Jesus hid." "Consider thy soul as a life, immortal and invisible, which has in itself the power to know the sovereign truth, and love the sovereign goodness, which is God. Seek thyself in no other place."

But he is no merely passive mystic, satisfied with contemplation, and for ever engaged in hunting for the "lost groat" within the dark of his own soul. He calls the Christian to a life of "busy rest" and energetic love, which loves every man, "be he ever so sinful," for in comparison with love, he says, "there is no great excellence in watching and fasting till thy head aches, nor in running to Rome or Jerusalem with bare feet!"

Less mystical, less of an adept in the inward way Godward, but much more practical and influential with the common people of England, was William Langland, the writer of *Piers Plowman*—probably, though not certainly, an Oxford man, like his contemporaries in literature. He was no hermit like Rolle, no recluse monk like Hilton, but he glowed with no less religious passion than they, though his ideal was a moral and spiritual *society* rather than the achievement of untroubled contemplation of God. He is the voice of the common people crying, in vivid alliterative verse, against the hollow shows and mockeries and hypocrisies of outward religion, and for a genuine religion of heart and life.

"It is not so much," says Milman,[2] "in his keen, cutting satire on all matters of the Church, as in his solemn installation of reason and conscience as the guides of the self-directed soul, that he is breaking the yoke of sacerdotal domination: in his constant appeal to the plainest, simplest Scriptural truths, as in themselves the whole of religion, he is a stern reformer. True religion was not to be found, it was not known by Pope,

[1] George Fox says the same thing in his *Journal*: "The woman that lost the piece of silver was seeking it without. But when the candle was lighted, and the house swept, she found it in her own house." Francis Howgil has a still closer parallel. He says: "Return home to within; sweep your house all; the groat is within!" (*A Lamentation to the Scattered Tribes*, 1656).

[2] *Latin Christianity*, Book XIV. chap. vii

Cardinals, Bishops, Clergy, Monks, Friars. It was to be sought by man himself, by the individual man, by the poorest man, under the sole guidance of Reason, Conscience, and the Grace of God, vouchsafed directly, not through any intermediate human being, or even sacrament, to the self-directing soul."

This voice from the Malvern Hills, the voice of the people, speaking in their own tongue, was a cry of heart for the religion of Christ—a yearning for a religion of new life and new motives—an "ill life is an ill life, whether in pope or peasant." Everywhere in this great poem of the people, the thing that counts is *right-doing*, a life that squares with faith and conscience: "If you had a bag full of pardons and provincial letters, though you be in the fraternity among the four orders, and have indulgences double-fold, I would not give a magpie's tail for your pardon *unless Do-well help you*."

He, too, though no mystic in the strict sense, has his *spiritual ladder* or scale of the religious life. This comes out in his three visions of "Do-well," "Do-bet," and "Do-best." "Do-well" religion is founded on moral uprightness and the fear of God. It is a good, plain, straightforward type of religion, observant of doctrine, playing fair with conscience, and deeply concerned over the everlasting issues of life. "Do-bet" religion is religion according to the "law of Christ"—the religion of love like that of the Good Samaritan, a religion whose ideal is realised in Christ, Who redeemed us by love. "Do-best" religion is the highest type of all—it is the Christ-spirit realized in a living Church, whose members are inwardly free, fed by Grace, united to Christ and embodying Him in the daily work of life—for at the last Piers Plowman is seen as Christ, typifying human nature joined to Divine Grace, and doing God's will in the midst of the busy world. It was a beautiful insight of the poet that made the figure of his Piers Plowman melt away into the Divine-human Christ, and the vision of a world with conscience as king and under the sway of love is good for any age of humanity.

But the greatest spiritual force of this period was

embodied in the patriot and reformer John Wyclif, who was born about 1320, of North of England parentage, in the Richmond district of Yorkshire.[1] His life and work are closely bound up with Oxford, which was his chief place of residence and of intellectual activity from about 1335, when he entered the University, to within three years of his death, which occurred at Lutterworth in 1384.[2]

He was most probably a fellow, and, for a short period, master of Balliol College. In 1361 he was presented by that College to the living of Fillingham, in Lincolnshire, though he continued to reside mainly at Oxford. In 1368, in order to be nearer Oxford, he exchanged this living for the less valuable rectory at Ludgershall, about twelve miles from Oxford, and probably devoted himself mainly to University work. About 1372 he received the degree of Doctor of Theology, and entered upon the work of a University teacher.[3] From this time to the end of his life he was in the forefront of the great spiritual battles of England. We must try to see what those battles were.

The early part of the reign of Edward III. (1327-1377) had given England "a dazzling harvest of glory," and had established an Anglo-Saxon supremacy in the western world. The later years of the same reign saw the military glory fade away, saw this "Anglo-Saxon supremacy" broken, saw England sapped by continual war, dreadfully misgoverned through corrupt favourites, the country swept by famine and pestilence, and brought face to face with social and economic conditions which no statesman of the time understood,[4] with its medieval Church sick unto

[1] According to Leland, who wrote in the time of Henry VIII., Wyclif was born at "Ipreswel," now Hipswell, about a mile from Richmond, in Yorkshire.

[2] All the details of Wyclif's early life are in doubt. No other great Englishman, except Shakespeare, has his biographical records more completely obscured by time. There was, too, an Oxford contemporary by the same name—a certain John Wyclyve of Mayfield—whose history has been tangled up with that of the great reformer. We do not possess a single authentic letter written either from or to Wyclif.

[3] Many scholars give an earlier date for the attainment of the degree. Poole thinks that he became Doctor between 1361 and 1366. At any rate he was Doctor in 1374, when he was appointed a member of the royal commission to confer with the papal representatives at Bruges on the question of "provisions."

[4] These social and economic troubles came to a head in 1381 in the form of a

death with a multitude of ills, and with the new religion, that was to save the nation, hardly yet born. The condition of the Church in this age especially concerns us, for the questions of life and death with Wyclif were questions of religion.

In this period there was only one form of "religion" in England—that of the Church, and to be an Englishman was to be a Christian of the orthodox type. This Church, though in the broad sense a unity, was in reality divided into two parts—the Religious Orders, such as monks and friars, and the Church under the jurisdiction of the bishops. The friars in the early days of their history had been the leaders of a great spiritual revival. They had carried religion into the homes of the people, they had spread abroad a fresh religious enthusiasm, and they had made a powerful protest against worldliness in the Church and laxity in the monastery. But in the intervening years they had greatly degenerated. Once they had been as saving salt in a very corrupt Church, but in Wyclif's time they had lost their savour, and were themselves one of the most corrupt elements within the corrupt Church. Langland has impaled them with his satire; Chaucer, though untroubled with religious convictions, and telling what he saw without passion, yet with much humour, has shown them to us in their spiritual nakedness. The worst feature of the friar's work in the profession of "cure of souls" was his cheap and easy method of granting absolution. Repentance, confession, and penance were the three acts by which sins were purged, but it had become a fixed custom to commute penance into a fine. The friars, once "God's poor men," were now eager to gather in money for their Orders by this easy method of granting absolution. A window for a church or convent would cover the crime of a great man; a pair of old shoes or a dinner would obtain heaven's pardon for the peasant.[1]

peasant uprising of great seriousness, headed by agitators like John Ball and Wat Tyler. The young king, Richard II., saved the day by temporizing promises, but not until the mob had slain Archbishop Sudbury and other men whom they held responsible for the evils of the time.

[1] It has been estimated that there were 4000 friars in England at this time, and that they drew from the people not less than £40,000 annually. Wyclif says

Then, too, both men and women much preferred to confess to a wandering and irresponsible friar, who was here to-day and gone to-morrow, than to the parish priest, who would be a constant presence and a permanent witness of their lives. The friars were furthermore a menace to the peace and purity of households, for they ingratiated themselves with women, made themselves their authoritative guides and masters, and naturally aroused the jealousy of husbands.[1]

Trevelyan lays great emphasis on the influence of the friars with women, and says :

> "The friars were as much in the confidence of great ladies as of common people's wives. Those among the laymen who were not in the hands of these insinuating visitors hated them with the hatred of righteous jealousy." [2]

Lechler quotes the following passage from Richard Fitzralph's sermon on the mendicant Orders, giving the following reason why people preferred to confess to the friars :—

> "With regard to confession, the archbishop shows most convincingly that it is much more suitable and, on moral grounds, much more advisable that confession should be made to one's own parish priest *(sacerdos ordinarius)* than to a begging monk; for the former stands much nearer than the latter to any member of his own parish coming to confess, and has personal knowledge both of the man and his previous sins; and naturally such a man has more feeling of shame before one whom he sees every day, than before a stranger whom perhaps he sees face to face only once a year." [3]

The monks, too, had once embodied the purest type of religion of the times. They had in their spiritual prime made *religion* the sole business of their lives, and they had called men, by a startlingly bold example of complete surrender, to leave all and follow Christ. But, like Jeshurun, they waxed fat and kicked. They had been extremely skilful in securing endowments. Men

that the friars took more from England than Christ and all His Apostles took from Judea !

[1] Trevelyan, *Age of Wyclif*, pp. 146-48. [2] *Age of Wyclif*, p. 148.

[3] Lechler, *John Wycliffe*, trans. by Lorimer, p. 58.

who had been weak and profligate while living were readily induced when dying to leave their fortunes to persons who were believed to have the keys of the next world at their disposal. They found out how to work this morbid fancy to its full, and through this and other means they became rich and increased in goods.[1] And at the same time they became fat and lazy. They, too, had the bad habit of absolving sin for gain and endowment, and though with a long list of good services to their credit, they were, on the whole, a burden to the people and a disgrace to the Church of Christ.

The national Church, with its array of clergy and "clerks," was under the jurisdiction of bishops, with a Primate at Canterbury. The bishops were, as a rule, selected by the King. The Statute of Provisors, passed in 1351, forbade any person to receive appointment by papal *provision*, but, as no one could actually become bishop without the confirmation of the Pope, the King found it necessary to act in alliance with the Pope, and in *practice* the Pope supported the royal candidates for bishoprics, while the King allowed the Pope to appoint his foreign cardinals to other places in the English Church.[2] The bishops of the time were all native Englishmen. Most of them had worked their way up from the poorer classes, and they were, as a rule, able men. The main trouble with them as officials of the Church was their worldliness. They had become the leading administrators and politicians of the kingdom. Trevelyan says that out of the twenty-five bishops between 1376 and 1380, *thirteen* at one time or another held high secular offices under the Crown. The principal offices in the nation were held by bishops, and what we now call the "civil service" of the country was monopolized by clerics.[3]

[1] Fully one-third of the land in England was in the hands of ecclesiastical Orders or ecclesiastical persons in the reign of Edward III., and all this enormous Church property was very inadequately taxed as regarded the property of the secular clergy, while the wealth of the friars was not taxed at all. The Pope's revenue from England at this period was five times that of the King.

[2] *Trevelyan*, p. 108.

[3] There was a great "reform wave" in 1371, which swept many of the clerical officers from their positions and put laymen in their places.

The natural result was that political ambitions, absorption in the affairs of the world, chances at great riches, took the attention of the leaders of the Church away from the business for which they existed.

This entire army of *clerics*, by a privilege known as "benefit of the clergy," were exempt in cases of felony from the criminal law of the land. "Criminous clerks" were taken from the King's courts and tried before "spiritual tribunals," from which they generally made an easy escape. These "spiritual courts" had a monopoly of the probate of wills, and were used as a ready means of extortion. Before these courts came the cases for collection of tithes, and the administration of *fines* imposed as commutation for penance for sins. It was an opportunity for "graft" and corruption on a gigantic scale.[1] The spiritual courts pressed hard on the poor, and they were bitterly hated by the people. Where the Church in its spiritual capacity touched the life of the people most closely, namely in its shepherding of the flock, it was weakest and least efficient. A system of *absenteeism* had grown up which proved a fine source of revenue but starved the flock. The cardinals and archdeacons who controlled many of the best benefices were foreigners appointed by the Pope, and they used their "charges" for revenue purposes only. Several benefices were often conferred upon one person, who then, under this plural system, farmed out "the cure of souls" to underlings. The parish priests, who at the end of the long chain finally came into immediate touch with the people, were generally poor, uneducated, and inefficient. The parsonage and tithes under the system of "appropriation" belonged either to the bishopric, to a monastery, or to some high benefice, and only a very small stipend came to the hands of the local priest or vicar who did the work. This was the worst possible division of the spoil. Those who were to live among the people, and raise them to higher spiritual levels, were too poorly paid to live

[1] Those who were rich sometimes gave a lump sum annually to the more corrupt courts to prevent inquiry.

decent lives, and generally men unfitted for these high tasks drifted into them, while their superiors treated the "cure of souls" as a comfortable source of income, and lived at their ease in cities. The actual instruction which the parish priests gave their flocks was in most places but slight. Preaching was not unknown, but it was very infrequent, and even when there was preaching it was puerile in its range and power. The parish priests taught the people the Creed, the Ten Commandments, the Ave Maria, the Paternoster, and they inculcated the superficial moral system which had grown up in the Church: the six works of mercy, the seven virtues, and a knowledge of the seven deadly sins, but they hardly touched the *moral quick* in their flocks. There is overwhelming evidence of widespread immorality in all classes of society, both among clergy and laity.

The population of rural England was several times greater than that of all the towns together. The people were ignorant, poor, and preyed upon by their overlords and by the Church, and they endured their lot only because they had no imagination of any other possible lot to be attained.

At the top of this dual spiritual system, with its Orders of monks and friars; its cardinals, bishops, priests and clerks, was the Pope. The Pope, to the medieval mind, was an inconceivably august being, the Vicar of Christ, the successor of Peter, the bearer of the keys, with power to loose and bind for eternity, and, what was of still more *practical* importance, by his power to excommunicate, able to bring the mightiest monarchs on their knees before him. He had, however, never possessed the same undisputed power in England as in most continental countries. The pretensions of the papacy reached their climax in England under Innocent III., when King John gave his crown to the Pope and received it as a fief to the See of Rome, and promised in perpetuity the annual sum of one thousand marks; but the very next year the Barons, who wrung the Magna Charta from the King, in the same spirit of great patriotism, defied the

Pope and his excommunications, announcing in significant words the national principle: "The ordering of secular matters appertaineth not to the Pope."

In 1365 Pope Urban V. called upon Edward III. to pay the tribute promised by John, with all the unpaid arrears during the previous years of his reign, threatening in case of refusal to summon the King before him as feudal lord. Edward was king over a different England from that of John's day, and he laid the question of tribute to the Pope before Parliament. Both Houses were unanimous in refusing the papal demand, announcing that John's act was null and void, as no king, without consent of Parliament, had any right to subject the realm of England to foreign authority. And yet in spite of this national spirit the Pope's power in England was very great. The vast army of monks and friars was, as I have said, under his immediate control. Through his appointments of Cardinals and other high beneficiaries he always had great places at his disposal throughout the kingdom.[1] England's continental possessions forced the Crown into European politics, and made it necessary for the nation to keep on good terms with the papal court, not to speak of the terrors of a possible interdict which filled all good Catholics with awe.

As I have been trying to show in previous chapters, the great mystics had long felt that the Church was in the wilderness. This vast machinery, this secular power, was weakness, not strength. They felt that things were out of joint, and that the art of ministering balm to burdened souls was being lost—but they were not statesmen. They could only withdraw from "the heavy and weary weight of all the unintelligible world" in which they were, and build from within the spiritual ladder for the individual soul to mount to freedom, peace, and God.

[1] The Statute of Provisors was passed in 1351, making it illegal to obtain any benefice from the Pope, but the statute was not enforced; and the Statute of Premunire was passed in 1353, forbidding appeals to the papal court on questions of property, and affirming the right of the nation to prohibit the execution of papal bulls within the realm. This anti-papal legislation was partly due to the fact that the Avignon popes were in league with the French, with whom England was at war.

Their service is immeasurable, for they patiently felt out, "with toil of knees and heart and hands," the inward way to God, and taught the finer souls of their age how to dispense with the cumbersome machinery of the medieval system. But the times were ripe for a prophet-statesman, who, with a great spiritual vision, would throw himself into the task of breaking the yoke of bondage, and of guiding *the people*, *the nation*, to freedom, peace, and God. Wyclif was this prophet-statesman, and few men have ever undertaken a harder task, or done it in a more uncompromising and heroic spirit.[1]

His first recorded appearance as a champion of the secular power against papal encroachment was in the form of a tract, written in answer to the challenge of an anonymous monk.[2] The monk is a champion of the indefeasible right of the hierarchy. He contends that the clergy should never be brought before a civil tribunal, that the temporal power has no right to withdraw property from the Church or from churchmen, and that the Crown of England is a fief of the papal see, and should pay annual tribute to the Pope. Wyclif, writing "as a lowly and obedient son of the Roman Church," has yet no consciousness of the great fire his spark is to grow into, nor does he see to what lengths his logic is eventually to carry him. He answers his opponent by giving him a summary of seven speeches given in the House of Lords during the great debate concerning the tribute, and in the summary of the sixth speech he gives the germ of his dominion theory. He says that Christ is the Lord-Paramount, the Feudal Chief-Proprietor, of all the goods of the universe. All who hold goods or rights hold them from Him—the *Pope* as well as other mortals. In case the Pope falls into mortal sin, as he may do like other

[1] "Had it not been for the perverseness of our prelates, against the divine and admirable Wicklef, to suppress him as a schismatic and innovator, perhaps neither the Bohemian Huss and Jerome, no, nor the name of Luther or of Calvin, had ever been known. The glory of reforming all our neighbours had been completely ours" (Milton, *Areopagitica*).

[2] The title of this tract is *Determinatio de Dominio*, and is Wyclif's earliest view of *dominion*. The tract was probably written in 1366, though some authorities put it in the early seventies.

men, he then loses all right to dominion of any kind, and has no claim to the possession of England, which is held by the English themselves directly in fief from Christ.

Shortly after this discussion Wyclif brought out his great treatise on the Dominion of God (*De Dominio Divino*), and probably about five years later he finished his third treatise on Dominion, Civil Dominion (*De Civili Dominio*). These works are prolix and abound in the far-fetched logic of the schoolman, in form quite remote from our way of thinking to-day, but in his ponderous manner he arrives at conclusions which are profoundly significant: all dominion, lordship, and possession belong to God, Who is Lord-in-Chief of the universe. All right of dominion which any man holds, whether civil or spiritual ("natural" is Wyclif's word for spiritual), is conferred upon him by God, and is held *directly*, *immediately* from God; and this *right* of dominion continues only so long as the man who holds it continues in grace, and renders the *service* which God expects from him. No one living in sin, or failing in service, has any legitimate *right* either to rule or to possess—he incurs *forfeiture of dominion.* In real fact all possessions *belong to the good*, though it is expedient in this present state of society to submit to the temporary dominion of the bad—God seems for a time to endure the rule of the devil.

We are not here concerned with the social and economic bearing of Wyclif's theory of dominion, though it should be said in passing that his *communism of the Good* was only an interpretation of the Sermon on the Mount, and was far removed from the aims of the leaders of the peasant uprising. But the fundamental principle of the theory is what concerns us, namely, that *man, as man, depends directly upon God and upon none else.* The Pope, the King, the priest have no *rights* except as a gift from God, and on the condition of goodness and service; and the "common man" has the same direct relation to God that the official has. Apostolic succession rests on the real worth of the man, not on position or outward ordination; "for crown and cloth make no priest, nor the emperor's bishop with his words, *but power that Christ giveth, and thus by life are priests known.*"[1] The *real Church*, therefore, is not the ecclesiastical system with inalienable magic rites; it is the society of good persons holding their spiritual gifts from God, and rendering the service that belongs to a divine society. Thus, through his dominion theory, Wyclif arrived in the fourteenth century at the supremacy of the individual soul, as Luther did in the sixteenth through his doctrine of justification by faith.[2] By the time his dominion doctrine was fully developed, Wyclif was well under way toward a complete transformation of medieval Christianity. He appears for a time in the doubtful company of John of Gaunt, in an attack on clerical influence in State affairs, and in a movement to dispossess or curtail the property-holdings of the Church. The two men were seeking totally different ultimate ends, and Wyclif was moving in directions in which the arch-politician could not travel with him, and their ways were soon to separate. He had, early in his intellectual life, become convinced of the supreme authority of Scripture over all traditions of men and over all Church authority, and, guided by its teachings, and pushed on by virile moral and religious instincts, he soon began to move against the central idea of medieval piety, and to attack the fundamental doctrines of the "system." The evils which Chaucer ridicules with such fine satire became intolerable to Wyclif's finer moral sense, and he smote them with all the intense power of his feelings and his logic. From his chair at Oxford he levelled his glowing arguments against the type of religion represented by the useless monks and friars and the unspiritual clergy.[3] He declared that work and service and a life of goodness are dearer to God than the conventional prayer and praise which fill such a place in the prevailing system of piety. The Gospel,

1 Matthew, *English Works of Wyclif*, p. 467.

2 This whole subject of *Dominion* is very well treated in a chapter on "Wyclif's Doctrine of Lordship," in R. L. Poole's *Illustrations of the History of Mediæval Thought*.

3 Wyclif's hostility to the friars belongs only to this later period of his life.

he holds, gives no ground for two types of religion —the religion of the "Orders" on the one hand, and of "common Christians" on the other. Whatever belongs intrinsically to religion is for all men alike. There is but one "sect" provided for in the Gospel, and that is the "sect of Christ." The distinguishing mark of membership in that "sect" is the practice of the Christ-like life.

The only salvation for the Church is a return to the primitive ideal—a return to the *original religion of Christ*:[1] "Well I know," he says, "that the Church has been many a day in growing, and some call it not Christ's Church, but the church of wicked spirits. And man may not better know Anti-Christ's clerk than by this, that he loveth *this* church and hateth the Church of Christ."[2] He had already in his early theory of dominion reached the logical conclusion that Christ is the Head of all dominion, but by the late seventies he had risen, under the influence of the Scriptures, to a more spiritual view of that sole Headship. In his treatise on *The Four New Sects*, he says: "If thou say that Christ's Church must have a Head, sooth it is; for Christ is Head, and must be here with His Church until the day of doom."[3] With the insight that Christ is Head, and that the individual person has direct relations with Him without interventions, it is not strange that Wyclif moves on to the conclusion that there is no sharp line between clergy and laity—that there is in Christ's Church a priesthood of believers, though he never uses the phrase.[4] Though he does not actually formulate a *doctrine* of inner Light as a universal guide, he does recognise a Light which belongs to man as man—*a natural Light* he calls it, though Wyclif uses "natural" to mean *inherently bound up with man's relation to God.* This Light, he holds, has been weakened by the Fall, but it is not lost,

[1] See Lechler, p. 323; and Trevelyan, pp. 179-80.
[2] *English Works of Wyclif*, p. 467.
[3] *Select English Works of Wyclif*, iii. p. 242.
[4] See Lechler, pp. 305-308.

nor is it opposed to the special light of Grace. It is simply imperfect, and needs the assistance of revealed knowledge.[1]

The directness of Divine teaching to the individual soul is emphasized in one of his late tracts.[2] This tract was written to exalt the Bible as the ultimate authority in matters of religion, and to show that the Church which has set up its traditions and its authority in the place of Scripture is Anti-Christ, but there are passages in this tract which acknowledge an *inward* teaching also: "God," he says "is our best Master, and ready to teach true men all things profitable and needful for their souls." Again, in the same tract: "Christian men take their faith of God by His gracious gift, when He giveth to them knowledge and understanding of truths needful to save men's souls by Grace, *to assent in their hearts to such truths.* And *this men call faith*; and of this faith Christian men are more certain than any man is of mere outward things by bodily wit."

The *Trialogus*, in which he brings together his religious and philosophical views in systematic form, is apparently developed from his University lectures[3]; and from it we can see what he was teaching his students in these eventful years. One can here see the bold mind of the master moving on irresistibly toward a *religion of the Spirit*, which will in time burst the bondage and restraint of the ancient system. He scores prelates who know how to extort money for sins, but know not how to cleanse a man from them; who "babble" of the distinction between mortal and venial sins in order to make merchandise of pardons; and who "chatter of Grace as though it were something to be bought and sold like an ox or an ass." Then, with the swing of his intense moral nature, he smites this heresy in morals, with the announcement that morality is grounded in the very nature of things, is immutable and eternal—is deeper than and anterior to even the will

[1] This is treated in the *Trialogus*, I. chap. vi.

[2] *How Anti-Christ and his Clerks travail to destroy Holy Writ*, etc.

[3] Vaughan's *John de Wycliffe—a Monograph*, pp. 142-43.

of God, for God wills the right *because it is right*, therefore indulgences and pardons are but stupid and unavailing jugglery. On the same ground he struck at saint-worship, and the superstition that God could be won over by a multitude of intercessors. "The apostles, without any saint's day, loved Jesus Christ more than we do," is his significant comment, as usual putting the conditions of the heart above the mummery of the lips. His test of any rite or service in the Church is the way in which it ministers to real devotion of the heart, well expressed in the saying: "As oft as the song delighteth me more than what is songen, so oft I acknowledge that I trespass grievously."

About 1380 he moved on to attack the very citadel of medieval Christianity—the doctrine of *Transubstantiation* itself. In words as unambiguous as the multiplication table, he says: "I maintain that among all the heresies which have ever appeared in the Church, there was never one which was more cunningly smuggled in by hypocrites than this, or which in more ways deceives the people; for it plunders them, leads them astray into idolatry, and denies the teaching of Scripture."[1]

He indicates that he was led on metaphysical grounds to disbelieve that the bread and wine became actual body and blood of Christ, and with his scholastic bent of mind this is quite natural; but he had already arrived, along distinctly religious lines, to a type of Christianity for which the miracle of the Mass, even if it were real, was useless and meaningless. He came to realize that the miraculous eucharist was the foundation stone of a false priesthood, and it was easy and natural for him to conclude that it had been invented for material purposes, and that its celebration was idolatry. But whatever Wyclif thought about it, the Church of his day considered Transubstantiation essential to its very existence, and in attacking this doctrine, and in pointing out another road to salvation, he was calling down upon himself all the bottles of wrath which the visible Church

[1] *Trialogus*, IV. chap. ii.

had in its keeping. He was now burning every bridge behind him and venturing his life and all on his soul's insight. He was challenging the very supremacy of the Church, in behalf of man's direct approach to God.

Wyclif had already come into collision with the hierarchy. In 1377 he was summoned before the Convocation of Canterbury at St. Paul's, but he had behind him the support of John of Gaunt and Lord Henry Percy and the people of London. The same year the Pope, Gregory XI., issued five Bulls against Wyclif, reciting his errors in nineteen articles of accusation. More than a year, however, passed before he was finally summoned by the Archbishop at Lambeth to answer the charges. Here again he had the people with him and the powerful influence of the royal family, so that once more his enemies stumbled and fell. Meantime the "great schism" arose, for a time paralysing the papal arm, and at the same time developing into sudden maturity Wyclif's anti-papal views. But now, in 1381, when Wyclif revealed the startling extent to which he was ready to change the religious beliefs of the nation, the situation was quite altered. The peasant rising had produced a great conservative reaction. An effort was made to hold Wyclif responsible for the extreme socialistic views of the leaders.[1] Then, by the murder of Archbishop Sudbury, Bishop Courtenay, Wyclif's great enemy, the stern foe of heresy, had become Primate. The Court and the nobles, who in the period of the political attack on Church privileges had been on Wyclif's side, were shocked at his doctrinal heresies, and John of Gaunt hastened to counsel him against the dangerous course he was taking. But Wyclif was a prophet, and not a politician, and the compromiser's words had no effect upon him. Early in 1382 a Council at Blackfriars' Convent, in London, condemned a long list of Wyclifite heresies, and for the first time dealt with the Lollard preachers. While the Council

[1] John Ball, in his "confession," declared that he had learned his popular doctrines from Wyclif, but this testimony is discredited by facts. John Ball was excommunicated for his views as early as 1366.

was coming to its decisions, a terrible earthquake shook the building and struck panic into the hearts of all present except the redoubtable Archbishop Courtenay. Wyclif's friends seized on the omen and made much of it, but Courtenay moved on to strike a powerful blow at the centre of Wyclif's power. He determined to drive him from Oxford. It was no light task, for Wyclif was the greatest figure in the University, and Oxford was very jealous of its liberty of thought and freedom of speech; but the union of the ecclesiastical and royal forces, with the far-reaching influence of the friars, formed too powerful a combination to be resisted, and in the summer of 1382 Oxford was closed for ever to Wyclif. With this loss of intellectual freedom, the University lost also its intellectual power and influence.

Wyclif himself was, however, wholly unmoved by the blow which fell upon him. He flung himself without a sigh into the greater work which was already opening before him—a work more important even than teaching Oxford scholars. He had for some time seen the necessity of teaching the truths of spiritual religion to the *people* of England, and to this task he now devoted all his powers. He withdrew from the storm centre, and settled down in the quiet parish of Lutterworth, which had been his living since 1374, and with almost incredible activity set himself to the crowning work of his life—the translation of the Bible, the development of a popular evangelism, and the writing of evangelical sermons and tracts for the people.[1]

It has been generally assumed that Wyclif was summoned to Rome in 1384, the year of his death, and that in a bold letter he declined, saying: "If I might with God's will travel to the Pope, I would, but necessity saith the contrary, and teacheth me to obey God rather than men." There is no reliable evidence that he was actually summoned; and Wyclif's famous letter, which throughout names the Pope in the third person, was probably written

[1] It is quite probable that Wyclif had largely withdrawn from his University work of his own accord, at least a year before the King's mandate was executed, and was mainly devoting himself to his work for the English people.

by him somewhat in the form of a popular tract, on hearing a rumour that he was *likely* to be summoned before the Pope. The letter, in any case, lets us see the great reformer's latest views of the Pope: "*He* is the highest vicar of Christ, who followeth Christ more than other men in virtuous living, for thus the Gospel teacheth. . . . I believe that no man should follow the Pope, no, nor any saint that is now in heaven, except inasmuch as *he* shall follow Christ."

At the time of his death, in 1384, Wyclif had come up to a very simple and untrammelled type of Christianity. It consisted of *following Christ according to the Gospel*, of living by "the law of God," *i.e.* the Scriptural revelation of truth. It put no superstitious emphasis on sacraments, holding that the benefit from them was wholly subjective and dependent on the spiritual attitude of the recipient; and none on Church systems—"any man following Christ is as much Christ's vicar as any other man."[1]

Wyclif put a value on the Bible wholly novel to medieval Christianity. It was for him, as it was not for other Christians of his time, the supreme and sufficient rule of life, and to him belongs the honour of having translated it into English speech. This honour was unchallenged until recent times, but through the publication of a critical essay by Dr. Gasquet, in the July number of the *Dublin Review*, 1895, maintaining that the so-called Wyclif Bible is neither Wyclif's nor even Wyclifite, the whole question was thrown open.[2] Dr. Gasquet has, however, not made out his case. Great Wyclif scholars

[1] The simplicity of Wyclif's final view of Christianity is well seen in the *Opus Evangelicum*, edited by Loserth, London, 1895. He put little value on music and on church architecture, and preferred the simple appeal of truth to the soul. Vaughan, in his summary of Wyclif's opinions (*Monograph*, chap. xii.), says: "Concerning the sacraments, he retained the ordinance of baptism, but without receiving the doctrine of the Church in respect to it as being necessary in all cases to salvation. In like manner he retained the ordinance of the Lord's Supper, but without the doctrine of Transubstantiation, . . . according to his general language the value of a sacrament must depend wholly on the mind of the recipient, not at all on the external act performed by the priest; and contrary to the received doctrine, he could not allow that infant salvation was dependent on infant baptism."

[2] See also Dr. Gasquet's *Old English Bible*.

like F. D. Matthew[1] and Vaughan,[2] have gathered such an array of indirect and circumstantial evidence in favour of the Wyclif claim, that it still holds its ground. It seems probable that between 1381 and 1384, Wyclif with a band of efficient helpers, of whom Nicholas of Hereford was the foremost, turned the Vulgate into English, Wyclif doing the New Testament and Hereford doing the Old, and that this first translation was revised and improved under the direction of Wyclif's friend and assistant in the Lutterworth parish, John Purvey, whose edition was probably issued four or five years after Wyclif's death. There is one famous testimony to the fact that it was Wyclif who gave the Bible to the people, and that his work was regarded in high places as a mischievous innovation:

"Christ," says Knighton in his Chronicles,[3] "delivered His Gospel to the clergy and doctors of the Church, that they might administer to the laity and to weaker persons, according to the states of the times, and the wants of men. But this master, John Wyclif, translated it out of Latin into English, and thus laid it out more open to the laity and to women who could read, than it had formerly been to the most learned of the clergy, even to those of them who had the best understanding. In this way the Gospel-pearl is cast abroad and trodden under foot of swine, and that which was before precious both to clergy and laity is rendered, as it were, the common jest of both. The jewel of the Church is turned into the sport of the people, and what had hitherto been the choice gift of the clergy and of divines is made for ever common to the laity."

The other great practical service of Wyclif's later life was his preparation and organization of a band of popular preachers—"evangelical men" he called them—and this step, like that of the translation, is extremely important, for through it Wyclif continued to influence the people of England long after his voice was hushed, and his ashes were thrown in disgrace into the tributary to the Avon; and thus his positive impact on the nation never ceased

[1] *English Historical Review*, January 1895.

[2] In his *John de Wycliffe*, pp. 331-59.

[3] *Chronicon Henrici Knighton*, edited by J. R. Lumby, vol. ii. pp. 151-52.

until his views triumphed in the Reformation and in the rise of the Commonwealth sects.

Unfortunately, we *know* extremely little of the precise part which Wyclif took in the organization of this popular itinerant ministry, known in history as the Lollard movement. The word "Lollard" was first applied, so far as we have record, to these itinerant ministers by an Oxford opponent of Wyclif, Henry Crump, in 1382. But the word Lollard, as a religious nickname, had been in use on the continent for more than a hundred and fifty years. Much labour has been bestowed on the effort to trace the origin of the word, and a good deal of ingenuity has been shown. The most probable supposition is that it comes from *Lollen*, to mumble or babble. It was usually given to members of the semi-monastic orders who worked among the people, and it was a kind of fling at persons who, though heretical, made pretensions to unusual piety, humility, and poverty. It was often applied to Beghards.[1]

It is evident that these *itinerant preachers* must already have become numerous in England by the year 1382, for they not only received a name of reproach at Oxford, but they also were made a distinct object of attack, under the name of "unlicensed priests," at the "Earthquake Council" of that year.[2] It is certain that the movement to establish itinerant preaching was already well under way before this date. It seems likely, from contemporary testimony, that Wyclif, in the later years of his Oxford life, had been preparing and sending out

[1] The name Lollard appears for the first time in the Chronicles of Joannes Hocsemius in 1309 (see Du Cange, *Glossarium*, vol. v. p. 138). It was at first used to designate associations of laymen who devoted themselves to the care of the sick and insane and to the burial of the dead, and it has been suggested that the name was derived from their low, soft singing of funeral chants (see Lea's *History of the Inquisition*, vol. ii. p. 351). They were also called Alexians from their patron St. Alexis, and Cellites, from the fact that they lived in cells. As lay Orders developed and spread this name took on a wider signification and became a general term, as did Beghard, to cover the members of lay Orders, and was used in official circles as a word of opprobrium.

[2] "Certain unauthorised itinerant preachers are setting forth erroneous, yea, heretical, assertions in public sermons, not only in churches, but also in public squares and other profane places" (Mandate of Archbishop to the Bishop of London, Mav 1382).

travelling preachers, and he seems to have been the central figure of a group of men, mostly young, who were devoted to the proclamation of evangelical religion in England.[1] At first the itinerant ministers were "priests" and men of good learning who had come under Wyclif's influence at Oxford, but after the eventful years of 1381-82 he seems to have made no distinction between priests and laymen, and he no longer calls the itinerants "poor priests," but rather "apostolic men" or "evangelical men," and he positively insists in these latter years of his life that *the Divine call and commission are entirely sufficient for ministering; that when God has installed a minister, the imposition of Bishop's hands is of no consequence.*[2]

As time went on the Lollard missionaries were less and less from the priestly and educated classes. There was nothing to gain and everything to lose for these unauthorized preachers. Their course was along the line of greatest resistance, and not many rich, not many learned, not many with great names were ready for such a hazardous calling. Of the early group we know the names of John Ashton, Nicholas Hereford, John Purvey, William Swynderby, John Parker, and Walter Brute. Some of them lacked staying power, and were drawn back into the Church again as the stress of persecution increased and the dangers of independency loomed before them. In fact, the early Lollards were not very good martyrs, but we must remember that the spirit of martyrdom has to be cultivated; it is not a natural tendency, and the need for it in England was new. There came in time a race of Lollards whose faith rose to the sticking-point, and whose spirit was equal to the fiery test to which it was put.[3]

[1] See testimony of William Thorpe, in *Acts and Monuments* of John Foxe.

[2] See Lechler, p. 196.

[3] It must, however, be admitted that the whole history of Lollardry is seriously marred with "recantation." Foxe has preserved a very harrowing record of a "great abjuration," near the end of the fifteenth century in the parish of Amersham, where there was a Lollard "conventicle" of sixty members and three preachers. William Tylesworth, one of the preachers, was seized and carried to the stake for burning. The members of his flock abjured their faith, and were

A decided group-spirit prevailed among these preachers. They wore a common garb—long russet-coloured gowns with deep pockets; they had a similarity of manner and style in preaching; they dwelt with peculiar fondness on "God's law," *i.e.* Scripture, as the basis of their argument; they were uniformly opposed to image-worship, and they were hostile to the Mass; they abhorred, like the Waldenses whom they resemble in many ways, the common oaths of the day.[1] They used simple, direct language, with much illustration; they avoided dogma and insisted on a practical, ethical religion. They had a vigorous way of dealing with the evils and vices of "official" Christians, and they indulged in biting satire on the followers of "Anti-Christ." They, however, were the bearers of a positive message—a gospel, with many real apostolic notes in it. They have been compared to Wesley's itinerant preachers, but a nearer parallel is found in the itinerant lay ministry of Gerard Groote, whose preaching in Holland in this same century was extremely like that of Wyclif's "evangelical men."

They were from the first popular, and had the common people with them. They also found favour at the first with the knights and wealthy citizens, who welcomed and supported the poor preachers on their rounds; and in the early stages of the movement the House of Commons was plainly in sympathy with their efforts. By the end of Richard's reign Lollardry had become a powerful influence in London, in Leicestershire and Nottinghamshire, in Sussex, Berks, and Wilts, in Herefordshire and Gloucestershire.[2] The people in all these sections of England were growing familiar with attacks on the entire medieval system, were becoming used to lay-preaching and the language of Scripture, and their ears had grown accustomed

ordered to "bear the fagots for his burning," which they did, and his own daughter, herself a Lollard, was compelled to set fire to the wood! It is a picture of awful barbarity, and unrelieved by any touch of heroism on the part of the flock. All three of the preachers, however, died for their faith (Foxe, folio edition, vol. i. pp. 877 *seq.*).

[1] William Thorpe, who bore a good testimony to the Lollard faith before Archbishop Arundel, in 1407, declared that "he preached that it was not lawful to swear by creatures and so not by a booke" (Foxe's *Acts and Monuments*).

[2] Trevelyan, p. 331

to the distinction between "Christ's Sect" and "Anti-Christ's Church."

Foxe has preserved a remarkable document from the early period of Lollardry, which vividly shows the character of the movement. It is written in the spirit, though not in the style, of *Piers Plowman*, and is called the *Plowman's Prayer and Complaint*.[1] The writer, a sort of fifteenth-century Quaker, is full of passion for the spiritual rights of man, is opposed to calling a "house" a church, and prefers good deeds to singing psalms.

> "Lord God," he cries out, "men maketh stonen houses, full of glasen windows and clepeth thilke thine houses and churches. And they setten in these houses mawmets (idols) of stocks and stones, and before them they knelen and maken their prayers, and all this they say is thy worship and a great herying (worship) to thee. But Lord God, what herying is it to build thee a church of dead stones and robben thy quick churches (living men) of their bodilich lives? Lord, I see thy image gone in cold and in hete, in clothes all tobroken, without shone and hosen, anhungered and athurst. . . . *Lord, we lewd (unlearned) men have a belief that thy goodness is endless, and if we keepen thy hests then ben we thy true servants.* Men singen thy words and that singing they clepen thy service, but Lord, I trow that the best singer herieth (worshippeth) thee not most."

In 1401, the second year of Henry IV.'s reign, the famous statute "for burning heretics" was passed by Parliament, and William Sawtrey (or Sautre or Chatrys) was its first victim. He had once recanted, as the fashion then was, but in 1401 he kept the faith, and was burned for teaching that "after consecration by the priest, the bread remaineth true material bread." The next victim, in 1410, was John Badby, a tailor, of Evesham—a lay-preacher—who declared that "Christ sitting at supper could not give His disciples His living (*i.e.* literal) body to eat." He stood by his faith, and went to the stake. The Prince of Wales, afterwards Henry V., was present at Smithfield when Badby was burned, and vainly offered him life on the condition of his recanting.

[1] Foxe, vol. i. pp. 453 *seq.*

"It was a remarkable and significant scene. The hope and pride of England had come in person to implore a tailor to accept life, but he had come in vain. At last the pile was lit. The man's agonies and contortions were taken for signals of submission. Henry ordered the faggots to be pulled away, and renewed his offers and entreaties, but again to no effect. The flames were lit a second time, and the body disappeared in them for ever."[1]

The next great event in the history of Lollardry is the hunting down of Sir John Oldcastle, Lord Cobham. He had been a friend of the young King, Henry V., had rendered on the Welsh border great service to the throne, but he had become thoroughly imbued with the new form of religion, and was the powerful protector of Lollard preachers. He was brought before "the spiritual court" by the intervention of the King, and here he made a clear confession of faith in the Lollard tenets. He was condemned as a heretic, and given over to the secular arm to be burned. He made, however, his escape from the Tower, and his Lollard friends resolved to save him. An insurrection was in all probability planned. At any rate it was suspected, and the Lollard meeting-place in London was surrounded by the King's troops, and many Lollards were seized and hung on the spot. Sir John Oldcastle escaped, and evaded capture for three years. At length he was caught, and executed with all the barbarity known to the period. He died like a hero and a saint, asking God to forgive his enemies, saying that to God only would he confess his sins and pray for forgiveness. As the crackling flames drowned his words of praise the people wept and prayed with him, and counted him a martyr to the truth.

From this time on Lollardry had scant patronage from the knights and gentry. It became the religion of the middle or lower classes, and its professors were shown no mercy. There were, however, in spite of the danger, many large congregations gathered by itinerant preachers

[1] Trevelyan, p. 335. There is a book in the muniment room of Colchester Castle which contains the account of the burning, "in the flame of fire," as a "manifest example to other Christians," of a tailor named William Chivelyng, who was a Lollard leader in the city of Colchester. He was burned in 1428.

down to the middle of the fifteenth century. One preacher, going to the stake, told his judges that he had converted not less than *seven hundred* persons during his life. They had their own schools, met to hear the Bible read, discarded the superstitious practices of the clergy, and appear to have been called by their opponents "the lay-party."[1]

During the second half of the fifteenth century this unofficial lay-religion seemed to be a losing cause, and likely to be stamped out. It was, however, moving on like a subterranean stream, and filtering down into the life of the people, and in the reign of Henry VII. there came, after a long incubation, a deep revival of Lollardry.[2] There were, as formerly, groups or congregations of them, with blacksmiths and tailors for preachers, who believed themselves "the only true priests." Their schools had been broken up, their founder's writings destroyed,[3] their Bibles burnt, and yet they flourished and grew. Foxe gives us a fine picture of their zeal:

> "Although *public authority* failed then to maintain the open preaching of the Gospel, yet the secret multitude of professors was not much unequal; certes the fervent zeal of those Christian days seemed much superior to these our days and times, as manifestly may appear by their sitting up all night in reading and hearing; also by their expenses and charges in buying of books in English, of which some gave five marks (about £40 of present value), some more, some less, for a book. Some gave a load of hay for a few chapters of St. James or of St. Paul in English."[4]

This zeal for the truth, this eagerness to barter hay for Scripture, continued on down into the reign of Henry VIII. There were "known men," as the Lollards came to be called, *i.e.* "Known of God," at work in a silent way in scores of English parishes on the day that Luther rode into Worms, and there was an unbroken succession of truth-bearers between the great "Evangelical doctor" of

[1] See Bishop Pecock's *The Repressor of Overmuch Blaming of the Clergy.*

[2] Trevelyan, p. 347.

[3] They seem to have preserved only Wyclif's Tract, called the *Wicket*, written against *Transubstantiation.*

[4] Quoted from Summers, *Our Lollard Ancestors*, p. 96.

Oxford and the Protestants of the Reformation period.[1] Lollardry was never extinguished; it merged into the great spiritual revival which remade the modern world. "Once the party of the Wyclifites was overcome by the power of the Kings," wrote Erasmus to Pope Adrian VI., "but it was only overcome, not extinguished." The Bishop of London was right in the opinion which he expressed to Erasmus, that the doctrines of Luther were no novelty in England.

There came to light in 1530 a number of pieces of anti-Church literature which gathered up in a popular way the *message* of the Lollard preachers. These tracts in the reports of the Ecclesiastical Commission bear the titles: "The Wicked Mammon," "The Obedience of a Cristen Man," "The Revelation of Anti-Crist," and most important of all, the "Sum of Scriptures." This latter tract bears strong marks of Anabaptist influence, though it may be only the inward development of Lollardry. The following passages give the character of the message embodied in these tracts:—

"There is noo warke better than another to please God—to wash dishes and to preche is all oon as towching the dede to please God."

"Cereymonyes of the Churche hath brought the worlde from God."[2]

---

[1] Foxe (*Acts and Monuments*, ii. p. 29) gives us a graphic picture of Lollard activity in England, the very year Luther was nailing his theses on the door of the Wittenberg church: "In the deposition of one Thomas Risby, weaver, of Stratford Langthorne, against the martyr Thomas Man, it appeareth by the Register, that he had been in divers places and countries in England, and had instructed very many, as at Amersham, at London, at Billerica, at Chelmsford, at Stratford Langthorne, at Uxbridge, at Burnham, at Henley-upon-Thames, in Suffolke and Northfolke, at Newbery and divers places more: where he himself testifieth, that as he went westward, he found a great company of well-disposed persons, being of the same judgment touching the Sacrament of the Lord's Supper that he was of, and especially at Newbery, where was (as he confessed) a glorious and sweet society of faithful favourers, who had continued the space of fifteen years together, till at last, by a certain lewd person, whom they trusted and made of their counsel, they were bewrayed; and then many of them, to the number of six or seven score, abjured, and three or four of them were burnt. From thence he came then (as he confessed) to the Forest of Windsor, where he, hearing of the brethren that were at Amersham, removed thither, where he found a godly and a great company, which had continued in that doctrine and teaching twenty-three years."

[2] The book of "The Wicked Mammon," Wilkins' *Concilia Magnae Britanniae et Hiberniae*, vol. iii. p. 728.

"Every man is a priest, and we nede noon other priest to be a meane [mediator]."[1]

"The Temple of God is not stones and wood, neither in the time of Pawle was there any *house* that was called the temple of God."[2]

"We think that when we beleve that God is God and *can* [know] owr crede, that we have the faithe that a cristen man is bound to have, but so doth the divill believe."[3]

"Every man *doth* as much as he believeth."[4]

There is a very strong social note in the *Sum of Scriptures*, and it carries on the best social spirit of the Lollards:

"He that is rich and liveth of his rents, may not use or spend his goodes as he wille, but thy goodes belong as well unto the poor as to thee."[5]

"A man shall be reproved for noo other thinge at the day of judgment but for forgetting the poor."[6]

"Men of warre are not allowed by the Gospel, the Gospel knoweth peace and not warre."[7]

Simultaneously with the growth of Reformation principles in England, advocates of Anabaptism began to appear, and this "heresy," feared everywhere by those who claimed the right to be vicars to the absent Christ, began to spread.[8] It is an interesting fact that it found its strongholds in the very districts where Lollardry had most flourished and where the people were familiar with anti-clerical sentiment. "God made not priests," the Lollards had taught, "for in Christ's time there were no priests"—"what need to go to the feet (*i.e.* to priest or to saints), when we may go to the Head?" The soil in which such teaching was sown was just the soil for Anabaptism to grow in, and we shall see in a later chapter how close the historical bond was.

Lollards and Quakers, too, had much in common.

[1] The book of "Obedience of a Cristen Man," *Conc. Mag. Brit.* p. 728.
[2] "The Revelation of Anti-Crist," *Conc. Mag. Brit.* p. 730.
[3] "Sum of Scriptures," *Conc. Mag. Brit.* p. 731.
[4] "Sum of Scriptures."
[5] *Conc. Mag. Brit.* p. 732.
[6] *Ibid.* p. 732.
[7] *Ibid.* p. 732.
[8] The earliest record of Anabaptists in England is in 1534. Mentioned in *Conc. Mag. Brit.* pp. 776-79.

The very founders of Quakerism were "of the stock of martyrs"—martyrs directly or indirectly for their faith in Lollard views. But the real connection is still closer than that. George Fox and his followers, consciously or unconsciously, were the genuine *apostolic successors* of Wyclif's "Evangelical men." They proclaimed anew to their age truths which England had already heard; that "God made not priests"; that *man*, and not "stonen houses with glasen windows," is the true divine temple; that the simplest person may go directly to *the Head* of the Church. The Lollard had already borne a valiant testimony to simple garb and plain speech; he had given his body to be burned in his protest against idolatrous sacraments; he had refused to "swear on a book," and he had called men away from "Anti-Christ" to simple membership in the "Sect of Christ."

> "The English mind," writes Trevelyan, "moves slowly, cautiously and often silently. The movement in regard to forms of religion began with Wyclif, if it began no earlier, and reached its full height perhaps not a hundred years ago. England was not converted from Germany; she changed her own opinion, and had begun that process long before Wittenberg or Geneva became famous in theological controversy. If we take a general view of our religious history, we must hold that English Protestantism had a gradual and mainly regular growth."
>
> "Apart from questions of doctrine and ritual, the importance of Lollardry was great in formulating the rebellion of the laity. That rebellion was directed against the attempt of the Church to keep men in subordination to the priest, after the time when higher developments had become possible. Lollardry offered a new religious basis to all. In the reign of Richard the Second, many laymen had thought the existing power, property, and privileges of the Church to be an evil, but a sacred evil. The Lollards asserted that ecclesiastical evils were not necessarily sacred. The triumph of that view was the downfall of the governing Church."[1]

Who can measure the reach of the spiritual influence of a great man's life and teaching! Wyclif dies; his dust is thrown into the river, and a college is built at

[1] Trevelyan, pp. 351-52.

Oxford to counteract his teaching. Statutes are passed to annihilate his followers, and all the might of the visible Church gathers itself to extinguish the flame which he had kindled. We have seen that it never *was* extinguished in England. But the kindling power of this Wyclif flame gets its most remarkable revelation in Bohemia. The story has all the surprises of a romance. Bohemian students came in large numbers to Oxford in Wyclif's time and later, and they imbibed the ideas of the great Oxford teacher, and patiently copied his manuscripts and took them back to their native land. Richard's Queen, Anne of Bohemia, became affected with Wyclif's views, and through her and her court circle the influence passed over to her home country. The main work, however, was accomplished through the scholars and the manuscripts. John Hus, in his own University of Prague, made copies of Wyclif's philosophical writings, and his friend Jerome, about the same time, came back from Oxford with the theological writings. It was like a spark in tinder, and in a brief time Wyclifite ideas had permeated Bohemia. Hus, from the pulpit of the Bethlehem Chapel, became a powerful preacher of righteousness, and a fearless opponent of the evils and corruptions of the Church, with almost the whole nation for his audience. Once more the visible Church girded itself to put out the fire which had leaped from England to Bohemia. The Council which decreed that Wyclif's bones should be burned at Lutterworth, also decreed that Hus should die at the stake in Constance. "The chief aim of my preaching," said the martyr, as the faggots were heaped about him, "has been to teach men repentance and the forgiveness of sins according to the truth of the Gospel of Jesus Christ, therefore I am prepared to die with a joyful soul."

The spiritual flame was not extinguished by the decrees of Constance; it spread more rapidly than ever, and when Luther was ready to speak, he found Europe ready to hear him; and from the continent, the truth, which Wyclif had done so much to spread, came back to swell the native flame which had never ceased to burn. "It is no pernicious *novelty*," declared the Bishop of London, when the Lutheran teachings began to disturb his peace; "it is only new arms being added to the great band of Wyclifite heretics!"

CHAPTER XVI

THE ANABAPTISTS

I

JUDGED by the reception it met at the hands of those in power, both in Church and State, equally in Roman Catholic and in Protestant countries, the Anabaptist movement was one of the most tragic in the history of Christianity; but, judged by the principles which were put into play by the men who bore this reproachful nickname, it must be pronounced one of the most momentous and significant undertakings in man's eventful religious struggle after the truth. It gathered up the gains of earlier movements, and it is the spiritual soil out of which all nonconformist sects have sprung, and it is the first plain announcement in modern history of a programme for a new type of Christian society which the modern world, especially in America and England, has been slowly realizing—an absolutely free and independent religious society, and a State in which every man counts as a man, and has his share in shaping both Church and State.

This distinct movement toward a radically new type of religious society—later named Anabaptism [1]—was launched at least as early as was the movement to reform the old Church. In fact, it is practically certain that "the Spiritual groups," which I have been studying in these chapters, had an unbroken existence; that the

[1] The term is an opprobrious nickname given by the enemies of the movement. It means *re-baptism*, but, as we shall see, questions of baptism were by no means the vital questions in the movement.

bands of "Brethren" who quietly gathered in homes and in out-of-the-way meeting-places to foster personal religion and to express their disapproval of the "system," had a continuous descent down to the times of the Reformation, and that they were gathered up by the glowing leaders of the sixteenth century into this great, though somewhat chaotic, movement, which ran parallel with the more rigidly organized Reformation.

I say "practically certain," because there is very little documentary evidence at hand to prove the direct connection between Anabaptism and the earlier mystical and evangelical societies.[1]

What we actually know is that there suddenly appeared, just at the dawn of the Reformation, in almost every Christian country, little groups of men and women, who were determined to reconstruct Christianity after the New Testament model, who were bent on reviving primitive Christianity. These groups had the same characteristic marks that have become familiar to us in these studies, with the addition of other peculiarities due largely to the social conditions under which they lived. They put, too, a peculiar and novel *emphasis* on certain aspects of truth, largely as a result of their greater knowledge of Scripture, and they felt, more intensely than any of the groups of "Brethren" before them, the social passion—the aspiration for a society in which men might be free from every kind of tyranny. But they present every appearance of having evolved from the social and religious groups which we know existed throughout Europe before them, and that, too, in the very centres where Anabaptism later flourished at its best.

It was perfectly natural that this freer, intenser, more radical type of Christianity should break forth simultaneously with the Reformation. The same tendencies which pushed Luther and Zwingli to take their bold stand for a reform in the Church, pushed these other groups

[1] Dr. Ludwig Keller, in his *Altevangelischen Gemeinden* (Berlin, 1887) and his *Die Reformation und die alteren Reformparteien* (Leipzig, 1885), has gathered much material which points in the direction of direct influence, but it is not generally admitted that he has made good his case.

of Christians into unwonted activity. They had alike measurably shaken themselves free from the spell of tradition, and had been appalled at the spiritual bankruptcy of the Church. They had alike rediscovered Christianity in the Bible; and the new vision worked within them like new wine. Those who had this vision, and with it had the power of restraint, and the gifts of statesmanship to see what would *work* and what would not work in the world as it actually was then, became the leaders of the Protestant Reformation, and have their renown in the pages of history. Those who had this vision and who were resolved to *make the world fit the vision*, with no shade of levelling down and with no hairsbreadth of a compromise, became the leaders of Anabaptism, risked everything for the cause they believed in, flung out ideals which have been guiding stars for us ever since, went to death in terrible fashions, and fell on almost total obscurity. It is a story well worth telling, and quite worth reading.

Whatever may have been the influence of the previous mystical and evangelical societies in producing this new religious outbreak, there can be no question that the circulation of the Bible among the people was the deepest spring and occasion of it. The priests were right when they announced that it was dangerous for "common men" to have the Bible. It was even more dangerous than they knew, and everybody now realizes that putting the Bible into the hands of peasants and craftsmen wrought one of the greatest spiritual revolutions in the history of the race, and marked the doom of an exclusive priesthood. The finer spirits had, in the earlier centuries, been able to feel out an inner way to God, and they knew in their own souls of a Divine fellowship, independent of priest or sacrament, but their message was vague and unformed, and did not grip the rank and file with reality. In the early part of the sixteenth century the actual message of the New Testament was beginning to filter down into the lives of the people themselves. There were many labouring men who had read the very words of Christ; there were many simple homes in which a copy of the wonderful

Book was owned and possessed. Men and women with slender culture and with no wealth but their hands of toil, were reading and pondering, and as they read and pondered they saw a new heaven and a new earth. With his open Bible, the "common man" became his own priest, and in a measure his own prophet. He suddenly found himself in strange new relations to God, and possessed of a picture of the Church wholly different from the actual Church which he knew. He awoke to the fact that he had been pitiably deceived by the priests, and led off into the wilderness instead of into the promised land. Under the powerful inspiration of the Bible, with its vivid prophecies and its luminous ideals of a pure and spotless Church as the Bride of Christ, there broke forth a great surging of spirit toward emancipation and toward the realization of the splendid vision which the Bible had opened.

The powerful challenge of Luther and Zwingli to the old system, and their championship of evangelical Christianity, stirred all Europe and kindled new courage in the hearts of those who were waiting and praying for the morning to break. The early utterances of Luther voiced the passionate yearning of multitudes of patient men and women who had been thinking deeply, but who were themselves unable to make their voices heard in high places, and his hammer strokes woke many more to sudden activity. Simultaneously, but by independent steps, Zwingli was moving toward a sweeping Reform, and was carrying with him the enlightened men of the Swiss Cantons and of Southern Germany. Already, by 1520, under his influence, the Council of Zurich issued an order directing all pastors and preachers in the Canton to declare the pure word of God. And by the time Luther was at work in the Wartburg, on his translation of the New Testament, Zwingli had declared the principle that the *Church must reject in doctrine and practice everything not positively enjoined by Scripture.*[1]

[1] Luther's own principle is much more conservative, namely, that the Church should retain whatever is not contrary to Scripture: "Whatever is not against Scripture is for Scripture, and Scripture for it."

But it soon became manifest that Luther and Zwingli had a very different aim in view from that which inspired the men who had hoped at first that a "root and branch" transformation was beginning. It quickly developed that both Luther and Zwingli, however they might differ in their personal views, were depending on the help of the secular arm, and were going no farther with their reforms than they could carry their respective States with them. They had no conception of a Church independent of secular princes and powers, and they were ready to sacrifice ideals and compromise principles to carry with them the persons whom they supposed essential to the formation of a winning, successful Church.

There appeared as early as 1523 a wing of the reforming force, composed of persons who saw then, as in the light of history we see to-day, the glaring inconsistencies of these great reformers. In *principle*, Luther and Zwingli announced the sovereignty and priesthood of the individual. They proclaimed the ideal of a Church on the New Testament model. In *practice* they put personal faith in jeopardy, under an authority almost as rigid and almost as unspiritual as in the system they were overthrowing, and they constantly levelled their ideal of a Church down to the standard which custom and tradition had made familiar. It is a nice question, which we are not debating here, whether the moderate reformers who compromised and "succeeded," or the radicals who died for their ideals, and "failed," were right. We are only concerned now with the fact that there quickly did develop a radical wing, resolved on constructing a Church of the apostolic type, and that Luther and Zwingli were among their most persistent opponents.

The first leaders of the radical wing of the reform movement were young Swiss scholars who were intimate with Zwingli and had worked zealously with him in the earliest stages of the Evangelical revival. The best-known names in this Swiss group are Conrad Grebel from one of the leading families of Zurich, educated in the Universities of Vienna and Paris; Felix Mantz, a first-rate Hebrew scholar; George Blaurock, a converted monk of Chur, a man who from his eloquence was popularly called the "mighty Jorg" and "the second Paul"; Simon Stumpf, the first priest to be publicly married in Switzerland; and Ludwig Hetzer, also a Hebrew scholar, and who with the German Anabaptist, Hans Denck, made the first Protestant translation of the Old Testament Prophets.[1]

The real issue, which finally led to a sharp cleavage between the Swiss reformers, was on the question of the type of Church to take the place of the old Church. As Philip Schaff well puts it, "the Zwinglian reformers aimed to *reform the old Church* by the Bible; the Anabaptists attempted to *build a new Church* from the Bible."[2] The radical wing demanded "a pure Church, separated from the Godless," "a congregation of believers conceived by the word of God and born of faith." It should have in it as members only those who had an *experience of religion*, "the saved," and it should have as practices only what was plainly enjoined by Scripture. They believed that the old Church had been swamped by its alliance with the world, that instead of overcoming the world it had been overcome by it, and that the time had now come to set religion free from all entangling alliances, and to form a Church which should be composed of members who were ready to make it their sole business to realize the kingdom of God. To them the centuries intervening between their time and the apostles formed a period of "apostasy," and they proposed leaping over the chasm and restoring the apostolic Church. They further maintained that both within and without the Church a man's conscience must be absolutely free to follow the best light he had. "Do not lay a burden on my conscience," said Hans Müller, an Anabaptist, when brought before the Zurich magistrates, "for faith is a gift given freely by God, and is not common property. The mystery of God lies hidden, like the

[1] The movement begun by these young Swiss leaders found its noblest expression in two young German scholars, Balthasar Hübmaier and Hans Denck, whose teachings will be given later on.

[2] Article on Swiss Anabaptists in *Baptist Quarterly Review*, vol. xl. p. 266.

treasure in the field, which no one can find but he to whom the Spirit shows it. So I beg you, ye servants of God, let my faith stand free."[1]

The advocates of the "pure, separate Church" first came into collision with the moderate reformers on the question of the basis of authority. It was in October 1523 at the "Second Zurich Discussion." The "Discussion" was on the celebration of the Mass and the use of images. Both groups of reformers agreed that there was no ground or place for either Mass or images in a Church of the apostolic type, but Zwingli and the moderates urged that the decision as to further practice should be left with the civic Council of Zurich. The radical party protested against such a course. "You have no authority," one of them cried out, "to leave the decision with them. The decision is given already. The Spirit of God decides. Should the men of the Council give a decision contrary to the word of God, imploring Christ for His Spirit, I will teach and act against it."[2]

This declaration perfectly fits the fundamental contention of the Anabaptists. The decision in spiritual matters does not belong to civic councils; it belongs alone to the group of *Spiritual persons who compose the Church*, and who have the leading of the Spirit. From the time of this "Discussion," those who united in this view of the Church began to meet in the houses of the "brethren" to study the Bible together and to mature their views. They were men, as even their fiercest opponents admit, of marked purity of life, of deep sincerity and simplicity, and they were ready to follow the light as soon as it broke upon them.[3]

As they pored over the Scriptures they failed to find that the New Testament gave any ground for infant

[1] Egli, *Die Züricher Wiedertäufer*, p. 98. Quoted in Lindsay's *History of the Reformation*, vol. ii. p. 441.

[2] Burrage, *Anab. in Switzerland* (Phila. 1882), p. 69.

[3] Bullinger in his *Rise of the Anabaptists*, though unfriendly to their views, says: "They denounced luxury, intemperance in eating and drinking, and all vices, and led a serious spiritual life." Kessler of St. Gall says: "Alas! what shall I say of these people? They move my sincere pity, for many of them are zealous for God though without knowledge." The testimony, even from their enemies, shows them consistent followers of Christ.

baptism, and they put their finger on this custom as one of the most objectionable inventions of the "apostasy." As in the Galatian controversy Paul focused the whole complex issue over the two kinds of Christianity on *circumcision*; so with a profound insight these young Swiss leaders saw that the whole question of the kind of Church they were to make was bound up with the question of infant baptism. Infant baptism implied at once, they believed, that there was some saving power in baptismal water. The baptized child was in some mysterious way put on a different spiritual level by the application of it. The child himself being wholly unconscious, had contributed nothing, had put forth no faith, and yet before baptism it was assumed that the child was *lost*; after baptism it was assumed that the child was in the class of the *saved*. If so, then he was saved entirely by something done for him by a priest, without the exercise of any faith on his own part. This was the very essence of sacerdotalism, and, as they concluded from their Scripture study, bald superstition. It gave the priest the fulcrum for all his power, and it opened the door for bringing the world into the Church, since the mere act of receiving baptism made one a member of the Church, quite apart from the exercise of personal faith, or a spiritual attitude of soul.

It was on this issue that the line of cleavage was drawn. The radicals cared little for baptism. They conceived in it no saving power. It was neither the use nor the non-use of it that primarily mattered or availed. Their contention went much deeper, and dealt with really vital matters. They were determined to lay the axe at the root of every superstition, and to destroy utterly sacerdotalism and priestcraft. Then, plainly, this was the place to strike.

But more than that was involved. They were determined to maintain the principle that no spiritual change can be wrought in the soul except by voluntary choice. Against the view that *God chooses* some to be "saints" and some to be "damned," they set the view that each man *by his own choice* is made spiritual and saintly, or unspiritual and damned. The Church, they held, should be the congregation of those who chose to be Christ's followers, and who were conscious of a living relation with their Lord. Then, of course, it followed that no baptism could be tolerated unless it were taken as an act of faith and as an act of personal obedience to the command of Christ.

"Water," said one of their leaders,[1] "is not baptism, else the whole Danube were baptism and the fishermen and boatmen would be daily baptized."

For a time Zwingli himself wavered on the question of infant baptism, and was on the point of declaring against it as unscriptural, and Oecolampadius, too, felt a similar halt in his mind in reference to it. But the deeper issues involved finally carried them against this insight. The ideal of a Church composed only of believers, a fellowship of the faithful, seemed to them impracticable for earth, and they swung over to the old plan of a Church of wheat and tares, and Zwingli became the most stubborn defender of infant baptism[2]

The progress of events steadily pushed the two groups of reformers, with their different ideals of the Church, farther apart and into sharper differentiation. The radicals —"spirituals," or simply "brethren," or "Christians," they called themselves — continued to meet in little groups. Their "apostles" were full of enthusiasm, restless, resistless, heroic, and the movement spread with an astonishing rapidity. Little societies of "believers" sprang up almost spontaneously in Berne, Basle, Appenzel, St. Gall, and in other places. The movement, even in Switzerland where it was thoroughly *sane*, had a powerful social aspect as well as a religious aspect. Its leaders had an intense humanitarian spirit, a passionate love for the "common man," and they "spoke to the condition" of the oppressed and the heavy-laden. Even their enemies admitted that

[1] Balthasar Hübmaier.

[2] He defended it on the analogy of circumcision enjoined in the Old Testament; on the ground of Christ's treatment of little children; and on the strength of Acts xvi. 15 and 33; 1 Cor. i. 16; and 1 Cor. vii. 14.

by the *test of life* they rang true. Bullinger, in his *History of the Reformation*, says:

"They had an *appearance* of spiritual life; they were excellent in character, they sighed much, they uttered no falsehoods, they were austere, they spake nobly and with excellence, so that they thereby acquired admiration and authority or respect with simple pious people. For the people said: 'Let others say what they will of the *Dippers*, we see in them nothing but what is excellent, and hear from them nothing else but that we should not swear and do no one wrong, that every one ought to do what is right, that everyone must live godly and holy lives; we see no wickedness in them.' Thus they deceived many people in this land."[1]

Finally, in 1525, they took the step which gave them their name, and which separated them completely from the moderate reformers. At one of their "brother-meetings" in Zurich, while all were bowed in prayer that God would grant them power to fulfil all His will, Blaurock stood up and asked Grebel to baptize him on his personal confession of faith. He then fell on his knees, and Grebel baptized him, and he (Blaurock) thereupon baptized all who were present. Similar scenes followed in the houses where the "brethren" met in the various Swiss cities. Baptism was thus adopted as a *sign and seal* of their faith and their membership in the Church of Christ, and in adopting it as an act of faith they proclaimed the nullity of infant baptism. Their enemies called them henceforth *Anabaptists*, *i.e.* re-baptists. They protested against the name as inapplicable, for they held that their first "baptism" was no baptism at all, but only mere water poured over a child incapable of faith, and that therefore the baptism of a believing adult was not re-baptism. Their protest, however, was in vain, and almost immediately the pitiless storm of persecution, which was pushed almost to annihilation, broke upon them.

To grasp the profounder meaning of the movement, we must now turn to its two greatest exponents, Hübmaier and Denck.

[1] Quoted from *A Martyrology of the Churches of Christ commonly called Baptists* (London, 1850, vol. i. p. 7).

II

Balthasar Hübmaier was born in Friedburg, about five miles from Augsburg, probably in 1480. He received his education in the University of Freiburg and Ingolstadt, under the famous Dr. Eck, Luther's antagonist, receiving in succession the Master's degree and the degree of Doctor of Theology. His great gifts as a preacher gave him wide fame, and he was induced to leave Ingolstadt, where he had become vice-rector of the University, to become chief preacher in the city of Regensburg (Ratisbon). This was in 1516, and he remained in this city five years. During this period he seemed thoroughly entrenched in the theology and practices of the old Church. There was no sign of the great radical leader, slumbering and potential, in the zealously devoted Catholic preacher.

In 1521—the year of the Diet of Worms—he became pastor of the church at Waldshut, on the Rhine, in Austrian territory, but near the Swiss border. Here he took up the study of Paul's Epistles, and went seriously to work to discover what the *primitive conception* of Christianity was. Through his study he came into a personal experience of salvation through Christ. He wrote to his Regensburg friends in 1524: "Within two years has Christ come for the first time into my heart to thrive." He entered into sympathetic relations with the Swiss reformers, and conferred with the great leaders of the new learning, Erasmus, Oecolampadius, and Vadian. By the autumn of 1523 he was thoroughly settled in the new faith, and had carried his congregation at Waldshut with him, and in the famous Zurich "Discussion," already referred to, he took his place on the side of the radical reformers. He was baptized—"re-baptized," as his opponents would have it—in 1525, by William Roublin, and shortly after he (Hübmaier) baptized from a milk-pail three hundred of the people of Waldshut. Only three years later—10th of March 1528—he was burned at the stake in Vienna as a martyr to his faith, but during the five years of his evangelical ministry he led a large number of serious men and women into the type of apostolic religion which he professed.[1]

He was a powerful preacher, and as a lucid and vigorous writer unmatched among the reformers except by Luther, and, though he temporarily wavered *on the rack*, on the whole he was one of the noblest spirits of the German Reformation. There are few finer testimonies than Hübmaier's to an absolute confidence in the power of the Truth. Again and again he closes his addresses and his treatises with the words, "Truth is immortal." In a letter asking for a Discussion with Zwingli on the subject of baptism, he says: "If I err, I will gladly retract. If Master Ulrich (Zwingli) errs, he should not be ashamed to forsake his error, *for the truth will ultimately conquer him*." In the Zurich "Discussion" he had already said: "I can err, for I am a man, but I cannot be a heretic, for *I am willing to be taught better* by anybody."

He made a fundamental point, as was true of all the Anabaptists, of the necessity of personal faith and individual experience. "You tell me," he wrote in his *Dialogue with Oecolampadius*, "of the faith of another, it may be of father or mother; of the faith of a godfather, or of the faith of the Church; but all of this is without foundation in Scripture, *for the just must live by his own faith*." This necessity of personal first-hand faith was his test of value for every religious observance, and it was on this ground that he threw over the Mass, which in his Regensburg days had been a central feature of his religion. "*As I cannot believe for another*," he said in his address before the Zurich Council, "so it is not permitted for me to celebrate the Mass for another." It is because of this fundamental insight that he was so determined to abolish infant baptism. To baptize a child, he says, is to perform a "ceremony"—it is not an intelligent act of faith.[2] One may as well expect, he says, to "save" a Turk or a Jew by pouring a little baptismal water over him. And

[1] During the closing year of his ministry, which was in the city of Nikolsburg, in Moravia, it is estimated that no less than 6000 were added to the ranks of the Anabaptists in that region (see Vedder's *Balthasar Hübmaier*, p. 152).

[2] See his treatise on *Christian Baptism of Believers*.

in answer to the claim that the child is baptized as a future believer, he says: "To baptize a child as a future believer is like hanging out a hoop as a sign of future wine!"[1]

Hübmaier was more distinctly evangelical than Denck, who was the great mystic of the group, and yet there was a decidedly mystical strain in Hübmaier, as there was, furthermore, in the entire Anabaptist movement. All the sane leaders of the movement held that true religion is an act and attitude of the person's own spirit, and that *nothing whatever is wrought* by magic, by sacerdotalism, by rite, or by ceremony.[2] Salvation is a change of nature within the soul, and this change is wrought alone by a personal transaction between the soul and God. To such an experience Hübmaier has given a powerful testimony: "*I believe and trust that the Holy Ghost has come in me* and the power of the most high God has, as with Mary (the Virgin), overshadowed my soul, to conceive in me the new man; so that in the living, indestructible Word and in the Spirit I might be born again, and see the kingdom of God. For Thou, Son of the living God, didst become man in order that through Thee we might become children of God."[3]

It is true that he founded his entire message on the teaching of Scripture, and he patiently spelled out the word for his age from the Word of the ages. And yet he emphatically insisted as well on the importance of a *direct, inward work*. "God draws men," he wrote in his *Table of Doctrine*, "in two ways, inwardly and outwardly. The outward drawing takes place by the public proclamation of His holy Gospel, which Christ commanded to be preached to every creature, and is now made known everywhere. *The inward drawing is wrought by God,* who enlightens the soul within, so that it understands the undeniable truth, and is so thoroughly convinced by the

[1] See his treatise on *Christian Baptism of Believers*.

[2] Hübmaier says in his *Form of Baptizing* that there is nothing sacramental in baptism. These are his words: "Water baptism is an external and public testimony of the inward baptism of the Spirit."

[3] Hübmaier's *Twelve Articles of Faith* (Vedder, p. 131).

Spirit and the preached word, as to confess from the conscience that these must be *so* and not otherwise."[1]

When he was face to face with the trial by fire he bore a personal testimony to this inward leading: "Whatever I have either written or taught hitherto was not for my own advantage, but simply from the conviction that the Spirit of God was leading me to do it."[2] Hübmaier holds that the true Church is a spiritual organism, made up of those who have been born from above and joined to Christ, so that they live in the Spirit as sons of God. The authority of this Church is *in itself*. It cannot depend on temporal rulers, or on any secular power, for its support. It deals only with the affairs of the soul. "The Church," he says in his *Table of Christian Doctrine*, "includes all men who are congregated and united in one God, in one Lord, in one faith and one baptism, and confess the faith with the mouth wherever they may be on earth. That is the universal Christian Church, the body and communion of saints, that meets only in the Spirit of God." And in his *Twelve Articles of Faith* he says: "I believe and confess a holy Catholic Church, which is the communion of saints and a brotherhood of pious and believing men."

Hübmaier's treatment of singing as a religious exercise throws much light on his conception of a Church and its positively spiritual function. It is well known that the Anabaptists made much of congregational singing, and that they produced some of the finest of the early Protestant hymns, but Hübmaier expresses the feeling, which prevailed pretty generally among them, that whatever was made a part of worship must be done intelligently and with spiritual intention. He says in his *Short Apology*:

> "With singing and reading in the Churches I am well contented (but not as they have been hitherto conducted), when it is with the Spirit and from the heart, and with the understanding of the words and edification of the Church as Paul teaches us. But, otherwise, God rejects it *and will have none of our Baal cries.*"

Hübmaier was one of the noblest spirits of his

[1] Vedder, p. 199. [2] From an interview in prison in Vienna (Vedder, p. 227).

time, but he was the herald of a message for which the world was not yet ripe, and he met at every turn the pitiless hate and persecution of a world that was resolved to seal his lips. He learned in a hard school the profound truth which he spoke: "Faith which flows from the Gospel fountain lives only in contests; and the rougher they become, so much the greater becomes faith."

III

Hans Denck has been rightly called "an apostle of Anabaptism,"[1] and as a scholar, leader and spiritual prophet he is Hübmaier's equal. His contemporaries, however hostile to his doctrines, recognised his great gifts. Bucer called him "the pope of the Anabaptists"; Haller, "the Anabaptist Apollo"; and Vadian wrote in 1523: "In Denck, that most gifted youth, all excellencies were present." Sebastian Franck says that he was "the President and Bishop of the Anabaptists."

He is a "priest" quite after the order of Melchizedec, for he has no traceable lineage. His place of nativity[2] and the date of his birth are unknown. He studied in the University of Basle, where he heard the lectures of Oecolampadius, though he never became his disciple. His main intellectual interest was in the prophets and mystics, in whom he was deeply read. He was not a revolutionary leader, but gentle in spirit and with a single passionate aim, to build up a spiritual fellowship of good persons.

He became headmaster in St. Sebald's School, in Nuremberg, in 1523, but he soon came into collision with the Lutheran theologians there, and was forced to leave the city. Instead of shaking off the dust of his feet against them he wrote a Tract called *A Protestation and Confession*, in which he shows himself to be a mystic and a *seeker* after a live faith. "I would fain possess," he wrote, "that faith which works

[1] Keller, *Hans Denck, ein Apostel der Wiedertäufer* (Leipzig, 1882).
[2] Probably in Bavaria.

salvation and leads to life, but I do not find it in me. Nay, if I said to-day that I had that faith, to-morrow I should accuse myself of lying; for an inner Voice, a Spark of Truth which I partly feel in me, tells me that I have not yet in me that faith which works life."

Denck's Nuremberg *Confession* is still in the archives of that city, and has been put into modern shape by Dr. Keller.[1] His leading question in the *Confession* is "Who gives me faith? Is it inborn, or is it *won*? Is it communicated by parents, or is it an elemental *condition of the soul*?" His answer is that it is a native condition of the soul. It is a *tendency* grounded in the very structure of the soul, which pushes man after a better, purer life, and which makes him resist the *lower* natural tendencies. This situation involves battle, struggle (*Seelenkampf*) as long as one lives in the body, but the victory is well in sight when one "sets his will towards God's will through Christ." He says that the higher convictions which make man truly religious cannot have their *origin* from the Bible, as they are *pre-supposed* in any acceptation of the Bible as a Word of God. Therefore the true and primary faith must rest on "facts of experience, directly given"; on what he rightly calls "an inner witness which God, by His grace, plants in the soul." The supreme *test* of the Word of God in the Bible is its power of speaking to this "inner witness." "It [the Bible] is an echo of what is being uttered deep in my own bosom," "it is the light and guide on the way of Faith, and without it the best of us would stumble and go astray, but it is not the primary Word of God." This "inner" Word, which perfectly fits the "outer," is, he says, "a spark of the Divine Spirit." Without *this* within him, a man would neither seek nor find God, for "he who seeks Him, in truth already has Him, and without this inner Spirit to guide and direct him, one cannot find Him, even in the Bible."[2]

1 *Ein Apostel der Wiedertäufer*, pp. 49-62.

2 Compare this view with Luther's doctrine of total depravity—the absence of all impulse toward Good: "I find nothing pure or holy in me, nor in any man,

During the next six months after his *Confession*, the awful six months of the peasant revolt, Denck's movements cannot be traced, but he finally comes to light again in June 1525, at St. Gall, in Switzerland, where he wrote a Tract with the luminous title: "He who really loves the truth can herein examine himself, so that none exalt his faith by reason of personal experiences, but knows from whom he should ask and receive wisdom!" He soon received a call to teach in Augsburg, where he found a group ready for his spiritual message. It was apparently under the influence of Hübmaier, who visited Augsburg on his way to Nikolsburg, that Denck became convinced of the distinct views on baptism held by the Anabaptists, though he had already arrived independently at the spiritual conception of Christianity. In fact, he went further than any of the other leaders in his teaching of a Light within. He flatly denied the *depravity* of man as we have seen, and asserted that there is something divine in every man—an upward impulse or conscience which he believed to be "a spark of the Divine Spirit." Consistently with this view he held to the freedom of the will, man's personal power to obey or disobey this Divine Light in the Soul. Christ, he taught, was the Eternal Word or Spirit, incarnate; this same Word, or Spirit, is in some measure in all true believers, and the Church is the company or fellowship of these spiritual souls, united to their Divine Head: "All who are inspired with the Spirit of love are one with Christ in God." He had an intense love for the Bible, and in conjunction with Ludwig Hetzer he made a translation of the Prophets, but he would not consent to make the Scriptures the sole source and foundation of faith. God was, he said, before the Scriptures, and they are only instruments to bring men to Him.

but all our works are (if I may be allowed the expression) mere lice in an old filthy hide, from which nothing good can come, because neither hide nor hair is any good any more."

"The Holy Scriptures," he wrote, "I esteem above human treasures, but not so highly as the Word of God, which is living, powerful, and eternal, and pure from the elements of this world, since it is God Himself, Spirit and not letter, written without pen and paper, so that it can never be blotted out. Therefore, blessedness is not bound up in Scripture, however useful and good it may always be in that direction. It is not possible for Scripture to make better a bad heart; but a good heart is bettered by all things. A man who is chosen by God may attain to blessedness without preaching, without Scripture."

During his stay in Augsburg, he threw himself with great earnestness into the task of forming a "Spiritual fellowship" in the city, "an apostolic brotherhood"—"an embassy of God," he called it—and he was so successful that more than a thousand persons were in a short time brought into the fellowship. But under the fire of opposition he withdrew from Augsburg and went to Strasbourg where another "fellowship" was being formed. Here the opposition was led by the great reformer, Bucer, who had Denck driven into exile.

Homeless, penniless, the object of fierce attack, hunted like a dangerous wild beast, he wandered about on foot from town to town, telling his message to those who were ready for it, and organizing the scattered Anabaptists into local brotherhoods. He seems also to have drawn together the leaders of the movement throughout Germany into a sort of "general meeting," over which he presided in Augsburg in 1527. Broken in health, and "dying daily," he found his way to Basle, where he hoped to spread the truth, but his worn-out body soon gave way entirely and he finished his course in faith.

He was one of the first in the modern world to proclaim consistently the plain, simple Gospel of the infinite love and fatherhood of God. He had no sympathy with far-fetched schemes of theology. He threw himself unreservedly on the goodness of God. "The voice of my heart," he wrote, "the voice of my heart, of which I assuredly know that it renders the truth, says to me that *God is righteous and merciful*, and this Voice speaks in every good heart distinctly, and intelligibly, and it speaks the more distinctly and clearly the better one is."

There were great diversities of view among the Anabaptists, and it is not safe to make any universal statements about their views or practices, but nearly all these early leaders of Anabaptism were radical in their opposition to the keeping of *fasts*, to the payment of *tithes*,[1] the taking of *oaths*, and a very large number of them opposed the performance of any *military service*. As early as 1524 Grebel and his friends wrote:

> "The Gospel and its followers shall not be guarded by the sword. . . . Truly believing Christians are sheep in the midst of wolves, sheep ready for the slaughter; they must be baptized in fear and in need, in tribulation and death, that they may be tried to the last, and enter the fatherland of eternal peace, not with carnal, but with spiritual weapons. They use neither the sword of the world nor war, for to kill is forbidden."[2]

They had discovered the fatherhood of God, and they had a firm belief in human brotherhood.[3] They opposed the fiction that from all eternity some were God's men and some were Satan's men, and they hoped to bring about a transformation of society, so that all men might actually live as children of God and as brothers. Sebastian Franck, the Chronicler, though himself not one of them, says that "they taught nothing but love, faith, and crucifixion of the flesh, manifesting patience and humility under many sufferings, breaking bread with one another in sign of love and unity, helping one another with true helpfulness, lending, borrowing, giving, learning to have all

[1] Some of the early Anabaptists strongly objected to a salaried ministry. Denck's disciple, Eitelhans Langenmantel, attacked the reformed clergy on the ground of its "hireling" feature. He condemned the grasping avarice of ministers who "will do nothing for the poor except for money," and he denounced the administration of ordinances for money (see Newman, *History of Anti-Pedobaptism*, p. 169).

[2] Letter to Thomas Münzer.

[3] One of the errors charged against an early English Anabaptist was his affirmation: "I am bound to love the Turke from the bethome (bottom) of my heart!'

things in common, calling each other 'brother.'"[1] There was a wing of the Anabaptists which pushed this idea of brotherhood to its limit in complete communism. "The highest command of God," said Eitelhans Langenmantel, of Augsburg, "is love. 'Love the Lord thy God, with all thy heart, and thy neighbour as thyself.' In the Community no one ought to say 'mine, mine,' it is also the brother's. A community where one is rich and another poor belongs not to Christ." In similar vein Ulrich Stradler, of Auspitz, taught: "All those who truly believe and have wholly given themselves up to Christ have all God's gifts and possessions in common. In the house of the Lord there is no mine, thine, nor his."[2] But the *apostles* of this great spiritual movement—the men whose views I have been studying—were simply bent on following Christ in the spirit of love, and on transforming society by *practising* the Gospel of the kingdom. Hübmaier wrote before he left Zurich:

> "I am accused as if I would have made all things in common, which yet I have not done, but I have called *this* a Christian community of goods, namely: that when one have, and see his neighbour suffer, he should give him alms, in order that the hungry, thirsty, naked, and imprisoned may be helped; and that the more a man practise such works of mercy, the nearer would he be to the Spirit of Christianity."[3]

But it was bound to happen, at that stage of history and of education, that such large principles of free and spiritual religion as those which this movement expressed could not be presented without producing extremes and divisions. There was throughout the primitive period of Anabaptism a fanatical wing which greatly hampered the sane leaders, and which gave a strong pretext to the authorities for their merciless attack on the whole move-

[1] *Chronica*, p. 164. Quoted in Lindsay's *History of the Reformation*, vol. ii. p. 437.

[2] The most successful of all the Communistic leaders was Jacob Huter, to whom belongs the chief credit for the organization of the Moravian Communities, which have survived through baptisms of blood and fire, and through many migrations, to the present time.

[3] *Vedder*, p. 139.

ment. There are always in any given group of men a certain number of psychopathic persons in whom *suggestions* will work with abnormal coerciveness. If new ideas are "in the air" these persons will be powerfully *infected* with them, obsessed with them. If their unstable nervous systems are organized and constructed under the control of the new insight, these persons will be the prophets and heroes of the movement; if they are unstrung and overwrought by the contagion they then become the fanatics and wreckage of the movement. Anabaptism had its full quota of psychopaths of both types. It had powerful prophets, and it also had its flotsam and jetsam.

IV

It has been customary among historians to reckon the "Zwickau Prophets" among Anabaptists, though strictly speaking they do not belong to this class. They were, however, considered a part of the movement by their contemporaries, and they well illustrate the new ideas that were abroad, and that worked like leaven in the ranks of the Anabaptists. "Zwickau Prophets" is a name given to a little group of ultra-evangelical reformers who came into prominence in Zwickau while Luther was in the Wartburg (1521-1522). Their leader was Thomas Münzer (born about 1490), a Master of Arts, a profound student of the mystics, and a fervent sympathizer with the people, burdened with wrongs and sufferings. While he was pastor at Zwickau he was greatly influenced by Nicholas Storch, an itinerant weaver, who in his travels had come under the influence of the "Bohemian Brethren." He had picked up a ready knowledge of Scripture, and had become strongly imbued with millenarian doctrine, a doctrine which prevailed in a branch of the "Bohemian Brethren." He was decidedly psychopathic, given to "visions" and conscious of immediate "inspiration." Like Münzer, he had a passion for the emancipation of the people. They both came to the conclusion that infant baptism was useless and not founded on Scripture, and they considered baptism with the Spirit the only important baptism ; but they did not confirm this view by their practice, for in "the model Church," which he set up after he was driven from Zwickau, Münzer still provided for the baptism of children.

While Luther was in the Wartburg, Storch and some of his disciples resolved to visit Wittenberg and win the University to their cause. It was a bold stroke, and in it they succeeded to the extent of gaining the rector of the University, Carlstadt, and of deeply impressing even Melanchthon. Luther hurried home and broke the spell of the "prophets" in Wittenberg. Meantime Münzer was carried farther and farther into millenarian and revolutionary views. His preaching became denunciatory and menacing,[1] and finally he conceived himself as a new Gideon, commissioned with "the sword of the Lord" to lead the people to victory over all princes and into complete freedom. He infused a fanatical spirit into the peasant revolt, and he did much to wreck the cause he championed. Against the warnings of the Swiss Anabaptists, he took the sword, and he perished by it. But he left a heavy legacy behind, for he and his group of disciples had spread widely abroad the extreme supernaturalism of this Zwickau movement, the eager expectation of an imminent millennium, and a passion for the sword to hasten religio-social ideals.

Soon after the death of Münzer, Hans Hut, an illiterate but powerful preacher, who firmly believed himself a divinely inspired prophet, played a remarkable rôle. His millenarian views, which he drew from the apocalyptic sections of the Bible, spread like contagion wherever he went, under his infectious preaching.

Melchior Hoffman was another leader of the "apocalyptic type." He had pored over the Scriptures, especially the apocalyptic chapters, until he became convinced that he had the key to all mysteries. He interpreted Bible texts by far-fetched allegory, and formulated a marvellous mil-

[1] "If princes act not only against the Gospel, but also against the natural rights of the people, they should be strangled like dogs," is one of his "sayings."

lenarian dream. He was opposed to a salaried ministry, and supported himself at his trade. He opposed all distinction between clergy and laity, except a difference in *gifts*. He was opposed to all oaths, and he held that it was inconsistent for a Christian to fill the office of magistrate.

His "Church" was as unecclesiastical as that of the primitive Quakers. He says:

> "God's community knows no head but Christ. Teachers and ministers are not lords. The pastors have no authority except to preach God's word and punish sins. A Bishop (*i.e.* overseer) must be elected out of the community. . . . A true preacher would willingly see the whole community prophesy."

He believed himself divinely inspired. He had a "revelation" that the New Jerusalem was to come in the City of Strasbourg, and though thrown into prison there he continued to set date after date for the "coming." Before his imprisonment he had been the "apostle" of Anabaptism in the Netherlands, where there was a great "convincement." His "message" *reached* the people, and he kindled the highest hopes in the popular mind wherever he went. This "message," though without the powerful magnetic personality which was behind it, is preserved in his Tract on "The Ordinances of God," an extract from which is herewith given:

> "Christ, King in heaven and on earth, sends His friends and servants to teach all nations that He has sacrificed Himself for the whole world, and taken away its sins. It is the work of a true apostle, not only to proclaim this Gospel of the Crucified, but also to bring to all people the joyful kiss from the mouth of the Bridegroom, who has been made by His Father king over all creatures in heaven and earth, and to deliver the message that all those who serve Him and will acknowledge Him as Lord can come to Him freely and surely, and that He will keep them with Him eternally. And the messengers of the Lord are furthermore commanded to unite to Christ through baptism all who have thus given Him their hearts. To the Bride (the holy community formed of those who have thus given themselves in baptism) the Bridegroom gives Himself in bread and wine, as an earthly bridegroom gives himself with a ring; and the Bride

receiving the bread and wine, through faith becomes with the Bridegroom one body and one flesh, one spirit and one mind."

Unfortunately the Dutch leaders, Jan Matthys and Jan Bockelson (often called John of Leyden), adopted the less spiritual side of Hoffman's teaching, and pushed his millenarian ideas to their extreme limit. They concluded that the time had come for the "believers" to take the sword and *hasten* "the coming of the Kingdom," and they swept along with them a band of followers who credited them with infallible divine guidance. The result was the maelstrom of fanaticism in the "Münster Kingdom" which shocked the civilized world.[1]

V

Even before the fanaticism of the "Münster Kingdom" had broken out, or the excesses of millenarianism had become apparent, the imperial authority and the officials of the Church had resolved on the extirpation of Anabaptism at whatever cost. It can be safely said that no other movement for spiritual freedom in the history of the Church has such an enormous martyrology.[2] Almost all the Swiss leaders suffered martyrdom while the movement was in its infancy. As early as 1528 the Suabian League sent out four hundred, and later eight hundred, and then a thousand armed troopers to scour the districts under their rule, and the leaders of the company were given authority, *at once and without trial or law*, to put to death Anabaptists wherever caught, and to hunt them down like wild beasts. Keller says that not less than 2000 were put to death in a few years,[3] and Sebastian Franck records that 2000 Anabaptists had been executed by 1530. At

[1] The story of this "Münster Kingdom" is well and fairly told for English readers in Belford Bax's *Rise and Fall of Anabaptism*, also in Heath's *Anabaptism*, chap. vii.

[2] *The Martyrology of the Anabaptists* was compiled by a Mennonite teacher named Tieleman Jans van Braght, and published in Dutch in 1660. It gives the memorial and dying witness of the leading martyrs "who suffered and were put to death for the testimony of Jesus their Saviour." It was translated into English by Benjamin Millard, edited by Edward Bean Underhill, and published in two volumes by the Hanserd-Knollys Society, in 1850, London.

[3] Keller, *Ein Apostel der Wiedertäufer*, p. 12.

the imperial Diet of Speier, in 1529, an edict was passed for the absolute eradication of Anabaptism. It decreed that "re-baptizers and re-baptized, all and each, male and female, of intelligent age, be judged and brought from natural life to death, without antecedent inquisition of the spiritual judges." This edict was ruthlessly carried out in almost every part of the empire. The records show that in Görz and the Tyrol alone the number of executions in the year 1531 number one thousand, in Enisheim six hundred, while seventy-three suffered martyrdom in Linz in six weeks.[1] An eye-witness of the persecution in the Tyrol, Conrad Braun, an assessor to the Imperial Chamber, wrote:

> "I have seen with my own eyes that nothing has been able to bring back the Anabaptists from their errors or to make them recant. The hardest imprisonment, hunger, fire, water, the sword, all sorts of frightful executions, have not been able to shake them. I have seen young people, men and women, go to the stake singing, filled with joy; and I can say that in the course of my whole life nothing has moved me more."

The slaughter in the Netherlands was almost beyond belief. Buckle estimates that by 1546 thirty thousand persons had been put to death in Holland and Friesland alone for their faith in Anabaptism.[2]

It was the sight of the pitiless murder and martyrdom of three hundred Anabaptists in West Friesland, near his own home, and one of whom was his own brother, which finally brought Menno Simons to the definite step of allying himself with the movement. He became the leader and organizer of a new stage of Anabaptism, and the prophet of the type out of which the modern Baptist

[1] See Lindsay's *History of Reformation*, vol. ii. p. 449; Cornelius, *Geschichte des münsterischen Aufruhrs* (Leipzig, 1855), vol. ii. p. 58.

[2] Buckle, *History of Civilization*, vol. i. p. 189.

Driven to frenzy and desperation under terrific persecution, the Anabaptists sometimes showed fanatic traits, as has happened in all eras of persecution. Who can read except with pity the account which relates how some Anabaptists in Amsterdam stripped off their clothes and ran through the street crying: "Woe! woe! woe! The wrath of God! The wrath of God!"? Brought before the magistrates they refused to dress. "We are," they said, "the naked truth." They were hurried to the scaffold in barbaric fashion. Blok, in his *History of the People of the Netherlands* (New York and London, 1899), thinks that Buckle's estimate is too large. Vol. ii. p. 317.

sects sprang—a type of Christianity which profoundly affected the religious life of Holland, the inner life of the religious societies of the English Commonwealth and the spiritual destinies of America. Menno Simons was born in Whitmarsum, in West Friesland, about 1496, and while still a young man was settled as priest in the near-by village of Pingjum. He was well-educated for his time, but had no first-hand knowledge of the Bible, and performed his priestly duties in a perfunctory fashion, living a worldly life with apparent unconcern.

One day, without any conscious reflection on the subject, he found himself arrested in the consecration of the Mass with the over-mastering suggestion that what he held in his hands was mere bread and wine, not Christ's flesh and blood. He thought at first that it must be a suggestion of the devil, but the impression would not leave him. He took counsel with other priests, and began to read his Bible and the new writings of Luther which were just appearing. A wonderful change came over his spirit. He discovered, to his surprise, that many of the practices of the Church had no foundation in Scripture, and that especially was this true of the practice of baptizing infants. The edicts for the suppression of the Anabaptists brought their views forcibly to his attention. In 1533 he was deeply stirred by the martyrdom of an Anabaptist near by, and two years later occurred the moving event already referred to. This spectacle, instead of arousing fear, fired his own faith to the point of conviction. In his own account of it, he says:

"I thought within myself, wretched man that I am, what do I, remaining in this position and not confirming by my life the word of the Lord and the knowledge that I have received? If I do not lead the ignorant, misguided sheep, who are so anxious to do what is right, as much as in me lies, to the true fold ot Christ, how then will the blood shed in error rise up against me in the judgment of Almighty God? My heart trembled in my body at this contemplation of myself. I implored God for grace and the pardon of my transgressions, and besought the Almighty that He would create in me a pure heart, that He would endow me with frankness and manly power in order that I might preach His unfalsified word."

Forthwith the die was cast, and he threw himself with the fervour of an apostle into his mission, which seemed to him a heavenly calling. He resolved from the outset to have done with dreams and fancies; to turn away for ever from the follies and fanaticisms of the "false prophets" of Anabaptism, and to organize the scattered forces of the great movement into a solid society, on the fundamental spiritual truths revealed in Scripture. He opposed all oaths, all war, and every form of capital punishment. He utterly refused to have anything to do with a salaried ministry; he insisted on a personal faith, a birth from above, and a new life in Christ as necessary conditions of membership in a Christian Church,[1] and he made a complete separation of State and Church.

[1] "Let no one trust," he wrote, "in the fact that he is a baptized Christian, nor upon the long usage of the times, nor upon papal decrees, nor upon imperial edicts, nor upon the wit of learned men, nor upon human counsels and wisdom, for he must be born from above and transposed from evil nature to good nature, from which a new life follows."

CHAPTER XVII

ANABAPTISM IN ENGLAND

I

THERE are two well-marked stages in the development of Anabaptism in England. The first stage, speaking roughly, covers the sixteenth century. During this period frequent refugees from Holland and Germany introduced, into different localities of Great Britain, the doctrines of the continental Anabaptists, and there was simultaneously a steady maturing of the ideas and teachings which the scattered groups of Lollards had kept alive. The early movement was, however, never allowed to have free development, nor did it achieve distinct national characteristics or produce a prophetic leader who was able to organize it into a national movement. Throughout the entire century it was regarded with disgust and horror by all sections of the Church, and it was subjected to a persistent campaign of "extermination."

The founder of the *new* Anabaptism—the Anabaptism of the second stage, more properly named the "General Baptist" movement—was himself an Englishman, a Cambridge scholar, a noble spirit with a great religious vision, and this movement was from its origin thoroughly English, with an early promise of national significance.

It is extremely difficult to fix the date of the first appearance of Anabaptism in England, because, as I have said, it had very many traits in common with the Lollards, who were secretly nursing a spiritual religion. We get glimpses in the early years of the sixteenth century of little groups of "brethren" in England who had views very similar to those of the continental Anabaptists. Proceedings were instituted in the court of Bishop Wareham, in 1511, against persons who were teaching that the sacraments of baptism and of confirmation are not necessary or profitable to man's soul.[1] They were probably Lollards who had come, independently, to the position which characterized the Anabaptists. Wareham succeeded in terrifying them into a renunciation of their "errors," and compelled them to "wear the badge of a fagot in flames on their clothing during the rest of their lives or till they were dispensed with for it." [2]

A commission appointed by Henry VIII., in 1530, consisting of the Archbishop of Canterbury, the Bishop of Durham, and others, found "divers heretical erroneous opinions," among others "the unlawfulness of all war." The commission declared that it had found a group of people who taught that Jesus Christ "hath not ordeyned in His spirituall kingdom—which is all trewe Cristen people—any sworde, for He Himself is the King and Governour without sworde and without any outward law. Cristen men among themselves have nought to do with the sworde, nor with the lawe, for that is to them neither needful nor profitable. The secular sworde belongeth not to Crist's kingdom, for in *it* is noon but good and justice. Crist saith that noo Cristen shall resist Evil, nor sue any man at the law." [3] This has the hall-mark of Anabaptism, but it is quite possible for such views to have developed from Lollardry without any foreign influence from the continent.

The name "Anabaptism" does not, so far as I am aware, appear in English documents before 1534. Two proclamations were issued in 1534, in which

[1] Evans' *Early English Baptists*, vol. i. p. 41; Crosby's *English Baptists*, vol. i. p. 30.

[2] Burnet's *History of the Reformation*, vol. i. p. 27.

[3] Quoted from Barclay's *Inner Life of the Religious Societies of the Commonwealth* (London, 1879), p. 14.

Anabaptists were denounced by name, were spoken of as being both of foreign and native origin, and they were accused of "lurking secretly in divers corners and places," and of increasing "naughty printed books."[1] But they were almost certainly "lurking secretly in divers corners" before that date. In an address issued by Bishop Wareham, in 1530, a statement is made which indicates that persecuted Anabaptists from the continent had already begun to seek refuge in Great Britain. It says that "many books in the English tongue, containing many detestable errors and damnable opinions, are printed in countries beyond the seas, to be brought into divers towns and sundry of this realm in England, and sown abroad in the same, to the great decay of our faith, and the perilous corruption of the people unless speedy remedy were provided."[2]

One of these books, full of "detestable errors and damnable opinions," was the *Sum of Scriptures*, which contained this "opinion": "The water in the font has no more virtue in it than the water of the river; the baptism lies not in hallowed water, or in any outward thing, *but in the faith only.* The water of baptism is nothing but a sign that we must be under the standard of the cross."[3] This "opinion" contains the very essence of Anabaptism, and was most probably written by a person who had been influenced by the continental movement.[4]

The terrible persecution of the Anabaptists in the Netherlands drove many of them across to England to try their fate under Henry VIII. The result was that the prevailing strain of teaching in Early English Anabaptism was of the "Hoffmanite" or "Melchiorite" type—due to the influence of Melchior Hoffman, the "apostle" to the Netherlands. There are many evidences of the presence in the kingdom of these Anabaptist

[1] Wilkins' *Concilia Magnae Britanniae et Hiberniae*, vol. iii. p. 776.

[2] Evans' *Early English Baptists*, vol. i. p. 42.

[3] The "Sum of Scriptures" is printed in Wilkins' *Concilia Magnae Britanniae et Hiberniae*, vol. iii. pp. 730-33 (see chap. xv.).

[4] It is, of course, possible that such opinions are only a native development of English Lollardry.

refugees, especially of the artisan class. The proclamation of 1534, already referred to, says that "divers and sundry *strangers* of the sects and false opinions of the Anabaptists . . . are lately come into this realme, where they lurke secretely in divers corners and places, minding craftily and subtilly to provoke and stir the King's loveing subjects to their errors and opinions." They are ordered to leave the country within eight days.

Again, in 1535, more "strangers" fell into the hands—one cannot say the "tender mercies"—of the Church authorities. A contemporary chronicler[1] gives the following account of the occurrence:

"The 25th day of May, were—in St. Paul's Church, London—examined, nineteen men and six women, born in Holland, whose opinions were—first, that in Christ is not two natures, God and man; secondly, that Christ took neither flesh nor blood of the Virgin Mary;[2] thirdly, that children born of infidels may be saved; fourthly, that *baptism of children is of none effect*; fifthly, that the sacrament of Christ's body is but bread only; sixthly, that he who after baptism sinneth wittingly, sinneth deadly, and cannot be saved. Fourteen of them were condemned; a man and woman were burnt in Smithfield; the other twelve of them were sent to other towns there to be burnt."

The chronicler further says that the above "damnable errors" were drawn from "the indiscreet use of the Scriptures."

Latimer, in one of his sermons, shows the indomitable spirit of these martyrs:

"I should have told you here of a certain sect of heretics. They will have no magistrates nor judges on the earth. Here I have to tell you what I heard of late, by the relations of a credible person and a worshipful man, of a town in this realm of England that hath about 500 of heretics of this erroneous opinion in it." "The Anabaptists that were burnt there, in divers towns of England, as I have heard of credible men (I saw them not myself), met their death even *intrepid*, as you will say; without any fear in the world. Well, let them go. There was, in the old times, another kind of poisoned heretics, that

[1] Stow's *Chronicles of England*, p. 1004.

[2] These opinions marked "first" and "secondly" are evidently "Hoffmanite" opinions.

were called Donatists; and those heretics went to their execution as they should have gone to some jolly recreation or banquet."[1]

Barclay, in his study of the *Inner Life of the Religious Societies of the Commonwealth*, which contains a large amount of valuable though badly digested material, gives an interesting account of a great gathering of Anabaptists on the continent in 1536, to which the English societies sent a deputation. He says (quoting Dr. Nippold's *Life of D. Joris*[2] as his authority):

"In that year (1536) certain Baptist societies in England sent a deputation to a great gathering of the Anabaptists near Buckholt, in Westphalia, which was held after the fall of Münster, to compose their differences upon the subject of the bearing of arms, in order to further the interests of the kingdom of Christ, and respecting some other matters. The violent party were represented by Battenburg, who approved the views of the Münster faction, and it is well to note that this man regarded *the tenet of adult baptism as quite unimportant* compared with the extirpation by the sword of the enemies of the 'Kingdom of God,' and had abolished it (*i.e.* water baptism) among his followers previously to this meeting. The party in direct antagonism were represented by Ubbo Phillips (although he was not present), who opposed all war and revenge as anti-Christian, and maintained the purely spiritual character of Christ's kingdom. The third party represented was that of Melchior Hoffman. David Joris, the originator of a fourth party, acted the part of mediator, and subtilely maintained that even if the Battenburgers were right, *the time was not come* to set up the 'Kingdom of the Elect,' and that for the present, therefore, the power must be left in the hands of the hostile and unbelieving magistracy. This meeting at Buckholt

[1] Latimer's Sermons (*Parker Soc. Pub.*), vol. v. p. 151. Froude has commemorated these unnamed heroes in a passage full of beautiful sympathy: "The details are gone—their names are gone. Poor Hollanders they were, and that is all. Scarcely the fact seemed worth the mention, so shortly is it told in a passing paragraph. For them no Europe was agitated, no courts were ordered into mourning, no papal hearts trembled with indignation. At their death the world looked on complacent, indifferent, or exulting. Yet here, too, out of twenty-five poor men and women were found fourteen who by no terror of stake or torture could be tempted to say they believed what they did not believe. History for them has no word of praise; yet they, too, were not giving their blood in vain. Their lives might have been as useless as the lives of most of us. In their deaths they assisted to pay the purchase money for England's freedom" (*History of England*, vol. ii. p. 365).

[2] In *Zeitschrift für die historische Theologie* for 1863, pp. 52-55.

was the commencement not only of the disentanglement of the Baptist Churches from political aims, but of the active propagation of the great idea concerning the entire distinction between the province of the Church and that of the State. This view was later developed by Menno, who was a follower of Ubbo Phillips.

A certain Englishman of the name of 'Henry' was very active in promoting this meeting, and himself paid the travelling expenses of the deputies. (Krohn's supposition that this 'Henry' was Henrick Niclaes is quite beside the mark, as may be seen by comparing the dates.) England was represented by John Mathias, of Middleburg (who was afterwards burnt at London for his adhesion to the tenets of Melchior Hoffman). It is interesting to notice that the representatives of England were very indignant at the loose views of the Münster party. The result of this conference was that the power of the unruly Anabaptists was completely destroyed."[1]

"The Pilgrimage of Grace," in 1536, which was an attempt on the part of Roman Catholics to overthrow the Reformation, included Anabaptism among the "new doctrines" that were to be extirpated. The list of heresies which the "pilgrims" laid before Henry VIII. ended with the words: "Heresies of Anabaptists, clearly within this realm, are to be annihilated and destroyed,"[2] and the Articles of Religion, drawn up by the Convocation which met in June 1536, show that Anabaptist opinions were on the increase in England.[3] The same year, in July, the Lower House laid before the Prelates in Convocation a portentous collection of sixty-seven erroneous doctrines which were then being publicly professed and preached in the country. In the list are found many tenets which are distinctly in line with Anabaptism. For example:[4]

"Item 5.—That all ceremonies accustomed in the Church, which are not clearly expressed in Scripture, must be taken away, because they are men's inventions."

"Item 8.—That it is preached and taught that the Church

---

[1] Barclay, p. 76 *note*.

[2] Froude, *History of England*, vol. ii. pp. 156-57.

[3] Crosby, *History of English Baptists*, vol i. p. 33.

[4] These "items" are taken from Fuller's *Church History of Britain* (London Edition, 1868), vol. iii. pp. 81-86.

that is commonly taken for the Church is the old synagogue; *and that the Church is the congregation of good men only.*"

"Item 12.—That all religions and professions (*i.e.* all established religions), whatsoever they be, are clean contrary to *Christ's religion.*"

"Item 17.—That it is as lawful to christen a child in a tub of water at home, or in a ditch by the way, as in a font-stone in the church."

"Item 34.—*That it is not necessary or profitable to have any church or chapel to pray in or to do any Divine service in.*"[1]

"Item 35.—That the church was made for no other purpose, but either to keep the people from wind and rain, or else that the people upon Sundays and holy-days should resort thither to have the word of God declared unto them."

"Item 41.—That it is as much available to pray unto saints as to hurl a stone against the wind; and that the saints have no more power to help a man than a man's wife hath to help her husband."

"Item 52.—That the singing or saying of Mass, matins, or even-song, is but a roaring, howling, whistling, mumming, tom-ring, and juggling; and that playing at the organ is a foolish vanity."

"Item 56.—That by preaching the people have been brought in opinion and belief that nothing is to be believed except it can be proved expressly by Scripture."

"Item 61.—That water running in the channel or common river is of as great virtue as the holy water."

The King was from the first resolved to "repress and utterly extinguish these persons," who, "whilst their hands were busied about their manufactures, had their heads also beating about points of divinity"; and from the year 1538, "by the exercise of the royal prerogative in the imposition of dogmas of faith on the consciences of his subjects,"[2] he set the machinery in operation to exterminate both the Anabaptists themselves and their books. The hated "sect," however, steadily increased, and Strype says that their "opinions were believed by many honest, well-meaning people."

[1] It is not possible to decide in the case of some of these views whether they have a Lollard or an Anabaptist origin. Strype records (in *Eccl. Mem. under Henry VIII.* vol. i. p. 288) how a converted friar taught that "Christ would dwell in no church that was made of lime and stones, but only in heaven above and *in men's hearts on earth.*"

[2] Tracts on Liberty of Conscience, Intro. by Dr. Underhill, p. xlvi.

Burnet, in his *History of the Reformation*,[1] makes it plain that the "extermination" policy was not succeeding. He says: "At this time (1549) there were many Anabaptists in several parts of England. They were generally Germans whom the Revolution forced to change their seats." Burnet further says that

> "the Reformers made the Scriptures the only rule for Christians, and thereupon many argued that the mysteries of the Trinity and Christ's Incarnation and sufferings, the fall of man and the aids of Grace, were indeed philosophical subtilties and only pretended to be deduced from Scripture, as almost all opinions of religion were, and therefore they rejected them. Among these, Baptism of Infants was one. They believed that our Saviour, commanding the Apostles to baptize, did join *teaching* with it, and they said that the great decay of Christians followed from this way of making children Christians before they understood what they did."

The county of Kent was especially infected with Anabaptist teaching, and an ecclesiastical commission, consisting of Cranmer and six other prelates and divines with various distinguished laymen, was appointed in 1549, "for the examination of the Anabaptists and Arians that now began to spring up apace and show themselves more openly."[2] The first martyr under this commission was the famous Joan Boucher, a member of a small congregation of Anabaptists in the town of Eythorne.[3] Strype says[4] that these sectaries in Kent and Essex were

> "the first that made *separation from the reformed Church of England, having gathered congregations of their own.* The congregation in Essex was mentioned to be at Bocking, that in Kent at Feversham, as I have from an old register. From whence I also collect that they held the opinions of the Anabaptists and Pelagians (free-willers); *that there were contributions made among them for the better maintaining of their congregations; that the members of the congregation in Kent went over to the congregation in Essex, to instruct and to join*

[1] Vol. ii. p. 202.

[2] Strype's *Life of Sir Thomas Smith*, p. 37.

[3] Strype calls her an Arian, and she probably did hold "heretical" views on the nature of the Incarnation.

[4] Strype's *Memorials of Reformers* (Oxford), vol. i. p. 369.

them; and that they had their meetings in Kent in divers places besides Feversham."

Strype has gathered some of the tenets of these sectaries as follows: "That the doctrine of predestination is meeter for devils than for Christian men"; "that children are not born in original sin"; "that there is no man *so chosen* but that he may damn himself, neither any man so reprobate but that he may keep God's commands and be saved." He further records a great dispute which arose among them, "whether it was necessary to stand or kneel, bareheaded or covered, at prayers." Their wise conclusion was "that the ceremony is not material (*i.e. counts for nothing*), *but that the heart before God is required, and nothing else*."[1]

The Cranmer commission, which was renewed in 1551, burnt George van Pare, evidently a Dutch Anabaptist, and forced from another Dutchman a recantation of the opinion that "there is no priest but God only; that no priest has power to take away sin; that no bishop can make one ground holier than another; that no man ought to keep any day holy but the Sunday."[2]

The sufferings of the "Reformers" during the reign of Mary have bulked so large that historians have given little thought and attention to "the root and branch Reformers," the Anabaptists, whom these very "martyrs" of "Bloody Mary's" reign had harried and done to death. All through Mary's reign the "extermination of Anabaptists continued, always needing, however, a repetition of "extermination" immediately after. It is with sadness that one reads of Ridley's condemnation of these noble "heretics" just before he himself was called to the stake in Oxford — to "light such a candle in England as by the grace of God was never to go out." He condemns them because they regard the sacraments as "only *badges and tokens* of Christian men's profession"; because they "make no difference between the

[1] See Strype's *Life of Parker*, vol. i. pp. 54-55; vol. iii. p. 413; and *Mem. of Cranmer*, vol. i. p. 337.

[2] Evans, *op. cit.* vol. i. p. 81.

Lord's table and their own"; because "they refuse to attend the ministry, or submit to any Christian rite from any clergyman, however regular his succession, *who was not known as a man of God by his holy life and the fruits of piety.*"[1]

During Elizabeth's reign not only the existence but the wide diffusion of Anabaptist principles is acknowledged on all hands. Marsden says,[2] speaking of this period:

> "But *the Anabaptists were the most numerous,* and for some time the most formidable, opponents of the Church. They are said to have existed in England from the early days of the Lollards; but their chief strength was now derived and their numbers reinforced from Germany."

Contemporary writers bear witness to the prevalence of the sect.

Bishop Jewel, in his correspondence with the Swiss divines, complained: "We found at the beginning of the reign of Elizabeth large and inauspicious crops of Arians, Anabaptists, and other pests," and Bishop Cox wrote to Gaulter: "You must not be grieved, my Gaulter, that sectaries are showing themselves to be mischievous and wicked interpreters of your most just opinion. For it can not be otherwise but that tares must grow in the Lord's field, and that in no small quantity. Of this kind are the Anabaptists, Donatists, Arians, Papists, and all the good-for-nothing tribe of sectaries." Bishop Aylmer was especially embittered, saying:[3] "The Anabaptists, with infinite other swarms of Satanists, do you think that every pulpit may be able to answer them? I pray God there may be many who can. . . . And in these latter daies the old festered sores newly broke out, as the Anabaptists, the free-willers, with infinite other swarms of God's enemies." And Dr. Parker, in his letter, declining the Archbishopric of Canterbury, says:[4] "They

[1] Underhill, *Liberty of Conscience*, p. cxxv.
[2] Marsden's *History of the Early Puritans*, p. 145.
[3] Bishop Aylmer's *An Harborowe for Faithful and True Subjects*, etc. (1559), p. A. 3.
[4] Burnet's *History of Reformation*, vol. ii. p. 359.

say that the realm is full of Anabaptists, Arians, libertines, free-will men, etc."

Many natives of the Low Countries, exiled by religious persecutions at home, had settled in Norfolk and Suffolk by 1560, and in the fourth year of Elizabeth's reign a proclamation was issued by the Queen,[1] commanding "the Anabaptists and such like heretics, *which had flocked to the coast towns of England* from the parts beyond the seas, under colour of shunning persecution, and had spread the poison of their sects in England, to depart the realm within twenty days, whether they were natural-born people of the land or foreign, upon pain of imprisonment and loss of goods." Many were forced to wander in other lands, and probably fell victims to the persecuting power. Collier says: "Several secured themselves with their Protestancy, and joined the French and Dutch congregations, both in London and the coast towns."[2]

A sect came to light in the diocese of Ely in 1573, which gave the "ecclesiastical commission" great trouble, and which seems like a small Society of Friends three-quarters of a century before their time. "They maintain and defend," the report of the commission declares, "that it is not lawful by the word of God to take any kind of oath, for any cause, before any person"; "that it is not lawful for any magistrate to put a malefactor to death"; "that every man may, without lawful callings, leap into the Church of God, and, as his furious brain moveth him, preach and interpret! Whose voice all men are bound to hear, as well as the ministers of God"; and finally, "they meet in privy conventicles, with the doors shut upon them: intromitting no man but him that will join with them in their mysteries, as they call them. *Their preacher is some one of their company; a private man called and moved, as is above said.*"[3]

There is overwhelming evidence from contemporary

[1] Camden's *Annales of Elizabeth* (edition of 1625), p. 64.

[2] Strype, in his Annals, gives a long account of these commotions, which he professes to draw from Dutch MSS. Evans (vol. i. p. 151) says: "These (MSS.) we believe still exist, and as yet unpublished. Their publication is much to be desired."

[3] Strype's *Life of Parker*, vol. ii. pp. 287-88.

writers to prove that Anabaptism never was "exterminated" in England. Such confessions as: "Now began the Anabaptists wonderfully to increase in the land";[1] and "There are several Anabaptistical conventicles in London (1589) and other places, and some of this sort have been bred at our universities,"[2] show that "the infection of England," as it was called, went on unchecked by "ecclesiastical commissions" and "martyr fires."

II

The second stage of English Anabaptism begins with John Smyth, the "Se-Baptist," or self-baptizer.[3] There is an amazing confusion of John Smyths (or Smiths) in this period of history. *Our* John Smyth received his Master's degree at Cambridge in 1593, was probably ordained a minister of the Church of England in 1594, and certainly became lecturer and preacher of the city of Lincoln in 1600, a position which came to an end two years later. He soon after wrote two books, *The Bright Morning Star* and *A Pattern of True Prayer*, and by 1606 he was a member of the "Separatist Church" of Gainsborough, a part of the famous congregation which assembled at Scrooby Manor House in 1602, and "formed themselves by covenant into a Church of the congregational order," and soon "afterwards he was chosen their pastor." Under the pitiless fire of persecution, a large band of this Gainsborough congregation resolved to migrate to Holland with their leading spirits, John Smyth, Thomas Helwys (or Helwisse), and John Murton (or Morton), to secure

[1] Fuller's *Church History of Britain*.

[2] Dr. Some's *Treatise Against Barrow*. Dr. Some gives interesting light on the views of the Anabaptists of the period. "They held," he says, "that ministers of the Gospel ought to be maintained by voluntary contributions of the people"; "that the civil power has no right to make or impose ecclesiastical laws"; "that the people ought to have the right of choosing their own ministers"; "that no man ought to arrogate to himself the title of Doctor of Divinity"; and "that though the Lord's Prayer be a rule and foundation of prayer, yet it is not to be used as a form; and that no forms of prayer ought to be imposed on the Church."

[3] The movement inaugurated by John Smyth is the beginning of what is historically known as the "Society of General Baptists," and the term Anabaptism gradually fell out of use.

freedom of faith, and thither they sailed, in all probability, toward the end of 1607.

Smyth was one of the most able of the Separatists, and, as Bishop Creighton says, none of them had "a finer mind or a more beautiful soul." He was broad and open-minded, and just the type of man to carry the separation idea to its logical issue, which he did by enunciating the principle of complete and perfect freedom, as opposed to a partial *toleration* by the State of certain "tolerable opinions."

It must be admitted, however, that with all his "open-mindedness" Smyth was, by a fundamental trait of nature, prone to put over-emphasis on unimportant scruples. This trait, in spite of his genuine honesty and sincerity, made him a disturbing element in the new Church, and the leader of separatist tendencies within "the separation." For example, in the interest of "spiritual worship," he insisted that it was a sin to use the English Bible in the worship of God, and he thought that the preachers should bring the originals, the Hebrew and Greek, and out of them translate *by voice.* "A *written* translation," he claimed, "was as much a human writing as a homily or written prayer."[1] Under the influence of the Mennonite teaching about him in Holland he came to see that "infants ought not to be baptized, (1) because there is neither precept nor example for it in the New Testament, and (2) because Christ commanded to make disciples by *teaching* them and then baptizing them."[2] This conclusion carried with it the necessity of re-baptism (for Smith did not adopt the Quaker position that baptism with water is no necessary part of the Christian dispensation), and the question therefore arose, as it had arisen with the primitive Swiss Anabaptists, who was qualified to give the leader the new baptism? The decision reached was novel and unique. It was decided that Smyth should baptize himself, which he did. He then baptized Thomas Helwys and the rest

[1] Ainsworth's "Reply" to Smyth's *Differences of the Churches of the Separation*, p. 108.

[2] Smyth's *Character of the Beast.*

of the company,[1] defending his action on the ground that he had "as good warrant for baptizing himself" as his critics had for "beginning a new Church," namely, "the true Church of the separation."

He, however, later looked on his act as an error and blunder, since, on further consideration, he came to the conclusion that the Mennonites were already "a true Church with a true baptism," and that he should have joined himself to that Church. On this ground he, with thirty-one others, asked for membership in the Mennonite congregation of Amsterdam;[2] but before the decision to receive them was reached Smyth had already joined the great company of those "who have washed their robes and made them white in the blood of the Lamb."

Before leaving Smyth, to follow the development of the larger movement which grew out of this initiation of the English Baptist Society, I must gather up the important religious principles which were more or less clearly enunciated by him.

The following passage from his *Long Confession* is remarkable for the boldness of its insistence on "freedom," its absolute rejection of "original sin," and for its declaration that the "atonement" means *the reconciliation of men to God*:—

"God created man with freedom of will, which was a natural power or faculty in the soul. Adam, after his fall, did not lose any natural faculty, but still retained freedom of will. Original sin is therefore an idle term. Infants are conceived and born in innocency without sin, and so dying are undoubtedly saved, and this is to be understood of all infants under heaven. All actual sinners bear the image of Adam in his innocency, fall, and restitution to grace. As no man begetteth his child to the gallows, nor no potter maketh a pot to break it, so God doth not pre-

[1] The form of baptism used by Smyth is unimportant, but it is generally thought to have been affusion, as was the custom of the Mennonites of the time, and not immersion (see Newman's *History of Baptists*, p. 41).

[2] The application for admission to the Mennonite Church runs as follows: "The names of the English who confess this their error and repent it, viz. that they undertook to baptize themselves contrary to the order appointed by Christ, and who now desire on this account to be brought back to the true Church of Christ as quickly as may be suffered." (Evans, vol. i. p. 209, and Appendix D.)

destinate any man to destruction. The sacrifice of Christ's body doth not reconcile God unto us, Who did never hate us nor was our enemy, but reconcileth us unto God. The efficacy of Christ's death is derived only to them who do mortify their sins, being grafted with Him in the similitude of His death; and every regenerate person hath in himself the three witnesses of the Father, the Word, and the Holy Spirit. Repentance and faith are wrought in the hearts of men by the preaching of the Word; but the new creature which is begotten of God needeth not the outward Scriptures, creatures, or ordinances of the Church; yet he can do nothing against the law and Scriptures, but rather all his doings shall serve to the confirming and establishing of the law. All penitent and faithful Christians are brethren in the communion of the outward Church, wheresoever they live, by what name soever they are known; and we salute them all with a holy kiss, being heartily grieved that we which follow after one faith and one Spirit, one Lord, one God, one baptism, should be rent into so many sects and schisms; and that only for matters of less moment. The outward baptism of water is to be administered only upon penitent and faithful persons, not upon innocent infants and wicked persons. The sacraments have the same use that the Word hath: they are a visible Word, and teach the eye of them that understand as the Word teacheth them that have ears to hear. The outward Church visible consists of penitent persons only, and is a mystical figure of the true, spiritual, invisible Church. The separation of the impenitent from the outward Church is a figure of their eternal rejection, but is reserved for those who forsake repentance and deny the power of godliness. There is no succession in the outward Church, but all succession is from heaven, and is of the new creature only. The magistrate is not by virtue of his office to meddle with religion or matters of conscience, to force or compel men to this or that form of religion or doctrine, but to leave (the) Christian religion free to every man's conscience, and to handle only civil transgressions, injuries, and wrongs of man against man, in murder, adultery, theft, etc., for Christ only is the King and Lawgiver of the Church and conscience."[1]

Some of the positions taken by Smyth in his book called *The Differences of the Church of the Separation* are of great interest for the light they throw on the teachings of the General Baptists and the practices of the Society of

[1] John Smyth's *Last Book*, which contains his "Confession of Faith" in one hundred propositions, was found in *The York Minster Library*. It has been printed in full in Barclay's *Inner Life*, as Appendix to chap. vi.

Friends. The three following principles have special bearing:—

"First—We hold that the New Testament, properly so-called, is spiritual, proceeding originally from the heart, and that reading out of a book (though a lawful ecclesiastical action) is no part of spiritual worship. Second—We hold that, seeing prophesying is a part of spiritual worship, therefore in the time of prophesying it is unlawful to have the book as a help before the eye. Third—We hold that seeing singing a psalm is a part of spiritual worship, it is unlawful to have the book before the eye in time of singing a psalm."[1]

In his *Short Confession* Smyth announced principles which are entirely in line with the doctrines later promulgated by Friends. Two or three specimens of these principles will suffice:—

"They that are redeemed of the Lord do change their fleshly weapons, namely their swords, into shares, and their spears into scythes, do lift up no sword, neither have nor consent to battle." "Yea, rather they are called of Him (whom they are commanded to obey by a voice heard from heaven) to the following of His unarmed and unweaponed life and His cross-bearing footsteps." "It is not permitted that the faithful of the New Testament should swear at all."

John Smyth died in the autumn of 1612,[2] and shortly before his death his old associate, Thomas Helwys, whom he had baptized, and who had refused to follow him into the Mennonite Church, returned to England, accompanied by Murton and a great part of their fellow-members, and established a Baptist Church in London, on Newgate

[1] The full title of this book, which was answered by Ainsworth, is *The Differences of the Church of the Separation: containing a description of the Leitourgie and Ministrie of the Visible Church, annexed as a Correction and supplement to a little treatise lately published, bearing title "Principles and Inferences respecting the Visible Church."* By John Smyth, 1608. Copy in the Bodleian.

[2] A footnote to p. 95 of Barclay's *Inner Life* says: "Smyth's burial is registered in the register of the New Church of Amsterdam, on the 1st of September 1612, where he was buried, and at the time of his decease he lodged in the hinder part of the 'great bakehouse' then belonging to John Munter, where religious meetings were held by the English who joined the Mennonites. I am indebted for this to Dr. Scheffer, who has, by searching these registers, established a date of great importance in the history of the English Separatist Church in Holland. The date of the death of Smyth has been variously stated, and no authority has hitherto been given for the date."

Street—the first General Baptist Church on English soil.[1] Helwys was actuated by the highest motives in his perilous undertaking, and in his courage and devotion to truth deserves to rank with the "Pilgrims," who eight years later began their experiment at Plymouth. He braved persecution in his homeland because he felt, as he says, that "thousands of ignorant souls in our own country were perishing for lack of instruction." He was fiercely attacked by some of those still in "exile" for his "return," and he was charged with an exhibition of "natural courage" and "vain-glory." His *Short Declaration* is a sufficient defence of his course.[2] There are, unfortunately, no extant "records" of this famous church, but there is no question that the ideas embodied in this little "society" in Newgate Street spread rapidly, for by 1626 there were five Baptist churches besides the original church, namely, in London, Lincoln, Sarum, Coventry, and Tiverton, in correspondence with the Mennonite Church of Amsterdam.[3] There was, too, a society of Baptists in Yarmouth in the year 1624.[4] There was also, as early as 1625, a Baptist society at Stony Stratford, which met for some time as a congregation without any settled minister.[5]

Taylor says:[6] "There is some reason to believe that in 1626 there was a General Baptist Church at Amersham, in Buckinghamshire. In the first page of an old church book belonging to that ancient church, there is an imperfect entry in this form: 'Brother David, 26 April, 1626,'" which affords a strong presumption that there was a church in that town at that early period. And we

[1] They were called "General Baptists" because they were Arminian in faith, *i.e.* they held to the general salvability of mankind.

[2] Helwys' writings are as follows: (1) *An Advertisement to the New Fryelers (Freewillers) in the Low Countries*, dated 1611; (2) *A Declaration of Faith of the English People at Amsterdam* (1611); (3) *A Proof that God's Decree is Not the Cause of any Man's Sin or Condemnation* (1611); (4) *Declaration of the Mystery of Iniquity* (1612); (5) *A Short Declaration* (1614); (6) *Persecution for Religion, Judged and Condemned* (1615). This last work may be from the pen of Helwys' associate, John Murton. It is, in any case, one of the most explicit expositions that had yet appeared of the doctrine that *the soul of man should be absolutely free in matters of faith.*

[3] Barclay, *Inner Life*, p. 95.

[4] See Stoughton's *Church of the Commonwealth*, vol. ii. pp. 232-34.

[5] Evans, vol. ii. p. 54.

[6] Taylor's *History of Baptists* (1818), vol. i. pp. 96-97.

have Dr. Featley's authority for stating that *two years prior to this* (*i.e.* to 1626) *they had many converts in Southwark.*[1]

Thomas Helwys seems to have died in 1616, and upon his death John Murton apparently became the leader of the movement.[2] By the year 1626 the society had grown to 150, in spite of the fact that it had had two years earlier a secession of eighteen members under the leadership of Elias Tookey. The most notable spiritual contribution of this little group of returned "exiles" was their splendid promulgation of liberty of conscience.

"It was," says Masson,[3] "from their little dingy meeting-house, somewhere in Old London, that there flashed out first in England the absolute doctrine of Religious Liberty. *Religious Peace; or a Plea for Liberty of Conscience*, is the title of a little tract first printed in 1614, and presented to King James and the English Parliament by 'Leonard Busher, citizen of London.' This Leonard Busher, there is *reason to believe*,[4] was a member of Helwys' congregation; and we learn from the tract itself that he was a poor man, labouring for his subsistence, and had had his share of persecution. He had probably been one of Smyth's Amsterdam flock who had returned with Helwys. The tract is certainly the earliest known English publication in which full liberty of conscience is openly advocated. It cannot be read now without a throb. The style is simple and rather helpless; but one comes on some touching passages. Thus: 'May it please your Majesty and Parliament to understand that by fire and sword to constrain princes and peoples to receive that one true religion of the Gospel is wholly against the mind and merciful law of Christ.' 'Persecution is a work well pleasing to all false prophets and bishops, but it is contrary to the mind of

---

[1] Daniel Featley's *Dippers Dipt*, dedication, London, 1645.

[2] A passage in *Truths Victory* (London, 1645) says: "Some thirty years ago Mr. Morton (Murton) was a teacher of a church of Anabaptists in Newgate. Then his confessions comprehended all the errors of the Arminians, which now of late many that go under your name in and about London dissent from."

[3] Masson's *Milton*, vol. iii. pp. 98-129.

[4] This cannot be *definitely proved*. See Underhill's Introduction to the reprint in Tracts for Liberty of Conscience. He was a citizen of London, and had been an exile from his native land at some part of his life, when he probably became acquainted with the Brownists and Mr. Robinson, to whom he refers. From them he differed on several important subjects, especially on Infant Baptism and Liberty of Conscience.

Leonard Busher's Tract was first printed in 1614. It is in the Bodleian Library.

Christ, Who came not to judge and destroy men's lives, but to save them. And, though some men and women believe not at the first hour, yet may they at the eleventh hour, if they be not persecuted to death before. And no king or bishop can or is able to command faith. That is the gift of God, Who worketh in us both the will and the deed of His own good pleasure. Set him not a day, therefore, in which, if His creature hear not and believe not, you will imprison and burn him. . . . As kings and bishops cannot command the wind, so they cannot command faith; and, as the wind bloweth where it listeth, so is every man that is born of the spirit. You may force men to church against their consciences, but they will believe as they did before when they come there.' 'Kings and magistrates are to rule temporal affairs by the swords of their temporal kingdoms, and bishops and ministers are to rule spiritual affairs by the word and Spirit of God, the sword of Christ's temporal kingdom, and not to intermeddle one with another's authority, office, and function.'"

Masson finely says that "the task of vindicating for England the idea of Liberty of Conscience" fell to "two of the most extreme and despised sects of the Puritans."

"The despised Independents," he continues, "and the still more despised Baptists, or thorough Separatists of the school of Smyth and Helwisse, were groping for the pearl between them; and, what is strangest at first sight, it was the more intensely Separatist of these two sects that was groping with most success. How is this to be explained? Partly, it may have been, that the Baptists were the sect that had been most persecuted—that they were the ultimate sect, in the English world, in respect of the necessary qualification of pain and suffering, accumulated in their own experience."[1]

The little band of English Anabaptists, sometimes called the "Smyth remainder," left behind in Holland on the return of Helwys and his Church, became thoroughly incorporated into the Mennonite Church. There was for some years an intimate relationship between the English societies and the Mennonite Church of Amsterdam, and it is evident from existing correspondence that the persecuted societies, struggling for their life, turned for recognition and support to their spiritual kindred on the continent. There were,

[1] Masson's *Milton*, vol. iii. p. 104.

however, some differences between the two groups which made complete union impossible.

"The English did not see their way to reject oaths, magistracy, and warfare *entirely*, and asked for toleration of slight differences of opinion in these matters. The Mennonites limited the administration of the ordinances to such as had received ordination; the English sought to explain their practice as substantially in accord with that of the Mennonites, *but they would extend the privilege of administering the ordinances, in the absence of an ordained minister, to teachers and evangelists recognized as such by the Church.* The efforts at union would seem to have been unsuccessful. The Mennonites were too inflexible in their positions to make compromises." [1]

III

These Baptist societies, of the Smyth and Helwys type, were, as we have seen, Arminian in their faith; that is to say, they rejected utterly the dogmas of original sin and predestination to wrath and salvation, and for that reason they are called General Baptists. We now come to the formation of another type of Baptist society, which was destined to have a great future: that was the Calvinistic, or "Particular," Baptist Society. The first society of this type was organized in Southwark, London, in 1616, under the leadership of Henry Jacob. Such a movement in the very nature of things was almost certain to appear sooner or later. Some person who accepted the Calvinistic theology was bound to ask on what Scriptural ground infants were baptized, and finding no satisfying ground was likely to start a "new Church." At any rate somebody did ask the question, and somebody did take the novel step, and that person was Henry Jacob. He was, like the other Separatist leaders of the period, a scholar, and a man with the genuine qualities of leadership. He was an Oxford graduate, and at first was disinclined to "separation," believing that the National Church offered sufficient scope for all genuine spiritual development. Time and events and the personal influence of the Separatist leaders in

[1] Newman, *Baptists*, p. 47.

Holland carried him over to the opposite view. He was for a time at Middleburg, in Zealand, where he collected a band of English exiles into a congregation, to which he ministered, and his experience in this congregation, together with the influence of John Robinson, with whom he conferred at Leyden, led him to adopt the "congregational idea."[1] And, in 1616, as stated, he decided to follow the bold course of Helwys, and organize a "congregation" in his home country. This Southwark congregation, often called the "Jacob Church," is the mother congregation of the Particular Baptists. Its founder went to Virginia in 1622, in the hope of founding a congregation under freer conditions than then prevailed in England. He, however, died before his contemplated "Jacobopolis" materialized. His successor in the mother congregation was John Lathrop, who, in his turn, surrendered the hard task of holding out against the organized forces of persecution, and sought relief in the New England colony. There are other great names associated either with this mother Church or with the daughter Churches which sprang from it: Samuel How, the "learned cobbler"; Praise-God Barebones, the "leather-seller," who gave the name to Cromwell's nominated Parliament; Henry Jessey, the "oracle" of his party; Hanserd Knollys, who "built on grace, not works"; and William Kiffin, "the strict communionist."

This Church was sadly prone to "separations." The first division came during Lathrop's pastorate, when a number withdrew "because the congregation kept not to their first principles of separation," and because those withdrawing were "convinced that baptism was not to be administered to infants, but only to such as professed faith in Christ." The inference is that the Church was too "broad," or open in its admission of members, to suit the seceders. One of the most interesting of the complicated separations was due to the adoption of "immersion." Richard Blunt had an "opening" that

[1] Barclay thinks he was influenced by Helwys (see *op. cit.* p. 98).

baptism ought to be "by dipping the body into the water," "though none had so practised it in England to professed believers." If Blunt had been a natural-born innovator like John Smyth, he would probably have immersed himself and, as a "se-immersionist," started a new line. But he rather inclined to follow precedents and to value channels of "succession." It was discovered that there was on the continent a body of immersionists called the "Collegianten," who were a branch of the Mennonites. To them Blunt went for what he had come to believe was "true baptism," and on his return in 1642 he immersed his fellow-believers, and "the new way of baptizing," as Praise-God Barebones puts it, "began to be practised—the particular of which opinion and practice is to *dip*." The "new baptism" was attacked and ridiculed as "a new leaven"; as "a new crotchet, that all who have not been dipt under water have not been truly baptized," and books against it abounded,[1] but the practice spread and came to be the approved method among the Baptist societies—"the fit symbol of Christ's death, burial, and resurrection."

By 1644 the sect of Particular Baptists had become a powerful influence, and, as Masson puts it, had "attained considerable dimensions." There were seven congregations in London, and forty-seven in the rest of England, with many vigorous adherents in the Parliamentary Army. They carefully defined their position in 1644, in a Confession of Faith of fifty-two articles, which impressed their contemporaries with the orthodoxy of their *theology*. Even Featley calls it "a little ratsbane in a great quantity of sugar." The permanent ground of objection, however, to all branches of the Baptists, on the part both of the Established Church and the Presbyterian Church, was the congregational form of organization, the complete separation of Church and State, the wide toleration of faith and practice, and the enormous expansion of the rights, privileges and functions of the *laity*. They were, therefore,

[1] See Featley's *Dippers Dipt, or The Anabaptists Duck'd and Plunged over Head and Ears*, London, 1647; and Pagitt's *Heresiography*, London (first edition), 1645.

throughout the formative period of their history, subject to persecution, and, when that ceased, to slander and abuse. Edwards,[1] with his drag-net spread all over England, gathered up a few stories of the extravagant practices of the Baptists in their conventicles and at "river-dippings," but there is no good evidence to show that the movement was not sane and morally sober. The famous Confession of Faith contained the injunction that at times of immersion "convenient garments be upon both the administrator and subject, with all modesty," and the fragments of truth in reported scandals are nothing more than "the occasions of offence" which attend any widespread movement.

They were frequently ridiculed for having illiterate preachers of mean origin. The charge was partly true; there were among them preachers who had been tailors, leather-sellers, soap-boilers, brewers, weavers, and tinkers, but the important point is that these preachers carried conviction and wrought righteousness and constructed spiritual churches to the glory of God. They did, in their generation, what herdsmen and vine-dressers did in the early days of Hebrew prophecy, what tax-collectors and fishermen did in the primitive days of the Church; and it was vastly to the credit of these primitive Baptists that they rediscovered how to bring the gifts of laymen and unschooled members into play for spiritual ends. Masson, in an interesting passage,[2] gathers up some of the important tenets and practices of the Baptists which were in the line of the expansion of the laity: "They put all Church power in the hand of the people"; "They give the power of preaching and celebrating the sacraments to any of their gifted members, out of all office"; "All *churches* must be demolished: they are glad of so large and public a preaching place as they can purchase, but of a steeple-house they must not hear"; "All tithes and all set stipends are unlawful; their preachers must work with their own hands; and may not go in black clothes."

[1] Edwards' *Gangraena, or Catalogue and Discovery of Errors, Heresies, and Blasphemies*, London, 1646.

[2] *Life of Milton*, vol. iii. p. 149.

According to Baillie,[1] also, the Baptists outwent even the Brownists[2] in the power which they gave to women in Church matters. There were many women preachers among them, of whom a Mrs. Attaway, "the mistress of all the she-preachers in Coleman Street, was the chief."

Baillie (p. 30) says further, that the continental Baptists allowed every one of their members, including women, to preach in public, and also to question the preacher on doctrine before the Church, and *that in England it was the same.*

We get more light on the famous "she-preacher of Coleman Street" from Edwards. In his gossipy way he gives testimony to the common custom of allowing women to preach among the Baptists, and incidentally he describes Mrs. Attaway:

"Among all the confussions and disorder in the Church," he writes,[3] "matters both of opinions and practices, and particularly of all sorts of mechanicks, taking upon them to preach and baptize as smiths, taylors, shoomakers, pedlars, weavers, etc., *there are also some women preachers* in our times, who keep constant lectures, preaching weekly to many men and women. In Lincolnshire, in Holland and those parts [*i.e.* the parts about Holland in Lincolnshire], there is a woman preacher who preaches (it's certain), and 'tis reported also she baptizeth, but that's not so certain. In the Isle of Ely (that land of errors and sectaries) is a woman preacher also; in Hartfordshire also there are some woman preachers who take upon them to expound the scriptures in houses, and preach upon texts as on Rom. viii. 2. But in London there are women who for some time together have preached weekly on every Tuesday, about four of the clock, unto whose preaching many have resorted. I shall particularly give the reader an account of the preaching of two women (one a lace-maker that sells lace in Cheapside, and dwells in Bell Alley in *Coleman Street*, and the other a major's wife living in the Old Bailey), who about a month ago, the second Tuesday in December (as I take it), did preach in Bell Alley in Coleman Street, the manner whereof is as follows (as I had it from a godly minister of this city who was there present, *an eye and ear witness*

[1] Baillie, *Anabaptism the True Foundation of Independency, Brownism, Familism, Antinomy, etc.*, London, 1646.

[2] The Brownists were primitive Congregationalists.

[3] *Gangraena* (edition of 1646, second division, p. 29).

of it): Three women came forth out of an inward room or chamber into the room where they used to exercise and where some company waited for to hear them. These women came with Bibles in their hands, and went to a table; the lace-woman took her place at the upper end of the table; the gentlewoman, the major's wife, sate on one side by her; the third woman stood on the other side of the table. The lace-woman at the upper end of the table turned herself first to this gentlewoman (who was in her hoods, necklace of pearls, watch by her side, and other suitable apparel), and intreated her to begin."

(Then follows a long account of their parleys and excuses, each trying to have the other speak.) Finally

"the lace-woman began with making a speech to this purpose, that now those days were come and were fulfilled which was spoken of in Scriptures, that God would pour out of His Spirit upon the handmaidens, and they should prophesy, and after this speech she made a prayer for almost half an hour, and after her prayer took that text, *If ye love Me, keep My Commandments*; when she had read the text she laboured to analyze the chapter as well as she could, and then spake upon the text, drawing her doctrines, opening them and making two uses, for the space of some three-quarters of an hour; when she had done she spake to the company and said if any had anything to object against any of the matter delivered they might speak, for *that was their custome to give liberty in that kinde*."

The gossipy account runs on and on until finally the minister who furnished the information had to leave the meeting "for fear the candles might go out." Edwards has heard that on another occasion a thousand persons came to hear these women preach! He says, too, that at a later meeting

"One Mrs. Attaway"—"the woman who before preached in Bell Alley (as he has described above), delivered many and dangerous doctrines: As (1) that it could not stand with the goodness of God to damn His own creatures eternally. (2) That God the Father did reign under the law; God the Son under the Gospel; and now God the Father and God the Son are making over the kingdom to God the Holy Ghost, and He shall be poured out on all flesh. (3) That there shall be a general restauration, wherein all men shall be reconciled and saved; and (4) that Christ died for all."

It plainly appears from this account of Mrs. Attaway's "dangerous errors" that this was a congregation of General Baptists, though the preaching of women seems not to have been confined to this branch of the movement. Edwards knows of "she-preachers in Kent, Norfolk, and the rest of the shires." Barclay quotes a vivid passage from *The Schismatics Sifted* (London, 1646), which is in line with Edwards' testimony:

> "Is it a miracle or wonder to see saucie boys, bold botching taylors, and other most audacious, illiterate mechanicks to run out of their shops into a pulpit? To see *bold, impudent huswifes* to take upon them to prate an hour or more; but when, I say, is the extraordinary Spirit poured upon them?"[1]

William Prynne adds his testimony that women not only have "decisive votes" in their congregations, but "liberty of preaching and prophesying." He further asks:

> "Whether Independents admitting women not only to vote as members, but sometimes to preach, expound, speak publicly as *predicants* in their conventicles, be not directly contrary to the Apostles' doctrine and practice, and a mere politick invention to engage that sex to their party?"[2]

Barclay has found in an "uncalendered State paper" an account of "an audacious virago" who preached for two hours in the Strand, and who "*claps her Bible and thumbs the pulpit cushion*" with much confidence.[3] Some one who was nourishing in his soul a rhymester's gift undertook to answer a letter written against Edwards, and has given a description in "poetry" of a woman preacher:

> "And that her zeal, piety, and knowledge
> Surpassed the gravest student in college,
> Who strive their human learning to advance;
> She with her Bible and concordance
> Could preach nine times a week, morning and night,
> Such revelation had she from New Light!"[4]

Henry Denne, who wrote a tract on *The Drag-net of the Kingdom of Heaven, or Christ Drawing All Men*

[1] Barclay, *Inner Life*, p. 157. [2] Quoted by Barclay, p. 157. [3] *Ibid.*
[4] From *Tub-Preachers Overturned* (London, 1647). Quoted in Barclay, p. 156.

(London, 1646), was one of the great exponents of lay-religion and of the doctrine of the indwelling of the Divine Light in all men. He was a Cambridge graduate, and an ordained minister of the Church, but in 1643 he joined himself to the Baptist congregation in Coleman Street, and he is "embalmed" in the pages of the *Gangraena* as "an antinomian and desperate Arminian," who was "re-baptized by a mechanick." He preached against tithes, which the "people" liked to hear. "He hath," mourns Edwards, "a kind of strain in his preaching which *affects and takes the people much*; as, for instance, he will say: 'Oh Lord Christ, if Thou wert now on earth and didst reveal the Gospel to men, they would call *Thee* Anabaptist, Antinomian, Independent, who now call us so.'" Edwards reports that "Mr. Denne preaches and prays, and after he hath done he calls to know if any be not satisfied, and then they stand up that will, and object, and he answers them." This seems to have been the settled custom in the Independent congregations. It is further reported that "others of the brethren that will, *meer mechanicks*, one, two, or more sometimes, do exercise (*i.e.* preach) after him." "This Mr. Denne delivered his opinions in such a manner *as if he had been an apostle from heaven.*" Edwards' whole account, in spite of himself, lets daylight enough through for us to see that here was a truly great soul. "Mr. Disbrough," he declares, "says of him that he is the ablest man in England for prayer, expounding, and preaching."[1] "His usual theme that he is upon is *Christ's dying for all*, for Judas as well as Peter. He often preaches this doctrine. This is the everlasting Gospel, *that Jesus Christ has died for all men, Turks, Pagans*; and men are only damned for not believing in Christ, and for nothing else."[2] A passage from Denne's *Drag-net*[3] will show that two years before George Fox began his preaching of the "Light within" there was an advocate of the same doctrine among the Baptists:

[1] "Mr. Disbrough" was James Disbrough, an elder in the famous Fenstanton Church, and a brother of Cromwell's major-general.

[2] Edwards, p. 23.

[3] P. 91.

"Now God is light, and God is spirit. If then Christ lighteth every man, God lighteth every man. The Spirit lighteth every man that cometh into the world. What is it for man to be lighted, but for the light of the glory of God, shining forth in the face of Jesus Christ, to shine in *darkness*? *For every man to be lighted is (as I conceive) for the manifestation of the glory of God to be showed forth in some measure to them.*

Lay-preaching greatly increased during the Civil War, and in spite of the Parliamentary Ordinance against it the practice was common in many parts of England during the Commonwealth. A prominent soldier of the period says:

"Many thousand souls besides me can testify that Christ hath been preached, and that effectually and to the comfort of many hearts, and I bid defiance to the devil and all his black-mouthed instruments (ordained ministers in black coats) to produce that even those who they call Sectaries in the preaching of the Lord Jesus did by that open a gap to profaneness."[1]

The Baptists not only opened the way for lay-preaching, and even women's preaching, but they vigorously opposed tithes, state-supported ministry, and anything that led to "hireling ministry." Many of their preachers gave their time and service freely to their congregation. Even as late as 1679 the practice of having "a set maintenance for preaching" is denounced.[2] Taylor thus describes the views of the General Baptists:

"The ministers of Christ, they say, who have freely received from God, ought freely to minister to others, and such as have spiritual things ministered unto them ought freely to communicate necessary things to the ministers upon account of their charge; but tythes or any forced maintenance we utterly deny to be the maintenance of Gospel ministers."[3]

They strongly protested against creating a worldly clergy for worldly ends. They were almost as positive as the Quakers were later in their assertions that human learning could not make a minister. Samuel How, a

[1] *Preaching without Ordination*, etc., by Edward Chillenden, Lieutenant of Horse. Quoted by Barclay, p. 171.

[2] Berkhamstead Church Book (1679). Quoted by Taylor in his *General Baptists*.

[3] *Ibid.* vol. i. p. 420.

minister of the Particular Baptists, says: "Human learning would never make a man a minister of the Gospel, or enable him to understand the mind of God in His Word."[1]

Barclay has collected much evidence to show that the Baptists originated the practice of *standing up in church* after the preacher had finished his sermon, and that this practice was current when George Fox began his ministry.[2]

"Our brethren in London" (*i.e.* the Independents), says Baillie,[3] "are for this exercise" (*i.e.* the exercise of prophesying), "but especially to hold a door open for them to preach in parish churches where they neither are, nor ever intend to be, pastors; only they preach as gifted men and prophets, for the conversion of those who are to be made members of their congregations."

Richard Baxter says there were "few of the Anabaptists that have not been the opposers and troublers of the faithful ministers of the land" (*i.e.* of the Presbyterians).

"On the 27th day of the ninth month, Henry Denne (the celebrated General Baptist preacher) declared the proceedings at Hawson. There was mention of a promise that I should go to Hawson the next first-day, and accordingly, on the 19th day of this present month, I went thither, and on the next day, it being the first day of the week, the priest and chiefest men of the town sent to me to come and preach in the public place (*i.e.* the church). Whereupon I went, intending to have spoken there unto the people, but as soon as I began to speak the rude multitude gathered together and would not suffer me to speak. . . . Whereupon I departed from them, and I spake in a private house."[4]

Edwards mentions that Lamb (of Bell Alley Church of the General Baptists) "preaches sometimes (when he can get into pulpits) in our churches." On 5th November, 1644, he preached at Grace Church in London, "where he had mighty great audience, and preached universal grace."[5] Hanserd Knollys preached "in the churchyard

[1] How's *Sufficiency of the World's Teaching without Human Learning* (1640).

[2] *Inner Life*, pp. 288-90.

[3] Baillie's *Dissuasive*, p. 175.

[4] Fenstanton Church Records, p. 81.

[5] Edwards, Part II. p. 35.

when he could not in the church, and getting up into the pulpits when the sermon or lecture had been ended, against the will of the minister, so that there were several riots and tumults by his means. He was complained against for this to a committee of Parliament, but he got off from that committee."[1] On another occasion Mr. Kiffin handed a letter to Edwards in the pulpit asking leave, "to declare against what you say when your sermon is ended."[2]

On the 14th July 1648, Edward Barber, a celebrated General Baptist, spoke at the "parish meeting-house of Bentfinck," London. Several of the inhabitants of the parish had invited Mr. Barber to come, promising that he should have liberty to add to what the minister (Mr. Calamy) should deliver, or contradict if erroneous. "I desired him," says Mr. Barber, "and the rest of the audience to add some few words. . . . Upon which he (Calamy) desired me to 'forbear till he had concluded, and I might speak.'" Mr. Barber then complains that he dealt with him as Calamy had before dealt with Mr. Kiffin, Mr. Knowles, and Mr. Cox, and charged him with "coming to make a disturbance in the 'Church of God.'" Mr. Barber was then sadly handled by the audience, who cried, "Kill him, kill him! pull him limb from limb!" and "a woman scratched his face." A constable, however, interfered in his favour, or he "might have been robbed or murdered." Some of the audience, however, spoke kindly to him, and wished him to "go to Mr. Calamy's house" and be satisfied, but Mr. Barber says that after this treatment he was satisfied that they were all anti-Christian ministers.[3]

The General Baptists, with their faith in universal

[1] Edwards, Part II. p. 39. [2] *Ibid.* p. 47.

[3] "A Declaration and Vindication of the carriage of Mr. Edward Barber at the parish meeting-house of Bentfinck, London, Friday, February 14, 1648. After the morning exercise of Mr. Calamy was ended, wherein the pride of the ministers and Babylonish carriage of the hearers is laid open, etc. . . . as also the false aspersions cast upon him, he doing nothing but what was according to the primitive institution, and is, and ought to be, in the best reformed churches according to the Protestation and Covenant" (Barclay, p. 290).

redemption through Christ, felt that the Gospel should be preached to every person under heaven, and that the work of "discipling all nations" should be seriously taken up. In fact, they had a vision of an apostolic mission. Says a quaint Baptist writer:

"It is most certain that there were several things proper and peculiar to the first and chief Apostles, not to be pretended at all by their successors, yet it is also true that many things pertaining to their office as itinerant ministers are of *perpetual duration* in the Church with respect to that holy function, and consequently to descend to those who were to succeed them as travelling ministers, to plant churches, and to settle them in order who are as sheep without a shepherd."[1]

They plainly had bands of travelling ministers, sometimes called "apostles," sometimes "messengers of the churches," who "travelled up and down the world planting new churches, edifying old churches, and seeing that good order and government was carefully and constantly kept up." The discipline, or Church power, in the Baptists' congregations was in the hands of the members themselves. Periodical meetings were held and officers were chosen "to look after the poor and the suffering," "to have care over the members in their respective districts," "to oversee their conversation and carriage," "to report on attendance of the members at meetings for worship and business."[2] They insisted, however, that Christ Himself is Head and Governor of the Church, and they made it a principle of the first importance that in order to "*restore the primitive way*" there must be "men professing and practising the order and form of Christ's doctrine who shall beautify the same with a holy and wise conversation in all godliness and honesty."[3]

[1] Grantham's *Christianismus Primitivus*, Book II. p. 119.

[2] Taylor's *General Baptists*, p. 435. If they absent themselves without sufficient cause, "they shall be looked upon as offending, and be proceeded with accordingly" (*Records of the Fenstanton Church*, p. 126, and *passim*, pp. 433-35). "As soon as any General Baptist Churches had been gathered, they united to support a periodical meeting—such meeting was called an association, and was usually held quarterly, half-yearly, or annually" (*ibid.* 437). The Travelling Ministers or Elders were most frequently chosen representatives.

[3] Grantham, *op. cit.* p. 69.

They were the ringing champions of a free conscience, a free ministry, a spiritual Church and a pure daily life. They were the beginners of a new order, which did much to prevent old customs from "corrupting the world." Their part in the great political transactions which were going on, as George Fox was starting out on his momentous journeys to enlarge the spiritual horizon of England, are beyond the scope of my work. I shall merely give one important passage from Skeats.[1]

"They protested against any *compulsory religion*, stating that 'the ways of God's worship are not all entrusted to us by any human power.' The Presbyterians, on the other hand, insisted on the establishment of their own religion only, upon 'a covenanted uniformity,' and upon the extirpation of the sects. A third party was represented by the King, who, after two years' treaty, consented to most of the views of the Presbyterians. It was at this period that the Army, seeing that everything for which they had fought, *including liberty of conscience*, was about to be wrested from them, sent in a remonstrance to the legislature. It was not attended to; Fairfax at once marched on London, and on December 6, 1648, Pride "purged" the House of Commons. From this time Cromwell and the Independents held the reins of government."[2]

---

[1] *History of the Free Churches of England*, p. 56.

[2] Skeats points out that it is remarkable that so few modern writers should have drawn attention to the intimate connection of the question of religious liberty with the events which led to Pride's "purge," the execution of Charles, and the establishment of the Commonwealth. Rushworth, and Neal following him, have clearly pointed it out.

CHAPTER XVIII

THE FAMILY OF LOVE

AMONG the obscure sects which came into existence during the opening period of the Reformation, none was more novel and unique, and none has been more vilified than the "Family of Love," or "House of Love," or "Familists." It was synchronous in origin with the rise of Anabaptism on the Continent, and, like Anabaptism, too, it had a great second flowering period in England during the early part of the seventeenth century, and on through the Commonwealth. It was, however, in origin entirely independent of the Anabaptist movement, and though its founder undoubtedly read the writings of Luther, the movement was in the main an isolated outburst, a sporadic upheaval, having its own course apart from the central stream which was breaking up the hardened crust of tradition and custom. It brought into public notice and gave wide vogue to many doctrines and practices generally supposed to have originated with the Quakers, and it was at its best the exponent of a very lofty type of mystical religion. Its founder was a very extraordinary character, and his voluminous writings contain spiritual insights and religious teachings which deserve to be rescued from the oblivion into which they have largely fallen.

This founder was Henry Nicholas (or Niklaes, or Niclaes), who was born of extremely devout and pious parents in Münster in Westphalia either in 1501 or 1502.[1]

[1] The data for the story of Nicholas are three unpublished manuscripts preserved in the Maatschappy Library in Leyden. They are (1) *Chronika des*

The boy was dowered with a constitution which made him susceptible even as a child to intimations and openings, and which turned him with an instinct like that of the homing pigeon toward Divine things. He was, like George Fox, a boy apart from the throng, solitary and brooding, full of vivid imaginations and unsatisfied with the ordinary, traditional explanations which were given to the boyish minds of the period. The whole atmosphere of the home was intensely religious. His father, a zealous Catholic, prayed to God every day "to be gracious to him, to give him a holy nature, and to give him holy offspring."[1] As little Heinrich was weak and delicate his mother gave him the first stages of his education, and thus he was in a peculiar degree penetrated and permeated with the religious spirit of the family. A special effort was made to cultivate in him reverence and love for the ceremonies of the Church. The child was taken to daily Mass, and his father took pains to talk with him freely about the holy things of his religion.

Under this nurture the highly susceptible boy advanced to a wisdom and insight unusual in persons of such tender years, so that by his eighth year his questions became too deep and puzzling for the simple pious father. The chronicler has preserved an incident from this period which seems to him to show that the Lord Himself opened the mouth of the child and touched his lips and tongue. He, so the account runs, naively asked his father one day what he thanked God for. The father replied that he thanked God for forgiveness of sins through Jesus Christ and for the true life of godliness established by Him. The child startled his father with the blunt remark that he could not see that sin in man had been bettered by Jesus Christ's coming, or that he was brought into actual godliness. The boy was told that he must not doubt or question the grace of God, but simply accept what was

Hüsgesinnes der Lieften, (2) *Acta H.N.*, and (3) *Ordo Sacerdotis.* Owing to an ambiguity in the *Chronika* it is impossible to decide whether he was born in 1501 or 1502, and also whether the birthday was the 9th or 10th of January.

[1] I have made large use of Nippold's excellent chapter on "Heinrich Niclaes und das Haus der Liebe" in *Zeitschrift für die historische Theologie*, Gotha, 1862. Nippold has drawn his material from the three MSS. mentioned above.

taught about it. Not easily hushed he still urged the point that he did not at all doubt that through the death of Christ the door to the kingdom of God was opened for all, but that for him faith was meaningless without an imitation of Christ's passion, and that he could think of no restoration to the perfect state of *godliness until sin itself was destroyed.* So far he could not see that this had taken place among men, therefore God must intend to destroy sin and establish perfect righteousness *in some other way than men generally thought.* This seems like an advanced position for an eight-year-old lad, but some such brooding is by no means unnatural or impossible in such a child. He was next brought to a Franciscan monk confessor for counsel, and to dispel "the strange whimsies in his head." He was told that he was much too young and too small to search into the deep, profound mysteries of divine things, or to expect to fathom them. "Very true," answered the boy, "and that is why I have *asked*, and have not tried to search them out in my own power." And then with simple earnestness he laid his spiritual burden on the confessor. His trouble was that the very thing which Christ died to do was not yet done. He died, everybody told him, to redeem mankind, to bring men back into the condition of righteousness which Adam was in before he fell; but men all about were still living in sin and very far from that first condition! There was a discrepancy somewhere; something was lacking. Sin was not destroyed, and men were not perfect like the Christ who had died for them. The helpless confessor had no illumination for the strange boy, and a second monk was called to no better purpose. In the end the boy was severely scolded, and told that he had committed the greatest sin possible in his questionings about the hidden things of God, and that perhaps he could never be forgiven at all, which threw him into a great fright. To quiet him he was finally promised absolution if he would repent. He came home far from satisfied with the "instruction of the two love-brothers," and he "went up and down with a sad heart." He now kept his musings to himself. He shrank from companions and playmates, and dwelt much on his spiritual problems. In his ninth year a marvellous vision came to him—the beginning of a series of visions. It came at daybreak when he was in a half-sleeping, half-waking state—a borderland condition—and when he was deeply troubled over the sinful condition of men. A great light suddenly surrounded him, the light of the splendour and glory of the Lord, in shape like a mountain rising from his bed up into heaven, wrapping him wholly about and illuminating him in mind and spirit through and through, until he was absolutely one being with the shining mountain. He felt himself penetrated with the divine Spirit, and, to use his later phrase, raised to "a begodded man." In this unity of being he discovered, says the chronicler,[1] the true fulfilment of redemption in Jesus Christ. When the vision departed he awoke in a weak and nervously exhausted state, and soon fell into a trance condition in which he saw a multitude of saints of God, to whom he imparted this glorious life for which men were created, and into which Christ had redeemed them, and this vision was taken as his *call* to be a prophet of the new revelation.[2] He early became a constant and careful reader of the Scriptures, and his later works show an extraordinary familiarity with them. Before he undertook his studies of the Bible he already had read the writings of Luther, but disapproved of them, first because of their attack on the priesthood of the Roman Catholic Church (to which he was still loyal), and secondly because Luther did not, to his mind, teach the ground of true righteousness and the fulfilment of real godliness in Jesus Christ, and did not insist on a Church composed of transformed persons.[3] He was married at twenty to a "virtuous lady, of a plain and simple family," who made him an excellent wife, and he took up a mercantile business in which, strangely enough, he was very successful. He was

[1] The discovery is, however, certainly the outcome of later reflection, and the whole account shows expansion in the light of later experience.

[2] Compare this vision of the "multitude of saints" with George Fox's vision in Wensleydale: "The Lord opened unto me, and let me see a great people in white raiment coming to the Lord" (*Journal*, London edition, 1901, vol. i. p. 110).

[3] Nippold, p. 349. In this particular he was like the Anabaptists.

early suspected of holding "unsound views," and partly on account of these prevailing suspicions he moved with his family to Amsterdam (about 1530), where he allied himself with persons "who had fallen away from the Catholic Church, though they were persons who earnestly sought after righteousness." It was, however, not till his thirty-ninth year that he received the revelation which at length made him the founder of a new sect. He had during his nine years in Amsterdam prayed unweariedly that God would "reveal His perfect truth on the earth." Suddenly one day "God appeared to him, enwrapt him, became one being with him, and communicated to him the hidden things of His Divine nature and of the spiritual nature of man. The Holy Spirit of Love was poured out upon him, and he felt himself chosen to be the revealer of the Word." With the revelation there came the command to write and publish what had been revealed to him.

A further vision of similar character came to him later (in Emden, whither he had removed his home). He had an enwrapping experience which so expanded his heart and mind that he comprehended the perfection of God and the heavenly host, and the things as well of the earthly kingdom, and he was definitely called to be the prophet of the Holy Spirit of love.[1] From now on he gathered adherents about him, and organized a society called the "House, or Family, of Love."[2] It spread slowly but steadily in the towns of Friesland, Holland, Brabant, Flanders, and later in England and France. He and his supporters were everywhere harried, and though he himself appears somewhat unheroic under the onset of persecution, his practice of allowing all abuse, slander, and enmity to go unnoticed was highly dignified, and was wholly unique at that date of the world. In the "House of Love," he insisted, there is to be no violence, no bluster, no wranglings.[3]

[1] Nippold, p. 354.

[2] From now on he always used the initials H. N., which may, and very likely do, stand for *Homo Novus* (New Man), as well as for his old name Henry Nicholas.

[3] "Brawling and discord do I not hold for any Christian fight, seeing men do thereby forsake love. Therefore such a fight doth nothing further the life" (Introduction to *Glass of Righteousness*, chap. xi. p. 21).

The organization of the "House of Love" was formed more on the basis of the Roman Catholic hierarchy than on any Protestant model. It had a highest bishop, twenty-four elders, and three lower orders of priests, but, notwithstanding his cumbersome hierarchy, it was the supreme purpose of Nicholas, through his writings, to raise the *entire membership* of the "House of Love" to "full-grown men in Christ," so that each member should attain to the experience of "a begodded person."[1] These "writings" were very numerous and voluminous, though they are now extremely rare.[2] They were originally in a Low German dialect (called by the English translator *Basse Almayne*), and they were all, or nearly all, translated into English. The works of chief importance were *The Glass of Righteousness*,[3] *An Introduction to the Glass of Righteousness*, *The First Exhortation of H. N. to his Children*, *The Evangelium Regni* (Gospel of the Kingdom), *Epistles*, *Cantica*, and *Terra Pacis: or Spiritual Land of Peace*, which is a spiritual pilgrimage quite like *Pilgrim's Progress* in germ.[4] The central idea in all Henry Nicholas's writings is his insistence on *real righteousness* and *actual holiness* as contrasted with the fiction of a merely imputed righteousness and a forensic holiness, or holiness based on a transaction outside the person himself. He maintains that the

[1] He says in *Introduction to Glass of Righteousness*, chap. xxv., that "Every father of a family under the Love hath the liberty in his family to use services and ceremonies as he perceiveth out of the Testimonies of the Holy Spirit of Love, that they are profitable or necessary for his household, to the life of Peace, and the true righteousness which God esteemeth. If any have any heavenly revelation, or use any service of the Priestly Ordinance, let him do it to concord and not to strife, dissension, or schism." He made much of the *Elders*, and frequently urged the members to obey them and take counsel of them. It is not improbable that the Elders in the Family of Love had an influence on the formation of the Quaker Eldership. He writes: "Give care to the Elders of the Holy Understanding, follow not the will or counsel of your own mind, but under the service of Love follow the counsel of wisdom and keep with the Elders in the Family of Love, to the concord and multiplying in good of the peaceable Kingdom in all Love. Be not wavery, but if ye stumble or fall, yet rise again, stay not upon yourselves lest ye come not at any time to the light of life or day of Love. Subject yourselves to teaching and the service of Love, that ye come to the Freedom of the Children of God" (*Introduction to Glass of Righteousness*).

[2] Charlotte Fell-Smith in her excellent article in the *Nat. Dict. of Biog.* gives a list of twenty-three genuine works and five doubtful works commonly ascribed to him.

[3] The only English translation of this work, so far as known, is the manuscript fragment in the Bodleian Library.

[4] It was printed in English in 1649.

only righteousness that amounts to anything is one which *appears* in the person himself—one which bears witness to a new life in the person. And this righteousness, this new life, comes from a spiritual incorporation of the person into God's life, so that the person, once a mere man, becomes "godded," or made comformable to Christ, who was an absolutely begodded man.[1] "God," he says, "is a living God, a perfect, clear Light and Love itself. This God *manneth* Himself [*i.e.* reveals Himself humanwise], and we may become likewise, through His godly Light, *godded* and made a conformable willing spirit with Him."[2] It is through Jesus Christ that we are *renewed* in our human spirit and brought into "a goodwilling life," and when we become "incorporated into Christ as fellow-members with Him," then and only then does He become our *Saviour.* This experience involves a following after Christ, even to His death on the Cross, in perfect obedience to His Holy Spirit of Love, *to the actual vanquishing of sin, death, and hell,* to the burying of all iniquity, to the destroying of our old nature and ungodly being. "Those that do not even *so* become baptized in His name, and do not bear in their inwardness the death of sin through the death on the Cross of Christ, are no Christians."[3]

In a passage of the *Spiritual Tabernacle* (chap. v. 15) he expresses himself precisely as George Fox so often does on the inwardness of the Christ-revelation:

> "Behold this high Priest is spirit and life, the true King and faithful Lord, a peaceable Prince, and *not this or that without us, but He is in us all which believe on Him according to the truth.*"

---

[1] He appears to have held the orthodox view of Christ's divinity, though his conception is often expressed in words which sound extremely modern. For example, he says in one of his *epistles* that "the true Christ was the like-being of God, only begotten Son of God from eternity, born of the seed of David according to the flesh, delivered to death on the Cross, but risen again from the dead *for a perpetual conquering of sin and death, and making himself manifest unto the friends that love him.*" Quoted freely from Prof. Allen C. Thomas's excellent monograph on "The Family of Love," in *Haverford College Studies*, fifth mo. 1893, p. 31.

[2] *First Exhortation* (London, 1656), pp. 27-31.

[3] *Ibid.* pp. 35-37. He means by the atonement a vital and dynamic redemption by which we are brought into union with Christ, who "*manneth Himself with us to an implanting of us in Him* with the like death of His Cross, to crucify and slay even so, through His suffering and death, the sinful flesh with its lusts and desires" (*First Exhortation*, p. 156).

This same idea is expounded again and again in the writings. It is set forth with a fair degree of clearness in another section of the *First Exhortation*, which I have freely rendered:

"The true Light is the everlasting life itself and has its origin and forthcoming out of the lovely Being and true Mind of the eternal and living God. This Light shows itself (in the world) through illuminated, *i.e. godded* men, for through such persons the Most High is *manned* (*i.e.* humanly shown). The true Light, therefore, consists not in knowing this or that, but in receiving and partaking of the true Being of the Eternal Life, by the renewing of the mind and spirit and by an incorporation of the inward man into this true Life and Light, so that the person henceforth lives and walks in the Light in all Love."[1]

Nothing short of this experience, he holds, can make a man a Christian, and apart from such an experience, "ceremonies" and "God-services" are "mere vain husks." "Ye shall find," he writes to his "dear children," "*in experience* that God with His Christ and Holy Spirit and with the heavenly fellowship of all the holy ones will inhabit in you and live and walk in you, for He hath chosen none other house or temple for His habitation but you."[2] With this exalted conception of the religious life as an inward experience of Christ *incorporated in the soul*, was joined also an equally lofty conception of the moral life in daily walk and conversation. Henry Nicholas and his Family of Love have been frequently charged with libertinism and antinomian leanings. There is no ground in his writings for the charge, and there is no evidence that the society countenanced loose and immoral living.[3] Henry Nicholas's writings abound in wholesome counsel, and his moral injunctions have everywhere the ring of sincerity.

[1] *First Exhortation*, pp. 107-9. [2] *Ibid.* p. 151.

[3] It is quite probable that loose livers took advantage of the movement in its beginning, and, under the guise of a spiritual Family of Love, formed a Family of Love with low motives and so gave the Society a bad reputation. No such charges can be established against the founder himself or against the genuine members of the House of Love. Nicholas, while admitting that marriage is a proper ordinance, counsels those who are married to destroy the lusts of the flesh in themselves, and he urges that there shall be no sexual intercourse even in the married state except such as is consistent with pure love (see Henry Nicholas upon the Beatitudes under "Beatitude on Cleanness of Heart").

In fact the entire burden of his "prophecy" is the necessity of exhibiting a renewed and transformed life in which the righteousness of God is *realized.*

"If now," he says, "any man be a Christian, let him then have also a Christian nature and stand under the obedience of the love of Jesus Christ."[1]

And he continues:

"If he have no Christian nature and standeth not subject under the Love of Jesus Christ, then can he not assuredly be illuminated, neither can he be any Christian in the sight of God."

On the subject of Antinomianism, he is as clear as a bell:

"No one is ever released from law. Those who think the law is abolished have not the Love of Christ formed in them. The law is not abolished, it is fulfilled in Love. He that loveth doeth the will. No one ever transcends righteousness, for the entire work of God toward salvation has been making for the fruits of righteousness."[2]

There is a fine personal testimony in the *Introduction*, in which Nicholas impresses his "dear friends" with the importance of positive righteousness for the reception of spiritual experience:

"I (Henry Nicholas) held my own human nature straight unto all virtue and righteous dealings to do the Lord's will in all my doings. I passed under the obedience of love with my human nature to the intent to obtain the virtuous disposition of love and to be incorporated to the same with soul and body, and with all the senses and thoughts of my human nature, and so the Lord received me into the Grace of His love and gave me inheritance with Christ and His saints in His heavenly riches, and revealed His last will unto me."[3]

Like the Anabaptists and the Quakers, he called his followers away from oaths and war and capital punish-

[1] *Introduction to Glass of Righteousness*, p. 7.

[2] An epitome of chap. ii. secs. 1-5, *Introduction to Glass of Righteousness.* In a fine passage of the *First Exhortation*, he defines "the true freedom" as the "Unbinding" of the man from himself and his wicked nature, "through the ministration of the gracious word," and as the formation in him of a new and heavenly life conformed to "the lovely being of the true Life and Love," pp. 120-21.

[3] *Introduction*, chap. xii. sec. 57.

ment. Here is a clear announcement of his position from the "Introduction":

"In the House of Love men do not curse nor swear; they do not destroy nor kill any. They use no outward swords or spears. They seek to destroy no flesh of men; but it is a fight of the cross and patience *to the subduing of sin.*" [1]

Their attitude, again, toward the Scriptures and toward outward ordinances and ceremonies (Henry Nicholas's phrase is "God-services") is almost exactly that of the Friends. The following passage from the *Introduction* sounds as though it were taken from Fox's *Journal* or Barclay's *Apology*, though they were written a hundred years later:

"The written word of the letter is not *the Word itself*, that cleanseth and sanctifieth the man, or which procreateth the life. But it is a shadow or figuring out of the holy and true word, a serviceable instrument whereby we are made well-affected inwardly in our souls to the true word of vivification, to the end that through belief and love we might in the spirit of our minds be made of like-being with the nature and being of the Good Life; even as the words of Scripture witness." [2]

In his *First Exhortation*,[3] he says that "this Word of Life (which now inspires us with the holy Spirit of Love) hath in all ages, by figures, shadows, parables, words, written letters, been working men up to good will," but he constantly speaks of the danger of being led astray by those who are only "Scripture-learned." So, too, all rites and ceremonies are only shadows and figures for a low stage of religious progress.

"Alas," he writes, "how great contention and disputation hath there been among many touching baptism. The one would have the baptism thus, the other so. But while it was right with them, yet hath no man been able, before this day of love which is the true light and glory of God himself, to understand nor discern the baptism of John (the outward) nor the baptism of Christ (the inward)." [4]

---

[1] Chap. xi. p. 20. [2] Chap. vii. sec. 29. [3] Pp. 13, 14.
[4] *Evangelium Regni*, xix. 12; quoted in Thomas's Monograph, p. 32.

This teaching gets a clearer interpretation in the *First Exhortation* where he says that those upright (*i.e.* spiritual) believers that follow after Christ in death and life become baptized and washed through Christ in the pure living water of the holy Ghost.[1] In another passage of sweeping import he sets forth his principle, in words that are probably inspired by the Galatian Epistle:

"Not in anything whatsoever that is visible or feelable, nor in any factious God-services or ceremonies which are observed with men's hands in contention and *which do not require any life of righteousness*, consisteth either salvation or condemnation before God, nor can they bring any vantage or damage at all unto souls."[2]

It was his overmastering concern that the *life* should be put above forms and "God-services," and it may not be amiss to quote one more passage out of an abundance of similar utterances:

"Let no man bind his heart unto any outward thing, for here is the sum of perfect Righteousness. It is a humble heart that departeth from all earthly and corruptible things and with a lowly and meek spirit is incorporated with God in pure love, according to the Spirit, living in the form of Jesus Christ, in an unspotted conscience."[3]

Nicholas, like George Fox, made much of quiet waiting in silence.

"Grow up in stillness and singleness of heart," he says, "praying for a right sight in the truth, for that shall make you free. He urges his Family to break spiritual bread together *in stillness*, abiding steadfast in prayer, till all covering wherewith

[1] P. 20, see also pp. 41-43.

[2] *Introduction to Glass of Righteousness*, chap. xvi. sec. 35. There is an interesting passage in the *Evangelium Regni*, chap. xxxiii., which shows that he believed that no religious service is of value unless the person who performs it is *illuminated*: "Therefore consider now that no man by his knowledge of the Scripture can rightlie erect, teach, or set forth the Christian ceremonies. But they shall be administered and taught in their right form by them that are chosen or raised up thereunto by God, which follow after Christ in his death, become renewed with him in a new life, in whom the living God with His Christ hath even so then obtained his dwelling and shape. From whose bodies likewise the Words of God and Christ do then flow forth as living waters, which also concordably agree with the testimony of the Holie Ghost."

[3] *Introduction to Glass of Righteousness*, chap. xii. p. 25.

their hearts, after the flesh, are covered is done away, that is to say until the spiritual, heavenly, and uncovered being of Christ appears and comes to their spirit." [1]

He undoubtedly looked upon himself as a prophet of at least equal standing and inspiration with any in the Scriptures, and he always assumes that his new sect, founded on his own revelations, is the only true church.[2] "The House of Love" is God's latest stage of revelation—"the more perfect way," for which the world had waited long. It was, they believed, "the New Day of Life," "the fulfilment of God's Covenant of Grace"—the beginning of the Religion of the Spirit. "Now *in the last time*," writes Henry Nicholas,[3] "through the appearing of Christ, God hath raised up His community of holy ones," which is "the *only true seed and witness* of Jesus Christ in the world," or, as he says again, "the stool of Grace to an everlasting remission of sins"; though the benefit is promised only to such as "submit your hearts until that Love which is the being of Christ have a shape in you." [4]

It has often been assumed that both Henry Nicholas and his followers pushed their claims of holiness and perfection to a wild and dangerous extreme. It is probably true that they held a "perfection" that inclined them, or at least some of them, to believe in their own infallibility, and that ministered to an over-security in their attainments. The doctrine was, however, safeguarded by an unvarying insistence on purity of life, and by an emphasis on the truth that the final goal of perfection is "the measure of the stature of the fulness of Christ," or as Henry Nicholas puts it, growing up from

[1] *Introduction*, chap. xviii.

[2] "So at the last God remembered the desolate, heard the sighing and prayer of the poor, and to the end that his truth and will might be made manifest, he wrought a wonderful work on earth and raised up Henry Nicholas, the least among the holy ones, who lay altogether dead and without breath and life, from the dead and made me alive through Christ, anointed me with his godlie Being, manned Himself with me and godded me with Him to a living tabernacle or House for his dwelling and to a seat of his Christ, to the end that his wonderful works might now in the last time be known, the light of His glorie revealed with full clearness and instruction" (*Evangelium Regni*, chap. xxxiv.).

[3] *First Exhortation*, pp. 23, 24.

[4] *Ibid.* pp. 75-78.

"the youngnesse of the spiritual life unto the oldnesse of the Man Christ." He counsels his followers not to assume that they "have already attained," but "to look steadily for the Increase of God, abiding steadfast in the service of Love, until the lapsing away of the mortal body." They are to prepare like good soldiers "for hard battle, expecting to face bitter enemies and to suffer hurt, but are to go on in courage, not satisfied with any victory short of actual deliverance from sin and the manifestation of the fruits of God in the daily life."[1] And he further insists that the "perfection" which he teaches is not a perfect obedience according to the flesh, but a perfect obedience to the true Light of Life, revealed in the soul, as the following passage testifies:

"Also how grossly have certain overreached themselves who have taught the perfection according to the flesh, and applied the freedom of the children of God to elementish man, with a certain use of fleshlie dealings. Let every one look well to it that he run not forth according to the good thinking of his own spirit, nor believe any manner of knowledge which riseth up in his own heart—he that forsaketh himself in the obedience of the requiring of the gracious word of the Lord and his service of Love cometh to the true Light of Life."[2]

The sect, or "society," first comes to light in England about the middle of the sixteenth century. Archbishop Cranmer had his attention called to "a sect newly sprung up in Kent," which Strype thinks may have been the "Family of Love.[3] We get our first definite information of the spread of the movement in John Rogers' book, which fairly screams against these simple religious people.[4] He says that he has been told *by the members* that there are about 1000 of the Family of Love in England at that time (1579). Rogers gives a very interesting "confession," which he says was given by two members of the Family before Sir William Moore,

[1] An epitome of chap. xiii. secs. 22-36, *Introduction to Glass of Righteousness.*
[2] *Ibid.* chap. xxv.
[3] Strype's *Cranmer*, ii. p. 410 (Oxford, 1848). Quoted by Thomas, p. 16. (This sect was very likely a group of Anabaptists.)
[4] John Rogers, *The Displaying of an Horrible Sect* (London, 1579).

a Justice of Surrey, May 28, 1561. The "confession" is in substance as follows:

"They are all unlearned, save some who can read English and are made bishops, elders, and deacons, who call them to one of the disciples' houses, *thirty in number* assemble to hear the Scriptures expounded. They have goods in common, new members are received with a kiss, all have meat, drink, and lodging found by the owner of the house where they meet. They knock, saying, 'Here is a Brother or Sister in Christ.' The congregation does not speak until admitted so to do. They go to church, but object to the Litany that says 'Lord have mercy upon us miserable sinners,' as if they could never be amended. They may not say 'God speed, God morrow, or God even.' They did prohibit bearing of weapons, but at length allowed the bearing of staves. When a question is demanded of any, they stay a great while ere they answer, and commonly their word shall be 'Surely' or 'So.' When their wives are in childbirth they must use the help of none other but one of their own sect. If any die, the wife or husband that overliveth must marry again with one of their congregation or else the offence is great.[1] The marriage is made by the brethren, who sometimes bring them together who live over a hundred miles asunder, as Thomas Chaundler of Woneherst, Surrey, who sent for a wife from the Isle of Ely by two of the congregation. These had never met before, and in a year they, upon a disliking, did divorce themselves asunder before certain of the congregation. No man is to be baptized before the age of thirty. Until then he is an infant. Heaven and hell are present in this world among us. They are bound to give alms only to their own sect, bound to relieve him that decayeth. All men not of their congregation or revolted from them are as dead. Bishops and ministers should not remain still in one place but should wander from country to country. They hold there was a world before Adam's time. No man should be put to death for his opinions, and they therefore condemn Cranmer and Ridley for burning Joane of Kent. They expound Scripture according to their own minds, comparing one place with another.

They bragge verie muche of their owne sincere lives, justifying themselves, saying, 'marke how purelie we live.' If they have anything to do touching their temporal things they must do it by advice, viz. ask Counsell of the Lord through one of their

[1] I take it this is if he marry again at all, not that there is compulsion to do so. Obviously the Family had not in 1561 been long enough existing in England for the children of Familists to arrive at marriageable age.

bishops or elders. They give their alms by putting under a hat upon a table what they are disposed to give, and the money is secretly distributed by the Bishops[1] or Elders."

Rogers says that he has seen and tried to read a number of Henry Nicholas' books, but that he finds them "subtle and dark"; they "speak in riddle and dark speech," which means that Rogers did not penetrate the meaning of their deep mystical teaching. He admits that these Familists "show an outward face of holy conversation, like the Pelagians who believe in works!" This good life, however, he thinks, is only a pretence, "a visard and cloake to hide their grosse and absurd doctrine, and a bait for the simple." He brings up the old theological mallet: "They press the need of a good life, but what is this without a right fayth! Turks and Jews are diligent in observances." He charges Nicholas with getting his ideas from David Joris (or David George, as it is sometimes written). "H. N. was a scholler of David George"; "David George layde the egg and H. N. brought forth the chicken."[2] He tells how these pestilential doctrines are being spread broad-cast by a certain ignorant Dutch joiner named Christopher Vitells. This Vitells "trudges from country to country; has not been with his wife in London for two years, 'tis said; creeps in corners and dare not show his head, is a man utterly unlearned, more fit to be a scholar in Christ's school than an illuminated elder and teacher." His preaching, however, to the sorrow of the said Rogers, "appeals to novices"; "many have been snared by him, and not a few *ministers* have been entangled by the drowsie dreams of this doting Dutchman," told by "a rude and unlearned joyner."[3] In spite

[1] The Family never itself uses the word bishop.

[2] This opinion is very common, but without much foundation. Joris was born in Ghent or Bruges in 1500. He had extraordinary experiences of the nature of "revelations," and he held that God made, through him, the third of His great revelations to the world. The first was through David the Psalmist, the second was through the Son of David, the holy one of the Gospels, and he claimed to be the third David through whom God was giving the revelation of the Spirit to supersede the other two. His visions are told in a book published in 1536 with the sensational title, "Hark, Hark, Great Marvel! Great Marvel!!"

[3] This "rude and unlearned joyner," however, was sufficiently learned to translate Henry Nicholas' difficult books into his adopted tongue!

of himself Roger's picture of the "Horrible Sect" reveals many fine traits in the members of the Family of Love, and evidently Vitells was a great success as an "Elder" in the Family![1] The next witness to the existence of the sect in England is J. Knewstub, who rushed into print against H. N. and his "Family" in 1579, under the title "A Confutation of Monstrous and Horrible Heresies taught by H. N., and embraced by a number who call themselves the Family of Love."[2] He does not accuse Nicholas or the Familists of immorality, though he thinks that Nicholas' writings encourage undue liberty, and in his dedicatory epistle to his work he says that "the errors of the sect bee so foule and so filthy, as would force the very penne in passing to stay and stop her nose!" When these "Errours" are marshalled they do not look so "foule and filthy" to us as they did to Knewstub in the sixteenth century. He charges that "H. N. turns religion up-side-down. He buildeth heaven here upon earth; he maketh God man and man God" [what Henry Nicholas really said was that God could reveal Himself humanly, and man could be raised to a divine nature, which Paul also said]. He shows that Henry Nicholas taught that "our bodies are not ours to do therewith our own will, but the Lord's to use as instruments of His service to all righteousness," and he tries, though unsuccessfully, to give this teaching a libertine construction. A number of interesting tenets of the sect are brought forward as "monstrous heresies." For example, he points out with horror that Henry Nicholas says that "God hath raised him from the dead and anointed him with the holy Ghost, and chosen him to be a minister of the Word under the obedience of Love." Again he

[1] We learn from "A Confutation of Certain Articles delivered unto the Family of Love," by William Wilkinson, M.A. (Cambridge, 1579), that the chief Elders of the Familists were "weavers, basket-makers, musicians, bottle-makers, and such like." He declares that they "swarm and dayly increase in the Isle of Ely."

[2] John Knewstub (1544-1624) was a Cambridge Master of Arts and a famous divine with strong Puritan leaning. He translated sections of Henry Nicholas' *Evangelium Regni* with denunciatory comments.

argues that "H. N. makes Christ no one man, but a state and condition *in men*, by the reception of which state and condition men grow into perfection and so sin no more. This state he calleth the true Light, or Being, or Perfection."[1] He quotes the following passage to illustrate the point:

> "The true Light is the anointing of the Holy Ghost called in Hebrew 'Messias,' in Greek 'Christus.' The Jews say the Messias or anointed is the Sabbath day. These figures change out of the letter into the true revealing of the holie Spirit of Christ. Divers have cried 'Christ, Christ,' and 'We are Christians,' and attributed to themselves much Freedom ere ever the time of the appearing of Christ or the anointing of the Holy Ghost was come to pass in them."[2]

Knewstub has also heard that the members of the Family of Love do not believe that the tree in the Garden of Eden was a material tree, or that the fruit which Adam ate was material fruit, but that the transgression of Adam was in the *will*, and that true seed to Abraham can now be conceived by the Holy Ghost.

Thomas Rogers, another contemporary opponent, gives us some of the prominent traits of the "Familists."[3] He says that they "deny original sin." They teach that the regenerated (*i.e.* the godded persons) do not sin, that the water of baptism is only "*elementish* water" (*i.e.* is just water). They condemn all war; prohibit the bearing of arms; hold that no man should be put to death for his religion. They "deny all calling but the immediate call of God." They term professional ministers "scripture-learned," "letter-doctors," "teaching-masters." They call it presumptuous to preach unless the preacher receives a revelation, for the Word of God can neither be "learned" nor "taught." They call churches "common houses";

[1] Poor Knewstub does not remotely comprehend the mystical view which he is combating. Hooker in the Preface to his *Ecclesiastical Polity* implies that the Familists "have it in their heads that Christ doth not signify any one person, but a quality whereof many are partakers." Neither of these writers has penetrated Henry Nicholas' spiritual meaning.

[2] *Evangelium Regni*, chap. xiii.

[3] In his *Catholic Doctrine of the Church of England*, London, 1585 (first edition said to be 1579). Published by the Parker Society, 1854.

they hold conventicles; they contemn the Lord's Day (on the contrary, they held that all days are the Lord's days). They say that the promises of blessedness are for this life, and they declare that hell is in the heart and conscience.

Another opponent, Edmond Jessop, considerably later, attacked the Family of Love, as "the most blasphemous and erroneous sect this day in the world."[1] Jessop charges that they teach that "the same perfection of holiness which was in Adam before he fell is to be attained here in this life, and affirm that the members of their Family are as perfect and innocent as he." They say that "the resurrection of the dead, spoken of by St. Paul in 1 Cor. 15, is fulfilled in them, and they deny all resurrection of the body after this life."[2]

Henry Ainsworth, the famous "Separatist," published in Amsterdam in 1608, "An Epistle to two daughters of Warwick from H. N."[3] This epistle Ainsworth answers section by section in a preface, quoting also from at least nine of Henry Nicholas' books. He says that "Satan has never had a fitter religion for atheists and carnal hypocrites than that which Henry Nicholas out of his corrupt and fleshly hert hath set abroach"; that "he hath written more blasphemously than ever did Mahomet in Elkoran," and that "he labors to be obscure in his words that he may have for his last refuge the claim that *men understand him not*!" He charges that Henry Nicholas' teaching "maketh persons pure and without al syn, in their own foolish imaginations, yea, it deifieth them with God." He then proceeds to "manifest the impieties of his dark, delphick speeches and glozing allegories." Here are some of Henry Nicholas' "impieties": That ceremonies are "mere outward means set forth by God and His ministers to direct people to the inward life of Christ in the Spirit"; that "he that letteth

[1] "A Discovery of the Errors of the English Anabaptists," London, 1623.

[2] Compare George Fox's statement: "I was in the condition Adam was in before he fell" (*Journal*, London, 1901, vol. i. p. 28).

[3] *An Epistle sent unto Two Daughters of Warwick with Refutation of the Errors that are therein*, by H. A., Amsterdam, 1608.

himself think that he is a Christian before the Spirit of Christ is born in him is a thief and a murderer"; that "the confession of Christ must stand in greater force than to be confessed with the mouth in a ceremonial service which is a baptizing with water or some other *elementish* confession," and that "baptism with water and the taking of the sacrament are elementish and unfruitful unless the Spirit of Christ is served (*i.e.* promoted) by the Christian service let it be fashioned ever so much on the Scriptures."

John Etherington was a prominent Familist teacher in London in 1623, as we learn from a fierce sermon against him, preached in St. Paul's by Stephen Denison on Sunday, February 11, 1627. Poor Etherington was compelled to stand through the entire service—three hours long—with a paper on his breast declaring that "he had scandalized the whole church of Christ by saying that *it* was no true church."[1] The sermon divides "Famisticall wolves" into four "packs," the two most important of which are (1) Those who hold that the law of God may be perfectly fulfilled in *this* world, and that *men may be inspired with light and illumination as far as ever Paul or any of the prophets were.* (2) Those who hold that the Spirit is above Scripture, that all days are Sabbaths, that when God dwells in a soul He fills the soul so that there is no more lusting, and who boast that they have cast off saying prayers and repeating sermons and such-like long ago. Etherington was a box-maker by trade, but he found time to do an extensive "missionary" work along with his trade. Denison says that he drew many men and women from the Church of England into the "Family of Love." He charges him with "tampering with many tender consciences" in his (Denison's) parish, and with circulating his "linsey-woolsie books."[2] He says that Etherington holds that "no baptism has any virtue except a baptism in a thousand tears."

[1] The "White Wolf," a Sermon, London, 1627.

[2] Etherington wrote a book in 1610 in which he said that outward ordination does not make a true minister. He wrote from prison in 1627 a "Defense against Stephen Denison," which was published in 1641.

The most lamentable attack on the Familists is that made by Samuel Rutherford, for in this attack he lays aside his saintliness and sweetness, and writes in a spirit of bigotry and intolerance, and in ignorance of the real teaching of the persons whom he assails. From him, however, we learn that many Familists were in jail at the time, that they regarded outward worship and ordinances as traditions, and that they were spread through twelve counties of England. He quotes from their petition to King James, saying that they are "few in number and poor in worldly wealth," and ejaculates, Would God they *were* few in number, yet they are pestering twelve counties of England.[1] John Evelyn has an interesting reference to the sect, under date of June 16, 1687. He says that James II. received an Address from some of the Family of Love, and "His Majesty asked them what their party might consist of; they told him their custom was to reade the Scripture and then to preach, but did not give any further account, onely sayd that for the rest they were *a sort of refined Quakers*, but their number was very small, not consisting, as they sayd, of above three score in all, and those chiefly belonging to the Isle of Ely." There can be no question, for any one who carefully studies the facts, that there is much truth in their claim, as reported by Evelyn, that they were "a sort of Quakers." They had, for more than a hundred years, maintained in England a steady testimony to the spiritual nature of religion, to the fact of a Divine Light and Life in the soul, and to the unimportance of outward forms and ordinances in comparison with the inward experience of God's Presence. They had insisted on spiritualizing *this* life rather than on dogmatizing about the *next* life, and they had been practising, as far as they could, in the society in which they lived, the Sermon on the Mount. Their organization was cumbersome, their religious books were over-mystical and hard to penetrate, and their teaching on "perfection" was open to a dangerous application.

[1] Rutherford's *Survey of Spiritual Antichrist* (London, 1648), which contains a Petition of the Familists to King James in 1604.

These weaknesses of system and method hampered them and kept them from becoming a powerful people. By the middle of the century the Quakers, with clearer insight and with far wiser leadership, were presenting all that was valuable in the Family of Love, with a much wider spirit of common human brotherhood and with a still more positive insistence on the necessity of carrying religion into daily life. Many Familists must have joined with Friends, though there is little proof of the fact that they did. Some of them took the attitude of and position of the "Seekers," whom I shall study in the next chapter, and some drifted into the looser movement which goes under the name of "Ranters."[1] A remnant of the Family lingered on into the opening of the eighteenth century.[2] It is now a "dead sect," but the great contention of its founder, that salvation is no true salvation unless it delivers from sin and produces a new man, is a very live doctrine in the world to-day.

[1] William Penn makes no clear distinction between these three groups (see preface to Fox's *Journal*, p. xxv.).

[2] Collier in his *Eccl. Hist. of Great Britain*, published 1708-1714, says that Henry Nicholas' opinions "exist to this day in new modifications." Neal, writing in 1720, speaks of Familists as "something akin to the Quakers among ourselves" (see *Hist. of the Puritans*, vol. i. p. 227; quoted from Thomas' Monograph, p. 26).

CHAPTER XIX

THE SEEKERS AND THE RANTERS

ALMOST all contemporary accounts refer with more or less horror to the swarm of sects which appeared in England during the Civil War and the period of the Commonwealth. It was a period of social and political ferment; a time of religious upheaval, when the crust of habit and ancient traditions was broken through by a wave of strong religious emotion. The nation passed through a distinct crisis of incubation, a creative epoch in its life attended by an extraordinary release of energy. Milton in a classic passage has given a description of England in this creative epoch:

> "I see a noble and puissant nation rousing herself like a strong man after a sleep and shaking her invincible locks. Methinks I see her, as an eagle mewing her mighty youth, and kindling her undazzled eyes at the full mid-day beam, purging and unsealing her long-abused sight at the fountain itself of heavenly radiance, while the whole noise of timorous and flocking birds, with those also that love the twilight, flutter about amazed at what she means, and in their envious gabble would prognosticate a year of sects and schisms." [1]

Whether Milton was conscious of the fact or not, it is impossible for a nation to "unseal her long-abused sight at the fountain itself of heavenly radiance," without the noise and flutter of sects and schisms. A nation that throws off its settled habits and faces the issues of life with freshness and freedom must expect ferment and turmoil; and therewith novelties and peculiarities.

[1] *The Areopagitica*, first edition, 1644.

England had passed through the great Reformation period without much social or religious ferment. Her Reformation was an extremely mild one. There was no seething, surging ground swell of popular emotion. There was no great religious prophet to re-voice in fresh ways the elemental hunger of the soul of man. Abuses were corrected, a few superstitions were cast aside, a national head of the Church was substituted for the papal head, a new prayer-book was produced and the form of worship simplified, but there was no severance of continuity with the old Church. Everybody was compelled to "conform." There was no toleration, no provision for independent thought. The Anabaptists and Familists and other separatists took their lives in their hands and were always in jeopardy. The nation was not yet ready to risk the danger of "kindling her eyes at the full mid-day beam." The civil war was the first opportunity for the long-delayed religious revival to break forth in England, and break forth it did with a vigour and commotion seldom witnessed before or since. "Old Ephraim" Pagitt is not a very reliable authority, but he was an eye-witness of the commotion, which he saw "with great grief of heart." "Our people," he writes, "are becoming of the Tribe of Gad, running after seducers as if they were mad." His appeal to the Lord Mayor of London in 1645 is a vivid picture of the *infection* of new faiths and religious novelties:

"The plague is of all diseases most infectious: I have lived among you almost a jubile, and have seen your great care and provision to keep the city from infection. The plague of heresy is greater, and you are now in more danger than when you buried five thousand a week. You have power to keep these heretics and sectaries from conventickling and sholing together to infect one another." [1]

Edwards' *Gangræna* is a still more hysterical account of the swarm of sects, or as he puts it himself, "of the many errors, heresies, blasphemies, and pernicious practices of the sectaries of this time, vented and acted in England

[1] Pagitt's *Heresiography* (London, 1645), Dedication to the Lord Mayor.

in these four last years."[1] Marsden's account is not that of an eye-witness, but it faithfully reproduces the general impression of contemporary writers:

> "Absurd excesses of opinion now appeared, as exotics in a hotbed. The distractions of the times suspended the restraints of Church discipline; opinions monstrous and prodigious started up every day, and were broached with impunity in public and in private, and multitudes were led astray. The number of new sects, religious and political, with which England swarmed appears almost incredible. The sober Puritans were confounded. The state of England reminded them of the fabulous description of the sands of Libya, where scorching suns produce new monsters every year."[2]

These contemporary impressions must, however, not distort our judgment. *We* are accustomed to complete religious freedom. We do not expect the heavens to fall because men differ in their views. We have learned that churches can live and flourish without conformity. These impressions come from persons who are unused to religious freedom and who have not learned that health and growth demand the removing of swaddling clothes. We must, therefore, discount their tales of woe. Their stories of excesses and "blasphemies" and "lewdnesses" are highly coloured by their own imaginations. The epoch of the Commonwealth was a time of great ferment, but on the whole it was marked by a maturing of the national consciousness and a heightening of religious life and thought. Most of the "sects, heresies, and schisms" described by Edwards and Pagitt were not distinct "sects" in our modern sense of the word. They were rather special phases of the general religious movement, prevailing types of thought and local peculiarities, due to a sudden expansion of freedom. Some of them developed into great and influential denominations; others were only sporadic and temporary tendencies, destined to be absorbed in larger movements which ministered more genuinely to the entire religious needs and nature of man.

[1] Edwards' *Gangræna* (London, 1646), Title-page.

[2] Marsden's *Later Puritans* (London, second edition), p. 224.

The most significant of these latter sporadic and temporary tendencies were those of the Seekers and Ranters. They were not, strictly speaking, sects; they were more or less contagious *movements or tendencies of thought,* which affected groups of people in various parts of England without producing any unifying, cementing organization. No "founder" can be discovered for either movement; no "origin" of them can be traced. They were tendencies more or less felt and shared by all classes of the people of England who were not satisfied with the national Church or with the equally rigid system of Presbyterianism. "Seekers" were to be found among the Anabaptists, the Familists, the Brownists, and also among those who nominally remained inside the fold of the Church. William Penn speaks of people who

> "left all visible churches and societies and wandered up and down as sheep without a shepherd, and as doves without their mates; *seeking* their beloved, but could not find Him (as their souls desired to know Him), whom their souls loved above their chiefest joy. These persons were called Seekers by some and the Family of Love by others."[1]

Barclay[2] thinks that this confusion of sects shows William Penn's ignorance of the facts. I do not think so. It rather shows that there were "Seekers" among the Familists as there almost certainly were among all the other religious societies of the time.[3] Such persons always appear in epochs of religious unsettlement, persons who are "like doves without their mates,"[4] and who seek in earnestness for the Beloved of their souls. As soon as faith in the authority of the Church grows faint, and the sufficiency of established forms and rituals is seriously questioned, the primal right of the soul to find God Himself is sure to be asserted. "Seekers," under different names, we have found at every period of this history. Sebastian Franck in his Chronicles has

[1] Penn's Preface to George Fox's *Journal.*

[2] *Inner Life of the Societies of the Commonwealth,* p. 177.

[3] Baptist writers of the period admit that there were many Baptist "Seekers."

[4] This expression "like doves without their mates" appears occasionally in the Seeker literature of the period.

preserved an interesting record of "Seekers" in the tumultuous times when Luther was shaking the ancient system, and when Anabaptism was first spreading its new ideas through the world.

"Some," he writes, "desire to allow Baptism and other ceremonies to remain in abeyance till God gives another command —sends out true labourers into His harvest—some have, with great desire, a longing for this, and desire nothing else. Some others agree with these, who think the ceremonies since the death of the apostles are equally defiled, laid waste, and fallen—that God no longer heeds them, and also does not desire that they should be longer kept, on which account they will never again be set up, but now are to proceed entirely in Spirit and in Truth, and never in an outward manner, so that it is as unbecoming that we should come to the Wine, as that we should go back to the pointer when we have found the road, or that we should look behind ourselves to the statue. These people will not acknowledge the Baptists for brethren, but exclude them, and are against them with mouth and pen."[1]

This description by Sebastian Franck is an accurate account of the position of the English *Seekers* in the seventeenth century.

Ubbo Philipps, fellow-labourer with Menno Simons, the founder of the Mennonites, says that there were persons in his day who "served God in quiet simplicity after the manner of the Patriarchs and *who sought God from the heart*, served and clave to Him, without preachers, teachers, or an outward gathering."[2]

There was a wing of the Mennonite Church in Zealand in which these Seeker tendencies were nourished, even down into the seventeenth century. There continued to be little groups of serious people among them, who "sought God from the heart" and who "served Him in quiet simplicity." It is quite likely that influences from these little hidden societies reached England through the Anabaptists, and that the Seeker-attitude in England thus had a continental origin, though the tendency might easily have developed from the native religious

[1] Sebastian Franck's *Chronica*, 1536, p. cc. Part III. (quoted from Barclay, p. 410).

[2] Barclay, p. 174.

movements which were quietly at work beneath the surface.

The only actual link which can at present be traced between the English Seekers and these continental groups is Bartholomew Legate, the last heretic burned at Smithfield—a very slender bridge, it must be confessed. Legate was a dealer in cloth, and his business took him to Zealand where he became a preacher among the Seeker Mennonites. He became convinced that God was soon to make a new revelation through "myraculous apostles," and a "myraculous ministry"; and that until this new revelation appeared, there was no "true church," no "true baptism," and no "visible Christian."

It was his belief that

"the Church has been latent and invisible for many years, and there can be no more a visible Church till some notable man be stirred up of God to raise it again out of the dust."

He held that the learning of the University is unnecessary for ministry, that Latin, Greek, and Hebrew are "the languages of the beast" and not of the Spirit. He argued that true ministry must be initiated by men with miraculous gifts, saying:

"The men that began the frame of the Church of Israel were Moses and Aaron. The men that began the New Testament Church were the Apostles. All these were furnished with the gift of miracles, for the persuading of their hearers: for without miracles they could not be believed to come from God for establishing a new Church-polity. Now, father (addressing an Anabaptist), who were the first layers of *your* Church foundations? They must bring miracles with them or who (but madmen) will take them for new *Founders*?"[1]

The right attitude was, therefore, that of a waiter, expecter, or seeker. Legate adopted the opinion that Christ was "a meere man, onely borne free from sinne" and possessed "of the Spirit beyond measure" and termed God, in Scripture, not from "His essence but from His office."[2]

[1] Legate's views are given in dialogue form in Henoch Clapham's *Error on the Right Hand* (London, 1608). These passages are taken from pp. 30-31.

[2] Henoch Clapham's *Error on the Right Hand*, p. 44.

It was his "Arian heresy" which aroused the choler of King James so that on one occasion, "he spurned at him with his foot," and it was for such views that he was burned at Smithfield in the presence of a vast "conflux of people," March 18, 1612.[1]

We find, in the teachings of this Legate, the main idea of the English Seekers, namely, that there now exists no true Church, no valid sacraments, no person with apostolic unction, and that the sincere soul can only *wait* for a fuller revelation and a more efficacious ministry.

The first use of the word "Seeker" to designate a religious "sect" in England, appears in *Truth's Champion*, first published in 1617, and which bears the initials "J. M.," supposed to be John Morton (or Murton), one of the founders of the General Baptists. He writes:

> "Oh, ye *Seekers*, I would ye sought aright and not beyond the Scriptures calling them carnal; and ye speak also against Christ, and set Him at light, and are not ashamed to say that there is none saved by the blood of Christ, and that it is of no value at all, and that they look upon the Scriptures as nothing . . . by preaching up a libertine doctrine to the people, and that they need not hear preaching nor read the Scriptures, nor live in obedience thereto."

This characterization of the Seekers must not be taken too seriously. It bears the marks of misinterpretation and unconscious colouring. The early Seekers merely insisted that the *letter* of Scripture is carnal and insufficient; that *Christ after the flesh* and that *literal blood of Christ* do not save; that wordy-preaching, with spiritual experience absent, is empty and worthless. A truer witness of their views is John Saltmarsh. He himself had reached a stage beyond the Seeker-attitude, as we shall see in the next chapter, but he thoroughly understood them and is a sympathetic reporter of their position.[2]

> "The Seekers find that the Christians of Apostolic times were visibly and spiritually endowed with power from on high and

[1] See Article by Alexander Gordon in *Nat. Dict. of Biog.*

[2] The following passage is condensed from Saltmarsh's *Sparkles of Glory*, London, 1648, pp. 214-21.

with Gifts of the Spirit, and so were able to make clear and evident demonstration of God in the Churches, and all who administered in any office were visibly gifted. All was administered in the anointing or unction of the Spirit clearly, certainly, infallibly. They ministered as the oracles of God. But now in this *time of apostacy* of the churches, they (the Seekers) find no such gifts, and so they dare not meddle with any outward administrations, dare not preach, baptize, or teach: they find in the churches nothing but the *outward ceremony* of all administrations, as of bare water in baptism, bare imposition of hands in ordination, etc. Therefore, they "wait" for power from on high, finding no practice of worship according to the first pattern. They wait in prayer, pretending to no certain determination of things, nor to any infallible interpretation of Scripture. They wait for a restoration of all things and a setting up of "Gospel Officers," "Gospel Churches," "Gospel Ordinances," according to the pattern in the New Testament. They wait for an apostle or some one with a visible glory and power, able in the spirit to give visible demonstration of being sent."[1]

They urged, too, that *miracles* should attend true ministry, as in apostolic times, and that until such demonstration and power appeared, the perfunctory performance of outward rites, and the utterance of *mere words* were vain and hollow. There was nothing to do but "wait."

William Penn says that

"they sometimes met together not formally to pray or preach at appointed times and places in their own wills, as in times past they were accustomed to do; but they waited together in silence, and as anything arose in one of their minds that they thought favored with a Divine Spring, so they sometimes spoke."[2]

Ephraim Pagitt gives us a glimpse of them, with his "double horn-pane" lantern. He says:

"Many have wrangled so long about the Church that at last they have quite lost it, and go under the name of *Expecters* or *Seekers*, and do deny that there is any Church, or any true minister, or any ordinances; some of them affirm the Church to

[1] Saltmarsh gives a similar account of the Seekers in his other writings (see especially his *New Quere* and his *Smoake in the Temple*, London, 1646).

[2] Preface to George Fox's *Journal*.

be in the wilderness, and they are seeking for it there; others say that it is in the smoke of the Temple, and that they are groping for it there—where I leave them, praying to God to open their eyes."[1]

Edwards was too chaotic to devote a distinct section of his book to a distinct "error," "heresy," or "blasphemy," but there are a number of "errors" in his long catalogue which seem to be meant for "Seekers." The following passages appear to apply to the subject in hand:

"That to read the Scripture to a mixed congregation is dangerous (Error 10). That we did look for great matters from One crucified at Jerusalem 1600 years ago; but that does no good, it must be a Christ formed in us—the Deity united to our humanity (Error 29). That men ought to preach and exercise their gifts without study and premeditation and not to think of what they are to say until they speak, because it shall be given them in that hour and the Spirit shall teach them (Error 127). That there is no need of human learning or reading of authors for preachers, but all books and learning must go down. It comes from *want of the Spirit that men write such great volumes* (Error 128). That only persons who have an infallible Spirit, as the Apostles, should pray (Error 135). That Christians are not bound to pray constantly every day at set times, as morning and evening, but only such time that the Spirit moves them to it, and if they find not themselves to be moved in many days and weeks together, they ought not to pray (Error 137). That parents are not to catechize their little children, nor to set them to read Scripture or to teach them to pray, but to let them alone for God to teach them (Error 157)."[2]

Edwards sheds a little more dim light by three personal references to individual "Seekers." He says that

"Lawrence Clerkson (Clarkson) turned from Anabaptist and Dipper to be a Seeker and to deny the Scriptures to be the rule of a Christian. He denied that in doctrine or practice half of God's glory was revealed as yet."[3]

"There is one Mr. Erbury . . . who has fallen to many grosse errors and is now a *Seeker* and I know not what. . . . He said that within a while God would raise up apostolical men, who should be extraordinary to preach the Gospel. . . . He

---

[1] *Heresiography*, p. 128. [2] *Gangræna*, pp. 15-31.
[3] *Ibid.* p. 20, sec. 2, Part I.

spake against gathering in churches and said that men ought to wait for the coming of the Spirit, as the Apostles did. In a private meeting, the main scope of his exercise was to speak against the certainty and sufficiency of the Scriptures."[1]

"There is one Clement Wrighter (Writer) in London . . . an arch-heretic and fearful apostate, an old wolf and subtile man. . . . He fell to be a Seeker and is now an anti-Scripturalist, a questionist and sceptic, and I fear an atheist. This Wrighter is one of the chief heads of those that deny the Scriptures to be the Word of God. . . . He said that the Scriptures are not the Word of God, neither in translation, nor yet in the original tongues, so as to be an infallible foundation of faith. He further said that there is no Gospel, no ministry, nor no faith, nor can be, unless any can show as immediate a call to the ministry as the Apostles had, and can do the same miracles they did."[2]

One more hostile witness to the views of the Seekers must be heard from, namely, Richard Baxter. He says:

"The second sect which then rose up was that called Seekers. These taught that our Scripture was uncertain; that present miracles are necessary to faith; that our ministry is null and without authority; and our worship and ordinances unnecessary or vain; the true Church, Ministry, Scriptures and Ordinances being lost; for which they are now *seeking*."[3]

John Jackson, who was himself a Seeker, says that those who write against Seekers "comprehend under the term all those which differ from themselves touching the present exercise of visible administration."[4]

"Seekers, properly so called," he says, "are such as, not seeing a sufficient ground for the practice of ordinances are said to seek them."

"Persons called by the name of Seekers," he continues, "having compared the present ministry with the Word of God and not finding it to conform thereto dare not join issue in the present practice of it."[5]

---

[1] *Gangræna*, p. 24, sec. 2, Part I. This was William Erbury (or Erberie), whose collected writings were published in 1658, *A Collection of Writings for the Benefit of Posterity*. His wife Dorcas became a Quaker and walked before James Nayler in the famous Bristol procession. There is no evidence that this "Mr. Erbury" became a Quaker.

[2] *Ibid.* p. 27, sec. 2, Part I.

[3] Richard Baxter's *Narrative of his Life and Times* (London, 1696), Part I. p. 76.

[4] *A Sober Word to a Serious People* (London, 1651), Preface.

[5] *Ibid.* pp. 2-4.

John Jackson holds that if a person do entitle himself a *minister of Christ* he must either have an *immediate call* from Christ, "a powerful enabling" from the Bridegroom Himself, or a call by the Friends of the Bridegroom, *i.e.* the Apostles; but there are now, he thinks, no ministers of either sort.[1]

The real pith of the Seeker movement is thus clear. It was at heart a mystical movement; a genuine spiritual quest for something deeper than the empty show of religion, a search for what some of them happily call "an upper room Christianity." They were resolved that they would not call stones bread, and that they would not take the husks of religion for the real thing. They were for the most part unlearned, simple, labouring folk. They knew little of the history of the spiritual travail of the race, and they evidently undervalued external helps and outward revelations. They dwelt too much on negations, and found themselves unable to minister to striving, hungering souls, for they could not find the true bread and water of life. But they preferred to wait for God Himself to show His face rather than to bow down before the images which men had set up for them to worship.

There was something in the movement which impressed Cromwell—a soberness, an honesty of spirit, a possibility of finding some real satisfaction for the soul. He writes in 1646 to his daughter Bridget, and in the letter tells of the spiritual state of his favourite daughter, Lady Claypole:

> "Your sister Claypole is, I trust in mercy, exercised with some perplexed thoughts. She sees her own vanity and carnal mind; bewailing it, *she seeks after* (*as I hope also*) *what will satisfy*. And thus to be a Seeker is to be of the best sect next to a finder, and such shall every faithful, humble seeker be at the end. Happy seeker, happy finder! Who ever tasted that graciousness of His, and could go less in desire—less than pressing after full enjoyment?"[2]

---

[1] *A Sober Word to a Serious People*, pp. 16, 17.
[2] Carlyle's *Oliver Cromwell*, vol. i. p. 254 (New York, 1897).

Even more striking is Cromwell's testimony of sympathy with the Seeker attitude, as expressed in one of his speeches to the army council in 1647:

"Truly, as Lieutenant-Colonel Goffe said, God hath in several ages used several dispensations, and yet some dispensations more eminently in one age than another. *I am one of those whose heart God hath drawn out to wait for some extraordinary dispensations*, according to those promises He hath set forth of things to be accomplished in the latter time, and I cannot but think that God is beginning of them."[1]

Gerrard Winstanley, in one of his early pamphlets (*The Breaking of the Day of God*, 1648), bears witness to the existence of waiting, seeking people whom he addresses as the "Despised Sons and Daughters of Zion, scattered up and down the Kingdom of England." He even calls them "Children of the Light," and promises that the day of relief is near.

"If they (the people of the world) did truly know the power of God that dwells in you, they would not despise you. . . . It is your Father's will that it shall be so. The world must lie under darkness for a time. That is God's dispensation to them. And you that are children of the Light must lie under the reproach and oppression of the world; that is God's dispensation to you. But it shall be for but a little time. What I have here to say is to bring you glad tidings that your redemption draws near."[2]

This pamphlet concludes with the words:

"Wait patiently upon the Lord; let every man that loves God endeavour by the spirit of wisdom, meekness, and love to dry up Euphrates, even this spirit of bitterness, that like a great river hath overflowed the earth of mankind."[3]

"Think it not strange," he writes in another Tract, "to see

[1] *Clarke Papers*, edited by C. H. Firth for the Camden Society, vol. i. pp. 378, 379. Lord Rosebery has this to say of Cromwell: "He was a practical mystic, the most formidable and terrible of all combinations. A man who combines inspiration apparently derived—in my judgment really derived—from close communion with the supernatural and the celestial, a man who has that inspiration and adds to it the energy of a mighty man of action, such a man as that lives in communion on a Sinai of his own, and when he pleases to come down to this world below seems armed with no less than the terrors and decrees of the Almighty Himself."

[2] *Breaking of the Day of God* (London, 1648), Dedication, p. 3.

[3] *Ibid.* p. 126.

many of the Saints of God at a stand in the wilderness, and at a loss, and so *waiting* upon God to discover Himself to them." [1]

John Jackson, whom even Baxter admits was "one of the sound sort of Seekers," [2] gives a clear and illuminating account of the views and practices of the sane and moderate Seekers, which makes them much less negative than the unsympathetic or hostile accounts given above. He says:

"Firstly, they seek the mind of God in the Scriptures. Secondly, they judge that prayer and alms are to be attended to, and for this purpose they come together into some place on the First-days as their hearts are drawn forth and opportunity offers. They then seek, firstly, that they may be instruments in the hand of the Lord to stir up the grace of God in one another, by mutual conference and communication of experience; and secondly, to wait for a further revelation. Thirdly, to hold out their testimony against the false, and for the pure ordinance of ministry and worship. They behave themselves as persons who have neither the power nor the gift to go before one another by way of eminency or authority, but as sheep unfolded, and as soldiers unrallied, waiting for a time of gathering. They acknowledge no other visible teacher but the Word and works of God, on whom they wait, for the grace which is to be brought at the revelation of Jesus Christ." [3]

The documents printed in *The First Publishers of Truth* [4] have brought to light the existence of a large community of simple Christian people, who were plainly separatists, in and about Preston Patrick, Westmorland, in the middle of the seventeenth century. They are called in these documents "a seeking and religiously inclined people." These people, however, had ministers settled among them who "usually preached," though there was evidently opportunity given for others to speak besides the regular ministers, and they appear not to have had scruples against paying at least a support to those who ministered among them, as the letters from a kindred

[1] *The Mystery of God* (London, 1648), p. 39.

[2] Baxter's *Key for Catholics*, p. 332.

[3] John Jackson's *A Sober Word*, p. 3.

[4] "Being Early Records of the Introduction of Quakerism into England and Wales," edited by Norman Penney, London, 1907.

separatist community in Swaledale to those in Preston Patrick clearly indicate.[1] It is now a settled historical fact, as William Charles Braithwaite has pointed out in his article on "Westmorland and the Swaledale Seekers,"[2] that a separatist religious movement of a novel sort had spread over a wide area in Westmorland and the West Riding of Yorkshire. It was evidently a mild and serious form of Seekerism. The leaders of the movement appear to have been Thomas Taylor, Francis Howgil, and John Audland.

Thomas Taylor (who afterwards became a Quaker) is thus described in *The First Publishers of Truth*:

"He was bred up a scholar at the University and became a public minister or preacher, but, being a sincere and conscientious man denied to receive his maintenance by that antichristian and popish way of tithes, so became a minister to a people that were separated from the common way of worship, then at Preston Chapel in Westmorland, and *took for his maintenance only what his hearers were willing freely to give him*, and was for his sincerity and godly living greatly beloved and esteemed by his congregation which were many, until such time as there were endeavours used by the Presbyterians and Independents and others for uniting into one body or church communion. And the persons appointed for that work did so far prevail upon the said Thomas Taylor to go back and sprinkle several of his children, that he and his hearers had seen beyond and the emptiness thereof as an invention of man and not the one baptism of our Lord Jesus Christ—which condescension (*i.e.* return to the emptiness) his hearers could not bear. So he removed into Swaledale in Yorkshire, and became a teacher there to a separatist congregation."[3]

These Westmorland Seekers, with their ministers, came over to Fox, and became the powerful nucleus of

[1] See *Swaledale Papers*. The originals are in Devonshire House, London. The letters referred to above are printed in an article by William Charles Braithwaite in *Journal of Friends' Historical Society*, Jan. 1908, pp. 5-9.

[2] *Journal of Friends' Historical Society*, Jan. 1908, pp. 3-10.

[3] *First Publishers of Truth*, p. 253. Thomas Taylor's brother Christopher gives the following "Testimony" of him: "My deceased brother Tho. Taylor was a man who, in his tender years, had a sense of sin upon him and saw a necessity of coming and attaining to a state of righteousness and faithfulness to God that he might please Him; as for several years he was exercised under the spirit of bondage and great fears, lest he should miss of eternal salvation, and so came to be a *true seeker* and inquirer after best things, and the Lord was good to him in a preparatory work, as I may say, before he came to know the sabbath of eternal rest in Christ Jesus" (Introduction to *Works* of T. Taylor).

Quakerism in Westmorland and western Yorkshire. Their "convincement" to Quakerism proved the turning of the tide of that cause, and opened the way for its great spread through England.

The following interesting passage from *The First Publishers of Truth* throws considerable light on this community of Seekers, and it tells in very simple style the story of the great "convincement":

"And it having then been a common practice amongst the said seeking and religiously inclined people[1] to raise (*i.e.* to hold) a General Meeting at Preston Patrick Chapel once a month upon the Fourth day of the week,[2] to which resorted the most zealous and religious people in several places adjacent, as from Sedberg side in the county of York; Yelland (Yealand) and Kellet in the county of Lancaster; Kendal, Grayridge (Grayrigg), Underbarrow, Hutton, and in and about the said Preston Patrick, where F. H. (Francis Howgil), J. A. (John Audland), and several others did usually preach to the congregation there met. The said meeting (monthly General meeting) being there appointed that same day, thither G. F. (George Fox) went, accompanied with J. A. and J. C. (John Camm). J. A. would have had G. F. to have gone into the place or pen where usually he and the preacher did sit, but he refused and took a back seat near the door, and J. C. sat down by him, where he sat quietly waiting upon God about half an hour, in which time of silence F. H. (Francis Howgil, their preacher) seemed uneasy,[3] and pulled out his Bible, and opened it, and stood up several times, sitting down again and closing his book, a dread and fear being upon him that he durst not begin to preach. After the said silence and waiting, G. F. (George Fox) stood up in the mighty power of God, and in the demonstration thereof was his mouth opened to preach Christ Jesus, the Light of Life and the way of God and Saviour of all that believe and obey Him; which was delivered in that power and authority that most of the auditory, *which were several hundreds*, were effectually reached to the heart and convinced of the truth that very day, for it was the day of God's power."[4]

---

[1] They are called on an earlier page "A *seeking* and religious people there separated from the common way of National worship" (p. 242).

[2] This has very interesting bearing upon the origin of the "Monthly Meetings" of the Quakers.

[3] Which would seem to imply that he was not accustomed to such long periods of *waiting*.

[4] *First Publishers of Truth*, p. 244.

There was another large band of Seekers in Bristol who finally came over bodily to the Friends, under the powerful preaching of John Audland and John Camm, who, as we have seen, had been among the leaders of the Seeker community in Westmorland. Charles Marshall, who was among the first of the band to be convinced of the truth of the Quaker teaching, has given a good account of this Seeker Society of Bristol.[1]

"Now, as I advanced in years, I grew more and more dissatisfied with lifeless, empty professions and professors, feeling the burden of the nature of sin, which lay on my spirit; in the sense whereof, I became like the solitary desert, and mourned like a dove without a mate. And seeing I could not find the living among the dead professions, I spent much time in retirements alone, in the fields and woods, and by springs of water, which I delighted to lie by, and drink of."

. . . . .

"And in those times, viz. about the year 1654, there were many (in these parts) who were seeking after the Lord; and there were a few of us who kept one day in the week in fasting and prayer; so that when this day came, we met together early in the morning, and did not taste anything. We sat down sometimes in silence; and as any found a concern on their spirits, and inclination in their hearts, they kneeled down and sought the Lord; so that sometimes, before the day ended, there might be twenty of us pray, men and women; on some of these occasions children spake a few words in prayer; and we were sometimes greatly bowed and broken before the Lord, in humility and tenderness."[2]

---

1 *Life and Works of Charles Marshall*, pp. 2, 4.

2 The following interesting Letters from John Audland and John Camm to Edward Burrough and Francis Howgil, written in 1654, give much light on these Bristol Seekers:

"JNO. AUDLAND and JNO. CAMM to EDW. BURROUGH and FRAS. HOWGIL.

"BRISTOL, *9th 7 mo.* (*Sept.*)—*must be* 1654.

"Dear hearts we are now in Bristol—here is a pretty many convinced of the truth and the truth works and spreads—my soul is much refreshed for they are much come down into themselves since we were here and they are sensible of their conditions—they are the most noble of any that we have met withal. . . . The work of the Lord is great hereaway, the people hungers after life, they groan to be delivered, they meet every day—if we go into the fields they follow us, from us they cannot be separated, if we sit silent a long time, they all wait in silence. The Lord will do a great work amongst them and raise up a pure people to place his name in—J. A., J. C. (Written by J. A. within a day or two of J. A. and J. C. reaching Bristol and referring specially to their reception by the Seekers)."—*Devonshire House MSS.*, *A. R. Barclay MSS.*, No. 158.

There were other similar groups of Seekers in almost all sections of England, and in many places they formed the nucleus of the Quaker Society. The following references will be sufficient to indicate how very wide-spread the movement was: William Caton, writing to Margaret Fell (London, 19th January 1657) says, "a door was opened me in a corner of Sussex, where there were several seekers (so called), the most part of two meetings were convinced."[1] In his Journal, William Caton says:[2]

> "After that I had exceedingly good service in Sussex, especially among a people that were called Seekers, who were mostly convinced not far from Lewes."

In the account of Ann Camm, in *Piety Promoted*, reference is made to the Kendal Seekers (prior to 1652):

> "At Kendal there was a Seeking people who met often

"LETTER No. 157. J. C. to E. B. and F. H.

"BRISTOL, *13th 7 mo.* (*4th day of week*).

"... Here is the largest fields that ever I saw, all is full of clusters of grapes—This day the people in the city who are our friends (*i.e.* the Seeker community at Bristol) met together to seek the Lord as they call it, ... we bore them long till the power of the Lord took hold upon us both and I was forced to cry out amongst them my life suffered and if I did not speak I should be an example amongst them and in much tenderness I spake unto them and silence was amongst them all and much tenderness and brokenness and it is a glorious day—now they are come to see the serpent which hath beguiled them and robbed them of their simplicity; they have many of them cast off their beautiful garments which was without—For we are with them from six in the morning, they will come to us before we get up, and unto eleven or sometimes one at night they will never be from us, go into the fields they will follow us, or go into any house the house will be filled full, so that we cannot tell how we should get from them. The Lord hath subjected them all under us and they are as fearful to offend us as a child is to offend its loving father."

"LETTER under same number. J. A. to E. B. and F. H.

"(*Same date.*)

"We came 7th day of month—That night it was noised in the city and all was filled where we were—We have every day a meeting, yea I may say every day is but a meeting and we cannot help it, for let us go where we will all is full where we are, night and day, and as the work is great the power is greatest in us that ever we knew in us—We had a great meeting upon the First day morning, the house and all was filled and the street, so the voice went forth for a field and one there which was free had a meadow (Earlsmead, see Chas. Marshall's account) and we went to it like an army. My dear brother J. C. spoke, he is exceedingly grown since I saw you—I stood up and all my limbs smote together and I was like a drunken man because of the Lord and because of the word of his holiness and I was made to cry like a woman in travail and to proclaim war, etc."

[1] *Swarthmore MSS.* $\frac{1}{314}$ (in Devonshire House, London).

[2] Life of Caton in *Select Series of Biographies*, edited by John Barclay, 1839, p. 58.

together, sometimes sitting in silence, other times in religious conferences, and often in fervent prayer."[1]

John Lawson, writing to Margaret Fell in 1653, says:

"There are also a people about Malpas in Cheshire who was formerly separated from the priests and since we came among them they are separated, one part of them meet together and speak their own words as they did, another part of them separate from them and meet together to wait upon the Lord without words."[2]

They were also called "thirsty souls who hunger."

"About the year 1652, It pleased the Lord to visit this County of Chester By that faithfull Servant of his Richard Hubberthorne, who for his Testimony was put into prison att Chester, where severall Came to See him & Some were Convinced, amongst whom was Thomas Yarwood, who had been a great professor & A preacher amongst them; who sometime after his Convincment had his Mouth opened to Preach Truth, and was Moved of the Lord to visit a people who Sometimes met att the house of one Rich Yarwood, in Moberly in the said County (whose Custom was when met Together neither To preach nor pray vocally butt to Read the Scriptures & Discourse of Religion, Expecting a farther Manifestation);"[3] . . .

(Wigton) "About ye Year 1653, A few People were Gathered together from ye publique worship of ye Nation, and oftentimes sat together in Silence."[4] . . .

"The first yt Came into Boulton to declare the glad tideings of the Everlasting Gospell to A people thatt was then seeking after ye Lord, was Geo: ffox and Robert Widders."[5]

The Seeker movement took two quite opposite directions. It attracted men of large spiritual powers and insight, who quickly transcended it and became "happy Finders" on the one hand. On the other hand, "it ran out" into what William Penn calls "a monstrous birth," and ended downward in *Ranterism.*

Some of them, as John Jackson says, after long waiting on God, waxed weary and said: "Come, let us go back to

[1] Ann Camm, before her marriage to Thomas Camm, was the wife of John Audland (*Piety Promoted*, vol. i. p. 318).

[2] *Swarthmore MSS.* $\frac{4}{69}$ (in Devonshire House).

[3] *First Publishers of Truth*, p. 18.

[4] *Ibid.* p. 52.

[5] *Ibid.* p. 56.

Egypt for bread, it is better to take it at the mouth of ravens (*i.e.* the Presbyterian black-gowned clergy) than starve."[1] But there were many Seekers who did *not* go back to Egypt for bread; they went on into a spiritual Canaan where they found milk and honey, oil and wine, for their souls.[2] John Saltmarsh, William Dell, Gerrard Winstanley, and, foremost of all, George Fox, *found* the clear Light and present Spirit the Seekers were groping for. We shall leave their discovery for the present and briefly consider the dregs of the Seeker movement—the *Ranters.*

The Ranters got a bad name from everybody who came in contact with them,[3] and there is no question that it was a "degenerate" movement, though many of the so-called Ranters were honest, sincere persons, trying in their crude fashion to utter the profound truth of Divine in-dwelling. The *central idea* of Ranterism was the doctrine that God is essentially in every creature. There is, they taught, one and only one Spirit in the universe. This Spirit is revealed in measure in all that is—"in the tiny ivy leaf," and "in the most glorious angel." This Spirit flows out into finite channels and then flows back again into the mother sea, the ground and spring of all things.[4]

Richard Baxter says that "they (the Ranters) made it their business to set up the Light of Nature, under the name of Christ in Men, and to dishonour and cry down

[1] John Jackson's *Sober Word to a Serious People*, Preface.

[2] John Jackson says that "those who have got above and beyond the practice of all ordinances are very improperly called *Seekers*; for these are so far from seeking, that they are rather possessors, enjoyers, and attainers than Seekers properly so-called" (*A Sober Word*, p. 2).

[3] "Old Ephraim Pagitt" allows himself free rein in his account of the Ranters: "The Ranter is an unclean beast, much of the make of our Quaker, *sic*) of the same puddle, and may keep pace with him; their infidelities, villanies and debochments are the same, only the Ranter is more open, and less sowre; professes what he is, and as he has neither religion nor honesty, so he pretends to none. . . . He denyes that there are either God or devil, Heaven or Hell. . . . It is a maxim with them that there is nothing sin but what a man thinks to be so. They are above ordinances, hence it is that nothing is to be forbidden them, nothing can be unlawful," and much more in the same strain (Pagitt's *Heresiography*, p. 143).

[4] Masson rightly says (*Life of Milton*, vol. v. p. 18), "There were probably varieties of Ranters theologically. Pantheism or the essential identity of God with the universe, and His indwellings in every creature, angelic, human, brute, or inorganic, seems to have been the belief of most Ranters that could manage to rise to a metaphysics."

the Church, the Scripture, the present Ministry and our Worship and Ordinances, and called men to hearken to Christ within them."[1]

George Whitehead, the Quaker, has left us an "Impartial Account" of the James Nayler episode, and in it he has given an interesting report of one Robert Rich who supported James Nayler under his examination before Parliament, and stood with him in the pillory. Rich was a Ranter,[2] and later declared to George Whitehead that he was "one of the dogs that licked Lazarus's sores"!

He had a habit of coming to the meetings of the Friends in London and of "walking up and down therein in a stately manner (having a very long white beard), in his black velvet coat, with a loose-hanging one over it." "When he heard something declared that pleased him, he would cry, 'Amen, amen, amen.'" Whitehead had "some discourse with the said Robert Rich about the seed of God (the Eternal Word) in Man and the Soul of Man; and he could not distinguish them, putting no Difference between the Soul, or Spirit, of Man, and that which saves it; to wit, the Ingrafted Immortal Word, which is able to save the Soul. So that he seemed to leave no room for the Immortality of the Soul of Man, but only of the Immortal Seed or Word of God; but discoursing with him a little closely upon the point, he put me off with an evasive Slight, saying, 'Thou art wise in the Letter, but I am in that which is above thy Wisdom; to wit, in the Mystery, etc.'"[3]

Many Ranters apparently rejected faith in Immortality, as well as belief in a personal God. Masson quotes the following passage from the "Carol of the Ranters," preserved in the Thomason Pamphlets:

> "They prate of God! Believe it, fellow-creatures,
> There's no such bug-bear: all was made by Nature.
> We know all came of nothing, and shall pass
> Into the same condition once it was

---

1 Baxter's *Life*, vol. i. p. 76.

2 Rich "publickly licked James Nayler's wounds."

3 "An Epistle to the Serious Reader containing an Impartial Account, etc." Preface to James Nayler's *Works* (London, 1716), p. xvii.

By Nature's power, and that they grossly lie
That say there's hope of immortality,
Let them but tell us what a soul is; then
We shall adhere to these mad brainsick men."

"The allness of God" was no new doctrine; it had fascinated the mystics of the thirteenth and fourteenth centuries. Ranterism was to all intents and purposes a revival of the doctrines of the "Free Spirit," which have been studied in an earlier chapter. There was in England, in the Commonwealth era, a real *contagion* of the idea of God as indwelling. Some of the stronger minds who were *possessed* with the idea were able to hold it in balance with other ideas equally true; but some unstable, ill-balanced men and women were swept quite off the poise of sanity by it,[1] and large groups of the common people (this was essentially a movement of the common people) were carried into a cheap, half-digested "spiritualism," which bristled with dangers; as, in their ignorance of history and sound psychology, they were almost bound to be, at that stage of thought.

They fell into a vague pantheism which blurred the distinctions between good and evil, and which landed them in a moral (or immoral) topsy-turvey. The Seeker movement had under-valued objective religion, historical revelation, and outward helps. The natural result was that those who pushed the ideas of the Seekers to their extreme limit, and throwing overboard all outward systems, acknowledged nothing Divine except the Spirit in themselves, had no fixed authority anywhere, no criterion of morals, no test of spiritual guidance, no ground and basis for goodness. Being "taught by the Spirit," they claimed that all other teachings were of no use. They called the Scriptures "a tale, a history, a dead letter, a fleshly story, a cause of divisions and contradictions." They looked upon Christ as a "figure" or "type" of the *true dispensation of the Spirit*, upon which they claimed to have entered.

[1] There was an element of fierce fanaticism in the movement, and among the Ranters there were some real lunatics.

Samuel Fisher, the Friend, writing in 1653, gives an extremely calm and valuable account of the Ranters.[1] He says:

"They considered that in the present dispensation, which is that of the Spirit, since Christ had come again spiritually, they had no longer any need of lower helps, outward administrations, carnal ordinances, visible representations of Christ, and mere bodily exercises, as baptism and fellowship together in breaking of bread. The Church once saw Christ in these things, but they had become men, and put away childish things; and as for gathering congregations, people assembling in the Church bodies to preach, break bread, to build up one another in the faith, search the Scriptures, etc.—all these shadowy dispensations had their day; but now Christ, the Morning Star, had shined, all we had to do was to take heed to His appearing in our hearts, and the shadows would flee away. They promised to their converts, that when they left off reading the Scriptures, and those childish things, they would then have the liberty of the Spirit, and would enjoy an Angelical or Seraphical life." "Till Christ come," means, he says, for the Ranter, "His coming into men by his Spirit, or in such full measures and manifestations of his Spirit into men's hearts, that they may be able to live up with him in spirit, so as no more to need such lower helps from outward administrations, such carnal ordinances, such visible representations of Christ to the bodily eyes, such legal rites and mere bodily exercises as baptism and fellowship together in breaking of bread are.

"These things were used indeed, and ordained, as milk for babes in that meer nonage and infancy of the Church, when Christ was known as a child as it were, but now we are to know Christ as a man grown in us, risen up in us, and to have fellowship with him more immediately and intimately in Spirit, and not in such external and meer fleshly formes; we are to live higher than on such low, weak, empty elements and beggarly rudiments as these, which were used and imposed for a time to resemble Christ to us from without, but must be left when once Christ, the substance, that was set forth by those Shadows, is come *into us*. . . . That which is perfect is now come, and therefore what is imperfect, and in part only, as ordinances are, must be done away, and as for gathering of congregations, peoples assembling together in the Church bodies to preach, pray, break bread, to

---

1 "This is put into the mouth of a Ranter in Samuel Fisher's rambling dialogue style in the chapter on Anti-Ranterism in the volume entitled *Baby Baptism meer Babism* (London, 1653), pp. 511-12.

build up one another in the faith, search the Scripture, etc., 'twas a way of God for men's edification till Christ the morning star shined, to which men did well to take heed, as unto a light that shined in a dark place, but now the day dawned and the day starre arises in men's hearts, yea the day breaks and the shadowes flee away; and Christ comes as a swift Roe and young hart upon the mountains of Bether; for that now we are to exercise ourselves rather into Godliness for all bodily exercises as baptism, breaking bread, and Church order, etc., profit little: besides 'twas said there should be a falling away from all those forms of worship, and the way of ordinances, which was in the primitive times (2 Thess. ii. 3), and a treading down of the Holy City and Temple (Rev. xi. 1, 2) as to the form it then stood in, both which have fell out also accordingly, so that there hath been a taking of all that dispensation of ordinances in their primitive purity totally out of the way, therefore now we are to meddle no more with them at all; at least unless we had some extraordinary Prophets, as the Jews had after the treading down of their temple and worship, to satisfie and shew us that its the mind of the Lord we should set up that old fabrick and form again."

The Friends, in the early period of the Quaker movement, came into contact and frequently into rivalry with the Ranters. There are very many accounts of them in the Quaker Journals, Pamphlets, and Letters, and these accounts for the most part show a horror of Ranterism and a hostility to its exponents. But these accounts are almost without exception vague and general, with few actual sins specified, though with frequent reference to their "swinishness."

Richard Hickock, a Friend, writing in 1659,[1] evidently to some who had once been Friends and had afterwards become Ranters, tells them "*lovingly*" that they have "become like the sow that was washed and is again wallowing in the mire." He calls upon them to "bring down their imaginations, which are kept above the Light of Christ."

He makes a great point of their *swearing*, but he makes fully as much a point of their using "you" for a single person. He charges them with holding that

[1] Richard Hickock, "A Testimony Against the People called Ranters and their Pleads" (London, 1659).

"nothing is sin, if a man himself do not count it sin and so make it sin unto himself," and he reproaches them with the assertion that when they have done wickedly they "lay it upon the Lord as though He were mover and leader thereto": and "when you have done wickedly you say you have taken up the cross therein."

The Journal of George Fox contains many references to the Ranters, and he mentions by name, and gives some characterisation of two men who were leaders of their rather chaotic ranks, Joseph Salmon and Jacob Bottomley (or Bauthumley). He found Joseph Salmon in company with a band of Ranters in the gaol at Coventry. "They said they were God," Fox tells us, "but I asked them whether it would rain to-morrow and they could not tell. I told them God could tell!" He informs us that Joseph Salmon afterwards wrote a book of recantation, upon which they were all set at liberty.[1] In Swannington, Leicestershire, Fox had a "contest" with "the great Ranter," as he calls him, Jacob Bauthumley, "but the Lord's power stopt him and came over them all." A little later in the same locality Fox sent for the Ranters "to come forth and try their God." "Abundance of them came," he writes, "and were very rude, and sung and whistled and danced; but the Lord's power so confounded them, that many of them came to be 'convinced' (that is became Friends)."[2]

In London, in 1654, Fox says "there came to me one Cobb to see me and a great company of Ranters with him. They began to call for drink and tobacco, and one of them cried, 'All is ours'; another said, 'All

[1] Fox's *Journal* (edition of 1902), vol. i. p. 47. This Joseph Salmon seems to be the author of the pamphlet, "A Rout, a Rout or Some Part of the Armies Quarters Beaten up by the Day of the Lord" (London, 1649).

[2] *Journal*, vol. i. p. 199. This Jacob Bauthumley is the author of an extremely pantheistical book with the sensational title, *The Light and Dark Sides of God* (London, 1660). A short extract will show the trend of its teaching: "O God, what shall I say thou art, when thou canst not be named? What shall I speak of thee, when speaking of thee, I speak nothing but contradiction? For I say I see thee, it is nothing but thy seeing of thyself; for there is nothing in me capable of seeing but thyself. If I say I know thee there is no other but the knowledge of thyself, for I am rather known of thee than know thee. If I say I love thee it is nothing so, for there is nothing in me can love thee but thyself, and therefore thou dost but love thyself. My seeking thee is no other but thy seeking of thyself" (pp. 1-2).

is well.'" "How is all well," Fox replied, "while thou art so peevish and envious and crabbed?" Fox preserves an interesting testimony from a prominent Justice of the Peace to the wide-spread prevalence of Ranterism. He reports that Justice Hotham said, "If God had not raised up this principle of life and light which I [George Fox] preached, the nation had been over-run with Ranterism and all the justices in the nation could not have stopped it with all their laws."[1]

There is a very interesting paper in the Swarthmore Collection—a paper giving an account of Quaker sufferings at Leicester (dated incorrectly 1653; it should be 1655) in which George Fox adds the following incident. While in Prison

"there came in many of the light spirits, professors, dippers, separatists, ranters, and such like, whom I was made to judge, and speak to their condition and declare against their ungodly practices, though I never saw them before: for the Lord gave (me) to discern their spirits; and the witness was raised, and they could not deny but that I had spoken truly to their several conditions, insomuch that some of the unclean spirits said 'I was a witch'; others demanded by what power I knew these things seeing I knew none of them. I said it pleased God to reveal his Son in me, which knew all things; and they said, Was I the Son of God? I said, 'I was no more, but the Father and the Son was all in me and we are one,' so when there was silence I was made to speak to the light in them, and when there was silence Jacob Bottomley and many others did witness that what I had spoken was the eternal truth, and I warned them to obey that which witnessed in me, or else it would eternally condemn them."

Thomas Curtis, writing to George Fox from Reading in 1659, refers to a Baptist meeting, which had evidently turned into a meeting of Ranters, where "every man had his tobacco pipe in his mouth!" and he continues, "when we had ended speaking, like swine whose nose must still be in the 'troffe,' they with so much eagerness followed the tobacco pipe again as if they had been famished."[2] The Antinomian Ranters in colonial New England also

[1] *Journal*, vol. i. p. 95. [2] *Swarthmore MSS.* $\frac{3}{87}$.

apparently used tobacco to heighten their spiritual vision. Captain Underhill of Dover, New Hampshire, told Governor Winthrop of Massachusetts that "the Spirit had sent into him the witness of Free Grace while he was in the moderate enjoyment of the creature called tobacco!"

The Ranters felt no longer under obligation to "eye or mind a Christ who died at Jerusalem, but rather to *eye and mind the Christ in themselves.*" They said "they had no occasion to read the Scriptures or hear sermons, because Father, Son, and Holy Ghost were all in them." They would not call anything the Word of God unless it was revealed in them as well as in the Scriptures. They believed a truth not because "such and such writ it," but because "God saith so in me."

They admitted that Paul had the Spirit, when he wrote, but they said: "Have not *I* the Spirit, and why may not I write Scriptures as well as Paul, and what I write be as binding and infallible as that which Paul writ?"[1]

"They were above such weak and beggarly things as ordinances, which are for weak Christians who are under the teaching of the letter."[2]

Jacob Bauthumley, in his *Light and Dark Sides of God*, says:

> "It is not so safe to go to the Bible to see what others have spoken and writ of the mind of God as to see what God speaks within me and to follow the doctrine and leading of it in me."[3]

---

[1] See Barclay, p. 417-18.

[2] It must be remembered that these "views" are largely taken from persons who put the worst construction on the Ranter's teaching, though the author of the *Smoke of the Bottomless Pit* (London, 1650-51) from which these teachings are gleaned, professes to be an honest witness. His name was Holland Porter, and he says that he is "an eye and ear witness." In a postscript he further says: "Reader, I have not followed that orderly method I might have done, but have written the judgments of these men in a confused manner; but I do profess in the presence of the Lord who is the searcher of all hearts, I have done them no wrong in the matter of their judgment except it be in forbearing to repeat their bloody cursing and swearing—for this offence I hope that those who fear the Lord will excuse me, farewell."

[3] P. 77.

It is one thing to hold, in the interests of spiritual religion as the Seekers did, that "the letter" and "the history" and "the outward" are only *helps*, and not the ultimate substance of religion itself, and it is quite another thing to fall over the edge of the chasm and assert that, having the substance—the Spirit—secondary helps are of no account! The individual is thus left as sole authority, an infallible oracle and prophet of the Divine Spirit, irresponsible and untrammelled. This fatal step the Ranters took. They made their "oneness with God" absolute, and confused the *possibility of Divine Guidance* with the *assertion of personal infallibility*.[1]

The most extraordinary personal account of Ranterism *from the inside*, which I have found, is that of Joseph Salmon.[2]

His *experience* and his descriptions give a good idea of the mental condition of the Ranters, and I know no document more valuable for a diagnosis of the Ranter-attitude. He relates how, as he was coming to maturity, he "received some quickenings of a Divine principle in him." After going through many stages of religious experience, he heard "a voice that came from the throne of the heavenly Almightinesse (which said), 'Arise and depart, for this is not your rest.'"

Here follows his own account of his "great experience"; (the reader should notice the sidenotes, which are part of the text):

"I was made as truly sensible of this inwardly, as the eye is sensible of the light, or the ear of the outward sound. I was suddenly struck dead to all my wonted enjoyment. Stript I was of my glory, and my crown taken from my head, and I could see nothing but vanity (and that legibly written) upon all my former travails. I then had a clear discovery in my spirit, how far all my former enjoyments came short of that true rest which my

---

[1] "One Ranter made answer that he was *not the* God, but he was God, because God was in him and in every creature in the world" (see *Smoke of Bottomless Pit*"; quoted by Barclay, p. 419).

[2] His tract bears the title: "Heights in Depths, and Depths in Heights; or Truth no less Secretly than Sweetly, Sparkling out of its Glory," etc., by Joseph Salmon, London, 1651. British Museum, 270-E-1361. Barclay prints extracts from it in appendix to chapter xvii. *op. cit.* He gives his name as *John* Salmon.

soul had all along aimed at. Here I stood for a season weeping with Mary at the sepulchre: fain I would have found Christ where I left him, but alas, he was risen. I found nothing in form but a few signals of mortality; as for Jesus, he was risen and departed. Thus have I followed Christ from his babeship or infancy to his grave of mortality, running through the life form, in a bare knowledge of Christ after the flesh, till I expired with him into his death, and was sealed up in the grave of most dark and somnolent retires for a season. Loath, full loath was I, thus to shake hands with form, and to leave the terrestrial image of Jesus Christ; yet so it was designed that hee must goe to his Father, and (although I were ignorant of it) prepare a higher mansion in himself for me. When my three dayes (or set time) was expired, I begann to feele some quickening comfort within me; the gravestone was rolled away and I set at libertie from these deep and dark retires; out I came with a most serene and cheerfull countenance, and (as one inspired with a supernaturall life) sprang up farr above my earthly center, into a most heavenly and divine enjoyment. Wrapt up in the embraces of such pure love and peace, as that I knew not oft-times whether I were in or out of this fading forme. Here I saw heaven opened upon me, and the new Jerusalem (in its divine brightness and corruscant beauty) greeting my soule by its humble and gentle discensions. Now I certainly enjoyed that substance, which all this while I had groped after in the shadow. My water was turned into wine; form into power, and all my former enjoyments being nothing in appearance to that glory which now rested on my spirit. Time would faile to tell what joy unspeakable, peace inconceivable, what soul-ravishing delights, and most divinely infatuating pleasures my soul was here possest with. I could cast my eye no where but that presence of love presented itselfe to me whose beatificall vision at times dazzled me into a sweet astonishment. In a word, I can give you no perfect account of that glory which then covered me; the lisps and slipps of my tongue will but render that imperfect, whose pure perfection surmounts the reach of the most strenuous and high-flown expression. I appeared to myselfe as one confounded into the abyss of eternitie, nonentitized into the being of beings, my soul spilt and emptied into the fountaine and ocean of divine fulness, expired into the aspires of pure life. In briefe, the Lord so much appeared, that I was little or nothing seen, but walked at an orderly distance from myself, treading and tripping over the pleasant mountains of the

A few grave clothes, or such like stuff.

As many of you as have been baptized into his death.

Like the disciples, who were ignorant of the promise of the Spirit.

Viz. the carnal self.

heavenly land, where I walked with the Lord and was not. I shall be esteemed a foole by the wise world, through an over much boasting, otherwise I could tell you how I have been exalted into the bosome of the eternall Almightiness, where I have seene and heard things unlawful (I say unlawful) to be uttered amongst men; but I shall at present spare myself the labour, and prevent the world's inconsiderate censure. The proud and imperious nature of flesh would willingly claim a share in this glorious work for which cause happened a suddain, certain, terrible, dreadfull revolution, a most strange vicissitude. God sent a thorn immediately, hid himself from me by a sudden departure, and gives a speedy commission to a messenger of Satan to assault me. The Lord being thus withdrawn, and having carried away (in the bundle of his treasures) the heart and life of that new seed in me, there now remained nought behind but the man of sinne, who (for his pride) being wounded with the thorn of divine vengeance, began by degrees to act its part."

As to the weakness of many.

Note well what I say, that was reserved pure in the life of Christ, while the flesh acted its part.

Richard Baxter writes with some hysteria in his attack and it would not carry much weight if not otherwise well supported. After describing their *views*, he adds:

"But withal they conjoyned a cursed Doctrine of Libertinism, which brought them to all abominable filthiness of Life. They taught that God regardeth not the actions of the outward man, but of the inner heart, and that to the Pure all things are Pure (even things forbidden) and so as allowed by God they spake most hideous words of Blasphemy, and many of them committed whoredoms commonly.

"There was never sect arose in the world that was a lowder warning to Professors of Religion to be humble, fearful, cautelous, and watchful. Never could the World behold more loudly whither the spiritual Pride of ungrounded Novices in Religion tendeth; and whither Professors of Strictness in Religion may be carried in the stream of sects and factions. I have seen myself Letters written from Abington, where among soldiers and People this *contagion* did then prevail, full of horrid oaths and curses and blasphemy, not fit to be repeated by the Tongue or Pen of Man; and this all uttered as the effect of knowledge and a part of their Religion in a Fanatick Strain and fathered on the Spirit of God. But the horrid villanies of this sect did speedily extinguish it." [1]

Gilbert Roulston, who professes to have been for

[1] Baxter's Life, i. pp. 76-77.

seven years a "wicked Ranter," and who claims to have been converted by "the terrible voice of the Lord," speaking within his heart and saying: "Leave off thy wicked ways and return from whence thou camest," has left a very dark picture of Ranterism in his *Ranter's Bible.*[1] This gives seven types of Ranter doctrine, and charges some of the Ranters with immoral conduct. But it shows itself on its own face to be thoroughly unreliable, and its account of the Ranters' doctrine and doings is of little value, though it adds to the impression that there was a vast amount of moral and religious unsoundness afloat.

The records of Parliament, too, give evidence of wide-spread moral disease and religious fanaticism. The measures which were passed in 1649 and 1650 were, it is true, formulated under strong Presbyterian influences, and may be thought to be part of a "blue law" system, but they cannot be explained away on that ground, for we find Cromwell himself cashiering Captain Covell in October 1650, for asserting that "sin was no sin," and some months later he expresses his vehement detestation of "opinions destructive of the power of godliness."[2]

August 9, 1650, an ordinance was passed "for punishing blasphemous and execrable opinions." The ordinance reads:

> "That any persons not distempered in their brains, who shall maintain any meer creature to be God; or to be Infinite, Almighty, or in Honor, Excellency, Majesty, and Power to be equal and the same with the true God or that the true God or the Eternal Majesty dwells in the creature, or that shall deny the holiness of God, or shall maintain that all acts of wickedness and unrighteousness are not forbidden in holy scripture; or that God approves them. Any one who shall maintain that acts of drunkenness, adultery, swearing, etc., are not in themselves shameful, wicked, sinful, and impious; or that there is not any real difference between moral good and evil, etc., all such persons shall suffer six months' imprisonment for the first offence; and for the second shall

[1] Ranter's Bible (London, 1650).

[2] Gardiner's *History of the Common. and Protect.*, vol. i. p. 396.

be banished; and if they return without licence shall be treated as felons."[1]

The preamble to this ordinance says that

"though several laws have been made for promoting reformation in doctrines and manners, yet there are divers men and women who have lately discovered monstrous opinions, even such as tend to the dissolution of human society."[2]

It is not likely that any "mere creature" who was possessed of sanity, *i.e.* "not distempered in his brains," did maintain himself to be God, but there were many cases of the use of extravagant Messianic language which was greatly in vogue in these times. There were undoubtedly those who called themselves, or allowed themselves to be called, Son of God, and there was at least one woman who claimed to be the "Lamb's wife,"[3] but those who made these professions and claims were plainly distraught, or, to use the language of the time, not "in the use of their intellectuals." In fact, the outbreak in Bristol, when James Nayler rode into the city accompanied by a group of "disciples" crying "Hosannah to the Son of David," was only a single instance of the culmination of this Ranter tendency, and of the danger of the use of Messianic language at a time when there were so many unbalanced persons about.

It is at any rate perfectly clear, even when full allowance is made for sectarian misunderstanding and

[1] Scobell's *Collections of Acts and Ordinances*, Part II. p. 124.

[2] Similar action was taken in the American Colonies. The United Colonies, which included all the New England Colonies except Rhode Island, entered the following statute upon their books:

"That Anabaptism, Familism, Antinomianism, and generally all errors of like nature, which oppose and undermine and slight either the Scriptures, the Sabbath, or other ordinances of God and bring in and cry up unwarrantable revelation, inventions of men, or any carnal liberty, under a deceitful colour of liberty of conscience, may be seasonably and duly suppressed; though they wish as much forbearance and respect may be had, of tender consciences seeking light as may stand with the purity of religion, and the peace of the churches." (Plymouth, *Col. Rec.* ix. 81, 82). We learn from King's pamphlets, "The Ranters," British Museum, E 486, 10, that "one named W. Smith was hung for denying the Deity and several illegal practices against the Parliament."

[3] See case of William Franklin and Mary Gadbury in *Pseudo Christus*, or a true and faithful relation of the grand impostures . . . lately spread abroad and acted in the County of Southamptom. By Humphry Ellis, London, 1650. This is a most extraordinary book, and deserves a careful study.

exaggeration, that the Ranter movement was a serious outbreak of mental and moral disorder. The movement furnishes much information on the wide-spread existence, in the period, of unstable mental conditions, and it brings forcibly to light the dangers involved in *extreme* mystical doctrines, that is, doctrines by which the individual is assumed to be an infallible embodiment of God, to be superior to all previous revelation, and to be able to arrive at final truth without the help of the Church or the social environment.

It is very significant that Gerrard Winstanley, whose sympathies with the common people were intense, who cannot conceivably be charged with any antipathy to *sectaries*, and who was, too, himself a mystic,[1] looked upon the Ranters as a dangerous folk. He calls the "Rantering power" "a devouring beast," which will tear in pieces the kingdom of peace in and among mankind. But, in his usual strain of brotherly love, he strongly counsels against suppressing the "ranting power by the *punishing hand*." "It is the work of the Righteous and Rational Spirit within, not the hand without (the hand of secular power) that must suppress it. For the spirit within must shame them (the Ranters) and turn them and pull them out of darkness."[2]

Strangely enough, just this method suggested by Winstanley, was the method which worked, and which ultimately saved England from the unwholesome contagion of Ranterism. George Fox began his travels over England in 1649, proclaiming everywhere to the *people* his message of the Divine Light and Spirit, revealing the will of God and the power of Christ within man. His message was as clear as a bell on all moral issues, his life was clean and pure and spiritually virile, and he called men everywhere to *a new life in Christ*. In the early days of his ministry, he frequently encountered Ranters. In many instances he was able to impress the

[1] For Winstanley's religious views, see next chapter.

[2] "A vindication of those . . . called Diggers; or some reasons given by them against the immoderate use of creatures, or the excessive community of women, Ranting, rather than Renting."

Ranters themselves with the larger truth which they were groping after; and out of Ranter communities he built up strong meetings. In other instances he failed to win the Ranters, but revealed to the people in their neighbourhoods the difference between the Spirit of Light and Love, which he announced, and the Ranter spirit, so that the influence of the Ranters was checked and a strong counter-influence set in motion.[1]

Justice Hotham of Cranswick, "a tender man, one that had some experience of God's workings in his heart," said, as has been already noted, that, "if God had not raised up the Principle of Light and Life," which Fox preached, "the nation would have been overrun with Ranterism, and all the justices in the nation could not have stopped it with their laws." "But," says Justice Hotham, "this Principle of Truth overthrows their principle and the root and ground of it."[2]

William Penn reports a similar testimony from Dr. Gell, whom he calls, "a person of worldly quality." This Dr. Gell said that "had not the Quakers come, the Ranters had overrun the nation."[3]

Baxter says, undoubtedly with some truth, "the horrid villanies of the sect did extinguish it," but there is no question that the positive message of the Divine in man did much to win the middle class English people away from the misguided views and practices of the Ranters to a sounder and more constructive spiritual religion.

[1] Trevelyan (*England Under the Stuarts*, p. 312) rightly says that Fox "had an overwhelming, perhaps an hypnotic, power and presence, like one of the ancient prophets."

[2] Fox's *Journal*, vol. i. p. 92.

[3] *Judas and the Jews*, Penn's *Works* (London, 1726), vol. ii. p. 208.

CHAPTER XX

INDIVIDUAL MYSTICS IN THE PERIOD OF THE ENGLISH COMMONWEALTH

ALL the great spiritual concerns of the race have their periods of flood and ebb, influenced by currents too subtle and too deep for scientific analysis or calculation, and religion, the most commanding of these spiritual concerns of humanity, is no exception to the rule. It, too, has had its flood and ebb periods, its flowering times and its barren stretches.

One of these flood-currents, a ground-swell of religious earnestness, came to its height in the period of the English Commonwealth. There was much in the movement that was chaotic and abortive, but there was also much that was creative and constructive. I have already studied some of the most significant *religious groups* which flourished during that important epoch. I shall now consider some of the men of the period who have a good claim to be called religious prophets, because they voiced this primary spiritual concern of the race in fresh and vital ways.

George Fox (born 1624, died 1691) is unquestionably the foremost of these "prophets," and he has the distinction of being the founder of a religious sect which has for two centuries and a half continued the mystical type of Christianity which he initiated. The rise of this movement and the history of its progress will be told as a continuation of this present volume, so that, for the moment, I pass by George Fox, with his message of Divine Light and his practical attempt to revive "primitive Christianity."

The next name to concern us is that of John Saltmarsh, a Yorkshire mystic, whose message is quite worth our attention. His birth date is unknown; his death occurred in 1647.[1] He received a degree of M.A. from Cambridge (Magdalene College) sometime before 1640,[2] and, also before that date, he became a rector of Heslerton, in Yorkshire, a preferment which he resigned in 1643 on account of his scruples against taking tithes. His period of literary activity as a religious reformer came mainly in the last two years of his life (1645-47), while he was occupying the rectory of Brasted, in Kent.

"He was," says Fuller,[3] "a man of a fine and active fancy, no contemptible poet, and a good preacher, as by some of his profitable printed sermons doth appear."

This is very fair of Fuller, for Saltmarsh "wrote a book" against the former's sermon on "Reformation," and a spirited controversy followed.

In 1646 he became an army chaplain, and, to the grief of Richard Baxter,[4] he had a large place with the soldiers.

It is interesting to note that Saltmarsh was subject to ecstatic, or trance, experiences. I quote the following from Alexander Gordon's account of him in the *National Dictionary of Biography*:—

> "On Saturday, December 4, 1647, rousing himself from what he deemed a trance, he left his abode at Coystreet, near Great Ilford, Essex, and hastened to London. Thence, after twice missing his way, he rode on horseback (December 6) to head-quarters (of the army) at Winsor. *Retaining his hat in Fairfax's presence*, he 'prophesied' that 'the army had departed from God.'"

Fuller further says that "he died in or about Winsor (as he was riding to and fro in the Parliament army) of a

[1] Baxter wrongly says 1650. It is thus only by using the term "Commonwealth" loosely that Saltmarsh comes in that "period."

[2] The college records do not begin until 1640.

[3] *Worthies of England*, London edition, 1840, vol. iii. p. 435.

[4] See *Life of Baxter*, Part I. p. 56.

burning fever, venting on his death-bed strange expressions, apprehended (by some of the party) as *extatical*, yea, *prophetical*, raptures, while others accounted them to the acuteness of his disease which had seized his intellectuals."[1]

Saltmarsh shows in all his controversies a beautiful spirit of charity and humility. He is profoundly convinced that he has seen a great Light, or, as he puts it: "The Light and Glory of Christ has dawned upon me." "I have seen the morning star of righteousness, the brightness of the glory, in my heart; that heart of mine that once lived in the region and shadow of death."[2] But he well knows that there is some of his own human colour mixed with the pure Radiance. "You may single out," he writes in his dedication to Lord Viscount Say and Seale, "something of the Lord's from what is mine, and discern some beams of God amongst many things of the man (the human). I know the candle of the Lord cannot shine anywhere with more snuff than in me. However, *since the Lord hath lighted* it, I dare not but let it shine (or rather glimmer) before men."[3]

He apologizes for the lack of finish in his writings: "I have no libraries beside me to put into my margins," and "I have more of myself in what I do than I ought," but he nevertheless insists that he is writing "not in the authority of man, but of God," and he modestly says that "if any of the Glory of Christ breaks out while he holds up the Glass (the Mirror) let Him have the glory who hath chosen the weak things of the world."[4]

He quietly says to "Master Edwards" of the *Gangræna*, into whose dragnet of Heresy Saltmarsh was drawn, "you set your name to more than you know!" And with a touch of that spirit which disarms controversy, he closes his brief reply to Edwards with this challenge: "I can freely challenge you, and thousands more such as you, to say, write, do, work, or print any-

[1] Fuller, vol. iii. p. 435.
[2] *Some Drops of the Viall*, London, 1646, p. 149.
[3] *The Smoake in the Temple*, London, 1646. Dedication.
[4] Quoted freely from *A Vindication*, London, 1645.

thing; and I hope I shall in the strength of Christ, in whom I am able to do all things, *give you blessings for cursings, and prayers for persecutions.*"

His style of writing is uncouth. Many of his tracts are so hurried that the sentences are utterly confused, and he does not often attain to lucid, powerful composition. As a writer he is by no means the equal even of George Fox, while he falls far below the level of his contemporary mystics, William Dell and Gerrard Winstanley. His most famous book, *Sparkles of Glory*,[1] is pervaded throughout by a pure and lofty spiritual tone, and is far superior in style to his more hasty tracts. I shall largely draw upon this for the material to present his mystical message. His primary idea is *the progressive revelation of God through men.* God has, he says, at each stage of humanity submitted to the limitations of the period, and made such revelation of Himself as man could then grasp. He appeared first under the external law, revealing Himself by visions and dreams, through a system of priests, sacrifices, and ceremonies. He next revealed Himself in an Immanuel—a heightened and much more glorious revelation than the one preceding. But even this revelation was in limitations. Those who experienced it were dependent on the fleshly presence, and on miracles, and they still needed a form of prayer—they attained to "few discoveries of Him in Spirit." Finally, God gave a "most naked unveiling of Himself in Spirit" to the sons of God, who are beginning to appear, and who henceforth will be His only Temple.

As there are three stages of revelation, so, too, there are three stages of ministry. First, there was the ministry of priesthood, conducted under law, and limited to one tribe. Next, came a far higher ministry through Divine *gifts* and "direct unction," committed, however, to only a few. This soon degenerated into a ministry of anti-Christ, a ministry acquired by art and study—an

[1] *Sparkles of Glory; or, Some Beams of the Morning Star*, London, 1647. Reprinted in 1811 and 1847.

artificial rather than a genuinely spiritual ministry. The third stage of ministry, now dawning, is to be that of Christ Himself, who shall be in *all* His saints and people, *shining in them as an inward Light and Glory*, for the immediate revelation of truth—no longer confined to one tribe, but in all his people, no longer a ministry through *gifts*, but rather with the actual presence of Christ in the believer.

The true Church is thus the body of Christ, which is baptized into one Spirit through incorporation into Christ. The true spiritual government of the Church is Christ reigning in the saints by His Spirit, ordering them in thought, word, and deed. The true ordination is the hand of Jesus Christ laid upon such Christians as preach or prophesy. The true test of prophecy is found when the spirit of the prophet is subject to the prophets, that is, when the gift by which any one speaks is witnessed to in the hearts and spirits of the other believers.[1]

All rites and ordinances are but passing *figures*, and are done away in the final spiritual dispensation. Baptism in water was a legal washing suited to the stage of John's ministry. The Baptism of Christ is a spiritual ministration by which true Christians are brought into vital fellowship and oneness with Him, becoming thereby *new men, new creatures.* By *His* Baptism Christ administers His own nature upon His followers. By it He brings them into His own sufferings and death, and by it they are made One Spirit with Him. Every other Baptism is a figure or shadow of *this real Baptism.*[2]

All the world-stages of religion are still to be found in the visible Church. There are some who are still under the law and under priesthood and under ordinances, some who are still bound and limited by systems that were only suited to the swaddling period of the race; but there are others who have been born of the Seed and Word of God, and who are living in the freedom of the Spirit of Christ. These two types of Christians are to be found everywhere; "they are grinding at the same

[1] See especially pp. 32-60.

[2] See especially pp. 21-32.

mill, *but one shall be taken, and the other left*!" God has His times of winding up a dispensation and of laying it by to make way for a more spiritual ministration, a way of more Spirit, Light, and Glory, until humanity shall finally be made into one Temple of the Spirit.

To this lofty teaching in *Sparkles of Glory* may be added a few points from his other works. He says that *the way to see Truth is by living in the power of Truth, by first obtaining Jesus Christ to live in us, and so to incarnate Him over again*."[1] He maintains that true spiritual ministry is higher than the miraculous signs of apostolic times, because (1) Truth needs nothing added to its own spiritual shine and brightness to convince the soul; (2) every Truth is a beam of Christ Himself and has light in itself; (3) the Spirit within us is far superior to anything outward, however glorious, and (4) the transforming power of the living Word is, in itself, such "a constant and standing miracle," that we need no "ministry with miracle."[2]

He insists that in the spiritual dispensation which God is bringing in, war is done away,

> "To be a man of war means," he says, "to live no longer than the life of the world which is perishing; but to be a man of the Holy Spirit, a man born of God, a man that wars not after the flesh, a man of the Kingdom of God, as well as of England . . . that means to live beyond time and age and men and the world; to be gathered into the life which is Eternal."[3]

No passage in his writings is more interesting than the following one on qualifications for ministry, for it contains a statement which has an exact parallel in George Fox's *Journal*:

> "For surely it is not a University, a Cambridge or Oxford, a Pulpit and black Gowne or Cloake, that makes one a true

---

[1] *The Smoake in the Temple.* Introduction.
[2] See *Smoake in the Temple*, pp. 14-15.
[3] Quoted loosely from Dedication to *Some Drops of the Viall* (see also *Sparkles of Glory*, pp. 112-15).

minister of Jesus Christ . . . for the mystery of Iniquity hath deceived the world with a false and artificial unction for *that true one of the Spirit.*"[1]

William Dell has often been taken for a Quaker. His works are frequently catalogued in lists of Quaker books, and they have been published by Quaker publishers and widely circulated among Friends. In his own lifetime he was charged with being a Seeker, an Antinomian, and a leader of "the bold and insolent fanatical ministers" who "poisoned the army," and who "offered their unhallowed services to the blessed martyr" (King Charles) when he was brought to the scaffold. He was, however, never a Quaker. There was probably no man living in England in the early days of Fox's ministry who would have become a more powerful leader in the Quaker movement if he had been brought into it. He had already, independently, won the insight into the truth which formed the central idea of Quakerism, and he possessed unusual gifts of interpretation. But the path of Dell and Fox never crossed, more's the pity! He does not, either, belong among the Seekers. He was not an Antinomian, and he is far removed from fanaticism.[2] In his early period he was a loyal Churchman, and filled the position of secretary to Archbishop Laud. The date of his birth is unknown. He received his B.A. degree at Cambridge (Emmanuel College) in 1627-28, and his M.A. in 1631.

It is not known under what influences he underwent the great changes in his religious views, which appear between his years of service to Laud and his connection with the Parliamentary Army, where he is found as a "preacher" in 1645. "Saltmarsh and Dell," writes

[1] *The Divine Right of Presbytery* (London, 1646). *Some Drops of the Viall,* p. 112. See for Fox's "Opening" *Journal,* vol. i. p. 7.

[2] He plainly, however, shows his sympathy with the small dissenting sects. In his sermon on "Right Reformation," preached before the House of Commons in 1646, he urges Parliament "to suffer the assemblings of the saints, both publicly and privately, as occasion serves, seeing this can be no prejudice to the state, but a great advantage. . . . Those who are anointed with the Spirit of God are the flesh of Christ and the prophets of God, and therefore you touch them and harm them at your own peril" (*Select Works,* pp. 140-41).

Richard Baxter, "were the two great preachers at the Head-Quarters."[1] Baxter further says:

"Mr. Dell, the chaplain of the army, I think, neither understood himself nor was understood by others any further than to be one who took Reason, Sound Doctrine, Order and Concord, to be intolerable maladies of Church and State, because they were the greatest strangers to his mind!"[2]

He preached his sermon on "The Building and the Glory of the truly Spiritual Church" before Fairfax and the army officers in 1646, and his sermon on "The Reformation of the Church of the New Testament in Gospel Light"[3] was preached before the House of Commons November 25 of the same year. On petition of the Fellows of Caius College, Cambridge, he was appointed by Parliament as Master of the College in 1649, a position which he appears to have occupied until 1656. He died in 1664, having two years before been ejected from his living at Yelden, in Bedfordshire. Calamy calls him "a very peculiar and unsettled man," who preached against infant baptism and yet baptized his own children; who preached against universities while he himself held the Mastership of a College; and who preached against tithes while he was himself receiving £200 a year from his living in Yelden.[4]

These seeming inconsistencies are not very serious when one realizes that William Dell was slowly moving from the settled positions of a lifetime, and was following the Light as fast and as far as he saw it. The only real inconsistency in the list was the acceptance of a *living* after he had seen that tithes were no part of the Christian religion, and if he did this, it is a blemish on him. His sermons were collected and published in 1773, under the title: "Select Works of William Dell, Master of Gonvil and Caius College in Cambridge, London (Printed for John Kendall in Colchester)." The sermons in this

[1] Baxter, Part I. p. 56.

[2] *Ibid.* p. 64. One would surely not get that view from reading Dell's printed sermons.

[3] Called hereafter "Right Reformation."

[4] Calamy's *Nonconformist's Memorial*, i. p. 201.

volume were preached between the years 1645 and 1653. I shall use them as the data for my account of his religious message.

The ruling conception in all his teaching is the direct and immediate inspiration of the Spirit of God in man, the revelation of spiritual truth by an inward Light. He contrasts religion of form or religion of externals with *religion in the power of the Holy Spirit.* The former he finds to be very fashionable and easy, as it leads its *professors* to think themselves "safe and happy," as being "near the suburbs of the Kingdom of God and close neighbours to the saints"; but, in the stress and strain of life, on the perilous edge of spiritual battle and moral duty, it leaves them "unanointed" and "as faint and languid as a snail." Religion of the Spirit, on the other hand, is the product of "the operation of God Himself in man," who thus "begets the man unto God," "unites him in one spirit unto Christ," "informs him with a spirit of truth," and "anoints him for ministry and service." The results of this "operation" are: (1) "It makes the man strong and mighty for every duty"; (2) "It makes the man inflexible in the ways of God, able to go straight toward the mark, not to be bended by fears, favours, frowns, nor flatteries";[1] (3) "It makes a man invincible by the evils and powers of the creature, for, with the power of God in him, he can no more be overcome than God Himself can be overcome."[2]

Like all exponents of mystical religion, he insists on experience. He demands a religion which "changes the very nature of men"—a religion which "finds men birds of prey and makes them doves; it finds them flesh, it makes them spirit; it finds them sin, it makes them righteousness."[3]

"It lays hold upon the heart, the soul, the inner man, and changes, alters, renews, and reforms that, and when the heart is

[1] It is difficult to believe that the man who wrote this would have accepted *tithes* if he saw that it was contrary to "the ways of God to take them."

[2] This is, in the main, a summary of the Epistle Dedicatory, with one or two quotations added from *Christ's Spirit a Christian's Strength.*

[3] *Select Works*, p. 117.

reformed, all is reformed. . . . When God undertakes to reform the Church He begins with the heart, and intending to reform the heart He puts His Word there; and that living Word put into the heart reforms it indeed."[1]

This is a primary position of all his teaching, that an inward change must occur, and that this inward change is wrought by the Divine Word, Light, Life, or Spirit.

"Christ," he says, "dwelling in our hearts by faith, discovers, reproves, condemns, and destroys sin: because Christ, the judgment of God in the soul, must needs, in the end, prevail against every sin of man."[2]

Again, in the same sermon,[3] he says:

"The living and Eternal Word dwells in our hearts, and this Word dwelling in us by faith changes us into its own likeness, as fire changeth iron into its own likeness, and takes us up into all its virtues. . . . This is not a word without us, as the word of the law is, but the Word within us. If thou live under the Word many years, and it come not into thy heart, it will never change thee."[4]

In a fine sentence he says: "The heart cannot be forced by outward power, but by the inward efficacy of truth."[5] "One single man," he elsewhere says, "*one single mean man with the Word* may very justly contradict the whole world without it; truth is not to be judged by multitudes but by the Word."[6] He cuts away, root and branch, the legal, external, carnal forms of Christianity. They are, to his mind, dead and done with. Man has, in the past, he says, understood the Church carnally; the law of it carnally; the liberties of it carnally; the power, authority, government, glory, officers, and so following carnally; but all outward religion is now abolished.[7] The time has come to "lay by all those opinions we have sucked in from our very cradles, and which are now become even a natural religion to us," and "to come immediately to the pure and unerring Word of God, and to the voice of Jesus Christ Himself by His Spirit."

[1] *Works*, p. 115. [2] *Ibid.* p. 113. [3] *The Right Reformation.*
[4] *Works*, p. 128. [5] *Ibid.* p. 135. [6] *Ibid.* p. 392.
[7] See pp. 110-11.

Illuminated by this "unerring Word of God" and by the Spirit of Christ in his heart, he discovers that nothing has any efficacious religious function unless it can help give "a new birth, and to make a man *new*, that is, a spiritual, holy, heavenly creature"—but, he continues, "external baptism," "material water," cannot do this.

> "After all the washing of the body with water, the soul still remains as full of filth, sin, and corruption as ever." "The baptism of Christ is alone efficacious, because it is a baptism of soul—it reaches the man's spirit with the Divine Spirit and attains to the soul, the conscience, the inner man, to purge and purify them."[1]

He is, however, no revolutionist; he has no desire to reform and change the Church by lopping off the age-grown customs. He would simply ask the State and all external powers to take their hands off and let the Divine Spirit, the Word of God, have unhindered way in men's hearts. He says, with fine wisdom: "Ceremonies are best laid down, and old customs best laid aside, by the efficacy of the Spirit."

> "The truth must eat out the ceremony, and the substance the sign; the more the baptism of Christ comes in, the more the baptism with water will go out; the ministry of the Son shall swallow up the ministry of the servant, as the sunlight doth the moonlight. The baptism of fire shall devour" (he elsewhere says, "lick up") "the baptism of water, and Christ's spirit-baptism, by degrees, shall put an end to water-baptism."[2]

In almost the same language as used by Fox and Saltmarsh, William Dell declares that the University does not equip for spiritual ministry. "It is one of the grossest errors that ever reigned under anti-Christ's Kingdom to affirm that Universities are the fountains of the ministers of the gospel!"[3] They are "false teachers" who suppose that "titles and degrees in the University, and pretended knowledge in divinity," make men able to reveal and teach Christ as the true life of the Spirit. "Sprinkling sermons with Hebrew, Greek, and Latin" may be "a perfume acceptable to the nostrils of the

[1] *Works*, p. 389. [2] *Ibid.* p. 398. [3] *Ibid.* p. 356.

world," but "the only sufficient unction for the ministry of the Word is the unction of the Spirit of God."[1]

There is no single passage in Dell's writings that better sums up his whole conception of religion than the one in which he declares that God is still writing His New Testament, writing it not in a book, but in the souls and spirits of men. It is a sentence which puts this truth as well as it has ever been put:

> "In the same Kingdom of Christ all things are inward and spiritual; and the true religion of Christ is written in the soul and spirit of man by the Spirit of God; and the believer is the only book in which God Himself writes His New Testament."[2]

Gerrard Winstanley, though not a University man like Saltmarsh and Dell, possessed greater fundamental capacity and original powers than either of them. He was the most like Fox in type of mind and bent of nature of any of the great Quaker's contemporaries. He was fifteen years older than Fox, having been born in 1609; a native of Wigan in Lancashire. As with most of the religious leaders of his epoch, his mind was mainly formed and nourished on the English Bible. Its teaching forms the very core of his thinking, and his style is plainly moulded by it, though, like Fox and Saltmarsh, he often falls into confused English, with long unlucid stretches.

It is not possible to trace the influences which shaped his mystical doctrine. He himself always attributes his doctrine to the direct "opening" of the Divine Spirit. In the *New Law of Righteousness*, written in January 1648, he says: "As I was in a trance, not long since, divers matters were *present to my sight*," and he heard definite words "spoken" to him. He continues:

> "After I was raised up (*i.e.* after the trance passed away) I was made to remember very fresh what I had seen and heard, and did declare all things to them that were with me, and I was filled with abundance of quiet peace and secret joy."

In his pamphlet entitled *A Watchword to the City of*

[1] See entire sermon on "The Stumbling Stone."

[2] From the sermon on "The Trial of Spirits" (*Works*, p. 438).

London and the Army, written in August 1649, he reports another ecstatical opening:

"Not a full year since," he writes, "being quiet at my work, my heart was filled with sweet thoughts, and many things were revealed to me which I never read in books, nor heard from the mouth of any flesh."[1]

The fact is, the environment in which Winstanley lived was full of mystical ideas. They had filtered in from many sources, and permeated the common life of England in the middle decades of the seventeenth century. I believe that the teachings of the Family of Love had as much to do with producing the general mystical atmosphere as any one influence had. I am inclined also to think that the writings of the great Teutonic mystic, Jacob Boehme, had much to do with it. His writings were put into English in successive volumes between the years 1644 and 1692, and they were widely read and even produced a distinct "Behmenite sect." I cannot agree with L. H. Berens that the founders of the Society of Friends "adopted almost in their entirety" the views and doctrines of Winstanley.[2] I very much doubt whether Winstanley in any degree influenced Fox. There is to my mind no sign of it. It seems to me rather that Saltmarsh, Dell, Winstanley, and Fox were all the product of peculiar social and spiritual

[1] It should, however, be said that these particular "openings" refer to his interesting views on the common ownership and use of land. For example, he says: "Amongst these revelations this was one, *That the earth shall be made a common Treasury of Livelihood to whole mankind without respect of persons.*" His main sociological tenet is that "all mankind ought to have a quiet subsistence and freedom to live upon earth; and that there be no bondman nor beggar in all his holy mountain" (*i.e.* anywhere). Lewis H. Berens, in his book on *The Digger Movement in the Days of the Commonwealth* (London, 1906), has given an able exposition of Winstanley's Economic Experiments. I am greatly indebted to this book, and I have in many instances made quotations from L. H. Berens' extracts from the writings of Winstanley, and I refer my readers to this book for an adequate account of this extremely interesting reformer, whose writings have long lain in "innocuous desuetude."

[2] A contemporary of George Fox held that Winstanley was the real founder of the Quakers: "The very draughts and even body of Quakerism are to be found in the several works of Gerrard Winstanley, a zealous Leveller, wherein he tells us of the arising of new times and dispensations, and challengeth Revelation very much for what he writ."—Thomas Coomber (Dean of Durham), *Christianity no Enthusiasm; or, the Several Kinds of Inspiration and Revelation Pretended by the Quakers*, 1678.

conditions, and that they came independently of each other to quite similar views and experiences. They were all, with the possible exception of William Dell, the subjects of extraordinary psychic experiences, and they were peculiarly responsive to the *suggestions* which were furnished by the small mystical sects of the time and the current mystical literature. Both Fox and Winstanley bear the marks of direct influence from Boehme. They both share with Boehme a belief in the infinite power of Light which is battling with the Dark Principle, a faith that in spite of the temporal "spoiling" of God's creation through the spirit and power of darkness, "the work of God shall finally be restored from its lost, dead, weedy, and enslaved condition,"[1] and they both hold with him the doctrine that man is an epitome of creation, a microcosm, or universe in small, possessed within by the same Spirit or Divine Reason that reveals Himself in large in the macrocosm or world system,[2] and they both show a marked tendency to allegorize and "spiritualize" the Scriptures in much the same fashion as Boehme does.[3]

Winstanley's central religious idea is the Divine Light within man's soul. He has passed completely and for ever away from the childish and pagan notion, or *imagination*, as he would call it, of a God who is far off in some distant sphere above the sky, to a Divine Being who is the inward power "by whom every one lives and moves and has his being." "Man," he says, "looks abroad for a God and doth imagine or fancy a God in some particular place of glory beyond the skies. But the Kingdom of Heaven is within you, dwelling and ruling in your flesh." The Spirit within (which he also calls that mighty man Christ Jesus) is to arise, not at a distance from man, but He will rise up *in men* and manifest Himself

[1] Winstanley's *Mystery of God concerning the Whole Creation* (London, 1648).

[2] See, for instance, the famous passage describing Fox's experience in 1648, *Journal*, pp. 28-29, and many other passages in the early pages of the *Journal*. Winstanley says that "Man is but a candle lighted by that living power of Light that is in all things."

[3] The careful reader will, however, note that the contrasts between Winstanley and Fox are fully as marked as are the similarities.

to be the Light and Life of every man and woman that is saved by Him.[1] "The Spirit of reason is not without a man, but within every man; hence he need not run after others to tell him or to teach him, for this Spirit is his Maker, He dwells in him, and if the flesh were subject thereto, he would daily find teaching therefrom."[2] He tells his little group of "Friends"—sometimes calling them "Children of the Light"—that they do not look for a God now,

"as formerly you did, to be in a place of glory beyond the sun, moon, and stars, nor imagine a Divine Being you know not where; *but you see Him ruling within you*; and not only in you, but you see and know Him to be the Spirit or Power that dwells in every man and woman, yea, in every creature, according to his orb, within the globe of the Creation. . . . You rise higher and higher into life and peace as this manifestation of the Father increases and spreads within you."[3]

He speaks of his old unillumined days as a period of darkness and tradition:

"I worshipped a God, but I neither knew who He was nor where He was, so that I lived in the dark. . . . I looked for a God without me, but *now* the true worshipper knows who God is and how He is to be worshipped as the Spirit and Power of Light shining within the man himself."[4]

He, however, does not set up some vague, undifferentiated, abstract "principle" to take the place of the God above the stars; he makes Christ the type and goal of the manifestation of God in the flesh, and he calls his "Friends" to an experience of this Christ rising up within themselves:

"Friends, do not mistake the resurrection of Christ. You expect that He shall come in one single person as He did when He came to suffer and die, and thereby to answer the types of Moses' Law. Let me tell you that if you look for Him under the notion of one single man after the flesh, to be your Saviour,

---

1 *The Saints' Paradise.* The passages above are quoted from *The Digger Movement*, p. 47.

2 *The Digger Movement*, p. 45.

3 *The Saints' Paradise.*

4 Given in substance, but not an exact quotation, from *The Saints' Paradise.*

you shall never, never taste Salvation by him. . . . If you expect or look for the resurrection of Jesus Christ, you must know that the spirit within the flesh is the Jesus Christ, and you must see, feel, and know from Himself His own resurrection within you, if you expect life and peace by Him. For He is the Life of the World, that is, of every particular son and daughter of the Father . . . for every one hath the Light of the Father within himself, which is the mighty man Christ Jesus. And He is now rising and spreading Himself in these His sons and daughters, and so rising from one to many persons till He enlightens the whole creation (mankind) in every branch of it, and covers this earth with knowledge as the waters cover the sea. . . . And this is to be saved by Jesus Christ; for that mighty Man of spirit hath taken up His habitation within your body; and your body is His body, and now His spirit is your spirit, and so you are become one with Him and with the Father. This is the faith of Christ, when your flesh is subject to the Spirit of Righteousness, as the flesh of Christ was subject. And this is to believe in Christ, when the actings and breathings of your soul are within the centre of the same spirit in which the man Jesus Christ lived, acted, and breathed."

He does not undervalue the Scriptures, though he does put them, as also Fox did, in subordination to the Spirit from whom they came forth, and like all mystics he regards a head knowledge of the Scriptures as a "moon-light stage" of illumination. He says:

"It is very possible that a man may attain to a literal knowledge of the Scriptures, of the Prophets and Apostles, and may speak largely of the history thereof, and yet both they that speak and they that hear may be not only unacquainted with, but enemies to, that Spirit of truth by which Prophets and Apostles writ. . . . It is not the Apostles' writings, but the Spirit that dwelt in them, that did inspire their hearts, which gives life and peace to all."[1]

It is the spirit within that must "prove these Scriptures to be true."[2] He says that "the Church now stands in its worship partly in the light and partly in the dark. It is in the light in so far as men have the anointing of Jesus Christ in them, ruling, teaching, acting, and dwelling in

[1] *The Digger Movement*, p. 58.
[2] From *Truth Lifting its Head Above Scandals* (London, 1648).

them, for the same anointing unites Christ and the saints, and makes them one mystical body."[1]

He looks upon outward ordinances precisely as Saltmarsh, Dell, and Fox did, as forms and customs which are to pass away as soon as men enter the stage of spiritual religion. He says:

"I have gone through the ordinance of dipping, which the letter of the Scripture doth warrant, yet I do not press any one thereunto, but bid every one to wait upon the Father, till He teach and persuade and then their submitting will be sound. For I see *now*, that it is not the material matter, but *the water of life—that is the Spirit in which souls are to be dipped*, and so drawn forth into the one Spirit; and all those outward customs and forms are to cease and be done away."[2]

Winstanley shows more of the "Seeker" tendency than does any of the other mystics studied in this chapter, though he possesses a far more virile and positive spirit than that which for the most part prevailed among the groups of "Seekers," as we know them. He puts a very strong emphasis on silence and on "waiting." As we have just seen, he would have no one to submit to an ordinance, even though it were warranted by the letter of Scripture, until he had "waited" and been persuaded by an inward teaching that "the submitting would be sound." He held the view, too, that no one should pray "until the Power within thee gives words to thy mouth to utter, then speak, for thou canst not but speak."[3] As soon as the true light shines into men's hearts the abundance of "talk" ceases, and "long discourses called preaching" also cease, and "men do not care to speak *till they know by experience within themselves what to speak, but they wait with a quiet silence upon the Lord*, till He break forth within their hearts and give them words and power to speak."

"Every one shall be taken off from seeking knowledge from without, and with an humble, quiet heart shall wait upon the Lord till He manifest Himself."[4] "You shall no longer feed upon

[1] *The Mystery of God*, pp. 39-40.
[2] *The Digger Movement*, p. 65.
[3] *Ibid.* p. 65.
[4] *Ibid.* pp. 65 and 66.

the oil that was in other men's lamps, for now it is required that every one have oil in his own lamp, even the pure testimony of truth within himself."[1]

One of his finest passages on silence and inward power comes in the *New Law of Righteousness*:

"There is nothing more sweet and satisfactory to a man than this, to know and feel that spiritual power of righteousness to rule in Him which he calls God. . . . Wait upon the Lord for teaching. You will never have rest in your soul till He speaks in you. Run after men for teaching, follow your forms with strictness, you will still be at a loss, and be more and more wrapt up in confusion and sorrow of heart. But, when once your heart is made subject to Christ, the Law of Righteousness, looking up to Him for instruction, waiting with a meek and quiet spirit till He appear in you; then you shall have peace; then you shall know the truth, and the truth shall make you free."

But it needs to be said that Winstanley was no passive Quietist, withdrawn from storm and stress of practical life. He is most like Fox in his strenuous determination to turn his visions into deed. He says:

"My mind was not at rest because nothing was acted (*i.e.* done); and thoughts ran in me that words and writings were all nothing and must die; *for action is the life of all, and if thou dost not act thou dost nothing*."[2]

His great "openings" all have reference to action and deed. His business in the world, as it was "revealed" to him, was to break yokes and set men free. Whatever one may think of his economic and social theories, one cannot fail to feel a thrill of sympathy with a man who flings himself, as Winstanley did, into the task of so changing the social conditions that "all mankind might have a quiet subsistence and freedom to live upon earth." This personal testimony of his which follows shows that the Divine Spirit in whom he believed had also wrought within his heart: "My spirit is made patient and is guarded with peace and joy, I hate none, I love all, I

[1] Sub-title to *Truth Lifting its Head Above Scandals.*

[2] *A Watchword to the City of London.* Quoted from *The Digger Movement*, p. 113.

delight to see every one live comfortably, I would have none live in poverty, straits, and sorrow,"[1] and this personal testimony confirms his saying that "whatever doth govern in you, that is your God."

There were many other fine souls, in this era, who struck out at least *fragments* of a true spiritual message, and who helped to hand on the torch which earlier saints and martyrs had kindled. I have selected these men as samples of the mystical teachers of the time. They are of a totally different type from the mystics who follow the negative path in a passionate search for the Divine Dark. They are primarily of the practical temper that belongs to the English character, and they introduce us to the new social spirit which is the very "hall mark" of the Quaker Fellowship, which will be studied in the succeeding volume.

[1] *The Digger Movement*, p. 104.

APPENDIX

CHRONOLOGY

I.—Classical Roots of Mysticism

Socrates	469–399 B.C.
Plato	429–347 B.C.
Aristotle	384–322 B.C.
Philo	*circa* 20 B.C.–between A.D. 41 and 54
Plotinus	A.D. 203–269
Julian the Apostate	A.D. 331–363
Proclus	A.D. 412–485
Emperor Justinian closes the Schools of Philosophy	A.D. 529

II.—Mysticism in the Fathers

Clement of Rome	d. A.D. 100
Ignatius	d. *circa* 117
Irenaeus	*circa* 130–202–3
Tertullian	b. *circa* 150, d. between 220–240
Clement of Alexandria	*circa* 160–220
Origen	185–254
Athanasius	296–373
Gregory of Nyssa	*circa* 332–5–395
St. Augustine	354–430
Fall of Rome	410

III.—Erigena and his Message

St. Patrick	*circa* 374–493
Columba	521–597
Aidan	605–651
St. Columban	543–615
St. Gall	551–646
Bede	673–735
Charlemagne	742–814
Charles the Bald	823–877
John Scotus Erigena	b. *circa* 800–815, d. 891(?)

IV.—St. Francis and the Brotherhood Groups

The Crusades—	
First	1096–1099
Second	1147–1187
Third	1189–1191
Fourth	1204
Fifth	1216
Sixth	1248
Seventh	1270
Popes of the thirteenth century—	
1. Innocent III.	1198–1216
2. Honorius III.	1216–1227
3. Gregory IX.	1227–1241
4. Celestine IV.	1241
5. Innocent IV.	1243–1254
6. Alexander IV.	1254–1261
7. Urban IV.	1261–1264
8. Clement IV.	1265–1268
Vacancy	1268–1271
9. Gregory X.	1271–1276
10. Innocent V.	1276
11. Adrian V.	1276
12. John XXI.	1276–1277
13. Nicholas III.	1277–1280
14. Martin IV.	1281–1285
15. Honorius IV.	1285–1287
16. Nicholas IV.	1288–1293
17. St. Celestine V. (abdicated)	1294
18. Boniface VIII.	1294–1303
Joachim of Floris	1145–1201–2
St. Francis	1182–1226
Dante	1265–1321

V.—The Friends of God in the Fourteenth Century

Babylonish Captivity at Avignon	1309–1377
Great Schism	1377–1418
Black Death	1340–1349
Eckhart	1260–1329
Tauler	1290–1361
Suso	1295–1365
Ruysbroek	1293(?)–1381

VI.—Age of Wyclif

Wyclif born	1320
Edward III. proclaimed King	1327

Edward assumes title of King of France	1337–8
War with France begun	1339
Black Death. Statute of Labourers passed	1349
First Statute of Provisors passed	1351
First Statute of Praemunire passed	1353
Victory of Poitiers and capture of John II. of France	1356
The Good Parliament. Death of the Black Prince	1376
Wyclif cited to appear at St. Paul's	1377
Death of Edward III. Accession of Richard II.	1377
Poll-tax imposed	1379–80
Rising of the Commons under Wat Tyler and Jack Straw Murder of Sudbury, Archbishop of Canterbury Return of John of Gaunt to Power	1381
Death of Wyclif	1384

VII.—Rise of Anabaptism

Luther born	1483
At Latin School at Magdeburg	1497
At Eisenach	1498
Enters Erfurt University	1501
Master of Arts	1505
Enters Augustinian Cloister at Erfurt	1505
Ordained Priest	1507
Becomes Professor of Philosophy at Wittenberg	1508
Visits Rome	1511
Doctor of Theology	1512
Controversy on Indulgences	1517
Publication of the Theses at Wittenberg	1517
Summoned before Papal Legate at Augsburg	1518
Leipzig Disputation between Eck and Luther	1520
Publication of the three great Reformation Treatises. Burning of the Papal Bull and Book of Decretals	1520
Luther at the Diet of Worms	1521
In the Wartburg	1522
First Edition of the New Testament in German published	1522
The Peasants' War	1525
Luther marries Catherine von Bora	1525
The Visitations	1528
Diet of Augsburg	1530
League of Schmalkald	1530
Augsburg "Confession" published	1531
Death of Luther	1546
Zwingli	1484–1531
Calvin	1509–1564
Hans Denck	d. 1527
Balthazar Hübmaier	1480–1528

Thomas Münzer	*circa* 1490–1525
Melchior Hoffman	d. 1542
The Münster Kingdom	1534–6
Menno Simons	1492–1559

VIII.—Anabaptists in Great Britain

Henry VIII. acknowledged as Head of the Church	1531
Act for restraining all appeals to Rome passed	1533
Act abolishing the authority of the Pope in England passed	1534
Act of Supremacy	1535
Fisher and More executed	1535
"Benefit of clergy" restricted	1536
English translation of the Bible set up in Churches	1536
Dissolution of the Monasteries	1536
Act of Six Articles	1539
Fall and execution of Cromwell	1540
Invasion of Scotland and France	1544
Death of Henry. Accession of Edward VI.	1547
Hertford made Protector	1547
Visitation, to order use of English in services and pull down images	1549
First Prayer-book of Edward VI. appeared	1549
Act for Uniformity of Service passed	1549
Second Prayer-book of Edward VI.	1552
Death of Edward VI. Accession of Mary	1553
Laws concerning religion passed in Edward's reign are annulled	1554
Rebellion of Sir Thomas Wyatt. Execution of Lady Jane Grey	1554
Mary marries Philip of Spain	1554
Persecuting statutes against heretics revived	1555
Cranmer burnt	1556
War with France. Loss of Calais by England	1557–8
Death of Mary. Accession of Elizabeth	1558
New Prayer-book prepared	1559
Acts of Supremacy and Uniformity passed	1559
Peace made with France	1559
Insurrection on behalf of Mary and Romanism	1559
Puritans in Parliament propose alterations in religion	1571
Jesuit mission to reconvert England	1580
Treaty between Elizabeth and the Netherlands	1585
Execution of Mary of Scotland	1587
Pope Sixtus V. proclaims a crusade against England	1587
Marprelate tracts circulated	1588
Defeat of the Spanish Armada	1588

Acts passed against Puritans and Romanists	1593
Insurrection of Essex; his execution	1601
Death of Elizabeth. Accession of James I.	1603
Hampton Court Conference. Authorized version of the Bible ordered to be made	1604
Gunpowder Plot	1605
Death of James I. Accession of Charles I.	1625
Sir D. Digges and Sir John Eliot impeach Buckingham on behalf of the Commons	1626
Petition of Right	1628
Sir John Eliot sent to the Tower	1628
Parliament dissolved, and eleven years of arbitrary government follow	1629
John Hampden refuses to pay Ship-money	1636
Prynne, Burton, and Bastwick condemned and pilloried for their writings	1637
Invasion of England by the Scots Council of Peers at York High Commission Court sits for last time Fifth Parliament of Charles I. meets and impeaches Strafford	1640
Triennial Act passed Strafford executed "Root and Branch" Bill read The Grand Remonstrance	1641
Hampden, Pym, Holles, Haselrig, and Strode charged with high treason, and escaping, are demanded in person by the King The King leaves London. Civil war begins Battle of Edgehill, October 23	1642
Solemn League and Covenant	1643
Self-denying ordinance brought in by Independents	1644
Battle of Naseby	1645
The King given up to the Parliamentary Commissioners at Newcastle The Westminster Assembly establishes Presbyterianism	1647
The Scottish Army enters England on behalf of Charles, and is defeated by Cromwell at Preston, Wigan, and Warrington	1648
Colonel Pride expels the Presbyterian majority from the House ("Pride's Purge")	1648
Charles is beheaded	1649
Commonwealth declared	1649
The "Barebones" Parliament meets	1653
Cromwell made Protector	1653
Peace made with Holland	1654
First Protectorate Parliament meets	1654
Second Protectorate Parliament meets	1656

"The Humble Petition and Advice"	1657
Death of Cromwell. Richard Cromwell declared Protector	1658
Richard Cromwell dissolves Parliament	1659
Remains of Long Parliament ("The Rump") restored by the Army	1659
The Long Parliament dissolves	1660
The Convention meets and invites Charles II. to return .	1660

INDEX

Absolute, The, in teaching of Plato, 63, 66
  of Aristotle, 67
  Plotinus, 72
  Proclus, 78
  Dionysius, 105, 111
  John the Scot, 124, 126
  Eckhart, 224-227
  Tauler, 278
  Suso, 289, 290
  "German Theology," 293-294
  Ranters, 469
Absolute, The, weakness of the doctrine of, 211-213, 215
Academy, Athenian closed, 77, 78, 102
Agape, 8, 21
Ainsworth, Henry, 445
Alain de l'Isle, 141
Albert the Great, 184, 192, 203, 217
  teacher in Cologne, 218
  mysticism of, 219
Albigenses, 136, 148, 183
Alexander of Aphrodisias, 68, 185
Alexians, 358
Amaurians, views of, 179-180, 186-190, 191
  discovered and persecuted, 180-181, 190
  highly trained men, 181
  charges of immorality, 189-190, 195
  influence on Strasbourg sects, 190
  and Waldenses, 191
  and Sect of the New Spirit, 192
Amaury (Amalrich), 179
  condemned, 182
  influenced by Erigena, 182, 186
  pantheism of, 186
  influence on common people, 202
Anabaptism, origin of name, 369, 378
  disuse of name, 407
  connection with earlier Societies, 369
  and the Reformation, 370, 371-378
  Social aspect, 370, 377, 387, 388, 389-392
  in England, 396-407
  second stage in England, 407
Anabaptism, and the Family of Love, 428, 431
  in New England, 479
Anabaptists, attempt to revive primitive Christianity, 370, 374
  views on Baptism, 375, 378, 380, 403
  theory of a church, 374, 375, 377, 382, 385
  theory of faith, 374, 384
  theory of basis of authority, 375
  views, 387, 399, 436
  persecution of, 378, 392-393, 399, 400
  and Zwickau prophets, 389
  gathering of, 400
  seek refuge in England, 398, 399, 406
  English, 440, 450, 452
  and Lollards, 364, 365, 396, 397, 402, 405
  first mentioned, 397
  of Hoffmanite type, 398
  represented in continental gathering, 400, 401
  in Holland, 407, 411, 412, 414, 416
  heresies of, 399, 401-402, 404, 407
  persecution of, 402, 403, 404
  separate from Reformed Church, 403
  spread of, 405, 406, 407
Angelo Clareno, 176
Anonymous of Passau, on Waldenses, 146
  on Sect of the New Spirit, 192, 193
Apollonius of Tyana, 77, 124
Apostolic Constitutions, 35
Aquinas, Thomas, 217
  influenced by Dionysian writings, 100
  on David of Dinant, 184
  in Cologne, 219
Arabians, interpreters of Aristotle, 185
Arians, 403, 405, 406
Aristotle, mysticism of, 67-69
  the doctrine of active reason, 67, 68, 185

Aristotle, the Absolute in, 67
mysticism of negative type, 69
books condemned, 182, 185
influence on David of Dinant, 184-186
writings restored through Arabians, 185
becomes buttress of Church, 186
and new scholasticism, 333
Arminians, 412, 413, 415
Asceticism, xxviii, 51, 284
of Cathari, 135
of Brethren of Free Spirit, 213
Ashton, John, 359
Athanasius, 83, 84
Attaway, Mrs., 419, 420
Audland, John, 462, 463, 464, 465, 466
Augustine, 80, 84, 98, 217, 291
father of Catholic mysticism, 87
mysticism of, 88-97
constructs authoritative Church, 87
Harnack on, 87
Doctrine of the Will, 91
influence of Platonic philosophy on, 95
Doctrine of Grace, 96
a Manichaean, 134
on freedom, 215

"Babylonish Captivity," 243, 299
St. Catherine and, 303, 304, 305
Bacon, Roger, 333
Badby, John, 361
Ball, John, 342, 354
Baptism, 356, 398
in second century, 32, 33
magical view of, 86, 88
John the Scot on, 122
opposed by Cathari, 135
opposed by Anabaptists, 398
in Family of Love, 437, 444, 446
sign of faith, 378
forms of, 409, 416, 417
infant, opposed by Cathari, 135
Wyclif, 356
Anabaptists, 375-378, 380, 403
Zwickau prophets, 389
Menno Simons, 394
Mennonites, 408
Particular Baptists, 415, 416
William Dell, 489
infant, defended by Zwingli, 377
adult, unnecessary, 400, 408, 453, 456, 492, 498
of Holy Spirit, 102, 135, 390, 438, 486, 492, 498
Baptists, General Society of, 393, 396, 407, 410, 455
first Church in England, 411, 412
Baptists, origin of name, 412, 415
and liberty of conscience, 414, 427
views of, 415, 420, 426
and Mennonites, 415
organization congregational, 417, 421, 426
missionary spirit, 426
Seekers among, 452
Baptists, Particular, organized, 415, 416
adopt immersion, 417
Confession of Faith, 417, 418
organization congregational, 417, 426
Barber, Edward, 425
Barebones, Praise-God, 416, 417
Basle, Earthquake of, 244, 265
Bauthumley, Jacob, 472, 473, 474
Baxter, Richard, 424, 458, 461, 467, 477, 481, 483, 489
Beghards, 176
origin of name, 198
organized, 199
degeneration of, 201
become heretics, 202, 222
change to Brethren of Free Spirit, 203
Edict against, 204, 205, 206, 207, 209-210
views of, 205-209
may join Tertiaries, 207
tendency to Pantheism, 210
doctrine of Absolute, 211-213
two tendencies, 212
spiritual freedom, 211-216
Eckhart and, 222, 223
and Friends of God, 245
called Lollards, 358
Beguinage, 198
classes of, 200-201
suppression decreed, 206
Beguines, 176 (*see* Beghards)
founded by Lambert, 197
origin of name, 198
Bernard, St., on vices of clergy, 132
Bible (*see* also Scripture), 139, 140
English, not to be used in worship, 408
reading of, not part of worship, 411
Bishops, first mentioned, 26, 27, 29
plurality of, 31
single, 31-33
in place of God, 32
supreme, 35
simony of, 131
English, 344
Black Death, 244, 255, 265
Blaurock, George, 374
baptized by Grebel, 378
Blunt, Richard, 416, 417
Bockelson, Jan., 392
Boehme, Jacob, xxvi, xxxviii, 494, 495
Bohemian Brethren, 389

Bonaventura, 338
Life of St. Francis, 153
on decline of Franciscan Order, 169
"Book of the Master of Holy Scripture," 259-263
Boucher, Joan, 403, 441
Brethren of Common Life, 301, 307, 308, 324
founded by Groote, 319-321
copy manuscripts and provide instruction, 320
Canons Regular, 323
Brethren of the Free Spirit supersede sect of New Spirit, 192
develop from Bequines and Beghards, 203
views, 203-209, 210-216
pantheism, 210
immorality of, 214
spiritual freedom, 211-216, 223
and Friends of God, 245
Bridget of Sweden, 301, 305
Brownists, 413, 419, 452
Brute, Walter, 359
Bucer, 383, 386
Burrough, Edward, 464, 465

Caesar of Heisterbach, 180, 185, 187
Calvin, 149, 348
Camm, Ann, 465, 466
Camm, John, 463, 464, 465
Canons Regular, 323
Capital punishment, 135, 142, 211, 395, 406, 436, 444
Carlstadt, 390
Cathari, 134-137, 140, 197
Catherine of Siena, 41, 301
Life, 301-305
Stigmata, 302
and "Babylonish Captivity," 303-304, 305
Caton, William, 465
Celibacy of Clergy, 130
Cellites, 358
Chaucer, 168, 342, 350
Christianity, weakness of, xiv
a legal system, 51, 148
and war, 51
and public office, 52, 391
of cloister, 110
in Ireland, 114-118
two types, 486, 490, 491
Church, early, a fellowship, 7, 20, 22
Holy Spirit in, 8, 21
House Church, 22
officials in, 21, 22, 23, 25-27.
Gifts, 8, 15, 21, 23
organization becomes fixed, 27-31, 36, 37
reaction against organization, 38, 42
Church, in Montanism, 45
authoritative, 80
Roman Catholic, organized by Augustine, 87, 88
only channel of Grace, 88, 97, 132, 133
world supremacy of, 130
existence depends on magic power, 148
attacked by Beghards, 206
attacked by Wyclif, 353, 354
power crumbling, 299
not a house, 45, 135, 361, 365, 366
not ecclesiastical system, 350
congregation of believers, 42, 135, 374, 375, 377, 382, 395, 402, 410, 431
English, 342-347
and state, separation of, 369, 373, 375, 395, 401, 417, 423
separation of, in England, 344-349, 366
Clara, Saint, 159-161
Head of Order of Clarisses, 159
Clement of Alexandria, 83, 84
reference to, in Dionysian writings, 100
Clement of Rome, Epistle of, 29
Clementines, 205
Clergy, authoritative, 34
magic power of, 130-131
and laity, 130, 391
vices of, 131-133, 264, 265, 268, 299, 303, 304, 313, 318
English, 345-346, 350
Clerkson, Lawrence, 457
"Cloud of Unknowing, The," 336, 337
Collegianten, 417
Columba, 116
Columban, St., 116
Communism in primitive Church, 8
of Waldenses, 144, 145
partial among Beguines, 200
Brethren of Common Life, 319
of Wyclif, 349, 354
of Lollards, 365
of Anabaptists, 388
of Family of Love, 441
Congregational methods, 407, 417, 421, 426
Council of Trent, 87
Constantinople, 98
Tyre, 98
Chiersey, 119
Valence, 120
Langres, 120
Lateran, 139, 140, 185
Verona, 140

Council of Paris, 182, 184, 185
Vienne, 201, 205, 206
Mayence, 201
Trèves, 204
Constance, 299, 306-307, 367
"Earthquake," 354, 358
Zurich, 372, 375, 380
Cranmer, 149, 403, 404, 440, 441

Dante, 107, 325, 327
David of Dinant, influenced by Aristotle and Erigena, 184-186
pantheistic views of, 184, 189
Dell, William, 467, 485, 494, 498
Life, 488, 489
Teachings, 490-493
Denck, Hans, 381
translates Prophets, 374, 385
Life, 383-386
mysticism of, 384, 385, 386
teaches fatherhood of God, 386
Denison, Stephen, 446
Denne, Henry, 421-423, 424
Devotion, New, 301, 308, 322 (*see* Brethren of the Common Life)
Didache, 24, 29
Diet of Worms, 379
Dionise Hid Divinite, 336
Dionysius, The Areopagite, writings first produced, 98
history of writings, 98-102
relation to St. Denis of Paris, 99, 100
pupil of "Hierotheus," 101
mysticism of, 104-112
influence on poetry, 107
influence on future mysticism, 110, 111, 202, 211, 217, 221, 224, 260, 300
translated by John the Scot, 123
translated by Grossetête, 334
translated into English, 336-338
Disbrough, James, 422
Doctrine, false, 33
of Love (Plato), 65
of Will (Augustine), 91
of Grace, 96
of Predestination, 118-120, 376, 387, 404, 409, 415
of Transubstantiation, 120, 353
of Free Spirit, 192-195, 203-209
of Divine "Spark," 229, 231-233, 241
of Inner Light, 276-278, 296, 351-352, 381, 384, 385, 423, 435, 446, 447, 480-484, 486, 490-492, 495-497
of Perfection, 273, 439, 440, 444, 445
Doctrine of Depravity, 384, 385, 404, 409, 415
of Divine Indwelling, 467, 469
Dominicans, 197, 209, 220, 221, 239, 274, 282, 301
Donatists, 400, 405
Duns Scotus, 204
leader of new scholasticism, 334

Ebner, Margaret and Christina, 244, 245, 255, 256, 257, 258
Eckhart, mysticism of, xxvi, 224-239
views of freedom, 212, 223, 224
views of Brethren of Free Spirit, 214
Life of, 218-224, 239-241
charges of heresy, 217, 239-241
not a pantheist, 225, 233-235, 240
doctrine of Divine "Spark," 229, 231-233, 241
and Kant, 229
and friends of God, 242, 274, 292
and Suso, 282, 289
Education of Children, 306, 307
of common people, 320
Elders in Family of Love, 433, 443
among Quakers, 433
Elizabeth of Schoenau, Saint, 242, 264, 268
Ellina of Crevelsheim, 271
Epiphanius, 47
Erasmus, 168, 364, 379
Erbury, William, 457, 458
Erigena, John Scotus (*see* John the Scot)
"Eternal Gospel," The, 171, 173, 174, 175
Etherington, John, 446
Eusebius, 55

Faith, 352
The, 27
a body of doctrine, 33, 34, 35, 36, 37, 80, 365
a condition of soul, xx, 384
to be free, 374
to be personal, 380, 395
Hans Denck on, 384
Familists (*see* Family of Love)
Family of Love, 428, 450, 452, 494
organized, 432, 433
in England, 440-448
not libertine, 435, 436, 443
latest stage of revelation, 439
claims of Perfection, 439, 440, 444, 445, 447
views, 441, 444
charges against, 442, 443-447, 479
and Quakers, 428, 447, 448
Fatherhood of God, 151, 157, 317, 386, 387

Fell, Margaret, 465, 466
Firmilian, 46
Fisher, Samuel, 470
Fox, George, 283, 316, 320, 330, 339, 422, 424, 427, 429, 431, 434, 437, 438, 462, 463, 466, 467, 485, 487, 493, 497, 498, 499
  on Ranters, 472, 480, 481
  founder of Quakers, 482
  reaches views independently, 494, 495
Francis of Assisi, 138, 317
  asks special Indulgence, 132
  character of, 150-153, 176, 177
  history, 153-167
  Lives of, 153
  psychic nature, 154-155, 165
  starts Order of Poor Little Brothers, 158
  starts second Order, Clarisses, 159
  starts third Order, Tertiaries, 161-162
  organization of first Order into Order of Friars, 163, 164
  Stigmata, 164-165
  traditional biography, 170
  view of later Spirituals of, 175, 176
  influence on literature and art, 153, 177
Franciscans (*see* Friars)
  Spiritual, 170-176
Franck, Sebastian, 383, 387, 392, 452
Fraticelli, 176
Free Spirit, doctrine of, 192-195, 203-209, 210
  two tendencies, 212
  weakness is its negative feature, 211
  Eckhart and, 214, 217, 223
  Ranters revive, 469
Freedom, spiritual, of Sect of Free Spirit, 193-195
  of Beghards, 209, 211-216
  Augustine on, 215
  Eckhart on, 212, 223, 224
  John Smyth on, 408
  true spiritual, 216, 412, 451
  of will, 385, 409
Friars, Franciscan, 197
  organized, 163, 164
  corruption of, 168-169
  corruption of English, 342, 343, 350
"Friend of God from Oberland," 245-254, 260, 273, 304
  writings of, 246, 266, 270
Friends of God, 210, 222, 242-245
  Leaders, 245
  writings of, 246
  Merswin and "Friend of God from Oberland," 245-254
  Characteristics, 254-259
  a lay movement, 254, 263
Friends of God hold Divine Diet, 267
  Book of Nine Rocks, 267-270
  ideals of, 270-274
  German Theology, 291-297
Friends, Society of (*see* Quakers), xxxviii, 296, 406, 410, 411, 437, 494

Gangraena, Edwards', 418, 419, 422, 424, 450, 457, 484
Gansfoort, John Wesel, 332
Gerard of San Donnino, 171, 174-175
Gerson, 188, 299, 301, 323
  and "Great Schism," 306
  mysticism, 306-307
  teacher of children, 306, 307
Gidding, Little, 324
Gifts, 8, 15, 21, 36
  of prophecy, 23
  give place to priesthood, 37
  succeed priesthood, 485
Gilbert of Gamblours, on vices of Clergy, 132
Gnosticism, 29, 33, 72, 134
  in Greek Fathers, 84
Grace, doctrine of, 96
  Church only channel of, 88, 97, 132, 133
  gift of God, 329
  universal, 415, 422, 424, 425
Grebel, Conrad, 373, 387
  baptizes Blaurock, 378
Gregory XI., 303-304, 305, 354
Gregory of Nyssa, 84-87, 98
Groote, Gerard, 308, 309, 314
  life, 314-323
  preaches new Evangelism, 317-319, 360
  founds Brethren of Common Life, 319-321
  mysticism, 321-322
  influence on Dutch universities, 321
Grossetête, Robert, 333-334
Grünenwörth, 249, 250, 252
Gui, Bernard, on Waldenses, 145
Guillaume le Breton, 179, 189
Guyon, Madame, xxvi

Haemerlein, Thomas, 323 (*see* à Kempis)
Helwys, Thomas, 407, 411-413, 414, 416
Henry de Kalkar, 315
Henry of Lausanne, 316
Henry of Nördlingen, 244, 245, 256, 257, 258, 274
Heresy, battle against, 33, 34, 119, 133, 140
  marks of, 143
  of John the Scot, 120
  of Catharism, 134-137

Heresy of Waldenses, 139-149
of Amaurians, 190
of Beghards, 202-206
of Brethren of Free Spirit, 203-206
of Eckhart, 217, 239-241
of Wyclif, 354-356
of Lollards, 361-365
of Anabaptists, 365, 401, 402, 404, 407
set forth in Edwards' *Gangraena*, 418, 419, 422, 424, 450, 457, 484
Heretics, Statute for burning, 361
how to recognize, 143
Hetzer, Ludwig, translates Prophets, 374, 385
Hickock, Richard, 471
Hierotheus, 101
mystical ladder of, 102, 106
Hildegarde, Saint, 169, 242, 264, 268
Hilton, Walter, 301, 323, 338-339
writes *Ladder of Perfection*, 338
Hoffman, Melchior, 390-392, 398
Hotham, Justice, 473, 481
House of Love (*see* Family of Love)
How, Samuel, 416, 422
Howgil, Francis, 339, 462, 463, 464, 465
Hübmaier, Balthasar, 374, 385, 388
Life, 379
teaching, 380-383
Hus, John, 149, 307, 348, 367
Hut, Hans, 390

Ignatius, Epistles of, 29, 31
reference to, in Dionysian writings, 100
Imitation of Christ, 291, 301, 321
authorship, 323, 338
negative aspect, 325-327
positive note, 327-330
not quietism, 331
not selfishness, 331
Independents, 414, 422, 424, 427, 462
Individual, supremacy of, 349-350
Indulgences, sale of, 132
opposed by Waldenses, 142
Wyclif, 353
Infant baptism, opposed by Cathari, 135
Wyclif, 356
Anabaptists, 375-378, 380, 403
Zwickau prophets, 389
Menno Simons, 395
Mennonites, 408
Particular Baptists, 415, 416
William Dell, 489
defended by Zwingli, 377
Irenaeus, 35
mysticism in, 81, 84
Harnack's summary of, 81
Irish Christianity, 114-118
Irish missionaries, 116
preserve classic learning, 116-118
foremost is John the Scot, 118

Jackson, John, 458, 459, 466
on Seekers, 461, 467
Jacob, Henry, 415
Jerome, 348, 367
Jessey, Henry, 416
Jessop, Edmond, 445
Joachim of Floris, 171
writings of, 172
"Three Ages," 172-173
disciples, 173
spurious writings, 174
compared with Amaury, 187
John, St., mysticism of, 16-19, 96
John de Brunn, a Beghard, 214
John of Parma, Minister General of Franciscans, 170, 171, 175
John the Scot, history of, 113-114, 118, 178, 183
translates Dionysian writings, 99, 111, 123
Tract on Predestination, 118-120
views of Sacraments, 121-122
of Progressive Revelation, 122
writes *On Division of Nature*, 124-128
books among Albigenses, 183
books condemned, 182
mysticism of, 124-129
influence on Amaury, 182-184
influence on Brethren of Free Spirit, 202, 211
later influence, 178-179, 217, 221, 224, 300
Joris, David, 400, 442
Julian, the Apostate, 77
Julian, Lady, 301
Justinian, 77, 79, 102

Kant, 229
à Kempis, Thomas, 291, 314, 317, 321, 322
Life, 323-325
Kiffin, William, 416, 425
Kingdom of God, a mystical fellowship, 6
in man, 321, 495
Knewstub, John, 443, 444
Knollys, Hanserd, 416, 424

Ladder, mystical, of Plotinus, 74-76
Stephen Bar Sudaili or "Hierotheus," 102
of Dionysius, 105, 107
in *Book of Nine Rocks*, 267-270, 273
in Tauler, 279

Ladder, in *German Theology*, 297
in "Ruysbroek," 310-313
in Piers Plowman, 340
of Perfection, The, 338
Lambert, founder of Beguines, 197
Langenmantel, Eitelhans, 387, 388
Langland, William, 168, 339-340, 342
Lathrop, John, 416
Lawson, John, 466
Lay preaching, in second century, 35
of Waldenses, 139, 140, 141, 147
Beguines and Beghards, 204
Friends of God, 263
Gerard Groote, 316, 360
Lollards, 357-360
Anabaptists, 406
Baptists, 418, 422, 423
in Family of Love, 446
Legate, Bartholomew, 454, 455
Liberty of conscience, 374, 410, 413, 414, 427
Light, inner, Eckhart's "Spark," 229, 231-233, 241
Tauler on, 276-278
in *German Theology*, 296
in Wyclif, 351-352
in Hübmaier, 381
in Denck, 384, 385
in Henry Denne, 423
in Henry Nicholas, 435
in Family of Love, 446, 447
in George Fox, 480, 481, 482, 483
in John Saltmarsh, 484, 486
in William Dell, 490-492
in Gerrard Winstanley, 495-497
Lollards, 354, 357-366
origin of name, 358
lay preachers, 359, 360
attacks on, 358, 361, 362
opposed to oaths, 360
to Mass, 360, 361, 366
revival of, 363, 364
message of, 364
and Anabaptists, 364, 365, 396, 397, 402, 405
and Quakers, 365, 366
Lombardy, poor of, 145
Lord's Supper (*see also* Mass and Sacraments), 17, 21
in second century, 32, 36, 37
administered by women, 46, 145
by laymen, 145
magic view of, 86
doctrine of transubstantiation, 120, 332, 353, 356
Lollards and, 360, 361, 364, 366
Love, St. Paul on, 15
Plato's doctrine of, 65
secret of St. Francis' power, 152, 167, 177
Love, Divine, 291, 296, 307, 311
practising God's, 313, 328
preaching God's, 317
eye of soul, 334
creed of Rolle, 335
Lull, Raimund, 138
Luther, 142, 149, 275, 291, 332, 348, 350, 363, 364, 367, 370, 372, 373, 380, 389, 390, 394, 428, 431, 452
on total depravity, 384
Lyons, poor men of, 139, 145
heretical sect in, 191

Magistrates, Tertullian on, 52
Melchior Hoffman on, 391
not to meddle with religion, 410, 414
Man, Thomas, 364
Manichaeism, 134, 136
and mysticism, 137
Mantz, Felix, 373
Marriage, Montanists on, 52
of a priest, 374
in Family of Love, 435
Marsh, Adam, 333
Marshall, Charles, 464, 465
Martin of Pologne, 182
Mass (*see* Lord's Supper, Sacraments, etc.), 130, 243, 360, 375, 380, 394
Matilda of Magdeburg, St., 242, 259, 264, 268
Matthys, Jan, 392
Maximilla, 41, 54
Melanchthon, 390
Mennonites, 408, 409, 412, 417, 453
and General Baptists, 414, 415
Menno Simons (*see* Simons)
Merswin, Rulman, 245-254
writings, 246, 251, 253, 266
life, 248-251
Millennium, 53, 389, 390, 392
Miracles, Seekers on, 454, 456, 458
John Saltmarsh on, 485, 487
Montanism, 35
origin of, 38
object, 39
value of, 42
dispensation of Paraclete, 42, 44, 45
foundation principle is development, 45, 122
type of prophecy, 40, 41, 47, 50
weaknesses, 50
a "new law," 51
regulation of marriages and fasts, 52
zeal for martyrdom, 53
expectation of millennium, 53
persecutions, 54
outcome, 55
stages of revelation, 43, 45, 46, 51, 122

Montanus, history of, 38
  character, 39
  sayings, 40
  claims of, 49
Mount St. Agnes, 323
  life in, 324
Münster Kingdom, 392, 400
Münzer, Thomas, 389, 390
Murton, John, 407, 411, 412, 413, 455
Mysticism, definitions, xv, xvi, xvii, xviii
  in all religions, xv, xvi, xxv
  normal aspect, xviii-xxv
  abnormal aspect, xxv-xxviii, xxxii
  value of, xxx-xxxiv
  temporal Element, xxxiv-xxxv
  two types, xxxv, 67, 500
  negative type, 69, 95, 108, 109, 211, 212, 219, 278-280
  in fourteenth century, 217, 242, 298, 334
  "new," 298, 300, 308
  and Manichaeism, 137
  and the "Church," 347-348
  of Gospels, 4, 5, 6, 57
  of Paul, 9-13
  of John, 16-19
  of Socrates, 58
  of Plato, 59-66
  of Aristotle, 67-69
  in Stoic philosophy, 69
  of Plotinus, 72-76
  of Proclus, 78
  of Church Fathers, 80-84
  of Gregory of Nyssa, 84-87
  of Augustine, 88-97
  of Dionysius, 104-112
  of John the Scot, 124-129
  of St. Francis, 151, 177
  of Joachim, 173
  of Amaurians, 179-180, 186-190
  of Sect of Free Spirit, 193
  of Brethren of Free Spirit, 206
  of Albertus Magnus, 219
  of Eckhart, 224-239
  of Friends of God, 268-274
  of Tauler, 276-281
  of Suso, 281-291
  of *German Theology*, 292-297
  of Gerson, 306-307
  of Ruysbroek, 309-313
  of Groote, 321, 322
  of *Imitation*, 325, 332
  of Richard Rolle, 335, 336
  of English translations of Dionysius, 336-338
  of Walter Hilton, 338, 339
  of Hübmaier, 381
  of Denck, 384, 385
  of Henry Nicholas, 431, 432, 444
  of Seekers, 459
Mysticism of George Fox, 482
  of John Saltmarsh, 484-487
  of William Dell, 490-49
  of Winstanley, 493-497
  of Quakers, 500

Nayler, James, 458, 468, 479
Neoplatonism, influence on mysticism, 70
  Plotinus, master mind of, 70
  later development, 77
  close of Academy, 78, 102
  influence on Greek Fathers, 83, 98
  on Augustine, 95
Nicholas of Basle, Beghard martyr, 210, 246
Nicholas (Niclaes), Henry, 401
  Life, 428-432
  organizes Family of Love, 432, 433
  writings, 433
  views, 433-440, 443, 444
Nicholas of Hereford, 357, 359
Nikolaus von Löwen, 245, 249, 252-253
Nine Rocks, Book of, 208, 246, 251, 253, 255, 267-270, 291
Norbert, Saint, 316

Oaths, opposed by Tertullian, 52
  opposed by Cathari, 135
    by Waldenses, 142
    by Beghards, 211
    by Lollards, 360, 366
    by Anabaptists, 387
    by Melchior Hoffman, 390
    by Menno Simons, 395
    by John Smyth, 411
    by Henry Nicholas, 436, 437
  not entirely rejected by General Baptists, 415
Occam, William of, 334
Oecolampadius, 377, 379, 383
Officials in early Church, 21, 22, 23, 25-27
Oldcastle, Sir John, 362
Order of St. Francis, 158, 163, 164
  of Poor Clares, 159
  Tertiaries, 161-162
  corruption of Franciscan, 168, 169
  schism in Franciscan, 170
  failure of Franciscan, 177
  decline of regular, 204
  of Beghards and Beguines, 200-202,
  of Beghards and Beguines abolished 206
  Dominican, 197, 209, 221, 239, 301
  of Saint John, 250
Organization, in early Church, 27
  reason for, 28
  becomes Ecclesiastical system, 36

Organization, reaction against, 42
of Franciscan Order, 163, 164
Origen, 71, 83, 84
Ortlieb, 202
founder of sect of New Spirit, 192, 195
an Amaurian, 192
Oxford, 178, 333, 334, 335, 338, 339, 341, 355, 358, 359, 367
Oxyrhynchus Papyri, 6

Pagitt, Ephraim, 450, 456, 467
Paris, Matthew, 169, 199
Parker, John, 359
Passion of Saint Perpetua, 43, 44, 48, 49, 53
Patrick, St., 115
Paul, St., development of, 2
mysticism of, 9-13, 96
central idea, 13-15, 21, 22, 111
Paulicians, 134, 136
Peasant revolt in Germany, 385, 390
in England, 342, 349, 354
Pelagians, 403, 442
Penington, Isaac, 296
Penn, William, 316, 448, 452, 456, 466, 481
Peter de Bruys, 316
Peter of Vaux-Sernai, 142, 145
Phillips, Ubbo, 400, 453
Piers Plowman, 339-340, 361
Pilgrimage of Grace, The, 401
Pistle of Private Cowncelle, 336, 337, 338
Plato, 98
father of speculative mysticism, 58
summary of his mysticism, 59-66
doctrine of Love, 65
Plotinus, 98, 224
mysticism of, 67, 72-76
life of, 70
Pope, The, and Tauler, 275
power in England, 344, 346-347
and Wyclif, 348, 355, 356
Porter, Holland, 474
Prayer, mystical element in, xix
to be only at moving of Spirit, 457, 498
Preaching, lay, 35, 139, 140, 141, 147, 204, 316, 357-360, 363, 406, 418, 422, 423, 446
in popular dialect, 317
without pay, 147, 317, 387, 391, 395, 418, 423
with pay, 461
without premeditation, 457
without university training, 423, 444, 454, 457, 487, 492
by women, 141, 419-421, 423
Predestination, John the Scot on, 118-120
Anabaptists, 376-377, 387, 404
John Smyth on, 409
Presbyterians, 424, 427, 452, 462, 478
Presbyters, 26
Pride's "purge," 427
Priesthood, of believers, 42, 46, 351
supplants prophecy, 29, 30
in Roman Church, 120, 122, 130-133, 148
Lollards' views on, 365, 366
doomed, 371
first stage of ministry, 485
Primitive Christianity, types of, 1
a mystical religion, 4, 57
becomes ecclesiastical system, 27, 36
persists in some localities, 38
attempts to revive, 1
by Waldenses, 133
by St. Francis, 150
in thirteenth century, 196
by Anabaptists, 370, 374
by George Fox, 483
Wyclif on, 351
studied by Hübmaier, 379
Priscilla, Montanist prophetess, 41
oracle of, 52, 54
Proclus, 77
mysticism of, 78
triads of, 106
Prophecy, in early Church, 23-25, 28, 47
supplanted by priesthood, 29, 30
in second century, 35
in Montanism, 40, 42, 47, 50
of Amaurians, 186
Psalms, translated into English, 335
singing of, 361
Pseudo Christus, 479
Purvey, John, 357, 359
Pythagoras, 58, 77

Quakers (*see* Friends), 391, 428, 436
views on baptism, 408
views on preaching, 423
Eldership of, 433
Monthly Meetings of, 463
Seekers become, 462-466
and Lollards, 365, 366
and Family of Love, 428, 447, 448
and Ranters, 471, 472, 473, 480, 481
founded by George Fox, 482
positive mystics, 500

Radewin, Florentius, 319, 320, 322, 324

Ranters, 448
degenerate movement, 467, 480
not a sect, 452
Pantheism of, 467, 469, 472
revive doctrine of Free Spirit, 469
and Quakers, 471-473, 480, 481
use of tobacco, 473, 474
Libertinism of, 477, 478
ordinance against, 478, 479
influence checked, 481
Reformation, The, 130, 149, 275, 308, 314, 370
in England, 364, 450
Religion, two tendencies in, xiii, xiv
mysticism in every, xv, xvi, xxv
mystics builders of, xxxii
a way of life, 152
two types of, 351
Revelation, dispensation of, 37
stages of, in Montanism, 43, 45, 46, 51
in John the Scot, 122
in Joachim of Floris, 172, 173, 174
in Eternal Gospel, 175
in Amaurians, 180, 187, 188
in Family of Love, 439
in David Joris, 442
in John Saltmarsh, 485
Rich, Robert, 468
Ridley, 149, 441
on Anabaptists, 404
Robinson, John, 413, 416
Rogers, John, 440, 442
Rogers, Thomas, 444
Rolle, Richard, 334-336, 338, 339
translated Psalms into English, 335
Roulston, Gilbert, 477
Rutherford, Samuel, 447
Ruysbroek, Jan, 245, 317
on Brethren of Free Spirit, 213, 214
Life, 308-310, 313-314
mysticism of, 309-313
spiritual ladder, 310-313

Sacraments, deification by, 86, 121
magical view of, 28, 36, 37, 86, 130-131
channel of Grace, 88
Doctrine of Transubstantiation, 120
John the Scot on, 120-122
Cathari on Baptism, 135
Waldenses on, 144, 145
Amaurians hold them unnecessary, 187, 188
sect in Lyons on, 191
Beghards on, 206, 208, 211
Eckhart on, 237, 241
Wyclif on, 353, 356
Lollards, 360, 361, 366
Sacraments, none valid for Seekers, 455
none valid for Ranters, 470
administered by lay persons, 415, 418
Salimbene, Brother, 168
Salmon, Joseph, 472
experience, 475-477
Saltmarsh, John, 467, 488, 493, 494, 498
on Seekers, 455, 456
life, 483
mystical views, 484-487
Sawtrey, William, 361
"Schism, Great," 243, 266, 299, 306-307, 319, 354
Scriptures (*see also* Bible), formation of canon, 38
translated by Waldo, 139
by Wyclif, 355-357
by Luther, 372
views of Beghards on, 208
of Friends of God on, 258, 259, 267
of Henry Nicholas on, 437
of Seekers, 455, 457, 458
of Ranters, 470, 471, 474
copied and taught, 320
foundation of true learning, 334
in hands of common people, 371, 372
not sole foundation of Faith, 258, 385, 386
reading of, dangerous, 457
authority above the Church, 332, 350, 352, 356, 372, 403
authority below the Spirit, 497
Sect of the New Spirit, founded by Ortlieb, 192
views, 192-195
charges of immorality, 194
superseded by Brethren of the Free Spirit, 192
"Seed," in John's Gospel, 17
Stoic doctrine of, 70
of God in man, 468
Seekers, 448, 488, 498
not strictly a sect, 452
on continent, 453, 454
in England, 454-466
undervalue objective religion, 469
views, 455, 456, 457, 458, 461, 469
mysticism of, 459
Cromwell on, 459, 460
become Quakers, 462-466
become Ranters, 466
in Westmorland, 461-463
in Bristol, 464
Severians, 98
"Shepherd of Hermas," 28, 29
Simons, Menno, 393-395, 401, 453

Simony, 131
Singing, not worship, 361
  part of worship, 411
  Hübmaier on, 382
Smyth, John, 414, 417
  Life, 407-409, 411
  teachings, 409-411
Socrates, a mystic, 58
Spirit, Holy, in early Church, 8, 21
  dispensation of, 42, 44, 45, 46, 123, 172, 174, 179, 187, 205, 420, 469, 470, 487
  baptism of, 102, 135, 390, 438, 486, 492, 498
  the soul of man, 191
  meetings at moving of, 210
  upper school of, 259, 270
  in heart, 330
  religion of, 352
Spiritual Franciscans, 170, 171-175
  or Zealots, 176
  Angelo Clareno on, 176
Spirituals (Montanists), 43, 52
Stephen Bar Sudaili, 101
  mystical ladder of, 102
Stephen, Sir James, on Albigenses, 148
Stewart, J. A., on Plato's mysticism, 66
Stigmata, xxvi, xxviii
  of St. Francis, 164
  Catherine of Siena, 302
Stoic philosophy, influence on mysticism, 69
  doctrine of the "Seed," 70
Storch, Nicholas, 389
Strasbourg, 190, 192, 218, 221, 244, 247, 249, 255, 274, 334, 386, 390
Stumpf, Simon, 374
"Sum of Scriptures, 364, 365, 398
Suso, Henry, 245, 308
  life, 282-289
  teaching, 289-291
Swynderby, William, 359

Tauler, John, 210, 245, 248, 255, 257, 266, 272, 273, 292, 308
  not "master of Holy Scripture," 263, 276
  life of, 274-276
  views on Free Spirit, 209, 214
  doctrine of inner light, 276-278
    of Absolute God, 278
  stages of self-dying and consecration, 279-281
Taylor, Thomas, 462
"Teaching of the Twelve Apostles," 24, 28, 29
  an early document, 30
Tertiaries, 248
  founded, 161, 162
  war forbidden to, 162
  and organization of artizans, 162
Tertullian, 39, 43, 46, 51
  on martyrs, 53
  on coming of New Jerusalem, 54
  mysticism in, 81, 82
Theology, German, 245, 291-297
  Luther on, 291
  author, 291
  "Absolute" in, 293-294
  on sin, 295
  on Inner Light, 296
  Spiritual Ladder in, 297
Thorpe, William, 359, 360
Tithes opposed by Anabaptists, 387
  by Baptists, 418, 422, 423
  by Seekers, 462
  by John Saltmarsh, 483
  by William Dell, 489
Transubstantiation, doctrine of, 120, 148
  views of Waldenses, 144, 145
  attacked, 332
    by Wyclif, 353, 356
Tyler, Wat, and peasant uprising, 342, 349, 354
Tylesworth, William, 359

Universities, Dutch, influence of Groote, 321

Vadian, 379, 383
Vaudois (*see* Waldenses)
Vitells, Christopher, 442

Waldenses, 197
  attempt to revive primitive Christianity, 133
  connection with Cathari, 134, 136
  history of, 137-140
  called "Insabbatati," 139
  under anathema, 140
  views of, 140-145, 208
  not strictly mystics, 146
  social views, 146, 147
  influenced by Beghards, 210
  and Amaurians, 191
  and sect of Free Spirit, 195
Waldo, Peter, 137-139, 147
  made translations from Scripture, 139
War, opposed by Cathari, 135
    by Waldenses, 142
  forbidden to Tertiaries, 162
  opposed by Lollards, 365, 397
    by Anabaptists, 387
    by Menno Simons, 395
    by John Smyth, 411

War, opposed by Henry Nicholas, 436, 437
by Family of Love, 444
by John Saltmarsh, 487
tolerated by General Baptists, 415
"Great Civil," 243
Wesley, John, 316, 360
Whitehead, George, 468
Wibald on Erigena, 178
Windesheim, 323
Winstanley, Gerrard, 467, 485
on Seekers, 460
on Ranters, 480
social views, 494, 499, 500
mysticism, 493-497
shows a Seeker attitude, 498
Woman, consecrates Eucharist, 46, 145, 191
Women may preach among Waldenses, 141
among Baptists, 419-421, 423
Wrighter, Clement, 458
Wyclif, 149, 333, 338, 342
life, 340-341
and the Pope, 348
theory of Dominion, 348-349, 350
and Individual Soul, 349, 350
and John of Gaunt, 350, 354
Trialogus, 352
on transubstantiation, 353, 356
charge of heresy, 354-356
translates Bible, 335, 355, 357
and Lollards, 357, 359
influence of, 366-368

Zurich, Council of, 375
"Discussion," 375, 379, 380
Zwickau Prophets, 389
revolutionary views, 390
Zwingli, 370, 372, 373, 380
and Infant Baptism, 377

THE END